MUSSOLINI'S
ITALY

MUSSOLINI'S
ITALY

Twenty Years of the Fascist Era

MAX GALLO

Translated by CHARLES LAM MARKMANN

Macmillan Publishing Co., Inc.
New York

Collier Macmillan Publishers
London

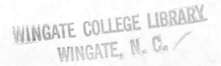

Contents

v

Preface to the American Edition

A HALF-CENTURY—that is precisely what lies between us and Mussolini's accession to power in Italy. At that time the word *Fascism* had barely been born. No one really knew that with the March on Rome on October 28, 1922, a new epoch of the twentieth century was beginning. Mussolini was seen as merely one of many leaders —more extreme, perhaps, more vehement; but it was assumed that he would blend into the parliamentary landscape after a few thunderous speeches. And, besides, gradually it had to be conceded that Il Duce had a new kind of politics.

Now fifty years have passed. Passions have not burned out, but it has become possible to look at that Fascist Italy with a view to understanding it rather than damning it or praising it. It is possible to X-ray the personality of Il Duce while avoiding peremptory judgments.

And the man Il Duce is fascinating. In the course of his life, which began at the most radical point of the extreme Left and ended in a summary execution, one encounters the pathetic side by side with the bombastic, the shrewdness of a great politician with the blindness of a fanatic. But one finds as well the mediocrity that is part of the normal man who, unlike Hitler, is not swept off balance by a political delirium.

Essentially, even in his worst moments, even at the peak of his cruelties, Mussolini was always a man torn. Torn between the drive of his desire for glory and his fear, his intuition of what was going to happen. For he sensed keenly, somewhere inside himself, that World War II could end only in defeat, that Fascist politics was

vii

chiefly a stage-setting, that the government that he instituted in 1943—that doomed Fascist Republic, the creation of the Nazis—had no reality.

In this complexity of Mussolini's character is the explanation why his story borders at the same time on tragedy and on farce. Here too is the explanation why that story, in the end, is closer to us than is Adolf Hitler's. When we look at Der Führer we are fascinated, as we are fascinated when we stand face to face with monstrosity, with Evil. When we look at Mussolini we are looking at a man. Great and commonplace. Perceptive and blind. Intuitive and limited. Criminal and victim.

A man who was drunk on power and who played with its appurtenances as if he were a child whose dream had come true: he appeared on balconies, he thrust out his chin, he paraded with raised arm between two rows of cattle at an agricultural fair. But he was also the man who put forth a few excellent ideas that would find realization in the years between the two World Wars: corporativism, that economic system that was meant to transcend both capitalism and Socialism and that was a Fascist propaganda success. It was he who brought into being those enterprises that still exist today in Italy and in which private investment and state capital are commingled.

And it was the same man again who was caught in the teeth of tragedy and cowardice when, at the end of the war, he sacrificed his own son-in-law, Count Galeazzo Ciano, who was executed by a Fascist firing-squad in Verona.

Here this scene blends with some of Verdi's operas, with a whole Italian tradition that dallies with violence, that shifts from the farcical to the heroic, from smiles to tears, from friendship to treachery. Mussolini has been called a hero and a villain of opera. He was thoroughly Italian. He embodied the defects—and also the qualities—of an inventive, warmhearted people that was still in the process of being born as a nation in the decades between the wars—and this in spite of the antiquity of a culture that is at the very source of western civilization.

But Italy had not achieved national unity until 1870. The First World War—the 1914 war—was her first great national war. And Mussolini appeared immediately afterward, a kind of Nasser of the years between the wars. He renewed Italians' pride in themselves.

That was why he was popular for so long in the United States, for example. No one who lived in a Little Italy, dominated for years, more or less contemptuously, by Irish and WASPs, could have any notion of the domestic reality of Mussolini's Italy. They knew only that the country ruled by Il Duce was respected, and that it was successful in some of its undertakings. When Italo Balbo arrived in New York at the head of an aerial squadron that was going around the world, his reception was hysterical. Italian-Americans reacted like men who had been wounded in their national pride.

But the war came, and eyes were harshly opened. Mussolini exposed his incapacities, his blindness.

Nonetheless, that ultimate failure cannot make us forget that he was an innovator, an inventor. The inventor of Fascism: a movement that proliferated in the world like a cancer. And, on October 28, 1942, Hitler could only acknowledge the accomplishments of Il Duce: "I am convinced that your historic March on Rome," he wrote to Mussolini, "created a turning point in the history of the world. When you were leading the Fascist Revolution to victory, Duce, I was still battling against fortune's reverses, and my struggle ended in a serious defeat and for myself, personally, imprisonment for more than a year."

In thus alluding to the failure of his beer-hall *Putsch* in Munich in 1923, Hitler clearly acknowledged that he had intended to emulate the March on Rome, as others sought to imitate it in Spain, in France, even in England, where there was a British Union of Fascists.

Moreover, it must be conceded that, until 1938–1940, Mussolini had succeeded in retaining control of his country without too much recourse to violence. The Fascist system, which forced thousands of opponents into exile, was a clear manifestation of an Italian reality. It was the war that sent the whole country into resolute opposition.

The story of Fascism in Italy and of Mussolini, then, is not a simple one. To understand it, one must attain to sympathy with a people.

I am of Italian origin through my mother. I was born in Nice, barely twenty miles from the Italian frontier. When the Fascist troops entered Nice in 1942, I was a child, but I remember those soldiers in their plumed helmets who paraded smiling through our streets.

From that moment forth I began to be marked by Italy, by her culture, by her traditions. Later I sought to understand how this nation—gay and solemn, optimistic and somber, frivolous and profound—could have fallen under the sway of the *fasces*. I began my investigation by questioning my relatives, my friends, strangers, notables. In newspapers and archives I discovered a reality that was neglected by historians too concerned with what goes on at the summit of governments. In short, I proceeded like a man who sets off in search not so much of great events as of other men and of a climate—political, psychological, social.

I plunged myself into Italy's past. As if I were seeking personal recollections in my memory. And to a degree that was the case, for as a child I had indeed traveled to Bologna and discovered children of my own age wearing black uniforms and playing already at being soldiers.

In long hours of talk with Italians abroad—anti-Fascist refugees in France and workers who had gone to find jobs far from their peninsula—I learned also what Fascist Italy had come to mean to them.

In such ways, I think, I have been able to get into the heart of a country and into the hearts of its people.

My greatest satisfaction has been the translation of this book into Italian and its reception by Italian readers and critics as an authentic study of those twenty years of the Fascist era . . . those twenty dramatic years that began fifty years ago.

October, 1972   MAX GALLO

Foreword

ON OCTOBER 28, 1942, in the midst of the war, Adolf Hitler sent Benito Mussolini a message of congratulations on the twentieth anniversary of Mussolini's seizure of power at the time of the March on Rome:

"I am convinced that your historic March of twenty years ago created a turning point in the history of the world," Der Führer wrote. "When you were leading the Fascist Revolution to victory, Duce, I was still battling against fortune's reverses, and my struggle ended in a serious defeat and for myself, personally, imprisonment for more than a year."

These remarks by Der Führer do indeed correspond to the reality, but who today remembers that reality?

The eruption of the Panzer into history, the SS, Naziism, its flames and its ashes, the hoarse voice of Der Führer, have all thrust the Italian precursors into the background, overshadowed those young men in black shirts who began to wield their clubs in 1920, who bombed the Ethiopians, who hailed the bombastic grandiloquence of Il Duce in 1922.

Yet, when Hitler came to power in 1933, the great "strong man" of Europe for the past eleven years had been Il Duce of Fascism, and the prestige of Mussolini and his movement was such that Goering, Hess, and Hitler turned to the Fascists for counsel, for money, and for arms. The Italian ambassador in Berlin played Lord Protector to the nascent Third Reich.

This alone would be a great deal for Fascism and its leader, but it was not all. In Greece and in Ethiopia, as in Spain, it was Mussolini's Italy that was the first to shake the structure of Europe and to hurl the most violent insults at the League of Nations. Here again Mussolini and Fascism made the breach in which Ribbentrop, Hitler, and their soldiers were to be swallowed. What is amazing is the fact that Mussolini's Italy, which evoked contempt and praise from 1922 to 1939 and remained at the center of European policy, should be buried today beneath so much ignorance, so many misjudgments, and, above all, oblivion.

Where once Churchill, Laval, Gandhi, and the world press acclaimed Il Duce's "handsome countenance of a peasant emperor" or that "Fascist movement that has rendered a service to the entire world" (Churchill), where once there was talk of nothing but "the new avenues opened by Fascist corporativism," transcending Socialism and Naziism, many people today view Fascism as a surrogate for Naziism. For some of them, Mussolini's Italy and the twenty years of Fascist rule were only the tale of a pallid clownish imitator of Hitler, a carnival Caesar devoid of historical significance, while for others those twenty years were a trivial parenthesis in the history of Italy.

Yet there is not a magazine in Italy that does not dedicate at least one article a month to Mussolini and Fascism; one party, the *Movimento sociale italiano* (Italian Social Movement), frankly avows Mussolini as its inspiration and even went to the extent of distributing photographs of him and recordings of his speeches in the electoral campaign of April, 1963.

These are significant indications: a system cannot survive for twenty-one years without impregnating, impressing, deeply marking a nation, even if its greatest imprint remains the resistance that it aroused.

In order to understand Italy, her past and her present, one must know Fascism; just as one must know it in order to grasp international policy during the period between the two World Wars and to uncover the origins of Naziism and of the war of 1939.

That is why I have sought to demonstrate the importance of Mussolini's Italy and of those twenty years of Fascist rule for the world and for Italy.

I have tried to sketch a complete but also a living history. Nor could it be otherwise, for that period of violence and unflagging passions—the history of a system, but also the history of a man who went from nothing to the seizure of power and whose corpse was tossed into a public square in Milan amid shouts, laughter, and spittle. Like, in an earlier time, the corpse of one of those gladiators or actors of that Roman Empire that, as Duce, he had professed to bring back to life.

M.G.

FREQUENT ABBREVIATIONS USED IN THE BOOK:

Popolo or *P.d.I.*: *Popolo d'Italia*, Mussolini's newspaper

CGL: Confederazione generale del lavoro (Italian Federation of Labor)

PNF: Partito nazionale fascista (National Fascist Party)

Acknowledgments

I SHOULD LIKE to thank Robert Aron and Marcel Jullian for their invaluable encouragement. Many Italian friends contributed to my work with their recollections and their documents, as well as their guidance through the vast Italian bibliography on Fascism. I have in mind especially A. Greborio, who made all the material in his private collection available to me. I hereby acknowledge my debt to all who have helped.

Part I
THE ORIGINS
OF FASCISM
AND THE
CONQUEST
OF POWER

(1883–October 30, 1922)

1

A Young Country, A Young Man
(1883–1914)

"Outside history, man is nothing."—MUSSOLINI (June 11, 1932)

AT ABOUT ELEVEN O'CLOCK in the morning of October 30, 1922, three taxis, trailed by a group of young men who shouted as they ran, stopped at the main gate of the Quirinal Palace in Rome. A crowd waiting nearby tried to identify the men who got out of the cars and were swallowed up under the portico. In a few seconds their silhouettes had vanished, and only the silent, braid-bedecked doorkeeper was left beneath the two statues by Bernini. The crowd had seen nothing, but a historic event had just taken place: Mussolini, black-shirted and bare-headed, was being received by King Vittorio Emanuele III, who was about to entrust the government of Italy to him. "The Fascist Era" was beginning.

Who was this thick-set, heavy-faced Italian who, at a resolute pace, had climbed the staircase framed by heavy bronze rails that leads from the square to the gate of the palace? The crowd of Romans waited outside the Quirinal as if hoping, at the sight of him, to identify the man and the meaning of the event. The crowd was curious rather than enthusiastic; it could not guess that for the next twenty-one years its fate and Italy's would depend on that thirty-nine-year-old man.

Young men in black shirts came and went with much gesturing in front of the peaceable spectators in their ordinary business clothes. In the distance, as if nothing were happening, the street-cars and the workers' bicycles continued on their way, and it is against the background of these contradictory fleeting images that

3

one faces the question of the country that was accepting a dictator in that Roman morning.

But a country is first of all a history that does not readily lend itself to being fragmented into isolated periods. If one wishes to understand Mussolini's Italy and to know the man, antecedents and points of reference must be traced far in advance of that morning; one must go back to the major characteristics of Italy's personality as she was at the time when the man who would profess to recreate her was born and grew up.

Mussolini was born on July 29, 1883; twenty-two years earlier, on March 23, 1861, King Vittorio Emanuele II of Piedmont had been proclaimed king of Italy after a vote by both chambers of Parliament; but the ceremony was performed in Turin, for that sober city, cloaked in the fogs of the Po, was still the capital of the kingdom. Rome was not conquered until September 20, 1870, and it was not until a year later that the king took up residence in the Quirinal. It was at that time, after a long struggle, almost an Odyssey, that Italy had at last achieved unity and a capital. Thus the *Risorgimento*, that resurrection whose stages had been established and whose accomplishments had been garnered by Cavour, and in which Garibaldi had represented the vital essence of the people, reached its conclusion on the banks of the Tiber as a monarchist, conservative triumph. It was only twelve years after the king's entrance into his Roman palace that Mussolini was born.

In the life of a nation, a dozen years are youth itself, even if, as in Italy's case, the citizens of the peninsula derived a feeling of Italianness from the language of Dante, their civilization, their history, their struggle for unity. And it was this nation, whose regional differences set Milan against Naples, whose unification had been achieved by Cavour, a man born to the French language who had never seen Sicily, Naples, or Rome, it was this nation, still as puny as an adolescent, that in 1914 was to be confronted with a European war that was at times to shake the foundations of nations whose histories were counted in centuries. If one loses sight of these essential premises, one cannot comprehend the magnitude of the crisis that carried Mussolini to power between 1919 and 1922. Nor can one then understand the man who "was born on a Sunday, July 29, 1883, at Varano dei Costa, a little cluster of old houses built on a height of Dovia, a hamlet in the commune of Predappio, near Forlì in the Romagna,"[1] this Benito Mussolini who was the son of an Italy still in the process of being born, a

[1] Mussolini's *Autobiography*.

nation whose youth was evidenced by the persistence and the vigor of its dialects as well as its illiteracy and its violent customs.

It is enough to consider these simple statistics: in 1882, one year before Mussolini's birth, the right of suffrage was extended to every citizen who had completed his elementary schooling, and these totaled one and a half million voters; in 1892, when Mussolini was ten years old, the total was three million, or 9.57 percent of the population!

Under such conditions, political circles were isolated from the people, of whose real problems they were ignorant, and they rejected Catholicism out of fear of the Vatican: since 1871, after all, the church had forbidden the faithful to take part in elections and the pope had regarded himself as a prisoner in unified Italy. Hence parliamentary circles were cut off, torn by clannishness, by personal rivalries, by corruption, and by self-interest, and thus incapable of breathing life into political parties.

Such was the kingdom in which Mussolini grew up.

The peasants around him in the Romagna spoke in dialect. If its use was forbidden in the Mussolinis' home, it was because Signora Mussolini was a school teacher. Her husband, Alessandro, was a blacksmith, boastful, garrulous, a wencher and a drinker, and also a correspondent for the pro-anarchist newspapers of Forlì; he preened himself on being a writer on Socialism and the revolution.

Now the political and social system was already being challenged in this Italy in which public opinion was composed of some seven or eight hundred persons, because public expenditures and taxes were increasing. Whether arrogant or paternalistic, the members of Parliament whose dream it was to forge a mighty state never boggled in fact at casting the whole burden of their ambition on the shoulders of a population that was not allowed to vote. Suffering persisted, and sometimes it grew worse.

The Mussolini family was always short at the end of the month. But the father had built a small threshing machine, which he rented out to peasants, and the mother, Rosa, born Maltoni, contributed her salary to the family funds. When she died at the age of forty-six in 1905, worn out by work and devotion, Alessandro moved to Forlì and set up as an innkeeper. There he lived with Anna Guidi, the widow of a penniless peasant, one of those innumerable peasants overburdened with debts and taxes who had lost whatever little they had owned and become members of the vast army of *braccianti*, those miserable day-laborers. By way of illustration: in a large Sardinian village, Ottana, the peasants owed eighteen years' taxes! And none of these *braccianti*, like Anna

5   *A Young Country, A Young Man*

Guidi's husband, ever earned more than one *lira* (about twenty cents) for a day's labor!

It is understandable that Alessandro Mussolini could assemble an enthusiastic audience when, before the marveling eyes of his son, he read aloud the articles that he wrote for such little newspapers as *la Rivendicazione* or *la Lotta*. His listeners applauded his forceful platitudes—"*bourgeois* society and justice are monstrous but crumbling structures"—and everyone had a drink on them.

Though in comparison to the miserable day-laborers Alessandro was privileged, he too experienced first-hand the hardships of his time. In his new household—Anna Guidi was already the mother of five daughters—the youngest girl, Rachele, who was born in 1892 and who was later to be Benito's wife, worked as a maid for a family named Chiadini in Forlì, earning three *lire* a month.

In the Mussolinis' home, as in many other Italian homes, there was one dish for the evening meal, *polenta*—maize flour—cooked in water: meat was a rarity, almost unknown. Yet the Mussolinis never suffered the hunger and the absolute destitution that were familiar then to many Italian families. Benito's childhood was sheltered from the hardships of labor and hunger. He was a quarrelsome, brawling boy, sharp in claiming his share in the petty thefts committed by the children who ranged through all the villages:

"Twenty-five years ago," he wrote later, "I was an arrogant and violent child. Some of my playmates still have scars on their faces from the stones that I threw at them. A nomad by instinct, I wandered along the river from morning until night, robbing birds' nests and stealing fruit. I went to mass. . . . I followed my mother. . . . I helped my father in his modest, difficult work. . . ."

At that time the Mussolinis lived in a house that was certainly simple—three scantily furnished rooms—but it contained the essentials: the iron bed, the sideboard, the wardrobe; one of the rooms, as long as Mussolini's mother was alive, was used as a school room. His mother, whom Benito loved devotedly, saw to it that he received a solid education. She enrolled him in the Salesian school in Faenza, where discipline was strict and inequality of treatment among the pupils was the rule: in the dining room there were three tables—one for the young nobles, one for the rich, and one for the poor. Arrogant and quarrelsome, Mussolini—who had told his mother: "One day Italy will be afraid of me"—chafed at the bit; he threw an inkwell into a teacher's face, he tried to run away, he was caught, he stabbed a classmate with a pocket knife. Nonetheless the school did not expel him: he was a good student. But his family had no money, and in the end Benito had to be withdrawn from the school when a request for a scholarship was refused.

He was then sent to a boarding school in Forlimpopoli, but he was soon forbidden to live in the school because of his behavior, though he was allowed to continue his studies as a day pupil, lodging in the house of an old woman. A penniless scapegrace, he developed a sudden passion for music.

To be a student in such a school was a privilege that was anything but common among Italians of his age. At that time almost 80 percent of the population in the south was illiterate; that *Mezzogiorno* has always been the cancer of Italy. Circumstances unfavorable by nature were aggravated by the burden of history: uncultivated estates owned by absentee landlords side by side with inadequate little plots in a region of arid soil where peasants endure lifetimes in prey to malaria, hunger, exhaustion, and ignorance. The Mafia and the Camorra control the country, and their "clients" are the voters: such was the start of Vittorio Emanuele Orlando, who became Premier of Italy at the end of the First World War. In contrast to such conditions, of course, the Mussolinis' Romagna seemed a land of privilege.

And yet, even though the south was stagnating, even though the growth in the population was making the situation still worse (in spite of emigration, between 1871 and 1914 the Italian population increased by more than eleven million to a total of thirty-seven million, and population density rose from thirty-four to fifty-two inhabitants per square mile), there was a sharp upsurge in the Italian economy at the time when young Benito Mussolini left the school at Forlimpopoli in order to start his training as a teacher.

The years between 1880 and 1910 were in fact decisive for Italian capitalism; the impetus was especially strong after 1900. In that year FIAT was founded with a capital of eight hundred thousand *lire* and by 1913 Italy was already exporting four thousand cars; the textile industry expanded so much that in 1908 its cotton sector was menaced by overproduction; powerful hydro-electric installations were established on the rivers. But this development was peculiar to northern Italy, and in large measure it was accomplished at the expense of the Italian small farmers who were sacrificed to trade treaties, especially in the Mezzogiorno.

It was a Sicilian who presided over this immolation of the south to the north: Francesco Crispi, a disciple of Mazzini and a participant in the expedition of Garibaldi's Thousand. It was said of him that he sought to copy Bismarck and Boulanger, and, like the Iron Chancellor, he wanted to leave his mark on his country. His long tenure of power—from 1887 to 1896—brought into the open the alliance that was being formed between the intellectual or agrarian middle class of the south and the industrial interests of the north.

One day Alessandro Mussolini said to his son: "You will be the Crispi of tomorrow."

Actually, regardless whether the elder Mussolini really said this, the remark has a certain validity, for Crispi's ideas and his style represent one of those deep-lying veins that exist in the history of a nation, revealing an aspect of its character, to which statesmen return at long intervals and under varying conditions, repeating, sometimes unconsciously, the language of remote precursors.

The Sicilian, Crispi, initially a revolutionary and then an authoritarian minister, the artisan of a policy of reaction and repression, projected himself as the defender of order against the extremist parties, even attempted a reconciliation with the Vatican, and, above all, undertook a program of prestige that culminated in an alliance with Germany and a colonial adventure in Abyssinia. In actuality Crispi was an admirer of Germany because he was a hater of France, but also because of the fascination in which he was caught by the strong state built by Bismarck.

The gradients that led from Crispism to Fascism were manifested thus in the field of foreign policy, in confirmation of the principle that the choices available to a nation are not infinite; and thus we can see what Fascism owed to Crispism and how, for all its appearance of being new, Mussolini's movement derived from a national tradition.

And Crispi, who loved to play at being chancellor, Crispi, who was so solicitous of the nation's honor, wore the chains of the Triple Alliance, accepted its contempt for Italy—"a whore who works the streets," Bismarck said in 1879—and led his country into the disaster of Adowa: five thousand men killed, including two generals and three hundred officers, and all the artillery left in the hands of the Abyssinians.

Standing erect with his companions in the school room, Benito Mussolini paid tribute to the dead of Adowa and swore to avenge them. This fact should be kept in mind because of what it demonstrates: the wound suffered by Italian national feeling at Adowa in 1896. But others reacted to the defeat at Adowa as a proof of the foolishness of colonial adventures. One of these was Alessandro Mussolini. He took up collections for the wounded and sick in the Abyssinian army; anti-militarist demonstrations broke out all over Italy. There were shouts of *"Evviva Menelik,"* and crowds tore up railway tracks in order to prevent the departure of troop trains.

This was how the energy of the new Socialist tendency expressed itself.

In August, 1892, the Italian Workers' Party was created in Genoa. But this party was the heir to a long tradition. Alessandro Mussolini aptly epitomized all the idle talk, the generosity of spirit, the anarchy, and the confusion that co-existed in the ancestors of Italian Socialism.

He was a member of the International and his house was the theater of unceasing discussion. It was in tribute to Benito Juarez, the hero of Mexican independence, that he named his son Benito, adding Amilcare and Andrea in honor of two Italian Socialists, Amilcare Cipriani and Andrea Costa. And yet this revolutionary, this man of violence, whose influence on Benito was indubitable but difficult to measure, was also a reformist, a legalitarian like all the "great men" in the party—Leonida Bissolati, Ivanoe Bonomi, Claudio Treves.

These Socialists, however, proclaimed themselves Marxists when it came to philosophy. About 1890 Antonio Labriola discovered Marxism and wrote to Engels; in 1891 a young Socialist, Filippo Turati, and his comrade, Anna Kulishova, founded a magazine, *Critica sociale*, in Milan for the propagation of Marxist ideas; above all, in 1896, still in Milan, Bissolati founded *Avanti!*, a Socialist daily whose editor in 1912 was to be Benito Mussolini.

In 1896 he was only a student in the Forlimpopoli school—where he played the trombone in the band—a turbulent pupil who watched one day as a party of emigrants was leaving for Brazil. Nine families loaded down with bundles, and without a thought of ever returning, were leaving *la terza Italia*, "the third Italy"—"the middle-class Italy that denies the poor workers a hunk of bread," Alessandro Mussolini wrote in *Pensiero romagnolo*. Like his father, Benito was deeply moved, and he always remembered the tragic spectacle.

Emigration in those declining years of the nineteenth century was increasing. While Crispi, with all the impulsiveness of an authoritarian southerner, was conjuring up the grandeur of Italy, whole masses of Italians were abandoning their young country, driven out of it by hunger; and this was taking place precisely when Italian capitalism was growing in the north. More than eight million Italians left their country between 1876 and 1914. Between 1900 and 1914 there were four hundred thousand departures every year. Alessandro Mussolini and his son were rightly disturbed, for these emigrants were packed together on decks and in gangways for an arduous journey from which there was no return.

There were those in the Veneto and the Romagna who, seduced by fraudulent advertisements, sold all that they owned in order to pay their passage and then, completely ruined, appealed across the Atlantic for help.

This hemorrhage of population, corroboration of the misery of the southern masses, explains many aspects of the Abyssinian undertaking, which was not so much an attempt to obtain raw materials, markets, and profits—Italian capitalism was far from having reached that stage of maturity—but rather an endeavor to export the misery by exporting the miserable.

Starting with Crispi, then, Italian colonial policy laid its stress on the necessity of finding areas to be populated by its proletarians. This was the origin of the idea of a "poor nation's colonialism" of a "proletarian Italy" guided by need, not by the desire for conquest that inspired the insatiable imperialist nations, Great Britain and France. These themes were to be those of Fascism.

The word *Fascio*,* furthermore, began to appear in Italian political life at this time—in Sicily, from which so many of the emigrants had gone. Workers' *Fasci*—Workers' Associations—were founded in May, 1892, first in Palermo and then throughout the island. The movement spread rapidly, spontaneously, and violently, demanding the redistribution of the land and reductions in taxes. Riots broke out in 1893. In 1894 Crispi proclaimed a state of siege in the whole of Sicily. Anarchist violence grew in the north. At the same time, in France, Sante Caserio, an anarchist, assassinated President Sadi Carnot on June 24, 1894. It was a time when, in the absence of legal representation, revolt was expressed through assassination. There were heated arguments in Alessandro Mussolini's house and Benito was present at excited discussions. The sections of the Workers' Party were dissolved. In 1897 another anarchist, Acciarito, attempted to assassinate King Umberto I. Social tension, heightened by the scandals and corruption of parliamentary circles, reached its climax in Milan. Crispi had been replaced by the Marquis di Rudinì when the outbreaks began on May 6, 1898.

The riot—a spontaneous, unarmed hunger riot—raged in the center of the city, which General Bava-Beccaris put under a state of siege. *Avanti!* and the *Osservatore cattolico* were suspended,

* Literally, *fascio* means a bundle or a sheaf. Its use in this political sense goes back to nineteenth-century Sicily, and the word was chosen to emphasize the extremely close bond that united all the members of the group. The *fasces*—bundle or sheaf of rods—carried by the *lictor* in ancient Rome became the official Fascist emblem.—Translator.

and their editors, Turati and Don Albertario, were arrested: manacled at the wrists and chained to each other, they were paraded through the city, where the rising was crushed with a minimum of one hundred dead, including women and children.

It is interesting to reflect that it was in Milan that the first demonstrations for participation in the war were held in 1914, it was in Milan that Fascism made its great start, Milan where in 1898 "the bourgeoisie thought for a moment that the end of the world was at hand, the authorities thought that they were not strong enough to resist, and the revolution that did not exist became in the end a real fact because everyone thought that it must exist."[2] Repression, however, did not prove fruitful: in the elections of June 3, 1900, the Socialists won fifteen seats.

A man of fifty-eight, a cautious Piedmontese with regular, delicate features, had led the opposition against Crispi. He was Giuseppe Giolitti, a native of Mondovì, whose personality was to dominate the history of Italy until Mussolini's seizure of power in 1922. A brilliant jurist, he had had a long administrative career before he became a deputy in 1882 and a minister under Crispi. His administration began in 1902 and lasted until 1914, with a few brief interruptions. But, as the final manifestation of the crisis of 1898, Gaetano Bresci, an anarchist chosen by lot among his comrades for the purpose, returned to Italy from Paterson, New Jersey, in 1900. Two years earlier, Umberto I had decorated General Bava-Beccaris for his achievement in Milan and his defense of civilization. On July 29, 1900, as the King was leaving Monza for his palace after having attended a gymnastic contest, Bresci, standing on a seat, fired four revolver shots at the King and killed him. The reaction was intense.

Benito Mussolini was now seventeen years old. He wore a flowing black tie, like the poets and the anarchists, and in Avanti! for February 1, 1901, there was a story that the student comrade, Mussolini, had paid tribute to Giuseppe Verdi in a much applauded speech.[3] With the twentieth century Italy acquired a new king, Vittorio Emanuele III; a new statesman, Giolitti; and, somewhere in the mass of her inhabitants, a thin young man who liked to recite poetry and who had just graduated brilliantly as a teacher.

"I too had a diploma . . . a diploma that made it possible for me to earn my livelihood," Mussolini wrote in his autobiography. "I was eighteen years old." This autobiography is the first of his writings that has come down to us. It shows him as he was then, a

[2] Villari, quoted by M. Vaussard, Histoire de l'Italie contemporaine, p. 59.
[3] Quoted by Paolo Monelli in Mussolini: The Intimate Life of a Demagogue, trans., Brigid Maxwell (New York: Vanguard, 1954).

nervous, temperamental young man, walking quickly along the paths of the commune of Predappio with a book in his hand, walking without raising his eyes from it, declaiming. He had joined the Socialist Party in 1900 and, to the despair of his extremely pious mother, he no longer went to church. One can picture him, ill-dressed, fueling his inner fire with heroic reading, proud of his brand-new yet superficial culture, overflowing with energy, and doing nothing. For in those early years of the twentieth century Italy had a plethora of teachers and a dearth of schools. Straining at the leash, Mussolini spent an entire year in the search for work. He was *disoccupato*: the Italian word is the best for that condition in which anger and violence accumulate little by little. He tried to get a job as a secretary in the town hall of Predappio. The mayor turned him down. "One day you'll accept him as your boss," Alessandro Mussolini threatened. But that accomplished nothing, and Benito went on trying to find some way of "earning his keep." For every job that became vacant—this happened to him in Ancona and again in Legnano—there were dozens of applicants, mature men but reduced, like Mussolini, to unemployment. What better soil for rebellion than a young intelligence confident of its achievements (these latter confirmed by a diploma), flattered by its scholastic successes—Mussolini had topped his class in Italian literature and history in the normal school—and feeling rejected by an established society that was unjust in its refusal to recognize either certificates or the worth that they represented.

Full of bitterness, his mouth acrid with sarcasms, the young "outsider" Mussolini, stripped of his class, talked of setting fire to his books and his diploma.

That was not enough to assuage his thirst for action, his thirst for being. He was eighteen years old; he threw himself desperately into amatory diversions, chasing girls and having them on stairways, quickly, brutally, trying to relieve himself of his desire and, in vain, to lose himself, to satisfy himself in the frenzy. He frequented village dances, he got into fights. In remembrance of this chaotic period he retained throughout his life a preference for quick copulations . . . and a syphilitic infection about which he did little. Fortunately for him, in February, 1902, the Socialist municipality of Gualtieri, near Reggio Emilia, was looking for a substitute teacher, and, out of political sympathy for the father and the son, it chose Mussolini. From February to June of 1902, then, he performed the duties and became familiar with the life of a teacher. It bored him. He was like an unused force. He became the lover of a married woman whom he dominated, he continued getting into fights, he went to dances; violence flashed from his eyes; even his attire was disturbing. He wrote a few articles for *la Giustizia*, the paper belonging to the Socialist, Camillo Prampolini, and he established contacts with the Socialists who had formed the local cooperative. There he found good, peaceable peasants who, just as in the whole Po Valley, had organized solidly based cooperative organizations that were beginning to centralize purchases and sales and that constituted the economic foundation of reformist Socialism. Young Mussolini was disappointed: here was no revolution, only legality and mutual help.

In contrast to these settled, mature men, he embodied the young man of uncertain fate, the unsatisfied semi-intellectual—he was earning fifty-six *lire* (about eleven dollars) a month—who is looking for a road to glory. He thought of going to Madagascar, and then in June, 1902, when his work as a substitute ended, he telegraphed to his mother, received from her the money that he had requested—forty-five *lire* (nine dollars)—and went to Switzerland.

Switzerland at that time was the haven of everything that Europe contained in the way of outlaws, Socialists, revolutionaries, anarchists. Pursued by the Okhrana, the Russians in particular were numerous: Plekhanov, Axelrod, Vera Zassulitcha, who had fired at the chief of police of St. Petersburg in February, 1878. They were concentrated in the Carouge quarter in Geneva, and they gathered at the Landolt beer saloon. It was from Geneva that the parcels of *Iskra*, the newspaper inspired by Lenin, were shipped to Russia. He and his wife, Natasha Krupskaya, moved to Geneva in April, 1903, less than a year after Mussolini's arrival. Young Benito wandered about that exiles' Switzerland. Just as he was crossing the border at Chiasso, he had learned of the arrest of his father, who, with several other Socialists, was wanted for having destroyed the voting urns in Predappio.

In Switzerland, Benito was a nobody who had to survive. He worked hard at a stonemason's job and yet he went hungry, and the lushness of the tourist palaces revolted him; he read the menu of a hotel: "enough to drive you mad, those swine. . . ." His clothes grew frayed and filthy. He took a certain satisfaction in fantasy: "I was filled with an immeasurable melancholy," he noted, "and on the shore of the Lake of Geneva I asked myself whether it was worth the trouble of living through another day." He spent one night in an empty packing crate under the arches of the big bridge in Lausanne and, as he came out in the morning, he was arrested for vagrancy. He had hit bottom. But not for long. Among the Italian emigrants there were few intellectuals. Very soon Mussolini acquired the stature of a daring rebel. He had arrived at the age

for military service and, since he had not gone home, he was sentenced *in absentia* to a year in prison as a deserter. He began to rise. He became secretary of the masons' union in Lausanne, he gave Italian lessons, he wrote a few articles. Rather than misery, it was a romanticized and disordered bohemianism that began for him.

On March 18, 1904, at a meeting in Geneva, he met a Russian revolutionary, Angelica Balabanova. An ugly little woman, she was quite cultivated and multi-lingual. She became interested in the young man, the worst dressed and dirtiest of all the exiles, a constant blasphemer, who at the same time kept thrusting out his jaw and assuming the postures of a leader. She thought him timid, initiated a friendship with him, and found work for him: every morning Mussolini pushed a wine merchant's loaded handcart through the streets. Above all, Balabanova made him study.

Actually, although he always wore a medallion bearing the likeness of Karl Marx, Mussolini had read nothing by Marx except *The Communist Manifesto*. Stimulated by Balabanova, he began to attend the university in Lausanne and to visit the library; he learned French and German. With Balabanova he translated Karl Kautsky's pamphlet, *Revolution on the March*, from the German, and Prince Kropotkin's *Remarks of a Rebel* from the French. He broadened his reading—Nietzsche, Max Stirner, Louis-Auguste Blanqui, Schopenhauer—and engaged in discussions with the exiles: the Russians, the Poles, and of course the Italians, including the Socialist, Giacinto Menotti Serrati. He was offered a job in New York on the staff of a newspaper called *The Proletarian*, but his mother was ill and he had to refuse. At last he had emerged from anonymity.

In that crucible of men and ideas that was Switzerland at the beginning of the century, Mussolini worked himself free of the "regionalism" that is so common among Italians. He had broken the chafing yoke of the Romagna. He would go back there, of course, but in Switzerland he lived and vibrated with all the revolutionaries of Europe. However superficial it might have been, he acquired a certain culture; above all, he met men, he held his own among them, occasionally against the most illustrious of the time. In a controversial lecture, for instance, he debated the Belgian Socialist, Emile Vandervelde, on the subject of Christ.

For this young man, who used to follow his mother to church, was extremely anti-clerical. On September 7, 1903, a pastor named Tagliatella spoke about God. Mussolini rose, pulled out his watch, and placed it on a table.

"God does not exist," he declared. "You want proof? Here. God, if you exist, you have five minutes in which to strike me dead. I spit on you. I curse you." He waited in silence, and then he said: "As you can clearly see, God does not exist."

This often-told tale is an excellent picture of him as he was in those days—and as he would always be: adept at finding the right gesture, the right attitude to cause surprise. There was much of the showman in him. There was also, in this young man who stood up in the middle of a lecture hall against accredited orators, a determination to push himself into the foreground, to achieve distinction, and it appears in that comic challenge to God: "Strike me dead."

He succeeded so well in acquiring a name that on April 6, 1904, he was expelled from the canton of Geneva after he had been denounced to the Italian consul as an anarchist. He moved to France, lingered briefly in Annemasse, and, if certain reports are to be credited, became a stool-pigeon for the French police. In Switzerland a Socialist councilor, Dr. Wyss, raised a question in the Grand Council of Geneva concerning his expulsion, and the Roman newspapers reported that "Geneva has gotten rid of the Socialist agitator, Mussolini."

Thus matured and imbued with the revolutionary climate of cosmopolitan Geneva, he returned to Italy in November of 1904. Under a new law an amnesty for minor offenses had been proclaimed, by way of celebrating the birth of Umberto di Savoia, but Mussolini remained in the police files as a "dangerous anarchist." And in truth he was no longer merely the young school teacher with inchoate aspirations. Undoubtedly his stay in Switzerland had confirmed him in the conviction that he could "succeed." He had written for foreign newspapers, he had given lectures, with Serrati he had founded an International Library for Rationalist Propaganda. He had already known prison and the exaltation of being chosen as a leader by compatriots; he had been the lover of exiles, including a Russian woman with whom he had gone to the French border. And he was only twenty-one years old.

He returned to Italy in order to perform his military service, but he could consider that in Switzerland he had completed his schooling as a revolutionary.

When Mussolini returned to Italy, the political situation had altered.

The Socialist tendency to which he adhered had broadened. In 1903 there were thirty-three Socialist deputies in the Italian Parliament. Paradoxically, however, although they had gained in impor-

A Young Country, A Young Man

tance, the leaders of the Socialist movement had in all essentials reinforced their reformist beliefs.

This was because in Giolitti they had found a statesman who had evolved a policy of collaboration. The problem was to win participation in the government for the Socialists. In 1903 Giolitti offered a ministry to Turati, who had been imprisoned in 1898. Turati refused it, but the significance of Giolitti's gesture was in no way diminished thereby: the Italian government was giving up violence and systematic repression and turning toward conciliation. Social legislation was enacted, and workers' cooperatives obtained the right to take part in enterprises of public utility. They were to assemble large financial contributions, run large enterprises, and distribute the profits among their members. Laws governing a weekly day of rest, night work, contracts, and workmen's compensation brought improvements in the lot of labor. Under Giolitti a middle-class Italy founded on a contented proletarian class strove to come into being. In the workers' houses the whitewashed walls bore two portraits: one of Karl Marx, the other of Giolitti.

If Giolitti was thus able to apply a social program that benefited certain sectors of the Italian proletariat, it was because the economic upsurge was vigorous and brought forth an aristocracy of labor that was cognizant of the advantages of Giolitti's government. This aristocracy was the rock on which the parliamentary Socialist group led by Turati, Bissolati, Treves, and Bonomi built. It would be impossible to under-estimate the importance of these men: as reformists, they were in effect accepting the monarchy, no doubt implicitly, but in fact they were united with the king, who was the personification of the nation. Hence it was clear that, thus interjected into the monarchist state, they could form a Socialist and national left wing in the face of crisis.

Young Mussolini was then at the opposite extreme from this deferential Socialism. After his military service—during which his mother died—with the Tenth Bersaglieri of Verona, from 1904 to 1906, Benito Mussolini obtained another teaching position. During his two years in uniform he had shown himself to be a good soldier: this young anarchist under police surveillance had made a show of practiced patriotism and consistent discipline. "Why," he wrote, "should a good soldier not at the same time be a fighter in the class struggle?"

Once he was discharged, however, Benito returned to a life of disorder. He taught in Carnie and Tomezzo, earning fifty *lire* (ten dollars) a month, but it bored him; he was often drunk and there were more and more one-night loves. At the end of this "year of brutalization," during which he even contemplated suicide—he learned now that he had syphilis—he went to France. He organized the Italian workers of Marseilles, from which he was soon expelled: the police escorted him to the border. He spent a few months in Predappio, then in Bologna, dabbling; he managed to acquire a certificate as a teacher of French literature and went off to teach French in a technical school in Oneglia, near Genoa. But everywhere he was either preceded or followed by his police record. In Oneglia, after he had gotten his job, he was described as "a dangerous revolutionary Socialist expelled from Switzerland and France, the organizer of insurrectional demonstrations in the Romagna." The prefect attempted, without success, to exert pressure on the director of the school to dismiss Mussolini. But the director stood firm, and Mussolini, who had met in Oneglia a son of Serrati, the Socialist whom he had known in Switzerland, wrote articles for *la Lima*, the Ligurian Socialists' newspaper. For the most part his articles were directed against the clergy, but he also expounded Georges Sorel's views on violence. For the twenty-fifth anniversary of the death of Karl Marx, on March 14, 1908, he wrote: "What we must do is not study the world but transform it. . . . The interests of the proletariat are opposed to those of the middle class. No agreement between them is possible. One or the other must disappear."

Thus Mussolini's antagonism to the reformists was borne out. What was important was the fact that, while his categorical position ran counter to the thinking of the parliamentary group and the Socialist leaders, as well as the privileged element in the proletariat, it voiced the feelings of many Italian workers and peasants.

For the benefactions of Giolittism had reached only a part of the proletariat—could it have been otherwise? Above all, they had been achieved only in the north of Italy and in the industrial sector, which distributed high pay within the limits of constant and protected expansion.

Many of the workers, especially those of the *Mezzogiorno* and all the *braccianti*, found little in Giolittism to interest them. Indeed, between 1900 and 1914 the rural proletariat increased by fifty percent, and Gaetano Salvemini, a southern intellectual, could write:

"For us in the south, social legislation is a phrase almost devoid of meaning, for we have nothing to do with those relationships that social legislation intends to regulate. Rather than being protected against exploitation, our proletariat still needs to be exploited.[4]

[4] Quoted by R. Paris in *Histoire du fascisme en Italie* (Paris: Maspero).

The general strike of 1904, which, moreover, had been preceded by a number of other walkouts, was to demonstrate the strength of this opposition to Giolittism. In April, 1904, the southern Socialists had proclaimed the necessity for the seizure of power by force, the general strike being the privileged weapon of the masses.

In Sardinia a striking miner was killed. In the Milan Labor Exchange, forty-five thousand strikers adopted a resolution proclaiming the general strike. This movement was to be marked by two facts gravid with consequences for the future. First, in many factories labor set up workers' councils, and Giolitti was careful not to interfere with this trend: strategic points were occupied by the army, but the government allowed the movement to "fall apart" in the factories. The general strike was a failure. Sixteen years later, in September, 1920, both the workers and Giolitti were to follow their tactics of 1904: workers' councils on the one hand and clever governmental watching and waiting on the other. It was indeed in this period before 1914 that the middle class, the government, and the proletariat adopted styles and solutions that they endeavored to apply after the war in a completely different situation. Besides, being in a position of strength, as he was after 1904, Giolitti knew how to exploit intimidating action. In 1908 it was decreed that strikes by government employes in all categories were tantamount to resignation.

In 1908 Mussolini left Oneglia for Predappio. Before his departure, he addressed an open letter to the authorities through *la Lima*:

> In a few days I am leaving, and, so that you can report me, I am giving you my exact address: the house stands on the provincial road at Rabbi, at kilometer-marker 15, in the hamlet of Dovia, commune of Predappio, province of Forlì. Make a record of it and think it over . . . perhaps it will be possible to throw me out of my own house too.

The month was June, and he arrived in the Romagna in the midst of an agrarian crisis, when the *braccianti* were battling the tenant farmers. It was a major problem: fifty-five percent of the Italian population still lived by the soil: there were only five million owners of land, and nine-tenths of them owned less than two acres each—in other words, there were fewer than seven million acres for twenty-two million farm workers. In order to live, the vast majority of the peasants had to become *braccianti* or else rent land from large or medium owners. The situation was most serious for the *braccianti* of the Po Valley (the region of Bologna, Ferrara, Cremona, Mantua, Piedmont itself in the area of Vercelli and Novara), who literally lived only by their "arms" and who represented the surplus manpower of the great estates. The conflict between these two social groups—landowners and *braccianti*—was simple and bitter. The landowners wanted "free" labor, so that the drifting mass of jobless men would enable them to dictate wages; the *braccianti* demanded that the employment offices be controlled by peasant leagues that would distribute work equitably over the whole year and establish wage scales, whatever the season or the economic conditions.

So there was fighting: over the threshing machines that the landowners refused to rent to the small farmers, over wages, over recognition for the freedom of labor; there was fighting between tenant farmers and *braccianti*. All this unrest was at its height when Mussolini arrived in Predappio in 1908: the organized peasants were battling the "yellows," the Krumirs—the scabs—and violence was built into all these peasant conflicts. Mussolini threatened a landowner with his stick and he was sentenced to three months in prison, but after two weeks he was set free on probation. Once again he had drawn attention to himself, and the Socialist newspapers lavished praise on him.

These agrarian conflicts in which he was thus for the first time engaged were a major theme of the Italy of the time. In 1911 and then in 1920 Giolitti recognized the right of the peasant leagues to organize and to control hiring, and thus protect the *braccianti*; problems, and violence, were to arise afresh after 1919, and it was in that same Po Valley, rent by the strife between farmers and *braccianti*, that Fascism took root. Certainly by 1920 Mussolini would have changed sides; but the fact remains that he served his apprenticeship in peasant problems in 1908.

Released on probation, Mussolini went back to Forlì. His father and Signora Guidi had a *trattoria*, the tavern called *Al Bersagliere*, in via Mazzini opposite the railway station.

For several months Benito spent his time waiting on customers, reading, and falling in love with Rachele, the youngest—she was sixteen—of the five daughters of Anna Guidi, born Lombardi. Rachele was blonde and graceful, and there was a rumor that she was Anna's illegitimate daughter by Benito's father, but this did not disturb the son. When he was about to leave Forlì, Benito staged a small family party. There were drinking and dancing. He played the violin and then, taking Rachele to one side, he asked her to wait for him. When he came back, he would marry her.

Mussolini was leaving Forlì for the Trentino. In 1909 that province was part of the Tyrol, which was in turn a province of the Austro-Hungarian empire. Mussolini established himself in Trento, a city of seventy thousand, to work with the *Popolo* and later with *l'Avvenire del lavoratore* (*The Worker's Future*), both Italian-language newspapers. Though administratively subject to Vienna, Trentino was inhabited by thirty-eight thousand Italians who submitted to Austrian rule but demanded reunion with Italy. The editor of the *Popolo*, Cesare Battisti, was the spokesman for the irredentist movement;[5] in contrast, though Mussolini openly proclaimed his anticlericalism—he engaged in controversy with Alcide de Gasperi, who was the director of the Catholic newspaper, *il Trentino*—he was not an irredentist. Collected into a pamphlet entitled *The Trentino as Seen by a Socialist*, his articles became the target of fierce attacks by Italian nationalist circles. Later, when he became Il Duce, Mussolini was to order the excision of these heretical texts from his official biographies and his collected works. Nevertheless the Austrian police kept an eye on him, and he was imprisoned after a number of demonstrations. He went on a hunger strike. In spite of the fact that a general strike was called by the Trento workers on his behalf, he was expelled. Leading Trentino Italians accompanied him to the border, where there were dramatic hand-shaking farewells across the markers defining the limits of the Habsburgs' empire. And again the Italian press devoted articles to Benito Mussolini.

It must be pointed out that irredentism had never died out of Italy since the *Risorgimento*. Indeed, at the beginning of the twentieth century it received a new impetus because it was based on a self-strengthening foundation: nationalism. Thus in 1903 the Trento-Trieste Association was formed, and its local committees multiplied throughout the peninsula, waving their banners at every public demonstration. Of course nationalist ideas were nothing new. When Crispi was in power, he sought to make them reality through his program of grandeur. What was new was the fact that these ideas were taken up, expanded, and propagated by groups of intellectuals who established publications, inspired little organizations, and gradually evolved a coherent nationalist ideology without which it would be impossible to understand Italy's entry into the war in 1915 or the later rise of Fascism. This ideology was the link that connected Crispi with Fascism: it was the foundation on

[5] *Irredentism* was the name given to the thesis according to which Italy should include, beyond her pre-1914 borders, all the areas that were connected with her by language and customs but separated from her by politics. These areas constituted *Italia irredenta* (enslaved or unredeemed Italy).

which the interventionist movement of 1914–15 and, later, Mussolini's party were based.

The themes of this ideology were simple, often quite literary and rhetorical, and well suited to the captivation of a lower middle class that had retained from its classical studies the memory of "the grandeur that was Rome," together with the exaltation of a few heroes of the *Risorgimento*—in short, the image of an idealized and aristocratic history.

Gabriele d'Annunzio, the theatrical, high-flown poet, fully epitomized the love of language, of spectacle, of antiquity, of empire that was the basic style of Italian nationalism and that foreshadowed the "Mussolinian gesture," his pomps, his bombast, his absurdities.[6] When Crispi launched his Abyssinian adventure, the novelist, Alfredo Oriani, declared: "All the millennial efforts of Italy to become a nation have been directed only to this day."[7]

Exaggeration already, and then above all the harsh lesson of reality with the disaster at Adowa on March 1, 1896. D'Annunzio too exalted Rome in his *Elettra* in 1904:

> O Rome, O Rome, only in thee alone,
> Within the circle of thy seven hills,
> The long divided multitudes of man
> Will find, sublime and broad, their unity,
> New aliment for body and for soul.[8]

When one recalls that d'Annunzio consistently peopled the stage with supermen acting beyond the law, interpreters of destiny, "leader[s] . . . breaker[s] of unknown paths . . . discoverer[s] of new planets," one sees how great a debt Mussolini and his movement owed to this precursor who later joined the ranks of Fascism. Enrico Corradini played a comparable part, but on the theoretical level. In 1902 he published a novel called *Julius Caesar* and a year later, with a group of loyal followers, he launched a magazine of minimal circulation, *Il Regno* (*The Kingdom*). Giovanni Papini and Giuseppe Prezzolini inspired similar groups through little periodicals. All of them declared themselves to be imperialists and championed the necessity of war: "The Roman reapers of men are sacred. Napoleon is sacred. Conquerors enjoy the sanctity of destiny."

They set the "great proletarian" Italy—in the words of the poet,

---

[6] An essential reference in this regard is M. Vaussard's *Évolution du sentiment nationaliste italien.*

[7] *Ibid.*, p. 149.

[8] *Ibid.*, p. 155.

Giovanni Pascoli—against the plutocratic nations. These were the constant themes in Crispi's time: Fascism was to enlarge on them. Other of Mussolini's utterances, too, seem to have been built on these fragments from Corradini: "we shall never be a nation without a war"; and "the inviolability of human life and pacifism are to be discarded with the old idols of the idealist and sentimental patrimony of the men of the past."

Such notions—which, in all honesty, were part of a general European tendency on the eve of the First World War—attracted the support of the "futurist" poets, who issued manifestos from both Paris and Milan. Filippo Tommaso Marinetti, who soon became a friend of Mussolini and a Fascist, announced that he wished "to sing of the love of danger, the habit of strength and boldness . . . to glorify war, the world's sole health, militarism and patriotism"; that "blood, you must know, has neither worth nor beauty but when it is set free by fire and sword from the prison of the arteries! And we shall show all the world's armed soldiers how blood ought to be shed."

The first futurist gathering was held in the *Teatro lirico* in Milan against a music of clamor and shouts. It was February 15, 1910, and the audience howled: "Up with war! Down with Austria!"

In December of the same year the first nationalist congress was held in Florence. A nationalist association was formed, and its members included Corradini, Luigi Federzoni, Minister of Colonies and president of the Senate under the Fascist government, and Francesco Coppola, all of whom we shall encounter again at Mussolini's side. Beginning on March 1, 1911, the movement had its own weekly, *l'Idea nazionale*, which was already talking about Nice, Corsica, Tunisia, Monaco . . . like Mussolini thirty years later. But, while it was the spokesman for imperialism, this weekly also showed the other side of Italian nationalism, which was also to be that of Fascism: the preference for a totalitarian doctrine that subordinated the individual to the nation defined as a whole. Corradini, who, like Mussolini, had come under the influence of Georges Sorel, wrote: "In thought and action nationalism was always anti-liberal, anti-democratic, anti-parliamentarian, anti-Masonic, its goal being the exaltation of the morality of man as soldier . . . and the creation of the cult of warrior morality in Italy."

Thus imperialism and war implied dictatorship within. Fascism was to receive the heritage of nationalism as well as that of Crispi.

But in 1911 everything was to set the nationalists against Benito Mussolini, who still represented the most violent, the most interna-

tionalist, and the most anti-militarist tendencies of Italian Socialism.

In October, 1909, after his expulsion from the Trentino, Mussolini had gone back to his father's house in Forlì and been reunited
with Rachele, the pleasant, much courted waitress. A young sur-
veyor from Ravenna, Olivieri, had just proposed marriage to her.
Furious, Mussolini prevented Rachele from going to work in the
tavern; then he had to overcome the opposition of their parents.
One evening, with his characteristic propensity for the melodramatic, he burst in on Anna and Alessandro in the girl's presence.
He tossed a pistol on to the table. "There are six bullets in it," he
shouted. "One is for Rachele, the rest are for me."

Alessandro and Rachele's mother gave in, and without either a
civil or a religious ceremony the young couple established residence in two gloomy rooms—a bedroom and a kitchen—whose
only luxury was Benito Mussolini's violin. On September 1, 1910,
Rachele gave birth to Edda, the future wife of Galeazzo Ciano. A
short time later Benito's father, Alessandro, died.

Living now with Rachele, Benito no longer looked for a teaching post. For one hundred twenty *lire* (twenty-four dollars) a
month he was the publisher, the editor, and the make-up man for
Forlì's Socialist newspaper, *la Lotta di classe* (*The Class Struggle*),
whose title alone stated its policy. His articles were violent, anti-
clerical, and anti-reform: "Socialism," he wrote, "is perhaps the
greatest drama that has stirred the human race."

He was the panegyrist of regicides and Russian terrorists. At the
news of the execution of Francisco Ferrer, a Spanish anarchist,
Mussolini made a speech to a large crowd and then led the demonstrators through the streets, hurling stones at the archbishop's
palace and knocking down a statue of the Virgin. He also took
part in the peasant conflicts that were so acute in the Romagna;
he castigated those who, "having been representatives of the Socialist Party, have become the shyster lawyers of a few little groups
and keep their mouths shut in Parliament so that they can speak
for their clients in the ministries. This is a harsh truth, but Truth
it is. Impotence is aggravated by baseness."

These attitudes and their inflexibility excited the devotion of his
Socialist comrades in the Romagna. He was offered a rise in salary,
but he refused the extra fifty *lire* per month: "I do not wish," he
said, "to become a parasite of the Socialist organization."

He made no attempt to husband his efforts. He was a correspondent for *Avanti!* and in addition, in the first three months of 1910,
he delivered sixteen lectures. As soon as he would appear on the
platform, a little knot of faithful comrades would burst into noisy

applause. Little by little, as he gave so abundantly of himself, he made an impression, driven as he was by his thirst for action and his hunger to be in the forefront.

Naturally, when the Socialist Party held its national congress in Milan in October, 1910, the Romagna group sent Mussolini as its delegate. For the most part the proceedings droned on routinely, but, when Mussolini's deep voice and violent tone erupted in the hall, the audience was impressed and momentarily taken aback. He went home disappointed, however, and, under his leadership, the Socialist federation of the Romagna declared its autonomy in order to break with the reformism and compromise of the national party. This break revealed the ambitions of the young Mussolini, already resolved to forge and wield his own political instrument. But no one paid any attention to him in October, 1910. Very soon, however, there occurred an event that seemed tailor-made for Mussolini's talents: the war over Libya, then a Turkish possession. For Italy Libya represented the mirage of colonialism. When a ship carrying ten thousand rifles left Constantinople for Tripoli, the Italian ambassador had his pretext: on September 28, 1911, he handed Turkey an ultimatum that sparked the Italian-Turkish war.

Giolitti had not listened to the experts who told him that Tripolitania was the poorest and most barren country in the world. He hoped that the war would satisfy nationalist circles, who considered that expansion in Africa was the basic pre-condition of existence for a country seeking to become a great power. But he thought it would also enable him to offer the *disoccupati* of the south, the *braccianti* of the Romagna—all the discontented in a country that was beginning to suffer from overproduction in certain sectors—the hope of populating a colony as the veteran soldiers of the Roman Empire had populated Rome's conquered territories. The press trumpeted the resources and history—Imperial Rome's granary—of those flat shores where the Arabs were waiting for their Italian deliverers.

That nationalism had taken deep root was demonstrated by the fact that certain Italian Socialists—Bissolati, Bonomi, Arturo Labriola—approved Giolitti's course. Deputies of the extreme left put the number of Italians who would be able to emigrate to Tripolitania at two million. The country must be conquered. But this Socialist support of the monarchy and the nationalists produced a serious crisis within the Socialist Party, for the mass of the people was intuitively hostile to the venture, and, wherever there was a strong leader to marshal it, this opposition was manifested.

Such was the case in Forlì, where the Socialist federation led by Mussolini waged an increasingly violent struggle against the war. It soon came to rioting. Mussolini had only one slogan: "The main thing is to fight!" Besides, the majority of the Socialist Party was opposed to the war, and so was the CGL (Confederazione generale del lavoro—Italian Federation of Labor): a strike call was issued, and there was a general cry: "Not one man, not one *lira!*"

Mussolini took that literally. He led the proletariat of Forlì in an attack on the railway station to prevent troop trains from moving. With him there was a young man of twenty, the secretary of the Republican Section of Forlì: Pietro Nenni. For three days the workers of Forlì were the masters of the streets. The telegraph lines were cut and the rails were pulled up. Mussolini himself was seen attacking the tracks with a pick. Three times the cavalry charged; barricades were thrown up and stones rained down on the troops. In *la Lotta di classe* Mussolini hailed the revolt: "The workers have shown that they understand the full revolutionary meaning of the general strike."

But a state of siege was declared in Forlì. On October 14, 1911, Mussolini was sitting on the terrace of the Caffè Garibaldi when he was arrested. The police chained his wrists. "Now I can finish my book on Jan Huss," he said. Nenni was arrested on the same day.

Two days later, during the prison exercise period, Nenni climbed the wall of the inner courtyard. In the neighboring courtyard he saw Mussolini, squatting and pouring water from a bucket over his freshly shaved head.

"Good God," Mussolini said, "I didn't think you were here."

"Are there any other comrades with you?" Nenni asked.

"I should think about a dozen."

"We'll cost quite a lot," Nenni said as he prepared to climb down.

"And to think of those cowards who won't pull a general strike!" Mussolini raged.[9]

That remark was already the complete portrait of the man. That resentment and that contempt characterized the arrogant individualist always ready to condemn.

Benito Mussolini was transferred to the prison of San Giovanni in Monte, in Bologna, and indicted on eight criminal counts, including incitement to an insurrectional strike, sabotage, and violently resisting arrest. A month later he went to trial in Forlì.

Mussolini faced his judges elegantly beside the young Nenni. He conducted his own defense with great skill, and it was surprising

[9] Pietro Nenni, *Six ans de guerre civile en Italie*, p. 12.

how he sought to minimize his own part in events, juggling words and reiterating a distinction between "moral" and "physical" sabotage. This was already an early indication of his tendency not to accept the full consequences of actions for which he was responsible when they threatened to burden him, as if Mussolini were led blindly by words, phrases, whatever was immediate, without considering the consequences of a decision. Nonetheless he behaved well throughout the trial, frankly stating his desire to build an Italy that would have none of conquests and empires, "a prosperous, free, rich Italy." He added: "I should rather be a citizen of Denmark than a subject of the Chinese Empire." Erect before his judges, he told them proudly: "If you acquit me, you shame me; if you convict me, you honor me."

Nenni was sentenced to one year and two weeks in prison, Mussolini to one year. An appeal was quickly taken, and Mussolini's sentence was reduced to six months, which he spent in the prison in Forlì. As a political prisoner he spent his time reading, and also writing an autobiography and the essay on Jan Huss.

The riot in Forlì, the arrest, the trial, and, a year before, the 1910 party congress, had drawn attention to him. To many he was now the incarnation of rigid, extremist Socialism. Therefore he took the Romagna Socialist federation back into the party when he came out of prison. He aspired now to become a national leader, and the Socialist congress that was held in Reggio Emilia from July 7 to 10, 1911, was to give him the opportunity.

Thin and in frayed clothes, he appeared there with the aura of his prison term about him. He appointed himself spokesman for the young and prosecutor of the reformists and all who had approved or countenanced the Libyan war. His favorite target was Leonida Bissolati: not only had Bissolati supported Giolitti; he had paid a call on the King after an anarchist had unsuccessfully made an attempt on his life. "How often, Bissolati," Mussolini shouted, "have you gone to pay your respects at the funeral of a mason who fell off a scaffold, or a cart-driver crushed under his vehicle, or a suffocated miner? For a king an assassination attempt is just an occupational hazard!"

Everyone in the congress who had grown weary of the pedestrian rhetoric of the usual leaders immediately recognized that he had found a spokesman in Mussolini. As Margherita Sarfatti, Mussolini's confidante and biographer, put it, he became, in Reggio Emilia, "the anti-pope of the official Socialism of Rome and Milan." His victory was assured when he cried to the congress: "Can Socialism be reduced to a theorem? We would prefer to think that mankind needs a credo."

This fresh wind swept the majority along. The young voted for him. Bissolati and Bonomi were expelled from the party and later founded the Reform Socialist Party. Others, such as Turati, Treves, and Modigliani, lost control of the leadership and, above all, of the party's daily paper, *Avanti!*, which was turned over to Bacci. Mussolini had won the battle: he had been able to seize the leadership of all those to whom Socialism in collaboration with Giolitti meant compromise. As against this Socialism that accepted bribes or nationalism in order, as Bissolati said, "not to leave the monopoly of patriotism in the hands of the enemies of Socialism," many preferred Mussolini's credo and gave him their unreserved confidence.

There were those, however, who did not trust him. Turati's nihilist comrade, Anna Kulishova, penetrated Mussolini's contrived mask in Reggio Emilia and recognized the individualist, the buccaneer. "He is not a Marxist at all," she cried; "he is not even a Socialist." And it was true that, in his speeches, even when he was talking of idealism, of "the religious soul of the party," Mussolini had betrayed flashes of the arrogant skepticism of the autocrat: "Illusion," he said, "is perhaps the only reality in life." But this remark, though already pregnant with "realism," with disenchantment, with superficial Machiavellianism, was forgotten by the majority, which regarded the young hero of Forlì as "the complete revolutionary" or "the man of the barricades."

After the congress, Mussolini returned to Forlì, but he did not remain much longer in the little town of the Romagna. The party leadership decided unanimously to appoint "Professor Mussolini editor of *Avanti!*." For Forlì it was a day of rejoicing and glory. The comrades gave him a banquet the night before he left for Milan. "He has been our Duce for three years," they said. On December 1, 1912, Mussolini took over control of *Avanti!*, the Socialist Party's daily and a newspaper of national stature.

At the culmination of a stormy, fiery youth he had finally reached the front rank. He was twenty-nine years old.

In 1912 the major newspapers played a decisive part in that Italy in which political formations still embraced only a small number of the citizens. Only the newspaper could reach the mass and disseminate ideas and slogans. *Avanti!*, therefore, gave Mussolini real power. He was not slow in increasing it and concentrating it in his own hands.

The newspaper immediately became his platform. Its old staff was dismissed, even the best-known members such as Claudio Treves, and Mussolini forced his own thinking on everyone. Angelica Balabanova, who had at first been appointed assistant to the editor-in-chief, was compelled to give up the post: Switzerland was already far behind Mussolini, and gratitude had never hobbled him.

Enriched by the experience he had acquired with *la Lotta di classe*, he remade the entire paper: he changed its format, its headline style, the tone of its writing; and vehemence paid off: the circulation of *Avanti!* rose from thirty thousand to one hundred thousand. It became one of the great Italian newspapers, side by side with that other Milanese newspaper, *il Corriere della Sera*, which, under the editorship of Luigi Albertini, set the tone for political circles and had a circulation of almost two hundred thousand. At *Avanti!* Mussolini had met Margherita Sarfatti, the paper's art critic. She was a Venetian of Jewish origin, blonde and elegant; welcome in every drawing-room, she introduced Mussolini into that world and discreetly schooled him in its workings; she took him to La Scala, and she tried to interest him in painting. It was no use: when he did have a moment to himself, Mussolini ran off almost furtively to the fencing schools—would the comrades understand that aristocratic sport? One of his fencing opponents described him as tense and hunched, seeking to win at any price and then, once the duel was over, slinking away, and always poorly dressed.

Rachele had moved to Milan with Edda, taking a small place in via Castel Marrone. They were no longer poor. Benito Mussolini was earning five hundred *lire* (one hundred dollars) a month, the rent was only a thousand *lire* a year, and there was plenty of money on which to live. But Mussolini, who had been anything but pleased by Rachele's arrival, was at the newspaper office more often than in via Castel Marrone. To *Avanti!* he gave himself completely. He denounced repressions, which he described as "the classic Italian butcheries, the police and the soldiers firing on the unarmed crowds." He was arrested. He told the court in Milan that he would repeat the offense. Nevertheless he was acquitted on the ground of freedom of the press, on which he had relied in his defense.

Mussolini's brushes with the law and his articles kept attention fastened on him, the more so because 1912 and 1913 were decisive and troubling years for the internal situation of Italy. Having completed the Libyan campaign, Giolitti had decided to extend the right of suffrage to all Italians over twenty-one years of age who had finished their military service or their elementary schooling: all others had to wait until they were thirty. This was certainly far from universal suffrage, but the number of voters rose from three and a half to eight million. Thus for the first time the Italian masses entered the political arena, and their mere presence raised the problem of enlarging the political circles that had ruled until then, as we have seen, with the support of a very constricted electoral base. This was necessarily to modify the world of politics, and the elections of 1913 underlined the importance of the change.

Mussolini entered his candidacy from the Forlì district. He carried on a vigorous anti-militarist campaign, citing his agitation against the Libyan war. He was defeated: only Predappio voted for him; but fifty-two Socialist deputies were elected. This was a success. But the major result of the electoral reform was the part taken by the Catholics, since the rural masses who turned out to vote—though it was true that there were many abstentions—were deeply loyal to the church. In order to win their votes, almost two hundred thirty deputies had signed a pre-election agreement introduced by Count Gentiloni: they promised to defend Christian principles in the Chamber. No one in Italy had any illusions: the first step toward the formation of a Catholic party had been taken.

Over a long period, moreover, men like Filippo Meda had already been "preparing in abstention" for the Catholics' entrance into the lists. They had formed Catholic professional unions, "white" leagues in opposition to the Socialists' "red" leagues. Consolidated in the Economic and Social Union, they represented more than a thousand associations and mutual-aid societies, which could provide a broad base for a Catholic Popular Party in the form in which, under that name, it was to be born in 1919.

The other lesson of the 1913 elections was the emergence of the nationalist deputies. Federzoni was elected from Rome, Bevione from Turin. Thus the lines were drawn in that October of 1913 for the forces that would carry weight after the war in the destiny of Italy and the future of Fascism.

But something else too was revived: the social agitation that foreshadowed that of after the war. The automobile workers of Milan went on strike in May and June of 1913. In *Avanti!* Mussolini congratulated them and proposed a general strike. It was called; it lasted only two days, but in labor circles those two words, "general strike," remained invested with illusions and hopes. In August, 1913, the general strike in Milan was resumed. This "magnificent creature," as Mussolini called it in his newspaper, paralyzed the city, arousing enthusiasm and discouragement at the same time, and causing anxiety in moderate circles.

These strikes were inspired by revolutionary syndicalists. They were publishing *l'Internazionale* in Parma; anti-parliamentarian, anti-reformist, often close to anarchism, they found their spokesman in Mussolini. This was recognized in 1914.

During the fourteenth Socialist congress in Ancona in April, 1914, Mussolini confirmed the hopes that the revolutionaries had placed in him. In order to amputate the party's moderate wing, he forced a vote for the expulsion of all Freemasons. In June of 1914 the full measure of the man was finally to become clear.

The port city of Ancona was red, anarchist, and Socialist. On June 7, 1914, an anti-militarist demonstration was held there. Its goal was the release of a soldier named Masetti who, in a moment of aberration in Libya, had wounded his colonel. The demonstrators gathered in front of Villa Rossa, which was occupied by Enrico Malatesta, an anarchist. The police reacted forcefully: three workers were killed and fifteen were wounded. A general strike was called in the Romagna and in the Marche, the provinces of Mussolini and Nenni. A general was arrested in Ravenna, officers were manhandled, Liberty poles were erected in the squares. This was the "Red Week." Pietro Nenni was the organizer of all the activities, signing requisition orders for wheat and decreeing "price ceilings." In Milan the Socialist Party and the CGL issued a call for a general strike. There was a demonstration in Piazza del Duomo. Mussolini was in the front rank. The cavalry charged. Mussolini stood fast, but a comrade tugged at his coat and pulled him into the safety of a carriage-way. *Avanti!* was in a fever. Mussolini wrote to his comrades in Ancona: "A hundred dead in Ancona and all Italy is in flames." In fact the general strike did spread to other areas. Clashes with the troops and the carabinieri multiplied. In Turin the young Socialist, Antonio Gramsci, took part in the fighting. In Ancona the sailors who were sent ashore to restore order were hailed by the women and girls. Was it a general upheaval? The cautious CGL issued an order for a return to work. As for Mussolini, he endeavored to prolong the rebellion. But in vain. The tide receded. On June 10–11 the strike ended everywhere. Mussolini had no choice but to postpone the final struggle for other battles. His article of June 12, 1914, was entitled "Fighting Suspended":

> We look on events with something of that legitimate joy that the artist must feel when he contemplates his work. If the proletariat of Italy has gained a new, more aggressive, more audacious psychology, that is the work of our newspaper.

Assuredly there was much exaggeration and self-satisfaction on Mussolini's part. In actuality he had insinuated himself into the insurrectional movement of the Romagna, which owed nothing to him initially. The fact remains, however, that he had expanded and supported it, and after the "Red Week" he emerged as the sole revolutionary leader with a national audience.

Now the Red Week might have been a failure, but it had given rise to anxiety. The masses of workers and peasants who had just been granted almost universal suffrage seemed not to have been pacified by that. Henceforth the fear of a revolution began to weigh on the ruling circles of Italy.

They remembered the Milan riots of 1898 and the general strike of 1904, and the wave of 1914 seemed to be mounting with the Socialist Party that was turning radical under the inspiration of Mussolini. Giolitti's whole policy was at stake in June, 1914, with his entire tactics, those of a "Giolitti *cunctator*," a temporizer. Giolitti himself, very intelligently, had chosen to withdraw for a while, turning over the government in March, 1914, to Antonio Salandra, a liberal of the right.

A small, bald, smiling man who always dressed with great care, Salandra had spent his entire political life in the shadow of Baron Sydney Sonnino, with whom he shared the political ideal of the restoration of the Statute granted by King Carlo Alberto—in 1848. In comparison with Giolitti, he represented a rigorous conservatism that was disturbed as much by universal suffrage as by the Red Week; he was the spokesman of the substantial segment of the Italian ruling circles that had reluctantly accepted Giolittism, with its progressive liberalism and its policy of concessions to and agreements with understanding Socialists. Sonnino and Salandra, backed by the *Corriere della Sera*, championed a different policy: that of a conservative liberalism directed by a restricted élite of enlightened statesmen. It was not surprising that these conservatives—though this was not true of Salandra himself—should often be as anti-clerical as the population was Catholic. The retreat from Giolittism began in 1914 with Salandra, and local elections throughout the country confirmed the new direction. Many municipalities were won by conservative nationalists. In Rome itself the Masonic mayor, Ernesto Nathan, the illegitimate son of Mazzini, lost his post to Prince Prospero Colonna, the candidate of the nationalists, the liberals, and the Catholics.

The fear born of the Red Week had made it possible for the conservative parties to consolidate. Was this a break between two sectors of the Italian ruling circles? was it the end of Giolittism or merely one of its eclipses?

Everyone knew that the crisis was real, but the reaction to it was postponed until Parliament reconvened in October. The summer was going to be hot. The politicians left Rome. In Milan, Mussolini wrote out his instructions for *Avanti!* and departed for a vacation on the Adriatic coast. It was the end of June, in the year 1914.

31   *A Young Country, A Young Man*

2

The Disappointments of a Victorious
War and the Birth of the Fasci
(1914—April, 1919)

"When in August, 1914, Germany embarked on her adventure of pillage and crimes. . . ."—MUSSOLINI (July 12, 1917)

USSOLINI'S VACATION was brief. One day in July, Michele Campana, a journalist, noticed him on the platform of the little railway station at Cattolica, a seashore resort on the Adriatic coast about a dozen miles from Rimini. Mussolini was striding up and down, striking at his legs with a Malacca cane. The cane was like a challenge, a striving for elegance, an esthetic retort to the wretched black suit that he was wearing on that summer day of 1914.

Both Mussolini and Campana had been urgently summoned back to Milan by their newspapers. Since Gavril Prinzip's assassination of Archduke Franz Ferdinand at Sarajevo on June 28, the crisis had been growing inexorably more intense.

"This means a European war," Mussolini told Campana. "The German Socialists will follow their emperor and the Socialist International will be shattered." He raised his voice. "But our goal is social revolution, and, if we fight bravely, we can take over the reins after the war."[1]

These predictions, including almost that of social revolution, were to be fulfilled. But while Mussolini was prophesying, the

---

[1] From Monelli, *Mussolini: The Intimate Life of a Demagogue.*

nations were arming, passions were erupting, nothing now could interrupt the implacable logic of alliances and economics. Serbia agreed to the Austro-Hungarian ultimatum of July 23 except for one point; on July 26 England suggested an international conference, but in vain. The decision to act had already been made in Vienna and Berlin. On July 28 Austria-Hungary declared war on Serbia. All the nations mobilized. The Socialists in the *Reichstag* voted in favor of credits for the war; a Sacred Union was formed in Paris and on July 31 Jean Jaurès was assassinated. The sparks of the first days of August were catching.

And what of Italy? Mussolini was back in Milan. True to his reputation as an anti-militarist, on July 26 he asserted the necessity of absolute neutrality under a large headline in *Avanti!*: "Down With the War." It was essential to choose, for Italy was still bound by the Triple Entente of 1882 (renewed in 1912) to the German chariot.

Unquestionably she had been a restraining element in this alliance. In July, 1913, when Austria-Hungary was already preparing to intervene in Serbia, Giolitti had resolutely declared that, in the event of aggression, Italy would remain neutral: and Austria had hesitated. But in July, 1914, Giolitti was vacationing in Piedmont and he was only one of many deputies; and Italy's diplomatic position was not so clear as a year earlier. Salandra and the Marquis Antonio di San Giuliano, the foreign minister, had begun on July 21 to restudy Article VIII of the Triple Entente treaty, which provided for compensation to Italy for any changes resulting from Austrian action in the Balkans. This diplomatic move might have incited Austria to act. Certainly Italy proclaimed her neutrality on August 3, but there was still some question as to the possibility of striking a bargain.

In fact, di San Giuliano, like Salandra, who was to succeed him, was favorable to the Triple Entente, and during that month of August, 1914, both men pressed for action on the side of Austria-Hungary. In this they were at one with the nationalist politicians, who, when the war began, trumpeted in *l'Idea nazionale* their desire for belligerency under the banner of the Germanic powers. Was not France a nation corrupted by liberalism? Alfredo Rocco wrote:

> Every man who admires the indomitable energy of the German race, its social and military organization, and the marvelous German culture . . . everyone who fears the malefic influence of the vices of the French on the social and political life of Italians, everyone who would prefer to see our national life model itself on

the much healthier and stronger pattern of Germany, is naturally drawn to oppose the Allies and to support Austria-Hungary and Germany.

This nationalist group that favored military action at Germany's side had little influence, however. The politicians' minds turned to the English fleet, which had Genoa and Leghorn under its guns, and the masses demonstrated their attachment to Belgium and, intuitively, to peace: the Socialist Party declared itself against the war and Mussolini pressed his vigorous campaign in *Avanti!*. "Not one man, not one *lira*," he had written in 1911 and now wrote again. Nevertheless the war fascinated everyone; never had the newspapers been so thoroughly read, and their contents were discussed in every level of society. On August 20 Pope Pius X died, and the election of his successor, Benedict XV, distracted attention from the front, but then in September the German drive on Paris put the war back on the front pages: the first Battle of the Marne was the major story everywhere.

Yet life went on: in the Vermo Theater in Milan there was a revival of Puccini's opera, *la Fanciulla del West* (*The Girl of the Golden West*). The performance began, and suddenly some thirty futurists, including Marinetti, whistled from the gallery and then shouted: "Down with Austria!" On September 16 eleven Austrian flags were burned in Piazza del Duomo and under the arcades, and there were scuffles with the people sitting in the cafés. For Italy the march toward war had begun.

The nationalists were the first to make a change of front. German superiority, apparently, was not conclusive, and the people would not support a war against France; but what mattered, in the view of the nationalists, was not so much the identity of the ally as a war, "the eternal vindicator of truth" (Coppola), a war that would make it possible to teach Italy "the value of international struggle." So it would be war on the side of the Allies. Victory might bring conquests—Trento, Trieste, Albania?—and so, having altered their course, the nationalists discovered an irredentist pretext for their war.

In this area they were joined by a democratic tendency that drew its inspiration from the *Risorgimento* traditions of the struggle against Austria and hoped to raise the torch of Mazzini and Garibaldi at the side of the great democracies. Between the nationalists and certain Socialists (Bissolati, Salvemini, Bonomi) a kind of "sacred union" was thus forged, and the government supported it. Actually, it was little by little becoming plain that the government had decided to intervene in the war.

Appearing before both chambers of Parliament on December 3, Salandra asserted: "Our neutrality must be not inert and weak, but active and alert, not helpless but strongly armed and ready for every eventuality." And both Chambers sent their greetings to Belgium . . . while Sonnino went on bargaining with Austria for compensations. Such an attitude—clumsy blackmail carried on by the rightist liberals—had to lead to a choice between the two sides and hence, in every way, to the renunciation of neutrality in favor of war.

"To tell the truth," Sonnino observed to Malagodi, "those who want war are very few. But, if we think it is necessary or beneficial for Italy, we shall have to—and we shall be able to—make our decision over the heads of the masses."

In order to learn what the masses thought, Mussolini initiated a massive referendum in *Avanti!* on September 22: "Do you want Peace or War?" And he himself wrote: "Those who are pushing you into war are betraying you!"

At that very time, however, it was he, Mussolini, who was suspected of betrayal by his comrades. Angelica Balabanova, who was keeping him under observation, caught him in conversation with Filippo Naldi. Naldi was a man well known to the Socialists: he was the owner of *il Resto del Carlino*, an interventionist newspaper connected with the Foreign Ministry and the large landowners in Emilia.

Other comrades had also noted a number of vacillations beneath Mussolini's stern pacifist mask: one day it was a tribute to Gustave Hervé, long an opponent of war, who had enlisted for combat duty; a few days later it was a panegyric to Marinetti, the futurist who was sowing disorder in Milan. There was a recurrent rumor that at a party meeting one evening in September Mussolini had shouted: "Only maniacs never change. New facts can call for new positions. . . ." In *Avanti!* he reprinted a letter from Cesare Battisti, whom he had known earlier in Trento and who, as the spokesman for the Italians in the Trentino, had written: "If Italy prefers no longer to remember us, so be it! . . . [but] do not say that we have no wish to be separated from Austria: that is a blasphemy! That is infamous!"

Criticism of Mussolini came also from Turin. He felt that he was under suspicion: he went to Switzerland, far from the supervision of his party comrades, to confer with Naldi. But, half launched as he was on a course of disavowal, he was in a delicate position. He was attacked in Naldi's paper, *il Resto del Carlino*—blackmail to compel him to choose, under the threat of revealing the initial talks? On October 10 he was branded "a man of straw who calls himself a man of bronze." Then, on October 18, on the third page of *Avanti!*, Mussolini burned his bridges in a long article entitled "From Absolute Neutrality to Active and Effective Neutrality." "Do we, as human beings or as Socialists," he wrote, "wish to be the lifeless spectators of this grandiose drama?"

It was done. Mussolini had taken a new road: that of interventionism. He had just committed his career; never again would he be able to be free of the machinery set in motion by the renunciations of that month of October, 1915.

On October 20 he went to Bologna, where the leaders of the Socialist Party were meeting; they rejected the resolution that he introduced and they relieved him of his post as editor of *Avanti!*. He resigned from the newspaper the next day, rejected the severance indemnity of one thousand *lire* that was offered, and told his wife: "Here we are back in the poverty of Forlì. I no longer have my newspaper. I do not have a single *lira*. . . . But I have made up my mind to go the limit in favor of intervention."

On November 14, however, this man without a single *lira* published the first issue of a new daily newspaper, *il Popolo d'Italia*, a Socialist organ of which he was the editor and that took as its watchwords two aphorisms—one from Napoleon: "Revolution is an idea that has found its bayonets," and one from Blanqui: "He who has a sword has bread." The anger and outrage in the ranks of the Socialists of Milan were in direct proportion to the faith they had invested in the young editor of *Avanti!*.

On November 24 the militants of Milan met in the Teatro del Popolo to discuss the matter. Mussolini arrived with some friends and was greeted with cries of "Judas!" and "Sell-out!" People flung handfuls of coins at him. The case for the prosecution was stated by an old fighter for Socialism, Costantino Lazzari: it was he who had proposed the appointment of Mussolini as editor of *Avanti!* and now he was calling for the renegade's expulsion. Unable to make himself heard, Mussolini smashed a glass against a table.

"The war will carry off the lot of you!" he shouted. "You hate me now because you still love me!" Jostled by the throng, he cried: "Don't think that by taking away my membership card you can root out my convictions or stop me from continuing to fight for the cause of Socialism and the revolution!"

He left the hall to the cadenced shouts of "Traitor! Judas!"

What was the truth of the matter? First of all there was the influence of Filippo Naldi, who procured Mussolini's initial capital, his newsprint supply, and two favorable contracts, one with the Italian Delivery Service Co., which handled newspaper distribution, and one with the advertising agency of Haasenstein & Vogler; in addition, Naldi promised to give Mussolini access to the foreign-news services of *il Resto del Carlino*. All this was considerable, but a Socialist commission of inquiry set up in 1915 on Mussolini's request absolved him of the charge of "venality." Yet there are considerable evidence and many presumptions that center on subsidies paid by the French government. Gaetano Salvemini, who was an interventionist in 1914 but later an anti-Fascist, calculated the money made available by Julien Luchaire, director of the French Institute in Milan, at twenty thousand francs; other prominent Frenchmen were supposed to have helped as well. The Socialists in Paris were part of the "sacred union" and had access to secret funds. It seems likely that they might have wanted to help Comrade Mussolini prepare the Italians for intervention. A courier—Marcel Cachin, the French Socialist who favored the war and later became a Communist—was reported to have gone to Italy from Paris with money sent by the Socialist minister, Marcel Sembat.

Were these payments made before or after the inception of *il Popolo d'Italia*? The question has never been resolved; in any event it is of minor importance, for Mussolini certainly did not adopt his position for mere financial reasons.

As director of *Avanti!* he had held a position of primary rank in the Socialist Party, and he had earned it by years of struggle. He could not have given that up for money alone. What then? Undoubtedly Mussolini was motivated by a complex of factors. There was, first of all, his love of the grand gesture, of verbal violence, difficult of reconciliation with a policy of neutrality; his preoccupation with being a leader also played its part. Now there was no one at the head of the democratic, *"risorgimentale"* intervention movement—the post was there for the taking. Perhaps Mussolini feared that others might prevent him from seizing the leadership of a turbulent movement whose style suited him. On October 5 such revolutionary syndicalists as Alceste De Ambris, Filippo Corridoni, and Cesare Rossi had issued an appeal in the name "of a revolutionary *fascio* of interventionist action": Thence to Mussolini the danger of being "passed on the left" seemed very real, and the more so because, like many others, he must sincerely have believed that the war could culminate in revolution. Then, after his negotiations with Naldi, Mussolini could be certain of having at least the good will of the authorities, even their material support, while at the same time preserving a revolutionary side in his life, or even, he might have believed, his revolutionary goals. Thus, in Mussolini's eyes, his turnabout was clothed in the tinsel of an exacting loyalty to action.

Now revolution to him was simply action, violence. His characterological tendencies emphasized the superficiality of his political development. In many respects his education was that of a self-taught man in a hurry, relying on instinct and confusing word with thought, activity with revolution. In addition he had been strongly influenced by the ideas of Sorel and Blanqui and by the example of the anarchists, all of which sharpened his taste for the spectacular and the rhetorical. So, at the age of thirty-one, when battle was raging from the Yser to Ypres and the face of modern war was making itself known, Mussolini brought out the first issue of *il Popolo d'Italia*, in which, in an article headed "Boldness," he stated his new position in his abrupt, concise style:

> In a period of general liquidation like the present . . ., propaganda against war is the propaganda of cowardice . . . leave that for the priests . . . the Jesuits . . . the bourgeois . . . the monarchists.
>
> Should it not be the task of revolutionary Socialists to awaken the sleeping conscience of the multitudes, to shovel quicklime over the faces of the dead—and there are so many of them in Italy— who persist in the illusion of being alive?

The conclusion was like a manifesto:

> It is to you, young men of Italy . . . that I address my call to arms . . . that cry, that word that in normal times I should never have uttered and that today I speak as loudly as I can, at the top of my voice. . . . It is a frightening, fascinating word: War.

In 1935, in 1940 the speeches of Il Duce were to be mere echoes of this cry of 1914.

On the evening of his ouster from the Socialist Party, November 24, 1914, Mussolini pulled himself erect when a reporter questioned him in the office of *il Popolo*: "As long as I have a pen in my hand and a revolver in my pocket, I fear no man." Then he added scornfully: "I am strong even if I am alone, and indeed because I am alone."

He was not alone in that interventionist movement that he had joined but that he had not created. As early as the autumn of 1914, Garibaldian volunteers were fighting in the Argonne, and the major part of the press—we have already cited its important role —from the *Corriere della Sera* to the *Messaggero* in Rome and the *Secolo* in Milan stood for intervention. *L'Idea nazionale* had become a daily on October 4, 1914, and thus nationalist propaganda had a forceful tribune at its disposal.

This press was allied with industrial circles: Filippo Naldi revealed, in an interview that he gave in 1960,[2] that *il Popolo d'Italia* had received subsidies from Esterle on behalf of the Italian Edison Company, from Bruzzone on behalf of the Unione zuccheri (Sugar Combine), from Giovanni Agnelli on behalf of FIAT, from Pio Perrone on behalf of Ansaldo. Moreover, in May, 1914, the Perrone brothers had bought *il Messaggero*, which became one of the most vociferous press advocates of intervention.

Now these men represented the most powerful firms in Italy. With the Ilva group and Breda, FIAT and Ansaldo were the great manufacturing companies—ships, rolling stock, automobiles, heavy machinery, armaments—that had overcome the economic depression of 1907 and gone on to dominate the market.

They were supported by the great Italian banks—the Banco di Roma, the Credito Italiano, the Banca di Sconto. Thus the interlocking of financial and industrial interests constituted the solid foundation of interventionism. Unquestionably they were concerned with war as an escape from over-production, but also with the prevention of a social revolution that to some of them seemed an imminent danger after the Red Week. On April 26, 1915, Alessandro Casati wrote to a deputy, Giovanni Amendola: "How could an army whose glory had not been refreshed confront an internal revolution tomorrow?"

Yet it was not such glacial calculation but national feeling, the enthusiasm of a minority of young men and intellectuals, that gave interventionism its color. Their ardor and their hatred for Austria were voiced in little student newspapers or in those of the Republican Party. They drew their inspiration from Garibaldi and from democratic ideals; they believed that this war would make it possible for Italy at last to attain the rank of a great nation. It was "Italy's first war. . . . It is not a war of savagery or of conquests, but a war for right and justice," Mussolini wrote in *il Popolo* on February 14. He had resolutely taken the leadership of the movement and his newspaper soon had a circulation of almost one hundred thousand. But this was not the limit of Mussolini's activity. He organized propaganda meetings, he threw himself recklessly into his work, passionately committed to follow his new road to the end. On December 13, 1914, he spoke in the courtyard of a school: "Neutrals have never dominated events. It is blood that sets the vibrant zone of history in motion."

The interventionist Socialists met in Milan on January 19, 1915. Six days later they created new Fasci of Revolutionary Action,

[2] In *il Paese*, January 12, 13, and 14, 1960.

which soon numbered five thousand members distributed throughout Italy and which included the men who would later become the first Fascists: Alceste De Ambris and Michele Bianchi. Mussolini concluded his address to the little group in Milan with these words: "The inevitable will come to pass. The old worlds of Italy's social and political life will crumble into dust."

And under his pressure the interventionist movement, supported morally and materially by the large newspapers allied with financial circles, took a violent, adolescent, noisy turn. But it was only a heterogeneous coalition in which nationalists formerly friendly to the Central Powers, like Alfredo Rocco, rubbed elbows with Socialists like Gaetano Salvemini: many inevitably would be fooled. In the wake of the war Fascism was to come to power: Rocco, the nationalist, would be a minister, and Salvemini, the Socialist, would choose exile.

In spite of all its ambiguities, however, the interventionist faction held the center of the Italian stage at the beginning of 1915. In order to appraise it accurately one must recognize that it represented only a minority of public opinion. Luigi Albertini, editor of the *Corriere*, and Salandra, the head of the government, said as much. Salandra wrote that war was "conceived and wanted by an active and courageous but, in all honesty, infinitesimal minority that the government could very easily have reined."

For the whole of the peasantry, the majority of the Catholics—on a number of occasions the Holy See had evidenced its preference for Italian neutrality; Austria-Hungary was a bastion of Catholicism—the Socialist Party and the workers who followed it all favored neutrality. In other words, the overwhelming majority of Italians. Hence, in terms of social groupings, the interventionists represented university elements of middle-class origin, a few syndicalists, a few nationalist or revolutionary intellectuals and—this was the essential factor—business and press circles. But even in this last category there was no unanimity. Light industry could still be satisfied with peace; the Catholic press, *La Stampa* in Turin, *Avanti!*, *La Tribuna*, and *il Mattino* in Naples were neutralist. Furthermore, the neutralist tendency had an impressive leader: Giolitti.

Here we come back to the rupture of 1913 between Salandra's conservative liberalism and Giolitti's progressive liberalism. Giolitti foresaw a long war; in addition, he said, "to go to war under the right auspices requires the enthusiastic endorsement of the great majority of the country." He was fearful of lack of preparation and economic disorganization; and, whereas the interventionists of the right hoped to kill off revolution by means of war, Giolitti, in contrast, was afraid that war might give birth to revolution.

Interventionist demonstrations became more frequent. On February 25, 1915, there were clashes between Socialists and interventionists in Mussolini's Milan; two men were killed in Reggio Emilia. On the pretext of a letter in which Giolitti had stated the possibility of obtaining "something (*parecchio*)" without war, the interventionists rained insults on him and accused him of connivance with Prince v. Bülow and Matthias Erzberger, the Catholic leader, who were representing Germany in Rome. Tension was mounting. A few days later, public demonstrations were prohibited and on March 29 Parliament adjourned for six weeks. Thereafter Salandra's government was at liberty to move.

Officially, Foreign Minister Sonnino had been negotiating since December 9, 1914, to obtain the Austrian "compensations." After long-drawn-out talks, the Austrians, under pressure from the Germans, agreed virtually *in toto* to the Italian demands. On April 4, 1915, *Avanti!* published a sensational special edition that contained the gist of these successful negotiations. It was too late. Since March 4 Sonnino had also been talking with the Allies in London, and on April 26 he signed the Treaty of London with France, England, and Russia. This treaty, which was secret—the Bolshevik government was to make it public in 1917—granted Italy's demand for a frontier at the Brenner, Trieste, Istria and the greater part of Dalmatia and the Adriatic islands, and in addition it alluded to a "legitimate colonial compensation." The gains were substantial, but the price was high: Italy promised to enter the war *one month*, at the latest, after signing the treaty—in other words, before May 26. Italy, in fact, was simply Sonnino, Salandra, and the King. For these three men were to keep the secret of the treaty: General Cadorna, chief of the general staff, was ignorant of its contents! Giolitti, the leader of the majority in Parliament, denied having been told about it.

But what was most important in the course taken by the government was the fact that, by committing Italy and the King, the treaty confronted the neutralist opposition with an impossible choice: either war or a government crisis, since the King was personally committed by the treaty: in telegrams to the King of England, the President of France, and the Tsar he had given his formal approval. The treaty left no escape road: it meant war before May 26. Henceforth, every day between April 26 and the fateful deadline counted for the government: at all costs it had to win the backing of the country and Parliament for a declaration of war.

The situation was all the more delicate in that the opposition, which knew nothing of the terms of the London treaty, clung to neutrality, and this opposition was growing.

From his Villa Malta on the Pincio, Prince v. Bülow amplified his advances, providing more information for the neutralists. Backed to the wall, the government and the crown let the streets do the job.

Earlier, on April 10, Mussolini had issued a proclamation in *il Popolo*: "Seize the squares tomorrow, regardless of everything! No one can stop us! You are the law, you are power!"

The next day he was in Rome, speaking in Piazza di Trevi at a demonstration organized by the interventionist Fascio. In a bowler hat, a black suit, and a butterfly bow tie, he finished his speech, and then he was dragged off by plain-clothes policemen who twisted his arms and manhandled him. He was kept in a cell until the end of the day.

On May 4 the Italian government denounced the Triple Alliance: the judgment day of May 26 was coming nearer. Then the "glowing month of May" began, one demonstration followed another as if in rehearsal for the Fascist Era, for only a minority— true, it was an impressive one—held the streets and the squares. D'Annunzio, the poet, who for months had been writing interventionist articles for the famous third page of the *Corriere della Sera*, made his farewells to his lying sources in France and went back to Italy. His purpose was to commemorate the March of the Thousand, which had begun on May 5, 1860, at the crag of Quarto, near Genoa. Mussolini and d'Annunzio: Fascism had already found its heroes.

Eugenio Baroni, the sculptor, had created a monumental bronze group on the rock at Quarto; Garibaldi's family was present at its dedication, as were many survivors of the expedition. Dozens of gaily decked craft, motorboats, and steamers furrowed the calm water of the bay with their wakes. Hatless, bald, surrounded by delegations from the universities, the poet delivered his oration as the crowd threw flowers and waved flags and handkerchiefs.

"Blessed are the young who hunger and thirst after glory, for they shall be satisfied," the poet said.

"*Abbasso l'Austria!*" the audience howled. "Down with Austria!"

In Genoa that evening there was a demonstration in front of the German consulate. Acclaimed by the crowd, Ricciotti Garibaldi stepped out on to the balcony of his hotel and cried: "War or revolution!"

Nonetheless the ceremony at the Quarto was a disappointment. The King and his ministers were supposed to attend, but at the last minute they sent their excuses. For the situation in Rome was grave. *La Stampa* had published the detailed record of the negotiations with Austria: Italy had obtained what she wanted, the paper argued, so why make war? Salandra, Sonnino, and the King were again at bay, and Giolitti was on his way from Piedmont. True, his journey was marked in Turin and Rome by shouts of *Abbasso il parecchio* (that "something" that could be had without war), but on May 9 *la Tribuna* reported that three hundred deputies and one h lred senators of all parties had been in communication with him. Apprehensive, Salandra made a quick recapitulation with Bissolati: altogether the advocates of war numbered some sixty members of Parliament. This was confirmation that "neither the real country nor the legal country wanted intervention" (Salvemini). But the streets were in the hands of the interventionists.

On May 9 there was brawling in front of the Milan office of *Avanti!*; three days later d'Annunzio arrived in Rome. A crowd bearing torches escorted his carriage along via Boncompagni, not far from the palace of Queen Mother Margherita, as ardent an interventionist as, later, she would be pro-Fascist. From the balcony of the Hotel Regina, d'Annunzio cried: "Tonight we intend to counter cowardice with heroism! Let Italy take up arms, and not for an absurd parade but for a bitter battle! Romans, behold the challenge!" And he tossed his white glove to the crowd.

On May 13 there was a rumor that Salandra had presented his government's resignation to the King. Again d'Annunzio spoke: "Hear me—heed me—treason is out in the open today. . . . They seek to strangle our country with a Prussian rope."

The press threw off all restraint. Mussolini wrote in *il Popolo*: "Are we to believe that a few dozen miserable German politicians in Italy are capable of halting the course of our destinies by their intrigues?"

Anti-parliamentarianism, thus sown, began to grow; d'Annunzio bawled: "Sweep, then, sweep away all the filth, shovel all the putrefaction into the sewers!"

Cartoons in the newspapers showed Giolitti as a Calabrian bandit setting an ambush for unhappy Italy, or else in his coffin while Wilhelm II and Franz Josef wept over him. Already the themes and the style of Fascism were emerging and for like ends: to enforce through violence, with the consent of the King and the government, what the country did not want, or did not yet want.

On May 13 Mussolini and Filippo Corridoni harangued the crowd in the Piazza del Duomo in Milan, a crowd in which the prevailing dress was soft hats and straw hats, white shirts and butterfly bows; a hostile demonstration was held at the archbishop's palace. Soon enough there was an incident: stones were thrown by neutralists, guns were fired, a mechanic named Luigi Gadda was killed by a bullet in the head, and eighteen wounded were taken to hospitals. In Bologna there were shouts of *Hurrah for the army!* and a counter-demonstration; in Florence *Down with the war!* was painted in large letters on the wall of the Uffizi.

War, however, was to triumph. The struggle against it was unorganized; often it was not undertaken until too late; and in addition interventionism had appropriated the insignia of patriotism and even of revolution. Mussolini declared threateningly on May 13: "We want war, and if you, Sire, who under Article V of the Constitution can send all our soldiers to the frontiers, refuse it to us, you will lose your crown."

A day later the news of Salandra's resignation was confirmed. Violence broke out; windows were broken in the offices of *la Stampa* in Turin and of *il Mattino* in Naples; little bands everywhere were howling: "War or revolution!" Barricades were thrown up in via del Viminale in Rome; the demonstrators regrouped before the Chamber of Deputies—Montecitorio—scaled the fences, entered the building (Salandra, supposedly, had assured the perpetrators of immunity), and streamed through the corridors. Taking neutralist deputies by surprise, they hooted at them, clubbed them, and spat in their faces. The German and Austrian embassies and Giolitti's villa were put under army guard. That evening, from his box in the Costanzi Theater, d'Annunzio loosed another tirade: "We are about to be sold like a flock of sheep. One is ashamed to say one is an Italian. See what the obscene scum of Dronero [Giolitti] wants to do . . . the leader of the criminals. The Italian Parliament will reconvene on May 20 . . . the anniversary of Garibaldi's magnificent march . . . let us close the doors of Parliament to the errand-boys of villa Malta [Bülow's residence]!"

This contempt, these charges of treason, this anti-parliamentarianism were all to re-appear with Fascism.

On May 15—and here it is likely that the resigning government had a hand—the personnel of all the ministries, in formal array under their directors-general and department heads, demonstrated in favor of Salandra. The same day the Perrone brothers' *Messaggero* wrote: "Royal cogitation cannot procrastinate. . . . Either the next government will faithfully interpret the national conscience by declaring war on Austria . . . or the people of Italy will declare war on those who betray its purest faith. War or Revolution!"

Vittorio Emanuele III told a senator whom he encountered: "I must make war; otherwise there will be revolution."

On the evening of May 16 the King sent for Salandra and announced that he was not accepting the Cabinet's resignation: the interventionists had won. Mussolini was gleeful, and on the next day, alluding to the events at Montecitorio, he wrote: "The irruption of the citizens of Rome into that sacred enclosure is a sign of the times. It is truly a stroke of luck that Montecitorio is not a charred heap of ruins today. . . ."

That sentence sums up the consequences of that "radiant May": Parliament was turned into a mockery, legality had lost its first battle. The price was to be high: it would be paid in 1922, when once again the streets would lay down the law.

In Rome there were cries of *Hurrah for the army!* and *Hurrah for Salandra!* Parliament was to reconvene on May 20: in a final act of intimidation, the secret police suggested to the neutralist deputies that they spend the night in a hotel across the street from Montecitorio and thus be safe from the mob.

When the Chamber assembled, its oldest member, Paolo Boselli, was in the chair. Rising, he strode somberly forward, his voice rich with tears: "Soldiers! sailors! Your banners are radiant still with the emblems of St. George and St. Mark, who hallow your enterprise. . . ."

The resolution that authorized the government to declare war was adopted by four hundred seven votes to seventy-four! Between May 9—when three hundred deputies had expressed their confidence in Giolitti—and May 20 the pressures and blackmail of the streets and the throne, of business groups and the press, had reversed the majority. The technique was not to be discarded. Giovanni Gentile, soon to become the official philosopher of Fascism, observed in connection with those May days: "All of us vibrate like strings under an artist's hand."

Mussolini clarioned—and in 1940 he was to return to the memory of that style, which he hoped was martial: "Italian bayonets, the fate of the peoples of Europe is entrusted, with Italy's, to your steel."

On May 17 the Turin workers called a general strike: too late. The Casa del Popolo—House of the People—was put to the sack. Peace was already lost. On May 24, two days before the expiration of the one-month grace, a state of war with Austria came into being.

So the glowing days of May came to an end. Italy's major cities had been the theaters of violence in which enthusiasm and patriotism were invoked to justify the violation of law and right. And the legal nation—the King, the Cabinet, the state, and the deputies—had proved either corrupt or passive; the real nation had shown itself to be unorganized, helpless, or bewitched; its economic forces had been instigators, approving or satisfied.

This May of 1915, when neither a Mussolini nor a d'Annunzio was lacking—a pleasant May, when in the streets of Rome young men in straw hats spat in the face of the Socialist deputy, Pietro Bertolini—foreshadowed and prepared another month, a rainy month: that of October, 1922, and the triumph of Fascism.

"Our war is a holy war!" Premier Salandra declaimed to a cheering audience in the Capitol in Rome on June 2, 1915.

On the front the Italian troops were advancing. The second day's communiqué announced: "We have occupied Caporetto." In July the Italians crossed the Isonzo and moved forward into the Trentino.

The interventionists went to war: Marinetti joined a bicycle unit and d'Annunzio was considering the air force, in which he was soon to be a colonel; Corridoni and the syndicalists joined the army; at the age of sixty the reformist Socialist, Bissolati, applied for service at the front. Mussolini, who was about to be drafted, did not enlist, and his enemies made a game of charging him with cowardice, but he was expecting to be mobilized, and on August 31, 1915, he was assigned to the Second Bersaglieri. Two days later he was at the front. He immediately began keeping a war diary. It was a self-portrait of a modest man among his modest fellow-soldiers in the front line, whom he was constantly urging to cry *Viva l'Italia!* Officers wanted to meet him, and invited him to their mess. On September 16 a staff captain sought him out in the ranks to say: "I just wanted to shake the hand of the editor of *il Popolo d'Italia.*" On that same day Mussolini crossed the Isonzo, noting in his diary: "Drank a big mouthful of the Isonzo, until yesterday an Austrian river, with tremendous emotion."

He did not mind recording the admiration expressed for him. Under the date of September 17 he reported with a certain smugness: "*A bersagliere* from Mantua came up to me and said: "Signor Mussolini, when you led us through the artillery barrage, we could see that you had plenty of guts. We'd like to be under your command.'" And Mussolini added: "*Sancta simplicitas!*"

That was the climate of the early days of the war. But very soon the tone changed. Mussolini had refused the suggestion of an understanding colonel that he be assigned to the rear to keep the regimental history. "For forty days," he wrote, "I have been shooting and been shot at continuously, day and night. I ate up the trenches. . . . My specialty is tossing back enemy grenades before they go off. It's a dangerous game." He elaborated on his courage: he would hold the grenade in his hand until the last possible second, amid the terrified silence of his fellows. "Poor little Italian soldiers," he wrote, "they have no pride." But one can understand them. For these peasants, shoveled brutally into the hell of a savage war that they had not wanted, were making acquaintance with death that strikes at random. They were deployed over a three-hundred-fifty-mile front, four-fifths of which was mountains, stretching from the peaks of the Trentino to the Isonzo and the Carso—that barren Karst—in exposed positions facing the Austrians who held the heights, dug in on inaccessible peaks or behind the barbed-wire defenses strung along the left bank of the Isonzo.

The soldiers were also becoming aware—often at the cost of their own blood—that on this inhospitable front the Italian army was the victim of shocking inadequacies. It was true that since 1914 General Cadorna had succeeded in increasing the number of divisions from twenty-five to thirty-five, but nothing had been done to prepare them for modern war. Their weapons were obsolete, their artillery was insufficient, their uniforms were highly visible, there was a shortage of officers, and sanitary and administrative services were badly organized. These words turned into tragedies in the merciless daily fighting: against the Austrian machine guns the Italians had nothing, and the cutters issued for attacks on barbed-wire emplacements could not get through the metal. And, in the face of these facts, the sharpening of sabers was being "expedited" and high officers were being posted to grenadier regiments! On top of this lack of preparation—which it was difficult to excuse, after a whole year of modern warfare on the French front —military doctrine consisted of compensating for deficiencies in equipment and leadership by launching frontal attacks and repeated charges. What the Italian General Staff was waging was the war of a poor country rich only in a peasantry for which it had little regard. In the first months of combat against the numerically inferior Austrians, the modest gains of the Italians cost them sixty-six thousand men killed and one hundred ninety thousand wounded. Naked, frozen ridges were captured and given up without reason, then captured again, the same units remaining constantly in the line without relief. Luigi Albertini said of Cadorna that "he knows nothing about men of flesh and blood; he always governs himself by the abstract formulae of duty and rules."

Giovanni Amendola, the deputy, observed in 1915: "Here we go on throwing ourselves to the butchers. . . . When our troops are not being led in a charge in the fashion that you know so well, they

are left in a demoralizing inertia in rotting, revolting trenches."
Mussolini himself wrote: "Throughout the year 1915 the Italian
soldier waged war under conditions of absolute inferiority. Battalion after battalion was thrown into assaults to open the way
through the barbed wire with spades, rifles, or bare hands. Regiment after regiment clung for months to mountainsides where
all the Austrians had to do to defend themselves was to roll down
rocks on them" (*il Popolo d'Italia*, November 12, 1917).

Thus thrust into the worst possible conditions, badly led and
subjected to harsh discipline, the fighting man soon lost his initial
fighting spirit. In November, 1915, Mussolini was returning from a
mission when a soldier stopped him: "Is that you, Mussolini? . . .
I've got good news for you. Corridoni [one of the earliest interven-
tionists] has been killed. That's fine—let them all croak!"

It was clever and easy to blame the rear for this development in
the state of mind, all the more so because the Socialists, hesitant
but loyal to their principles, had taken the initiative of convoking
the International Socialist Conference that was held in Zimmer-
wald, Switzerland, from September 5 to 8, 1915, and in which
Lenin took part. Mussolini was enraged. On September 14, in *il
Popolo*, he issued a violent call for repressive measures: "There
must be no saboteurs of our strength at the rear. . . . If they exist,
they must be killed." Now the theme of treachery was added to
that of *radiosomaggismo* (the-glowing-month-of-Mayism) and
marked another milestone on the road to Fascism. Mussolini went
on: "The corruption that we purged in May has not yet been wholly
swept away and scattered. . . . Maintain constant vigilance, strike
furiously, do not allow a moment's respite to the hyenas who are
getting ready to devour the gruesome banquet of the dead." And
Salandra, the head of the government, outdid him: "Repression is
a two-edged sword, but we will cut off our hands if we must, provided that we can cut off the heads of our country's enemies."

And the war went on for good or for ill, little by little eroding
the youthful body politic of Italy.

Mussolini was promoted to corporal for gallantry; according to
his citation, he was "the first for every detail and for dangerous
assignments," and undoubtedly he was a good soldier. In December, 1915, he fell ill with typhoid fever and spent several weeks in
the Cividale hospital; then, having received convalescent leave, he
went through a civil wedding ceremony with Rachele.

On September 27, 1915, his first son had been born: the boy
was named Vittorio in anticipation of victory. Before Mussolini
went back to the Carso front, he launched a new attack on the neu-

tralists in *il Popolo*. Its contemptuous tone was a poor disguise for Mussolini's uneasiness in confrontation with these opponents who had not laid down their arms and to whom the sufferings and the duration of the war seemed to provide vindication: "For some time now the slackers have been browsing on the flowered lawns of Arcady side by side with the gentle sheep of the Catholic flock and the goats of the official Socialist congregation. Benedict XV afflicts us with his encyclicals, his discourses, and his lamentations."

The echo of these lamentations was all the louder because Italy's losses were inordinate: from May, 1915, to October, 1917, the average monthly casualty figure was eleven thousand dead and twenty-seven thousand wounded, or almost thirteen hundred men put out of action every day. In three months of 1916 the Italians had four times as many dead and twice as many wounded as the Austrians. And in spite of that Italy brushed elbows with disaster on May 12, 1916: Marshal Conrad v. Hötzendorf launched his *Strafexpedition* (punitive expedition) on the plateau of Asegio: Venice was threatened and the entire Italian front was in danger of being turned. Fortunately the attack by Brusilov's Russians in Galicia and the resistance at Verdun imposed limits on the Austrians' successes, but the Italians had lost one hundred fifty thousand. This was already the shadow of the rout of Caporetto, darkening the country a full year before that catastrophe. Salandra could not stand up to defeat: a "sacred union" government was formed with two Socialists, Bonomi and Bissolati, and a Catholic, Filippo Meda, under the dean of the Chamber, Paolo Boselli. This cabinet imposed military psychology and discipline on the country. A new labor code made resignation from a job the equivalent of desertion from the army. Big industry grew rapidly even bigger: Ansaldo's payroll went from four to eleven thousand workers and its capital rose from thirty to five hundred million *lire* (from six to one hundred million dollars). Shell output was increased eight hundred percent and an aircraft industry was brought into being. But this upsurge in big industry was matched with growing restrictions: the war went on, the peasants were at the front, food rations were diminishing, and at the end of 1916 the financial position was difficult. And no end to the conflict was in sight. Granted, the Italians had taken Gorizia in August, but General Capello's forces still had their backs to the Isonzo under a punishing counteroffensive. Uncertainty and discontent were rising. The Socialists were hardening in their positions. From April 24 to 30, 1916, they had taken part in a second international congress, in Kienthal, and on May 1, at the height of the war, they issued a manifesto that declared: "The struggle for a lasting peace can be only the struggle for the achievement of Socialism."

The soldiers at the front had a song about Cadorna:

> "You want to see Trieste?"
> Our general asked the queen;
> "Go buy a picture postcard,
> That's where it's to be seen."

But discipline was devoid of mercy. Men were shot for the most trivial offenses. Consequently, Amendola observed, "our men are resigned now to remaining at the front, but they don't take any risks." Senator Olindo Malagodi, who made a survey of the front lines in January, 1917, reported: "As for morale, I was compelled to recognize an atmosphere of gloom and exhaustion, and here and there of repressed, silent anger and rebellion as well—and all the more impressive *because* it was kept in."

In March of 1917 the Russian Revolution broke out and Nicholas II abdicated. Alexander Kerensky, heading the Provisional Government, pledged to continue the war, but his armies disbanded. Gramsci, the most resolute of the Italian Socialists, viewed these as encouraging indications of an early Socialist revolution.

These were the ominous auspices under which the year 1917 began. It was also a difficult year for Mussolini.

On Hill 144 he was part of a crew assigned to range-finding with a trench mortar. Suddenly the weapon exploded and five men were killed. Mussolini was picked up with forty fragments of metal in his body. He was moved to Doberdò and then to the hospital in Ronchi. The news spread in interventionist circles and telegrams poured in, from the minister and from Corridoni's mother. Mussolini replied: "I have turned the road to Trieste red with my blood."

On March 7, the King, who was making more and more tours of inspection from his headquarters in Udine, visited the hospital. He stopped at Mussolini's bed.

"How do you feel, Mussolini?"

"Not too well, Your Majesty."

"Be brave, Mussolini. Try to resign yourself to your immobility and your pain."

Mussolini got out of the hospital in August. He was walking on crutches, and some people—as if he were the only wounded man, or the most seriously hurt—spoke of him only as "the wounded *bersagliere.*"

Mussolini received a medical discharge and resumed his work

at *il Popolo*, beside the blonde Sarfatti, at via Paolo da Canobbio, 35, where the newspaper occupied four rooms. In his own office, as remembrances of the front and by way of precaution, Mussolini kept a supply of grenades within reach.

For the climate was progressively deteriorating. There were anti-war demonstrations when men came home on leave; the military censors held up hundreds of postcards and letters in which men at the front urged their families not to sow any more crops in order to force the country to the edge of starvation and thus compel it to sue for peace. Nor was this all. On August 1, Benedict XV addressed his "papal letter for peace" to all the powers, describing the war as a "needless massacre." Giolitti came back to public life in Coni and made a speech, his first since 1915. On the same day, August 13, two emissaries from the Petrograd Soviet, Smirnov and Goldenberg—Mensheviki, supporters of the war—were greeted in Turin by fifty thousand workers shouting: "Hurrah for Lenin! Hurrah for the Bolsheviki!" This demonstration was the prelude to more important events. On August 23 insurrection broke out on opposite outskirts of Turin, at the Milan and Nice "junctions," and three or four times the workers tried to seize control of the center of the city. Barricades were built and networks of electrified barbed wire were strung. For five days the workers held out against attacks, but the troops did not go over to the rebels; Turin was not to be a second Petrograd.

Nevertheless what had happened in Turin was viewed with anxiety by the ruling classes. Now there was a new dread to fill the hearts of the conservatives and the moderates after the Red Week. What would happen after the war? For the moment the immediate situation must be faced. Promises to the fighting forces poured out. On August 30, 1917, Mussolini wrote: "Gentlemen of the government: . . . turn over the Germans' billions to the families of the fighting men! Land to the peasants! Even drastic reforms are still not enough in the face of the tremendous, eternal sacrifice of so many human lives!"

Italy, however, did not come to the end of her ordeals in that year of 1917. Superficially the military situation seemed favorable. Between May and September, General Capello's forces had attacked—there were, in all, eleven offensives on the Isonzo—and scored successes, and now they were preparing to start off again.

But then came the rout at Caporetto, at the same time as the October Revolution in Russia. On the morning of October 24, 1917, rain and fog engulfed the Isonzo valley, which was infiltrated by a German division, reinforced by Austrians. The Italian artillery was zeroed in on and reduced to silence with a few accurate attacks. The use of gas completed the disruption of the Italians, who fell back and then disintegrated. The outcome of the battle was settled in a few hours. The Fourth Army collapsed. The Italian troops on the other side of the Isonzo had to retreat in order to avoid being outflanked. On October 25, Cadorna telegraphed to the government: "I see a disaster taking shape."

The tragic flames of the rout threw the flaws of the Italian army into sharp relief. Generals acted as they pleased; orders were not transmitted. The roads were clogged with refugees and with soldiers retreating in confusion in the rain, their arms abandoned, their units commingled; they flung themselves down in the mud, embracing one another for warmth, to sleep and sleep, while on the road farm wagons went by with women in black shawls nestling their children in blankets. Impassive carabinieri, their rifles slung over their shoulders, stood motionless in pairs at their posts, watching in bewilderment as three hundred fifty thousand fleeing soldiers and four hundred thousand civilians packed the roads. The military disaster brought on a political crisis: Boselli resigned and was replaced on October 29 by Vittorio Emanuele Orlando; Francesco Saverio Nitti became Minister of Finance. The front went on rolling backward; on November 1 it was on the Tagliamento about twenty miles west of the Isonzo; eight days later it had been driven back twenty more miles to the right bank of the Piave. The King sent out a vigorous summons:

"Italians, citizens and soldiers! Form a single army. Every cowardice, every dissent, every accusation is treason."

For the search had already been launched to find the men responsible for Caporetto. Cadorna, who was soon to be replaced by Armando Diaz, wrote to Orlando on November 3, blaming "the insidious campaign for a strike in the army, the wind of madness blowing from one part of the country that has poisoned the spirit of part of the army."

So the army was clear; it had been betrayed by the defeatists. Mussolini had spoken earlier, on October 29, of "the vices of parliamentarianism" and of "Montecitorio and its dangerous charlatans." On November 9 he wrote: "The entire nation should be militarized. . . . Let us forget about the rights of individual freedom. . . . Invasion of our territory is a national grief."

He appealed to "unity of spirit," and, under the lash of defeat and invasion, Italy reacted. The winded Austrians were held at the Piave. On November 11 members of the Wounded War Veterans' Association applied for permission to go to the front. On November 14 the interventionist deputies formed the Parliamentary

Fascio of National Defense, the futurists formed Futurist Political Fasci, and these set the climate for a wave of arrests and convictions of Socialists charged with defeatism: Costantino Lazzari, Serrati, and Nicola Bombacci were sent to prison. As for Mussolini, he insisted more than ever on the opposition between Nation and Parliament. Speaking of Montecitorio on December 10, he concluded: "It is an appalling grotesque, for forty million Italians are nothing and four hundred deputies are everything."

In the Augusteo in Rome, he proclaimed on February 24, 1918, to an already frenzied crowd: "I call for savage men. I call for a savage man who has strength, the strength to shatter, the inflexibility to punish, to strike without hesitation, and the harder and oftener when the guilty are in high places." Who can help thinking of the image that Il Duce would later try to create for himself?

Meanwhile the war was continuing along the Piave—a hard war, without pity. Naked men, their bodies painted black, slipped into the frigid water every night to cut the throats of the Austrian sentries on the opposite bank. These were the "alligators of the Piave," the *Arditi*, soldiers of those Italian guerrilla-type forces whose exploits the press described with relish. Ardent young volunteers or convicts released in exchange for enlistment, they were the heroes of the sudden strangling, the grenade charge, the dagger battle. Well taken care of, coddled, relieved of all ordinary duties, of the cruel boredom of nightly guard details, they represented the "ideal" war, and Italy was fascinated by them. After every attack, every murder, they went back to the rear to live at their ease, daggers in the belts of their black uniforms: a sweater and a fez or a cap, and a flame sewed to their sleeves as an escutcheon. They lived from assignment to assignment, with nothing to lose, between relaxation and death. When they went into a shop, the shopgirls fled; the Arditi served themselves and outraged the population. They had acquired a taste for war, they loved its violence. Fascism would find them ready for it.

So the war brought the post-war dramas to maturity. On May 24, 1918, in the municipal theater of Bologna, Mussolini took the stage. It was the third anniversary of Italy's entry into the war. It was clear that he had found his program and his themes:

"Soldiers, ladies, gentlemen: Without the war our nation's valor would have been extinguished. Italy can no longer be portrayed in the apron of an innkeeper. . . . We are and we wish to be a nation of producers. . . ." Already he was putting forward his candidacy for power: "We who have survived, we who have come through, claim the right to govern Italy."

On March 29 he had shrewdly dropped the quotations from

Blanqui and Napoleon from his masthead, and in August the sub-title, "A Socialist daily," became "The newspaper of fighters and producers." In its very ambiguousness—who is not a producer?—the word was indicative of Mussolini's ambitions. It was time for him to clarify them, for he was aware that the war, "the pure fountain that has purified us," was coming to an end.

In June, 1918, a powerful Austrian offensive on the Piave failed: it was a great victory for Italy, "the sacred moment," as Mussolini called it. On October 24, one year after Caporetto, the Italian army attacked in its turn, and on November 1 Mussolini wrote excitedly: "It is the army of Italy that is ending the war with a triumphal march. Victory thus gained is beautiful, it is Italian, it is OURS!" Ours—*a noi*—the slogan of Fascism.

On November 3 General Enrico Caviglia's offensive culminated in the victory of Vittorio Veneto, and the next day, in Padua, the Austrians signed an armistice.

"Now is the hour of divine rejoicing!" Mussolini wrote. Against Caporetto, which he described as "the fruit of neutralist poison," he pointed to the army's triumph in Vittorio Veneto, and he did not boggle at adding: "It is through a victory that transcends all those of the other armies that Italy has struck the mortal blow against the enemies of the human race" (P.d.I., November 2, 1918).

On its deathbed the war gave birth to the myths of Fascism.

In Milan, via Paolo da Canobbio, 35, the office of *il Popolo d'Italia,* that "camping ground," was never empty: Arditi, bersa-glieri, officers, young men with decorations constantly filled the little rooms stacked with old copies of *il Popolo* and foreign newspapers. On the door of Mussolini's office there was a poster: "He who enters does me honor; he who stays out does me a favor."

It was there that Mussolini learned, as he was to write, that "peace had broken out." His editorials poured out one after another, fevered clarion calls composed at a corner of the desk, in clouds of smoke, while the ever-devoted Sarfatti ministered to him. To Mussolini victory represented the success of interventionism: "At last Italy achieves her unity and impresses the seal of the accomplished fact on the enormous toil of many centuries" (P.d.I., November 4, 1918). And indeed Italian troops, in pursuance of the London agreement, were occupying a long strip of the Austro-Hungarian empire: in Trieste and Trento—the home of Cesare Battisti, whom the Austrians had beheaded during the war—the Italians were received as liberators; flags decked the windows, and singing and dancing hailed the victory of irredentism. Fiume too, though it had not been included in the London accord, offered an enraptured welcome to the glorious soldiers of the Piave and the Carso. These occupations were the *a posteriori* justifications of the irredentism of the *Risorgimento* tradition, and on November 5 Mussolini wrote: "Our war was a people's war. There has been a tremendous clash between the forces of the past and those of the future. Italy, the nation of the future, has crushed the forces of the past; she has wrested the bars from the old prison of the Habsburgs: she has set the peoples free."

The victory parade in Milan on November 10 was remarkable in its extent. Crowds hailed the soldiers in the central-city streets, and men on leave, nurses, passersby were carried away by the collective frenzy; even priests threw themselves into the improvised mass dances that wove through the city in the sudden eruption of the joy of survival. After the parade, trucks loaded with Arditi coursed through the streets. These Arditi were the spoiled children of the war. Among the young men clinging to the platform of one of the trucks was Mussolini. The trucks stopped at every intersection, the horns blew madly, everyone shouted *Long live Italy!* The Arditi leaped down from their trucks and invaded the cafés; some of the customers applauded them, others watched with frozen smiles.

Suddenly, out of the hubbub, Mussolini's voice soared: "Arditi! Comrades in arms! I defended you when the cowardly Philistines slandered you. . . . The gleam of your daggers and the flood of your grenades will render justice to all the swine who would try to halt the march of greater Italy. She belongs to YOU [*a voi*]!"

"*A noi*—to US!" the Arditi repeated, linking arms. They raised their daggers high and shouted: "*Viva l'Italia!*" Behind the flag of the nation they strode out, knocking over chairs and drinkers like a rampaging river.

"After the war" was beginning.

On November 11 there was an armistice on the French front. The demonstrations began again. In front of the monument to the Five Days in Milan that commemorates the *Risorgimento*, a crowd clotted, and traffic was halted. Carried on the shoulders of his friends, Mussolini started to speak: "Brothers of the trenches, fellow-citizens, remember well that it was here that we held the first meeting in favor of the war—at this very place, with Francesco Corridoni."

Corridoni, the revolutionary syndicalist, had been killed at the front. There was a great ovation at the name of the man who had been Mussolini's rival and whom now the editor of *il Popolo* appropriated to his own purposes.

"Today the Italian flag flies from the Brenner to Trieste, to Fiume, to Zara, Italian of the Italians. . . ." He was interrupted by cheers and applause. "At home too, victory must accomplish the other purposes of the war: the redemption of the workers."

Men crowded round to shake Mussolini's hand, to embrace him; then, led by the younger men, the crowd formed into a new parade that wound through the streets of Milan again until late in the night. Mussolini, however, went back to his newspaper office and, modulating on his theme, drafted his editorial for the next day's editions: "Every man who has fought and bled is superior to the rest. . . . the good has triumphed. . . . Peace has come as we planned it: it is just . . ." (November 12, 1918).

Once the songs had stilled and the dancers had left the streets, peace had to be lived, to be looked in the face. Certainly it was a victorious peace: the empire of the Habsburgs had collapsed, and Trento and Trieste were Italian, but as early as November 13 a delegation arrived in Rome from Fiume to demand annexation to Italy: the Treaty of London had assigned the city to Croatia. Soon Allied detachments were to be dispatched to join the Italians in the Adriatic port, while nationalist circles called for the annexation of the entire Dalmatian coast and Admiral Millo's Italian fleet sent troops ashore at Zara and Sebenico, on the Dalmatian coast.

This first shadow on the nascent peace was not to be the only one. The end of the fighting was now part of the past, but still the carabinieri or the village mayors continued delivering telegrams announcing the glorious deaths of sons or fathers. For the victory had claimed a high, a very high price: six hundred thousand dead, nine hundred fifty thousand wounded; of the latter, two hundred fifty thousand were crippled for life. Unquestionably the nation had survived the blood-letting, and this was a proof of its unity, but it was weakened. Gramsci was to declare: "Italy has come out of the war a vast wound, and her blood pours in jets from a body covered with wounds."

However exorbitant it might have been, the tax in blood was not the only cost of the war. Expenditures had risen from two and a half billion lire in 1913–14 to 30.857 billion in 1918–19; the deficit had increased a hundredfold; money in circulation had gone up by one thousand percent. And the United States and Great Britain had announced that, as of the armistice, they were suspending their loans; worse, the question of repaying these had already been raised.

And yet no one took cognizance of this situation; quite the contrary. Once the fighting had stopped, the nation waited for prices to drop and abundance to return: had not industry expanded during the years of conflict? Everyone knew that heavy industry, called on to increase production and made absolute master of its workers, who were treated as soldiers, had erected all kinds of large new establishments. Turin, Genoa, and Milan formed the corners of an industrial triangle, and FIAT, Ansaldo, and Ilva were more than ever the giants of Italian production. In 1917 it was possible for Corradini to write: "Italy is an industrial nation. From her soldiers' uniforms to their guns, everything is of Italian manufacture."

War profits, moreover, had been huge, and conducive to concentration: speedily reinvested in order to keep them out of the hands of the tax collector, they formed the basis for increases in capitalization, the issuance of new shares and speculations on the stock exchanges, and they explained the invasion of the big banks by industrial capital. Ansaldo and Ilva (with, respectively, five hundred million and three hundred million *lire* in capital stock) gained control of the Banca Nazionale di Sconto; and other financial institutions, like the Credito Italiano and the Banco di Roma, were transferred in part or in whole to the control of the owners of heavy industry. Not only was this absorption an evidence of industry's power; it increased the fragility of the whole Italian economic structure by making the future of the banks and that of industry closely interdependent, and from 1921 on there was to be a series of spectacular failures that would rock both financial and industrial circles.

But the newly demobilized soldier of November, 1918, was hardly concerned with these deep and significant alterations of his country's economic structure; what he could see was the *pescicani* (sharks, profiteers) and the *imboscati* (slackers), middlemen who had been made rich by the war and who, in his view, were the incarnation of the problems and the outrageous fortunes of the home front.

At first, however, hope was stronger than resentment. People wanted to believe that restrictions were about to end and to forget that fifty-nine percent of Italy's merchant tonnage had been destroyed, that the British government had just reinstated the right of freedom of navigation for its own shipping, that Italy was poor. The word *victory* created an illusion, inflated hopes; did not victory bestow rights?

The National Association of Crippled War Veterans, the first such organization of former soldiers, had already issued its "postwar program." On November 12 it called on all veterans to organize throughout the country, "above and beyond the old political parties," in order to preserve the solidarity born under fire in the trenches. Now these former soldiers were extremely many; promises had been made to them; and already the first demobilization trains were beginning to arrive in the cities. They must be given consideration, and they demanded it. When the Chamber of Deputies reconvened in Rome on November 20, the *onorevoli* deputies filing into Montecitorio included a number still in uniform.

The hall and the galleries were filled with the honorables and with officers, ambassadors, and elegant ladies. Orlando, who headed the victory Cabinet, heightened the effect of his white hair and his heavy body by the emotion with which he spoke: the hour of triumph had sounded, he reiterated his allegiance to Woodrow Wilson's program, and, above all, he said that "this war, the greatest political and social revolution within the memory of history, should open the way to great social reforms."

The tone had been set. Political groups and leaders were to strive to channel and exploit this great hope, this thirst for renewal that, intensified by the sacrifices of the war and the promises of the government, had seized all Italy. No soldier returning home, not one man who had "come through," could believe that he had fought for nothing, that everything was going to start all over again in the same old way. Hence every political organization was evolving its own ambitious program. After the opening session of the Chamber, Salandra, the champion of intervention, presided over a ceremony in the Augusteo in honor of victory. This observance had been organized by the Parliamentary Fascio. The political purpose was obvious: to exploit the winning of the war in order to perpetuate the divisions born of entry into it and to isolate the neutralists, Giolitti in particular. In short, peace should complete the task of the "glowing May" and the war. To the applause of the crowd, Salandra declared: "Broad and bold reforms are required. Above all, the nation's highest representatives must no longer be manipulated in an old structure reinforced by old and new simonies."

Thus anti-parliamentarianism sought to survive the end of the war, and Salandra insisted, quite naturally, that the Fasci should not be dissolved, but should constitute "active, industrious phalanxes, open to all men of good will."

Il Corriere della Sera, for its part, clarified the purport of the speech when it said that "from now on, the Fasci represent the end of the old parties."

On November 26, in the name of the Parliamentary Fascio, Orazio Raimondo called on all honorable men—excluding the defeatists—to join in opposition to Bolshevism. A bridge had been built between May, 1915, and the post-war period, between interventionism and Fascism.

But the great effort and all the agitation of these last two months of 1918 were concentrated on the theme of the election of a Constituent Assembly by universal suffrage, the sole means of infusing new life into Italian institutions. This idea enjoyed the support of all points of view: the Crippled Veterans' Association, the Republican Party, the reformist Socialists, and especially the CGL and its competitor, l'Unione italiana del lavoro (Italian Union of Labor), in which Mussolini had many friends.

But this chorus lacked the voice of the massive Partito socialista ufficiale (Official Socialist Party), which Mussolini was soon to stigmatize scornfully as the PUS. This party had subscribed to an ambitious revolutionary program, which it made public on December 12, 1918; "The Socialist Party sets as its objective the establishment of the Socialist Republic and the Dictatorship of the Proletariat with the following aims: (1) the socialization of the means of production and exchange. . . ." The rest of the program carried on in this radical tenor, calling for universal disarmament, the collective distribution of goods, and direct management by the workers.

On December 22–23 the Socialist forces gathered in Bologna, in the heart of "red Emilia," where during the war processions of peasants and children had paraded as they sang:

> La bandiera rossa la trionferà,
> La bandiera rossa la trionferà,
> Evviva il socialismo e la libertà!
> (The red flag leads us on to victory,
> The red flag leads us on to victory,
> And long live Socialism and liberty!)

The old leaders were all there—Treves and Turati, whose broad, kindly face, grey beard, careless cravat and corpulence were memories of the end of the nineteenth century, of the parliamentarianism of the Third Republic of France. And there were also the young, whose opposition had cost them imprisonment and who were fascinated by the Bolsheviki, those "majoritarians" whose phraseology and even whose name—the meaning of which they transformed—they had adopted: these were the Maximalists—Serrati, Bombacci, and Amadeo Bordiga, who wanted to follow the German and Russian revolutionary examples.

For revolution seemed to be irresistibly overrunning Europe, from Petrograd to Berlin: why not, then, from Turin to Bologna?

The other factions in attendance (the Socialist Parliamentary Group, the CGL, the railway workers' union, the league of Socialist municipalities) endeavored to present a more immediate program of reforms: a democratic republic, the elimination of the Senate, the election of a Constituent Assembly. But the Maximalist tide was stronger, and the end in view remained the dictatorship of the proletariat, the decisive means to which would be the general strike: revolutionary language was beginning to reign in Italy. Arrested after the rioting in Turin, Serrati took over the editorship of *Avanti!* in Milan. The first processions appeared in the streets— workers and demobilized soldiers, who would soon create the Red War Veterans' Associations. Turning to the apprehensive crowds who watched them march, the demonstrators shouted: "Up the revolution! up the Soviets! up the Spartacists! up the Bolsheviki!" And the revolutionary song stilled since 1917 rang out again like a confident challenge:

> Avanti, popolo, alla rescossa . . .
> Bandiera rossa, bandiera rossa . . .
> (The people, forward! to the rescue . . .
> The red banner, the red banner . . .)

But what interested Italian governmental circles more than the marchers was national territorial claims. Undoubtedly these also embraced the concern, already felt at the time of the declaration of war, for contrasting conquest to revolution, the nation to Socialism, and as well the resurgence of the nationalist tendency that, as we have seen, was born before the war and was nurtured by the fighting.

In fact the nationalists had never been satisfied with the annexation of the "unredeemed" territories: of course a start must be made with Trento and the Brenner, but it was essential to look farther ahead, beyond this "irredentist pretext" that was the justification of the left interventionists. Even during the war—on June 5, 1917—Albania had been occupied; Socialists like Bissolati and Bonomi wanted to resign, but Sonnino reassured them with the declaration that Italy had no interest in assuming a protectorate over that country. Unity was restored among the interventionists in order to proclaim, in the Pact of Rome of April 10, 1918, the right of the peoples of the Austro-Hungarian empire to independence. In vain. The tendencies of interventionism remained fundamentally opposed to this, and victory was to shatter the ostensible unity of war time. Intoxicated by victory, by the warlike exaltation of armed action, by the cult of the hero, nationalism developed rapidly, and the question of Fiume became an abscess of fixation for the chauvinist passions to which it gave rise.

The port of Fiume, which contained twenty-four thousand Italian residents, sent delegation after delegation to Venice and Rome, all demanding annexation to Italy. In the city itself, Italian officers were greeted with joy; the nationalists' daily, *l'Idea nazionale*, fostered the campaign, backed by a new magazine, *Politica*, which had just been established—there was no lack of financing—by Coppola and Rocco.

When they published the nationalist program on December 15, 1918, the masks were off. The two theoreticians frankly asserted that the war had been merely a conflict between two opposing imperialisms, that democracy was only a form of decadence, that the right of conquest alone mattered, that expansion was the sole criterion of a nation's vitality. Those who had thought that they were fighting for democratic ideals had made a mistake, and the nationalists laid claim to Fiume, Dalmatia, Albania, territory in Asia Minor, natural borders for Libya, and free economic penetration of Ethiopia, Arabia, the Red Sea, West Africa, and the Far East, in addition to reparations, railway lines, and industrial concessions. Indeed, the prominence of the economic demands was revealing: Italian heavy industry, deprived of the war, was looking for a new field of growth; but what was also striking in this program was its lack of proportion, as well as names like Ethiopia and Albania, which foreshadowed Fascism.

Was this program to become the foundation of the government? Orlando was under powerful pressures; the press was divided: Sonnino, who was Foreign Minister, had a newspaper of his own, *il Giornale d'Italia*, and he joined the chorus of the nationalists. *Il Corriere della Sera*, on the other hand, aligned itself with the "abstainers," realists whose yardstick for expansion was the country's actual power and men of principle who hoped that peace would mean the dawn of a new era. In Milan they founded an organization in support of the League of Nations.

It was Dalmatia in particular that set the nationalists and the abstainers against each other, even at the center of the government, for old Bissolati rejected a policy of conquest. On December 28 there was exciting news in Montecitorio: Bissolati had offered his resignation. "The soldier of the alliance," a twice-wounded former sergeant in the Alpini, the symbol of democratic interventionism, Bissolati was walking out.

But on the evening of December 29, in counterpoint to his resignation, the auditorium of the Augusteo in Rome slowly filled with a crowd of young men, officers, and well-dressed intellectuals. The audience gave a standing ovation to a delegation from Fiume, shouting: "Dalmatia is Italian!" Other groups ran through the streets of Rome with the same cry, to which they appended: "Down with the abstainers! down with Bissolati!"

Thus, with the arrival of peace, interventionism was divided within itself, and Bissolati, one of the first to volunteer for the front, was cast out. Now that the war had been fought and the victory had been gained, he would have had to accept the new nationalist demands. He was too honest an old man to be capable of that.

Mussolini showed more understanding. On January 1, 1919, he attacked "that Croat" Bissolati, and added: "Imperialism is the eternal, the immutable law of life." But, well versed in disguising his vital meanings, he went on: "It can be democratic, peaceful, economic, and spiritual."

As a matter of fact, while he had been singing the same song of victory as the nationalists for two months, Mussolini was preoccupied also with recapturing a popular audience. He had compromised far too much to return to the Socialist fold, but he had not yet been finally accepted by the nationalists: his rhetoric was still that of a revolutionary.

So he vacillated, offering pledges to the one side and seeking to charm the working masses that yearned for radical upheavals and were thankful for the return of peace. And the man of peace was President Wilson of the United States, who arrived in Rome on January 3, 1919.

This was further evidence of the want of response to nationalist propaganda, for Wilson was opposed to Italian claims to Dalmatia. Therefore the official reception for him was chilly, in spite of a large state dinner at the Quirinal. When Wilson received the Roman officials in the United States Embassy, Palazzo del Drago, he remarked with considerable irony: "New York is certainly the largest Italian city in the world, but I hope that the Italians are not going to claim it."

Nothing could have been more direct, but Mussolini's headline read VIVA WILSON and he characterized the President as "the bringer of the new human gospels." No matter that the President had a long conversation with Bissolati at the Quirinal and went to confer with Benedict XV in the Vatican; that did not stop Mussolini from writing on January 5, when Wilson was to arrive in Milan: "Pay the greatest of tributes to Wilson, men of the Five Days!" A huge, enthusiastic crowd greeted him in Milan; many soldiers waved their caps; and the shouts were the same hope-laden cries as those of Rome: *La pace, la pace* (Peace, peace)! It was not yet time to attack the President.

So Mussolini proceeded, always looking for the strongest tendency without cutting himself off from the others. His position in these early months of 1919 was difficult, and his changes of partners showed that he was still on the outside. In spite of his manifestos, he was a kind of political *disoccupato* whom events passed by: he could only add his voice and his activity to movements already led by others. He was a follower, in his own way; but it was still following. Then he turned toward those who like himself, but for other reasons, were also outsiders. Already, on November 10, he had joined the truckloads of Arditi as they paraded through the streets of Milan. These men of violence had now been relegated to inaction, demoted from glory to oblivion, from sudden murder to the long training marches along the Po that the army command, determined to take them in hand, had prescribed for them. These aimless marches were humiliating; for the Arditi peace was a harsh break in the rhythm of life, the end of bad habits, and a time of resentment.

And so they came together for old times' sake and to recreate an atmosphere. They were available. On January 7, Mario Carli, a futurist, founded the first Arditi Association in Rome; in Milan they gathered round the poet, Marinetti, and former Captain Ferruccio Vecchi. This tall, slender young man with his goatee and moustache was the archetype of the Ardito who had covered himself with medals and ribbons for his daredevil actions. A typical story about this Don Juan had it that he had slipped into his sleeping colonel's bed to make love to the colonel's wife. He dazzled the middle-class youths who were too young to have fought in the war and who dedicated themselves to aping their elders: Vecchi or Marinetti, Bolzon, Brambillaschi, or that Alligator of the Piave, Albino Volpi. Before the end of January there was a National Association of the Italian Arditi, which had its seat in Milan in via Cerva, 23, in a very aristocratic neighborhood. The building was sumptuous, but the association's rooms were like a barracks: the walls were hung with the black flag bearing skull and cross-bones, the Arditi emblem; everywhere there were helmets, bayonets, firearms, and daggers, the favorite weapon of these men accustomed to carrying out their operations under the rule of *no prisoners*.

Mussolini delighted in mingling with the Arditi. To him their violence echoed his own anarchism, their unrest as men uprooted reflected his own anxiety as a politician without a flock; he shared the bitterness common to all who have been pushed from the foreground to the ranks; and, above all, in the Arditi Association he discovered the nucleus of an organization, a core of resolute men whom he could use, with whom he could act. An opportunity was very soon to arise.

In January the cold, dense fog of Milan embraces the city by five in the afternoon. On the eleventh day of this ungrateful month in 1919, the Caffè Cova was constantly filled. This was the meeting place for jobless young men and demobilized officers. Mussolini, his head shaved, had just left, surrounded by three bodyguards. Piazza alla Scala and Galleria Vittorio Emanuele were clogged with a dense crowd that coagulated outside the Teatro alla Scala. Leonida Bissolati was scheduled to speak at six o'clock under the auspices of the Association for the League of Nations, and the theater was full. People were still arriving in via Manzoni. Suddenly there were songs from the center of the square, at the foot of the statue of Leonardo da Vinci: songs of war in bellicose voices modulated by the fog:

> Il Piave mormorò
> Non passa lo straniero
> (The River Piave murmured:
> "No foreigner shall pass.")

The singers were Arditi, in numerous groups that called to one another: "Arditi? *A noi*—it's all ours!"

Daggers at their sides, decorations on their chests, they had come to demonstrate against "the Croat," Bissolati. Soon another band entered the square, and Vecchi broke out the *"Gagliardetto,"* one of their fringed black flags, at the end of a long staff. He assumed the leadership of the column, which made a path for itself through the astonished crowd, taken aback by the resolve of these men in fezzes or black caps who dared to flaunt their weapons. The crowd could not know that this January 11 marked the cynical introduction of violence into post-war Italian political life, of violence that had already adopted the black flag.

Teatro alla Scala was a little world of heat, glare, and shouts. Marinetti and the futurists were waving their arms. Officers' widows in their boxes, their faces flaming with passion, applauded, and in his own well-guarded box Mussolini stood alone and erect, looking down on the hall as if from a pedestal. Insults flew from orchestra to gallery. When the aging Bissolati appeared on the stage, his voice was drowned out by shouts: "Down with the Croat! Hurrah for Italian Dalmatia!"

The audience was progressing from insults to brawls, and soon

Bissolati had to abandon any attempt to speak. The brawling spread to the fog-enveloped streets; then, with Vecchi and Mussolini in the van, the Arditi re-formed their lines and, arms linked, headed for Galleria Vittorio Emanuele amid the cheers of the customers in the fashionable cafés and their own chant of *Non passa lo straniero*.

Italian nationalism had taken possession of the war and the victory, gagging the voice of the "soldier of the alliance," the old *"risorgimentale"* interventionist. The violent determination of the minority had just imposed its will on the unorganized throng. As for the police, it stood aside.

Later Mussolini was to go back to *il Popolo d'Italia* and then to his fourth-floor apartment on the Foro Bonaparte. He had learned a great deal in that damp, cold evening of January 11, 1919. In the days that followed he sang of victory in *il Popolo*. On January 13 he published d'Annunzio's *Letter to the Dalmatians*.

During the war the poet had played his part as a legendary hero with theatricality, and courage. He had flown a bravado raid on Vienna; with Costanzo Ciano and three motorboats he had ventured out into the Bay of Buccari and, in three bottles dropped into the waves, hurled a "challenge" at the Austrians. Now, with his rank of colonel and his five silver medals, he was the incarnation of Arditism in the new era of peace, and he took up the fight for the notions of nationalism. In *il Popolo* he wrote of the opponents of Italian expansionism: "Not a bone, not a stump, not a rag. . . . We will face the new conspiracy in the manner of the Arditi, a bomb in each hand and a knife between the teeth."

But, though he was making *il Popolo* the platform for the demands of the nationalists, Mussolini had no intention of neglecting social problems on that account. Every new day was eroding the illusion of a return to pre-war prices. The price level of January, 1919, was six times that of 1914, and it was mounting steadily. Certain foodstuffs were difficult to obtain as post-war hunger increased; there was a shortage of shipping and speculation was rampant.

The most resentful victims were the middle classes. During the war they had subscribed more than fifteen billion to the various loans; they had contributed their sons, those young reserve officers who had constituted the great majority of the cadres and who had acquired the habit of command. They regarded Italy's victory as their own, and now the return of peace was burying them in oblivion while the rise in prices was strangling them. Some sectors were disturbed, too, by the rise of those large corporations that were stifling competition—powerful, anonymous monopolies against which the small business man and the working man sought some defense.

But above all there were the returning young officers—they numbered almost two hundred thousand in 1919—who had to find employment, and competition among them was acute everywhere, for, while heavy industry had expanded, it was still too young to have developed a large tertiary sector that could offer a prospect of use for those ambitions, those claims, that taste for authority that had been born of the war or invigorated by it.

Very often the returning warrior had no graduation certificate, and then all doors were closed to him and his decorations could not unlock them; younger men who had not gone to war had acquired the necessary qualifications and established themselves. He might have been in the trenches, but what else did he know? Those who could went back to the universities, but they found their studies useless and they grew bitter. Sometimes, when they were talking of their wartime deeds, they were laughed at. In the workers' quarters of Genoa and Turin some officers had even been insulted, struck, and stripped in the street.

All these skilled workers, abetted by the growth of industry and the shortage of labor, had been able to keep their wages high during the war. Furthermore, the expansion and concentration of industry had been determining factors in the entrenchment of a skilled, aggressive, politically oriented proletariat, particularly in Turin, where the revolutionary tradition had never been smothered. The proletariat could fight the rise in prices with the weapon of the strike (it was employed almost seventeen hundred times in 1919 alone), but it was looking beyond mere purchasing power. According to Federico Chabod, an Italian historian, Turati called a meeting on Janaury 28, 1919, and declared: "We must prepare men's minds for the installation of a Socialist society, but at the same time we must proceed by gradual stages in the transformation of society."

"Too slow," someone shouted from the audience.

"If you know a faster way," Turati said, "tell me."

"Russia's," a number of voices shouted. *"Viva Lenin!"*

Undoubtedly not all the proletariat had been won over to this view, but there was a widespread desire for change. The peasants back from the war wanted land and labor contracts, and all the former soldiers wanted jobs. The government had promised them a bonus of ten *lire* (one dollar in 1919 *lire*) for each month spent in combat areas; in February it legalized the eight-hour day. Mussolini projected himself as the spokesman for these veterans in *il Popolo*. On January 16 he wrote:

> Above all, the excessive promises made to the fighting men must be fulfilled. . . . Demobilization has just begun: fifteen classes of conscripts have been discharged. The soldiers are denied even the esthetic and moral satisfaction of being welcomed in triumph. . . . The military trains unload their human cargoes in our cities. The soldier puts aside his uniform and becomes a citizen again. And then his problems begin. . . . Gentlemen of the government, gentlemen of the ruling class, listen to us!

In January Mussolini backed the postal and railway workers in their demands for higher pay and the right to strike. But at the same time he endorsed the industrialists who were clamoring for the restoration of economic liberalism. On January 30 they gathered in Bergamo and called for the end of all state controls; on April 3, 1919, the landowners and the industrialists met in Genoa, where the shipbuilders were all-powerful: they forged an alliance to combat state monopolies, the war economy, and Bolshevism. Mussolini cheered.

To every man, opportunist or demagogue, he offered his hand, seeking the springboard, the opportunity, yet emphasizing that his basic premise was "the soil of the Nation, the war, victory" (P.d.I., March 18, 1919). And there can be no doubt that, among all his variations, the national theme was the only fixed point in his thinking, as his prime source of strength was ambition. In all other respects he was groping.

On March 17 he was informed that, at the instigation of l'Unione italiana del lavoro, in which he had many friends, the workers in the Franchi & Gregorini factory in Dalmine (in the province of Bologna) had gone on strike. Even better, they had occupied the factory—this was the first such action after the war—and for three days they continued to operate it on their own. Mussolini acclaimed the creation of this "Workers' Council." He went to Dalmine from Milan; eyeing the Italian flag that the workers had raised, he concluded his speech by saying: "You have taken your stand on the basis of class, but you have not forgotten the nation."

That was indeed the essence of his program in those early months of 1919: to seek to merge the nationalist tendency and the Socialist aspirations of the masses for his own benefit.

These masses were also the target for a new group. Huge white posters had gone up in the major cities of Italy on January 18, 1919. At the top of each was the word *Libertas*, inscribed in a shield bearing a cross. This was the emblem of a new party, the Partito popolare italiano (Italian Popular Party), and the posters reprinted its first manifesto, "inspired by the principles of Christianity that will hallow the great civilizing mission of Italy." It called on "all free, strong men" to build "a truly popular state," and the party held itself forth as the first organized political expression of the Catholic forces. Among the many signatures on the manifesto —those of Bertini and Count Santucci, for example—that of the party's political secretary stood out: Don Luigi Sturzo.

This Sicilian priest, born into a family of the old nobility in 1871, had gained distinction as mayor of Caltagirone and then as secretary general of Catholic Action. For him, as for the Vatican, the goal was to make the Catholic masses definitively a factor in political life. Thin, nervous, his aquiline face always creased by a smile, Don Sturzo soon dreamed of a large party that would be the voice of the Catholics even more effectively than the Gentiloni Accord.*

In November, 1918, he had requested an audience with Cardinal Gasparri, Papal Secretary of State, to whom he expounded his thinking. When he had finished, the cardinal asked: "Assuming that the pope would approve, what policy would you adopt toward the church?"

"None that would be antagonistic," Sturzo replied; "that goes without saying; but no particular policy as a party."[3]

Benedict XV gave his consent and Don Sturzo could then proceed with the manifesto of the Popular Party. The new organization was to assemble the most varied Catholic elements—Roman aristocrats, social Catholics, and veterans of the agrarian leagues. This diversity was to be at the root of the ambiguity of its policy, the more so because, while it was not a religious organization, its preoccupation with the defense of Christian values "in opposition to the Socialist democracies that seek to materialize ideals, in opposition to the old sectarian liberalisms," was often to make "the rectory the second headquarters" of the new party.[4] In any event it grew rapidly: by June of 1919 it already had eight hundred fifty sections (which soon increased to twenty-seven hundred) and fifty-six thousand enrolled members. From the start, of course, it had

* In 1913 Giolitti had sufficiently tempered his anti-clericalism to enter into an election agreement with Count Ottorino Gentiloni, president of the Catholic Union. This agreement provided that anti-Socialist liberals who signed a declaration stating that they opposed divorce and favored the religious orders and private schools would receive Catholic votes.—Editor.

[3] Quoted by Carlo Sforza in L'Italia del 1914 al 1944 quale io la vidi (Rome: Mondadori, 1944).

[4] A. C. Jemolo, Chiesa e stato in Italia negli ultimi cento anni (Turin: Einaudi, 1948).

many strong backers: twenty daily newspapers and some fifty weeklies.

The birth of the PPI made a radical change in Italian political life: Socialism now had an opponent of stature; as for Mussolini, the emergence of this new force made his position seem only the more precarious. He went into action, nevertheless, resolved to rally his followers.

Arditi groups were established throughout Italy in February, 1919. In Milan, with Mussolini's support, Carli and Ferruccio Vecchi founded a newspaper, *l'Ardito*, which formed a bond among the various groups. But Mussolini wanted to go farther, and, above all, to gain the leadership of the movement.

On March 21 he assembled some sixty of his followers in Milan. They must form an organization, he said; having been won at the front, the war must be carried on within the country. His audience included a number of Arditi, one of them being Vecchi.

The meeting resulted in the foundation of a *Fascio milanese di combattimento* (Milanese Battle Fascio). Mussolini, Vecchi, and Michele Bianchi were among its officers. The organization's name made it quite obvious that it was establishing its roots in the war and its future in fighting. A general meeting was planned for the evening of March 23.

On the appointed date 119 men met in the second-floor reception room at Piazza San Sepolcro, 9, that belonged to the Industrial and Commercial Society. The attendance included Marinetti, Carli, and young Roberto Farinacci, who had come from Cremona for the purpose.

The presidency of the new group was assumed by Ferruccio Vecchi. Its task was defined as the creation of a national organization to be called the *Fasci italiani di combattimento* (Italian Battle Fasci). Mussolini made a long speech and then presented a three-point declaration, the first charter of Fascism, which was not to be published until June. The March 23 meeting pledged itself to "support with vigor the material and moral demands that would be made by the associations of war veterans." It declared its opposition to imperialism, but, it emphasized, "Italy has to achieve fulfillment in the Alps and on the Adriatic by demanding and annexing Fiume and Dalmatia. . . ." And Mussolini shouted: "We say: let all be idealists, or none."

Then, amid applause, he offered the third declaration: "The March 23 meeting calls on Fascists to sabotage the election campaigns of all parties by whatever possible means. . . ." As a complement to these three principles that carried on the spirit of nationalist interventionism, a very detailed program was laid down, in the form of precise points, demanding: (1) a constituent assembly; (2) a republic; (3), (4), and (5) the abolition of the Senate, of titles of nobility, and of compulsory military service; . . . (10) and (12) a census of wealth, the distribution of land to the peasants, the management of industry by the trade unions; (13) the abolition of secret diplomacy. . . .

As Mussolini wrote in *il Popolo* on March 23: "We allow ourselves the luxury of being aristocrats and democrats, conservatives and progressives, reactionaries and revolutionaries, legalist or illegalist, depending on circumstances of time, place, and situation. . . ."

It was as good as a confession that the original Fascism was primarily opportunism. Besides, the first meeting was characterized by lack of preparation and even by confusion. In order to staff the new organization's executive committee, Mussolini chose those in the front rows of the room who had given him the warmest applause: two of these "elect" were convicted common criminals. . . . After the meeting, the "sansepolcrist" program was signed by fifty-four men—the "*Sansepolcristi.*" Its bold language allowed no illusions. On March 24 the nationalist newspaper, *l'Idea nazionale*, declared: "Since the next attack by Bolshevism is imminent and will be directed against Milan, Turin, and Bologna, . . . it is logical that there above all we should concoct the counter-poison to the danger that threatens the security of our country. . . . Mussolini has moved from the negative side to the positive side."

The night before, in the deserted meeting room, a number of young men, most of them Arditi, had gathered round their black banner. Ferruccio Vecchi drew his dagger and stretched out his arm above the flag, and his friends joined their hands to him. "We swear," he intoned, "to defend Italy. For her we are prepared to kill and to die."

Fascism was born. That night Mussolini had said: "I have the feeling that in Italy the road to the replacement of the current system is open."

The Italian Battle Fasci were a national organization. At the March 23 meeting Mussolini had predicted: "In two months a thousand Fasci will have sprung up throughout all Italy." A day later he noted: "The Fasci are coming to life! Our call has been heard. Genoa, Verona, and Turin are marching in the van. In other cities our friends are at work. All that is needed is the will. Battle Fasci will spring up everywhere. . . ."

Though in fact the Fasci were increasing—notably in Genoa,

Verona, Naples, Parma, Bologna—with Pietro Nenni and Dino Grandi on April 10—and then in Florence with Amerigo Dumini and Italo Balbo—their growth was not so rapid as Mussolini had hoped. Above all, at no time did the Fasci attract large masses. Most often they were formed round a nucleus of Arditi reinforced by a few students. Soon, however, an organization of students exclusively was created. Mussolini was well aware that he had made no impression on the workers and peasants who adhered to the Socialist Party or the new Catholic Popular Party. So he attacked, on March 28:

> We must get it firmly into our heads, we must believe and make others believe that the only party in Italy that is reactionary today is the Official Socialist Party, the PUS. Therefore we are the enemies of the PUS, but we are in no way the enemies of the proletariat, whose legitimate demands we recognize and for which we are prepared to do battle.

This appeal to the workers and efforts to detach them from the Socialist Party were constantly repeated by Mussolini, who tried to seduce them by playing on the word *revolution*. "Revolution in Europe is a direct and unchallengeable result of Italian intervention . . ." and therefore, he was ostensibly saying with this statement, the revolutionists should join the interventionists: since "it was we who began in 1915, we have the right and the duty to finish the job in 1919" (P.d.I., March 28, 1919).

These maneuvers demonstrate both the opportunism of the man and the vigor of revolutionary aspirations in the Italy of 1919. They also show his attempt to depict May, 1915, as the first step of the revolution in order to bring the Italian masses over to the interventionist position or, better, by brandishing the word revolution, to create at last a broad popular audience for Italian nationalism. In this "seduction campaign," Mussolini published the Socialist and Republican programs in *il Popolo* and concluded: "We desire the unlimited progress of the working masses, but never the dictatorship of politicians" (P.d.I., April 18, 1919).

Even with this confection of demagogy, nationalism, and anti-parliamentarianism, and in spite of his Fasci, Mussolini still seemed in mid-April to be well outside the major trends of his country. Suddenly attention was to be concentrated on him and on the Fascio of Milan.

Socialist demonstrators and troops of the cavalry and artillery confronted each other on April 13 in via Borsieri in Milan. There were shouts, there were pushing and shoving, and then all at once there were shots. The demonstrators fled, except for those who lay dead or wounded before the soldiers. That night the Socialist Party and the Labor Exchange proclaimed a general strike for April 15.

At dawn on that day the carabinieri and the soldiers took up positions in the streets at all strategic points. The whole city was marked off by patrols, but the strike was completely effective. The apprehensive Fascists gathered in the offices of *il Popolo*, which were protected by barbed wire. Arditi stood guard at the windows and on the roof. They were not short of revolvers and grenades. In the afternoon a huge crowd of strikers met in the stadium called the Arena, in the center of the city near the park in which Castello Sforzesco stands. There were almost a hundred thousand strikers at the demonstration; in spite of the anarchists, they voted to return to work the next day.

The Fascists, the futurists, and the Arditi were ready. Lieutenant Chiesa had trained and asembled three hundred student officers from the Polytechnic; they set out in good order and marched along Corso Venezia to Piazza del Duomo. The soldiers did not interfere.

Arrived at the square, the armed Fascists ignored the carabinieri and formed a knot round Marinetti, Vecchi, and a poet named Pinna at the foot of the monument to Vittorio Emanuele. There was a long series of speeches, songs, and chants of *a noi*; then, with the student officers, the Fascists marched on Piazza della Scala, which was also being guarded by carabinieri.

At the same time, the strains of *Bandiera rossa* were coming closer and closer. At a given signal the Fascists charged. The carabinieri made way for them. Their target was the strikers in via dei Mercanti, led by three women in red blouses and two children carrying a portrait of Lenin; behind them marched the anarchists, with red flowers in their buttonholes. Gunfire crackled and clubs split heads. The surprised marchers fell back; some dropped to the street, some fled, some died. Marinetti knocked down a young Socialist and then helped him to rise, adjuring him, as the poet afterward told it: "At least say *Viva Serrati*, you idiot, not *Viva Lenin*."

Then the procession of Arditi and students, swollen by other young men, headed for the offices of *Avanti!* in via San Damiano. Marinetti himself reported that the troops made no resistance. Nevertheless, the soldiers posted outside the newspaper were ordered to defend it. A shot from the marchers felled a soldier named Martino Speroni, and his comrades left their posts. Chaos followed. The doors were forced, the printing equipment was thrown out the windows, the printers were driven out, the paper's records were set on fire, and soon the entire building was in flames. The attackers marched away shouting: *"L'Avanti! non c'è più (Avanti!* no longer exists)."* In the lead, the Arditi flourished the paper's emblem, wrenched off the building. In via Paolo da Canobbio, under the windows of *il Popolo,* the mob applauded Mussolini and then broke into little groups and dispersed.

The Fascists were to celebrate this April 15, 1919, as a glorious victory. The lunch at *il Popolo,* in anticipation of the afternoon's action, became known as "the mess-kit of April 15," the attack on the strikers was baptized "the battle of via dei Mercanti," and Speroni, the soldier, was canonized as "the first Fascist martyr."

And indeed it was an important event.

Marinetti recounted that on the next day General Caviglia, the victor of Vittorio Veneto and Minister of War, sent for him and Ferruccio Vecchi and congratulated them: "In my opinion you won a decisive battle yesterday in via dei Mercanti." This sympathetic praise by the general was representative of all the forces of order. It was an evil omen for the future.

Mussolini quickly recognized this fact and, with his acute feeling for tactics, he concocted the arguments that he would go on employing until he had seized power. In an interview with *il Giornale d'Italia* on April 18, he said: "Everything that happened at *Avanti!* was the product of a spontaneous mass action, action by the soldiers and the people, fed up with Leninist blackmail." Thus he sloughed off his own responsibility, but he added: "We of the Fasci did not plan the attack on the Socialist paper, but we accept full moral responsibility for the incident."

The whole man was incarnate in this guile with which in turn— depending on whether danger or gain was to be expected—he would minimize or emphasize the part played by the Fasci. On April 19, addressing the Socialists in *il Popolo,* Mussolini said frankly: "He who plans an attack can be attacked sooner. Surprise is the strongest card in the deck."

To turn the aggression of an organized and armed band into the spontaneous action of the people, to award the palm of glory to that attack carried out with the connivance of the authorities, to hold the victims guilty for the blows that they had suffered— these were Mussolini's objectives.

Within a month of its creation, Fascism had found its arguments, its confederates, and its tactics.

3

The Shadow of Revolution
(April, 1919—June, 1920)

"But meanwhile 'navigare necesse est,' even if shipwreck awaits the proud and lonely missionaries of our heresy."—MUSSOLINI (January 1, 1920)

ON APRIL 19, 1919, the same day when Mussolini was proudly explaining the lessons of the "battle of via dei Mercanti," the atmosphere was fevered in the Hôtel Edouard-VII in Paris and on the boulevards. The hotel was the temporary residence of the overwhelming majority of the Italian delegation to the Peace Conference: Orlando, the Premier; Sonnino, the Foreign Minister; and General Diaz, chief of the general staff. This was the day when Orlando was finally to state the Italian position before the council of the Big Four.

Finally, because, though they had been sitting since January 18, the Big Four had not yet been able to give any but superficial consideration to Italian problems. And little by little the climate had deteriorated. In the Italian view, victory should have opened a splendid road for Italy: the Austro-Hungarian empire having been destroyed, she demanded payment of the price for her entry into the war: a border in the Alps, Fiume, Dalmatia and the Dalmatian islands, a broad sphere of influence in Albania, the Aegean Sea, and Asia Minor, and, of course, colonial advantages. This program differed little from that of the nationalist circles; the Italians defended it by relying on the Treaty of London in 1915 and the conversations that had been held in April, 1917, in St.-Jean-de-Maurienne.

As he left the Hôtel Edouard-VII on April 19 to confer with

74

President Wilson, Premier Georges Clemenceau, and Prime Minister David Lloyd George, Orlando might have been recalling the speech that he had made to his Senate on December 15, 1918. The eminent Italians chosen by the King to be Senators had applauded deliriously when, as the interpreter of Italian post-war psychology, Orlando declared:

> Italy is truly a great power today, not by reason of some patronizing diplomatic concession but because she has demonstrated a capacity for action and resolution that genuinely identifies her with the great states of history and of the present. This, in my view, is Italy's primary and major gain, a gain that cannot be subject to any debate round an international table, that cannot be challenged or diminished or taken away.

But since January there had been no respite in the irritations and the disillusionments of the Italians. Orlando, who spoke French badly, was a sitting target for Clemenceau's ironies; French officers adopted an attitude of superiority and even of poorly disguised mockery, for to them the shadow of Caporetto blacked out the battles of the Piave; and, above all, the Big Three were not disposed to concede merit to Italy's demands. Wilson had not signed the Treaty of London; Allied troops were in Fiume, and the city, which had not been included in the treaty, was viewed by the Quai d'Orsay as essential to Yugoslavia's existence. French destroyers were even patrolling off the Dalmatian coast, and Wilson, forgetting the welcome that the Italians had given him, was defending those Serbs and Slovenes and Croats to whom peace had just given a nation.

When Orlando finished his statement on April 19, it was Wilson who replied. He accepted a frontier at the Brenner and the annexation of Trieste and a large part of Istria, but he would never give in on Fiume and Dalmatia. Orlando and Sonnino exerted pressure. There were certainly differences and disagreements between these two men—Sonnino was the more rigid—but, confronted by rejection, they joined forces. Sonnino rose: he had done so much to bring Italy into the war and was he now to be condemned to repentance, was Italian intervention to be robbed of all its meaning? Wilson's face, that intelligent clergyman's face, showed no reaction.

Then Orlando spoke again. If the nation should be humiliated, he said, if its war had been for nothing, then revolution might break out. And it was true that the press in Italy was taking a sharper tone. But Wilson refused to yield. Meeting without him two days later, the Big Three strove for a compromise: Dalmatia

The Shadow of Revolution

would be given to Yugoslavia, Fiume to Italy. But Sonnino insisted on Dalmatia, on the subject of which he cited the terms of the Treaty of London and prepared to denounce it as soon as Fiume was in issue.

Thereafter events tumbled over one another.

Orlando threatened to go back to Rome. Arthur Balfour, the British Foreign Secretary, spoke: "Have you considered the consequences of a rupture between Italy and the United States?"

"We are a frugal people," Orlando replied, "and we know the art and the style of dying of hunger."

In Italy the nationalists and, first, Mussolini, then the entire press let it be understood that the conference had reached a deadlock. Feeling rose high.

On April 23 there was amazing news: Wilson had issued an appeal directly to the Italian people over the head of its government. It was reported that Orlando had replied, but no texts were made public. That was enough, however, to incite the organization of a demonstration in Rome, led by the municipal officials: Wilson's name was hooted; a military guard was placed round Palazzo del Drago, the United States Embassy; carabinieri and an infantry detachment took up positions outside the French Embassy, and others were assigned to the British Embassy. So national passions were reborn and embittered, and they were to mount, providing a fertile soil for Fascism.

Wilson's message was made public on April 25: "Fiume should be a port of ingress and egress for the commerce not of Italy but of the countries to the north and the northeast of that port. . . . To grant Fiume to Italy would create the conviction that the port . . . had been deliberately given by us to a power of which it does not constitute an integral part. . . ."

Nothing could be clearer, and Italian resentment and disappointment could not be assuaged by declarations of principle: "America is the friend of Italy. Millions of her citizens were born in the beautiful Italian countryside . . ." or: "It is a question not of interests but of the sacred rights of peoples and of states both new and old. . . ." Granted that it was the nationalists, the Arditi, the Fascists, the students who demonstrated in Milan, Naples, Bologna, Turin, and Genoa; but the whole nation approved.

Side by side with Wilson's message, the text of Orlando's reply was also made public; it accurately reflected the Italian state of mind: "The practice of directly addressing a people . . . is one that has thus far been applied to enemy governments." But what fired emotion to its peak was the announcement that on the evening of April 24 Orlando and General Diaz had left Paris for Rome.

The atmosphere of May, 1915, returned. Prince Colonna, the mayor of Rome, called for demonstrations; the nationalist press and Mussolini's *Popolo* attacked the Allies and spoke of a "supreme moment."

For Mussolini it was a splendid opportunity to denounce the "abstainers," to continue the battle of the "glorious May," the assault on *Avanti!*. In some quarters there was open anticipation of a resumption of hostilities. Only the Socialists preached caution. Federzoni for the nationalists and Mussolini for the Fascists called on the people to demonstrate in the squares; since Italy had once again been isolated and "the ill-fitting mask of a great ideological and universalist war has at last fallen" (Federzoni), Italy must fight again. The nationalists and Mussolini saw what had happened as corroboration of the Fascist leader's axiom: "Imperialism is the eternal and immutable law of life" (January 1, 1919).

They also recognized a magnificent platform for agitation.

And so, on April 26, huge crowds of Romans invaded Piazza dell'Esedra, via Nazionale, and the Stazione Termini. Soldiers in close-order array blocked the streets leading to the United States Embassy. Everyone was waiting for Orlando. His train had evoked tremendous demonstrations at every stop along the way. Rome was filled with enthusiasm—indeed, with fervor.

The train came into the station at ten-thirty. Orlando, Diaz, and Barzilai were surrounded by the throng, which carried them to their waiting cars. Standing erect in his automobile, Orlando began a brief dialogue with the crowd.

"Has the Italian delegation in Paris, acting as it has done, honestly and properly represented the thought and the will of the people?"

"*Sì!*" The roar was deafening.

Tears in his eyes, Orlando went on: "For four years we made sacrifices beyond description [here there was a pause]; perhaps we shall have to impose new sufferings and hardships and sacrifices on ourselves." Did this mean a new war? Carried away, Orlando added: "I know that Italy's army and navy are more ready at this moment than they were in May of 1915!"

General Diaz rose too and confirmed that the "army is ready to do its duty." An enormous popular procession took shape and accompanied Orlando all the way to the Quirinal. There the King and the royal family came out on the balcony and were hailed.

That evening it was learned that the national council of Fiume had renewed its "solemn oath": "The people of Fiume will stand firm to the end to enforce respect for its unshakable desire for union with Italy!"

On April 28 Prince Colonna organized a large popular rally at the Capitol to demand Fiume, Spalato, and Trau; on the same day the Battle Fascio met in Milan under the chairmanship of Mussolini. Thus the feeling that Italy's victory had been "mutilated" fed the Fascist agitation.

That evening Sonnino arrived in Rome and a new procession was formed to escort him; he too delivered a patriotic address. The next day the Chamber held a solemn session and, by three hundred eighty-two votes to forty, "declared its solidarity with the government, to which it pledged anew its full confidence for the defense of the supreme rights of the nation and for the creation of a just and lasting peace."

It was a proud retort to Wilson; but what then? In Paris the three great powers continued their talks. Italian troops having landed at Adalia in Anatolia on April 2, Wilson suggested sending the battleship *George Washington* to Asia Minor. Furthermore, in spite of Italy's absence, the Big Three were preparing to sign the peace treaty with Germany and Austria-Hungary. Must Italy return to Paris? Her diplomats thought so, and they dispatched urgent telegrams pressing Orlando to confer with the Big Three without delay.

Meanwhile nationalist agitation was rising and, as five years before, d'Annunzio was at its head. Embracing the flag that had been carried by a hero, Randaccio, who flourished it even as he fell, d'Annunzio spoke in the Augusteo on May 4:

"Our epic month of May begins again. . . . There on the roads of Istria, on the roads of Dalmatia, on those roads that are all Roman roads, do you not hear the cadenced rhythm of an army on the march? With the Eagles and the Tricolor . . . once more Italy sets out from the Capitol. *A noi!*"

Then, commenting on the report that Orlando would return to Paris, he added: "If our leaders went back to that bank, all would be lost, even our honor."

Two days later, however, Orlando and Sonnino did leave for Paris. In *il Popolo* on May 7 Mussolini headlined: TO PARIS, NOT TO CANOSSA, and guilefully he remarked two days later: "The great proletariat that has given the blood of ten of its flowering generations can take its revenge on the battleground of the class struggle." He established the tone, seeking to direct social demands against foreign countries—France, England, or the United States, which, as the Roman Battle Fascio put it on May 10, represented "the imperialism of the banks . . . the alliance of the plutocracy."

It is obvious how international rivalries were helping and, especially, would in the future help Fascism. For it was true that Orlando had been humiliated in Paris. Crespi, a member of the Italian delegation, observed: "One would have thought he was an interloper. His attitude was that of a man who feels that he is just barely tolerated and who is profoundly mortified by that fact. Orlando hurt me deeply."

For Wilson could not be moved; Lloyd George or Clemenceau would pay only lip service to the Italian position. Hence Italy's undeniable and substantial gains—the Brenner frontier, the destruction of Austria-Hungary, the annexation of Trieste—were pushed into the background by the nationalists and the Fascists, who devoted all their emphasis instead to the Allies' rejections. Thus the "mutilated victory" became a major propaganda theme that encouraged every extreme. The nationalists talked of going back to an alliance with Germany. Mussolini denounced—with what violence!—the men in power: "This group of pestilential syphilitics who hold the destiny of Italy in their arteriosclerotic hands today, this group of men who call themselves ministers, deserves no other definition than that of bastards or idiots or swindlers."

Thus the "mutilated victory" emerged for what it was above all, a springboard for an adventure in internal policy.

On June 19 Orlando's government resigned, having received only seventy-eight votes against two hundred sixty-two.

The situation was critical. The "national" crisis was aggravated by the "social" crisis: in May alone there were three hundred sixteen strike calls, more than ten per day. All industries and all areas were affected, from printers to metal workers, from Piedmont to Naples. The strikes were overwhelming. Fifteen abreast, the teachers of Milan paraded on June 11 behind a red flag. At La Spezia on the same day there were violent clashes between strikers and police: two were killed. Most dramatic of all, the priests of the Basilica of Loreto stopped performing the liturgy on June 16 and demanded more pay!

For the cost of living was rising inexorably. Foreign-exchange controls had been lifted on March 25, and the *lira* tumbled just when imports were vital for the country. But there was also a political element in the strikes: in Turin a strike was called in honor of the memory of Rosa Luxemburg; and the former soldiers in quest of work also sought a political solution to their problems. Mussolini, who was hopeful of winning them over to his side, had headlined on May 1: GENTLEMEN OF THE GOVERNMENT, MAKE UP YOUR MINDS TO GRANT THE DEMANDS OF THE WORKING MASSES; nevertheless, he added, "we warn the Italian workers that they are going to fall victim to a new tyranny that is merciless and also absurd"—by which he meant the Socialist Party; and he denounced that "new idol, the party card": "Proletarians, shatter the tyranny of the politicans of the card!"

Italy was without a government.

On June 20 the Fascists demonstrated in Piazza del Duomo in Milan: "no neutralists in the government!" A day later the Parliamentary Fascio in Rome adopted the same position. Francesco Saverio Nitti was the man who was meant, and he denied that he was an "abstainer"; he established contact with every faction, from Giolitti's friends to the Popular Party's Catholics and the members of the Parliamentary Fascio. This group refused to accept cabinet posts. In spite of all obstacles, Nitti succeeded in forming a ministry on June 23, but the atmosphere was still tense. D'Annunzio and Mussolini were in Rome for the first convention of the National Veterans' Association in the Augusteo.

Rumors of a nationalist and military *coup d'état* were flourishing. General Giardino and Federzoni pledged their collaboration to d'Annunzio and Mussolini. Unquestionably the national crisis was a vital matter in army circles. The Third Army's propaganda section published a bulletin inspired by the nationalists. Until July the army was under the command of Emanuele-Filiberto, Duke of Aosta, a cousin of the King, whose ambitions, popularity, and noble bearing were matters of common knowledge. His duchess, Hélène of France, was also a devotee of nationalist ideas.

So the situation grew more and more strained as June of 1919 merged into July. Even before Nitti could present his cabinet, there was a sudden outbreak of unrest. On June 30 shops were looted in Forlì—Mussolini's town. Soon the act was being repeated all through Italy: shop windows were shattered and interiors were rifled—two hundred in Milan in a single day. Nitti was uneasy; the situation seemed extremely serious. The prison attendants announced that they were prepared to set all their prisoners free if their own demands were not granted. The army could not be relied on: fraternization with demonstrators was common. There were only twenty-five thousand carabinieri. A Soviet Republic was established near Florence and local soviets were created, but the Socialist Party nowhere took over the leadership of any of the activities, which thus remained disorganized, anarchic, local, and devoid of any precise revolutionary purpose.

Il Popolo and the Battle Fasci proclaimed their "solidarity with the people of the different provinces of Italy who rise up against those who would starve the nation." In an article entitled "The People's Justice" and published in *il Popolo*, Alceste De Ambris called on the people to strike at the criminals "not only in their property but in their persons." In Milan Mussolini acted: he created a "Committee of Alliance and Action" in which he conbined Fascists, Arditi, war veterans, and members of the Italian Labor Union. During the night of July 6–7, Arditi from the Pietralata fort near Rome attempted to seize control of the city in order to occupy Montecitorio and the Ministry of the Interior in Palazzo Braschi, overthrow Nitti's government, and proclaim a Constituent Assembly.

Thus it seems evident that, when Orlando's government fell, nationalist and Fascist circles endeavored to capitalize on internal as well as foreign problems in order to seize power. In Nitti's accession the army, the navy (General Giardino and Admiral Thaon di Revel), Mussolini, d'Annunzio, the Duke of Aosta—all seem to have feared the restoration of a normal situation and the liquidation of the war, which would establish harmony among the various ruling groups in Italian society and force out the adventurers and the extremists. Nitti appeared before the Chamber on July 9; the outbreaks had ended, but the situation was to continue to deteriorate.

The government had barely obtained a vote of confidence (257 to 111) when a general strike was called by the Italian Socialist Party (PSI) and the CGL. It was based on an effort by the British Labor Party to put an end to foreign intervention in the recently created Union of Soviet Socialist Republics. The question was not merely one of "principle." Even in Italy there were those who were advocating such intervention. "Occupy Georgia," Lloyd George had told Orlando, and Sonnino had dispatched a certain Colonel Gabba to that Russian province.

Carlo Sforza, then Under-Secretary for Foreign Affairs, relates that he was ordered to establish contact with Russian exile groups and that, on his advice, Nitti abandoned the project of an expedition, but, in order to establish this new position, he had to break "the combination of military and financial interests" and defy the powerful Banca di Sconto. In spite of that, Nitti was confronted with the political strike of July 20–21, which was not a complete success. Nenni, who had become a Socialist, observed that "the masses showed a great apathy" and *Avanti!* admitted that "at present a conquest of power through an insurrectional general

The Shadow of Revolution

strike is impossible." Mussolini, on the other hand, was exultant: "The Socialist Party [has been] liquidated by the re-awakened conscience of the working class."

In fact, both this strike and the protests early in July against the high cost of living made it clearly apparent that the Socialist Party was incapable of organizing or leading any broad-scale movement. New forces, however, had emerged within it: in Turin, around the group that since May 1, 1919, had been publishing *l'Ordine nuovo* (*The New Order*) with Gramsci, Palmiro Togliatti, and Tasca; in July this group issued "the program of the Communist fraction" and Gramsci proposed the idea of "factory councils" that would make it possible for the workers to take a direct hand in production. In Naples another group under the leadership of Amadeo Bordiga established *The Soviet*. But, in spite of these efforts, as Gramsci was to write, "this poor Socialist Party that declared itself the leader of the working class was nothing but the impedimenta of the army of the proletariat."

Meanwhile the strikes were resumed in Rome, Turin, and Trieste. They were especially effective among the farm workers. On September 11, 1919, the *braccianti* called general strikes in several areas, and they were often backed up by the *mezzadri* (tenant farmers); what frightened the government and the landowners even more was the steady rise in seizures of land. Peasants discharged from the army, prominently displaying their decorations and carrying red flags, marched into private estates, often to the sound of church bells. And the soldiers fraternized with them while the Catholics followed—or led—the movement, providing moral support for a "white Bolshevism."

Some regions were plagued by banditry, for they were the hiding places of deserters. Nitti's government had to give way: on September 2 the Visocchi decree legalized land seizures under certain conditions and on the same day amnesty was granted to deserters.

These measures helped to complete the isolation of Nitti, who, in addition, was a remote, intelligent teacher incapable of communicating with public opinion. He found it necessary to make the trip from his home to Parliament in an armored car, and his children had police bodyguards. His enemies on the right began to conspire against him; Mussolini was to write: "On top of everything else, in August, 1919, the report of the commission of inquiry on the painful episode of Caporetto was published. I said to myself: 'This is pouring oil on the fire.' "

And in truth the wartime conflicts were revived. The report made it unequivocally plain that the disaster was the result of military mistakes and not of defeatist propaganda. Hence all to whom the army was sacrosanct—military men, nationalists, and Fascists—felt that they had been shamed, accused, and threatened. In *il Popolo* Mussolini damned "the jackals of Caporetto." An Italian air force ace who had been d'Annunzio's pilot in the bravura raid on Vienna flew low over Montecitorio and dropped a chamber pot on the Parliament building.

It might seem laughable. The Fiume incident was to show the gravity and the depth of national problems.

August 24, 1919. The city of Fiume was seething. The Sardinian grenadiers departed. In June there had been brawls between Italians and Frenchmen, and an inter-Allied board of inquiry had found the Italians at fault. They had to leave. The Fiume volunteer corps was disbanded; the English would take over police duties. On August 23 a crowd of Italians had bidden farewell to the grenadiers, who waved and shouted: "Fiume or death." The grenadier regiment was re-assigned to Ronchi and Monfalcone.

August 31, 1919. The grenadiers' camp was in darkness. Second Lieutenant Riccardo Frassetto had gathered six of his fellows in his room. He drew his dagger and said in a low voice: "In the name of all who have died for the unity of Italy, I swear fidelity to the sacred cause of Fiume.... Fiume or death."

September 8. Lieutenant Grandjacquet met Gabriele d'Annunzio in Venice and informed him of the plan laid down by the young officers: a March on Fiume, the occupation of the city and its annexation to Italy. D'Annunzio agreed to take over the leadership of the expedition.

For three days the conspirators refined their tactics. The military authorities looked the other way. D'Annunzio sent letters to the newspapers, requesting that they be withheld from publication until the day of his entrance into Fiume. One of these letters was addressed to Mussolini, but the rivalry between these two men was already so acute that d'Annunzio preferred not to give *il Popolo* exclusive rights to his dispatches.

"My dear comrade," he wrote to Mussolini, "the die is cast, I am setting out. Tomorrow I will seize Fiume, sword in hand. May the God of Italy stand by us. I am in a fever. But it is impossible to delay. Once more the spirit shall triumph over the miserable flesh.

"Make a summary of the article that will be published by *la Gazzetta del Popolo*, but reprint the peroration *in extenso*. And give us strong support while the conflict is in progress.

"I embrace you.

"Gabriele d'Annunzio

"September 11, 1919."

September 11. D'Annunzio arrived in Ronchi, wearing the uniform of a lieutenant colonel of the Novara Lancers. At the last moment Captain Salomone, who was in command of the Palmanova motor pool, refused to hand over any of his trucks. Some of the Arditi threatened him, and he gave in.

The expedition set out by moonlight. The main body of the column was made up of grenadiers and Arditi, but along the road d'Annunzio was joined by other groups, some with armored cars. At dawn of September 12 they encountered General Pittaluga's regular troops near Castua. The general wanted to order his men to fire, but d'Annunzio stepped forward.

"If that is how it is, General," he said, "you have two targets: my gold medal and my serious-wound decoration. Order your men to shoot."

General Pittaluga stepped aside.

September 12. At 11 A.M. d'Annunzio entered Fiume. Church bells pealed, a siren shrieked, men shouted with joy. This was the beginning of the time of speech-making. At six in the evening d'Annunzio bade the assembled citizens repeat their plebiscite in favor of annexation to Italy; then he quieted their cheers and declaimed: "Fiume is like a shining lighthouse that gleams above a sea of baseness. . . ." He waved the famous blood-stained flag that had been carried by Randaccio, the foot soldier, and then he cried: "I who volunteered, I who fought, I who was wounded, call upon the France of Victor Hugo, the England of Milton, the America of Lincoln and Walt Whitman, and I speak for the will of the whole sacred nation of Italy when I proclaim the annexation of Fiume to Italy."

The first post-war pronunciamento had just succeeded. Mussolini's March on Rome now had its overture, its model, and its style.

What were Mussolini and the government going to do?

Mussolini could only approve. And with ice in his soul, for once more he was only Number Two. Fiume may have been—for some it definitely was—the starting point for a March on Rome. Volunteers poured in from all branches of the service; the cruisers *Dante Alighieri* and *Emanuele-Filiberto* refused to leave the harbor in spite of orders to do so; contingents of sailors joined d'Annunzio; Admiral Casanuova was arrested aboard the *Dante.*

In short, the Fascists and nationalists could henceforth put aside theories and go over to action. D'Annunzio, as in 1915, was the herald of their passions. *Il Popolo* published his proclamations and his letters to Mussolini:

"My dear Mussolini,

"I have risked all, I have given all, I have conquered, I am the master of Fiume . . . if half the Italians had the spirit of the Fiumesi, we should be the rulers of the world. . . ."

And there were his manifestos:

"My Italian brothers:

"The spirit has conquered the oppressor.

"Italians!

"Against everything and against everyone, remember that the fire was kindled in Fiume and that all discussion can be reduced to two words:

"Either Italy or death!"

This was on September 15, 1919. In other words, it was a matter of launching the conquest of Italy from Fiume, and Mussolini wrote: "The Italian government is not in Rome but in Fiume. It is that government to which we owe obedience."

For on September 13 Nitti had reacted vigorously in Rome. Round-faced professor of economics though he was, he held the Chamber in rapt attention to the hammered phrases of his forceful speech. The news of d'Annunzio's expedition had reached him the day before, in the newspapers and in private.

"What has been done," he said, "has filled me with grief and shame, for sedition has made its appearance for the first time in the Italian army. . . ." He threatened to invoke the code of military justice, and finally, amid applause, he concluded: "I turn therefore to the anonymous masses, the workers and peasants, so that the great voice of the people may boldly lead everyone into the path of renunciation and duty."

Nitti was the more apprehensive because the behavior of the Duke and Duchess of Aosta made plain their thorough endorsement of d'Annunzio. Was there a fresh conspiracy? The likelihood seemed sufficient to impel Nitti to ask the duke not to leave Rome without his permission. In any event, the request by the head of the government created a sensation.

Mussolini voiced his anger in *il Popolo* on September 15: "We summon Saverio Nitti to resign. . . . His speech was appallingly cowardly. . . . Nitti's bitter, bestial anger is the fruit of his insane fear of the Allies."

This hatred was to give Nitti no respite. It did him no good, on the following day, to deliver another speech, very largely a recantation, in which he appealed no longer to the proletarians but "to the soldiers"; he sent General Badoglio to parley with d'Annunzio; it was useless. To the poet, Nitti had become a *cagoia*, a passive pederast and the butt of the most revolting jests. Moreover, d'Annunzio was setting himself up in Fiume as master. He commanded almost twenty thousand legionaries, and the blockade maintained by Badoglio's troops had little effect on his supply system. He had the support of Captain Giulietti of the Italian Seafarers' Federation, and in *il Popolo* Mussolini was taking up a collection . . . the proceeds of which, the editor of *il Popolo* later admitted, were allocated *in toto* to the maintenance of his own private armed guard!

On September 20 d'Annunzio had himself appointed "Commander of the Citadel of Fiume," with full powers. He joined the Fiume Fascio, writing on his application: "Profession: man at arms." While it is undeniable that many of his posturings were risible, they nonetheless did much to widen the audience of the Fasci and especially, by popularizing the poet's "gesture," to set the style that would be characteristic of Fascism in power.

Almost daily d'Annunzio and his legionaries marched for miles through the countryside, feeding their enthusiasm with his questions and their responses:

"Whose is Italy?"—"Ours, *a noi!*"

"What do our enemies make us feel?"—"They make us puke."

It was d'Annunzio's dream to stage a landing at Ravenna or Rimini and from there, along Caesar's road, to march on Rome.

"What will we make out of the deputies?"—"Sausages."

"No, they would poison us."—"Then we'll beat their bottoms in Piazza Colonna."

Fascism was to borrow the *Eîa, eîa, alalà*—the war cry of d'Annunzio's old squadron—that answered the Arditi's shouts of "For Gabriele d'Annunzio!"

"For the people of Fiume?"—"*Eîa, eîa, alalà!*"

Sometimes the legionaries would repeat the old watchword of the Arditi, *Me ne frego* (Fuck it all), and then, when their leader had finished his oration, they would wander off arm in arm, cheering General Sante Ceccherini, who had joined their cause:

> I nostri bersaglieri
> con Ceccherini in testa
> andranno da Cagoia
> e gli faran la festa.
>
> (With Ceccherini leading
> Our fighting men in line,
> They'll go see the old queen
> And give him a hot time.)

Nitti and d'Annunzio were maintaining contact through the intermediary of Badoglio, however. When the Allied troops evacuated Fiume, the government let things take their own course.

On November 26 the "Commander" held a plebiscite on the question of annexation. Of the 10,331 enrolled voters, 7,155 turned out, and 6,199 supported the single party on the ballot, Unità nazionale (National Unity). Once more annexation was proclaimed against a counterpoint of songs.

Thereafter, between speeches, it was a matter of awaiting and welcoming guests, from Marinetti to Guglielmo Marconi and Arturo Toscanini. Toscanini was supposed to conduct a Wagner concert in a natural amphitheater among the hills. The excited legionaries burst out, shouting, in a mock charge, and they were soon followed by the musicians. . . . D'Annunzio signed a multitude of proclamations and drafted writs imprinted with his seal: a spider web ripped by a dagger. Through the streets of Fiume the handsome, white-gloved young men of his legions strolled hand in hand, like the Greeks in another time. . . . Everyone competed for the right of sitting at the "Commander's" table in the Golden Deer restaurant. Fiume became the stage of a theater in which nationalism provided the settings and d'Annunzio played the hero.

This state of affairs did not please Mussolini. He had no choice but to cheer, but the poet was robbing him of that public of Arditi and the young on whom the Fascist leader was relying. Mussolini often went to Fiume by plane. He did as much spying as supporting. In his view the March on Rome should not take place as yet, because d'Annunzio would naturally be its greatest beneficiary. He dissuaded the poet, urged him to be patient, and tried to turn the Fiume adventure to the advantage of Fascism.

Besides, d'Annunzio's expedition had launched a major political battle whose stake went far beyond the question of Fiume. As the Foreign Minister acknowledged to François Charles-Roux:[1] "The government is powerless against d'Annunzio; if we attempted to resort to force, we should be obeyed by neither the army nor the navy."

On September 25, therefore, for the first time since the *Risorgimento*, the Crown Council met, bringing together the most eminent Italians. Was the Chamber to be dissolved? That would mean the first elections to be conducted under universal suffrage and proportional representation (enacted on August 14, 1919), the beginning of a new political system, and hence the unequivocal verdict of the people on the war and its consequences.

The nationalists were opposed to elections. During the September 28 session of Parliament at Montecitorio, Socialists and deputies of the Fascio punched one another until the sergeants-at-arms

[1] François Charles-Roux, *Une grande ambassade à Rome* (Paris: Fayard). p. 77.

pulled them apart. The next day, however, a royal decree was issued: the Chamber was dissolved and new elections were set for November 16. The political campaign began at once. The parties immediately scheduled conventions. The Socialists met in Bologna from October 5 to 8. Adherence to Lenin's Third International was voted by acclamation. As the Maximalists saw the situation, the elections would initiate a period of revolution.

The Fasci convened in Florence on October 9. They claimed one hundred forty-eight branches with forty-five thousand members; the true figures were only fifty-six Fasci with seventeen thousand members. This was the first Fascist congress, and it was dominated by Mussolini. He announced in Florence that he had just arrived from Fiume—"a little joke on His Indecency, Nitti"—and the delegates bawled: "Down with the *Cagoia!*" Then Mussolini spoke of Fiume, where, he said, he had found "an atmosphere of marvel and miracle."

Thus accepting the spiritual patronage of d'Annunzio, Mussolini stated the creed of Fascism: "We are against premises, against doctrines; we are for posing problems, we are dynamic, we have neither a monarchist nor a republican bias." He added, however, that "the monarchy has undoubtedly outlived its usefulness," since the King had permitted Nitti to "deliver a speech that was a transparent call to the Bolshevist forces in the nation."

The poet, Marinetti, for his part, called for "the expulsion of the Pope and the devaticanization of Rome"; the other speakers enjoyed themselves with the "PeePees" of Don Sturzo's PPI and the Socialist "Poopies" who, Mussolini said, could be "identified by their physical cowardice. They do not like to fight; fire and sword scare them." With extreme arrogance he concluded: "We Fascists should recognize that we stand alone, we should come out [of the elections] set apart, numbered, and, if we are few, it must be remembered that we have been in being only six months."

The realities were quite different. Well aware of their weakness, the Fascists went in search of allies, but in vain. In Milan, after fruitless endeavors, Mussolini put together a single slate that included Marinetti, Toscanini, Piero Bolzon, and Guido Podreca, a rabid anti-clerical. Actually the Fascists took no part in the election campaign beyond disturbing meetings, administering beatings, and performing their responsive rituals:

"Honor to whom?"—"To Fiume."

"Long live who?"—"D'Annunzio."

"Down with whom?"—"*Cagoia.*"

They also hurled signal rockets, held uniformed parades, and turned trucks into mock armored cars.

The dominant factor in the electoral campaign, however, was the return of Giolitti, who presented a governmental program on October 12 in the little Piedmontese town of Dronero; this was in a sense an expansion of his pre-war "Giolittism." He called for an investigation of Italy's entrance into the war, exalted "labor," and, in connection with the World War, criticized "the ruling classes that led humanity into disaster and could now no longer stand alone in ruling the world, this world whose destinies were henceforth in the hands of its peoples."

This "progressivism" of Giolitti set new fires to passions. *Il Corriere della Sera* branded the statesman a "Bolshevik of the Annunziata," for Giolitti had been decorated with that order and therefore ranked as a cousin of the king. To the nationalist papers and *il Popolo*, as in May, 1915, he was a bandit, the "highwayman of Dronero."

It was up to the people to decide.

The decision came on the night of November 16. *Il Popolo* was enveloped in silence, and in Mussolini's office, to which the first edition of *Avanti!* had just been brought, no one spoke a word. Mussolini, who headed the only Fascist slate in Italy; Mussolini, who had carried the burden of *il Popolo* for five years and breathed life into the Fasci with his oratory, Mussolini had amassed barely forty-eight hundred votes in Milan, where the Socialists had rolled up one hundred seventy-six thousand and the PPI had seventy-four thousand.

"The Italy of the Revolution is born!" *Avanti!* headlined.

Throughout the country, the Socialists received 1,840,593 of the six-and-a-half million votes cast, and, to everyone's surprise, Sturzo's Popular Party totaled 1,175,000. There were now one hundred fifty-six instead of fifty-one Socialist deputies in the Chamber, and one hundred three Popular deputies. Two blocs had been created, seizing the majority of the seats from the old parties, which now had only two hundred fifty-two of the total of five hundred nine. The Socialist triumph was very clear-cut in the north: the party received more than forty percent of the votes in Tuscany, Lombardy, Umbria, and Piedmont and reached sixty percent in Emilia.

The next morning the red flag was raised over the town hall of Bologna while the bells rang from the tower; Mayor Francesco Zanardi greeted the crowd. A cab made over into a hearse for the landowners crossed the square amid laughter. In Milan a gay procession in Corso Venezia escorted a catafalque bearing the effigies of Mussolini and Marinetti as far as the Naviglio, where they were thrown into the canal. The next day *Avanti!* ran a one-paragraph story: "A body was recovered yesterday from the Naviglio. It was identified as Mussolini's."

The atmosphere at *il Popolo* was acrid. Alternately Mussolini sat speechless, his head in his hands, or walked up and down talking to the silent Sarfatti. "The war and the trenches—those were the good days," he muttered. Then he talked of "dropping everything." He added:

"I can be a mason again— I'm a very good mason—or I can be a pilot: you know I'm learning to fly. I can even be a wandering musician, with my violin—I'll give up the paper, I'll leave what's owing to me for my family: I can always get by. Bocca has made me excellent offers for my book on *Myth and Heresy*—I can write it in two weeks. And Talli would take me on as an actor: all I have to do is finish my play, *Lamp without Light.* . . ."

Mussolini would even have asked Nitti to help him leave Italy. He was not exaggerating when he declared in *il Popolo*: "The outcome of the elections is painful from the moral point of view."

But, while a Socialist parade was winding through the streets of Milan on November 17, a gang of Arditi hurled a bomb that wounded nine persons. The police immediately searched the offices of *il Popolo*, and in that hide-away, known as The Lair, grenades and revolvers were discovered. Mussolini, Marinetti, and Vecchi were arrested, but after forty-eight hours Mussolini was released. Luigi Albertini, editor of *il Corriere*, had telephoned Nitti: "He's only a has-been now, don't make a martyr of him." The military circles that protected the Arditi also exerted pressure on the government.

These circles were to show their hands more and more. On November 22, in fact, while the red flag was still flying over Socialist-dominated town halls, the Stefani news agency announced that on November 14, just before the elections, d'Annunzio had landed at Zara on the Dalmatian coast: Admiral Enrico Millo, the commander of the area, had offered no opposition and, even better, he had promised d'Annunzio that he would never give up Dalmatia. Thus, at the very time when the elections were unequivocally condemning the war and its consequences, when the Popular Party and the Socialists, the whites and the reds, were triumphing over the interventionists, the armed forces were openly advertising their sympathies with nationalist rebellion. An admiral on active duty made a rebel officer the judge of his conduct and welcomed him to occupied Dalmatia as the incarnation of all the patriotic virtues. This was a serious matter.

But the electoral victory overshadowed the anxieties of the closing days of November. *Avanti!* prepared a program for the government. It must recognize Soviet Russia, reach an understanding with
her, disband the standing army, confiscate large fortunes and war
profits, inaugurate a republic, and so prepare for the advent of
Socialism. The Socialist Party announced its readiness to accept
the responsibilities of power: was it not the largest body?

On December 1 the one hundred fifty-six Socialist deputies in
Montecitorio formed a compact bloc that included Treves, Turati,
and Modigliani, as well as many new names. As the deputies were
taking their seats, the royal procession, escorted by mounted troops
and preceded by the *battistrada*, the royal groom, was leaving the
Quirinal for Montecitorio: the King was to deliver the speech from
the throne to the new Chamber. All along the route there were
large numbers of monarchists, students, nationalists, officers, and
Fascists; three times the royal family had had to step out on the
balcony. It was essential to impress the King and the numerous
deputies with the loyalty and the intensity of monarchist feeling.

When the little King, laced into his uniform, entered the Chamber, the deputies were all on their feet. The center and the right
cheered; suddenly the Socialists shouted: "Hurrah for Socialism!
Up the Socialist republic!" With a great stir, they left the Chamber.
They exchanged congratulations with one another, and some left
the building. But the monarchists who had watched the royal procession, and who were waiting outside Parliament for the King to
leave so that they could display their loyalty again, had already
heard of what had taken place inside. They launched a pursuit of
the Socialist deputies, insulted them, showered blows on them, and
ran after them again through the narrow streets. The reaction to
this outrage was forceful throughout Italy.

For the next two days general strikes reigned in Rome, Milan,
Genoa, and Naples. Officers and students were put to rout wherever they appeared. In Turin, where Gramsci's group had organized the workers on a factory-by-factory basis, 120,000 workers
were mobilized within an hour and an attack was made on the
Technical Institute. There was considerable disorder elsewhere: in
Mantua the railway station, warehouses, and arms factories were
sacked and the prison set afire. Feeling ran extremely high. In
Milan and Turin the funerals of a carabiniere and a student took
on the appearance of anti-Socialist demonstrations.

It was completely obvious to all observers that the elections had
resolved nothing and that the twenty-fifth Parliament, which was
beginning its sessions in a climate of disorder, would have a difficult
life. On December 3 the Socialist, Treves, spoke of "the parliamen-

tary revolution of November 16, threatened by the violent revenge of the streets prepared by the conservative and militarist parties." He added: "We feel as if we were caught up in an ominous wind of counter-revolution before the revolution."

There would be no need for Mussolini to change trades.

So he stayed as editor of *il Popolo d'Italia*. In December he even announced that henceforth his publication would have "the typographical facilities necessary to a great newspaper." With what assistance? Perhaps this was mere boasting. Be that as it might, *il Popolo* went on, but the defeat at the polls and the brief stay in prison had upset its editor, especially since there was still an open charge against him for "having created during the summer and autumn of 1919 an armed group intended to commit offenses against persons." In this situation, he could only move forward—*"navigare necesse est,"* he wrote on January 1, 1920. Besides, with his political intuition, he soon recognized that there were better occupations than self-pity and that "the victorious avalanche of Socialist votes" (P.d.I., November 21, 1919) was not conclusive.

He made this point in several articles at the end of the year. As for the Socialist victory . . . "There are victories that are as crushing as defeats. The latter crush with the burden of losses, the former with the sometimes greater burden of responsibilities."

And it was true that Italian Socialism, with its ambitious program and its seeming strength, would be judged by its real capabilities. Mussolini clearly saw that the Socialists "have promised too much and too soon: they have too often shouted *Viva Lenin* and *Viva la Russia*. . . . They have too often waved the program of immediate Communism in front of the masses, available the first Wednesday after election day." And Mussolini offered a glimpse of his own hopes: "If the Italian Maximalist does not make good on his promissory note, the lower classes will protest it, and then will come the lousy part, as we used to say in the trenches. It is obvious that Maximalism will wear itself out in the effort to replace the impossible revolutionary fact with the facile revolutionary phrase."

Mussolini's analysis was not devoid of insight, the more so in that, as he emphasized, the Socialist Party, the "PUS," was divided. The old deputies like Turati, the men who had come from trade-union circles, were a "pacifying" element opposed to those disciples of Lenin, like Nicola Bombacci and Bordiga, who hoped to be "the wild men of the new parliamentary group." Furthermore, among the one hundred fifty-six Socialist deputies, there were only ten genuine working men.

But the Socialists' conflicts were deeper than those in the parliamentary group. Elected by masses whose state of mind at that time was revolutionary, the deputies dared not imagine a revolutionary course or a broadly reformist program. To trumpet their resolve was in their minds to keep formal faith with their electors and at the same time to retain their confidence. But, even at the risk of powerlessness, they must go farther than words. They did not know how; often they did not want to. Were they able to? Socialist voters were a minority in the nation (32.3 percent of the total), Don Sturzo's Popular Party was a competitive force, and the state was evolving its own means of action: in January, 1920, Nitti created the *Regia Guardia*, the Royal Guard, to which the carabinieri with their expanded ranks were added. Thereafter it was difficult to conceive of "a democratic alternative to revolution" and to find allies, for violence had become daily and enforced. Deputies were beaten as they emerged from Montecitorio, and the most trivial strikes were paid for in dead and wounded: between April, 1919, and April, 1920, one hundred forty-five persons were killed and four hundred forty-four were wounded even before Fascism had yet come on to the stage.

Violence and disguised war were firmly entrenched, and the Socialists were caught up in them even though they had not incited or desired them, though they did not know how to deal with them, and could not or—in some instances—would not find a way out.

At the beginning of 1920 all this was only faintly perceptible, but Mussolini, who had had personal experience of violence—had he not presided over the sack of *Avanti!?*—intuitively sensed it.

Meanwhile, a few weeks after the elections, the Socialist tide swept in again, and Mussolini retreated into himself, returning to the quasi-anarchist bed-rock of his upbringing. It was a time of bitter skepticism for him, after the Socialism that he had abandoned in 1914 and the Arditism and the nationalism that he had vainly championed in the elections, and all that welled up in him now was personal ambition. Here, perhaps, was the decisive turning point in a personality, when, in the disillusion of a defeat, frenzied ambition decided that only success, no matter what it cost, could satisfy it. Viewed in that light, Mussolini's articles of January, 1920, reflect his arrogance and his masked declaration that all that matters is the ego.

> We do not believe in programs . . . in the promised land. . . . We go back to the individual. We will support everything that exalts and aggrandizes the individual, gives him more freedom, a better life, a broader life; we will fight everything that oppresses or degrades the individual.

This apologia for individualism, which was first of all a defense of Mussolini's own ego, was invested with a political content by the Fascist leader. "Encyclicals are issued today by two Vaticans: one in Rome, the other in Moscow. We are the heretics of both these religions. We alone are immunized against their infection." And, with that coarse elaboration that was characteristic of him, he particularized: "We have torn up all the revealed truths, we have spat on all the dogmas, rejected all the paradises, mocked all the charlatans who offered miraculous drugs to provide 'happiness' to the human race."

Taking this line when the old anarchist, Malatesta, returned to Italy at the age of sixty-seven late in December, 1919, Mussolini hailed him, and, with him, that Captain Giulietti who was putting his Seafarers' Federation at the service of the Soviet Union and d'Annunzio. These contradictions, this return to his sources, were clear proof that in his Lair in Milan, with his little bodyguard of Arditi armed to the teeth, Mussolini was waiting and watching. But it was an anxious wait, and his nervousness was reflected in the tension of his bony face, the extremely prominent cheekbones, the thin lips, that whole lower face in which Sforza saw "a savage, animal vulgarity."[2]

That tension was also, perhaps, the tension of anger and fear; cut off from Socialism, Mussolini could only fear, watch, and hope. Malatesta aptly described what was at stake: "If we let this auspicious moment escape us, we shall have to pay one day in tears of blood for the fear that now we inspire in the middle class."

For the middle class was frightened. Its emotions had been sharpened by the nationalist campaign based on the "mutilated victory," and it had been stunned by the results of the elections. Had not Nitti himself, on the eve of the voting, reiterated that the elections would be "governmental and conservative"? The workers' parades and the red flags, the oratory and the songs, the words *revolution* and *soviet* injected into every discussion ultimately threw conservative quarters into panic. Suffering under the collapse of the *lira*, which by the end of 1920 would have lost three-quarters of its 1919 value, and beset by inflation, they blamed the strikes, the *scioperomania*—strike fever—and the weakness of Nitti's government.

And it was true that 1920 began with strikes. Prices had risen so high that in 1920 real wages were lower than they had been in 1913: hence there were 1,881 strikes in 1920 against 1,663 in

[2] Sforza, *L'Italia dal 1914 al 1944 quale io la vidi.*

1919. January and February were marked by strikes of the railway workers and the postal staffs. The government yielded, even granting pay for time spent on strike. Anger ran riot against the concessions made by Nitti, who was to cry out against "this rotten, corrupt middle class of ours, which is not even aware of the risks that it runs and lacks even the instinct of self-preservation. . . ."

But it had that instinct, and in abundance; it was simply that it was not attracted by the road of concessions. On February 9, 1920, for example, the Senate was in session. This Upper House met in Palazzo Madama, an elegant Renaissance structure adorned with the fleurs-de-lys of the Valois. It was a place where the speeches were marked by style and burdened with quotations. Senator De Cupis had the floor to discuss the strikes in the public services.

"Does it not seem to you," he said, turning toward Nitti, "that the time has come to say *basta* (enough) to all these disturbances? . . . It is the spirit of disorder that is abroad among us, arousing that sentiment that, among all human feelings, is the easiest to entice: cupidity, which is insatiable. . . . Cicero himself offers you the proof of that." The honorable senator then read a long extract and, without a smile, with no idea what a confession of blindness he was making, he went on: "In these words of the great orator of Rome you will find the explanation of our present social unrest in all its causes and all its effects. . . ."

Anachronism, archaism, academicism—all of these, undoubtedly; but, above all, conservatism, and Nitti made no mistake when he asserted realistically: "While the railway strike is deplorable, what is even more deplorable is the fact that men who think they are serving their country are led to commit unspeakable acts. . . ."

The cobblestone of Fiume had been hurled into the placid pool of the Senate. It is easy to understand that Nitti was soon detested.

Strikes, moreover, were lengthening and spreading, from the textile mills to the sulphur mines of Sicily (in February). The *braccianti* went out in March. Incidents were frequent: in Milan strikers and nationalists clashed; there were dead and wounded everywhere. A new kind of action was taking root all through Italy: the sit-in strike. On February 28 the Mazzoni textile mills in Ponte Canavese were occupied and the red flag was raised when the management refused to obey the regulations prescribing working conditions. In the Mezzogiorno the peasants occupied estates: for several days the Duke of Bevona was surrounded in his castle and he was not set free until he had granted the demands made by the peasants; one can imagine the thoughts of that Grandee of Spain!

But these unanimous manifestations that affected all sectors of

The Shadow of Revolution

industry and a large part of the peasantry seemed to be a kind of purposeless round-robin carried on by the Italian workers and peasants. The Socialist Party made no effort to break out of the circle and lead these movements in a predetermined direction. In Milan on February 29 the party's leaders suggested that studies on the timeliness of soviets be continued until the April party congress; and yet certain organizations had adopted clearly revolutionary behavior on their own initiative. The railway workers refused to move troops, and this refusal spread to the merchant seamen. When military detachments disembarked from warships, they came into conflict with the dock workers. Officers were harassed. The town of Viareggio was gripped by insurrection in May; in Leghorn the prefecture of police was bombed. For the police, the *Regia Guardia*, had very quickly earned a reputation for brutality. Firing without a warning was not uncommon. The forces of law and order were reinforced by the first *squadre* (squads), groups of volunteers who delivered the mail when the postal workers struck and who then offered themselves as auxiliary police. It is to be observed that most often the squadre were created outside the Fasci, even though the majority of the Fascists joined their ranks; above all, they had the open backing of the state. In February the prefect in Milan formally decided to recruit a "corps of volunteers" for the defense of "property and persons."

So, once their initial panic had abated, the forces opposed to Socialism began to organize.

The most prominent industrialists of Italy gathered in Milan in March. Their first session was held on March 7 under the auspices of the *Confederazione generale dell'industria* (General Confederation of Industry), the famous *Confindustria*, as it is still called. Under the chairmanship of an industrialist named G. Silvestri, this sober convention, sitting amid the climate of social crisis that was paralyzing the country, evolved the program and the methodology to be followed by big business in Italy. Its proposals were unequivocal, ranging from the rejection of the eight-hour day to political problems; in the latter connection the congress called for a strong government that would foster the development of individual initiative within the framework of discipline and respect for the laws; the execution of this program demanded new men and new methods. Thus a general management strategy was elaborated, and it became clear that Nitti no longer enjoyed the confidence of the ruling circles of industry: he had increased his concessions and in April he instituted foreign-exchange controls, which did not accomplish any improvement in the situation—quite the opposite.

Food-ration cards had been re-introduced on March 4, and

prices went on rising: the index was 639 in January, 701 in February, 825 at the end of the year. The price of bread was stabilized only through state intervention: five hundred million *lire* per month in 1920 was allocated to this purpose, thus abetting the course of inflation and the escalation of prices.*

Hence the government's back was against the wall. The Popular Party deserted it. On March 13 the Cabinet was "patched up." On March 30 Nitti told the Chamber: "I fear the violence that is erupting on the revolutionary side, but I fear even more the tendencies on the other side."

On the same day the Socialist deputy, Treves, took the floor: "Revolution is an era, not a single day. . . . We are in the midst of it and we shall remain there for many years. . . . It is terribly long and painful. . . . Gentlemen, this is our Expiation!" In a letter to Turati, Anna Kulishova summarized the speech: "Let us all commit suicide and have done with it"—a kind of Socialist apocalypse.

It was true that the Socialist leaders were paralyzed by a messianic fatalism; it was true that a wind of tragedy was beginning to blow through Italian history when Nitti, who saw a menace to himself in the decisions taken by Confindustria, warned of the emergence of other dangers besides those of Socialist revolution.

Accounts of clashes and battles filled the newspapers: eight men were killed near Bologna in April, and food was either unobtainable or priced beyond reach. In FIAT's Turin plants the workers struck to protest the adoption of official time, which differed from the solar time that thirty-five thousand of them preferred. The factories were closed, and a test of strength began in Italy's largest industrial city: the first conflict to follow Confindustria's program. Communist tendencies were strong in Turin and within the Socialist Party. There was a Communist nucleus in every factory, and these ninety thousand union members took their inspiration from Gramsci. They occupied the factories and raised the red flag, but soldiers moved into the plants and the strikes broadened; for ten days they involved four million workers. But a return to work was ordered on April 24 after a major conflict, for there had been a large-scale confrontation between workers' factory councils and the lockout, and Gramsci's followers had received no support from *Avanti!*, the Socialist Party, or the CGL. On May 8 Gramsci issued a disturbing warning in the name of the Socialist section of Turin: "The present stage of the class struggle is the stage that precedes either the conquest of political power by the revolutionary prole-

* In 1914, the *lira* was worth approximately twenty cents; in December, 1919, it was worth about eight; in April, 1920, four and a half; and in December, 1920, three and a half.—*Ed.*

The Shadow of Revolution

tariat . . . or a fearful reaction by the propertied class and the governmental caste."

In Rome, at the same time, fashionable young students were reporting for work as substitutes for the striking streetcleaners; in Bologna, in April, the parties and the leading citizens had called for the organization of a "citizen volunteer corps for the defense of public order."

As this new force took shape, Mussolini seemed to be retreating. He had even, in very general terms, taken a position against the official time change and against "that Moloch, the state," adding: "Down with the state . . . yesterday's state, today's state, tomorrow's state. . . . All that is left for us, in the present darkness and the shadowy future, is the momentarily ridiculous but always consoling religion of *Anarchy*" (P.d.I., April 6, 1920).

He could not have made it clearer that he stood outside the two major currents, the opposing forces. From May 23 to 25 he held a convention of the one hundred twenty Fasci in Milan, but no major decisions were arrived at. Actually he was waiting for all the bets to be placed. He saw the situation accurately: in May, 1920, the great explanation had not yet been undertaken.

At the end of the month, however, the Trieste Fascio formally set up its first action squadre, but these were directed against those elements hostile to Italian influence. As we know, Mussolini had never relinquished his patriotic themes, and at this time the ideology of his movement could be described as quasi-Socialist, or, better, demagogic, nationalism.

The best evidence of Mussolini's nationalist tendencies was the part played by d'Annunzio. The "Commander" was still in Fiume; it was impossible to allow him to retain the monopoly of patriotism, particularly when great interests were at stake on the shores of the Adriatic. The shipbuilders—the Cosuliches and the Sinigaglias—who ruled Trieste could not permit Fiume to become a competing international seaport. As Bissolati had remarked, "We must take care not to play the game . . . of four Levantines in Trieste who would like to stifle Fiume as a seaport for their own advantage."

Mussolini did not share these scruples. *Il Popolo*'s needs were great, and d'Annunzio looked kindly on it, since the proceeds of the fund drive launched by the paper had been allowed to remain in its editor's hands for his own use. D'Annunzio had accepted this. Had he not, after all, his own resources? These were the pirates that he had organized, the *Uscocchi*, who swarmed over the Adriatic, and the taxes that he levied on the city.

The position was deteriorating nevertheless. Granted that the blockade was often no more than nominal. D'Annunzio's numerous aircraft pilots had been granted the right to use the royal airdrome at Mattuglie, about eight miles northwest of Fiume. Every morning the gates were opened to admit their truck. The tragedy, one observer remarked,[3] was turning into a musical comedy. But the population was fed up. On December 18, 1919, d'Annunzio had held a plebiscite on the government's proposed measures: some tampering began, but he had to accept the facts: the result of the plebiscite was hostile to the "Commander." The ballots were quickly destroyed and the plebiscite was declared invalid.

D'Annunzio went into seclusion and began to draft the "Charter of the Carnaro,"* the constitution of the first corporative republic, with the inspiration of Fascist thinking. Picture the poet, in his white gloves, his neck shaved, followed by the cohort of his followers, on his way to the old Golden Door restaurant, now renamed The Duck-Billed Platypus, where his favorites were called to his table. Then Malatesta, the anarchist, arrived, in order to work with d'Annunzio in the preparation of an armed insurrection that would bring down the strike-paralyzed state.

How many different streams were flowing into Fiume! Mussolini was informed of the insurrection plan. He did not hesitate: on February 17, 1920, he unmasked the conspiracy in an article in *il Popolo* under the headline: OPERETTA AND EPIC. For under no conditions could he assist an impetuous rival; but, cleverly, he exonerated d'Annunzio; the poet was still a strong factor.

Nitti too had to reckon with him. On May 9 Nitti was once again in the minority in Parliament; his government was overthrown and on May 21 he formed his third Cabinet. Three days later came the anniversary of Italy's entry into the war.

Nationalist and Fascist students gathered at the University of Rome and tried to parade along via Nazionale to the Quirinal. The Regia Guardia blocked them: it was feared that there would be provocations. Soon guns were fired. One demonstrator and four policemen were killed. Citizens of Fiume who had gone to Rome as a delegation were arrested. Nitti was still *Cagoia*. In Fiume itself d'Annunzio revived enthusiasm, and in Milan, in the *Teatro lirico*, Mussolini cried: "In a short while . . . the whole people will honor its defenders . . . the whole people will honor the Arditi."

Once more Nitti was in a difficult position. Even in other countries he was hardly respected: the French, in particular, accused

[3] Nino Valeri, *Trente ans d'histoire italienne* (Turin: Einaudi).

* The Carnaro is that portion of the Adriatic that lies between the Istrian peninsula and the islands of Cherso and Veglia.—*Ed.*

The Shadow of Revolution

him of pro-Germanism—had he not requested the recall of Ambassador Camille Barrère? The end of May and the beginning of June were like a hunters' kill.

Giolitti gave interviews and held himself out as the successor, with the support of an astonishing conservative unanimity: his return was envisaged as an escape from Nitti, as a means of wiping out the war and its divisions, which were undermining the Italian ruling class, as a basis for the reconstruction of a peaceful Italy under his highly respected name. Mario Missiroli, a journalist, wrote on June 2, 1920: "Reading the Roman newspapers gives one the feeling of being present at the end of a banquet that has become an orgy, when everyone babbles nonsense and tries in vain to find his way out of the room."

Two days later Nitti issued a decree-law raising the price of bread to one and one half *lire* per kilogram (about three and one half cents a pound). Thus he provided his combined opponents with their issue. All parties rose up against the decree. Bloody demonstrations broke out in Milan and Bari; troop movements were blocked. On June 9 Nitti rescinded his decree and resigned. He was to remark in his *Rivelazioni*:

> It was the major figures in the Banca Commerciale, the big war profiteers, who made the greatest efforts to prevent a small increase in the price of bread, which they themselves had suggested and for which they called again immediately after my resignation. . . . I was in a strange position: the most advanced elements, who voted against me and to whom my program must have seemed dangerous, had confidence in me; they knew that I was laboring in behalf of a democratic monarchy not in words alone but in substance; they knew that I was striving for economic reconstruction.

Nitti fell—Nitti-*Cagoia* to the end. Mussolini was exultant in *il Popolo* of June 10: "Yesterday, at last, that fetus, half legislative and half bureaucratic, was finally taken out of circulation forever."

Such hatred added weight to Nitti's plea in his own defense. With his fall the hope of a democratic monarchy vanished.

4

The Decisive Months

(June, 1920 — May, 1921)

"This, my dear sirs who take to the pulpit to lecture us on morality, is the way it was. Fascism was born after 'PUSist' [Socialist] extremism and as a very logical, very human reaction to it."—MUSSOLINI (November 24, 1920)

AT THE AGE of seventy-eight "the traitor of 1915," "the highwayman of Dronero," "the Bolshevik of the Annunziata"—Giovanni Giolitti—returned to power on the shoulders of those who had insulted him and against the misgivings of the Socialists who had once supported him. The situation of May, 1915, had been reversed to the advantage of the old master of Italian politics. He did not look his age: tall, very slender, his face divided horizontally by a thick white moustache, he had preserved all his quickness of mind, and the years had enhanced his natural distinction with a kind of detachment like that of an esthete or a good loser. He was summoned to form a cabinet on June 11, 1920, and four days later a brilliant group was seated around the huge table in the new office of the Premier in Palazzo Viminale. Benedetto Croce, the philosopher, held the Ministry of Public Education; Filippo Meda, the Catholic, had the Treasury; Ivanoe Bonomi, the former Socialist, was Minister of War; a former syndicalist, Arturo Labriola, was Minister of Labor—a new post created by Nitti.

Count Carlo Sforza was Minister of Foreign Affairs. Giolitti had first known him at the Frascati beach, and the two men regularly traveled back and forth together, quite simply, in the train between the resort and the capital. When Giolitti was made Premier, he asked Sforza to join his Cabinet.

"Are you aware that I was one of the first interventionists?" Sforza asked.

"That," Giolitti replied, "is exactly why I want you."

The Cabinet did indeed have the significance of a reconciliation: it was, or hoped to be, the end of the discord between neutralists and interventionists: 1915, that incision in the Italian ruling class, had to be closed, and one of Giolitti's first acts was to go to Palazzo Farnese to pay a call on Ambassador Barrère of France: the days of v. Bülow must be erased. In his task of reconciliation, moreover, Giolitti had the advantage of not having been branded or compromised by the war, whereas, as the Fascist philosopher, Giovanni Gentile, acknowledged, "victory was turning into defeat, and the Italian people was being infected with the mentality of the conquered: hatred for war and for those responsible for it, even for the army, which had been its instrument."

From this point of view, in spite of his seventy-eight years, Giolitti was a new man in politics: he gave the history of Italy a fresh start as if the war had never taken place.

His first policy speech was much awaited; he made it short and technical, like the efficient man that he was, and it was centered on financial and economic problems: for no matter what anyone did, the war could not be forgotten like a backdrop that is removed to make room for its successor . . . or its predecessor.

The deficit had reached eighteen billion *lire* and the currency was steadily declining in value, thus leading to price rises. Giolitti proposed drastic measures: from the registration of all securities and the elimination of bearer instruments to the control of war profits and the requisitioning of property. He hoped too, he said, to give back all its power to Parliament and to eliminate legislation by decree.

Debate began; but Montecitorio, these discussions, that old man and the deputies seemed isolated in an Italy of violence. On June 24, the very day when Giolitti presented his program, the Royal Guard was shooting in Milan and Piombino; a general strike was called in the province of Belluno, the neighbor of the glorious Piave. Two days later serious news reached Bonomi, the Minister of War: the 11th Bersaglieri Regiment, which was scheduled to depart for Albania from Ancona, had mutinied.

This was the first major military rising in post-war Italy. Giolitti was uneasy. The insurrection had spread from the barracks to the city, and then to the towns of Forlì and Pesaro. The disturbances overflowed into Umbria, and soon there was a general strike in Rome.

There the leaders of the Socialist Party and the CGL conferred. These were two strong forces. In addition to the one hundred fifty-six deputies, two thousand municipalities, three thousand sections, and two hundred thousand members of the Socialist Party, there were the 2,150,000 members of the CGL. The Confederazione italiana dei lavoratori (CIL—Italian Workers' Federation), which was allied with the Popular Party, had 1,161,238 members.

These forces increased in the social climate of the summer of 1920, but they remained more potential than dynamic. On June 29 they rejected the idea of a general strike even though they issued a forceful statement:

"At the first sign of a new war, your duty, whether you be soldiers or proletarians, is solely this: Revolution. If the middle class wants it, we will accept the conflict and it will be carried on to the end."

In actual fact the struggle was already being waged—unclear, difficult, composed of withdrawals and attacks, never acquiring that "ideal" character of a social Fontenoy: "Gentlemen, you may fire the first shot."

The struggle was also taking place on the patriotic level. Humiliated officers and disillusioned nationalists, who were angered by the return of Giolitti, held the Socialists responsible for their incapacities. On July 11 Italian naval officers were attacked in Spalato (Split) by Croats and the commander of the corvette *Puglia* was killed. Two days later, in retaliation, the squadre of the Trieste Fascio attacked the Hotel Balkan and the houses belonging to Yugoslavs, including the consul's. The Fascists destroyed and burned. This was the first punitive expedition with a "patriotic" purpose, but soon its targets were extended to include the Socialists: the Casa del popolo in Pola (Pulj) was destroyed. In Rome, after a transport strike, the street-cars started running again on July 20, but many of them flew red flags. Arditi, students, and Fascists grouped their forces, attacked the street-cars, ripped off the red flags, and mauled the drivers and conductors. Then the attackers regrouped and headed for the printing plant that put out the Roman edition of *Avanti!*, which they sacked. An unlimited general strike was called: it lasted only one day. Socialist deputies were beaten up; after all, one of them, Misiano, was an amnestied deserter. At no time did the police lift a hand: it was obvious that its sympathies were all with the young men who were helping it to maintain order and who backed the Tricolor against the Red Flag of the Revolution. At the beginning of August nationalism and anti-Socialism were to become even more clearly identified. On August 3 Giolitti announced that he was withdrawing Italian troops from Albania and the city of Valona (the Albanian Selenica) was being given up. Only the island of Saseno (the Albanian Sazanit) would be retained. Were there diplomatic reasons behind this decision? There were rumors that the evacuation had been made necessary by the mutiny of Ancona and that the general staff's requests for reinforcements had elicited this response from Bonomi: "Internal conditions in the country make it impossible to detach any troops. . . ."

CAPORETTO IN ALBANIA was Mussolini's headline of August 5; he pointed out that Misiano, the deserter, had a seat in Parliament; and he added bitterly: "As long as the Italian people puts on such charming shows as the beating and lynching of officers . . . it is certain to have a brilliant future. . . ."

From neutralism to defeatism, from Caporetto to Valona, from desertion to the red flag, Socialism was encircled by its enemies, put under the nation's interdict. On this battlefield—regardless of the facts—it had already lost its fight. What was left to it was the social struggle.

The decisive test was to begin at the end of that summer of 1920. On August 13 the negotiations that had been dragging on in Milan between the Italian Federation of Metal Workers and the analogous employers' association were suddenly broken off. The employers adduced their economic difficulties in support of their refusal to grant the wage increases requested, and it was indeed true that their profits had a tendency to diminish, precisely because of the amount of capital invested and also because of the economic crisis of over-production that had begun in the United States in the spring of 1920 and taken the world by surprise after the lush days of war time. And undoubtedly the employers' refusal was also part of a general battle strategy against the labor movement.

When the union called a slow-down strike on August 17 and announced its readiness to occupy the factories, the employers retaliated with a lockout, hoping thus to bring in government troops on their side. On August 28 the management of Alfa-Romeo closed the Milan factories, which were occupied by the police. The test of strength was under way.

Two days later the workers took over factories in Milan; the movement spread to Turin and then throughout the peninsula. As we have seen, it had had its precedents, but its national scope was a shock to the strategists of Confindustria. A frontal opposition to such a wave was dangerous, the more so in that labor and its defenses were well organized everywhere. At FIAT, for example, the workers' factory council met in the directors' conference room under a red flag bearing the hammer and sickle; in the factory, workers' meetings were called to discuss production, courts were instituted, and everywhere there were red flags and revolutionary posters: "Long live the Soviets! Long live the Revolution!" The movement reached even the smallest companies; workers on sentry duty and sandbag barricades testified to the will to resist. Workers' cooperatives provided raw materials, occasionally transport was requisitioned, safes were opened, factory production was put on the market and wages continued to be paid under the direction of the *consiglio di fabbrica*—the workers' factory council.

As far as the Italian middle class was concerned, revolution held full sway in the factory areas. On September 7 the French Embassy telegraphed to the Quai d'Orsay: "The Italian metalworking and machine industry is in the solid grip of Bolshevism."[1]

Meanwhile seizures of land were continuing, in spite of the united front put up since August 18 by the landowners' creation of the Confederazione generale dell'agricoltura (General Confederation of Agriculture), better known as Confagricola. These seizures spread out from the south to the Po Valley, the rich districts. Catholics and Socialists, whites and reds, were rivals in them. Miglioli, a deputy of the Popular Party, was at the head of this "white Bolshevism," which demanded the establishment of *consigli di cascina* (farm councils), the creation of collective enterprises, the direct management of the land by the peasants. The "reds" were thinking of the landless peasants, the *braccianti*, who primarily were asking the landowners for jobs. Hence the two courses of action differed in their objectives and were addressed to different categories, but very often they shared the same style in that summer. From the fields to the factories, Italy seemed to be bathed in a pre-revolutionary climate.

Ever provident, Mussolini sought to form new ties with the Socialists. He went to see Bruno Buozzi, the president of the metalworkers' union. "It's all the same to me," Mussolini said, "whether the factories belong to the management or the workers. We Fascists will stay out of it unless there's an uprising with a Bolshevik base."

There were those who feared such a rising; the workers had control of the arms factories and in Turin they had established relations with the troops. Giolitti did not intervene. He had gone off to his home in Bardonnecchia in the Susa Valley near the French border, and he was waiting. He was "letting things fall apart of their own weight." Later he was to write: "As in 1904, the enter-

[1] Charles-Roux, *Une grande ambassade à Rome*, p. 129.

The Decisive Months

prise had to be allowed to go its own way up to a certain point. . . .
The workers would see that it was just a dream [to try to continue production] and that would cure them of all dangerous
illusions."

But industrialists were insisting that the head of the government
see them. One of them demanded the use of force. With a serene
irony Giolitti replied: "Would you like us to start by bombing your
factories?" Then he laid bare what he was really thinking. "If I
order the police and the army to occupy the factories, who will
keep watch on the areas that are really decisive for the life of the
country?"

To this end he ordered the factories surrounded and the garrisons of the industrial cities reinforced; he kept ready in his desk,
already signed by the King, a decree mobilizing the railway workers. But to a shrewd politician like Giolitti, waiting and erosion
were an essential part of the game. And then he was counting
above all, as he was to write, on "the common sense of the great
organizations that represented the working masses."

The CGL met in Milan on September 10–11. By 591,241 votes it
approved a motion by its secretary, Ludovico d'Aragona, calling for
recognition of the principle of trade-union control of enterprises;
an opposing motion, which would have made the current operations the springboard for a political struggle for governmental
power, received 409,569 votes. D'Aragona was to reflect later:
"Perhaps we are to blame for having made over-large verbal concessions at the time of the Bolshevik hysteria. But our honor and
our virtue lie in the fact that we opposed the explosion of the revolution that the extremists were planning."

On September 12 Giolitti quietly boarded a train for his meeting
in Aix-les-Bains with the French Premier and Foreign Minister,
Alexandre Millerand. There was no question that management
circles in Italy were critical of his inaction, but the political results
obtained by the old man of Piedmont were probative: he had not
gambled in vain on the understanding of trade-union circles. In
Turin on September 15 he presided at a meeting among d'Aragona,
Bruno Buozzi, and the leaders of Confindustria, Angelo Olivetti
and Conti. In exchange for the workers' evacuation of the factories,
the employers agreed to accept the principle of worker participation in them. During the conversations Giolitti outlined the proposal for a law setting forth the provisions of such participation,
which he promised to endorse. But the proposal was never to be
made. On September 27 the workers evacuated the factories and
on October 4 work was resumed. Observers were not mistaken: a
decisive event had just occurred. According to *Il Corriere della*

Sera for September 29, 1920: "Italy was in danger of death. If there has been no revolution, it is not because it encountered obstacles but because the CGL did not want it." However debatable it may be, this view was significant. Indeed, everyone felt that revolution had failed or been narrowly averted.

Within the Socialist Party men like Gramsci thought that the reformism of the party and the CGL was responsible for the defeat. A great number of the workers, after this last battle, had wearied of these struggles that were waged in vain, in a vicious circle of strike after strike. After the great surges of the spring and summer, the autumn of 1920 clearly showed the end of their enthusiasm and the rise of skepticism and revulsion among the masses.

These tendencies born of so many badly led and futile struggles were to be aggravated by economic conditions. The crisis of overproduction was growing worse. Soon price declines, bankruptcies, and deflation increased the number of the unemployed (it exceeded six hundred thousand in January, 1921). The worker who had a full week's work was a man of privilege, and in such circumstances the labor struggle could most often be only defensive. In 1921 there were only one thousand forty-five strike calls affecting only seven hundred twenty thousand workers—no more than in 1915.

The defeat of labor all over Europe since the spring, furthermore, was universal, from the Ruhr to Budapest. Retreat had begun on all fronts. The seizures of factories in September, 1920, were the last offensive actions carried out in Italy. And so everyone who had been frightened was to raise his head again and listen to Mussolini, who said of the Socialist leaders in Trieste on September 20: "I have known them all, I have had dealings with them. I know very well that when they play the lion they are all rabbits."

At six o'clock in the afternoon of September 28, in the middle of via Grossi, in the heart of Milan, a Captain Bruno, wearing all his many decorations, drew a revolver and took aim at a red flag displayed at a second-floor window. He fired at the flagpole until his gun was empty, then calmly reloaded without leaving the street and resumed firing until the flag fell.

The occupations of the factories had ended the day before. A few days later the Maximalist leader, Serrati, was assaulted in the street by members of the Fascio. In this first attack they restricted themselves to cutting off his beard. Just a joke of young fellows with a sense of humor, some Milanese smiled. Mussolini, however, made no jokes. On September 20 he had pointed out: "The Fascio is called a Battle Fascio, and the word *battle* leaves no room for doubt: battle with peaceful weapons but also with weapons of war." Strange though the phraseology might be, the meaning was clear.

Weapons—rifles, bombs, grenades, revolvers, even a machine gun—were always available at *il Popolo d'Italia*. On Mussolini's desk his glass of milk always had the company of a revolver and two grenades. The cellar was a veritable armory, where rifles lined the walls. As for the room next to his office, Mussolini had turned that into a fencing arena.

But it was not only in the offices of *il Popolo* that there were weapons. Virtually ever former officer had kept his revolver, and the same was true of the Arditi. Thus in the autumn of 1920 every Fascio in the country had its little group of armed men.

Now, about the same time, a colonel assigned to the War Ministry was traveling all through Italy with the duty of setting up reliable groups intended to defend the country in the event of revolutionary action. As we have seen, this project was already several months old.

In his report to the ministry the colonel suggested the "formation of a militia of idealists, composed of the most experienced, the bravest, the strongest, and the most aggressive men, who could stand with the police and the army in carrying out resistance operations and political actions." It was hardly surprising, then, that on October 20 a bulletin dealing with the Fasci was circulated by the chief of the army general staff to all unit commanders, and that the officers took it as an invitation to join such groups, whereas the circular appeared merely to ask for information. Some historians, indeed, state that another circular, issued by Bonomi, the War Minister, called on the fifty thousand officers then being demobilized to join the Fasci and act as their staffs: they would then receive four-fifths of their former army pay. Whether there ever actually was such a circular and whether Bonomi thus *directly* contributed to the birth of the Fasci is still debated.

What is certain is—and we have already seen the emergence of the reasons for it—that the Fascists were to receive the overt support of the local authorities, the army officers, and the police. Relations between any reserve captain at the head of a Fascio and any lieutenant of carabinieri or of the Royal Guard could not be other than congenial: they were allied by the same hatred. In these circumstances—and the government, by its entire attitude, raised no hindrances—the squadre would never be short of weapons. Nor of men.

The men were former officers, Arditi, students, lawyers, white-collar men, manual laborers, unemployed, city-dwellers all—true; but they were to acquire more and more open support from owners of land, however large or small their parcels. For the end of 1920, in the Po Valley, in Emilia and Tuscany, was to bring the birth of an "agrarian Fascism" that would give urban Fascism the transfusion of its riches, its men, and its violence.

Under the impetus of the activities of the *braccianti* organized into their agrarian leagues, many landowners in this rich agricultural area had sold property to share-croppers and *mezzadri* (tenant farmers). Hence, between 1911 and 1921, the number of landowners had risen from twenty-one to thirty-six percent of those working the land, while the number of wage workers on farms had dropped from forty-eight to thirty-eight percent.[2] Smaller than their predecessors, these new landowners were ruthless in defense of their property. Socialism had no agricultural program to offer them, apart from socialization or cooperatives. Furthermore, to these men absorbed by their land, the agrarian league was a yoke, a burden, with those *braccianti* who had to be hired in unnecessary number just when, as a result of the economic crisis, farm prices were dropping. Now these Socialist agrarian leagues were based on Socialist municipalities—such as Bologna—and this alliance of city and league was to be reflected in Fascism: agrarian Fascism-urban Fascism, the city providing the momentum and the leaders, the countryside furnishing the favorable environment.

This agrarian Fascism began to come to maturity after October, 1920. For this, from Tuscany to the environs of Ferrara, Reggio Emilia, and Bologna, was the month of agrarian conflicts: the *braccianti* belonging to the Land Workers' Federation went on strike in order to obtain collective labor contracts. The landowners had to give in on October 25, but already their association was beginning to finance those little groups that had survived in inactivity since the war, composed of violent *disoccupati* lounging under the arcades and in the cafés of Ferrara or Bologna around men like Italo Balbo and Leandro Arpinati.

Those in Florence were grouped in the *Squadra disperata* (Desperate Squad), which went into action on October 22 with an attack on a Socialist town hall. Its members included Tullio Tamburini, whose past was questionable; Amerigo Dumini, a former Ardito with staring eyes and little to say, who had been born in St. Louis, Missouri; Banchelli, Frullini. All of them were paid by

[2] Mario Bandini, *Cent' anni di storia agraria italiana.*

The Decisive Months

the landowners and industrialists of the Florence area under the cover of an "Alliance for Civic Defense."

A "Fascio of Education and Social Defense" was formed in Mortara, in the province of Pavia. Landowners belonging to the association were assessed two to four *lire* (about seven to fourteen cents) per acre; industrialists contributed whatever they wished. Thus the squadristi were paid thirty-five to forty *lire* per day— double the average earnings of a white-collar worker.

These groups prepared for the municipal elections of October 31 and November 7, 1920, the first since the war.

The outcome was important: in the difficult social ambience that continued in spite of the end of the factory seizures, what was the voter going to do? He had a choice among three groups: the Socialists, the Popular Party, and the nationalists, for—and this was the major factor—"national blocs" had been set up with the patronage of the government, and at the last moment the Fascists joined them. Their number, true, was not high, but it was one more evidence of the tacit alliance that was taking shape between the government and Mussolini—Mussolini, who had been arrested in the wake of the elections of 1919. This was a new source of backing for the Fasci, and the representatives of authority who, on the local level, attended the meetings among the "liberal" lawyer, the representative of the government and the Fascist leader saw fresh encouragement to offer no barriers, if not indeed to provide material assistance, to these young men, the fervent inspiration of the patriotic blocs.

But the municipal elections resulted in surprises: while the blocs scored great successes, the Socialists held on to two thousand twenty-two communes, including Milan and Bologna[3]—Socialist Bologna in the heart of turbulent Emilia, like a challenge to the best interests of the nation. Between the two sets of elections, on November 4, the anniversary of the Austrian capitulation, there was an ostentatious victory celebration, the first since the war. In the presence of the King and Giolitti, all the flags of the glorious regiments were massed in Rome round the Altar of the Nation. Officers, nationalists, monarchists, and Fascists from Salandra to Sonnino, from Giolitti to Mussolini, celebrated the anniversary. The instigator of this display was Bonomi: it was the symbol of the national bloc, the unanimity and the bond of sympathy that already extended, from the King to the premier and his war minister and even to the commanders of the squadre.

[3] The Popular Party won 1,613 communes.

Was d'Annunzio going to break the chain thus forged? He was still in Fiume, in that unreal, chaotic setting in which grotesquerie, ardor, and corruption rubbed elbows. In September, with Captain Giulietti's help, his pirates had succeeded in bringing into Fiume a ship called the *Cogne*, whose cargo included a large amount of currency. D'Annunzio ordered his men to open the cases filled with bank notes, thrust his white-gloved hand among them, shuffled the bank notes, and then drafted a letter to the ship owners and signed it: "The Great Pirate." The money arrived with perfect timing, for Fiume was now gripped by a real blockade. Giolitti and Sforza wanted to put an end to the situation, but d'Annunzio held out. On September 8, 1920, he announced: "I, Gabriele d'Annunzio, first legionary of the legion of Ronchi, proclaim Italian regency for the Carnaro."

Four days later, on horseback, he attended the great parade that marked the anniversary of the city's liberation beneath the flag that he had designed: on a dark red ground it bore golden emblems—a serpent biting its tail, as a symbol of eternity, and the seven stars of the Great Bear, the constellation of September. Mussolini went through the motions of approving this patriotic spectacle, paying tribute to d'Annunzio in the poet's own style: "The one man who for twelve or thirteen months has held all the forces of the world at bay is Gabriele d'Annunzio with his legionaries. Against this man of pure Italian lineage all the cowardly are leagued, and that is why we take pride and glory in standing with him even though the vast tribe of idiots rage against us."

Once more Mussolini concealed surrender in bombast. During this period he was received by Sforza at the Foreign Ministry, for he knew that talks were under way with the Yugoslavs and he wished to contribute his own, very governmental point of view.

On November 12 the treaty of Rapallo with Yugoslavia was formally signed. Italy received the whole of Istria and gave up Dalmatia, with the exception of Zara; Fiume became an independent state. The treaty was profitable, but it ran counter to nationalist demands. Mussolini approved it: he abandoned his years-old positions with a disconcerting suppleness. The day after the signing he wrote: "Italians should not be hypnotized by the Adriatic or certain shores of the Adriatic. There is also—unless we are in error—a vast sea of which the Adriatic is a mere gulf and that is called the Mediterranean, in which the opportunities for vigorous Italian expansion are great."

In effect he had recognized that the political battle had moved from Fiume to the Po Valley; that, if Giolitti let him alone in Italy, he must let Giolitti alone in Fiume; was this not moreover, a means for Mussolini to be rid of his embarrassing rival? Was this exchange of courtesies a real agreement? Many Fascists who were also genuine supporters of d'Annunzio believed so. It made little difference. The coincidences of events were impressive. And events multiplied. For example, in Bologna.

The first session of the city council of Bologna was scheduled for Sunday, November 21. The council was to elect a mayor and his colleagues. The population was urged to celebrate the occasion, which marked the success of the Socialists in the elections.

Thursday, November 18. Pedestrians were perplexed and disturbed by typewritten posters pasted on walls. There was nothing ambiguous about them:

"On Sunday, women and everyone else who likes peace and quiet should stay at home. Those who wish to deserve well of the Nation should deck their windows with the Italian Tricolor.

"On Sunday there should be only Fascists and Bolsheviks in the streets of Bologna. This will be the test, the great test in the name of Italy!"

The Battle Fascio led by Arpinati had decided to act.

Sunday, November 21. It was three o'clock in the afternoon. As the city councilors arrived for their meeting in Palazzo Accursio, twenty thousand persons stood in the public square, blocked off by the soldiery, and sang Socialist anthems to the accompaniment of two bands. The newly elected mayor, Ennio Gnudi, a railway worker, came out on the balcony of the town hall, followed by Socialist councilors displaying the red flag.

The barricades erected by the troops to block via Rizzoli were overthrown. A resolute detachment of soldiers moved forward, firing at the balcony and the crowd. Some persons were able to huddled together under the balcony; the rest tried to flee. Grenades were thrown from windows. In the council's meeting room there were shouts, and then suddenly shots. An anti-Socialist lawyer named Giulio Giordani, a wounded war veteran, died where he sat, killed by a bullet; another anti-Socialist, Cesare Colliva, was seriously wounded. The final count was nine dead and almost a hundred wounded. The press seized on the episode, making it appear a Socialist conspiracy intended to drown the national opposition in blood. Who actually did kill Giordani? The answer was never allowed to emerge from any official investigation. Had Fascist provocateurs entered the meeting room? It was not impossible.

Whatever its origins, the Bologna episode was a decisive turning point. It marked the real start of the rise of Fascism and its brutalities.

In July, 1920, there were one hundred eight Fasci; by the end of October there were one hundred ninety; by the end of the year eight hundred; by the end of May, 1921, one thousand six hundred. After Bologna, the Fasci became the rallying points for everyone opposed to Socialism: landowners, officers, and the industrialists who were to provide generous financing for the movement and its squadre.

Mussolini, of course, was at the confluence of all these currents; but, as we have seen, he was carried along by them; he was the man who was to accomplish the merger of the parallel lines, for, as a result of his past, his newspaper, and his ability, he had a reputation. And he committed himself without reservation. On November 24 he wrote: "We are speaking loud and clear to let all the world know that henceforth we have enough 'tools' to overcome and shatter every kind of violence by the extremists of the PUS."

"Enough tools": the statement was frightening, but it was the truth. The barracks would open and arms would flow out of them. And trucks and sometimes men as well, for mixed forces became a commonplace: carabinieri and squadre acting in concert as they sang the same hymns.

Adroit at presenting the Fascist attacks as purely defensive reactions—it must be added that this was the attitude of all the major newspapers—Mussolini wrote: "We are not drinkers of blood or esthetes of violence. . . . But we are ready to accept a civil war if it is forced on us" (P.d.I., November 24, 1920).

But the young Fascist lawyer of Bologna, Dino Grandi, was more outspoken. On December 1 he founded a newspaper called l'Assalto (The Attack), and his first editorial concluded: "For the glory and the welfare of the whole people, the Fascists are issuing today their second declaration of war: no armistice and no quarter."

On December 21 the Fascists launched an attack on the town hall of Ferrara, the Castello. Three of them were killed, but their action gave birth to new squadre, which were headed by Italo Balbo and which were soon to dominate the entire province and even to be equipped with machine guns.

For major undertakings the truck-borne squadristi wore helmets, and their column on the march was very much like an army, a "parallel" army in the process of being built up. As Gentile was to write, "the action squadre are the force of a potential state that is moving to become a reality."

For Giolitti and those who followed him, the liberals and the constitutionalists, this development of the squadre, which they at least fostered by their permissiveness, represented the height of shrewdness. They made use of Fascist violence and they diverted it against Socialism, and they reckoned on gaining from every point of view: Socialism would be neutralized and smashed, and Fascism, absorbed in accomplishing this work and tied to the government by the assistance that the government offered it, would be distracted from international matters. As an admirer of Giolitti wrote: "It was a shift of Fascist activity from foreign to domestic policy by directing it . . . against Bolshevism."[4]

It was a dangerous and highly theoretical Machiavellianism, but in the beginning it seemed successful.

In spite of defections, indeed, d'Annunzio stubbornly held out. Weeping, Admiral Millo, who was still in command in Dalmatia, had given orders to evacuate the territory handed over to the Yugoslavs. His oath of obedience to the King was paramount to his pledge to the poet. Thereafter, d'Annunzio and his legionaries stood alone against General Caviglia, who had been instructed to carry on to the finish. On November 30 the "Commander" sent word to the general: "I do not recognize your authority. . . . I am waiting for you to send your people to rout the legionaries. Your people will receive a warm welcome."

Caviglia tightened the blockade still further. Mussolini remarked in *il Popolo* on December 2: "The blockade may be the prelude to a civil war for which the responsibility will rest on the government in Rome." But in the days that followed he issued no appeal for solidarity. Four warships, including a battleship, however, placed themselves under d'Annunzio's command. On December 22 d'Annunzio summoned Captain Arturo Marpicati to his government mansion. "Go at once to Mussolini with this message," d'Annunzio ordered.

Marpicati managed to get through and to deliver the message to Mussolini. D'Annunzio had written: "Are you ready to blow up the prefectures and the police stations? Are we or are we not going to make this revolution?"

Mussolini was swept away by rage against everyone—Giolitti, Daviglia, and d'Annunzio. "Your poet is undoubtedly a great poet," he said to Marpicati, "but he is mad, utterly mad." Then he summoned several Fascist leaders. Their conference was short and their answer was negative. "We all have Giolitti's cops at our heels," Mussolini said by way of excuse.[5]

On December 24, however, he wrote: "Fiume is absolutely right in opposing the fulfillment of the Treaty of Rapallo," which, it will be remembered, called for the creation of a Free State of Fiume. That same evening Caviglia's soldiers moved forward. The legion-

[4] Ciccoti, *L'Italia in rissa.*
[5] As reported by Marpicati in Valeri, *Trente ans d'histoire italienne.*

aries had plastered up huge posters bearing a message from the poet: "If your leaders blind you, may the God of Italy bring you light."

But the posters did no good. The first victims of the "Bloody Christmas" were already falling. D'Annunzio filled the air with radio appeals: "To Italy of the mutilated victory I send this watchword, which will he heard: Insurrection-Resurrection." But these calls to combat aroused no echo. Mussolini filled his newspaper with "Eîa to Gabriele d'Annunzio and Italian Fiume." This was a mockery of help, and d'Annunzio had no illusions about it: "Dishonored for ever," he said, "Italy . . . will not raise a finger."

At dawn of December 26 the guns of the battleship *Andrea Doria* fired on his government mansion. A 152-mm. shell struck the cornice of the window next to the poet's. Showered with rubble, d'Annunzio made his decision: "A hundred and one times have I offered my life with a smile during my war, but it would be absurd to throw it away today to serve a nation that cannot, even for a moment, interrupt the gluttony of its holiday festivities."

Two days later the armistice was signed at Abbazia. Before he evacuated Fiume, he paid solemn tribute on December 31 to the bodies of the thirty-five men killed, legionaries and regular soldiers laid out together in the frozen shapes of wasteful death. To the last of his followers, gathered round him, he proclaimed: "The night is dark, but each of us has a flame in his hand. . . . Soon the new year will begin. . . . A death's head crowned with laurel clenches its teeth over the naked dagger and stares fixedly from its deep eye-sockets into the unknown. To whom does the unknown belong? To us—*a noi.*"

The poet was allowed to retire unmolested to the shores of the Lago di Garda. Italy had not stirred. This was still another proof of the minimal impression that had been made by nationalism, but how would the Fascists react? There were mutterings, and in Florence there was a split, but nothing decisive was done because Fascism was now living on its squadre.

The mutilated victory, national passion, and the question of Fiume had been able to prevent the dissolution of Fascism by providing it with propaganda themes, but none of this would ever have been enough to swell its ranks with the thousands of recruits that it needed. After the surrender of Fiume, Fascism continued to grow: d'Annunzio's legionaries enlisted in its squadre, bringing with them their hatreds and their Arditi uniforms—black shirts and tasseled black fezzes; after the evacuation of Dalmatia, Fascism mounted steadily from Tuscany to Venezia, from Pavia to Bologna, and the squadre, the armed forces of social conflict, inspired, as the conservative *Giornale d'Italia* pointed out, a broad "middle-class terrorism."

Money and support were anything but lacking. There were rumors (some historians challenge them) that secret orders from Luigi Fera, the Keeper of the Privy Seal—Minister of Justice— called for acquittals in cases of "crimes committed for the good of the nation." Such crimes multiplied, and for many years they would be part of the everyday life of both city and countryside in Italy. The labor exchanges, the cooperatives, and the peasants' leagues were the first targets.

The Fascists would strike without warning at night, surrounding the residence of the *capolega*, the peasant who headed a league. They would beat him, often they would kill him; his house would be burned, and the other peasants would flee. If there was resistance, the telephone and the trucks—two of the trump aces of the squadre, the two others being money and weapons—would be put to work to assemble a "punitive expedition" composed of the squadre of several cities, and the village would be overrun. The press automatically described these brutalities as proper reactions to "cowardly Bolshevik attacks."

In Florence it was the Marquis Dino Perrone-Compagni who directed the outrages; in Cremona it was Farinacci. The beatings were inflicted with the *manganello*, a solid bludgeon that the government was said to have imported by the carload. Peasants would be left chained naked to trees dozens of miles from their homes, while the attackers would file back into the city in the early morning, singing:

> They killed Giovanni Berta,
> Fascist of the *Fascisti*,
> So vengeance, we'll take vengeance
> On all the *Comunisti*.

or else:

> To arms, to arms—
> We are the *Fascisti*,
> Death to *Comunisti*.

In fact the Communists were far from being the only targets. The leagues of the "white Bolsheviki" were destroyed the same as those of the reds, and the Catholic deputy, Guido Miglioli, escaped the squadre only with the utmost difficulty. In Piacenza and Parma, "interventionist" and pro-d'Annunzio groups were attacked; in Padua totally non-political cooperatives suffered the same fate.

Cultural associations, libraries, newspapers—whatever had any connection, however remote, with peasant or worker organizations was threatened, and invariably labeled Communist. Castor oil was forced down the victims by the quart. A woman school teacher would be forced to drink the castor oil after her head had been shaved and then, her skirt tied above her knees, she would be made to jump up and down until the purge took effect.

The violence was systematic: in two months four hundred labor exchanges, cooperatives, and Socialist clubs were destroyed, twenty town halls were invaded, sixty-eight regional and municipal councils were forced to resign. At least two hundred fifty persons were killed, of whom only forty were Fascists.

Sandro Carosi, a pharmacist, soon became notorious in the Pisa area. He never went out without his Mauser. One day he and two other squadristi went into an *osteria* that was a meeting place for Socialist and Communist peasants. There was an uneasy silence. In the spirit of fun, Carosi lined a peasant against a wall, placed an apple on his head, and fired at it. He killed the peasant. No one dared to intervene, or even to testify in court, and Carosi continued his career. His invariable remark when he introduced himself was: "Sandro Carosi—fifteen political murders."

In the province of Mantua, where Giacomo Matteotti, when he was a deputy, warned the peasants: "Stay in your houses, don't reply to provocations; even silence, even cowardice can sometimes be heroic," several dozen persons were killed and four to five thousand were wounded or tortured.

Defensive action existed—ambushes of Fascists' trucks, for instance—but it was difficult. The distances among houses, confusion, surprise, the lack of equipment were grievous handicaps. Mussolini remarked: "The PUS . . . is a colossal elephant without a soul"—and it was breaking.

The party's 1921 congress opened on January 15 in the Teatro Goldoni in Leghorn. Gramsci, Umberto Terracini, Togliatti, Bombacci, and the Communist faction (58,753 votes) demanded the expulsion of the reformists (14,695 votes) from the party, in conformity with the directives embodied in Lenin's twenty-one points. But the "unitarian" Maximalists (98,023) under Serrati flatly refused, even though pledging allegiance to the Third International.

Thereupon the Communists left the Italian Socialist Party, but this did not make it any more united. Furthermore, half the membership (one hundred thousand) left the party without making a choice between the "old house" of the Socialists and the new Italian Communist Party.

This could only facilitate matters for the Fascists' offensive. It was steadily growing in scope, deriving its strength, as the Socialist deputy, Giovanni Zibordi, wrote at the time, from the fact that it "combined in itself all the resources of an extra-legal organization and extra-legal activity with all the protections and the passive complicities of the law." Quite often the complicity lay in the very way in which the law was applied. In Ferrara, for example, the carabinieri regularly searched and disarmed everyone who went into the labor exchange, but they never touched visitors to the offices of the Fascio.

Under these conditions Mussolini felt that he could go the limit, that this "posthumous and preventative counter-revolution" [i.e., after the first and before the next revolutionary wave] that was under way could carry him into power if he won the official support of Confindustria. Men like Cesare Rossi and Michele Bianchi acted as his liaison agents with financial circles, and Mussolini, the former anarchist and former Socialist, suddenly discovered the virtues of the liberal economic system. On January 14 he wrote: "Capitalism . . . is a hierarchy . . . a scale of values that had been developed over the centuries. These are values that are irreplaceable today. . . ."

Nonetheless he was not forgetting to gather in the peasants. When their leagues had been destroyed in Emilia, the landowners repudiated their labor contracts and refused to hire anyone who was not enrolled with the Fascio. The first Fascist labor union was founded on February 25 in San Bartolomeo in Bosco, in the province of Ferrara. Rather than suffer destruction, the surviving peasant leagues thereupon often went over in a body to Fascism: in one day seventeen of them became autonomous unions and each was solemnly presented with its gagliardetto. In order to expedite the business, some landowners even leased land to the peasants, thus making it appear that they were facilitating the upward move to tenant farming and ownership. As for the Socialists, they were still talking of collectivism. In the next few months they were to lose provinces that they had taken thirty years to win over, and many of their militants enrolled in the Fasci. Mussolini could now take another tone.

"Fascism," he wrote on March 23, "is a great mobilization of material and moral energies. What is its goal? To govern the nation. . . . In a few months the whole of Italy will be in our hands."

On April 3 he spoke in the municipal theater in Bologna. The audience was enthusiastic. The squadre of the whole province had gathered at the summons from Dino Grandi. On the previous day a cabinet decree had dissolved the Socialist city government "for reasons of public order." With what assurance, then, Mussolini addressed his public: "Fascists of Italy and the Romagna! Citizens of Bologna! I offer my thanks to Counselor Grandi, whose introduction was far too flattering. I accept his praise, and I think I have never committed the sin of pride. . . ."

The entire hall applauded. "That Mussolini!" people laughed contentedly. He was so sure of himself that he continued: "We should act in this way, led by a column of fire, because others reviled us and refused to understand us. And, even though violence may be deplorable, it is obvious that in order to instill our ideas into some minds we shall have to make refractory heads ring with the sound of the cudgel!"

The shouts of *Bravo!* were deafening—this was the triumph of the squadristi. Mussolini added: "The violence required by Fascism must preserve a line, a clearly aristocratic, or, if you prefer, clearly surgical style."

Giolitti, having made use of this violence, wanted now to domesticate it, to "parliamentarize" it, and the old magician of majorities, as he still believed himself to be, thought that he would be able to find support among the most opposed groups, even—why not?—from the Socialists, brought back to reason by the presence of Fascist deputies. This was all the more important to him because Giolitti was contemplating a daringly liberal program: had he not already created a commission to investigate the costs of the war, required the registration of securities, and broadened the rights of inheritance? But it was precisely these measures that had alienated Confindustria from the old leader: with his prestige untainted he had been extremely useful in June of 1920, but with his "neo-Giolittism" he could now become a stumbling block.

Giolitti indeed felt that he was endangered on the right as on the left, which reproached him for the support that he had given to Fascism. In the belief that he was playing a shrewd game, he dissolved the Chamber on April 7 and announced new elections for May 15, 1921.

Giolitti's intention was the creation of "national blocs," Tricolor blocs that would be joined by the Fascists and through which he would shatter the mass parties that were least amenable to parliamentary deals: the Popular Party and the Socialist Party. Sforza was disturbed by the alliance with the Fascists. With a thin smile and in a calm tone, Giolitti explained his plan: "Wait and see: the Fascists' candidacies will be like fireworks: they will make a great deal of noise, but they will amount to nothing but smoke. . . ."[6]

Sforza remained skeptical, but Giolitti insisted on his point of

[6] Sforza, *L'Italia dal 1914 al 1944.* . . .

The Decisive Months

view: Fascism could be reduced to legality and transformed into "something decent once it got into the Chamber." Had not Giolitti himself brought off the same thing with the Socialists before 1914?

The elections were enveloped in an atmosphere of violence. Dino Grandi, the Fascist leader in Bologna, was to say in November, 1921: "The elections were held between two punitive expeditions. For the Fascists they were no more and no less than an incident in their civil war. The election campaign was carried on without a program; it was simply an anti-Socialist campaign."

A Socialist school teacher was assassinated in the presence of his pupils in Pisa; two deputies, Matteotti and Modigliani, were attacked. To quote Grandi again: "The Battle Fasci became protective squadre for the old liberal candidates who . . . accepted the symbol of the Fasci as their election symbol and who joined in the shouts of *Eîa, eîa, alalà* for Commander d'Annunzio and Benito Mussolini."

In spite of that, the elections were a surprise for Giolitti: the Socialists retained one hundred twenty-two seats, the Communists won sixteen, and the two parties together received 1,861,505 votes —twenty thousand more than in 1919. With considerable optimism and short-sightedness, *Avanti!* headlined: "The Italian proletariat has swamped Fascist reaction under an ocean of red ballots."

The Popular Party increased its representation from one hundred to one hundred seven seats; the "national blocs" won two hundred seventy-five of the five hundred thirty-five seats in the Chamber. It was certainly a majority, but purely a theoretical one, for these two hundred seventy-five seats had been transferred from the reformists to the Fascists.

Mussolini was elected twice: in Milan with 124,918 votes and in Bolonga with 172,491. This was revenge for November, 1919, and all the more because he went to Montecitorio at the head of a group of thirty-five Fascists that included Grandi and Farinacci. At the age of thirty-eight he finally saw the road to power really opened.

Giolitti had a kindly welcome for these Fascist deputies. They were "young, for the most part, and animated by an aggressive spirit. . . . I regarded that as a great advantage, because now Fascism represented a real force in the country," he observed in his memoirs.

Was Mussolini, as Giolitti hoped, to become a "Turati" of Fascism? As soon as he learned that he had been elected, the Fascist chief proclaimed: "We will be not a parliamentary group but an assault squad and a firing squad."

5

Fascism in the State
(May, 1921 – August, 1922)

"I tell you frankly that no government whose program includes machine guns against Fascism can keep its feet in Italy."—MUSSOLINI (speech in Parliament July 19, 1922)

ONSERVATIVE QUARTERS looked forward with curiosity to the arrival of the young Fascist deputies, several of whom were less than thirty years old: everyone from Salandra to Giolitti was prepared to serve as their mentor when, a few days before the inauguration of this thirty-sixth Parliament, *il Giornale d'Italia* published an interview with Mussolini: "Fascism," he said, "has no monarchist or republican predisposition, but it is republican in tendency."

Therefore the Fascist group would take no part in the session at which the speech from the throne would be delivered. This created a great scandal. Cesare De Vecchi, a Fascist and a devout monarchist, protested, and Mussolini had to admit that he was stating "personal views that should not and could not bind Italian Fascism as a whole or even the new Fascist deputies" (May 27, 1921).

Thus he was backing down, and in fact he was one of the few deputies who did not attend the solemn session of June 11. Was this interview a mistake on Mussolini's part? More subtly, no doubt, it was a means of voicing a disguised threat to the crown and at the same time of asserting himself dramatically.

The day after the speech from the throne, all the Fascist deputies took their seats together on the benches of the extreme right, where no one else wanted to be seen. It was indeed an assault and firing squad that had entered the Chamber. On June 13, Francesco Misiano, who had become a Communist deputy, was encircled by the Fascist deputies, who threatened the "deserter-deputy"; frightened, he drew a revolver, but then he changed his mind and handed it to Roberto Farinacci, who was the leader of his assailants.

"This pistol was used in an attempt to assassinate Italian deputies!" Farinacci shouted, and he went up to Giolitti and gave him the weapon. "I turn it over to you."

"Really," Giolitti replied, "I have no permit to carry a gun."

The deputies protested against the attack, but nevertheless Misiano was expelled from Montecitorio. Then the debate began. It went badly for Giolitti: his financial proposals were still making the right apprehensive, and Don Sturzo's Popular Party criticized him for the law requiring the registration of securities, which was embarrassing for the Vatican's treasury and its rich congregations; as for the Socialists, they endorsed Don Sturzo's conviction that "Fascism [under Giolitti] was given arms, organized militarily, and brought on to the Parliamentary scene."

On June 21 Mussolini rose to speak. Curiosity silenced everyone. Here then was the man whose squadre were sowing violence across the countryside of central Italy. He appeared at Montecitorio smiling, somewhat tense and arrogant, his fist on his hip, his neck concealed in a white wing collar that emphasized the heaviness of his face.

"I warn you at once, with the sovereign contempt that I flaunt in the face of all proprieties, that I am going to stand here for reactionary principles. . . ." There was a burst of laughter from the left. ". . . I am sufficiently lacking in modesty to state that my words can be heard with some profit by all groups in the Chamber. . . . I ask you not to interrupt me. . . ."

It was a martial beginning, but, Mussolini went on, "I am coming to my subject. . . ." And then, to the great astonishment of many deputies, the tone was moderate and the ideas were simple —even simplistic; the ideas of the national right. To Giolitti, to whom he owed so much, Mussolini—like Salandra—addressed reproaches for a foreign policy conducted by that Count Sforza who was a "world-weary diplomat . . . devoid of all feeling"; he attacked the Communists: "between them and us there can never be anything but war"; but he offered dialogue with all other groups. He proclaimed himself a liberal first of all: "The state must be reduced to its juridical and political manifestations," he repeated, knowing very well that business groups favored this point of view, which would doom Giolitti's plans. Then, turning toward the Socialists,

Mussolini continued: "We deny that the history of mankind can be explained by economic determinism."

Vigorous applause came from many benches. Then Mussolini launched into a panegyric for the CGL which, like Fascism, had remained patriotic. To the Popular Party he declared: "Fascism neither preaches nor practices anti-clericalism. . . ."

Who still remembered the Mussolini who had challenged God in Geneva? In his speech he emphasized the areas of agreement: "Basically I am no advocate of divorce. . . ." He stood for the freedom of the schools, but, beyond the Popular Party, he addressed himself above all to the Vatican: "The imperial and Latin tradition of Rome is represented today by Catholicism. . . . Profane or secular Italy should provide the Vatican with material help, give it the facilities to build schools, churches, hospitals. . . ."

This was the first hint of the agile maneuvering that Mussolini would carry through to its conclusion, which would be the conciliation of the Vatican in order to neutralize the Popular Party. Mussolini ended his speech on a solemn note: "For us," he said, facing the Socialists, "violence is not a system . . . it is not a sport. . . . We are ready to lay down our arms if you too will disarm, and especially disarm your minds."

Mussolini returned to his seat amid considerable applause, but some of the Fascists, especially young Dino Grandi and Farinacci, were upset. At the head of their squadre they had thrust Fascism into the flesh of Italy; must they now disarm? Doubt began to fester: was Mussolini going to desert them? Certainly the man was capable of doing so: insanely individualistic, he was concerned primarily with power, and for himself. The highly favorable reaction of the deputies at the end of his speech in Montecitorio had made it clear to him that he could undoubtedly have his way with them within Parliament, and, beginning on June 21, he launched the search for "his" majority.

Two days later Giolitti resigned, and on July 4 he was succeeded by Bonomi, the former Minister of War who was constantly accused of being pro-Fascist and who had been elected from Mantua on a "national bloc" ticket with Fascists as fellow-candidates and the fasces as his symbol.

How could Mussolini not try to work his way into some Parliamentary scheme? But, in order to do so, he would have to establish firm personal control over Fascism, which was still, as Grandi told Mario Missiroli, "in spite of all the central committees in the world, nothing but a chaotic aggregation of local reaction phenomena." Mussolini would have to enforce obedience on each of the local leaders, each *ras* who, like the Ethiopian feudal chiefs whose title they had taken, acted with his own squadra at his own whim, with no understanding of the danger to which he was exposing Fascism: that of forging, through Fascist outrages, a union between the Socialist and the Popular Parties, Italy's two mass parties. Furthermore, for some time new groups had been taking shape, the Arditi del popolo (People's Arditi), bold men who, rejecting Turati's slogan—"Be good, be holy, be cowardly"—were setting traps for the Fascist squadre. Nothing was clear-cut in these bands: one of their two leaders went over to Fascism and in 1926 the other was accused of being a provocateur; but they represented a force nonetheless. On July 6 they marched through Rome armed with clubs and daggers. When they went into action, they roused the workers and peasants out of their lethargy. Mussolini felt it necessary to arm himself against this peril too, and what happened at Sarzana at the end of July confirmed his belief in the necessity of maneuvering.

Dominated by its castle, and nestled behind its fifteenth-century walls, the town of Sarzana in the southern tip of Liguria was holding out against the squadre of Carrara and Florence. A Defense Group, which embraced every party from anarchists to republicans, had been established and had exerted enough pressure on the carabinieri to force the arrest of a whole squadra of Fascists. During the night of July 20–21, Amerigo Dunini, Banchelli, and the Florentines moved out with five hundred young men to free their comrades. Sarzana was ready for them. The anarchists entrenched in the Gothic tower were prepared to hurl a kitchen pot filled with dynamite on Piazza Mazzini. The Fascists arrived, following the railway tracks. A carabinieri captain, Jurghens, was waiting for them with eleven of his men. Dumini set up a shout: "Hurrah for the carabinieri! Long live the King!" But his followers surrounded the captain, someone fired and wounded a carabiniere, and his fellows fired back: ten Fascists fell. The others ran away, ignoring the captain's shouts: "Halt! Don't try to escape, you'll be killed."

And indeed the Fascists were hunted down in the fields; some were killed with farm implements and some were tortured. They left eighteen dead and thirty wounded at Sarzana. The episode created a great sensation and was the talk of all Italy: it was the first time that the forces of law and order had met the Fascists in a blood-letting clash. Was this the signal for Bonomi's government to change its course?

There was always the danger that, having made use of the weapon of Fascism, the liberals might smash it. It was true that in other areas the Fascists killed and burned with impunity, as, for instance, the Tuscan group did at Roccastrada on July 24 under Marquis Dino Compagni; but such outrages cost them all their popularity in the area. That was the real danger, and Mussolini confronted it cleverly. In *il Popolo* of June 23 he had already gotten his own skirts clear: "It has been said many times that our violence should be knightly, aristocratic, surgical, and hence, in a certain sense, humane. It was said in vain."

On July 23 the Chamber was discussing the recent outbreaks. Mussolini's statement was awaited impatiently. The Fascist chief castigated the government for putting his movement, "with its outraged patriotic idealism and its goal of vigorously reestablishing the authority of the state," on the same plane with that Socialist movement "that clashes with the state in order to destroy it."

For Bonomi and the "constitutionalists" this was a discreet reminder of services rendered, coupled—for Mussolini always played several cards at once—with the threat: "The great forces recognized today are three: Socialism, which will have to discipline itself and which has already begun to do so; . . . the Popular Party . . . Fascism. . . . It is my belief that a coalition of these three forces based on a joint program . . . might be able to govern Italy."

The deputies examined this new tripartite approach, of which there had been not the slightest advance hint: another of Mussolini's tricks to disarm his opponents? Yes, but undoubtedly, too, a means of pressure on Bonomi's government; in any event the maneuver was to be successful. On August 3, under the august auspices of Enrico De Nicola, the President of the Chamber, a treaty of peace was signed by the Socialists and the Fascists. Outside Montecitorio the great Socialist deputy, Tito Zaniboni—who was later to organize an attempt on Il Duce's life—was observed in conversation with the elegantly dressed squadrista deputy, Giacomo Acerbo. In the agreement the Socialist Party declared that it had nothing to do with the People's Arditi, and the CGL, over Gino Baldesi's signature, made itself a party to the statement.

Coming in the wake of all that Italy had seen of the work of the squadre, after what the Socialists themselves had said—Turati himself, on March 22, 1921, had proclaimed: "Fascism is anti-civilization!"—such an accord could only bewilder, the more so in that neither the Popular Party nor the Communists had signed it.

On this level, then, Mussolini had won. But had he not lost the confidence of the squadristi?

"If Fascism does not follow me," he said on August 2, "no one can make me follow Fascism." But he took it almost for granted that he would be obeyed. Already he was Il Duce, and there was a song about him:

> He's an electric current,
> His voltage runs up high—
> Lay hands on Mussolini
> And probably you'll die.

On August 3 he wrote: "I have the right to look down from a mountain peak . . . on a panorama that is not Bologna or Venice or Cuneo, but Italy, Europe, the world."

But this accomplished nothing. Not one *ras* followed. The dark, slender, resolute Farinacci, and Balbo and Grandi, wanted to go the limit. They felt securely backed up; their squadristi were eager for the assaults, the songs, and the unpunished violence. The industrialists and the landowners had invested substantial amounts of money in Fascism, and not for the purpose of becoming part of a team with the Socialists. Unquestionably there had been initial successes: in one year of the squadre, wages on the farms had been forced down fifty percent and those in industry almost fifteen percent, but the economic crisis persisted. Large companies like Ilva, Ansaldo, and the Banca di Sconto were in trouble: they called for succor to Bonomi's government, which very perceptibly relaxed Giolitti's financial rigors; but to Confindustria and banking circles Fascism was still a means of pressure, a last resort that they could not and would not give up. And it became clear to Mussolini, to his surprise, that he was being "let down."

On August 16, five hundred forty-one Fasci of Emilia and the Romagna gathered in Grandi's home city of Bologna and refused to recognize the political peace pact. Posters went up, saying: "Revenge and revenge again on Mussolini, the traitor" and: "Once a traitor, always a traitor." The next day Mussolini created a sensation by resigning from the movement's executive committee; but he explained: "It is not I who am resigning, but the others who are forcing me to leave."

On August 19, however, the central committee of the Fasci refused to accept Mussolini's resignation and he agreed to return to the executive committee's meetings. This in itself did not mean the end of the crisis, but Mussolini had felt the chill wind of solitude, and in these last weeks of August he had quickly to reorient himself.

First of all there was the political accord. Its assets vanished the moment when it was signed and some of the enemy were demobilized. Besides, the attitude of Bonomi's government was little different from that of Giolitti's: Captain Jurghens, for whom an award had been suggested after his stand at Sarzana, was now forgotten. Finally, and this was the determining factor, the squadre were receiving massive backing: in money on the part of the land-owners and in equipment on the part of military circles. For these groups this was a means of inducing Fascism to "be itself."

Thereafter all Mussolini had to do was merely to drape the squadre in the comfortable cloak of a political label, and on September 7 the Fascist deputies whom he had summoned to Milan proposed that the movement be converted into a political party. In this Mussolini saw a triple advantage: he would be able to regain control of the movement and thus he would have available for his own use a stable instrument of political action. And this party would be in a position to become what the squadre could not be: a mass party.

At this time the forces commanded by Farinacci, Balbo, Dumini, Cesare De Vecchi (Turin), and Achille Starace (Trento) were launched on operations of unprecedented scope, still with the ap-proval—or the benevolent passivity—of the representatives of au-thority. A march on Ravenna by three thousand Fascists was planned, beginning on September 12: these were the "columns of fire" which converged on the city under Grandi, Balbo, and Arpinati. In celebration of the six-hundredth anniversary of the death of Dante, foreigners had poured into the city. Everyone had to remove his hat when the Fascist emblems and banners went by, and some priests who did not react quickly enough were beaten until they bled. In the middle of the night of September 25, two carriages entered the main square of Mola di Bari, after a day dur-ing which Giuseppe Di Vagno, a Socialist deputy, had held a meet-ing. Out of the shadow of the arcades an informer approached the carriages: "There's where he is," he told the men inside. They knocked at the door of a small house, and Di Vagno opened: there were three shots, the explosion of a grenade, and the sound of horses' hoofs.

Obviously the assassination of the deputy meant the abrogation of the peace treaty. But this was also accomplished more formally. Marquis Compagni sent a telegram to the Premier saying that the squadre were re-asserting their freedom of action. On September 27 the government leisurely drafted a very rigorous decree-law against possessors of weapons. . . . Mussolini wrote: "There can be no peace as long as the Fascists are called killers."

He was again on good terms with his people, but it was he who had followed them. On October 10 he stated precisely the goals of the political party that was to take the place of the Fascist move-ment: "To channel and consolidate a cluster of young forces round an outstanding individual force that can make use of them as a driving mass for his own ends conceived in harmony with the real interests of Italy."

"The outstanding individual force," obviously, was himself.

The congress of the movement was to open in Rome on November 7, and the date had not been chosen at random.

Three days earlier there had been huge celebrations throughout Italy in commemoration of the victory of 1918: the body of an unknown soldier was buried beneath the Altar of the Nation, and everywhere, in all the observances, the Fascists and their gagliardetti were in the front ranks; in Milan Archbishop Achille Ratti (the future Pope Pius XI) agreed that the gagliardetti, like the regimental standards, should be paraded into the cathedral and blessed. The congress of November 7 began in the Augusteo, and in his first speech Mussolini declaimed: "Without Fascism the Unknown Soldier would not be sleeping today in his coffin at the Altar of the Nation."

He had chosen at the outset the theme that could assure the unanimity of his audience. Ten or fifteen thousand or even more Fascists had poured into Rome from the whole country, at a cost of about three hundred *lire* per man to the movement's treasury, or at the very least a total of three million *lire* (one hundred thousand dollars). The movement must have been rich.

This influx of bellicose young men was not unaccompanied by violence. The railway workers forced their special trains to stop at some distance from the station platforms; whereupon the Fascists broke out their guns and killed a worker. A "Committee of Proletarian Defense" called a general strike. Parading through the center of Rome, the Fascists used their canes to bare the heads of those spectators whose hats had not been removed in homage to the gagliardetti. The shops were closed, and the coldness of the reception was unmistakable. In the poor quarter of San Lorenzo four Fascists were found dead at a street corner, their chests ripped open.

Mussolini was apprehensive. He sat in the first row in the great hall of the Augusteo, his legs crossed, and, with a rose in his hand, he observed the speakers. He was solemn. This movement of three hundred twenty thousand members was to become his party. The evening of November 8 was painful. The city was paralyzed by the general strike; Balbo was calling for direct action: "We are an attack force," he cried, with the endorsement of Grandi.

Mussolini and Giuseppe Bottai were on the side of caution. Finally Grandi and Mussolini embraced in full view of a cheering, reunified convention. Over and over again the hall rang with the anthem, *Giovinezza* (*Youth*):

> The years of youth, the years of youth,
> Beauty in its flowering spring,
> Fascism is salvation's truth
> And our freedom's armored ring.

Then the convention resolved to consider itself besieged in the Augusteo, and it was in the oppressive atmosphere of a barracks that the Partito nazionale fascista (PNF—National Fascist Party) was born at eleven o'clock in the evening of November 9, 1921. After a theatrical abdication—"I should like to disappear into the new organization, because you ought to heal yourselves of me and walk alone"—Mussolini was put at the head of the party, with Grandi, among others; Michele Bianchi became the party's secretary-general.

Mussolini's program speech had emphasized the "liberal" aspect of the movement: "In the economic sphere we are liberals. . . . I will turn back the railways and the telegraph services to private companies. . . ." In an allusion to his past that brought general laughter, he had added: "It is not a question of turning to Socialism but of turning away from it."

Hailed with an ovation, carried in triumph, presented with flowers, Mussolini was indeed the leader of this new party, which officially repudiated the peace treaty on November 15, retained its armed squadre, and proclaimed: "We will take the place of the state whenever it shows itself unable to give battle . . . to the causes and the components of internal disintegration."

Bonomi tried to react against this position, but his own past bound him to Fascism. In an effort to win the release of Fascists in prison in Florence, the city's Fascio announced its readiness to give the names of those "functionaries of Bonomi" who had afforded unqualified support, providing arms and information and inciting to arson and murder, for the Fascist assaults. When it was announced that Bonomi was planning to dissolve the squadre, the PNF issued a call to arms: "To all sections of the party! To all battle squadre! An imminent offensive against Fascism is reported planned. . . . As of December 15, all members of the party are members of the battle squadre." The challenge was clear: now let the government dare to declare the PNF outside the law!

The militarization of the party was soon complete: the squadre became a Militia, a veritable army. The black shirt became the general uniform. Mussolini, in order to stand out from the rest, was to be one of the few who would refuse to wear it. Within the Militia, the *principi* (from the classic Roman army's *principes*, first-line infantry) were the active force, the *triari* (rear guard) were the reserves. This Militia was organized by centuries, or hundreds, cohorts, and legions. In addition there were the *Avanguardia* for boys ten to fifteen years old and the *Balilla* for those under ten, as well as the "women's groups": thus the PNF was made a parallel state, an army ready for war.

On January 19, 1922, Mussolini wrote: "We must destroy the enemy's vital centers. We must wipe out the seats of the infection of anti-Fascism." In the same month, however, he left Italy for Cannes in order to observe the inter-Allied conference in which French Premier and Foreign Minister Aristide Briand and Prime Minister Lloyd George were taking part. One evening, under the lights of the Croisette, he encountered Pietro Nenni, who had become a journalist on the staff of *Avanti!* These two men, who had already clashed so often, eyed each other.

"Your friends are going to have to understand me," Mussolini said. "I am as ready for war as for peace."

"You've lost the opportunity of choosing," Nenni replied.

"In that case it's war."[1]

Mussolini turned away in anger; it had always been intolerable to him that anyone should stand up to him. Besides, he was constantly galled by his experiences ever since his arrival in France. At the border he had changed the ten thousand *lire* that his brother, Arnaldo, had lent him, and he had received only fifty-two hundred francs.

"This is an insult, a slap in the face," he said, deeply wounded in his vanity, for his was a parochial nationalism very like that of the lower middle class that followed Fascism in such great number. Later, at the Carlton, when he was told that Briand would grant him an interview, he was ashamed of the state of his shoes and he had to run from one shop to another, finally buying a pair of white spats that would hide the breaks in the uppers. Thereafter he adopted the habit of wearing spats, even with clothes to which they were least appropriate.

During this time he became acquainted with a rich Italian landowner who became his devotee and drove him everywhere in an Hispano-Suiza. Mussolini let himself be persuaded to go to the Casino, where he gambled and lost: always superstitious, he swore, and damned luck's desertion of him. One morning, in an Italian barber shop, he was compelled to listen to the anti-Fascist com-

[1] Nenni, *Six ans de guerre civile en Italie.*

ments of the barber who was shaving him and who, not recognizing him, was amazed that no one in Italy had settled the score with "that traitor, Mussolini."

One is entitled to wonder what had drawn Il Duce to Cannes. Had he gone in order to report the conference for *il Popolo*? If so, why had he taken along his secretary, Arturo Fasciolo? Why had he left Italy at the height of the political battle? Perhaps he had it in mind to establish contacts with foreign groups: reporting and interviewing were excellent excuses for meetings.

This hypothesis seems to derive some confirmation from the fact that in March, 1922, Mussolini went to Berlin. He stayed at the Hotel Hessler. Once again Fasciolo was with him. In the beginning he hardly left the hotel; *Die rote Fahne* (*The Red Flag*), the Communist newspaper, had appealed for a demonstration against him. Mussolini gave interviews to journalists in his room, where they could see the glass of milk—Il Duce was already complaining of stomach troubles—side by side with the customary revolver. Then Mussolini had a long conference with the Foreign Minister, Walther Rathenau. Dazzling receptions in his honor were given by the Italian Embassy. This was considerable deference to an ordinary deputy, even if he was the leader of a party. It seemed much more like an official visit by a future Prime Minister.

Obviously Mussolini was seriously preparing himself to assume that position. On January 25, in Milan, he published the first issue of a theoretical journal, *Gerarchia* (*Hierarchy*), which was to serve as the display case for Fascist thinking. This marked his first efforts at making Fascism part of a general historical trend. Thus, he remarked: "It is possible that in the nineteenth century capitalism needed democracy; today it can get along without it. . . . The process of the re-establishment of the right is already visible. . . . This century demonstrates that it will be the antithesis of the previous century" (*Gerarchia*, January 25, 1922).

In the second issue of the magazine he summarized this view in one sentence: "If the nineteenth century was the century of revolutions, the twentieth is the century of restorations" (February 25, 1922). Fascism, a "new hierarchy," represented in Mussolini's thinking the restoration that had been made necessary by the bankruptcy of liberalism.

Bonomi's government was in fact tottering. The Banca di Sconto had been dragged into the bankruptcies of Ansaldo and Ilva; the depositors stormed its counters in order to liquidate their accounts, and the bank had to close, causing the ruin of many small savers. These became so many new enemies of parliamentarianism and of the government that, in spite of the pressures exerted in financial circles, refused to save the bank: they were fresh recruits to Fascism. They did not know that the failure had been brought on—in part—by a number of the men who had financed Fascism and sought thus to force the state to reimburse the money that they had invested in Mussolini's movement. It was to be to the interest of these financiers in every way to bring Il Duce to power, and naturally they were opposed to Bonomi's government. One such was the all-powerful Banca Commerciale Italiana, which was very close to the royal court and which had very profitably bought up the large investments of the Banca di Sconto in Italian heavy industry.

Thus, while Mussolini was in Cannes, events, men, and the dominant groups in the Italian economy were working for him. On February 2 Bonomi resigned: only Don Sturzo's Popular Party still supported him. Political quarters turned at once to the old magician, Giolitti.

These constant re-appearances of the great pre-war statesman were in themselves sufficient evidence of the temporizing of the Italian ruling class and its inability to resolve the crisis. Giolitti agreed to serve, but Sturzo interposed his veto: Giolitti was the man who had required the registration of securities, boggled at conversations with the Vatican, and, in addition, compromised himself with Fascism.

Blocked as he was by Sturzo, was Giolitti the only man who could have saved Italy from Fascism in February, 1922? This thesis has been advanced, thus making Sturzo and his followers responsible for the downfall of Italian democracy. In fact, the whole of Giolitti's previous record demonstrates that he wanted to collaborate with Fascism which, he wrote, "can contribute to the re-activation of constitutional forces."

At the very most Giolitti's return to power would have meant different externals. Meanwhile, no successor having been found, the King called on Bonomi to present himself again before the Chamber. But in Rome and Florence the Fascists reacted; there were demonstrations and cries of "Down with Parliament." Young Fascists in Bologna gathered outside the headquarters of the Army Corps to cry: "Hurrah for military dictatorship!" In *il Popolo* of February 12 Mussolini wrote: "Today, in the light of recent political and parliamentary events, the possibility of a military dictatorship ought to be seriously considered. . . . It is possible that tomorrow the cry of the Fascist demonstrators in Bologna may be the overwhelming and irresistible chorus of the entire nation."

On that February 12, 1922, the nation was looking toward

Rome. The walls of the nave and the chancel of the Basilica of St. Peter's were decked with long hangings of red damask striped with gold, and a hundred thousand persons were waiting for the arrival of the *Sedia gestatoria*, for on this Sunday morning the new pope, Pius XI, was to be crowned. Benedict XV had died on January 22 and on February 6 Monsignor Ratti, archbishop of Milan, had been elected. Mussolini had hailed the new pope with joy: had he not blessed the Fascist banners in the Duomo three months before? He was known as a fervent patriot, and he was suspected of being a political pope determined to settle relations between the Vatican and Italy. Everyone knew what, when he was archbishop, he was supposed to have told the writer, Luca Valti, in confidence: "Mussolini is making great progress and he is going to invade everything with the strength of a natural force. Mussolini is a remarkable man . . . he has the zeal of the novice that pushes a man forward. . . . The future belongs to him. . . ."[2]

For the first time since 1870, a pope stood in the Loggia of St. Peter's and blessed a throng assembled in the splendid setting of Bernini's colonnade. All round the square Italian soldiers presented arms.

Mussolini was to play on the predilections of His Holiness to the limit. He had already suggested that the Chamber pay solemn homage to the late pope, the same Benedict XV whom in 1915 he had accused of every cowardice. Times had indeed changed.

In every direction, with a political instinct that he has often been accused of lacking, Mussolini laid his plans for action, and the speech of February 17 was an indication of his confidence. When he took the floor that day, Bonomi's government was already doomed, and so it was no longer Bonomi but his successor who was Mussolini's target. He was contemptuous and arrogant, but he was listened to attentively by the constitutionalists whom he was castigating.

"Form a government or don't form a government," he said; "create it from the left or don't create it from the left. Let one point, however, be made clear, in order to avoid a perilous plunge into the unknown: it is impossible to go against Fascism, it is impossible to crush Fascism."

On this same February 17 Bonomi was overthrown by two hundred ninety-five votes to one hundred seven; the crisis was apparent; but Mussolini's veto of any anti-Fascist Cabinet, this challenge that no "constitutionalist" politician dared to accept, showed that the crisis was also the first symptom of the final agony of a system.

[2] *L'Illustration*, January 9, 1937.

Fascism in the State

On the surface, however, the crisis was quickly resolved. The same names appeared again: Giolitti, Orlando, De Nicola; but Sturzo stood by his veto. Finally Luigi Facta was agreed on, as the least of the evils. A disciple of Giolitti, like him a Piedmontese, this smiling, honest little round-faced man was a sixty-one-year-old deputy whom it has pleased his contemporaries to ridicule. To Sforza, "it is possible that he was not an agent of Fascism: he was worse—he was a nullity." To Barrère, "in politics he is what is called in the theater a super." Today, in the light of the most recent studies, it is open to question whether Facta was not the resigned scapegoat of the Italian ruling class and whether the accusations should not be diverted from him to that class as a whole and its foremost representative, Giolitti, as the lieutenant of whom, after all, Facta was introduced. Besides, it was more than a man, it was a whole policy that was doomed to defeat. On March 3, before Facta had obtained a vote of confidence, there were new disorders in Fiume: Francesco Giunta, a Fascist deputy, assisted by the city's carabinieri and Fascists, took the government's offices by storm. Once again the annexation of the free city to Italy was proclaimed. Facta's government agreed that the city should be entrusted to the Italian military command: Giolitti's accomplishment was undone by his lieutenant!

Then there began for Fascism what Mussolini called *la fiumana* (the flood). Enrollments—more or less voluntary, it must be admitted—piled up. On January 25 a National Confederation of Corporations was formed in Bologna as a trade-union arm of the PNF. By June, 1922, it had four hundred fifty-eight thousand members; by the end of July, almost seven hundred thousand. These corporations embraced above all the peasants, the white-collar workers, and also the growing ranks of the unemployed. They were all given training and shipped by truck from one province to another; the unemployed were put to work as strike-breakers wherever the peasant leagues were still holding out. Everywhere there were parades of squadre preceded by their gagliardetti and bands that played the rousing, strident Fascist marches. The men wore helmets and black shirts with grey-green trousers, boots, or leggings; each carried a heavy cane. Behind them marched the women's Fasci: cloche hats, short bobbed hair, open-necked black blouses, grey skirts, black stockings. And in the middle there were the peasants, the workers of the Fascist unions in their Sunday suits and their wide-brimmed hats; they took the oath of allegiance to their leaders as they raised their banners. Occasionally, as in Cremona, Mussolini was in attendance, his face stern above his wing collar and white shirt, his feet in spats, a white pocket handkerchief standing out against his dark suit. He would watch the parade as a *Balilla* stood near. On March 26, twenty thousand Fascists paraded in Milan; on May 1, "that Socialist clownishness," as Mussolini called it, a general strike was called, but the Fascists gathered in Bologna and Rovigo. Clashes and deaths were many. In Ferrara on May 12 Balbo's Fascists assembled sixty-five thousand persons, took over the city, and proclaimed a general strike in order to win a monopoly of employment in public works (two and a half million *lire*) for the Fascist unions. On May 19 there was a similar rally in Rovigo. Balbo could soon write: "We are the masters of the situation. Not only have we shattered the resistance of our opponents; the public agencies are under our control. The prefect has to do our bidding, which I impose on him in the name of the Fascists."

The last of these mobilizations—which were so many rehearsals for a general action—was the occupation of Bologna. Cesare Mori, the prefect, who had shown his opposition to the arrival of the unemployed Fascists, was besieged. On June 1 the military authorities took command of the situation, and the commanding general at once entered into negotiations with Italo Balbo. The next day Mussolini telegraphed: "My dear friends, your splendid activity must be interrupted for a time, which will be quite short. . . ."

The government, once again, had just capitulated: Mori, the prefect, was transferred to Bari. Obviously Mussolini could only increase his demands. "There is no doubt," he wrote, "that Fascism and the state are destined to become identical in a relatively short time. In what way? Perhaps in a legal fashion?"

These question marks epitomize his shrewdness. With one hand he waved the squadre into action, with the other he reined them back; he asked them to halt their activities, but *after* the government had yielded. And the government's weakness was at the same time the military strength of the squadre and the political strength of Mussolini, who was winning on both the chessboards on which he had decided to play simultaneously: that of insurrection and that of parliamentary bargaining.

The activities of the squadre increased in the beginning of July, 1922. In Cremona, on July 3, Farinacci and two men slipped into the town hall, took over the official seals, and then demanded that Farinacci be appointed mayor. Facta declared the municipal government of Cremona dissolved. But the city's Fascists multiplied their acts of violence; they ravaged the residences of Guido Miglioli, the Popular Party deputy, and Giuseppe Garibotti, his Socialist colleague. The news reached Montecitorio on July 15. The deputies protested; Facta's government was in danger, accused of being "an accomplice or a eunuch." Cautiously, Mussolini wrote to

Fascism in the State

Farinacci two days later: "It would be better to make a show of discipline again and not to force situations in a way that will back us into a dead-end street."[3]

The fall of Facta's government, if it came about, would have a clearly anti-Fascist significance. A serious turn was the attitude taken by *il Corriere della Sera*, which called the atmosphere of Montecitorio polluted just when, for the first time in many months, the deputies resolved to take a firmer stand. Attacked in the person of their colleague, Miglioli, the Popular Party deputies were determined to provoke the crisis. Facta, on the other hand, was still calmly repeating: "Everything is quiet; I have full confidence."

In a resolution of July 18, which the Socialists also endorsed, the Popular Party condemned Facta. But the surprise was provided by Mussolini. He announced that his group would vote for the resolution against Facta—a rather ingenuous attempt to disguise the anti-Fascist tenor of the crisis; but on July 19, when he rose to speak in Montecitorio—for the last time before he seized power—he cynically showed his hand. His confident rhetoric deserves attention, for Mussolini knew the strength of his support and his accomplices: "I warn you frankly that no government whose program includes machine guns against Fascism can keep its feet in Italy."

As in February, Mussolini went on to make this interdict plainly clear. By July, Fascism, which had fed on the weakness of the constituted authorities in the spring of 1922, was an organization with seven hundred thousand members that had been able, in its seizures of cities, to assess the conniving good will of the majority of the officials.

"If, by some chance," Mussolini continued in Montecitorio, "the current crisis should end in the formation of a government of violent reaction against Fascism, . . . we will counter that reaction with insurrection." The word had been spoken; immediately Mussolini sought to soften it. "I should prefer that Fascism attain to participation in the life of the state by legal means, but I must also take into account the other possibility." Dropping his tone, he proceeded: "Let every man among you reflect on these declarations that I have offered for your scrutiny and your consciences. I have finished."

As he resumed his seat, there were as many protests as cheers; but that same evening, by two hundred eighty-eight votes to one hundred three, Facta was overthrown. What would, what could happen next?

During the voting it had been observed that a Popular Party

[3] Roberto Farinacci, *Squadrismo*.

deputy, Don Francesco Boncompagni Ludovisi, who had good connections in the Vatican, had broken away from his party to support Facta. This immediately gave rise to a rumor that the Vatican was opposed to the party's position. One thing certain was that Mussolini had established relations with the papacy. Cardinal Pietro Gasparri, the Papal Secretary of State, had had a secret meeting with Il Duce (as he had reported to François Charles-Roux)[4] in the residence of a senator, Count Carlo Santucci, at Ara Coeli; the Senator was also one of the directors of the Banco di Roma. In these conversations Mussolini had pledged himself to recognize the Pope's temporal sovereignty in Rome.

"But you cannot prevail on the Chamber to vote for that," the cardinal protested.

"Very well; there will be a new Chamber," Mussolini said. When the cardinal raised another objection, Mussolini retorted: "Then the election law will be changed."

As a result Cardinal Gasparri concluded that, "if this man did come into power, one could do business with him."

In these circumstances, the crisis that had taken an anti-Fascist direction was difficult of resolution. It was as if, having had the temerity to face the facts honestly—to overthrow Facta—the politicians had been frightened by their own audacity and by its implications. Every opposition, every personal antipathy, every sectarianism broke to the surface again. Orlando was sounded out, but he refused to serve. Mussolini was called to the Quirinal for consultations. He arrived for the meeting in a rented car, with Aldo Finzi, later a Cabinet member, and Bottai. The carabinieri saluted as he arrived. Relaxed and smiling, wearing a straw hat and carrying a cane, Mussolini felt that power was within arm's reach. He said afterward that he had suggested a new Giolitti cabinet. Always Giolitti! The old man of Piedmont was in Aix-les-Bains, but he sent a letter advising against any anti-Fascist government: "What benefit for the country can come out of a union among Sturzo, Treves, and Turati?"

L'Ordine nuovo, the Communist paper, was scathing on July 27: "The sleazy tyrant . . . that will have one face and three names . . . Turati, Don Sturzo, Mussolini."

During this interval a new Fascist offensive had been unleashed at Magenta and at Ravenna, where the cooperatives' headquarters, Palazzo Byron, was burned. Balbo prevailed on the prefecture of police to lend him twenty trucks. Loaded with squadristi, they left Ravenna at eleven o'clock on the night of July 29, a "column of

[4] François Charles-Roux, *Huit' ans au Vatican.*

fire" that in one night, "one terrible night," as Balbo called it, ravaged the whole province.

In Rome, one potential Premier after another was approached, but in vain. Again there was talk of Orlando, then of Bonomi. On July 29 the Social-Democratic leader, Turati, agreed to confer with the King and to support a Bonomi Cabinet. Mussolini was ironic: "Since they cannot build barricades, they go to the Quirinal. . . ."

Suddenly it was learned that the "Alliance of Labor," which had been formed on February 20 by the major trade unions, had scheduled a general strike to begin at midnight of July 31. At the same time the King was informed by three prefects that the Fascists were preparing a *coup d'état*. Fast action was essential.

Arriving at home on July 30 after a walk through Tivoli, Facta found a message from General Arturo Cittadini, the King's aide-de-camp, requesting him to go to the palace. The next day Facta formed his second Cabinet. With its second personification in the lackluster person of this Piedmont deputy, the existing system merely confirmed its impotence. In the heat of the late Roman evening, when the news of Facta's return was being received with anger, indifference, or disgust, when the workers' quarters were completing their preparations for the general strike, Mussolini left the Hotel Savoia and took a taxi out to the Castelli Romani for the cooler air of the Alban Hills, where he was engaged in an affair with a rich Roman woman. Was he so unaware or so unconcerned on the eve of the strike? It would seem rather that he was confident that, with a second Facta government, he could let things take their own leisurely course while he relaxed in the delights of Frascati.

"Workers, arise! Defend what is most sacred to every civilized man: freedom!"

This was the concluding paragraph of the strike call, a strike "within and for the rule of law [*sciopero legalitario*]," as Turati called it. But things went wrong from the start. The strike order was supposed to have been a secret, but *il Lavoro* in Genoa printed it on the morning of July 31. The Fascists had twenty-four hours in which to mobilize their troops. On August 1 the PNF issued a manifesto to the nation:

> Fascists, Italians! The anti-national parties . . . have hurled the gauntlet at Fascism and the nation. . . . The Italian Fascists have mobilized from the Alps to Sicily. . . . We give the state forty-eight hours to offer proof of its authority. . . . Once this deadline has passed, Fascism . . . will replace the state, which will once more have demonstrated its impotence. . . .

The instructions given to the Fasci were precise: (1) mobilization of all forces; (2) occupation of provincial capitals; and (3) Fascist replacement of all prefects. . . .

Thus the launching of the strike contributed to the identification of the state with Fascism. In addition, it was a confrontation between a Fascism in full strength and masses that had been weakened and harshly tried for two years, demoralized by unemployment (FIAT, for instance, was working only thirty-two hours a week), and bewildered by this unexpected movement that seemed to have been developed as a support for Turati's parliamentary dickerings.

An enterprise so badly begun could only fail. Everywhere the Fascists took the initiative in the battle, and they pursued it even after the Alliance of Labor had called for the resumption of work on August 2. The military authorities cooperated with the squadre, and a front came into being from Ancona to Genoa. In Parma, however, the Fascists ran into the resistance of the People's Arditi under Guido Picelli, who was later to be killed in Madrid. Balbo concentrated twenty thousand Black Shirts round the city; the fighting lasted for five days, and the whole population took part in the defense. The orders were simple: "Resist or die where you stand." Balbo telephoned to Mussolini, who advised him to give up the battle: the Fascists' losses were heavy—thirty-nine killed and one hundred fifty wounded. The squadre suffered similar setbacks in Forlì and Bari, but these anti-Fascist victories came too late; and in addition the military authorities were instructed to maintain order.

The most typical events occurred in Milan. On August 1 the strike was completely effective. Armed Fascists, led by Cesare Forni, went out on patrol, stopped cars, requisitioned them, occupied strategic points, and soon had the street-cars running again—at high speed and in the utmost confusion—and filled with Black Shirts singing *Giovinezza*. On August 3 the squadristi massed in Piazza della Scala outside Palazzo Marino, the premises of Socialist Mayor Filippo Filipetti's municipal offices. Mounted Royal Guards were in plentiful attendance, but they waited for orders. A shout went up: "Italy to whom?" "*A noi!*" And again: "Hang whom?"—"Hang Filipetti!"

A truck was driven full tilt into the closed gates of the building; they fell, and soon the banners of the Fascio and the national flag were raised to the trumpet call of *Attention*. Suddenly a car appeared in the crowd, and a name ran from lip to lip: d'Annunzio!

A vast ovation hailed the poet's appearance on the balcony: "Citizens of Milan—men of Milan, as indeed a captain of the days of the sword would say—this is the first time that I have spoken from a balcony since the glorious days of Ronchi. . . ."

Indeed, since "Bloody Christmas" d'Annunzio had manifested nothing but contempt for Fascism, which, from his seclusion in Cargnacco, he harshly defined as an "agrarian slave system," and he answered every visitor who hinted at a Fascist *coup d'état* or a Giolitti Cabinet: "Rome, noble Rome, will you give yourself to a butcher?" Yet there he was, on the balcony of Palazzo Marino, looking down on the throng of Black Shirts. Was it by pure chance? There was a story that he had happened to be in Milan on August 1 to confer with his publisher and that Cesare Rossi of the Fascio had thought it worth-while to ask him to speak. That may be. But it was certain that d'Ann nzio had never relinquished the idea of personal action; a few weeks earlier he had in fact advanced from plans to practicalities.

At the end of July one of his emissaries had established relations with . . . Nitti, Nitti-*Cagoia*! The theme was that of "rallying the living forces," and on August 1 Nitti wrote to the poet:

> Dear and glorious friend,
> We have long been antagonists. . . . You believe, as I believe, in the salvation and greatness of Italy. . . . You can influence the young by inflaming them and bringing them back to the right road. . . . One is never so strong as when one speaks as you can speak to men drunk on prejudices and blinded by violence. . . .

Thus strange combinations were forged in that troubled Italy where the squadre were the law. Mussolini was also involved in this one: Nitti had insisted that Il Duce be kept informed. A conference was to be held in Tuscany on August 15. Nitti's car would be driven by a Fascist armed with a safe-conduct issued by Mussolini.

In the light of these facts it is understandable that d'Annunzio would have agreed to speak in Milan. But he pleaded his own case, careful never once to mention the word *Fascism*.

"Italy," he proclaimed from the balcony of the building that the Black Shirts had seized, "will be saved by me, because I am the center of convergence for all those forces, at the moment separated and disbanded, that work with death and misery. . . ."

By thus assuming a position above all factions, d'Annunzio hoped to be the "peace-maker," but, while he was addressing the crowd and giving his mere presence—whatever he might say or omit to say—a Fascist meaning, the squadre were besieging *Avanti!* in via Settala, which had been rebuilt through a fund drive that had raised four million *lire*.

The staff had dug a trench in the courtyard and strung electrified barbed wire. Nenni, who had been editor-in-chief since April, was waiting for the Black Shirts to attack. The premises had been searched by the police, who had confiscated what few weapons they could find there. Soon the captain of the Royal Guard went to Nenni.

"It is not possible for me to guarantee the newspaper's defense," the captain said.

"I never thought you would," Nenni retorted.

"I am under orders not to fire."

"I don't doubt it."

"I advise you," the captain concluded, "to place yourselves under the protection of the police."

The captain withdrew his men and the Fascists cheered. They then got down to business and the building was quickly captured and burned.

Similar scenes were reproduced all through Italy. Filling column after column with place names, il Popolo detailed the exploits of the squadre. On August 4 it published a triumphant communiqué: ". . . The Fascist counter-attack has been lightning-like and inexorable. Labor exchanges, Socialist clubs, Socialist town halls have been occupied by the Fascist squadre, and retaliatory action has also made it necessary to destroy some headquarters of labor organizations. . . ."

During these activities Mussolini had remained in Rome, detained by romantic commitments and also, perhaps, by caution. On August 6, after the battle, he wrote: "The retaliatory actions that you have taken have my unqualified approval . . . if I had been in Milan, I would have helped to prepare reprisals on an even greater scale. . . ."

Intoxicated by their victories, his lieutenants in Milan increased the number of their projects. Aldo Finzi, Mussolini's confidential assistant, told Luigi Albertini in the beginning of August that a coup d'état was imminent. The Chamber would be dissolved by force and a Directory would be installed under d'Annunzio, Mussolini, Nitti, and two major industrialists, Giovanni Agnelli (FIAT) and Alberto Pirelli (rubber). D'Annunzio denied this on August 9. "Every word should be weighed," he wrote, "every act meditated."

There were rumors of contacts between Fascists and the highest military officers, including, of course, the Duke of Aosta. Italy was embarked on a period of intrigues and conspiracies that were evolved in the twilight zone of the half-secret, for almost everything was already smashed or conquered, corrupted or dissolved, favorable or apathetic.

Formally, however, though drained of its powers by Fascism, the government remained in office, under siege on all sides, often yielding, ready for any compromise, but still continuing to function: on August 9 the man who always "had confidence," Facta, received two hundred forty-seven votes to one hundred twenty-one. Under the Constitution, Mussolini was merely the parliamentary leader of a group of thirty-five deputies that formed part of the opposition. True, it was an opposition that had long ago crossed its Rubicon; on August 9 the Fascist deputies, Giunta and Arpinati, arrived armed at Montecitorio and on the same day their colleague, Lupi, declared that "the state will swallow Fascism or Fascism will swallow the state."

And indeed, in this month of August, the question was already in the past, for, from the police sergeant to the captain of the Royal Guard, from the prefect to Vincenzo Riccio, the Minister of Public Works—of whom Mussolini was to say that he had been invaluable during the crisis of the summer and autumn of 1922—Fascism was already present in every component of the machinery of the state from the expendable to the most important.

From now on the only question was *how* Fascism would go about becoming the state. On August 13 Mussolini went to Milan and presided at a meeting of the National Council of the PNF. Faithful to his old tactics, he moved a pawn on each of his two chessboards: the parliamentary and the insurrectional. The party council demanded the dissolution of the Chamber and new elections, but *at the same time* it analyzed the military position of Fascism and established a supreme command of three men whose purpose was the execution of all necessary military moves. This was the first milestone of the March on Rome.

But Mussolini had the wariness of a cat; before he moved, he concentrated on the elimination of obstacles. On August 14 he learned that d'Annunzio, who clung tenaciously to his rôle of peacemaker and rival, had been seriously injured in a fall from his balcony in Cargnacco. The fall was said to have resulted from a private quarrel with Loisa Baccara. In any event, for a few weeks Mussolini would be rid of the poet. The plan for a three-sided meeting with him and Nitti in Tuscany was dropped.

There was still Don Sturzo. The thin, smiling priest, in spite of pressures from the Vatican, stood firmly on his anti-Fascist position. On August 19, in *il Popolo*, Mussolini openly stated the conditions of his blackmail: "Is not Don Sturzo the anti-pope, the instrument of Satan? It is clear now that a thousand tempests will sweep over the horizon of the church if the Popular Party persists in its entanglement in a materialist, tyrannical, and anti-Christian policy. . . ."

At the crucial moment the Vatican would not forget these threats. In other directions Mussolini extended himself in favors: he joined the Freemasons, which granted him a credit of several million *lire*; he called on the CGL to divorce itself from the "PUS" if it "wanted to save itself from total ruin" (P.d.I., August 2, 1922); he was especially cordial to the monarchy, and that was a major question.

In fact, the army officers were still loyal to the King and in their view Fascism could not and should not go against the crown. They supported Fascism as a nationalist and anti-Socialist movement, but, if the necessity arose, they were capable of defending the monarchy against it. Mussolini was not a man to run this risk. On August 22 *il Popolo* printed a paragraph that marked the end of a "Fascism of republican tendency." Its key sentence said: "The crown is not at issue, provided that the crown does not of itself choose to put itself at issue."

It was now the end of August. On August 28 the government ordered the dissolution of the municipal administration of Milan. *Il Popolo* headlined: STATE RATIFIES FASCIST MEASURE OF AUGUST 3 OVERTHROWING FILIPETTI'S RULE. It seemed that it would not be long before, in a paraphrase of *il Popolo*, "the state would ratify the Fascist measure overthrowing the state."

But Deputy Luigi Facta and his wife left Rome for a vacation at Pinerolo, in Piedmont, and there was gossip that Signora Facta, "Madamina di Pinerolo," would like to outdo Signora Giolitti.[5]

---

[5] Sforza, *L'Italia dal 1914 al 1944.* . . .

6

The March on Rome

(September, 1922 — October 30, 1922)

"The liberal state is nothing but a mask behind which there is no face. It is a scaffolding behind which there is no structure."
—MUSSOLINI (October 4, 1922)

September 4, 1922. The town of Civitavecchia was occupied by the squadristi. The Socialist city government was forced to resign. The Fascists took over the city, taking it outside the national government's control as well. It commanded one of the three access roads to Rome.

September 12. Back from his Piedmont vacation, Facta presided at a Cabinet meeting. Senator Carlo Taddei, Minister of the Interior, suggested the recall of one class of conscripts in order to strengthen the army. The Cabinet was against it.

September 14. Antonino Anile, Minister of Public Education and a member of the Popular Party, was attending a dinner in Ancona. Suddenly it was invaded by squadristi, who manhandled the minister. He was forced to leave without having been able to deliver his speech. Ancona was taken out of government control. It was an important military base and a stronghold of anarchism. The town of Terni, which commanded the Rome-Ancona railway, fell under Fascist rule.

September 19. Senators belonging to the Popular Party made public a letter to the party secretariat condemning "certain alliances that contravene the most sacred principles." What was meant was Sturzo's anti-Fascist policy.

September 20. Mussolini was in Udine. Since the beginning of the month there had not been a day without good news for him. This evening he was speaking to the Fascists of Friuli. He felt himself on the tide of power and in the voice of this man of thirty-nine there was confidence—a studied confidence, granted, but it had its basis in the progress of events. There were songs and cheers. He interrupted: "You do not expect me to make a speech that is not completely Fascist—that is, strong-boned, sharp, open, hard."

Then he reiterated his deferences to the monarchy, which, since he was about to act, he must dramatically enlist on his side: "I believe that the system can be radically revised without infringing on monarchical institutions. . . ." Interrupted by cheers, he raised his voice: "I believe that the monarchy has no reason to oppose the Fascist revolution. . . . If it did so, it would become our target."

He oscillated between open threats and kind words for everything and everyone: the nationalists, who had set up "Blue-Shirt Squadre"; the industrialists, who wanted to throw off state controls. "We wish to strip the state of all its economic functions," Mussolini said. "There must be an end of the state as railway worker, the state as letter carrier, the state as insurer. . . . We will not permit strikes in the public services on any ground."

This speech was indeed the preface to action, when the masks were dropped. After a pause Mussolini concluded in his hoarse voice: "Our program is simple: we want to govern Italy."

The audience broke loose: *"Viva Mussolini! Evviva il Duce!"*

That same evening was cool in Rome. A few men arrived at the offices of the Federation of Cooperatives in via Monte d'Oro. One of them was Michele Bianchi: the March on Rome was about to begin. The participants had reached agreement on the purposes of the enterprise: to give Italy a government that would eliminate the parliamentary system but would not affect the monarchy, and, above all, to win the neutrality of the army.

Events were moving more quickly and details on the projected march were leaking fast. Aboard a crowded train in September, the Belgian ambassador, who had a compartment to himself, offered a seat to a prominent Italian industrialist, Baron Blanc. The baron confided to him that a *coup d'état* was being prepared and that in a few weeks the Black Shirts "would be mobilized, equipped with rifles and machine guns," and assembled in a congress in Naples, whence they would march on Rome.[1]

While confidences of this nature were being offered on trains, Facta was celebrating his thirty-year parliamentary career in Pinerolo. In the riding ring at the Military School he presided over

[1] Baron Beyens, *Quatre ans à Rome* (Paris: Plon), p. 139.

The March on Rome

a magnificent banquet for thirty-two hundred guests, who included seventy-one senators and one hundred seventeen deputies. His white moustaches meticulously waxed, Facta, as usual, was smiling. Giulio Alessio, the Minister of Justice and a determined anti-Fascist, made a speech in which he called for resistance; it was useless. "I have confidence," Facta repeated. "What could Mussolini want? He has never been even a Secretary of State!"

In Cremona, meanwhile, in the Po Valley, where Fascist brutalities were continuing, Mussolini reviewed a parade of thirty thousand Black Shirts. Everything here was in sharp contrast to the feast of Pinerolo, and it is understandable that, caught up in the intoxication of the songs, the uniforms, the rhetoric, and this huge spectacle, some of the young should have overlooked the basic reality of Fascism and preferred to see in it only the appearance of a new Italy. It is understandable that, rather than the aged countenance of the *onorevole* Facta, they should have preferred the profile of a new leader even if, as Sforza was to say bitterly, he was "only a Facta with the manners of a savage."

The town of Cremona was ablaze with flags, from the streetcars to the cafés with black-shirted waiters. This was one of the first cities in Italy to be subjected to Fascist rule. Mussolini reviewed a parade and then addressed the crowd in Piazza del Comune, in a medieval setting dominated by the high Gothic tower of the Torrazzo: "*Principi, Triari, Avanguardisti, Balilla*, Fascist women, working masses of Cremona and the Province! The march on which you have embarked cannot stop until it has reached the supreme goal: Rome!"

Thus his demands became clearer with every speech, as if Mussolini were testing the government's power of resistance. Symbolically he embraced his "old and loyal friend, Farinacci," before his audiences. For Mussolini the time for divergences was over.

September 24. Salandra, the leader of the liberal group, which included Alfano Benni, a deputy and president of Confindustria, proclaimed his regret that his age (sixty-nine) made it impossible for him to put on the Black Shirt. In any event, he concluded, "I regard myself as an honorary Fascist."

September 28. In Merano the handsome Duke of Aosta reviewed the Fascist squadristi parading behind their banners. *Giovinezza* was played by the regimental band of the 231st Infantry.

October 3. The Italian news agency distributed the first detailed news that a "March on Rome" was in preparation.

October 4. In the Italian Socialist Party's congress in Rome the

Maximalists decided to expel the social democrats, who founded the Unitarian Socialist Party.

In the evening of October 4 Mussolini went to the quarters of the Fascio Antonio Sciesa in via Senato in Milan. There he paid tribute to Fascists who had fallen in the assaults on "the criminal dens of the cowardly Communists." But something else was looked for. In fact, matters had begun to come to a head since the beginning of the month. The squadre were concentrated in the Trentino under the leadership of Giunta, Farinacci, Alberto De Stefani, and Starace. Was this the start of decisive action? The Milanese Fascists knew too that the Fascist high command had drafted "a code of discipline for the Fascist Militia" on October 3. The regulations were signed by four men: Michele Bianchi, Cesare De Vecchi, Italo Balbo, and a general on active duty, Emilio de Bono.

What next? It was still on October 4, when Mussolini was speaking in Milan, that De Stefani appeared on the balcony of a building in via Belanzani in Trento, which the Fascists had just taken over. He was cheered when he came out, he was cheered even more when he announced: "This is the first step of the March on Rome."

And in Milan Mussolini seemed at first to be echoing him: "A clash seems inevitable. . . . The liberal state is nothing but a mask . . . it is a scaffolding behind which there is no structure." Was this then the attack? Abruptly, lowering his voice, he turned ironic: "If they have not all gone soft in Rome, they will have to convene the Chamber for early November, have an election law enacted, and set the elections for December. But, if the government chooses another road, then Fascism will attain its objectives by other means. . . ."

Thus, in the face of the mounting evidence that Fascism was organizing a March on Rome, in the face of the detailed reports competing for public attention, Mussolini shrewdly (though his shrewdness seems to have consisted above all in the blindness of the other players in the game—it is difficult to conceive of them as his opponents) continued to propose two courses, as if Facta or Giolitti could hesitate between them. By preserving the semblance of an alternative, Mussolini paralyzed what resistance might still survive in the state, at the same time setting his lures for Italy's political leaders, even as high as Facta.

For negotiations were multiplying during these early days of October. Every faction was hoping to enlist Mussolini in an important Cabinet post; some planned to accede to his demand for the dissolution of the Chamber, some to offer him one or even two Cabinet posts. Impelled by an ambition that he had long suppressed, old Facta played his card: relying on one minister, Vincenzo Riccio, he consulted first Michele Bianchi and then Grandi and opposed the anti-Fascist measures suggested by two other ministers, Alessio and Amendola. Giolitti, of course, was pursuing his own personal intrigues, making use of Alfredo Lusignoli, the prefect of Milan, as his intermediary. But Giolitti conducted himself with perfect good form, scorning to abandon the practice of Cavour and offering only two portfolios, whereas Mussolini—what had he to lose?—was demanding five. Salandra, who could be sure of the confidence of nationalist circles and the court, was also scheming. As for Nitti, he conferred in Calabria with Ambassador Baron Avezzana, Mussolini's emissary. An agreement was reached: Nitti would call for new elections and then he would form a new Cabinet that would include Mussolini. Whoever could do so would "capture" Fascism. It was believed that the King had reservations against a Mussolini Cabinet. Asking Marcello Soleri, the Minister of War, to join him in his car on October 7, Vittorio Emanuele said to him of the Fascists: "Bear in mind that I do not want those fellows in Rome, and take all possible steps to avert this danger."

It was essential, therefore, that Mussolini compromise with the various political groups. What was overlooked was the fact that Il Duce was also playing the card of insurrection at the same time. Moreover, the Fascist leader had decided to move quickly, for Luigi Facta had just cleverly gained the allegiance of Mussolini's eternal rival, d'Annunzio.

The poet had recovered from his fall, and he was visited by a steady stream of emissaries. It was said that, even when he was delirious, he had raved of the salvation of Italy, and Facta suggested that he go to Rome as a peacemaker to address a large rally of war veterans on November 4. The government precipitately proclaimed a national holiday for that date and announced a patriotic demonstration in Rome. The unacknowledged purpose was to exalt the monarchy and undermine Mussolini. Was he going to allow himself to be left behind? Still maneuvering, he signed an accord with the Seafarers' Federation of Captain Giulietti, d'Annunzio's friend, that was advantageous for the federation. But this was not enough: Facta had contributed large sums to the captain. D'Annunzio withdrew of his own accord when he began to feel that he was serving as a hostage for the return of Giolitti. "What dealings could I have with the man who fired the naval guns?" he wrote, recalling the bombardment of Fiume. But in the meantime (according to Tom Antongini), Mussolini's anxiety had led him to offer d'Annunzio—in vain—the command of the forces of insurrection.

For insurrection had been resolved on after October 16, and especially after Mussolini had learned of the government's plan to have d'Annunzio lead the November 4 celebration.

Mussolini, Balbo, De Vecchi, Attilio Teruzzi, Michele Bianchi, and Generals De Bono, Fara, and Ceccherini met secretly in via San Marco in Milan. Gustavo Fara and Sante Ceccherini, who were on active duty, were not party members. The meeting got off to a bad start. De Bono would have preferred to keep the two other generals out of the secret. The army should maintain neutrality. Mussolini interrupted curtly: "I think it is necessary, in a revolutionary operation, to have generals in uniform at the head of insurgent groups." In considerable detail he explained that the dickering with Giolitti had led to nothing and that the government would not yield. "So we must make the masses act in order to create an extra-parliamentary crisis and gain power for ourselves," he concluded. He added that Giolitti's return must be prevented at any price: "If he ordered d'Annunzio fired on, he could order the Fascists fired on."

When then would action begin? De Bono wanted to know. He needed time in order to "work over the army." For the army was indeed the great bogey of the plotters. In their inmost thoughts they were not too skeptical of the remark supposed to have been made by Badoglio: "Five minutes' shooting and the whole of Fascism will fall to pieces."

De Vecchi and Generals De Bono and Fara wanted forty days for preparation. Mussolini, Balbo, and Ferruccio Vecchi opposed this: it was essential to move quickly, to exploit the Fascist congress scheduled for October 24 in Naples in order to group the Fascists and attract attention. But on the appointed day the actual leadership of the party would be taken over by a secret quadrumvirate composed of De Bono, De Vecchi, Balbo, and Bianchi.

The conspirators talked until late in the night. In relative secrecy there was a subsequent meeting in the Hôtel du Parc in Bordighera: the participants were De Bono, the old general and ultra-typical Italian nobleman with his white moustaches and beard; De Vecchi, the Piedmont landowner, bald and heavy-set, his square face bisected by a black moustache; and Balbo, the slender young squadrista. Their purpose was to complete the plans for the March on Rome: Italy was divided into twelve zones, each of which would have an inspector (such men as Teruzzi, Bottai, etc.). As soon as the rising was announced, the Fascist forces would have to be mobilized everywhere and strategic points would have to be occupied, but actual conflict with the army would have to be avoided. The march was to begin from three points near Rome—Santa Marinella, Mentana, and Tivoli—and the command headquarters would be set up in Perugia, where a strategic reserve would have been established. The three men were assigning command appointments when they received an invitation to dinner with Queen Mother Margherita, who was living in Bordighera.

De Bono and De Vecchi accepted the invitation. The dinner conversation was purely social until the guests were leaving. "May all your plans be fulfilled," the queen mother whispered. "They have only one goal, the salvation and the glory of our nation."

It was in this strange climate that the theoretically insurrectionary "March on Rome" was prepared. While it was true Mussolini had managed to make the march appear to be an operation to be carried through to the finish, he had always conceived of it as one of the cards—an indispensable card—in the political game that he continued to play in order to gain power—complete power. For the bargaining, which had been briefly interrupted, was under way again. Giolitti had discreetly had soundings taken in the Popular Party, and there had been a meeting on October 4–5 between his agent, Camillo Corradini, and Don Sturzo.

"Is Giolitti still willing to form a ministry with the Fascists?" Don Sturzo asked drily.

"Yes."

"And without them too?"

"That does not seem possible," Corradini replied.

Sturzo had a final question: "And against the Fascists?"

"No, that is impossible."

"In that case," Don Sturzo concluded, "Giolitti will not form a Cabinet."

But, in the face of this anti-Fascist firmness on the part of Don Sturzo, Giolitti turned to Mussolini. Again there was a stream of emissaries covering the triangle of Rome, Milan, and Turin, where Giolitti had his headquarters. Later Michele Bianchi remarked ironically: "I kept my mind on the March on Rome that Il Duce was preparing and dragged things out."

As for Nitti, he lived up to his agreement with Mussolini. On October 19 he was the chairman of a dinner in Potenza, where he asserted that "the ideal element in Fascism, which has been the source of its growth, must be accepted," and he called for new elections. Obviously he did not know that Balbo had written in his diary: "The old pirate has nothing to hope for from Fascism but a firing squad."

October 19. A circular letter sent by Cardinal Gasparri to the bishops reminded them of the duty of the ecclesiastical authorities to preserve their neutrality in political conflicts. This was an indirect repudiation of Don Sturzo's stand.

On his way to the Naples congress, Mussolini broke his journey in Rome on October 23 for a meeting with Salandra. He and Giolitti were Mussolini's strongest opponents. The two old politicians represented the two faces of the Italian ruling class; hence Mussolini gave Salandra every possible assurance: he insisted that he wanted to stay out of the new government so that he could disband the squadre! Having thus drugged the liberal leader's suspicions, he boarded a train for Naples.

Special trains from every part of Italy had carried forty thousand Black Shirts to the October 24 assembly. That morning, in the presence of the prefect and Benedetto Croce, Mussolini delivered a threatening speech in Teatro San Carlo: "We Fascists do not intend to enter the government through the service door . . . the problem is one of relative strengths."

In the afternoon the Black Shirts staged a huge parade. Children were released from school to join the spectators. Dressed entirely in black except for a sash across his chest with the colors of Rome, Mussolini shouted to his troops arrayed in Piazza San Ferdinando: "I announce to you in all solemnity that the moment is at hand: either they give us the government or we go to Rome and take it."

Balbo, standing among the Emilian squadristi, began to bellow: "Rome! Rome!" Soon the whole square was bawling with him. When the tide began to ebb, Mussolini resumed: "Now it is a matter of days, perhaps only of hours. . . . We must seize the vile ruling class by the throat!"

That evening Premier Luigi Facta telegraphed to the King: "The Fascist meeting is proceeding quietly. . . . I think the planned March on Rome has now been abandoned."

At ten o'clock the same evening Mussolini and the quadrumvirate—Balbo, De Bono, De Vecchi, and Bianchi—conferred in the Hotel Vesuvio in Naples with Starace, Teruzzi, and Bastianini. Mobilization was scheduled for October 27 and the March on Rome for the following day. "The operation of October 28," Mussolini said, "should be undertaken in advance of the maneuver planned for November 4. We can wait no longer."

As he was returning to his hotel, Balbo was embarrassed by encountering General Federico Baistrocchi, who reassured him with an air of knowing all about the plans: "The army in the south is favorable."

That night Mussolini returned to Milan.

151   *The March on Rome*

De Vecchi, Grandi, and Costanzo Ciano, who had left Naples with Mussolini, went only to Rome. It was their task to spy out the target area. They instructed Salandra to convey the Fascist ultimatum to Facta and the King: "Resignation by the government or a March on Rome."

In the afternoon of October 26 the ministers gave Facta their resignations: the old man thought that this would assure him the mastery in the struggle. Under the constitution, he himself had not resigned, and yet he no longer had any ministers. Hence he could call on Mussolini. But Mussolini did not answer.

Facta thereupon asked the King, who was in San Rossore, near Pisa, to return to Rome. When he arrived by train at about eight o'clock in the evening of October 27, the King seemed firm. Facta had gone to the station to meet him, and the King bade him proclaim a state of siege. Facta said to Alessio, in Piedmont dialect: "I will not form a government under duress. I will throw up the whole thing. I'm going off to the country with my wife and son." And he went back to the Quirinal.

A few hours later the Black Shirts began to mobilize all over Italy. De Bono, Balbo, and De Vecchi had signed a note for the equivalent of more than one hundred thousand dollars to cover the costs. The Quadrumvirate's proclamation was posted everywhere:

> Fascists of all Italy! The hour of the decisive battle has struck. . . .
> The army of the Black Shirts reminds you once more of the
> mutilated victory. . . . The martial law of Fascism is now in ef-
> fect. . . . the army, the nation's reserve and safeguard, should not
> take part in the struggle. . . . Nor does Fascism wish to contend
> against the forces of public order. . . .

The new offices of *il Popolo* in via Lovanio in Milan were converted into a small fort, barricaded at every aperture by rolls of newsprint stacked one on another. Actually, enjoying excellent relations with the prefect, Lusignoli, Mussolini feared no serious attack, but he made a considerable show of emerging every now and then with a rifle in his hand. . . . In Rome, moreover, it was reported that General Diaz and Admiral Paolo Thaon di Revel, the two idols of the armed forces, would have portfolios in Mussolini's Cabinet.

At eleven o'clock on the night of October 27 the Ministry of War was informed that the March on Rome had begun. Some cities were occupied without much trouble. In Trieste, Padua, and Venice the military authorities openly collaborated with the Black Shirts. But other cities, including some of the most important, held back. In Florence, where one squadra was under the command of Curzio

Malaparte, the journalist and writer, the Fascists held all strategic points. Young men wearing pointed goatees like Balbo's, helmets painted red, death's heads sewn on their black shirts, and daggers thrust into broad leather belts marched singing through the rain.

For it was pouring: this was the central Italian October, whose skies in the grip of Mediterranean storms drenched the cypresses bent beneath the wind with a whole year's rain in a few hours. The squadre tried to keep their weapons dry as they moved through the downpour; the sodden gagliardetti clung limply to their poles. The Tuscan Fascists marched through Prato early in the morning of October 28 as twenty-five thousand workers were on their way to their jobs, as usual, for the two hundred textile mills in the area had reopened.

How many men did the Fascist army include at this time? According to the detailed studies of Rapaci, the exact figure was five thousand! Soon it would be twenty-five thousand, but they were poorly armed, soaked to the marrow, and, above all, halted without any effort on the part of the military authorities: four hundred carabinieri and two railway stoppages had sufficed, and the squadre that had been counting on reaching Rome by train quickly scattered in search of shelter from the rain.

Established in the Hotel Brufani in Perugia, the Quadrumvirs were uneasy: the military failure of the March on Rome was already obvious when, early on that morning of October 28, they received word that Facta's government—which had resigned the day before—had proclaimed a state of siege. It had made a strong appeal to the country: "In the face of attempts at insurrection, it is the duty of the caretaker government to maintain order by every means and at all costs."

In Rome, where he had twenty-five thousand well-armed soldiers, General Emanuele Pugliese ordered barbed-wire barricades set up on all the bridges and sandbags placed round all official buildings. Their rifles slung muzzles down beneath the protection of their short capes, soldiers stood guard at strategic points. But the Black Shirts and the nationalist Blue Shirts patrolled the streets at will.

At 9 A.M. Facta went to the royal palace to obtain the King's signature to the proclamation of the state of siege that the King himself had urged. Dramatically, Vittorio Emanuele III refused to sign. "I have been compelled to recognize," he said, "that the situation is quite different from what had been expected."

The King stood firm on his reversal despite a second visit from Facta. Undoubtedly he had given in to pressure from nationalist leaders—Armando Diaz, Luigi Federzoni, Admiral Paolo Thaon di

Revel, and General Arturo Cittadini. Undoubtedly too he had feared some action by the King's cousin, Duke of Aosta, who had gone to see the Quadrumvirs in Perugia, and probably the King had hoped that his unexpected decision would, as in 1915, enable him to appoint a Salandra government in which Mussolini and the Fascists would hold a few ministries.

At 11:30 A.M. the Stefani News Agency announced that the decree of the state of siege had been rescinded; three-quarters of an hour later, the news was given to the press. At 6 P.M. the King designated Salandra to form a Cabinet, apparently unable to comprehend that there was no longer anything for Mussolini to fear and that the time for talk was over.

In the evening, furthermore, Salandra received two detailed messages: one, from Confindustria, Confagricola, and the Banking Association, warned that the only possible solution to the crisis was a Mussolini government; the other, from Senators Luigi Albertini (of *il Corriere della Sera*) and Ettore Conti (a dominant figure in the electrical industry), took the same view. Salandra was also aware that, just before the March on Rome, Alfano Benni and Gino Olivetti, both deputies and members of Confindustria, had gone to Milan and played major parts in the political negotiations there; it was said that the Banking Association had advanced some seven hundred thousand dollars to finance the march. Salandra, however, hung on throughout the night. There were constant telephone calls between Rome and Milan. Salandra offered four portfolios; Mussolini replied curtly: "I do not accept," and broke the connection.

At 10 A.M. of October 29 Salandra went to the Quirinal and urged the King to call on Mussolini to form a government. *Il Popolo* headlined: FASCISM WANTS POWER AND WILL HAVE IT.

The army went to work to take over the squadre still immobilized in the Rome area. De Vecchi went to confer with the King and then telephoned to Mussolini, requesting him, in the name of the King, to come to Rome.

"It's a trick," Mussolini said. "I want it in writing." Now he could speak frankly. About two o'clock in the afternoon he received a telegram: "Very urgent. Absolute priority. To Deputy Mussolini, Milan. From Rome, Quirinal. His Majesty the King wishes to confer with you and desires you to come to Rome. Respectfully, General Cittadini."

At three o'clock on that Sunday afternoon Mussolini telephoned to the prefect, asking that a special train be made ready. The train, consisting of a locomotive and one car, was made up, but Mussolini changed his mind. He wanted a demonstration; he would leave later. He put out a special edition of *il Popolo d'Italia*, announcing that he would leave for Rome that evening by sleeper. He issued orders: "*Avanti!* is not to publish; otherwise tomorrow they'll trip me up with a general strike."

This was not an easy matter. A similar suggestion by the Communist Party brought the reply from the CGL—to one of whose leaders Mussolini had offered a Cabinet portfolio—that this was a political maneuver. The premises of *Avanti!*, however, were attacked. In Rome, pro-Nitti newspapers—*il Paese, l'Epoca*—were also ravaged. *Il Corriere della Sera* was unable to publish, the Turin Labor Exchange was burned, and so was the office of *l'Ordine nuovo.* There was fighting in the workers' quarters in Rome.

Meanwhile Mussolini went to visit his wife. Thunderstruck at seeing him head of the government, she began to weep. "I felt that the family and I were losing him," she said later.

Masses of flowers were presented to Mussolini at the Milan railway station. "I want the train to leave on time," he told the stationmaster. "Everything will have to go off perfectly."

The train started amid a chorus of *Evviva il Duce!*

At 10:42 A.M. on October 30 the train stopped beside the platform in Rome. A guard of honor presented arms. Mussolini and Bianchi entered a taxi, his staff filled two others, and the three cars set off for the Quirinal.

A half-hour later he stood before the King in his Fascist uniform. He apologized at first for his attire, but, he explained, "I have come straight from the battle, which, fortunately, was won without bloodshed."

The King appointed Mussolini to form a government. The letter of the constitution was not infringed. But Il Duce had ordered the squadre to move back into Rome by rail; the military would see to the feeding and housing of the Black Shirts.

The spectacular parade of the squadristi would provide a cloak for the web of conspiracies, compromises, desertions; the legend of a seizure of power through a mass rising by the people would become a political force in the future. Undoubtedly all this had gone through Mussolini's mind before he disguised himself as a valiant fighter for his meeting with the King.

Part II

MUSSOLINI
IN POWER:
THE SUCCESSES
OF FASCISM

(1922–1936)

7

The Time of the Last Illusions
(October, 1922 – April, 1924)

"We wish to give the Italian people five years of peace and fruitful work. Let all factions, even our own, perish, but let our fatherland be great, let it be respected, let it be strong."—IL DUCE (April 10, 1924)

WHEN MUSSOLINI emerged from the Quirinal at noon on October 30 after his first conference with the King, he was met with an ovation. The crowd in front of the palace had swollen; it called for the King, who appeared on the balcony. Then, as the cars drove away, the crowd headed for the Hotel Savoia at via Ludovisi, 15, where Mussolini was staying. Little by little the throng of Fascists and the merely curious outside the hotel grew, and there were cries of "Mussolini! Mussolini!" He appeared on the balcony and shouted back: "I can assure you that in a few hours you will have not a ministry but a government."

It was a clever phrase, and it appealed to the expectations of that average opinion that constituted the pliable fabric of a nation and that since 1919 had been rubbed raw by political uncertainty and violence, that average opinion that is always on the winner's side not out of weakness but out of "realism" and a yearning for internal order. It placed its hopes in Mussolini, it wanted to invest rational hopes in this man who was backed by everything that counted in the country. Thus began what Sforza called "the honeymoon between Italy and Fascism."

Rome was quiet that afternoon of October 30. Mussolini's words to the King stood out on the front pages of the newspapers: "I bring to Your Majesty the Italy of Vittorio Veneto, consecrated anew by victory, and I am Your Majesty's loyal servant," he was reported to have said.

The newspapers were already publishing the names of his ministers when Mussolini was preparing, in a tight-fitting frock coat and a top-hat, both borrowed from friends, to return to the Quirinal to present his program to the King and take his oath of office. How could the new ministry not have brought reassurance to all those for whom a sound policy meant first of all the total absence of political events? True, Mussolini had reserved for himself, as Premier, the Ministries of the Interior and Foreign Affairs—as Crispi had once done—but among the thirteen ministers there were only three Fascists, holding the portfolios of Justice, Finance, and Liberated Territories, and one nationalist, Federzoni, who was made Minister of "Colonies."

Side by side with this nucleus of marked men, all the groups in the Chamber except those of the extreme left were represented in the government. Don Sturzo's Popular Party received two important portfolios, the Treasury and Labor; the architect of victory, Marshal Diaz, was Minister of War, and the eagle of the sea, Admiral Thaon di Revel, was Minister of the Navy; the philosopher, Giovanni Gentile, held the portfolio of Education. It was said even that, had it not been for the opposition of the right, Gino Baldesi, a Socialist deputy and leader of the CGL, would have been in the Cabinet. Was this not the national ministry of rebirth, the ministry of union, the great ministry of pacification, the ministry of normalization for which Italy had been waiting to bring her out of the long after-war sickness? The majority hoped it was. Of course there had been the attempt to march on Rome, but, as Giolitti declared, "it cannot be said that the crisis was resolved by parliamentary means, but it was done within the limits of the constitution."

Thus the blindness and the easy solace of some, the ingenuous hopes of the majority, the calculations of others concealed from most of the nation the fact that the King, the Italian ruling class, and its political institutions had yielded to an armed faction or become its confederates. Events would make it their business to bring the fact home to Italians.

An initial close study of the composition of the Cabinet showed that behind the three Fascist ministers there were numerous secretaries of state who had built their careers in squadrismo: De Vecchi, Acerbo, De Bono, Finzi, Costanzo Ciano. In addition, the frankness of certain official statements clarified the significance of Mussolini's government. General Luigi Cadorna, who had been beaten at Caporetto, did not hesitate to descend into the political arena in order to give voice to a harsh anti-parliamentarianism: "It was not possible for Italian youth . . . , which has suffered for the greater fatherland, to tolerate any longer the submersion of our country in all the rottenness of a corrupt parliamentarianism and a sordid political life."

Above all, Confindustria, with unprecedented brazenness, admitted on October 31 that it had "exerted a direct and urgent influence in favor of the Mussolini solution. . . . The nation needed a government prepared to make decisions and to act. This government was promised to us by the man who has been summoned to create it with the confidence of the King."

Thus far there were only announcements, but in the morning of October 31 the Fascist legions of the March on Rome, still inactive in the countryside, marched into the Eternal City, where the main streets were decked with banners. In the working-class quarter of San Lorenzo, Bottai's squadre attacked: seven persons were killed and seventeen were wounded; others were killed in the Trionfale quarter; Nitti's and Labriola's apartments were invaded and the offices of newspapers and the Socialist Party were attacked and devastated; young Palmiro Togliatti was manhandled, the face of a Communist deputy's secretary was painted green, white, and red—the national colors—and he was forced to go through the streets shouting: "Viva il Fascio"; after that he was forced to drink several quarts of castor oil. Yet there was nothing that resembled a systematic seizure of the city: the innumerable incidents were localized and quickly suppressed.

Meanwhile, at Villa Borghese, Mussolini reviewed the march of fifty thousand Black Shirts; then the long procession broke up and groups made their way through Piazza del Popolo, the Corso, past Piazza Venezia and the Altar of the Nation, to the Quirinal and the railway station. The march was led by a detachment of bersaglieri from the regular army; they were followed by the Quadrumvirs, several generals, and officers of all ranks; after them came the Fascist legions: groups of bare-headed young men marched in irregular order; now and then a regular army unit was sandwiched between two squadre, symbolizing the union of Fascism and the military; the Rieti legion was led by a priest, the Pavia legions by a countess. The spectators were not particularly demonstrative; they were curious more than anything, and there was no great number of them except at the Quirinal. From the balcony the King and Queen, flanked by Marshal Diaz and Admiral Thaon di Revel, observed the march and were hailed by the Black Shirts, who dipped their gagliardetti in salute as they passed. Some observers believed that the period of violence and unlawful acts was over because Fascism had bent its head before the constitutional monarchy.

Then Mussolini went to the Central Station to watch the Fascists depart: during the night of October 31—November 1 fifty special trains left Rome amid songs and cheers under the vigilant eye of Il Duce. Everyone was delighted with this proof of the good faith of the chief of the government, who had just demonstrated his ability to "avoid the worst" and his desire to "normalize the situation" and "parliamentarize Fascism": the few murders in Rome were, after all, merely the negligible price of the preservation of peace and the social order. Politicians had every ground to entertain the highest hopes.

One of these politicians resoundingly dissociated himself, with a shock: Sforza. Mussolini had made indirect overtures to the highly respected former Foreign Minister, by this time ambassador in Paris. Sforza replied with a telegram of resignation that the Roman newspapers printed on November 1. The signer of the Treaty of Rapallo was afraid that "the foreign policy of the new government amounts to no more than a mere collection of sentiment and resentment."

The afternoon newspapers printed Mussolini's "proud" response under big headlines. "I officially call on you," Mussolini said, "to retain your post and not to create obstacles for the government that at this time represents the highest expression of the national conscience."

The matter did not end there. There were more messages between the two men. Sforza adopted a more conciliatory tone, but reiterated his decision; he was summoned to Rome and at ten o'clock on the morning of November 6 he was ushered into the little waiting room adjoining the Foreign Minister's state office, where Mussolini was expecting him.

Mussolini stared hard at Sforza and said in a low voice: "I could have had you shot." The ambassador did not blink. Mussolini was quite well aware, besides, that he had no choice but to accept the resignation: he would have to sham again, to convince Italy and the world of his good will and his respect for rules. Even after his threat he confided to Sforza that he wanted "to govern with a democratic program."

In the same spirit the press reprinted the telegram that he had sent from Rome to each provincial Fascist *ras*: "We should maintain discipline and we should never violate personal liberties."

In these early days the same moderation obtained in foreign affairs. Mussolini had set up his office in the quarters of the Foreign Ministry, the *Consulta*, which rises opposite the Obelisk and the Dioscuri and overlooks Rome. With its eighteenth-century façade, its Fuga architraves, and its monumental staircase, it was the symbol of the diplomacy of Cavour conducted by elegant aristocrats. These men were apprehensive: what was their new minister going to do? Raffaele Guariglia, Baron di Vituso, who had served in turn in Paris, London, St. Petersburg, and Brussels, was among the men who received Mussolini in the Umberto-style rooms of the *Consulta*. "From the first instant," he remarked of his new chief, "with his oxlike look, his ways of moving and speaking, contrived but with a certain lack of skill, . . . the man offended me."[1]

But these superficial aversions soon vanished. The higher officials—except Sforza and the ambassador in Berlin, Alfredo Frassati—followed the King and, therefore, Mussolini. Il Duce, moreover, made a show of docility: he accepted the lessons in protocol and elegance that were given to him by a young man in the Foreign Ministry and he seemed to be observing the counsels that were lavished on him by Salvatore Contarini, the secretary general of the *Consulta*. Hence his first act was to call on the Fascists of the Free City of Fiume to cease all activity: henceforth the avenues of normal diplomacy must be followed. With relief and satisfaction Guariglia observed: "I must admit that, once invested with the responsibilities of government, the new minister was able in a few minutes to strip off the disguise of the demagogue and to give quite reasonable instructions on a problem that he had contributed to complicating."[2]

In actuality, even though he was wearing his frock coat again and carrying his top-hat, Mussolini had not abandoned the "disguise of the demagogue." On November 4, the anniversary of victory, he went with the King and all the members of the government to a solemn mass at St. Mary of the Angels. This was his first official ceremony. Throughout the mass he remained standing, his face frozen; afterward, with a resolute step, he put himself at the head of the notables. Flanked by Admiral Thaon di Revel in full-dress uniform and Marshal Diaz, and followed by a host of gentlemen in top-hats, Mussolini led them through the streets to the Altar of the Nation. There everyone halted and knelt. The ranks of eminent dignitaries under the grey November sky made a rather curious spectacle. It is not impossible that Mussolini had this first ceremony in mind when he remarked later: "The state is a solemn, irregular, melancholy procession of sixty top-hats that are gathered together on great occasions."

This pompous tribute marked the inception of his rule. To Baron Beyens, the Belgian ambassador, Cardinal Gasparri observed with satisfaction: "He ordered that everyone kneel in prayer for one

[1] Raffaele Guariglia, *Riccordi 1922–1946* (Naples: Edizioni scientifiche italiane, 1950).
[2] *Ibid.*, p. 3.

The Time of the Last Illusions

minute, which must have seemed quite long to many of the free-thinkers present; but everyone bent the knee." The Cardinal, Secretary of State of His Holiness, added with a smile: "Let us give him a few months' time before we sit in judgment on the revolutionary *coup d'état* that he carried out so masterfully. What we know of him is that he is a remarkable organizer—Fascism is here to prove the point—and a great character."[3]

A few months' time? Receiving Paolo Orano, a Fascist journalist, on November 2, and complacently showing his comrade the formal office in which he was installed, Mussolini brought the palm of his hand down on his desk and said: "I am not here as a visitor: I am here to set up a government in Italy and to govern. What did not exist before exists now: a government." He struck himself on the chest and added, throwing back his head: "*I* am here."

He widened his eyes and stared at Orano, a habit that he was acquiring in order to impress. He seemed older than his thirty-nine years, and his very obvious baldness emphasized his big convex forehead. "The Italians," he went on, "have never obeyed. . . . When we have established a government that governs all Italians, everything that is now wrong will be well. I will keep this promise implacably against any enemies and against myself. You shall see."

Orano was taking notes. Mussolini put in a telephone call to Cesare De Vecchi, one of the Quadrumvirs. "You wanted a marshal's bâton right away, didn't you?" he bellowed. "Well, be satisfied with a fountain-pen." Then he hung up.

There was the man, already drunk on power and yet still accessible. He was still living in the Hotel Savoia, converted now into a staff headquarters guarded by armed squadristi and visited by a steady stream of seekers of favors, Fascist chiefs arriving as if for a distribution of booty, admiring women already dreaming of the brutal maleness of Il Duce. Already there was a rumor that during a large part of the squadrista parade Mussolini had been closeted in an office of the *Consulta* with one of them.

These details give an authentic feeling of the atmosphere of Rome at the beginning of November, 1922. It seemed that, as long as he did not disrupt the social order, Mussolini could do as he liked, supported as he was by all the hierarchies, political, economic, and religious, even profiting by the acquiescence of the bewildered masses, and having to confront only a few adversaries —Turati, Piero Gobetti, Sturzo, Gramsci—who struggled desperately in their isolation to maintain their footing.

[3] Beyens, *Quatre ans à Rome*, pp. 136–137.

The powerful newspapers, however, busied themselves in drowning out their voices while every column supported "the Mussolini experiment" and contributed to the creation of the myth of "the exceptional man." Every morning, on the second page, every paper ran a laudatory diary entitled "Benito Mussolini's Day." Of course these papers reflected the views of those who controlled them. The world of business was highly enthusiastic over the chief of the government: on November 6 fourteen financiers and industrialists, all in regulation black frock coats, elegant and respectable, their gloves in their hands, were received in the *Consulta* and clustered round Mussolini. He was wearing riding clothes, and a double-breasted grey jacket emphasized his weight; his leather boots, his flaring trousers, and that tight jacket made him look like a circus animal trainer, and undoubtedly that was just the thought that he wanted to implant. Nevertheless, four days later a decree-law abrogated the registration of securities and eliminated all plans for agrarian reform. A few days later the parliamentary investigation of war profits was dropped. Mussolini's fierce manner in the midst of these well-bred gentlemen of business, evidently, could hardly worry them.

But the chorus of praise or relief that accompanied Mussolini's advent to power was not limited to business groups. On November 7 the CGL's publication, *Union Battles*, rejoiced that "the workers' organizations have remained aloof from both contesting factions" and declared that Mussolini's accession was "the way to clarify a situation that was becoming more and more untenable."

As for Giolitti, that figurehead of the world of politics, he was writing letter after letter to urge his friends to support Mussolini's government. On November 15 *il Popolo d'Italia*, the management of which had been transferred to Mussolini's brother, Arnaldo, splashed a sentence of Giolitti's across its front page: "Mussolini's is the only government that can restore social peace." Giolitti was further quoted: "The Cabinet must be supported. The country needs a strong government that looks beyond living from day to day. Italian political life needs new blood, new energies."

Giolitti's position unequivocally symbolized the general attitude of the Italian ruling class, an attitude reminiscent of that of 1920–21: accept Fascism, utilize it as a counterweight—essentially against Socialism—unite with it and, if possible, parliamentarize it, "normalize" it.

These obstinate arguments, exactly as on the eve of the March on Rome, were brought out once more by Salandra, Giolitti, and a large part of the Popular Party, and again the politicians were ready for any compromise. This became clear on November 16.

That was the day when Parliament reconvened. This was essential to the legalization of Mussolini's government. Now, even though there were only thirty-five Fascist deputies in the Chamber, no one entertained the least doubt that the government would win a comfortable majority. Who would dare to withhold confidence and full powers from the man formally chosen by the King and factually forced into office by the collective abdication of the ruling class and by the March on Rome? The only question was how Mussolini would handle this Chamber already resigned to submission.

In Montecitorio, where the galleries were filled with Black Shirts, Mussolini was contemptuous, threatening, building the legend of a Fascism born of revolution. "Gentlemen," he began, "What I am performing in this chamber today is an act of purely formal deference to you, for which I ask of you no sign of special gratitude. I declare that revolution has its rights. I have refused to carry my victory to its final conclusion. I could do so."

Mussolini paused for a moment in the heavy silence. Then he raised his voice: "With three hundred thousand armed young men . . . prepared for everything, ready to obey me in almost mystic blindness, I could chastise all those who have slandered and sought to sully Fascism. I have set myself certain limits."

Thus Mussolini sired the legend of the "three hundred thousand" of the March on Rome. He went on: "I could make this grey, silent hall a camp of foot soldiers!"

"*Evviva il Parlamento!* Long live Parliament!" Giuseppe Modigliani and Giacomo Matteotti, Socialist deputies, shouted as they rose. For a few moments there was utter chaos in the Chamber; when silence returned, Mussolini resumed his speech: "Let no one have any illusions as to the brevity of our time in power," he began. Alluding to the fact that fifty-two deputies had put down their names as speakers, he said sarcastically: "Let us not throw any more empty babble at the nation, gentlemen! . . . Fifty-two speakers are too many." He concluded on a religious note: "May God help me to carry my arduous task to its victorious end!"

In the corridor Modigliani sought to persuade Giolitti to rise against the insult to Parliament embodied in this "barrack-room tirade." Unruffled and calm, Giolitti said again and again: "I wholly approve of the speech made by the Premier."

The Senate gave Mussolini an ovation. But on November 17 Turati quickened the debate in the Chamber. The Socialist leader, smoothing his thick beard from time to time in his characteristic gesture, looked calmly at two deputies who had risen to interrupt and denounce him; then he turned toward Mussolini and listened with a half-smile as the Premier addressed him with arrogant, cynical self-confidence.

"The Italian Parliament," Turati began, "has ceased to exist." He threw out his arm toward the Fascists. "We deny any revolutionary aspect to your accession to power."

"You shall see," Mussolini interrupted.

"When all flee or yield," Turati continued, "from the crown to the lowest policeman, victory is easy. . . . Your ideal is that of enlightened despotism."

In spite of all the talk, the game was over. In the evening, by three hundred six votes to one hundred sixteen, the Chamber adopted a resolution: "Having confidence in the destiny of the nation, the Chamber approves the government's statement and proceeds with the agenda."

Giolitti, Bonomi, Orlando, Salandra, Alcide De Gasperi, Giovanni Gronchi, and Meda voted confidence in Mussolini with the Fascist, nationalist, liberal, and Popular groups. Nitti and Amendola were not present. Only Matteotti, Turati, and the Socialist and Communist groups voted against the resolution. On November 24 and 29, without debate, full powers were conferred by two hundred seventy-five votes to ninety in the Chamber and by one hundred ninety-six to nineteen in the Senate. The letter of the constitution had been obeyed and, legally, nothing had changed in the government of Italy. The deputies had voted a cover of legality for the *coup d'état*.

A few days after the vote of confidence, a special train carrying Premier Raymond Poincaré and Lord Curzon arrived in Lausanne, where the Allies' conference on Turkey was to be held. Poincaré had already gotten out of the train when he was told that Mussolini, who was supposed to represent Italy in the conference, had not arrived. "Where is the swine?" Poincaré shouted.

Wearing a black frock coat and white spats, carrying a heavy cane, surrounded by young men in black shirts, Mussolini was waiting for the statesmen in the lobby of the Grand Hotel in Territet, a dozen miles out of Lausanne. Outside the hotel, a band composed of the little town's Italians was playing *Giovinezza*. Such was Mussolini's entry into foreign policy, forcing the representatives of the British Empire and the French Republic to go to him, the political adventurer turned chief of government. This was his first official journey outside Italy, and he wanted to make it impressive. When he was closeted alone with Curzon and Poincaré, the Italian diplomats sighed and worried.

"Contarini is crushed. . . . His contacts with Mussolini made a frightful impression on him," Ambassador Barrère observed.[4] What did that matter to Mussolini? In actuality he had attained his goal. Italians would know that the representatives of France and England had gone to him, and there was no question of his gain in prestige.

As a matter of fact, the powers held no grudge against Fascism and indeed reinforced it with their approval. To Lord Curzon, former Viceroy of India and a typical English aristocrat, Mussolini was "a young man, a great character and a great force." To *The Times* of London, Fascism was "a salutary reaction against Bolshevism." This was the general view, moreover, and it was readily forgotten that in large part Fascism had built its success on the exploitation of nationalist themes; that it regarded France, England, and the United States as "the plutocratic nations . . . three moneybags who had devoured the universe in Paris" (*il Popolo*, February 22, 1920); that it exalted "Rome, the magic word that has filled the whole of history for twenty centuries"[5]; that for this rebirth of the Roman Empire it had already brought up "Tunisia, which we gave up in a moment of colossal idiocy": in short, everyone forgot that Mussolini had made himself the mouthpiece of all the nationalist ideals. French and English statesmen reasoned like Giolitti or Guariglia. The latter had written quite bluntly: "It was therefore necessary to use the fact of Fascism economically if it could be of use in resolving our foreign-policy problems. Certainly this resulted in a perceptible increase of strength for the new government, but also in a substantial advantage."[6]

This state of mind explained the attentions that were lavished on Mussolini. When he arrived in London in December, Colonel Waterhouse went to Claridge's to offer the personal welcome—an extraordinary occurrence—of His Majesty, George V. The British press vied with the Fascist in its praises; it emphasized "the forceful profile, the manly features, the broad chest, the determined, sparkling eyes" of Il Duce. In spite of all this there were the London climate, the fog, a few demonstrations by Italian exiles, and in the last analysis Mussolini was to leave with an unpleasant memory of England and the English: "They are Germans who have traveled," he was to say. He had hardly appreciated English humor, which had enjoyed pointing out that every Italian on the payroll of Claridge's had been made a *cavaliere* of the Italian crown on Mussolini's personal order.

[4] Charles-Roux, *Une grande ambassade à Rome*, p. 222.
[5] Trieste speech, September 20, 1920.
[6] Guariglia, *Riccordi 1922–1946*, p. 5.

The favorable welcome that, on the whole, Mussolini had enjoyed abroad during this journey in the winter of 1922 had certainly enhanced the prestige of the Fascist government in Italian eyes. On his return to Rome, Il Duce decided first of all to move the Foreign Ministry to Palazzo Chigi. The tradition-steeped *Consulta* was abandoned for the elegant structure at the end of the Corso on Piazza Colonna; at the other end was Piazza Venezia with its palace, which provided the setting for the receptions that Mussolini gave and at which he wore his new decorations: the big green cord of SS.-Maurice-et-Lazare, the Order of Malta, and the grand cross of the *Légion d'honneur*.

But this man whose vanity was enlarged with every new day, who established himself in the "victory room" of Palazzo Chigi, a huge chamber embellished with magnificent Flemish tapestries, was still a political leader at grips with difficult problems. On December 13 he had had to send a telegram from London to Farinacci, the *ras* of Cremona: "Fascism, which conquered by attacking its enemies frontally, is too intelligent and too strong to be betrayed or swindled. Such vague illusions as persist will be dissipated and such enemies as have not disarmed will be inexorably, definitively crushed."

Such violence at the very start evoked astonishment: the government had been granted full powers; the banks, the factories, the crown, the army, and the church had approved it; the people had accepted it: what more was wanted? In actual fact, while the strength of Fascism was real, elements of weakness were not absent. First of all, the parliamentary forms were still in being: Parliament and the constitution were still there. Granted that these were convenient shelters; but they were also obstacles, however feeble, to the totalitarian power of Fascism.

There was more. The Fascists were still a tiny minority in Montecitorio. In the event of some grave occurrence, would the "morass," that colorless mass of deputies, follow Il Duce? Must the Chamber be dissolved? Undoubtedly, but how to manage the votes? If Fascism suffered a defeat at the polls, what would happen? In this connection Mussolini was well aware that he had triumphed only through the consent of the King and the army, that the real country had submitted to Fascism but might well turn against it in its heart; what would Vittorio Emanuele III do then? Of course there was still the National Fascist Party, but the squadre were being torn by rivalries.

The veteran Fascists clubbed the new adherents, and every *ras* behaved as he chose. Farinacci was the leader of those for whom "the revolution was still to be completed," and the squadristi—

they numbered tens of thousands—were suddenly idle after having fought hard and collected their reward. For nothing had altered formally: a Mussolini Cabinet had simply replaced a Facta Cabinet, but the carabinieri, like the King and the nobility, were still there. Parties, even if they were persecuted, continued to exist legally. The old squadristi, furthermore, were embittered when they saw the victor's camp thronged with those *signorotti*, those dapper little gentlemen who were taking the leading places in the party organizations, and Mussolini seemed to be siding with these late arrivals who advocated a return to legality.

And the brutalities went on: first against the enemy, Socialists and Catholics (the bishop of Brescia was compelled to protest). No matter that in Rome there was collaboration; outside there was fighting. The violence spread to new areas: Piedmont, Sardinia. There was also fighting between Fascists and nationalists in the Mezzogiorno and in Genoa. Cautious journalists stopped reporting the outbreaks. After all it was essential to help Mussolini to "normalize" Fascism and, therefore, to mask Fascist illegality in silence and instead to adulate Il Duce, the man in the best position to shatter the squadre, the reasonable and indispensable man.

So the illusions persisted, and moreover with a certain basis of truth, for Mussolini, the chief of government, needed order, even if only, as Sforza said, for the sake of his personal prestige. But in truth the Italian leaders—those, at least, who were conservative yet liberal and were not yet ready to accept open dictatorship— were making another gamble on Mussolini . . . the same gamble as in 1920, 1921, and 1922, and it was already lost.

On December 15, 1922, Mussolini announced during the afternoon that he was convoking the leading figures in Fascism for a meeting at ten o'clock that night in the Grand Hotel in order to establish the Fascist Grand Council. Some twenty men gathered in the rococo meeting room; they included Acerbo, Finzi, Michele Bianchi, Francesco Giunta, Achille Starace. The new body, which was extra-constitutional, was to meet regularly at 10 P.M. on the twelfth day of each month in order not to interfere with the normal course of government work. Its creation was an indication that Mussolini was beginning to "Fascistize the state."

The most important of the decisions made that night was the establishment of a Volunteer Militia for National Security (MVSN), directly under Mussolini's orders and not taking an oath to the King. It was to be composed of squadristi. Officially now Mussolini had his pretorian guard. Some optimists argued that the enrollment of the squadre in a militia was tantamount to eliminating or at least to controlling them. Two days after the Grand Council's meeting, events in Turin were to show the true face of the future militiamen.

On December 17 two Fascists were killed during a private quarrel in Turin, the city of Gramsci and the young anti-Fascist liberal, Gobetti. Piero Brandimarte's squadre decided to avenge them: twenty-two persons were summarily murdered with clubs and rifle butts, either because they were anti-Fascists or because they had publicly voiced indignation at the wave of violence. The Labor Exchange was set afire; Pietro Ferreio, the secretary of the metal-workers' union, was recognized by the light of the flames and beaten to death at the foot of the monument to Vittorio Emanuele; his body was then attached by the feet to a truck and dragged through the streets at high speed to a chorus of songs and shots. In an interview Brandimarte boasted that he had selected his victims from a list of three thousand revolutionaries in order to "give the anti-Fascists a terrible lesson."

The revulsion—though, it is true, it was silent—was general. Mussolini ordered the dissolution of the Turin Fascio: was this then the normalization that was so eagerly awaited? At the same time he entrusted its re-creation to Cesare De Vecchi, who had publicly congratulated Brandimarte, and both men were appointed generals in the Volunteer Militia.

Normalization was only a front. This became all the more apparent as the violence continued. The punitive expeditions were now augmented with the "bando fascista"—the "Fascist banishment" of an opponent from a given area. In addition Mussolini was constantly making harsher and harsher speeches. "What has happened is irrevocable," he said on January 8, 1923; "The Fascist state not only defends itself but attacks," he added on February 10.

While the Volunteer Militia was being organized and the squadristi were finally receiving regular salaries and a uniform—grey-green trousers, black shirts, Alpini hats without the feathers—the Royal Guard was dissolved. In his magazine, Gerarchia, Mussolini commented cynically: "Fascism has already trampled, and, if necessary, will calmly trample again, the more or less decomposed body of the goddess, Liberty."

Socialists were arrested, workers' associations were dissolved, the freedom of movement of anti-Fascist deputies was curtailed, the wives of militant anti-Fascists were stripped naked and painted red. Between January and April, 1923, the government adopted a whole set of measures tending in the same direction as the violence: more than fifty thousand railway workers were dismissed because during 1919 and 1920 they had taken leading parts in a number of worker actions; the May 1 celebrations were officially

The Time of the Last Illusions

abolished and replaced by the "Roman Christmas" on April 21. On that day the Militia paraded through the Eternal City. The Ministry of Labor was eliminated. The telephone and life-insurance industries were returned to private hands by the state. A decree-law recognizing the eight-hour day could not alter the resolutely conservative orientation of the government.

On February 26, 1923, furthermore, the nationalists merged with the PNF; the Blue Shirts loyal to the King joined the Militia, and through them the ideology of anti-liberal and totalitarian nationalism climaxed its invasion of the Fascist Party, through which it was to attempt to win over the nation.

Enrollments in the Partito nazionale fascista had soared, especially after its victory: the lower middle class, merchants, minor officials, for the most part, but also peasants, workers, students wearing the lictor's *fasces* in their buttonholes—enlistments born of conviction, necessity, hope, or neighborhood or office politics, and in such number that in April, 1923, the influx of candidates for membership was so great that the party's secretariat closed the membership books. By then the PNF had more than five hundred thousand members.

Outside the party the press evangelized the "national-Fascist" ideology: there were dissertations on "the Fascist ethic," the Fascist state, Fascist obedience. Indeed, an adverb was coined for application to the most varied activities carried out *"fascistica-mente*—Fascistically." In spite of this more and more frankly totalitarian development, the political class continued to lend its "moral guaranty" to Mussolini's government. At its congress in Turin on April 12–13, in spite of Don Sturzo, the Popular Party adopted a resolution in which it reaffirmed "its confidence in the government. . . . Therefore, as in the past, the collaboration of the Popular Party with the government will be inspired by total loyalty to the head of the government."

But to Mussolini, whatever resolutions it adopted, the Popular Party led by Don Sturzo remained an obstacle: he threw its ministers out of his government. At the same time—in a tactic already proved—he increased his gestures toward the Vatican; the educational reform of April 27, 1923, satisfied the preference for religious schooling; crucifixes were restored to schools and courtrooms. This brought him to his goal. The Italian Popular Party split into a left and right wing. On June 20 the walls of Rome were plastered with posters signed by a number of leading Catholics who affirmed their "complete harmony with Fascism, which honors the religious and social values that constitute the foundation of any healthy political system."

On July 10 Don Sturzo resigned the leadership of the party. Once more Mussolini had won. He then carried his political plan to completion with a proposal to the Chamber to ratify an electoral reform worked out by his friend, Acerbo. Acerbo's was a clever scheme: two-thirds of the seats in the Chamber would be awarded to the national ticket that won twenty-five percent of the votes. Mussolini entered this decisive combat—the electoral law was to give Fascism the absolute majority—with some hesitancy: there were at present only thirty-five Fascist deputies. He ordered units of the Militia to converge on Rome. The air in the capital was oppressive; again there was talk of civil war and of vengeance against any deputies who might oppose the reform.

On July 15 Mussolini spoke in Montecitorio. Defying those who interrupted him from the left, he cried: "You are forgetting one very simple thing: the revolution has the right to defend itself. You who support the Russian system have no right to protest against mine." Then, alluding to his direct contacts with the people, he added: "Well, so far the population has not asked me for its freedom!"

By three hundred three votes to forty the deputies approved the election law that doomed them. When the result was announced, Mussolini laughed in triumph as he left the Chamber, slapping his fellow-Fascists on the shoulder. He had just won a major hand, and already he was thinking of the next.

Three days earlier the Cabinet had issued a harsh decree-law on the press. Day by day, violence by violence, decree by decree, law by law, Italy's freedoms were being destroyed.

During the same month, shortly after the adoption of the new election law, the Foreign Ministry was in an uproar. On July 24 Italy was officially awarded the Dodecanese Islands, and Mussolini had decided to send his warships in battle formation to take solemn possession of islands that had been in Italian hands for ten years. Contarini and Guariglia saw the absurdity and the exaggeration of such an act. Guariglia arranged an appointment with Il Duce and put forth common-sense arguments: Mussolini strode largely up and down the Hall of Victory. He was in his riding clothes. Without a word he sent Guariglia packing. The fleet did not sail, but Mussolini's resolve to make a dramatic show of success in foreign affairs was clearly confirmed.

In January, 1923, he had supported the French and Belgian occupation of the Ruhr, while at the same time trying to appear— "with consummate journalistic foolishness," as Sforza put it—as the leader of a continental bloc against England. He envisaged the creation of a French-German-Italian "common market" in coal and steel under the pressure of industrial circles, and above all he pushed for a last-resort policy: the cellars of the *Reichsbank* were full of gold ingots, the Allies had only to go and seize them. This was followed by denials, already showing those two faces of Mussolini's tactics, which consisted in carrying a hazardous attack or an outrageous idea to a great length and then quickly organizing a withdrawal; thereupon the other face was offered, conciliatory and almost bland after the drama of the initial moves. The harm, however, had most often been done already.

So on May 7, 1923, forgetting all about the continental bloc, Mussolini welcomed Their Britannic Majesties to Rome with great pomp. For several days there was a succession of receptions, parades, and speeches. The Order of the Bath was conferred on Mussolini, and Lord Curzon extolled the work of Fascism. But Mussolini could not be satisfied with the splendors of the royal travels. He wanted a grand, a "Cyclopean" policy, for his personal glory and because nationalism had been at the root of Fascism from the start.

At about nine o'clock in the morning of August 27, 1923, a car containing five Italian officers sent by the ambassadors' conference to mark out the Greek-Albanian border was stopped by a tree across the road from Janina to Forty Saints, in Greek territory. Guns began to fire and the Italians tried to flee. They were killed. When the bodies of General Enrico Tellini and his companions were recovered, their faces had been smashed with rifle butts. Feeling in Italy was intense; *Il Messaggero* called the event a "political assassination without precedent in the contemporary history of Europe."

Demonstrations were staged in front of Greek consulates; newspapers reported that Mussolini had labored in Palazzo Chigi until one o'clock in the morning. What was certain was that Il Duce now had the incident that would enable him to act. (Some Italian diplomats later offered Sforza documents tending to show that the crime had been staged by Mussolini himself; but Sforza was skeptical.)

On August 29 Italy issued a public ultimatum that would have forced Greece into shameful capitulation; two days later a squadron of warships commanded by Admiral Solari shelled and then seized the unoccupied fortress of Corfu.

This was Italian Fascism's first aggression against an independent state. The matter was put into the hands of the League of Nations, which was vilified by the Fascist press as a ridiculous, infantile institution, a nineteenth-century fossil in the pay of England and the Swiss owners of the buildings it occupied. Fascism had been in power less than a year and already, as *The Daily News* of

London remarked, "Italy shows the peculiar symptoms of a rapidly growing war fever."

The English newspaper did not know how accurate it was. Recently published diplomatic documents[7] are eloquent: in 1923 Mussolini and Admiral Thaon di Revel examined the possibility of a war against England and gave it up only after they had analyzed relative strengths. All that he could do now was to re-embark the troops that had landed with their bands playing at Corfu and content himself with an indemnity of two and a half million dollars. A stinging defeat, the diplomats said. Of course; but also a shrewd demagogic success. The lower-middle-class jingo was satisfied with the appearances: the crime had been avenged. Mussolini's Italy was an Italy that counted, that was talked about; it was no longer Giolitti's Italy evacuating Valona. What was more, Mussolini had learned that the democracies were far from harmonizing their policies. Understanding, kindly France opposed resolute England because Mussolini had backed the occupation of the Ruhr. Thus as early as 1923 the fire of the naval guns at Corfu symbolized the whole of Fascism's foreign policy, which led to Ethiopia, to Munich, and to action against Albania and which ended in the Second World War—a policy that sought expansion and glory through aggression.

And the smaller nations gave in: on January 27, 1924, under the convention of Nettuno, Yugoslavia restored the city of Fiume to Italy: this was a great success for Mussolini, and on his initiative a royal decree conferred on Gabriele d'Annunzio the title of Prince of Monte Nevoso. In Fiume the King himself made Mussolini his cousin by dubbing him a knight of the *Annunziata*. The atmosphere in Rome was one of triumph.

But other events foreshadowed a future of which no one could yet conceive all the sinister developments. In conquered Germany the Nazi movement had recently come into being, and at once it turned toward Italy, regenerated by Fascism, which had momentarily been able to contemplate a war against England.

As early as the end of September, 1922, before Mussolini had yet seized power, Adolf Hitler had begun following his career with absorption. Hitler's personal emissary, Karl Ludecke, was sent to Milan to establish contact with the Fascist leader; he returned full of enthusiasm and announced to the little group of Nazis conspiring in Bavaria that the success of Fascism was assured. Therefore Hitler was fascinated by the Fascist experiment. He aug-

[7] *Documenti diplomatici italiani*, Seventh Series (1922–35).

The Time of the Last Illusions

mented his plan for a *Putsch* in Munich with a "March on Berlin."
In August, 1923, Ludecke went back to Italy, collected funds for
the now imminent *Putsch*, and, in exchange for this help, promised
that the Nazi movement would make no claim for the South
Tyrol.[8] In mid-October Hitler gave an interview of the same tenor
to *il Corriere italiano*, arousing protests among the Tyrolean nationalists.

Thus tenuous bonds were created between the two movements.
But the Nazi Party was still very weak; and the beer-hall *Putsch* of
November 8, 1923, in Munich collapsed. What then was Hitler to
onorevole Mussolini, who was dealing with Curzon and Poincaré
as if he were their equal? An unlucky little adventurer. A disciple,
Hitler declared. Arrested after his *Putsch*, he took the occasion of
his trial in March, 1924, to hymn Mussolini's Italy, which was
combatting "the Jewish hydra," "Freemasonry," and "Marxism."
Imprisoned in the old fortress of Landsberg, he dictated *Mein
Kampf* to Rudolf Hess: he officially relinquished the South Tyrol;
that apple of discord must not be left between Naziism and Fascist Italy. After the failed adventure of Munich two important
Nazis escaped arrest: Hermann Goering and Hans Frank. They
took refuge in Italy, where they formed a number of friendships.

Dangerous in the immediate—and for the future—this foreign
policy in no way lowered the prestige of the government and its
chief; quite the contrary. Many Italians in 1923 shared the views
that Pius XI confided to Ambassador Beyens during a conference:

> Mussolini is no Napoleon, nor perhaps a Cavour, but he alone
> had a proper understanding of what was necessary for his country
> in order to rid it of the anarchy to which it had been reduced by
> an impotent parliamentarianism and three years of war. You see
> that he has carried the nation with him. May he be able to regen-
> erate Italy! What is lacking for the establishment of peace is pre-
> destined men. God grant us some of these luminaries so that they
> may guide and enlighten humanity![9]

Even Nitti wrote to Amendola: "The Fascist experiment must be
carried out without interference: there should be no opposition
from our side. I cannot adhere, but I wish to put nothing in its
way."

[8] *Revue d'histoire de la deuxième guerre mondiale*, April, 1957; Marc
Langereau, *La question du Sud Tyrol* (Paris: CDU, 1961).
[9] Beyens, *Quatre ans à Rome*, p. 169.

Under such conditions it is understandable that the years that followed the March on Rome should have been the finest that Mussolini experienced.

He was alone in Rome. He had left Rachele and the children in Milan. He concerned himself, however, with regularizing his family situation: during the summer of 1923 he had his three children —Vittorio, Bruno, and Edda—baptized at home, but this belated concession to the exigencies of his position was obviously purely *pro forma*. In actuality he continued to live as if he were not married.

His apartment was on the second floor of Palazzo Tittoni, looking out on the narrow, quiet via Rasella. The owner of the building, Baron Fassini, often sent up a frugal meal to his tenant; Mussolini, whose stomach trouble was chronic, ate it in solitude, served by a dynamic and authoritarian woman of fifty, Cesira Carroci. She had formerly worked in the Grand Hotel and had been hired for Mussolini by Signora Sarfatti. "She wants to make a lord of me," Mussolini said.

Mussolini's home was really a gloomy bachelor apartment crammed with gifts, amulets, a *prie-Dieu*, three violins, and a player-piano. There he received his mistresses. Sometimes he took them savagely on the red carpet, with the haste of one who seeks his pleasure rather in conquest than in possession or in the symphony of sensations. One evening he summoned one of his mistresses, who arrived in haste and found him ready to go out, wearing evening clothes with all his decorations. "I look handsome, don't I?" he said. And he made love to her as he was, out of vanity.

When he went out, he used a red sports car that he drove fast and recklessly, and in these simple satisfactions that he allowed himself one could already discern the man drunk on his own success, amazed to have made his dream an even larger reality than all his imaginings, astonished at being the equal of the greatest. The feeling of being the incarnation of destiny, already quite intense in him, became a firm conviction, shored up by the opinions of the most varied notables and by the newspaper campaigns—and those not only in Italy. In such a climate, such a man, with his past and his aspirations to totalitarian power, could no longer tolerate opposition and opponents.

He himself examined the subscription lists of anti-Fascist publications, circled the names in red pencil, and sent them to the various Fascist federations with a curt note: "Are there still Fascists in your province?" Thus he expressed not only his violence and his spirit of revenge but also his narrowness of mind and the

fact that he conceived politics, Fascism, and the state to be his personal property. He insisted that "life should be made impossible"
for certain of his enemies. In connection with Gobetti he wrote to
the prefect of Turin: "I beg you to keep me informed and to see to
it that life is made difficult for this stupid antagonist of the government and of Fascism."

Such an attitude, certainly characterological but important in
its political manifestations, could only illustrate the thought that
he himself voiced: "Any attempt to separate Mussolini from Fascism or Fascism from Mussolini is the most futile, the most absurd,
the most ridiculous effort that could be imagined."

And yet even within Fascism there were some—Alfredo Misuri
and Massimo Rocca—who strove to preach "normalization," a return to strict legality. Later they would be expelled from the party
and beaten. Outside the party, however, it was still assumed that
Mussolini was ready to "constitutionalize" his rule.

On January 25, 1924, the Chamber was dissolved, elections—
under the new system of the majoritarian electoral law—were set
for April 6 and the first session of the new legislature was scheduled for May 24, the anniversary of the declaration of war. Two
days after the Chamber had been dissolved, the Italian Popular
Party issued a statement summing up the situation: "The new electoral system . . . puts the independent parties into a situation of
complete inferiority . . . the expression of the popular will is made
a mockery."

It was all the more so because, in their eagerness to enter Fascism, to draw it to their own side, but also to be elected, many
Italian politicians inscribed their names on the *listone*, or big list,
the immense election ticket organized by the Fascists. For Mussolini had appealed to the most varied personalities: to men, not to
parties, he insisted. He had even offered thirty places, in vain, to
Giolitti's followers. Orlando, Salandra, former members of the Popular Party, men from the universities and the arts . . . altogether
some hundred allies were commingled with Fascism's own candidates.

The other parties joined the battle in scattered array. Now the
majoritarian electoral system made this a guaranty of defeat.
Giolitti had haughtily drawn up his own ticket, as had the Popular
Party, the Socialists, and the Communists: the Communists had
suggested the formation of a bloc with the Socialists, but Matteotti
had retorted sharply: "We are fighting Fascism for freedom: we
cannot fight Fascism in the name of another dictatorship." Besides, the Fascists had made it very clear that, though they toler-

ated opponents who were divided, they would not accept a single opposition front without violence.

Outbreaks of violence continued in any event, and it would be impossible to list them all. Mussolini set the tone on January 28. At nine o'clock that evening the Fascists held their first meeting in Piazza Venezia. It was the first official manifestation of everything that was to become part of a rite: the high officials massed in the outstretched-arm salute, the cries of *"Eîa, eîa, alalà"* and "Duce! Duce!" Carried away by the crowd of the faithful, Mussolini did not mince words: "Let it be noted once and for all: whoever touches the Militia will be shot." He concluded: "As far as we are concerned, when it is a question of the fatherland, when it is a question of Fascism, we are prepared to kill and to die."

Prepared to kill? Mussolini was not lying. Antonio Piccinini, a Socialist candidate from Reggio Emilia, was killed by three bullets in the back; journalists were beaten and cities were placed in a state of siege; Turati and Amendola were prevented from holding meetings; Matteotti was kidnapped and left in an open field; newspaper offices were destroyed, candidates were prevented from filing their papers; others could not get ballots printed; Nitti's house in via Farnese in Rome was looted and its contents were sold at auction. Sforza related that, in the little village where he was staying, the first fifteen persons who voted against the *listone* were savagely beaten while the carabinieri ran off into the woods so that they could not see what was going on. It was in the countryside, furthermore, that the vote frauds were the worst; ten or twenty Fascists voted several times each in election premises guarded by the Volunteer Militia. In the Mezzogiorno Fascism had surrounded itself with all the traditional authorities: it was not so much the Fascist Party as the government party, and it made use of the local notables—including Orlando—who took part in political life. Undoubtedly the Fascist success was to be explained in large part by the rôle played in the *listone* by these "liberals." For there was success: three hundred seventy-five government deputies, two hundred seventy-five of them Fascists, were elected, and the *listone* received sixty-five percent of the votes. The Popular Party elected thirty-nine deputies, the Socialists twenty-four, the Communists nineteen. Amendola and Giolitti were elected; Nitti and Facta were not candidates.

Impressive as it was in terms of seats gained, the Fascist victory should be seen without illusions: while there were 4,305,936 votes for the *listone*, its opponents as a whole received almost three million in spite of the brutalities and the money of the government party. Don Sturzo pointed out that more than one million dollars was spent by Confindustria, which had established a scale of "voluntary contributions" for all its member firms. It would be erroneous, however, to attribute the success of the *listone* to the violence alone. Actually, in spite of the brutality of the squadre, in spite of his own speeches, much hope was still invested in Mussolini; it was thought that the majority that the nation had just given him would be used for the best interests of Italy. On April 10, ten days after the election, Mussolini himself said from the balcony of Palazzo Chigi: "We want to give the Italian people five years of peace and fruitful labor. Let all factions, even our own, perish, but may our nation be great, may it be respected, may it be strong!"

The reception was enthusiastic. There were even those who thought that Mussolini was preparing to dissolve the Fascist Party!

On May 5, however, Mussolini asked a crowd in Palermo: "If it is necessary to clear away everything that has no further reason for being, are you ready to march?" The crowd, naturally, howled back: "Yes!" Mussolini went on: "Rome is ours by right of revolution, and it cannot be taken from us without a bitter battle."

His verbal ambiguities persisted. But once again there could be no doubt as to the real choice: in the provinces the Catholics were assaulted and their last cooperatives were destroyed; one by one the Socialist newspapers were suppressed. And yet there were men who still preferred to hope: Fascism was now—and thanks to them—the majority party in Parliament; henceforth, they said again and again, it could only become "parliamentary."

8

The Risk of Total Loss:
The Matteotti Affair
(May, 1924—January 3, 1925)

"Only one of my enemies could commit this crime that fills us with horror and stirs us to cries of anger."—IL DUCE to the Chamber (June 13, 1924)

THE ATMOSPHERE IN MONTECITORIO was stormy on May 30, 1924. Black-shirted Militiamen, flaunting their weapons, circulated among the galleries and the corridors. The benches were occupied by the compact mass of the Fascist deputies, whose whole bearing showed an "exceptional nervousness" (Sturzo) and the arrogance of the victors. Six days earlier, when the Chamber opened, the King had paid homage in his speech from the throne to "the generation of victory that leads the government and constitutes the great majority of the assembly." He had extolled the "Fascist Militia that complements the armed forces"—that Militia that took no oath of allegiance to him. But on this May 30 the majority was angry and outraged. The president of the Chamber, Alfredo Rocco, an outstanding nationalist, had just announced: "A resolution has been offered by the deputies Labriola and Matteotti. . . ."

The resolution was a pure and simple demand for the invalidation of the elections and therefore for the mass expulsion of the Fascist deputies. With a gesture the president of the Chamber stilled the clamor and granted Matteotti's request to speak.

A slender man of average height, Matteotti strode with a firm step to the speaker's well. His regular features beneath the high forehead showed the inner serenity of a man who lives his life in accordance with his principles. His eyes were deeply sunk in their sockets; there were hollows in the cheeks and at the temples, as if this man of thirty-nine were being eroded by an illness or a passion. And it was indeed a passion that was at work in him. In spite of his properties in Rovigo, Giacomo Matteotti had dedicated himself to Socialism. This "millionnaire," as Mussolini called him, had been convicted of defeatism in 1916; vindicated on appeal, he had served throughout the war as a private soldier. After the war he was the inspiration of the peasant leagues of Rovigo; he was elected a deputy in 1919, 1921, and 1924. Secretary of the PSU, he was a man of facts, restricting himself to bare truths, excluding all flights of rhetoric from his speeches as a matter of modesty and principle. In a book entitled *One Year of Fascist Domination* he had collected all the episodes best fitted to portraying the violence of the system, with the long forgotten pro-anarchist articles written by Mussolini in his youth, quoting them with precise references, and, in each instance, setting Il Duce against his own past. Now, heedless of interruptions, Giacomo Matteotti began to speak.

"No one has been free," he said, "because every citizen knew *a priori* that, even had he dared with majority support to express his opposition, the government had a force at its disposal that would have nullified his words. . . ."

Farinacci rose from his bench. "All you had to do was make a revolution," he shouted.

Matteotti: "There is an armed Militia. . . ."

A voice from the right: "What about the Red Guards?"

Matteotti resumed speaking. Standing calmly, he waited for each storm of interruption to pass; he catalogued all the irregularities of the election and he rapped out sharp answers to the Fascists.

Farinacci: "It will come to pass that we will really do what we have not done. . . ."

Matteotti: "You will ply your trade. . . ."

President Rocco: "If the honorable deputy wishes to speak, he may continue, but with prudence."

Matteotti: "I am not asking to speak prudently or imprudently, but parliamentarily."

Before the speech was concluded, tempers had risen so high that some of the Fascists were shaking their fists and others were walking out of the Chamber.

Deputy Giacomo Suardo: "On its knees my city hailed Il Duce, Mussolini. I challenge the honorable deputy Matteotti to prove his charges. My dignity as a soldier compels me to leave this Chamber."

Deputy Attilio Teruzzi: "The honorable Deputy Suardo wears the gold medal. Shame, Deputy Matteotti!"

Matteotti: "I can cite details and facts."

Various voices: "We'll teach you respect with a shot in the back. . . . Go to Russia."

Matteotti: "We are defending the sovereign freedom of the Italian people . . . by demanding the nullification of the elections."

Throughout the two hours of Matteotti's speech—which, without the interruptions, could have been delivered in thirty minutes—Mussolini had sat motionless in his place. Leaving Montecitorio, Matteotti said to his friends: "Now you can start drafting my funeral oration."

On June 1 *il Popolo* headlined: MAJORITY SHOWS EXAGGERATED TOLERANCE TOWARD MATTEOTTI'S SPEECH. Three days later Matteotti repeated his offense. This time he assailed Mussolini directly; with the record in his hand, he showed that in *il Popolo* Mussolini had formerly approved the amnesty granted to deserters. This cut Mussolini deeply, and on June 6 he interrupted a Communist speaker to show that he was morally prepared to go very far indeed. "In Russia," he said, the words coming out like bullets, "there are excellent teachers, and we are wrong in not following them completely, because by this time you would not be here but in a cell. You would have gotten some lead in your back. . . ."

The Fascist deputies applauded heartily. "But we have the courage for that," Mussolini went on, "and we will prove it to you. There is still time, and that will happen sooner than you think."

On June 7, by three hundred sixty-one votes to one hundred seven, "the Chamber expressed its full confidence in the government." Mussolini had won handsomely, but he was not the man to forget Matteotti. Moreover, the press reported that Matteotti intended to question the government on the matter of the financial speculations with which Fascist circles were involved.

June 10, 1924. An afternoon session in Montecitorio. Matteotti was not present. No one in the Chamber was concerned. But the news of his absence struck terror into his family. He had left his house early in the afternoon to walk to the Chamber.

June 11. In the morning Mussolini's private secretary, Fasciolo, brought him news of a very serious incident: the assassination of Giacomo Matteotti.

On the previous day, when Matteotti was walking from via Pisanelli, 40, to Montecitorio, the policeman who usually tailed him and guarded him did not follow him. Coincidence Number One. It was a hot day, and the quay along the Tiber was deserted. A car was parked at Lungotevere Arnaldo da Brescia—a Lancia with the license plate 55-12169. As Matteotti came abreast of it, its passengers sprang out and leaped on him. He fought them off, tried to flee, was pursued, was struck, was dragged into the car. It started quickly. Matteotti broke one of its windows with a kick; he was immediately stabbed. His blood poured down in the car. It drove aimlessly through the countryside until nightfall; then, at Quartarella, about fourteen miles from Rome, the killers hastily made a shallow ditch with a hammer and the jack from the car and trampled the body down into it.

Later that night Fasciolo met the killers at the Caffè Picarozzi: they included Amerigo Dumini; a squadrista hero, Alvino Volpi, and a Pole named Thierschwald, who had been released from prison for secret operations of this character. Still later that night Fasciolo went to the office of *il Corriere italiano*, whose editor, Filippo Filipelli, a friend of Mussolini, had provided the car. Filipelli listened to the whole story, fainted, and then informed General De Bono, the Quadrumvir, who was now chief of police and who assured him that everything would be arranged. Indeed, the gang that had done the job was well known to him. Its members lived in the Hotel Dragoni and worked under Dumini's direction (it was responsible for at least twelve political murders).

On the morning of June 11 the leading Fascist groups had their story about Matteotti's disappearance ready. Listening to Fasciolo's account, Mussolini had been angered by the fact that no one had thought to change the car's license plates. "Good God," he shouted, "all they had to do was piss on them!"

Later that day, opposition circles grew apprehensive at what might have happened to Matteotti.

1 P.M., *June 12*. Informed by a concierge who had written down the car's number, the police picked up Filipelli. This was the first link in the chain that made it possible step by step to identify those who were guilty of the crime. Amerigo Dumini was arrested at the station just as he was preparing to flee.

7:30 P.M., *June 12*. Mussolini—who, as we have seen, was completely informed—took the speaker's well in the Chamber. "I believe," he said, "that the Chamber is concerned with what has happened to Deputy Matteotti, who disappeared suddenly on Tuesday afternoon in circumstances of time and place that are not yet altogether definite but that can support the hypothesis of a crime that, if it has indeed been committed, can only arouse the indignation and the grief of the government and Parliament."

June 13. It was no longer possible to conceal the fact of the murder; as the news spread, it dismayed and enraged the great masses. Matteotti dead was a greater danger than Matteotti alive. His cold-blooded murder in broad daylight and the connections that it laid bare between Mussolini himself and the actual executants present a brutal epitome of all the Fascist crimes. For a few days Mussolini and his followers were cut off and disarmed, at the mercy of any sudden onslaught. For a few months they were to remain weakened. Forever they would be stained with Matteotti's blood.

This June 13 was a day of prime importance. In the morning the opposition groups decided to withdraw from the Chamber "and to reserve the right to observe what action the government would take." This position, this withdrawal from Parliament, was called the Aventine, for it was reminiscent of the decision of the Roman *plebs* meeting outside the city on the Aventine Hill.

On the same day the Fascist deputies voted to suspend the Chamber's labors after an address by Mussolini. Only his majority was present when he delivered his speech in a low, solemn voice. "If there is anyone in this room," he began, "who more than all the rest has the right to be moved and angered, it is I. Only one of my enemies . . . could commit this crime that fills us with horror and stirs us to cries of anger."

Mussolini was pale; at times there was even a tremor in his voice; several deputies had the impression that he was frightened. But he regained his self-control and his voice grew firmer as he proclaimed his unshakable intention of retaining power regardless of the cost: "If anyone is thinking of initiating some gamble of a political nature with the aim of besieging the government, let him be clearly put on notice that the government will defend itself at all costs, that it has an immeasurably clear conscience and will adopt the necessary means. . . ."

This was the inception of a political battle whose stake was the fate of Fascism. But would the Aventine deputies be worthy of Matteotti? Public opinion was unquestionably on their side and those deputies who had raged against "the submissive masses" had lost the foundation of their argument.

Within two or three days a desert spread round Mussolini. First of all, he had abandoned those of his followers who were too compromised. Filipelli was arrested when he tried to flee from Genoa aboard a motorboat; Volpi also was arrested. All that were left were a journalist and two squadristi, Dumini having already been jailed. But then Finzi, Under-Secretary of State to the Ministry of the Interior, resigned; General De Bono was replaced as chief of police; a fugitive warrant was issued for Cesare Rossi, the head of Premier Mussolini's public-relations staff. Rossi was arrested on June 22. Meanwhile Giovanni Marinelli, the Fascist Party's secretary, had also been imprisoned.

Mussolini had jettisoned his ballast. But this was not enough. He was brought under direct accusation; it was said that he had set up a "*Cheka,*" a secret political police that, on his instructions, gave "lessons" to his opponents. Had he issued orders that Matteotti be murdered, or merely frightened into silence? Or had his henchmen made their own interpretation of his thinking and his statements?

Of course he took great care not to be directly implicated in the murder; but he had ordered action taken against Gobetti and against dissident Fascists like Alfredo Misuri and Cesare Forni. In any case his moral responsibility was total, and his direct responsibility, though it could not be proved, was probable. It was reported that after Matteotti's speech Mussolini had said to Rossi and Marinelli: "What kind of party do I have, then, if it leaves the enemy's hands free to such an extent? What are the squadristi doing?"

What more was needed to set the killers to work? After the murder Mussolini said with a contemptuous smile to Rossi: "Now let them go look in the sewers."

In any event, during the days from June 12 to 16 he was crippled. According to his intimates there were times when he bit his nails and spent long solitary hours in the Hall of Victory. There were other times when his colleagues found him, staring and banging his head against the back of the chair in which he sat. For his waiting-room was empty; he was well aware that thoughout Italy, in offices, in schools, in villages, the Fascists were ripping down their emblems and repeating: "We didn't know." And often this was the truth. It was only after the murder of Matteotti that a large part of the press campaigned against Mussolini as it had never done before: and so, side by side with *Avanti!* and the Communist *l'Unità* (founded on February 12, 1924), there stood *il Corriere della Sera* and *la Stampa*. The press published accounts of what had happened in Turin and had been suppressed in December, and editorial comment was angry. It was supported by public opinion.

As the Roman police watched, the opposition deputies were spontaneously acclaimed in Piazza Colonna and the crowd called for "*luce e giustizia* (light and justice)." The Fascist Militia did not obey its mobilization orders; the Fascist deputies themselves were ready to call on Mussolini to resign. And yet, once the first days of bewilderment were over, Mussolini was to be the victor. Why?

Power, first of all, meant more to Mussolini than anything else, more even than his fear; for his fall might mean going on trial for his life. On June 14 he said, as he was often to repeat: "There are attempts to strike, to fight Fascism and the government. This cannot be tolerated, and the government will know how to cope with it."

He knew too that he could rely on the more determined element in the Militia. In the event of the overthrow of Fascism, he need not fear that he would stand alone in the dock. On June 22, in Cremona, Farinacci announced "the second Fascist wave" and the party's press spoke of "the firing squads that we made the mistake of not assigning to every public square in Italy in October, 1922."

Leandro Arpinati, the Bolognese Fascist, went to Rome with a number of squadristi in mid-July in order to encourage Mussolini. Palazzo Chigi was empty. Wan and defeated, Mussolini sat alone in his office. "My position is untenable," he told Arpinati; "it is impossible to remain in power with a dead man at one's feet." Arpinati urged him to defend himself: "Punish the man who committed that idiotic murder and then forget about it."

That evening the Bolognese squadristi mingled with the silent crowd that was waiting to see Mussolini leave. They cheered, but they were the only persons who did so, and they were soon isolated in a hostile curiosity.

During those months of June and July the decisive support could not yet appear from the squadre, even disguised as they were in the Volunteer Militia. The most valuable help that Mussolini got came first from the King. Returning from Spain on the evening of June 16, Vittorio Emanuele took no steps, posed no questions to Mussolini. In fact, he advised the Premier to give up the Ministry of the Interior to Luigi Federzoni, the former nationalist; this, the King said, would be a reassuring move. Fortified by the King's backing, Mussolini confronted the Senate on June 24. He reminded this conservative body of "the Socialist outrages" and proclaimed his resolve of national pacification. Albertini and Sforza rose to speak against the government. That same morning a number of men had gone to Sforza's house and told his wife: "If you do not wish to be a widow this evening, advise your husband not to speak."

Countess Sforza had not even mentioned the matter to her husband. In the Senate he made a forceful speech. Turning toward Mussolini, he declared: "You have the choice: either you are guilty as no man has ever been or you are incompetent as no man has ever been."

But the Senators sided with the liberal philosopher, Benedetto Croce, who—though he was later to be one of the firmest opponents of Fascism—concluded his address by saying: "We must allow time for Fascism to complete its process of change; our vote will be prudent and patriotic."

The Senate voted its confidence in the government by two hundred twenty-five to twenty-one; there were six abstentions. Once more the élites, in the blindness of their conservatism and their illusions, left Mussolini a free hand.

This vote gave Vittorio Emanuele his excuse: he was only a modest constitutional monarch, he said; he followed the opinion of the majorities in the two Houses of Parliament, and what could he do when they voted in favor of the chief of the government? In fact Vittorio Emanuele III did not wish to dismiss Mussolini under any conditions. He regarded Il Duce as the best defender of the crown. When Amendola and then Bonomi presented the King with the memorandum that had been prepared by Mussolini's former collaborator, Cesare Rossi, and that contained serious charges against the Premier, the King leafed through it and then said: "May I ask you a favor? Don't make me read it; take it back." And to Sforza he said: "I cannot judge, I am not qualified." Then, when the organized war veterans sent a deputation to him to read their resolution against Fascism, His Majesty turned pale and murmured: "My daughter shot two quail this morning."

This attitude on the part of the King, reflecting the choice made by court and army circles, was all the more serious because the opposition assembled in the Aventine was still looking to the sovereign for all its support. The Aventine leaders were thus standing firm on constitutional ground, and in all the great tides of opinion that shook Italy while Fascism was in the grip of disorder they made no suggestions.

Some unknown hand had drawn a black cross on the spot from which Matteotti had been abducted, and every day fresh flowers were laid there. The deputies had knelt there in tribute on June 27, and, at Turati's apostrophe to Matteotti, "young, strong, armed with all the forces of civilization, unsparing in his courage, and volunteering for death," the streets that led to the Tiber were packed with a crowd that was waiting for a word of command that was never spoken. Sforza was one of the few men who insisted that force must be used, Palazzo Chigi must be invaded, and Mussolini must be arrested. But legal procedures prevailed: the nation should have confidence in the King and the government. Thus the accomplishments of the Aventine were reduced to a courageous enterprise of journalistic denunciation carried out in the parliamentary and moral arenas.

In fact the Aventine was powerless for reasons that went deeper than its choice of means. The Popular Party, for example, in spite of the action of men like Giuseppe Donati, the journalist, continued to be swayed by the warnings of the church. *L'Osservatore romano* worried lest, if Fascism fell, there be a "fatal leap into the dark"; the conservative liberals worried over the constant possibility of a Socialist resurgence—had not Italy in 1919 escaped revolution through Fascism? Even if this argument was not founded on fact, it made for reflection. Besides, the Communists had just appealed to the Socialist Parties and the CGL: "We propose the proclamation of a national strike in order to clear the political stage of the specter of Fascism. Proletarian greetings."

Gramsci further stiffened the reservations of the members of the Aventine when he wrote: "The revolutionary proletariat has no reason to place its confidence in middle-class groups to carry on the struggle against Fascism. . . . Hence this is not the time to join hands and deliberately shut off possible revolutionary protractions of the crisis."

Thus the Aventine was undermined by its own contradictions. For the members of the opposition, genuine democrats who had not understood that Fascism represented a radically new element in political life, there was no choice but to await the constitutional monarch's pleasure and to continue making broad-minded statements. Therefore, and as much in order to avoid frightening the King as out of fear of revolution, they rejected the call for a general strike and the proclamation of the Aventine as the sole legal Parliament of the country. Thereupon the anti-Fascist tide receded. As early as June 24, Turati wrote of the members of the opposition: "All of them have the feeling of the little parliamentary environment, but none of them has the feeling of the country, of the entire civilized world, of the history of tomorrow, which calls on us us not to be inferior, not to be clever."

Again on July 13, and his lucid inner anguish was implicit, he noted: "We feel that it is essential to do something, but we cannot decide on anything positive. We feel that with the passage of time the enemy is catching his breath and that without doubt the Matteotti affair has now been drained of its possibilities."

Essentially this was true. It was true too that all through Italy anti-Fascist war veterans' organizations had come into being, such as those of *Italia libera* (Free Italy), and that for the first time anti-Fascists of every tendency had come together at the level of a neighborhood, a street, even an apartment building, and that these were seeds for the future. But Turati was not deceived: after July, 1924, the last-chance battle against Fascism had been lost.

July 10, 1924. A decree-law on the press made virtually any newspaper subject to seizure on the government's decision.

August 1. The Fascist Militia swore an oath to the King, but remained under Mussolini's personal orders. This was a purely formal gesture toward Vittorio Emanuele III, changing nothing in the character of the Volunteer Militia, but, on the contrary, emphasizing the "legal" and constitutional character of Fascism. "This is a tremendous step forward toward the Fascistization of the state," *il Popolo d'Italia* declared.

August 16. The government now felt secure enough to allow Matteotti's corpse to be discovered accidentally by a carabiniere officer on vacation. The body was nude and decapitated. Again feeling rose high throughout the country. In spite of the restrictions imposed by the government, the funeral was deeply moving and the crowd in the village of Fratta Polesine was impressive. Covered with flowers and carried by the dead man's comrades, surrounded by carabinieri, the coffin seemed as if supported by the entire throng, so closely did the mourners press about the simple black wooden box.

August 31. "The day when our enemies give up their boring jabber for concrete action," Mussolini roared, "will be the day when we make them the dungheap of Fascist camps."

During that same month Fascists had been arriving in Rome from the provinces in the old trucks of 1922, armed as they had been at the time of the March on Rome, under Arconovaldo Bonaccorsi of Bologna and Tullio Tamburini of Tuscany. They paraded through the streets of the capital to the roll of drums and the blare of trumpets to show the Romans and Mussolini the resoluteness of provincial Fascism. Farinacci led the operation from his citadel in Cremona. His newspaper headlined VIVA DUMINI and pointed out that "all that is needed to resolve the Italian problem is a few thousand deaths."

In Milan a Socialist worker called Oldani was murdered and the killers were acquitted because Oldani had had "an abnormally thin skull." Malaparte extolled the "Fascist savages" in his poem that began "*O Italiani ammazzavivi*" . . .

> Italians, killers of the living,
> Heroic times are here again. . . .
> The evil times have passed away,

Now the traitors have to pay,
Peace to the dead, war on the live. . . .

September 6. Vittorio Emanuele III received Mussolini, who showed a certain uneasiness over the activities of the opposition. The King drew him into the bay of a window. "You attach too much importance to those obsolete debaters," the King said. "Carry on with your work. You are a blunt man."

Now Mussolini had won the game. On September 12 a workman killed Armando Casalini, a Fascist deputy, in a Roman street-car. Thereafter any violence could be justified. An anti-Fascist bar owner in Rome was bayoneted to death as his customers watched; there was a wave of murders, beatings, banishments.

November 4. Victory Day. All through the country there were innumerable clashes between the war veterans of *Italia libera* and the Fascists.

November 11. "Either smash all opposition or smash Fascism," Farinacci wrote.

November 12. The Chamber of Deputies began its session. This was to be the last battle by the opposition. In the Senate the Catholic journalist, Giuseppe Donati, accused General De Bono of complicity in the murder of Matteotti and demanded that he be tried by the Senate.

December 27. Il Mondo, owned by the deputy, Amendola, published long extracts from Rossi's memorandum on the Matteotti case. It was too late. Rossi said in his memorandum: "Everything that has been done has always been done on the direct wish or with the complicity of Il Duce." The liberals of the Aventine thought that this indictment would be read by at least *one* person, the King. They hoped to bring about a Cabinet crisis and the dismissal of Mussolini. It was now December, seven months after the murder of Matteotti, and the Aventine moderates had not yet learned that on the parliamentary battleground Mussolini was bound to win because the King was determined to uphold him and a comfortable Fascist majority in the Chamber supported him. Furthermore, the battle was already lost because disillusion had swept the Italian masses once roused by hope and rebellion. In addition, the Fascists everywhere were arming themselves and reinforcing the Militia.

December 31. Luigi Federzoni, Minister of the Interior, ordered the seizure of all opposition newspapers and searches in the residences of all anti-Fascist leaders.

On the same day thirty-three consuls of the Militia marched into Mussolini's office without having been announced. They were under the command of a Tuscan squadrista, A. Tarabella. Was this a visit on impulse or had it been planned in order to create the appearance that Fascism was exerting pressure on Mussolini on the threshold of grave events? Whatever the answer, one of the squadristi, Francesco Giunta, supposedly tossed his dagger on Il Duce's desk and said: "If you want to go under, all right; we don't." Tarabella added: "Either we all go to jail, you included, or we all stay out."

Still on December 31, Farinacci's newspaper headlined across six columns: NEW YEAR'S RESOLUTION: A CLUB WITHIN REACH.

January 3, 1925. Mussolini was scheduled to speak in Montecitorio. In the morning Paolo Orano visited him and tried to learn what turn the speech would take. "I'm going to put my balls on the table," Mussolini replied. That afternoon, when Mussolini rose to speak, there were only twenty-eight opponents in the Chamber.

"The speech that I am going to make," he began in a low voice, "may not be classifiable, perhaps, as a parliamentary speech." Then he attacked. "I tell you here, in the presence of this assemblage and before the whole Italian people, that I alone assume the moral and historical responsibility for everything that has occurred."

"And all of us with you!" the Fascist deputies shouted amid the handclaps.

"If Fascism has been only a business of castor oil and beatings," Mussolini resumed, silencing the deputies' cries of protest with a gesture, "and not, in contrast, the superb passion of the élite and the youth of Italy, the fault is mine. If Fascism has been a band of malefactors, I am the leader of that band."

Equivocation was at an end: henceforth Mussolini could dispense with it, for he had won the battle. He waited for the frenetic cheers to subside and continued: "This Aventine sedition has borne consequences . . . a revival of Communism all along the line; but Fascism, at once a party and the government, is at the height of its power, and so the moment comes to say *enough*, to turn for a solution to force. Gentlemen of the Aventine, you have deluded yourselves."

When the Chamber rose, three "liberal" ministers resigned and, it was reported, the King criticized the speech for its lack of constitutional spirit. That was all.

"You may be sure," Mussolini concluded, "that within the next forty-eight hours everything will be clarified."

More than two years had elapsed since the March on Rome.

9

All Power to Fascism
(1925–1926)

"The day of the little Italians who had a thousand opinions and none is over."—IL DUCE (June 22, 1925)

"WITHIN FORTY-EIGHT HOURS everything will be clarified," Mussolini had said. In fact everything had been clarified since December 30. The police had made hundreds of arrests and carried out searches, and in Florence, for example, the province's squadristi, armed with machine guns, manganelli, rifles, had leaped from their trucks crying: "Mussolini the Dictator! . . . Let's finish off the enemy. . . . Duce, untie our hands."

On January 3 it was all done. The Militia was officially mobilized. Federzoni ordered the seizures of newspapers and the arrests of "subversives." As the deputies of the Aventine wrote on January 8, 1925, "the mask of constitutionalism and normalization has been dropped."

And Mussolini, having now chosen open dictatorship, wrote in *Gerarchia*: "Fascism is not able, does not know how, and, I add, ought not to become parliamentary. Better the legions than the electoral colleges!"

To emphasize the choice, Fascism's strong-arm man, Roberto Farinacci, was appointed secretary of the party on February 12. This former railway clerk turned leader of the squadre of Cremona had in a few months become a lawyer. His doctoral thesis was a perfect copy of one already published in Turin, but then who in the climate of 1925 would have dared to challenge the qualifications of

Counselor Farinacci? A man of heavy, common features, he was only thirty-two years old, and he was ambitious.

Now it was in 1925 that Mussolini suffered his first serious attack of gastric ulcer. For almost two months he was compelled to curtail his activities. Rachele wanted to join him in Rome, but this was prevented by the party hierarchy, lest public opinion be alarmed. It was Cesira, the servant, who tended Mussolini, spending thirteen days at his bedside without rest. During this illness Farinacci sought in his own interests to raise the question of the succession to Mussolini. But he found himself opposed by Federzoni, the Minister of the Interior, who represented the conservative and nationalist clan that had rallied to Fascism. Farinacci symbolized the thousands of squadristi and adventurers who were indispensable in difficult moments but who were also elements of disorder. Federzoni, in contrast, represented the hierarchical structure of a society that accepted Mussolini and provided him not only with ruffians but also with a social order, an ideology, and laws. It did Farinacci no good to complain to Mussolini that, although Federzoni was never mentioned in the graffiti of the public toilets, Party Secretary Farinacci was covered with insults; in the end he was doomed nevertheless.

But the time for that was not yet at hand. First the *"seconda ondata* (second wave)" of Fascism had to be used to sweep away all opposition until a legal apparatus of repression could be set up. And for this task Farinacci was the ideal man. If he became the target of everyone's hate, it would be easy to get rid of him later, and it would be advantageous as well; hence Mussolini had every reason to let the party secretary act freely. Farinacci threw himself body and soul into the politics of force: "Fascism should laugh at all agreements," he said; "Fascism in Cremona spits on democracy and liberalism. . . ."

In order to put an end to the rumors that he was on his deathbed, Mussolini made a speech from the balcony of Palazzo Chigi on March 23. "Black Shirts of the *Urbs!*" he bawled. "The spring is coming. . . . For you and for me it will be a total, integral surge of Fascist action always and everywhere, against anyone. Do you want that?"

Arms and voices rose in approbation: for Mussolini this was the equivalent of the voice of the people. He received the same endorsement in Parliament, where the Fascist majority had received its orders: in one day, January 14, more than two thousand decree-laws were ratified. But, in order to complete the image of national unanimity centered on Fascism, the intellectuals had to be rallied. Giovanni Gentile, the Hegelian philosopher, took over this task and on March 29, 1925, he convoked a "Congress of Fascist Intellectuals." Curzio Malaparte was one of two hundred fifty prominent persons in attendance, including the nationalist, Alfredo Rocco; Margherita Sarfatti, and the poet, Marinetti. Luigi Pirandello joined the congress. The most diverse themes were discussed, from "the theory of national syndicalism" to "the rejuvenation of choral singing in Italy." Farinacci sent a telegram to the congress: "You are demonstrating that in addition to faith and muscles Fascism has a brain."

All honor was paid to the totalitarian state and to Il Duce. On the "Roman Christmas," April 21, a *Manifesto of Fascist Intellectuals* was issued, affirming the "religious" character of Fascism, rewriting its idealized history, and linking it to Mazzini and the *Risorgimento*. It was a great success, but it did not last long.

Amendola called on Benedetto Croce to draft a *Counter-Manifesto*, which was published on May 1 and drew hundreds of signatures. It energetically attacked the "verbose Fascist *Manifesto*." Not all the intellectuals of Italy had bent the knee. But there were still the weapons of violence and arrest.

On June 22 a huge Fascist rally was held in the Augusteo in Rome. Mussolini was on the platform. "I am going to make an admission to you that will fill your souls with horror," he began sarcastically. "I have never read a single page of Benedetto Croce. . . ." There was a tide of laughter. What matter that Croce was one of Italy's greatest philosophers? "The day of the little Italians who had a thousand opinions and none is over," Il Duce continued. "To me violence is completely moral, more moral than compromise and bargaining."

The Fascists did not need this encouragement. Amendola, the leader of the Aventine, was driven out of Montecatini, where he was staying. In spite of the official protection of the prefect and an escort composed of two Militiamen, the Fascists, who for good reason knew in advance what roads the deputy would take when he obeyed their orders to leave the city, ambushed him and beat him: he died of the consequences of the attack on April 7, 1926, in Cannes. Sforza's house and later Croce's were looted and burned. Under these conditions the opposition was driven underground. The Communists organized and began publishing little newspapers. In Florence and Milan young liberal students, such as the Rosselli brothers, Nello and Carlo; Ferruccio Parri, Ricardo Bauer, Ernesto Rossi, joined by Professor Gaetano Salvemini, clandestinely issued little publications like *Non mollare* (*Do Not Flinch*) or *Il Caffè* (*The Café*), with such aphorisms as these: "The Italians boycotted the Austrians from 1848 to 1859. The Fascists are today's

Austrians: boycott them. . . . He is conquered who admits that he is conquered, but never he who still continues to fight."

These few and tiny groups poured out posters and graffiti, hanging huge portraits of Matteotti where they could not be torn down. Granted that these were only pinpricks, but the actions of these young men showed that anti-Fascism would not lay down its arms.

Angered by this clandestine opposition, the Fascists of Florence sought vengeance against the Freemasons. In a punitive expedition of October 3, 1925, Giovanni Luporini, a Fascist hierarch, was killed. Thereupon the reprisals began: the city was in the hands of the squadre, which roamed the empty streets. They invaded theaters and cinemas and drove the audiences out with their clubs; cars filled with Fascists were constantly racing away from their customary parking places outside Signora Saffo's brothel. The cars would stop at the houses of opposition leaders; the Fascists would storm their way in, destroying and murdering. The manhunt continued throughout the night, orchestrated by the sirens and bells of ambulances on their way to the hospitals. The violence spread to the entire province. On the afternoon of October 4 the secretary of the provincial Fascist federation issued an order: "In the name of our beloved Duce and of Deputy Farinacci, all reprisals should immediately terminate."

Everything had already been accomplished. Besides, if Il Duce was asking obedience, it was not so much in order to put an end to the violence as to bring the party under the rule of ". . . discipline . . . which should not be purely formal but typically religious: that is, absolute . . ." (*Gerarchia*, October, 1925).

His opponents clearly understood that, when he inveighed against "individual, private violence," it was in order to resort to the violence of the Militia, "the aristocracy of Fascism." Under these conditions, when in addition the field of legal activity was shrinking day by day, some of his adversaries could envisage only the smashing of Fascism by any possible means, including the assassination of Il Duce.

On November 4, 1925, Mussolini was to speak from the corner balcony of Palazzo Chigi. A police inspector repeatedly sent Navarra, Mussolini's combination butler and valet, out on the balcony as if to indicate that Il Duce himself would appear at any moment. The purpose was to trap Tito Zaniboni, the former Socialist deputy, *in flagrante delicto*: Navarra was the unknowing decoy. Zaniboni had indeed gotten hold of a rifle with a telescopic sight and he hoped to bring down Mussolini from a room in the Hotel Dragoni. Actually, thanks to a stool-pigeon appropriately named

Quaglia (quail), the police had been able to follow Zaniboni step by step in his ingenuous scheme. He was allowed to carry on in order that he might be seized on the hotel stairway just a few minutes before the speech. This would put the government in a position to make the best use of the attempt. A tremendous crowd was waiting in Piazza Colonna to hail Mussolini.

"People of Rome . . . your souls are in your voices," he shouted from the balcony. "I insist that there be no needless disorder."

The government took it upon itself to act. On November 26 it issued a law regulating associations, limiting their activities, and supervising their members, especially if the latter were employed by the state.

December 24, 1925. State employes who could not furnish complete evidence of their political acceptability were made subject to dismissal. The Chief of Government—a new title, deemed to be more martial than Premier or President of the Council of Ministers—was granted broader powers: parliamentary initiation of legislation and votes of confidence were abolished.

December 31. A journalists' society was established, making it possible to get rid of opponents.

January 31, 1926. Loss of Italian citizenship was sanctioned for opponents of Fascism. The government was given the right to legislate as it chose.

On February 4 and September 6 municipal councils were eliminated; each municipality was to be governed by an appointed *podestà* (chief magistrate). On April 6 the powers of the prefects were enlarged.

Legally Italy was no longer a parliamentary state in which the citizens enjoyed the rights guaranteed by the old *Statuto piemontese* (Statute of Piedmont). In a few months a whole body of authoritarian law was established. It drew its inspiration from ultra-nationalist ideals, and it was significant that the laws called *fascistissime* (ultra-Fascist) were drafted by Alfredo Rocco, the nationalist. This professor of political economy at the University of Padua, whose nationalist passion had made him even before 1914 a fanatical lawyer dedicated to the totalitarian state, was the Fascist intellectual *par excellence*, undoubtedly the closest in spirit to the high Nazi officials. Mussolini was to provide the unequivocal label for the legislative code conceived by Rocco: "Everything within the state, nothing outside the state, nothing against the state."

It clearly proved that Italy had become a dictatorship *de jure* and *de facto*: the world's first Fascist state.

This state, however, always enjoyed important backing. For-

All Power to Fascism

getting the Holy Father's criticisms of violence, the Fascist press made much of the fact that on December 14, 1925, His Holiness, Pius XI, speaking before the Consistory at the close of the Holy Year, declared: "We are pleased to express before this august Assembly our grateful satisfaction, and that gratitude extends also to all that has been taking place for some time in favor of Religion and the church." The press was pleased too to emphasize that Pius XI had denounced "the criminal attempt, the mere thought of which still saddens us, as its discovery rejoices us and makes us give thanks to God."

The Fascists also pointed out that the Holy Father had refused to receive Matteotti's mother and widow. "The Pope grieves for them," Cardinal Gasparri explained to Baron Beyens, "but it would be impossible for him to lend himself to a maneuver that has perhaps been suggested by the Socialist Party with a view to setting the Holy Father against Fascism."[1]

Mussolini himself was cleverly intent on bringing his own affairs into harmony with the church. On December 29 his religious wedding was celebrated in a private ceremony, and he told Rachele: "I will never allow divorce to be introduced into Italy." Thus the church and Fascism embarked on an adroit strategy, each seeking to get the most from the other.

It was true that in 1926 Fascism was by and large accepted by the country, and the attitude of the church reflected that of the Italians. Certainly the ultra-Fascist laws—coming after the election reform—demonstrated that the government placed only relative confidence in the sentiments of the people, but that affords no ground for concluding that it was isolated.

In the beginning of 1926 Fascism was sternly structuring a country that submitted, that adjusted itself to the system in the belief that Mussolini genuinely sought greatness for Italy. When now and then Il Duce went out alone into the streets, he was at once surrounded by enthusiastic crowds. In Florence, in fact, in 1925, he actually had to flee. "Give me a drink," he gasped, "the crowd is a terrible mistress."

Held in check by the police, his opponents were hampered even more by the apathy of the great masses, and they began to go abroad: Piero Gobetti, Gaetano Salvemini, and Giuseppe Donati left in 1925. This was the beginning of the massive exodus that was to take thousands of *fuorusciti*—exiles—to France. But the isolated, hunted opposition pulled itself together and reflected. The third congress of the Italian Communist Party was held in Lyon. The

[1] Beyens, *Quatre ans à Rome*, p. 235.

statements of principle drafted by Gramsci defined Fascism as certainly a specifically Italian phenomenon but one linked to the capitalist system: Fascism, he argued, was the reaction of the ruling class to the age of imperialism under the peculiarly weak conditions of Italian capitalism. These arguments carried little weight in 1926. The Communist Party had barely twenty thousand members and its militants were under surveillance. Much more than the party, the last strongholds of the workers were the labor unions, and in most of the northern factories in 1924–25 the elected delegates belonged to the CGL (in twenty-four factories the Fascists received only six hundred five votes to 8,887 for the CGL). Of the eighteen thousand workers at FIAT, not one voted for Mussolini's partisans!

Hence Il Duce wanted to smash the unions. Fascist corporativism was embodied in a law of April 3, 1926, known as the Law on Corporations, the author of which, again, was Alfredo Rocco. Speaking in the Senate, Mussolini himself described this "educative syndicalism" that "recognizes the historic function of capital and capitalists . . . those men who are great organizers . . . on whom the fate and the pay, the welfare of tens of thousands of workers depend. What can these men ask? The success of their industries. Their success is that of the Nation." To the applause of the Senators, Mussolini concluded: "Fascist syndicalism stands for class collaboration . . . capital and labor are not two contradictory terms, they are terms that complement each other." Soberly he added: "A single hour—only one, I tell you—lost from work in a factory is already a grave injury of a national character."

Nationalism, set thus in opposition to the strike, and the exaltation of the fatherland were always the most constant elements of Fascism. This was dramatically shown in foreign policy.

Mussolini was coldly received at the Locarno Conference in October, 1925. Emile Vandervelde, the Belgian Socialist, refused to shake hands with him; the journalists avoided him. Mussolini made an effort to convince Aristide Briand, the French Foreign Minister, of his good faith and his concern with legality, but the old statesman, with an allusion to the murder of Matteotti, replied coldly: "It is difficult to cross the Rubicon twice, especially if it is running with blood."

Hence 1925 ended in an outburst of anti-French violence. "Italy does not tolerate insults," Farinacci screamed. In the Chamber of Deputies Mussolini issued his own warning on November 18: "In some of these countries there are individuals and political groups that have the absurd notion of erecting a kind of barbed-wire

All Power to Fascism

fence round Fascist Italy on a moral basis. . . . They must recognize that tomorrow two million young men will march at my order."

Two months later, in January, 1926, Salvatore Contarini, the former collaborator of Sforza, resigned as secretary general of the Foreign Ministry. He was replaced by the former squadrista, Dino Grandi. Mussolini exclaimed: "May it be granted to us to establish the unshakable foundations of this century that I have named, and that shall be, the century of Italian power."

Such eruptions, already significant, clearly marked the dangerous course that was being taken by Fascism's foreign policy. Gramsci was led to predict that Italy would throw herself into "a war that in appearance will be waged for the expansion of Italy but in which, in reality, Italy will be a tool in the hands of one of the imperialist blocs that are contesting for world domination."

Today that makes one think of 1940. But in 1926 Mussolini was still anti-German. He reiterated that "Fascism will never haul down its flag on the Brenner," that he might even "plant it farther forward if that is necessary," and in France there was applause from conservative quarters for this forceful policy.

Standing against Germany with France and with Germany against the others, Mussolini was in truth striving at every opportunity to fuel the fire of Italian nationalism. The newspaper *Impero* (*Empire*) said: "We need air to breathe, land on which to expand, coal . . . and waves for heroism and poetry. Our race today gives off so much physical power that its right to expand throughout the world is as beyond question as the right of the torrent to empty into the sea."

In March, 1926, Il Duce announced that "the hour of destiny is near." Speculation focused on some great undertaking with the benevolent support of England. It was known that Mussolini was to leave Italy for Tripolitania—his first journey to Africa.

Just before his departure, on April 7, Mussolini opened an international convention of surgeons. Out of the crowd a grey-haired woman came forward: she was the Honorable Violet Gibson, a sixty-two-year-old Irishwoman. She raised her arm. Il Duce saw her, he saw the pistol that she was aiming at him over the heads of the crowd; he stepped sharply backward, a shot rang out, and the bullet struck his nose. Everyone rushed to him; the wound was minor. Soon, his face bisected by a white strip of bandage, Il Duce was proclaiming: "If I advance, follow me; if I retreat, kill me; if I die, avenge me."

Miss Gibson, a half-mad mystic, was merely expelled from Italy. But her attempt had created a climate of emotion: the handkerchief spotted with Il Duce's blood was displayed under glass, the

Roman streets near Palazzo Chigi were filled with enthusiastic crowds, women knelt at Mussolini's passage, everywhere there were prayers for his safety, and once again Providence was mentioned.

In spite of his wound, he sailed next day, in the midst of ceremonial salvos, aboard the warship *Cavour*. On his instructions, the party directorate was also on board, in order to become acquainted with warships. There were ritual repetitions of *Eîa, eîa, alalà* for "the glorious Italian navy."

When Il Duce landed in Tripolitania, he was received enthusiastically. Someone in the crowd cried: "Whose is Tunisia?" and everyone shouted: "*A noi*—Ours!" Mussolini was on horseback, facing the castle of Tripoli. He delivered his speech from the saddle, like a Roman emperor, and no doubt he was thinking of Septimus Severus, the emperor born in nearby Leptis Magna. *Il Popolo d'Italia* spoke of "the eastern basin of the Mediterranean . . . Syria, which France will never colonize."

Without comment the French government announced on April 20 that its fleet would hold maneuvers, and its troops landed at Bizerte.

Thus Mussolini's foreign policy turned toward international tension, especially as internal political events might at any moment create new incidents.

As Mussolini's car was driving past Porta Pia at about ten o'clock in the morning of September 11, 1926, it was struck by a bomb. "Keep going, keep going!" Mussolini ordered his driver. "Someone's thrown a time bomb at the car."

The driver accelerated as Il Duce leaned out the window and gestured at the police. A few minutes later the bomb exploded, wounding four persons. An anarchist marble worker named Gino Lucetti confessed to having thrown it. He had just arrived from France without a passport. The press and the government loosed their anger against that country, the haven of the *fuorusciti*. "There must be an end of certain tolerances on the other side of the border," Il Duce cried from the balcony of Palazzo Chigi.

Anti-French outbreaks of violence increased, the more so as Italy was playing the English game. On September 30 Chamberlain and Mussolini met in Leghorn. On his return to London, Sir Austen said in his calm voice bathed in politeness not devoid of a certain condescension: "I have very great respect and very great admiration for Mr. Mussolini himself. He is a man with great strength of character and profound sagacity, and his personal conduct is marked by great charm and complete simplicity." When the reporters could not conceal their amazement at this flattery, Sir Austen looked at them coldly and said: "Whatever your views on his politics, he is a great patriot."

Thus the Fascist government was shored up by His Britannic Majesty's Foreign Secretary when it was heaping insults on France. Mussolini was in a position to stage a pompous celebration of the fourth anniversary of the March on Rome and to congratulate "the Italian people, who thirsted to obey, who thirsted for discipline, who wanted to be governed. . . ." And he brought his fist down on the railing of the balcony as he shouted on October 8: "The government is as solid as a mountain of granite!"

And yet three days later came the most mysterious of all the attempts on the life of Il Duce.

Mussolini was fired on in Bologna as he rode in an open car. One bullet cut through the ribbon of his Order of SS.-Maurice-et-Lazare and his uniform at chest level, but it did not reach the skin. In the street, as if on signal, some squadristi ran toward the prefecture while others threw themselves on a fifteen-year-old spectator, Anteo Zamboni, stabbed him, and threw him to the mob. Was he the assassin? It is doubtful. In any event, his death provided an easy solution for a number of people: a corpse can be made to confess to anything. But a day later well-informed quarters began attributing the attempt on Il Duce to embittered Fascists—Arpinati, or Farinacci, who had been made to give up his post as party secretary on March 30, 1926—or even to a combination of two actions: one, of police origin, intended to simulate an attempt at assassination (in order to provide a pretext for repressions), and the other of Fascist origin, woven into the first and really intended to kill Il Duce, thus converting a farce into a crime.

It is a matter of record that twenty-four hours before the attempt was made the possibility of it was considerably dwelt on. To reinforce the hypothesis of a police provocation there is the fact that in France a few weeks earlier the agents of the secret service had arrested a number of Italians—La Polla, Scivoli, Scala, Ricciotti, Garibaldi—on charges of enticing *fuorusciti* into the trap of a conspiracy against Il Duce. The French press ran such headlines as PLOTTER MUSSOLINI PLOTS AGAINST DUCE. To what end? The answer came in what followed the Bologna attack, which was fatal only to the unfortunate Zamboni: the attack was to be used as a justification for the repression and the revolutionary laws demanded by the chorus of the Fascist press. Mussolini wrote: "On the very evening after the trivial attack in Bologna it was I who personally dictated the measures to be adopted."

In fact Alfredo Rocco had prepared them long before. What

was lacking was a pretext; Bologna provided it. These "Laws for the Defense of the State" completed the transformation of Italy into a Fascist police state. They included: the dissolution of all political parties; deportation on mere administrative order for no more than the intention of committing an offense, even if it was only one of opinion; the rescission of the parliamentary mandate of all opposition deputies from Gramsci to Alcide De Gasperi (but Giolitti, Salandra, Orlando were not affected); a register of citizens "of bad reputation" as designated by "the voice of the people"; the creation of a special political investigation bureau, the OVRA (Volunteer Organization for the Repression of Anti-Fascism), under the control of an efficient minister, Arturo Bocchini. This edifice of ultra-Fascist laws was crowned with a Special Court for the Defense of the State, and the death penalty was restored (November, 1926). All these provisions were effective retroactively. Mussolini told the Senate without irony: "The Special Court . . . will be composed of persons chosen by me and absolutely above any suspicion."

In fact, headed by a general and five consuls of the Militia, the court was the archetype of a summary tribunal. Moreover, the Fascist government stated in its explanation of its motives: "The struggle that the state has undertaken against its enemies is similar to what it would have to wage in time of war."

Thus, established in power by the threat of a civil war, Fascism enacted undisguised war legislation four years after its accession. The avowal was important.

It was now the end of 1926, "the Napoleonic year of Fascism," as Mussolini wrote. The anti-Fascists were streaming out of Italy: Modigliani, Turati, Nenni, Togliatti—it was a mass exodus. The first deportees (there were already more than five hundred by November 30, 1926), bound to one another at the wrists with heavy chains, were arriving in the southern islands, Lipari or Ponza.

This time there could be no doubt that the Fascist system was in the saddle.

10

The Fascist System: Il Duce
(1926–1936)

"I have made my body a disciplined and controlled engine that functions with absolute regularity."—IL DUCE (March 9, 1937)

ON DECEMBER 30, 1926, the lictor's *fasces*, the symbol of Fascism, became the official emblem of the state, and Italians recognized that, with the year that was ending, a stage of their history was being concluded. Henceforth they would live under a new system that had been established through two years of intense legislative labor—the ultra-Fascist laws—and the indifferent, like the advocates and the adversaries, saw that Fascism "'was solidly entrenched behind the government" (Sforza).

"It would take us twenty years"—that was the phrase that recurred like a *Leitmotiv* in the conversations of the most clear-thinking anti-Fascists. Professor Salvemini, in exile in the United States, wrote in the spring of 1927: "The weak point of the Fascist system is its foreign policy; it is there that disaster will strike."

This was tantamount to saying that he considered it impossible to uproot Fascism from within. True, he added: "Dictatorships end in war . . . because in war they find an escape from their domestic difficulties."

From 1926 to 1935—almost ten years—Fascism limited itself to the exaltation of nationalism, to the proliferation of belligerent statements without, however, engaging in any military adventure. Certainly it was preparing for such action, but abroad, as in Italy, outspoken warlike intentions were ignored in favor of peaceful or reassuring actions. On May 26, 1927, however, Mussolini asserted: "At a given moment between 1935 and 1940, when Europe's situation will have reached its crucial point, we shall be able to make our voice heard and at last to obtain recognition of our rights. Our preparations still require several years."

It was a prophetic vision. It was to give the Fascist system ten years of peace, ten years during which Italians and the entire world, revolted or entranced, would accept or tolerate the Fascist state of Il Duce: ten years during which *Evviva il Duce* was not yet drowned out by *Heil Hitler* and the apocalyptic march of Nazi troops on the roads of Germany. In 1927 Adolf Hitler was still at the stage of begging Mussolini for an inscribed photograph, which was refused with these instructions: "Please thank the above-named gentleman for the sentiments that he expresses . . . but Il Duce was unable to grant his request."

This petition by the unknown Hitler is an indication of the extent of the changes that would take place in Europe between 1926 and 1935, the year in which Der Führer began to impose his policies and his ambitions on weaker nations. Until then the Fascist system would remain the magnetic pole of Europe and its chief would continue to be the continent's strong man.

That chief, Il Duce, was approaching the age of fifty at the same time when the régime was celebrating its *decennale* in 1932—the tenth anniversary of the March on Rome. By this time Mussolini had learned to strike an admirable *condottiere* posture. His head was always scrupulously shaved—a practice imitated by many of his hierarchs—in a clever exploitation of his baldness that gave him a "Roman head." Emil Ludwig, the German journalist who had almost daily conversations with him from March 23 to April 4, 1932, pointed out that one of his typical mannerisms was to thrust forward his chin and his lower lip; he clenched his teeth, kept his head constantly raised, and succeeded even in seeming taller than his five feet five and a half inches; and he had adopted his famous "magnetic look" with the widely staring eyes—all to such an effect that Ludwig asked: "Are you pleased at being compared with Colleone?"*

"He looked at me with his piercing eyes," Ludwig reported, "thrust forward his lower jaw, and said nothing. Now he really looked like Colleone."

By putting this question Ludwig was unconsciously making himself an accomplice, for by 1932 there was no longer anything natural about Mussolini. The man facing Ludwig was nothing but an

* Bartolomeo Colleone, a fifteenth-century *condottiere* and generalissimo of the Republic of Venice.—Translator.

The Fascist System: Il Duce

actor in whom everything was studied—his posture, his way of moving (head high, stride exaggerated), his carefully tended hands, his concealment of his age. In 1933 he saw to it that there was no mention of his fiftieth birthday; he tried even to avoid being seen by his servant, Quinto Navarra, when he was wearing his glasses: he would whip them off when Navarra entered his office. He even had a special typewriter made for him with letters three times normal size so that he could read his speeches to the hierarchs without the glasses. Naturally he watched his figure: he weighed himself every day and against the obesity that constantly threatened him he resorted to sports: from fencing to tennis, from riding to wood-chopping, by way of swimming. At the Adriatic coastal town of Riccione tourists vied for the honor of watching him run into the water in his bathing suit, his muscles rippling. He had kept an athletic figure: in addition to his sports, he disciplined himself to a rigid diet, which was dictated, true, by his stomach trouble in part but also by his determination not to grow fat. To young Ruggero Zangrandi, the friend of his son, Vittorio, he sang the praises of yoghurt. "The Bulgarians," he said, "enjoy exceptional longevity because they are great eaters of milk curds, especially those of mare's milk."[1] And indeed he never shared the young men's meals but limited himself to yoghurt and fruit. He did the same thing at official banquets, refusing the various courses in favor of a salad.

The concern that Il Duce devoted to his appearance was a significant indication of the dictator's conception of his relations with the crowd. He should be seen and admired. When he traveled in his six-car presidential train, Navarra would always tell Il Duce on which side of the tracks the crowd would be waiting, and Mussolini would appear at the appropriate window. "Everyone," he said seriously, "should have an equal opportunity to look at me."

"Then a dictator can be loved in spite of everything?" Ludwig asked him, and Mussolini replied: "He can be . . . when at the same time the crowd is afraid of him. The crowd loves strong men. The crowd is a woman."

Undoubtedly it was a contrived answer, but it explained that preoccupation with physical detail that haunted Mussolini. He wanted to please. Consequently he placed the greatest importance in the slightest portrayal of himself. He himself would examine every photograph in which he appeared, and he would select those that might be published by the newspapers. In Villa Torlonia,

[1] R. Zangrandi, *Il lungo viaggio attraverso il fascismo* (Milan: Feltrinelli, 1962), p. 22.

his residence, he had set up a projection room where he went meticulously through every frame of the *Giornale luce,* the newsreels or short films in which he was the major actor. Was he clearly enough visible in the midst of a group of hierarchs? If not, the film or the still was thrown out. Now he was to be shown smiling, relaxed; now vivaciously tasting a dish offered by some peasants; there were other times when he must be shown only rigid in a warlike stance, his face resolute: erect, bare-chested, his muscles standing out, his face immobile in the midst of a group of admiring peasants. All the official photographs of the Fascist period were in a certain sense posed, whether they portrayed him in command or in relaxation and private life. Hence there is not one photograph, one bust, one painting that shows the well-known wen on Il Duce's skull; so ridiculous and minor an imperfection should never be seen.

The happiest moments, of course, in the life—and the government—of Il Duce were those of his contacts with the crowd. These encounters between Il Duce and "his" people had lost all naturalness. More and more the staging became as stylized as that of a ballet: Piazza Venezia, in front of Palazzo Venezia, where Mussolini now had his offices; the crowd—that crowd of which it might be said, in that country so passionately devoted to opera, that what it loved best in Mussolini was precisely the actor, the tenor—the "oceanic" crowd would gather in order: battalions of the Volunteer Militia, then school children, then the claque of spectators marched out in ranks from their jobs, and then the crowd properly so called. Nor was the enthusiasm always factitious: Baron Pompeo Aloisi, who stood beside Il Duce at the celebration on October 28, 1934, reported that at about ten-thirty in the morning, "during a silence, a stentorian voice rose from the crowd: 'Duce, give us a smile!' Mussolini raised his arm in surprise and delight, with an unforgettable look on his face."[2] Face to face with the crowd, Mussolini handled himself admirably. He had a feeling for the apt phrase, he prepared his speeches meticulously, and in the piazza the hollow note of the big drums of a dozen orchestras and the songs and shouts of the *Balilla* created the atmosphere. "Music and women," Mussolini told Ludwig, "make crowds more malleable and gayer."

These speeches were great moments for him. He was tense to the point of paroxysm. He knew that a public-address system would carry his voice to every major square in Rome, but what fascinated

[2] *Journal du Baron Aloisi (25 Juillet 1932–14 Juin 1936)* (Paris: Plon, 1957), p. 228.

The Fascist System: Il Duce

him was the living crowd in Piazza Venezia. He often lost his temper: "Why are those guards pushing the people? Why don't those idiots play? People are bored with waiting, they ought to have some music," he would repeat with vexation.

For him governing seemed to consist essentially in "being," in "appearing to be" Il Duce. He played the part perfectly and so he governed perfectly. Soon, however, he lost all distinction between seeming and being. He would no longer tolerate the slightest joke, he dismissed anyone who showed any independence or whose success might dim his own luster. Air Minister Italo Balbo, his old comrade, who had led the mass transatlantic flight, was relegated to the governorship of Libya. In 1934 Balbo told Paolo Monelli: "Mussolini thinks he is God now. He has lost all contact with the country and no one can make him listen to reason any more."

And it was true that, apart from the artificial communion of his speeches, Mussolini lived in the sealed-off, pompous world of his own glory, imprisoned in his own postures, his arrogance, and the adulation of those round him.

He had moved his offices to Palazzo Venezia on September 19, 1929 This austere structure, built in 1455 with stones torn out of the Coliseum, guarded by a tower and adorned with mullion windows, had served as a residence for Pope Paul III and then for the Venetian and Austrian ambassadors to the Vatican. With its four entrances, its inner courtyard, its enormous halls and the great rectangle of Piazza Venezia stretching out below the rust-colored main façade, this building was admirably suited to Il Duce: was he not the heir of Machiavelli, the peer of a prince of the Renaissance? He evicted the institutes and libraries that had long had their quarters in the palace, gave their premises to his staff, and chose as his own office Room VIII, the so-called Mappamondo Room (Hall of the Globe): more than sixty feet long and forty feet high. In this vast hall, without furniture but rich in decoration—mosaics, reliefs, painted ceiling—Il Duce had a thirteen-foot desk installed at a window; a lamp with a yellow silk shade cast its light on a few objects such as three telephones and a bronze inkwell. The central ceiling lights were always burning; on a lectern there was an atlas; in a right-hand drawer of the desk there was a revolver; in a left-hand drawer there was money to be given to those who asked for it.

This theatrical room, this bareness, this void round the man who, against this glacial background, observed the progress of the visitor struck by the sound of his own steps on the stone floor, provide an excellent idea of the setting—verging on the absurd—that

Il Duce had contrived for himself. He had the Hall of Battles fitted as a reception room and created a *Regia* room in which a podium was installed from which he could address the two or three thousand persons who could be accommodated there.

Another room was reserved for the Fascist Grand Council. At ten o'clock on its meeting nights the members would gather in silence. The party secretary called the roll: each man was supposed to answer *Present* in a loud voice. Then the discussions began. But there could be no real exchange of ideas, no spontaneity: this gathering of men in uniform was handled by Il Duce as if it were a school class or an army squad. Abruptly Mussolini would rise: "The meeting is adjourned for ten minutes. Go smoke a cigarette."

In the corridors and round the buffet where the hierarchs crowded for refreshment the musketeers of Il Duce stood guard in their black uniforms with the death's head and cross-bones on their fezzes, daggers in their belts, and carbines on their shoulders. They were Mussolini's personal bodyguard: young volunteers of good appearance and fine Roman ancestry, they provided the final detail of the "Mussolinian style" of Palazzo Venezia.

Though that style may rouse a smile today (for almost forty years have gone by), it fascinated visitors then: hierarchs or high officials, deferential and obsequious to Navarra, anxious to know the master's mood before they traversed the long hall to the desk from which, sometimes, they would be dismissed by a mere gesture. Often Mussolini's angry shouts could be heard in the waiting room. Hence relations between chief and visitors could be only those of servility. If some Fascist were told that his shoes squeaked —a sound that Il Duce could not abide—he would ask for water and wet his soles while Navarra watched with a smile of amusement. Another might be told to cut his beard. Mussolini enjoyed striking these terrorizing attitudes. He told Ludwig, and the irony of the observation escaped both Il Duce and the deferential journalist: "The *podestà* of San Remo killed himself with a revolver in the catacombs and the director of civil engineering in Naples drowned himself, and both for no reason except that they had been asked to appear before me without having done anything wrong!"

This man who played at being terrible had also—and this too was part of his act—his paternal moments. Ludwig was present at one curious episode after a speech. Imploring cries of *Duce! Duce!* could be heard from outside the Mappamondo. Mussolini ordered the doors opened, and some sixty Fascist officers rushed toward him. He called each one by name and mentioned his home

The Fascist System: Il Duce

town; then he wanted them to leave. But they all shouted: "Photo, photo!" and soon Mussolini was posing in their midst.

The more the years went on the more the world of Il Duce betrayed its artificial character. Between Mussolini and reality there were not only his own blindness and the adulation of his intimates but also the host of policemen of the "Presidential Brigade" who became a kind of outside extension of the walls of Palazzo Venezia. Even Mussolini's barber was a policeman, Sciaretta: who else could be entrusted with so delicate a post? "Buck up," Mussolini said when he saw how Sciaretta was trembling the first time he was to perform his task. "Just pretend that you're shaving your father."

And this trivial daily act carried out by a policeman was the symbol of Il Duce's entire life, surrounded little by little by a ring of policemen. These were necessities imposed for Mussolini's protection. In the view of Arturo Bocchini, Minister of Police, dictatorships fell only when the dictators died. It was his job to prevent such a death.

Piazza Venezia, in front of the palace, soon acquired a reputation among Romans. Those who had to cross it did so as fast as they could, lest they be stopped and questioned by the innumerable policemen who surrounded and filled it. The adjoining Caffè Faraglia lost all its customers, and Mussolini regularly sent money to the unhappy waiters. There were policemen everywhere: on the route taken by Mussolini's car, in the garden of Villa Torlonia; Navarra, indeed, contended that during public ceremonies, "except for the hierarchs and the officials, within a radius of three hundred yards there was nothing but policemen in disguise." The miners, workingmen, peasants, swimmers, stonemasons, ordinary women who surrounded Il Duce in photographs were all police agents. Others followed Mussolini when he went to swim; more hid behind the trees; there were policemen to hand him the trowel when he laid a cornerstone. It was a sham world that surrounded Mussolini and that was held up to Italy. Occasionally Il Duce himself was not aware of all the precautions taken for his protection. When he was examined for his pilot's license, a retired flier was hidden, without anyone's knowledge, in the fuselage of the plane, ready to take over for Il Duce in his "solo" flight. Furthermore, the police did an excellent job: there were no more threats on the life of Il Duce and the least evidence of any plot was stifled at birth.

Even more effectively and more irreparably than the police, it was the cult of personality that isolated Il Duce from the real world. What was amazing was the growth of the man's prestige outside Italy. British journalists spoke of the "Mussolini miracle"; Emile Henriot remarked that "the great man is in the process of becoming God." To the Archbishop of Canterbury "Mussolini is the only gigantic figure in Europe." Gandhi confessed: "Unfortunately, I am not a superman like him." To Churchill he was the incarnation of "genius in person." To Ludwig he was "that powerful, nervous lion," the sound of whose voice was like "the tapping of a telegraph key."

In this light it is easier to forgive the Italians their adoration. Above all "Il Duce is always right," but more than this was within his competence: it was said that his look could stop the flow of lava, that he was "visibly protected by God" (His Eminence Merry del Val, the papal legate); a pamphlet series entitled *Mussolinia* was founded and each month it published such little essays as "The Two Marches on Rome," or "Caesar and Mussolini," or "Mussolini the Musician," for Il Duce still played the violin. Innocent of irony, this essay recalled young Mussolini, who "danced with the frenzy of a colt"; it emphasized "the exquisitely emotional depth of his soul"; it reported that a violin with five strings had been given to Mussolini and it pointed out that Il Duce was an "honorary academician of the Bologna Philharmonic" and of other equally august societies. . . . As for the newspapers, they always printed the word DUCE in capitals and used boldface for everything that concerned him. Gifts piled up at Villa Torlonia, from lion cubs to three hundred volumes containing two million signatures of Hungarian admirers, as well as a history of Rome written in Chinese. Busts and equestrian statues of IL DUCE multiplied; some, in order to give Mussolini greater pleasure, were equipped with eyes that at night flashed green, white, and red, the Italian national colors.

Such a climate of near-idolatry could only intensify a psychology already predisposed to megalomania. That was visible even in the family life of Il Duce. Rachele had moved into Villa Torlonia with the children. Symbolically, Prince Giovanni Torlonia had leased this sumptuous mansion in the midst of a huge park along via Nomentana to Mussolini for twenty *centesimi* (about one cent) a month. Il Duce maintained a separate suite of rooms in it, and he either had his breakfast in seclusion or walled himself in silence when he ate with the family. While Rachele behaved like a typical lower-middle-class housewife, always wearing an apron, serving the bread and butter when her son, Vittorio, had his friends in for tea, Il Duce spoke only and always in the oratorical manner, "like a Shakespearean actor," as if his audience were not two or three adolescents but a Fascist meeting or an "oceanic" crowd. Arrogance and lack of proportion gradually gained the upper hand in him, captive as he was to the legend that he had built round himself and the praises that were heaped on him. "I have never taken Napoleon as a model," he told Ludwig proudly: "he finished a revolution and I started one." Again, he would say: "I love Caesar," in so intense a tone that it was apparent that he regarded himself as the great Roman's heir.

Nowhere better than in these conversations with Ludwig did he show himself as he wanted to appear, as he imagined himself to be. "I do not like near-misses," he said often. "I never look for excuses. . . . Today I can no longer philosophize, I must act."

"Do you read much?" Ludwig asked; and Mussolini replied: "I read everything."

His propaganda portrayed Mussolini as the archetype of the universal man: he was a philosopher and a historian, competent to give lessons to the greatest experts on such subjects as "the Roman Empire and the sea," but also adept at threshing grain, piloting airplanes, delivering lectures on demography, directing gunfire from the bridge of a battle cruiser, dedicating a new village in the Pontine Marshes, playing a sonata on the violin, or translating French, German, and English. It was understandable that some Italians looked with awe at the lighted window in Palazzo Venezia that showed all Italy that in the enormous Mappamondo Room Il Duce was working and governing.

But Rome was soon filled with a rumor that this luminous square that broke the façade of Palazzo Venezia during the greater part of every night meant nothing. And the rumor was well founded. The room was empty, but the lights were burning, for everyone ought to think that Mussolini was watching over the nation there. Although he enjoyed heavy, regular, restful sleep, propaganda made him an untiring "insomniac." He himself was punctilious in living up to this part: in Libya, at the height of an official ceremony, he excused himself "to work." The hierarchs who wanted to pay him homage went to his room and found him lying on his bed, yawning and leafing through old magazines.

One may well wonder what then was the reality of Mussolini's governmental labors. First of all, he was there. He was up at six in the morning: gymnastics, breakfast—milk, fruit, whole-wheat bread. At eight o'clock in summer, nine o'clock in winter, he was in Palazzo Venezia. He read the party secretary's report and then, from nine-thirty to eleven-thirty, he received:

1) the commanding general of the carabinieri;
2) the chief of the political police (OVRA);
3) the chief of the criminal police;
4) the under-secretary to the Premier;

5) the Foreign Minister;
6) the Minister of Popular Culture;
7) the party secretary;
8) the Minister of the Interior.

The emphasis on police forces is noteworthy: a necessity of any dictatorship, which Il Duce raised to the rank of a philosophical system when he announced on May 26, 1927: "Gentlemen, it is time to make it clear that the police must be not only respected but honored. Gentlemen, it is time to make it clear that, before man felt the need for culture, he felt the need for order. In a certain sense one might say that the policeman preceded the professor."

Apart from this daily review of the police agencies, which was one of the essential aspects of Mussolini's governmental work, the other function consisted in giving audiences from eleven-thirty in the morning to two in the afternoon. At that hour he went back to Villa Torlonia; he lunched alone on pasta, fruit, and vegetables, read the newspapers, and returned to Palazzo Venezia, where he resumed his audiences from three-thirty to eight or nine at night. Paderewski, Churchill, opera singers, Mahatma Gandhi, explorers, diplomats, prefects, inventors, Pirandello, industrialists . . . a perpetually moving water-wheel carried into Palazzo Venezia everyone who mattered in Italy or the world. The total is said to have reached one hundred thirty thousand persons. If to govern means to receive, Mussolini governed splendidly.

Every visitor was supposed to carry away the conviction of Il Duce's competence. When Mussolini received Paderewski, he ordered two violins sent in; the day before Gandhi's visit, Il Duce sent for a teacher of Oriental languages. Often Mussolini would call for this or that volume of an encyclopedia and give himself a veneer of knowledge in preparation for the visit of a specialist. What was essential to him was to seem to be infallible in everything. Government was a great show. Telling Ludwig of the individual cases that were brought to his attention, Mussolini said: "Three years ago—in 1929—I ordered statistics kept on these cases. In seven years they totaled one and a half million. Every one was reviewed by me or under my instructions."

On March 10, 1929, during a large Fascist gathering in Rome, he had supplied other statistics, to much applause: "I have granted more than six thousand audiences, I have occupied myself with 1,887,112 petitions by citizens that came directly to my private secretaries . . . in order to keep up this effort, I have tuned my engine to it."

In this he seemed unaware—as did Ludwig and the Fascists too—that with this ingenuous statistical display ("I carry statistics to three decimal places," he often said) he was acknowledging that he was no more than a kind of emperor of detail, neglecting the reality of decisions for the appearance of power and in fact exercising power only in matters of spectacle, policing, and repression.

Answering Ludwig's questions on the lot of the imprisoned anti-Fascists, Mussolini shrugged: "It all seems logical enough to me," he said; "they began by throwing me inside and now I shove them in."

And yet one should not entertain illusions: there was nothing of the tyrant in the man. In actuality he governed in the armor of others' fear and submission, in that strange dialectic of authority by virtue of which power is power only to the extent to which it is recognized or submitted to. But sometimes an unforeseen event upsets the balance. On one occasion a prefect was summoned to be notified of his dismissal. As he approached Mussolini's desk, Il Duce sat rocking back and forth in his chair and rolling his eyes in menace. The prefect drew nearer and Il Duce, rocking harder, was carried away by his own momentum: he and the chair fell over backward on the floor. The prefect was petrified. Mussolini waved him out and he kept his post. Inevitably one is reminded of what Sforza said of "the splendid ideogram that the Chinese invented for this type of government: the man riding the tiger. He seems terrible and in reality he is dying of fear."

In any event, Mussolini was so concerned with appearances that he did not hesitate to send an emissary, Pietro di Scalea, to Sforza. His mission was to inform Sforza that nothing would happen to his estates in Italy if the former minister would only have the grace now and then to write: "But nevertheless it cannot be denied that Il Duce has genius."

The act was as revealing of the man as was his taste for the press. Even at the peak of governmental responsibilities, Il Duce was still a journalist, running through dozens of publications, from provincial dailies to the great international newspapers. He kept a constant eye on the image of himself and Italy that they projected. In the Italian press he would order changes in headlines or in the color of the cover of a women's magazine. Here again is that concern with show, with trivial detail; the same concern that made him lose his temper because he could no longer see the policeman on duty at a given intersection from his window in Palazzo Venezia, or because he had noticed that the gates of the Altar of the Nation were being closed earlier than normal.

In the crowded daily routine that he had imposed on himself, Mussolini made room for women. Navarra said that Il Duce had a new woman every day in Palazzo Venezia. Of course Navarra was exaggerating, but the reality was populated enough. A special staff sorted, classified, analyzed, and filed the innumerable letters that infatuated women sent to Il Duce. The police, of course, investigated each writer's background, and thus the file was kept up to date so that on the slightest demand Il Duce could be offered a new aspirant or supplied with the chronologically arranged letters of a mistress who for some time had been neglected. For Mussolini was not inhibited by fidelity or manners. He received his mistresses in the Hall of the Globe, and he had them on the floor or on the padded cushion on a marble bench in a window embrasure. These "private" audiences were arranged for the late afternoon. Mussolini never suffered from any complexes in this domain: to him it seemed perfectly natural to receive a prefect and then, in the same setting, a buxom lady who would have to run the gantlet of Navarra and his other visitors after a brisk coitus.

He had affairs with intellectual women (Margherita Sarfatti, Tanzi), but he really preferred the middle class, even though in this area he was extremely eclectic because basically extremely superficial. His mistresses knew that their tours of duty had ended when they telephoned Il Duce on his private line and were connected with one or another ministry, the number having just been changed. Thereafter they were no longer admitted to Palazzo Venezia and their letters were stored away by the secretariat. One poor woman, Ida Dalser, who had borne a son to Mussolini in 1915 and who lived on this past, was arrested in 1926 and subsequently committed in 1935 to an asylum in Venice, where she died. Her son also vanished into an asylum, at Monbello.

With his mistresses, obviously, Mussolini was not one to offer delicate attentions—no little cakes, no flowers, no perfume: occasionally cash, a few banknotes slipped into a book. Il Duce, as he told Ludwig, was convinced that "women can have no influence on strong men" and, in most middle-class fashion, that "the woman should be passive . . . she is analytic, not synthetic, she is alien to architecture, the synthesis of all the arts: that is a symbol of her destiny . . . in our state the woman should not matter."

It must also be pointed out that for some time Italy knew nothing of the diversions of Il Duce. Everyone thought of him as the father of a good-sized family: after Edda, Vittorio, and Bruno, Rachele had two more children—Romano, born in 1927, and Anna Maria, born in 1929. Virtually nothing was ever seen of Rachele, it was true, but that was quite in keeping with the subordination of the Italian woman. From time to time there were family photographs in the newspapers: Il Duce surrounded by his children at his estate at Rocca della Caminate, a solid castle near Forlì, which he converted into a huge residence. In a word, he led a respectable life.

On April 25, 1930, in the magnificently decorated setting of Villa Torlonia, Edda, the eldest of Mussolini's children, was married to Count Galeazzo Ciano, son of Admiral Costanzo Ciano, Mussolini's old comrade. The religious ceremony was followed by a princely reception attended by the Roman aristocracy, the diplomatic corps, everyone of importance in Rome. A few months later Ciano was appointed consul in Shanghai; in 1933 he began an impressive career by becoming head of his father-in-law's press department.

So Mussolini preserved appearances. A Jesuit, Father Pietro Tacchi-Venturi, his confidant, counselor, and, perhaps, confessor, busied himself in saving Mussolini's soul. But the respectable front was to crumble.

On the road to Ostia in April, 1932, a romantic adventure began that, contrary to all its predecessors, was to be known to all Italy. Driving an open Alfa Romeo and accompanied by an officer, Il Duce was moving quickly when he overtook a crowded car in which a girl stood up and rapturously shouted: "Duce! Duce!" Mussolini stopped and waved down the other car: the girl got out and ran toward him. She told him that she sent him letters and poems regularly. Il Duce asked her name, and she replied: "Claretta Petacci."

Now her family joined her—a good middle-class family: the father, Francesco, was a physician in the Vatican; the brother, Marcello, was one of Mussolini's musketeers; the sister, Myriam, was an actress. There was also Claretta's betrothed, Lieutenant Frederici. After a few questions, Il Duce drove off, leaving the Petaccis enraptured. When he returned to Rome, Mussolini had his staff get out any letters from a girl named Petacci, and he sent them back to her with flowers. The twenty-year-old girl could not imagine the efficiency of the staff of her Duce: she thought that she had been singled out. When, a few days later, "the gentleman from Ostia" requested on the telephone that "Signorina Petacci be kind enough to come to Palazzo Venezia," she was ecstatic.

She arrived with her sister, was admitted, and came home alone. But for almost four years it was assumed that all that went on between the athletic fifty-year-old and the girl with the bangs, the grey-green eyes, and the commanding bosom was weekly romantic and platonic conversations. "Ben," she is supposed to have told a friend, "talked to me about his struggles and hardships when he was young, his dreams, while we sat hand in hand watching the flight of the swallows in the deepening autumn twilight."

Pedestrians hurried through Piazza Venezia under the vigilant eyes of a swarm of policemen; cars moved rapidly without a single horn blast: Il Duce did not wish to be disturbed; the traffic police at the intersections directed the vehicles with precise gestures, for at any moment Il Duce might see them; in his waiting room be-medaled Fascist hierarchs harassed Navarra with anxious questions, while in the sixty-five-hundred-square-foot Hall of the Globe a man alone, already old, whispered his thoughts to an infatuated girl before returning to his hundred thirty thousand audiences, his reading of a newspaper, his draft of a speech, his consideration of an anonymous letter, or his choice of the picture that should be used next day in all the newspapers.

And yet the Fascist system existed, Italy was governed, and her chief, a prey to the demon of the flesh and to vanity, hung ominously throughout those years over the course of his country and the world, over the fate of millions of men.

11

The Fascist System: The Ideology, the State, the Party
(1926–1936)

"Everything is in the state; nothing human or spiritual exists outside the state."—IL DUCE (1936)

ON MAY 9, 1927, Augusto Turati, whose surname was the same as that of the Socialist leader but who was the secretary of the Fascist Party, addressed the Fascists of Florence. Tall and spare, angular of feature, with an aquiline nose and eyes sunk deep in their sockets, he was immaculately dressed in a Militia uniform; it was said that he had his black shirts made of silk. He spoke in a metallic voice. "Every day, in every square," he declared, "the thousand hearts of Fascism cry the same words: love, devotion, discipline, loyalty to the point of sacrifice." The Fascists cheered, and Turati concluded: "I will not speak to Il Duce of your cheers, but I will take him the pledge that, tomorrow as today, you will know how to serve in silence and to obey with humility."

In these few words Turati had just virtually summed up the Fascist state. Naturally that state could not officially be satisfied with an ideology built on obedience. Therefore, on many occasions Gentile, the philosopher, Mussolini himself, and everyone who was their echo strove to elaborate a Fascist doctrine. The efforts were great, the fruits minuscule.

In actuality Fascist ideology was composed above all of rejection: rejection of democracy, rejection of Socialism, rejection of the class struggle. The note of negation was sounded with vigor, but the declarations were derived from a rhetoric that was most often reduced to a few extremely traditional ideas: the cult of action, of violence, of virility, the cult of Il Duce and the state. So some Fascist teacher would assert that the French Revolution was feminine, whereas "nothing could be more male than Fascism," which was "the impetuous surge of a concrete and immediate will to conquer."

Very soon, however, Mussolini, Gentile, and Rocco placed their emphasis on the theme of the state, a totalitarian state: "The Fascist concept is anti-individualist and made for the state. . . . Everything is in the state; nothing human or spiritual exists outside the state. In this sense Fascism is totalitarian," Mussolini wrote with great clarity. Il Duce continued: "The state is the absolute. . . . There can be neither group nor individual outside the state. The Fascist state is a will to power and domination."

What is essential, of course, is to ask oneself what that state was and not to reply in the style of those days: "The state is Fascism because Fascism is the state."

Above everything else the state was a man in whom one must *believe*, for *faith—la fede*—was basic. Paolo Orano, now a Fascist deputy, declared in the Chamber: "The philosopher is an inferior mental type. . . . Mussolini-ism is faith."

On the white walls of the villages of the South, weary with sunlight and misery; beneath the slate roofs of the Val d'Aosta; between two advertising billboards; on the wall of a big building in Rome there were always the same legends: "*Mussolini ha sempre ragione* (Mussolini is always right)" or: "*Credere ubbidire combattere* (Believe, obey, fight)."

The Fascist state—"a spiritual creation" (Gentile), an "ethical state," an "idealist state"—was first of all, then, the celebration of the cult of the Chief. Here is Gentile again: "The Italian nation marches . . . without hesitation, without question, its eyes fixed on the heroic man of exceptional talents comparable to those of the great leaders of peoples." Soaring into mysticism, Gentile added: "Mussolini goes forward with confidence, in a halo of myth, almost chosen by God, indefatigable and infallible, the instrument employed by Providence for the creation of a new civilization."

For Fascism's claims attained to the altitude of a "civilization." Facing the "multitudes" in the squares of Turin or Milan, wearing his black uniform, his chin thrust out, his legs widespread, his hands on his hips, Mussolini stood on the podium adorned with the lictor's *fasces* and delivered his prophetic incantations: "I declare to you, O immense multitude, that the twentieth century shall be the century of Italian power, it shall be the century during which for the third time Italy shall be the guide of human civilization. Outside our principles there is salvation neither for individuals nor above all for peoples." Then came the menacing, inspired prediction: "Ten years from now Europe will be Fascist or Fascistized."

As far as Italy was concerned, by 1932 she was thoroughly Fascist. First of all there was the Fascist Party, a ubiquitous mass party: in 1933 it numbered three million members in addition to the youth organizations: the *Balilla*, the Little Italians (girls under fourteen), the *Avanguardisti*, and the Young Italians (girls between fourteen and eighteen). These groups had almost two million members in 1933. In May, 1932, the Fascist trade unions had 3.82 million members, and the Opera nazionale dopolavoro (National Recreation Organization) had 1.8 million. Thus ten million persons were organized. All kinds of Fascist operations from Fascist cultural institutes to Fascist vacation camps for the young made it possible to consolidate all activities around Fascism and Il Duce. Turati, the party secretary, was appointed "referee emeritus" of the nation's football and was given a golden whistle. Every year the *leva fascista* (Fascist levy) promoted a class of *Avanguardisti*, in a solemn ceremonial, into the ranks of the Militia. The school was of course the focus of every attention. Textbooks were supposed to emphasize the "Fascist soul"; teachers were checked on, retired on pension or expelled if their opinions did not conform. The Gruppi universitari fascisti (GUF—Fascist University Groups) devoted themselves to rowdyism against recalcitrant teachers, who were soon removed. More and more rallies, uniforms, songs, and annual competitions were created for the young: the *Littoriali* (lictorial competitions) in culture, the arts, and sports. The goal, Alfredo Rocco said, was "the radical transformation of the mind and the character of the Italian people. Thus, after centuries of indiscipline and idleness, Italy will be able once more to become a great military and warlike nation."

Indoctrination began at the earliest possible age: *Balilla* boys of six, mounted and helmeted, paraded in uniform before Il Duce; at the age of twelve they received scaled-down rifles and they stood guard, erect in their black gloves and short trousers, with fixed bayonets. According to a Fascist pamphlet, "We must create the Italians of Fascism, who will be for our time what the Italians of the Renaissance and the Latin period were for theirs."

The *Balilla escursionisti* (campers—aged eight to twelve), the *Balilla moschettieri* (musketeers—aged twelve to fourteen), the

Avanguardisti moschettieri (fourteen to sixteen), and the *Avan-guardisti mitraglieri* (machine-gunners—sixteen to eighteen), commanded by Militia officers, gathered every year in Mussolini's Forum, near Rome, for the *Campo Dux*, a national convocation of the young. A tank stood at the great stucco gateway; an arch of triumph was crowned with the word *Dux*, and inside the camp there were black panels bearing the same word and also such curt maxims of Mussolini's as: "War: a word that does not frighten us," or: "I am preparing the young to fight for life but also for the Nation." *Avanguardisti* were trained in the use of the machine gun, smaller boys paraded with their rifles, others carried shovels on their shoulders as they marched, and on each shovel was chalked *W il Duce.*

This dual exaltation of warrior energy and blind obedience to Il Duce formed the pillars of Fascist education from the *Balilla* to the party. As soon as a boy was eligible for the *Balilla*, he had to learn its credo:

> I believe in the genius of Il Duce and Our Lord Fascism,
> I believe in the Communion of the martyrs of Fascism,
> Lord, thou who lightest every flame,
> Lord, thou who rulest every heart,
> Revive in me each day
> My passion for Italy.

Songs played a large part in this training. This was the official *Balilla* hymn:

> For our Duce,
> For our blessed Duce,
> We are ready,
> We are ready with our guns,
> And with our,
> And with our flag,
> Forever forward,
> Forever forward we will go,
> *Alalà!*

The chorus of the schoolboys' song was still more indicative:

> Italians have been given a new life,
> Mussolini gave them their new life,
> For tomorrow's war.

The young Fascists also had their Ten Commandments, the second of which proclaimed: "He who is not prepared to give his body and his soul to the Nation and to serve Il Duce without question is not worthy to wear the Black Shirt."

The Fascist Militia, that "Fascist army" that was to mold generations of warriors, gave each new member a little pamphlet that also contained ten commandments:

1) Remember that the Fascist, and especially the Militiaman, must not believe in permanent peace.
2) Time in prison is always deserved. . . .
8) Mussolini is always right. . . .
10) One thing above all must be dear to you: the life of Il Duce.

When at last he had completed this *cursus honorum*, the Italian was eligible for the party. "If the party did not exist, I would invent it," Mussolini said. He added: "The party is the capillary system of the régime. . . . It is more than an authority: it is an apostolate."

The party was indeed the skeleton and the nervous system of Fascism, at least on the theoretical level. Every year the party secretary obsequiously presented Il Duce with *tessera* (card) Number One, for hierarchy was the very foundation of the party: "it is hallowed by the illumination of Genius . . . of him who knows all and sees all, who reads the hearts of men through closed eyelids" —in other words, Mussolini. Turati and Il Duce provided complementary definitions of the party. "We are an army of seers, not a mass of associates," the one said. "The party is an Order," Mussolini declared. "One enters it only to serve and to obey."

And in a certain sense it was indeed a return to the Middle Ages that was sought. Each member bought a copy of the party's by-laws for about seven cents. On page three, in bold type, there was an introductory chapter entitled *La Fede* (*The Faith*): "Fascism has always regarded itself as being in a state of war. . . . Fascism is above all a faith that has its confessors."

This was followed by thirty-five rules that defined the party's components. Number 27 declared: "New members shall take the oath in the presence of the secretary and in accordance with the following form: 'I swear to follow the orders of Il Duce without question and to serve the cause of the Fascist revolution with all my strength and, if need be, with my blood.'"

But this ideology of obedience and conquest, this rhetoric of violence and faith, this *mystique* of the leader, the hierarchy, and the state, this exaltation of nationalism, though they might dominate a minority, were not enough to mobilize large masses for long. That was why stress was laid on corporativism.

Introduced, as we have seen, in April, 1926, corporativism was soon to become the major theme of propaganda, the great illusion, the great hope, the great excuse, the great subject of discussions of Fascism both inside and outside Italy. It was also one of the last successful pieces of stage management by that able demagogue, Mussolini. Its basic principle was simple: the subordination of private interests to the general—that is, the national—interest and the subjugation of social classes to the national mass. These achieved, there could no longer be strikes or lockouts, or conflict among classes that had to collaborate with one another. The state as arbiter, the state as regulator organized the components of society. In 1926 a Ministry of Corporations was created; in 1927 the Charter of Labor was published. This was a long document containing thirty articles, which said, among other things: "Work is a social duty. . . . The whole productive system is a unit from the national point of view. . . . Its objective is the development of national power."

Thus—though only in the Charter—there were no more employers or employes; there were only producers reorganized in 1934 into twenty-two corporations. These were the meeting places of representatives of the workers and of the "organizers of production." Naturally, under the provisions of official regulations, these representatives "must meet the political requirements of the government"—in plain language, be Fascists. Furthermore, they were chosen by the government, not elected, and these corporate officials received much higher salaries than those of state officials. This system marked the end of any independent labor union. It was evolved, too, in the depths of the depression and it fostered the state's intervention in production and assistance to private capital while at the same time chaining the working masses in obedience.

But this policy of cold reality was camouflaged in the colors of a social revolution. Here again one must acknowledge Mussolini's talents as an orator, an inventor of phrases and concepts designed to charm and, for a while, to disguise the truth. On October 6, 1934, he addressed a workers' meeting in Milan: "Black Shirts of Milan, comrades of labor! Here, at this moment, you are the heroes of an event that the political history of the future will call 'the address to the workers of Milan.' "

He did not hesitate to denounce capitalism. "In 1929," he said, "the pillars of a temple that seemed to defy the centuries crumbled in a vast uproar. . . . The crisis through which we are passing is not a crisis *in* the system: it is a crisis *of* the system." Against that capitalist system in crisis Mussolini offered "the corporative solution, the solution of disciplined production entrusted to the producers . . . industrialists . . . employers . . . but by producers I mean workers as well." This solution would make it possible to transcend capitalism and Socialism, for "it inherits from each its vital elements." And on November 14, 1933, Mussolini told the general assembly of the National Council of Corporations: "Today we are taking a decisive step along the road of revolution."

This word, like so many others, was often employed. For Fascist ideology was, above all, words and phrases, a "public-address-system" ideology. Pronouncements *created* reality, just as omissions erased it: there were no more proletarians in Italy, no more unemployed, simply because they were no longer mentioned: never was there an ideology, a system so wholly one of words and illusion and rhetoric, so limited to vague generalities, such as its mottoes, like *Tireremo avanti*—We shall go forward. Just outside Naples, on a winding road, an especially tight corner was dominated by a large inscription: "We shall go straight ahead." For irony had vanished: Mussolini wanted to resuscitate Rome, but without Juvenal.

And yet the system survived. The ministers round Il Duce succeeded one another: Gentile, Bottai, De Vecchi, De Bono, Grandi, Federzoni, Renato Ricci, Arturo Bocchini. In actuality they were all footmen whose relations with Mussolini were necessarily those of servants with their master. Grandi wrote to Mussolini on December 14, 1927: "My loyalty is blind, absolute, indestructible."

The ministers were not kept informed even of decisions that concerned them: they learned by sheer chance that they had resigned or been transferred, and Mussolini was adept at producing obedience in them. "I do not forget," he observed, "those who leave when the time comes and are careful not to slam the door."

He was indeed the sole Duce of Fascism, Chief of Government and holder of as many as eight cabinet portfolios (particularly those of Foreign Affairs, War, the Navy, and the Interior). In December, 1928, the Fascist Grand Council was directed by law to provide for a successor to him. But Il Duce lost no time in pointing out: "I must assume the duty of governing the Italian nation for ten or fifteen years more. That is essential. My successor has not yet been born."

Nevertheless this highly personal government required the formal approval of the country: the 1928 election law reduced the number of deputies to four hundred, who would be chosen by the Fascist Grand Council from a list of eight hundred names submitted by employers' and workers' organizations. The voter's function would consist in saying *yes* or *no* to the roster set before him. This election law in the form of a sham plebiscite was approved, according to the party's publication, "in perfect Fascist style, without debate and with absolute discipline."

But the aging Giolitti, who was still a deputy, had the courage to speak the truth. "Any possibility of choice is eliminated," he said; "the voters will be presented with a single ticket." At last the statesman was acknowledging the fact that Fascism had officially abandoned any pretense of parliamentarianism and the further fact that the whole of his own policy had been a failure. When Giolitti had finished speaking, Mussolini observed sarcastically: "We will come to you to learn how to run an election." Aloof and mordant, Giolitti retorted: "Deputy Mussolini, you are too modest. I never dreamed of a Chamber like yours."

The plebiscites were held: on March 24, 1929, and again in 1931. The ballots bore the three national colors; buildings were draped from roof to pavement with huge black posters bearing in white letters the word *sì* (yes) and a stern, enigmatic portrait of Mussolini. The vote in 1929 was ninety percent favorable: 8,506,576 *yes* and 136,198 *no*; in 1934 it was ninety-seven percent favorable: 10,045,447 *yes* and 15,201 *no* (.15 percent). It was not, of course, a secret ballot, but the triumph was a real one.

"Anti-Fascism is dead," Il Duce proclaimed.

Indeed Fascism seemed to have profoundly impregnated everyday life. There were constant parades of *Avanguardisti*, soldiers, *Littoriali*, children in uniform; priests were kept busy blessing *Balilla* detachments; in every train the corridors were patrolled by two men of the Fascist Militia. There was even a "Fascist style," which developed gradually in an effort to imitate Mussolini's style, from the clean-shaven skull to the martial look. As Il Duce himself wrote, defining this new style: "Life as it is conceived by Fascism is sober, austere, and religious. Fascism scorns the easy life. It believes still and forever in sanctity and heroism." The Italian press reiterated Mussolini's maxim: "Better to live a single day as a lion than a hundred years as a sheep."

Italians strove hard to adopt a "fierce" manner, because, as Il Duce further wrote, "Fascism rejects the materialistic concept of happiness. Consequently it denies the equation of well-being with happiness, which would transform men into beasts with no thought but to eat and grow fat—reduced, in other words, to the pure and simple state of vegetables."

The epitome of the Fascist style was Achille Starace, who was party secretary from December 12, 1931, until 1939. This slender man of average height, always serious of manner and imbued with the importance of his mission, was a "southerner." Born in Apulia, he had been a captain in the bersaglieri and a squadrista; remarking on the decorations that covered his chest at every official function, Mussolini had nicknamed him "the walking medal factory." After his elevation to the post of party secretary, Starace soon made his love of uniforms and parades the way of life in Italy. Mussolini justly esteemed this Fascist stage manager who had the wit, when appearing with him, to take second rank, satisfied to deck himself in the most various liveries from a huge black cape to pajamas, it was said, that bore the insignia of his duties.

Actually Starace merely propagated and systematized the quirks of Il Duce; he was an excellent symbol of the Fascism of 1932 to 1939. Under his direction the party bulletins were crammed with rigid rules to be followed in order to give the slightest act a "Fascist style." First of all, greetings were to be exchanged *romanamente*— in the Roman manner—with the right arm raised at an angle. "Shaking hands has also disappeared among us," Mussolini told Ludwig without a smile; "the Roman greeting is more sanitary, more esthetic, and quicker." Starace issued a number of orders on this subject: "To give the Roman greeting while remaining seated is hardly Roman" (August 28, 1932); "The Roman greeting does not require the lifting of the hat; but the removal of the hat is mandatory when the greeting is given indoors" (June 12, 1933).

Starace concerned himself with appearances of all kinds. For example: "I absolutely prohibit official banquets and gala spectacles that resemble the old customs" (February 27, 1932); "The word *meeting* is to be replaced by *propaganda rally*; *meeting* is a relic from a time forever gone" (April 15, 1932); "I remind you that the black necktie worn in a loose bow is not permitted" (August 7, 1932); "Correspondence between comrades is to be addressed: 'to Fascist So-and-So'; when the adjective is used as a noun, it is to be written in capitals" (April 11, 1933); "It is strictly forbidden to starch the collars of black shirts" (May 23, 1932).

In addition to these social and sartorial rules, Starace dedicated himself to preserving the monopoly of all honors for Il DUCE. "All cheers should be given only for IL DUCE, regardless of which members of the hierarchy, including myself, are present" (July 13, 1932); "Occasionally branch secretaries introduce laudatory remarks about the party secretary into their reports to IL DUCE: this is improper. When the party secretary makes his report to IL DUCE, he should not be put into a position where he must either mutilate the document or read compliments on his own work" (July 31, 1932); "It has become a general practice to mark new buildings with inscriptions in which other names are added to that of IL DUCE: this is improper" (June 7, 1934).

Obviously Mussolini had nothing to fear from competition by Starace. What is really made apparent, when one reads some of these instructions, is the extent of the blindness of Il Duce and his whole political system from the party secretary to the most modest Fascist. The fact that the party secretary could devote his time to the elaboration of such rules tells us much in itself of the critical faculty of the Fascist leaders. Thus on September 26, Year XII E.F. (for it had now been made the rule to date everything from the March on Rome, the beginning of the *Era fascista*—the Fascist Era), Starace distributed an order that revived the old motto of the cities of the Hanseatic League: "The Federations of Battle Fasci and the Battle Fasci of coastal cities shall adopt the following legend: 'It is not necessary to live, but it is necessary to navigate.' "

In order to give these quotations their full value, it must be pointed out that they were brought together into a book entitled *The Vademecum of the Fascist Style*, whose fly-leaf was adorned with a picture of a war chariot and whose preface in bold type repeated the *Me ne frego* that Il Duce had called "an act of Stoic philosophy." The introduction concluded thus: "It is fine to march again, to fight, and, if necessary, it will be finer still to go forward against the unknown, illuminated by the light of an ideal continuity that has its most glorious emblem in faith and resolve and its *condottiere* of yesterday and today in MUSSOLINI."

But then one turns the page and finds that the burden of the book is neckties, stiff collars, mural inscriptions, and forbidden top-hats: and then it becomes apparent to what extent, after 1932, the Fascist Party, in spite of the number of its members, had become a cumbersome apparatus dedicated to pomps and ritual repetitions of absurd, lifeless rhetoric, a mere cardboard stage set.

Actually, the party owed its strength in 1932 neither to its ideology nor to the Fascist style, but quite simply to the fact that it was the official party. The *tessera*, the party card, soon became essential for the acquisition or retention of any job that was directly or remotely connected with the state: the fact was legalized on May 27, 1932. And so the *tessera* became (in the words of Pius XI himself) the *tessera del pane*—the bread card.

At the height of unemployment in May, 1934, for instance, Starace requested that party members be given priority whenever jobs were available. Naturally the number of members rose rapidly, though not to the point of any decisive importance. And, of course, the higher one mounted on the job scale, the more indispensable the *tessera* became; responsible positions were the monopoly of Fascists. In short, a man who wanted to build a career had to

have in his buttonhole the *distintivo*, the party emblem composed
of the lictor's *fasces* and the initials PNF. So the whole body of offi-
cialdom rushed frenetically into the embrace of Fascism: judges
spoke only of "Fascist justice"; every party hierarch, however low
his rank, was regarded as a public official. The universities followed
the same path. Unquestionably some rebellious teachers were still
to be found in the secondary schools, but the whole of the higher
educational institutions accepted the oath of 1931: "I swear to be
faithful to the King . . . to the Fascist system . . . to fulfill my duties
as a teacher with the purpose of training industrious, honest citizens devoted to the Fatherland and to the Fascist System. I swear
that I am not and will not become a member of any organization
or party whose activities would conflict with the duties entrusted
to me."

Only thirteen teachers out of twelve hundred fifty refused to
take the oath and resigned their posts. The others were compelled
to wear the black shirt at all official ceremonies. Certainly there
were those who were cautious rebels in the privacy of their own
living-rooms, professors who laughed when they pointed to their
buttonhole emblems because to them PNF meant *per necessità
familiare* (driven by family needs). But any Italian who wanted to
move ahead, any intellectual who wanted to publish, and in the
overwhelming majority of cases anyone who wished merely to stay
alive was compelled in one way or another to yield, to collaborate,
or at the very least to remain silent. For part of the strength of the
Fascist system derived from its continuity, and what lasts must be
adjusted to under the penalty of isolation, oblivion, or sometimes
suffering. Besides, Mussolini was adept at mixing threats, honors,
and rewards.

The vulgar bait of gain lured some. Mussolini said of one of the
Fascist syndicalists, Rossini: "He is a revolutionary who has definitely gone over to the side of order: hence he loves money."

The Fascist leaders demanded a price for their influence, and
this traffic, highly developed in Italy long before Fascism, rose to a
degree that roused apprehension. Starace's orders grew more
numerous: there must be an end of *raccomandazioni*—protection;
party hierarchs too deeply involved were dismissed, but corruption
was universal: everything from public-works contracts to decorations was based on price. In the isolation of his citadel of Cremona,
Farinacci asserted that the party had fallen into the hands of
thieves and opportunists. In his battle against this gangrene
Starace dismissed five thousand party officials—an average of
fourteen a day—in a single year (December, 1931, to December,
1932) and even so it was impossible to root out the disease.

But, in addition to those who were moved by the mere desire for money, there were all the others who were attracted by titles, glory, a professorship, or a simple promotion, all those who half-unconsciously accepted whatever advantages were offered to them in exchange for their toleration, their approval, or even no more than their silence. Mussolini increased the number of senators, of whom he appointed two hundred ninety-four between 1926 and 1934: politicians, cultural and artistic notables, soldiers were invited to sit in the Senate, and there was not one refusal. An Academy of Italy was created and each of its members received one hundred fifty dollars a month. They included such unchallengeable scientists as Marconi and Enrico Fermi but also other men whose sole qualification was the fact that they were Fascists, and the cleverly executed fusion served to commingle them in a common identity.

From 1932 to 1935 there was an annual Exhibition of the Fascist Revolution, and every year a guard of honor was posted before the Exhibition Hall in via Nazionale. The members of this guard were prominent citizens, academicians, and senators as well as Fascists of high rank: they were organized into sections, each with its chief and its stipulated tour of duty; Marconi, a historian, or an eminent man of letters, buckled into his uniform, stood at attention outside the hall and moved on command. In this connection the old quadrumvir, De Bono, noted in his diary in 1934: "It is no use, I will never understand some of these Fascist methods and customs! Posting senators, deputies, and generals on guard at the Exhibit of the Revolution!!!"

Now there was a great deal of purpose in the posting of these guards: Mussolini wanted to show off his Fascists; men who accepted the honors of the Senate, the Chamber, or the Academy were expected to pay for them to the greater glory of Fascism. After all, it mattered little to Il Duce what these honorable citizens might really feel in their inmost hearts. Mussolini had said to Ludwig: "To me the mass is nothing more than a flock of sheep as long as it is not organized . . . but, if it is led, it must be led with two reins, enthusiasm and self-interest." As we have seen, self-interest was shrewdly handled; as for enthusiasm, every time Il Duce left Stazione Termini in Rome, he was followed by fourteen trains loaded with cheering brigades.

But demagogy, stage management, and shrewdness alone were not enough to account for the genuine adherence or the benevolent or passive toleration of large sectors of the Italian people. In fact, as time went on, a generation—the pre-Fascist generation—began to die out. Giolitti died in 1928, Facta in 1930, Salandra in

1931, Turati in 1932, Treves in 1933. A new generation born about 1915 was coming to maturity: it was composed of young men who had no historical experience of anti-Fascism or of the violence of the squadre: they believed in the three hundred thousand Black Shirts of the March on Rome.

Some of them, of course, were bound by family ties to the men in exile and in prison, but others had been caught up since childhood by Fascist organizations and education, and they were Fascists because idealistically, under the hammering of official propaganda, they imagined Fascism as a social revolution that would lead to "the equality of men in labor through corporativism." They never heard the names of Matteotti or Sforza, of Gramsci or Gobetti, of Amendola or Nenni, of the Rosselli brothers; indeed, the greatest achievement of Mussolinian rhetoric was its imprisonment of these young men within Fascism.

Some students did found little magazines that were more or less orthodox, but they wanted to be Fascists, faithful to what they believed to be the objectives of the Fascist and corporativist revolution. They were the backers of the "left Fascists," men who, like Professor Ugo Spirito, proposed at the party congress in Ferrara in 1932 that ownership of everything be transferred to the corporations and that the capitalists be dispossessed. These young debaters within Fascism—young middle-class intellectuals, in other words— were tolerated by Mussolini in their restricted divagations from orthodoxy, for their discussions gave some reality to the demagogy of the system. With their illusions, their sincerity, and their youth they injected an appearance of life into the verbosity of the slogans.

Besides, in those years between 1932 and 1936, Fascism had no fear of them. It could claim a record of achievements that, presented in the proper light, seemed to answer any criticism.

There was first of all the success of the Lateran Accords with the Holy See, which included a treaty between Italy and the Vatican, a Concordat, and a financial agreement.

At noon of February 11, 1929, the feast day of the Madonna's apparition at Lourdes, Pietro Cardinal Gasparri and *Cavaliere* Benito Mussolini solemnly signed the documents that hallowed the sovereignty of the Pope over Vatican City and the official character of the Catholic religion in Italy. Article XXXIV of the Concordat was of special importance: "In the intent of restoring to the institution of marriage, which is at the base of the family, a dignity in accord with the Catholic traditions of its people, the Italian state recognizes the civil validity of the sacrament of marriage administered under canon law."

In addition to this legal validation of church marriages in Italy the government made other concessions: "Catholic doctrine is the foundation and the crown of public education." But what interested Italians above all else was the fact that at last Il Duce had achieved the accord with the papacy that Italy had sought since 1870. No one bothered to remember that that accord had been in sight since the days before the accession of Fascism to power. Everywhere postcards were distributed bearing the portraits of the King, Il Duce, and Pius XI; everyone quoted Francesco Crispi's prediction: "Italy's greatest statesman will be the man who resolves the Roman question."

Addressing the students of the Catholic University of Milan on February 14, His Holiness said of the accords: "We have also been nobly and abundantly seconded by the other party. And undoubtedly it required a man like him whom Providence has given us to encounter." In simpler terms, "the man of Providence" was Mussolini, who had "given God back to Italy and Italy back to God."

The country was filled with genuine enthusiasm and, at the same time, a joyous surprise. Prayers, however, were offered for the Holy Father by a few Catholics who agreed with the statement of the anti-Fascists: "The Pope has nailed down the lid on the coffin of Italian freedom."

Hence, the triumph of Il Duce was vast, and, after the Concordat, Fascism was undeniably at "the highest point of its curve."[1] Deputies and senators hailed Il Duce, "a prophet in word and deed"; they extolled the Lateran Accords, which "raise the cross of Christ still higher before the world on its rightful throne; at the same time they open vast domains to the flight of the imperial eagles of the new Italy."

Thereafter the church took part every day in the life of Fascism; and was not that life, after all, the only reality in Italy? The *Case del Fascio* (houses of the Fasci) were blessed by priests; pastoral letters were often full of praises for Il Duce; Ildefonso Cardinal Schuster of Milan was received by Starace in the *Casa del Fascio*; at official ceremonies it was no rarity to see priests and even bishops raise their arms in the Fascist salute alongside the hierarchs.

But, though it collaborated, the church did not abdicate. A few months after the Lateran Accords, Mussolini delivered a dramatic speech that was to arouse tremendous feeling, a three-hour address in which Il Duce reaffirmed the supremacy of the state. "The church is not sovereign in the state," he said; "it is not even free. . . . The Christian religion was born in Palestine, but it became

[1] A. C. Jemolo, *L'Église et l'État en Italie dua nos jouts* (Paris: Le Seuil).

Catholic in Rome; confined to Palestine, it would probably have been no more than still another of the sects that abounded in that troubled region, like that of the Essenes, for example, or the Therapeutae; it is quite likely that it would have been erased without leaving a single trace."

This was reminiscent of the anti-clerical Mussolini who challenged God in the old days in Switzerland. Il Duce added: "We have not resuscitated the temporal power of the Popes; we have locked it up. . . . The state is Catholic but it is Fascist; it is Fascist above all else, exclusively and essentially."

Pius XI forcefully condemned these "heretical utterances," but beyond Mussolini's speech there was the reality of the Lateran Accords. Other controversies, furthermore, were to arise between the church and the Fascist state, as in 1931 on the subject of Catholic Action, the Catholic youth movement. Pius XI did not hesitate to make it plain that "for a very large number membership in the party and the oath are the pre-conditions of their careers, of their livelihoods."

But the church had to take into account the Fascist state that furthered it on many levels, as Fascism had to reckon with the power that Catholicism represented. Hence the controversies ended in compromises. Jemolo, a Catholic historian, indeed believes that few of the faithful would have backed the church in a conflict with Fascism. Italy had no Emmanuel Mounier, no Georges Bernanos, no Jacques Maritain, and so the priests and the monks continued to parade past Il Duce. The church had opted, Jemolo says, for offending the lesser number.

In any event, for the greater number Fascism emerged the stronger, and its labors were as if sanctified. Cesare De Vecchi, the squadrista, was appointed Ambassador to the Vatican; and on January 9, 1932, Pius XI bestowed the golden spur on Il Duce. On February 11, Mussolini, the former anarchist, the man of the multiple mistresses, the orator to whom Christianity would have been only a sect if not for Rome, was received by Pius XI, and their conversation lasted for an hour and five minutes. The church too accepted realities.

The success of this reconciliation with the church was augmented by other triumphs of Fascism that were enlarged by its propaganda.

Il Duce had waged *la Battaglia del Grano*, *la Battaglia della Lira*, *la Battaglia della Bonifica integrale* (the battles for wheat, the *lira*, and land reclamation). He had begun the first of these on July 4, 1925: Italy must cease importing wheat and become self-

sufficient. And Mussolini went into the fields: he ran a threshing
machine and he plunged his hand into the sacks of grain. Competitions were established, with prizes of gold, silver, and bronze
stars for the Harvest Infantry. Mussolini even wrote a poem:

> Let us all love bread,
> The heart of every home,
> The perfume of the table,
> The joy of every hearth.
> Let us respect our bread,
> Let us honor bread,
> Let us not waste the bread of Italy.

In 1931 he won his harvest victory: the nation met its needs.
Fascism triumphed and propaganda thundered. Closer analysis
disclosed that more profitable crops, such as fruits and vegetables,
for which there were export markets, had been sacrificed, that
livestock breeding had been neglected, and, finally, that this pro-
tectionism in the sphere of wheat had redounded to the profit of the
great landed proprietors and the least developed sectors of Italian
agriculture. In actuality the policy of "Italian bread" could be justified only on the grounds of propaganda and a war economy. But
that did not become apparent until later.

Then Il Duce announced *la battaglia della lira.* On October 18,
1926, he swore: "I will defend the *lira* to my last breath, to the
last drop of my blood." In 1927 the exchange rate of the *lira* was
established at 92.47 to the pound sterling, the same as Poincaré's
franc: this was a policy of deflation and prestige from which the
middle classes benefited, but that led to reductions in salaries and
wages while prices dropped only very little. But the figures speak
for themselves. Between 1927 and 1939 (the 1913 level having
been taken as the index at 100), salary and wage payments shrank
from 120.8 to 105.7. Here again, in reality, the deflation and the
artificial exchange rate were justified first of all on the propaganda
level. Large companies, like Montecatini, the giant chemical trust,
swallowed the smaller firms damaged by the drop in prices. But
at the time no one looked beyond the rise in the reputation of the
Italian currency.

The third battle, for land reclamation, included the drainage of
marsh areas, reforestation, etc. New villages were built in the
Pontine Marshes: Littoria, Sabaudia, Pontinia. They were colo-
nized by war veterans while journalists and foreign observers
looked on. "This is where we have waged a veritable war," Mussolini declared in Littoria in 1932. "This is the war that we prefer."

Propaganda was to pour out panegyrics on an undertaking that was only partly completed at a cost of six hundred million dollars to the state and often to the greater enrichment of landowners the value of whose properties was increased by the investment of public funds in them. Meanwhile, covered with wreaths, Mussolini dedicated the colonists' little houses, on the walls of which were inscribed one of the aphorisms of Il Duce: "It is the plow that makes the furrow, but it is the sword that defends it."

In other areas there were bridges, roads, aqueducts, *autostrade* (express highways), beaches—like the Lido di Roma—stadia, forums, swimming pools to dedicate. In that period of economic depression the government emphasized public works of this kind that could take up some of the unemployment and redound to the glory of the system without any penny-pinching on credits, part of which went to the hierarchs.

New streets were laid out, and demolitions began in the medieval areas of Rome because, Mussolini said, "the two-thousand-year-old monuments of our history should rise and dominate in the solitude that they deserve." Excavations were started in the Forum and at Pompei.

In 1931 work began on the University City in Rome. From the *case popolari* (low-cost housing) to the villages in the reclaimed areas, from the Florence railway station to the *Case del Fascio* and the Aeronautical Exhibition, Fascist-built structures were characterized by their often daring architecture, which in the view of foreigners seemed to symbolize the face of a rejuvenating order.

This feeling was reinforced by such ventures as that of Italo Balbo, who undertook to fly the Atlantic in 1933 with twenty-four seaplanes. The whole country followed the stages of his voyage from Orbetello to Amsterdam to Reykjavik to Montreal to Chicago to New York. Each stop was the occasion for a demonstration and for a flood of messages. In Chicago, as in New York, Balbo played Duce to a chorus of acclamation. Eugenio Cardinal Pacelli (the future Pius XII), now Papal Secretary of State to Pius XI, cabled: "Please convey to General Balbo and his companions the felicitations of His Holiness and His Benediction, while He prays that the Divine aid invoked by the brave aviators on their departure be extended also to their safe return."

Balbo spoke at Madison Square: "Italians of New York, we bring you the greetings of Italy and Mussolini. . . . Be proud that you are Italians. . . . And especially you, workers of untiring hands and simple hearts . . . Mussolini has ended the era of humiliations. To be an Italian is a title of honor." Naturally the descendants of the immigrants thrilled to this playing on their national pride.

The return to Rome was a triumph. The fliers paraded on a

carpet of flowers. They marched beneath the Arch of Constantine. At the Palatine Il Duce delivered a magnificent oration. Balbo was made air marshal. It is clear how Fascism identified itself with the nation, adroitly emphasizing its own achievements as it exalted the Italian Fatherland and People.

In New York Balbo had declaimed: "It is you, workers, who enjoy the pride and the love of Il Duce because you are religious and fruitful." And it was true that in Mussolini's mind national greatness and a large population were closely connected. He launched a fourth battle, "the population battle," for which he offered himself as an example; when Romano Mussolini was born, a Fascist organization hailed "the confirmed proof of a virility that is a model for all Italians." In a splendid ceremony on November 30, 1933, a mass wedding rite was celebrated for 2,620 couples in Rome, and there was a "gift from Il Duce" for each. Just before being received that evening by the Pope, they sent a telegram to Mussolini: "A year from now each of us will present a little *balilla* to our beloved Fascist Italy." But, for all this play-acting, the birth rate continued its regular decline, from 27.5 per thousand in 1927 to 23.4 in 1934. Mussolini was irate. "If we continue to shrink, gentlemen," he warned the Senate, "we shall not build an empire: we shall become a colony."

A tax was imposed on the unmarried. Officials lost promotions when it was learned that they were childless. "How many party hierarchs are there," *il Popolo d'Italia* demanded, "who have large families—that is, at least five children—and where are they?"

In spite of the decline in births and the economic advances of Fascism, Italy's social situation continued to be difficult. There were still more than a million men unemployed (twenty-one percent of the total working force), for Fascist Italy had been affected by the depression of 1929–31 like other countries. Prices were falling, and salaries and wages dropped even more sharply: almost fifty percent for farm workers in Lombardy. Bankruptcies increased: among the 2,939 firms with capital of less than fifty thousand dollars in 1932, there were 1,216 failures. In 1931 the largest Italian banks (Banca commerciale italiana, Credito italiano, Banco di Roma, Credito marittimo) were in jeopardy and called on the state for help. Although he had championed economic liberalism until 1926, now—and this was also the time when corporativist theories were promulgated—Mussolini proclaimed the necessity for state intervention: semi-public agencies were established to employ state funds to rescue banks and large companies from failure. This was the origin of the Società finanziaria industriale italiana (Sofindit—Italian Industrial and Financial Co.), the

Istituto mobiliare italiano (IMI—Italian Securities Institution), the Istituto di ricostruzione industriale (IRI—Italian Reconstruction Institute); a complete osmosis between the state and the most powerful industrial and financial quarters, a homogeneity of fact (and of persons) embracing the top bureaucrats, industrialists, ministers, and Fascist hierarchs gradually came into being.

In the end the state was to compel concentrations of industry to the advantage of the largest components: concentration became mandatory in the metal industries in 1931, and every sector of industry was legally subject to supervision and direction by those who controlled seventy percent of its production (1932). This meant further strengthening of some of the industrial giants: FIAT, Biella, Montecatini, the hydro-electric companies. Mussolini extended himself to justify this policy of helping the largest capitalists: "Could the state," he asked, "repeat the gesture of Pontius Pilate?" His answer was negative, because these companies employed thousands of workers.

And the corporative institutions were at hand to disguise the real meaning of this policy. But, while the representatives of management in the corporations were actually Agnelli, the owner of FIAT, or Donegani, the owner of Montecatini, the representatives of the workers were generals of the Fascist Militia, lawyers, squadristi, some of the sons of d'Annunzio, interchangeable men moving from one corporation to another and representing only Fascism and not the workers.

Hence it was not surprising that, in spite of the cheering squads, Mussolini received a cold welcome at the FIAT plant or that the *braccianti* of Apulia and the Abruzzi sought to rebel in 1933. Nor had strikes been eliminated: the Special Court handed down one hundred one sentences for strike action in 1933, seventy-two in 1932, and sixty-nine in 1935. In order to provide a closer check on the worker, the mandatory Labor Card was introduced in 1934. Such measures made it impossible to forget that Mussolini's system, in spite of its successes and the active or passive support that it received from large sections of the country, was still a police state on a constant alert and that anti-Fascism, whatever Mussolini might say on the subject, was not dead.

The struggle against anti-Fascism, however, was carried on by the Special Court for the Defense of the State. It sat in the huge Palace of Justice in Rome behind a guard of the Fascist Militia. The judges wore dress uniform on the bench: most often the presiding judge was a consul general of the Militia, assisted by five consuls, and a platoon of armed Militiamen paid its respects to them in the courtroom. This was a military apparatus, a summary court in which judgments were framed in advance and any defense was a pure matter of form. The tribunal's production totaled fifty-one hundred fifteen sentences amounting to 28,116 years of imprisonment. Its first two cases were those of two men accused of insults to Mussolini, trivial comments for which the two men, made to sit in a cage facing the exalted jurists, had to pay with nine months in prison, fines of twenty-five dollars, and one year of special supervision.

Special supervision was the fate of all anti-Fascists and indeed of all Italians. After nine o'clock at night the police could ask for the *documenti* of anyone abroad in the streets of the large cities. Those whose papers were dubious were taken to a police station and kept there until morning for verification of their identifications. In practice, the police simplified the job by rounding up the first hundred or two hundred persons encountered each evening, thus establishing a quota for the entire night.

The system applied to opponents of the government or to those who were simply uninterested was a more serious matter: a Roman worker who had once been an Ardito and then refused to join the Fascio was arrested one hundred times in four years; others had to report every week to the police; on May 1 they were all locked up for twenty-four hours to make certain of their good behavior.

Repression became, in fact, the keystone of the state. In 1930 the Fascist penal code drawn by Rocco was promulgated: it defined those persons who were "socially dangerous." These could include anyone who "was commonly reputed to be habitually guilty of serious crimes . . . or commonly suspected of being capable of infringing public order."

It was the heyday of the informer, the gossip, the legalized stoolpigeon. The political police, the famous OVRA, kept its files up to date, making use of an army of more or less volunteer informers. From 1935 until his arrest in 1942, young Ruggero Zangrandi, Vittorio Mussolini's friend who became an anti-Fascist, was followed and spied on. Censorship of mail, of course, was the rule. Zangrandi and his young friends made it a habit to enclose a hair in each of their letters, but it was never there when the letter reached the addressee. They all adopted the same phrase to alert their correspondents: "I'm beginning to worry because I'm losing all my hair."

This was, of course, mere child's play. But the OVRA often worked more roughly: it did not have to justify its arrests, and its interrogations were severe: its men offered cigarettes, but they also tortured: fifty cockroaches on a prisoner's lower abdomen, confined by a glass cover, created intolerable itching; cord was drawn tight over testicles; prisoners were put through make-believe executions; others were made to drink iodine; and everyone, constantly, was beaten, wherever he could be hit, so that many were killed or driven insane. But, while these instances clearly demonstrate that Italian Fascism was not innocent of horrors, it could in no way compare with the universalization of an industry of torture that was to be developed by the Gestapo.

The difference was even more apparent in the area of deportation: Mussolini sent his opponents to the south. The islands of Ustica and Lipari, and the reef of Lampedusa became the *confini*—internment camps. Gramsci, Rosselli, and such writers as Carlo Levi and Cesare Pavese were held there among thousands of unknown militants from all over Italy. The prisoners arrived in chains, shocked by the misery round them and the cruel sunlight on the white limed walls after their voyage in the excrement-filled holds of their ships. Each prisoner received ten *lire* a day, and he had either to rent quarters from the citizenry or to live in a dormitory, subject to the tyranny or the cruelty of a Fascist Militia officer and side by side with the ordinary criminal who might rob or inform on him at any moment.

The political deportees, however, set up courses for one another and reorganized branches of their old parties. It was far from being the "kind and humane deportation" of which Mussolini boasted, but this kind of life, after all, was not so much more miserable than that of the islanders, themselves confined in what has been called a "Siberia on fire," though it had nothing in common with Buchenwald or the real Siberia of Stalin. Carlo Rosselli, one of the founders of the *Giustizia e Libertà* movement, provided an excellent description of his confinement on Lipari when he wrote: "The *confino* is a large cell without walls, a cell composed entirely of sky and sea. The Militia sentries are its walls, walls of flesh and blood rather than of lime and stone. The desire to blow them up becomes an obsession."

And there were escapes. One July night Rosselli, Emilio Lussu, and Francesco Fausto Nitti managed to reach a motorboat waiting for them offshore. By morning they were within sight of the flat coast of Tunisia, where they began their exile.

The exiles, the *fuorusciti*, formed the main body of anti-Fascism, living in large part in Paris: Nitti, Turati, Treves, and Sforza met there. An Anti-Fascist Confederation was formed, though it did not put an end to the old internal dissensions. The Communists looked on it as a reincarnation of the idealistic and impotent assembly of the Aventine, or, as some of them said more harshly, "a new political scheme inspired by the Freemasons."

The Communist Party was in actuality the only party that remained alive in Italy in spite of repression. It was kept under particular watch, however: of 4,671 convictions handed down by the Special Court, 4,030 were those of Communists—real or alleged. A worker was sent to prison for three years for having written *W Lenin* on the handle of his knife. On May 28, 1928, the state began the *Processone*, the show trial of the Central Committee of the Communist Party. Speaking of Antonio Gramsci, one of the defendants, the public prosecutor warned: "We must keep this brain from functioning for twenty years."

Gramsci, the Sardinian intellectual with the squat body and the astonishingly heavy head on fragile shoulders, was sentenced to twenty years in prison. For him this was tantamount to slow execution, for he had tuberculosis, and the prison doctors, Fascists or loafers, were to allow the disease to grow worse. Wasting away from his illness, Gramsci wrote to his wife in 1936. "The limits of my liberty have been reduced to my inner life, and my will has become merely a will to resist."

Mussolini had ordered a policeman to attend the trial and bring him a detailed report of it every evening; but Il Duce could not be moved by the numerous appeals that were made to him by the most diverse Italian notables. Gramsci died in 1937, leaving thirty-two notebooks filled with his fine script: incisive essays in which he analyzed the history of Italy, the philosophy of Benedetto Croce, and the nature of the modern state.

These trials and imprisonments, which struck blows of varying effect against the opposition, clearly show that anti-Fascism encountered major obstacles in Italy. First of all there was the question how the struggle should be waged: through force or through propaganda? The Communists opted for the latter: *l'Unità* reappeared clandestinely in 1927, and other underground publications were distributed door to door at great risk: *L'Avanguardia* (*Vanguard*), *Battaglie sindacali* (*Syndicalist Battles*), *The Red Cadet*. In 1934 *The Red Cadet* headlined: "War, misery, slavery? No! We want bread, work, and freedom."

It concentrated on specific demands and tried to win over the youth; clandestine labor unions were organized. In 1933 there were numerous more or less spontaneous demonstrations by the unemployed in the large cities under the slogan: "We want bread and jobs." When the plebiscite was held, the Communists called for a *no* vote, but, as we have seen, the results were pitiful: .14 percent voted *no*.

This was because there were many of those whom the militant anti-Fascists called the *dormienti*, the sleepers: workers or peasants whose anti-Fascist views were known, but who kept their mouths shut, reported regularly to the police, sometimes took out Fascist Party cards, or, since it could not always be avoided, joined Fascist unions; they let matters take their course, limiting their reactions to a thought or a look or a corner-of-the-mouth comment. Occasionally that was enough to awaken a young apprentice born under Fascism and ignorant of the past.

There were also all the intellectuals, all the trained men who "slept" in silence, refusing glory and accepting hardship rather than compromise themselves, a host of unknowns who will always remain unknown: journalists who became accountants or drugstore clerks, that whole base of inactive anti-Fascism that was to bring the greater part of Italy to its feet after 1943. But for the young anti-Fascists these years were long and onerous. For them, for example, it was not enough to read the distinguished opposition magazine directed by Croce, *la Critica*, which Il Duce tolerated. Giorgio Amendola, one of the sons of the liberal deputy, went to Paris in April, 1928. Claudio Treves, the Socialist leader, was living in a small hotel in rue de la Tour-d'Auvergne, near the Cadet subway station, and Amendola went to him for counsel. But Treves told him: "I am glad to see that there are young anti-Fascists in Italy who want to make their way and carry on the fight, but I tell you frankly: do not turn to us, we are beaten men, weak men; do not seek our help, but find your own way alone." As he spoke, Treves wept.

The young men did indeed find their own way. In November, 1929, they published the manifesto of the *Giustizia e Libertà* (Justice and Freedom) movement, which was led by Carlo and Nello Rosselli and Lussu: "a non-party revolutionary movement. . . . It is we Italians and no one else who will overthrow Fascism." The manifesto was a call for direct action. In 1929 young Ferdinando De Rosa tried to kill the Prince of Piedmont during his official visit to Brussels. In the Belgian court De Rosa declared: "Yes, I wanted to kill the Prince of Piedmont, the heir to the throne of a ruling house that has murdered freedom in my country."

Giustizia e Libertà also sponsored other activities. A few minutes after noon on July 11, 1930, a small plane appeared above Piazza del Duomo in Milan. It discharged a cargo of leaflets over the city: "Committees of *Giustizia e Libertà* have already been organized and armed in thirty cities." Then, piloted by a twenty-one-year-old teacher, Giovanni Bassanesi, the plane headed toward Switzerland. The repercussions were considerable.

In Italy the branches of *Giustizia e Libertà* (G.L.) thought in terms of acts of violence: seven tax offices in the major Italian cities were to be the targets. But the operations of the little knots of conspirators were soon infiltrated by spies and provocateurs, and Bocchini's police were past masters in the art of allowing a plan to grow to the point at which the greatest possible number of persons could be arrested.

On October 20, 1930, twenty-four leaders of the G.L. were arrested as a result of espionage: they included Ferruccio Parri, Riccardo Bauer, and Ernesto Rossi. Although they had abandoned their plan, the police tried to charge them with an attack that had killed twenty persons and wounded forty in Milan on April 28, 1928, when the King arrived in the city: in all probability that bombing had been the work of pro-republican Fascists. But the accusation by the police, even though it was later dropped, was enough to throw suspicion on the members of the G.L. One of them, driven mad by the accusations of the police, committed suicide in prison. Each of the others was sentenced to twenty years. But the struggle did not end, for, as Parri had said earlier, after a previous conviction by a Fascist court: "Your Honor, when a drumhead court condemns us, it pays us homage."

Everywhere the police were efficient. Michele Schirru, an anarchist who had sailed from New York to Italy with the intention of killing Mussolini, was arrested and shot in the back at 4:27 A.M. on May 29, 1931. He had time first to write a brief note: "My action will not be a crime . . . but, if I die without having attained the goal that for so many years I have hoped to reach, I am sure that someone else will take my place."

A week later a young man was arrested in Piazza Venezia. On examination his papers proved to be false, and he was questioned. His name was Angelo Sbardellotto, and he admitted his intention of assassinating Mussolini: he was shot in the back at 5:45 A.M. on June 17. Neither Schirru nor Sbardellotto had even begun to carry out his plan: both were shot for their intentions.

At the same time and on the same day as Sbardellotto, a young man named Domenico Bovone was shot for having exploded bombs in Turin, Genoa, and Bologna. The newspapers reported that the Black Shirts selected for his firing squad had behaved admirably, drawing their daggers and shouting: "*A noi!*"

In all three cases, Mussolini had been awakened in the middle of the night by subordinates more vulnerable than he to pity, but he had refused clemency: justice must take its course. He could not brook defiance. He was beside himself again when Lauro De Bosis flew over Rome at eight o'clock in the evening of October 3, 1931, in spite of Balbo's war planes, and dropped four hundred thousand leaflets over the Corso, Piazza Venezia, and the airport. "Have faith in Italy and freedom," the circulars said. "Italian defeatism is the real foundation of the Italian Fascist system. Communicate your faith and your ardor to others."

De Bosis vanished over the sea on his way back to his base. Before his flight, he had written a touching *Story of My Death*, showing that he had been prepared to sacrifice his life.

But idealistic acts and the statements of accused men in court were suppressed by the newspapers. Their examples were limited to a few groups loyal to old ideals, those ideals that the young would have to rediscover.

Besides, Mussolini granted many pardons in 1932: 22,173 persons were released and only three hundred thirty-seven were left in the government's prisons. Their number was to rise again, though remaining relatively small—evidence of the failure of an anti-Fascism oriented to the past or to isolated acts of individuals. The anti-Fascists were learning that other methods must be adopted.

One day, in prison, Giorgio Amendola, now a leader in the Communist Party of Italy, received a letter in which his younger brother announced that he was taking part in the *Littoriali* competitions organized by the GUF. Amendola was enraged, but his brother countered: "That is where the young are: they think they are Fascists, but they are not . . . when the young recognize that Fascism is not corporative Socialism . . . not patriotism . . . that is when the revolt will come."

Soon the Communist Party announced that "Fascist demagogy" must be employed "in order to mobilize the young." And indeed the anti-Fascism of the elders began to be revived and reanimated in 1934–35 by a party of young men, a party still tolerated by the government because it had not yet grown sufficiently. But, while all seemed somnolent in an Italy deluded and submerged by bombastic oratory, this was as it were the promise of new vigor for the opponents of the government. In 1934 the Communist and Socialist Parties concluded the first agreement for unity of action. Thus little by little the political situation was changing.

For Italy, like the rest of Europe, could now see the gathering of the international storm, that storm of 1935–40 that Mussolini had predicted in 1927. Italy would be able to fulfill her ambitions, "to win recognition of her rights," Mussolini had said. And the storm was closer: money and trucks loaded with arms had been crossing the Italian border for Bavaria since 1929. Nazi groups were being trained in Italy, and, as the result of successful elections (in 1930 and in March and July, 1932), Adolf Hitler, the unknown admirer of Il Duce, was emerging from obscurity. On January 30, 1933, he became Chancellor of the Reich.

12

Mussolini's Big Gamble and the Ethiopian War
(1933–1936)

"War is to man what motherhood is to woman."—IL DUCE (May 26, 1934)

AT EIGHT-THIRTY in the morning of October 4, 1932, Baron Pompeo Aloisi was ushered into the Hall of the Mappamondo to see Il Duce. This noble Roman, a naval officer and ambassador, had been serving since July 20 as Mussolini's executive secretary for the Foreign Ministry, which Mussolini had taken back into his own hands. Il Duce listened as the diplomat attempted to point out the dangers of German rearmament, but Aloisi noted that "not only was Il Duce not frightened; he wanted this rearmament in order to keep France in line." When Aloisi, a devoted exponent of alliance with France, voiced his astonishment, Il Duce explained with a certain smugness: "On the Rhine we are against France, on the Danube we stand with her."

When Aloisi made another visit the next day, he found Mussolini talking with Starace in extremely good humor. Aloisi completed his errand, and, as he was leaving the Hall of the Mappamondo, Mussolini called after him: "I will tell the press to say that we don't give a shit for anyone."[1]

These two incidents were characteristic of the style, compounded

---

[1] *Journal du Baron Aloisi*, published by Plon in 1957, is a highly valuable source for Italian foreign policy between 1932 and 1936, and I have relied on it *in extenso*.

244

of over-simplification and self-confidence, that Mussolini was to impart to Italian diplomacy in those crucial years of the world's history.

In fact it seemed that events were proving Il Duce right. Fascism was spreading vigorously. Hitler had been Chancellor less than a month when the Reichstag in Berlin was burned on February 28, 1933, and the era of persecution began. Mussolini deputized a personal representative, Major Mario Renzetti, to lavish advice on Hitler: advice concerning the Storm Troopers modeled on the squadre, on governmental problems, and on tactics. There seems to be reason to believe that after January 30, 1933, Hitler and Goering consulted Mussolini on the composition of their Cabinet, in which, like the Fascists in 1922, the Nazis were a minority. Vittorio Cerutti, the Italian Ambassador, was a kind of "lord protector" to the nascent Third Reich. It is not difficult to imagine Mussolini's pride and his sense of historical responsibility. On one point, however, Hitler turned his back on the counsels of Il Duce. "I have the utmost respect for Mussolini's character and work," he told the Italian Ambassador when Cerutti offered some suggestions looking toward moderation in "racial" policy, "but there is one subject on which I cannot admit that he has a clear view, and that is everything that concerns the Jewish question in Germany."

In spite of Il Duce, then, Hitler continued to persecute the Jews. Nonetheless the Fascist Grand Council paid tribute on March 9 to "the Fascist movement that is developing beyond Italy's borders . . . that has directly or indirectly been nurtured on that solid aggregate of doctrines and institutions thanks to which Italy has created the modern state."

Thus Mussolini annexed Naziism and its Adolf Hitler, who had written in 1923: "I have gained the keenest admiration for the great man who governs south of the Alps," and who had added in 1931: "Prussianism is a moral, not a geographical concept: Mussolini is a Prussian."

Such tributes, ideally suited to confirm Mussolini in his conviction that he was an unrivaled political genius, and naturally likely to impel him into international adventures, came also from such men as Winston Churchill. On February 18, 1933, the twenty-fifth congress of the Anti-Socialist League was held in the Queen's Hall in London. Churchill declared: "The Roman genius personified by Mussolini, the greatest living lawgiver, has shown many nations that the pressure of Socialism can be resisted; that spirit has pointed out the road that a nation can follow when it is bravely led." To eliminate any misunderstanding, Churchill added: "With the Fascist system Mussolini has established a central direction that countries engaged in a hand-to-hand battle against Socialism should not hesitate to take as their guide."

So from the banks of the Rhine to the banks of the Thames, by men as diverse as Hitler and Churchill, Mussolini was acknowledged as a guide in the beginning of 1933. As for France, she had sent Hubert Lagardelle to Rome on a semi-official mission. Lagardelle was a disciple of Georges Sorel and a personal friend of Mussolini. In Italy itself, the majority of the correspondents of the great foreign newspapers, like Paul Gentizon of *Le Temps*, did not conceal their admiration for Il Duce and his system. It seemed in truth as if Mussolini and Fascist Italy were surrounded only by obsequious courtiers in these privileged moments when Il Duce could play at being the master of Europe.

In 1932 Ludwig said, speaking as if to himself while Il Duce's staring eyes fixed him: "Mussolini, as the founder of a united Europe, you could be the greatest man of the century."

"Yes," Il Duce replied as if Ludwig's statement were a self-evident truth, "I am closer to that idea than I was five years ago, but the time is not yet ripe. The crisis must first be allowed to produce more drastic consequences. There will be new revolutions. It is they alone that will shape the new type of European."

Had the time come in 1933? In actuality there was no need to think in terms of the foundation of a united Europe in order to understand the attitude taken by nations and statesmen toward Mussolini and his régime. First of all there was that "hand-to-hand battle against Socialism" of which Churchill spoke; the depression, with its vast army of unemployed and bread lines, from Madrid to Paris, was stimulating the rise of Socialism and Communism, whose militants stood side by side in the riots in the streets and in the grounds of closed factories. Mussolini and Fascism offered an example, an apparently effective solution in the face of the growing Popular Fronts.

But there was also Hitler's Germany, which made Europe uneasy from the outset; here too Mussolini could be an ally: Fascism and its Duce could be the backfire, the antidote to Hitlerism and its Führer. This policy was something of a gamble: it placed Mussolini in a position of strength. Always admirably able to *sfruttare* (exploit) any situation, to play both sides, he was thus presented with the means of carrying out a peremptory, effective, and dangerous blackmail. For the sake of his own gain he could threaten to turn against France and England to the advantage of Germany, a Nazi Germany that was all the more useful to his game because it was stronger and disturbing. This policy of course ended in catastrophe for Fascist Italy, first of all, but in 1933 who could foresee that? Not Il Duce, in any event.

So once more his successes of the moment were to be built on the weakness and the acquiescence of others. But in 1933 the drama was not played in the setting of Montecitorio or the editorial rooms of *il Popolo d'Italia*, as in 1922; the stage was Europe and the Hall of the Mappamondo in Palazzo Venezia, and it was no longer the destiny of Italy but the fate of peace that was at issue.

In any case this situation, these congratulations and panegyrics, were like alcohol to Mussolini. On September 16, 1933, he received the French Ambassador, Count Charles de Chambrun, who told him: "You are too convincing, I am the mouse and you are the cat." Aloisi observed that "the joke amused Mussolini." Then Chambrun explained to Il Duce the problems faced by Premier Edouard Daladier, and Mussolini, extremely relaxed, pointed out to the Ambassador that in Daladier's place he would have done this and that. Complacently he wound up: "When I was young, I worked out ideas and let others copy them; now I do the work for other countries' Premiers."

This self-intoxicated man was steeped in nationalism, dedicated to expansion, prestige, conquest, and empire. "Tomorrow, with the dawn," he cried in 1930 in sun-bathed Florence, "the spectacle of our armed forces will show the world the serene warrior face of Italy." When the cheers subsided, he added, his face stern and his voice solemn: "Words are beautiful things, but rifles, cannon, ships, and airplanes are still more beautiful." And it was this Duce that was to be set up against Hitler; it was on him that London and Paris counted to bolster the peace of Europe.

Yet that policy seemed to be successful. Il Duce proposed a Four-Power Pact—Italy, France, Great Britain, Germany. At seven-thirty in the evening of June 7, 1933, the ambassadors affixed their signatures to the treaty in Palazzo Venezia: the four signatories pledged themselves to increase their "solidarity that would be able to strengthen confidence in peace in Europe."

Mussolini was radiant as he responded to the cheering throng gathered in front of the palace. In the Senate, still filled with the atmosphere of those great days, Il Duce apostrophized the ambassadors in the galleries: "I call upon you, representatives of all the governments, to fill the luminous breach that has just been opened, while the clouds were massing on the horizon, with not only the hopes but the certainties of the peoples."

Beyond such lyric flights Mussolini had also envisaged the treaty as a means of revising those of 1918, but, met by hostility from France, this project was little by little drained of all real substance and became a mere repetition of the principles of the League of Nations and a means for the glorification of Il Duce.

That the Four-Power Treaty had solved nothing and that its signatories, beginning with Mussolini, attached no importance to it soon became apparent. On November 14, 1933, Germany withdrew from the League, although that body had been taken as the model for the treaty; on December 6 the Fascist Grand Council resolved that Italy would remain in the League only if there were a "radical reform in that organization, and within a minimum time." This was tantamount to saying that Mussolini was denouncing the Mussolini Pact, but that did not matter; in foreign policy Il Duce had a few simple notions: to act in such manner as to gain attention and greater glory for himself and the Italy that was incarnate in him, to exploit the international crisis and the rivalries among nations for the satisfaction of Italy's territorial and colonial ambitions, and, if there should be a relaxation of tension, to heighten it again through dramatic actions, for it was through disorder that riches and growth were to be had.

On December 22, 1933, in the Julius Caesar Hall of the Capitol, he addressed the Asian students who had just held a congress in Rome. They included Arabs, Afghans, Indians, and Syrians. "In the evils of which Asia complains," Mussolini said, "we see the reflection of our own historical aspects. . . . But today, with the Fascist rebirth, a rebirth that is above all else spiritual, Rome and the Mediterranean are resuming their universal mission."

Loudly cheered, Il Duce left the Julius Caesar Hall; the Roman Empire, Asia, the mission of Fascism . . . such was the universe of grandeur, real and illusory, that daily shaped Mussolini's psychology.

In 1933 he resumed personal control of the Ministries of War, the Air, and the Navy and he decided to speed the equipment of the armed forces with the most modern matériel. The depression had not vanished, the country was still weighed down by unemployment, social conflict was resurgent, and hence vital necessities— jobs and profits—impelled Mussolini in the same direction as did his aspirations of conquest. Military maneuvers became frequent. Two thousand officers gathered after their exercises in a "mass report to Il Duce." In full-dress uniform, his helmet on the lectern beside him, Mussolini told them: "We are becoming, and we shall become still more, a military nation. And, since we are not afraid of words, let us add: a militarist nation and in the end a warrior nation."

There were other, later speeches, blending the theme of force with that of the universal mission of Fascism. "Fascist Italy," Il Duce cried at Cuneo, "is the only nation that has a language and a doctrine of salvation to give to all the civilized peoples of the earth."

In actuality, strangled by the depression and dragged one after another into the web of danger, "the civilized peoples of the earth" were throwing themselves into an arms race. It was all very well for Il Duce, on May 28, 1934, to utter a cry of alarm at the failure of disarmament, which threatened "the destiny of Europe and millions of lives" and "brought back to life the politics of blocs and alliances . . . and in the end it will be His Majesty the Artillery who will be called on to speak." How could it be overlooked that only two days earlier he had proclaimed with harshly confident finality that "war is to man what motherhood is to woman"?

A few days later, astounded and perturbed, Europe learned that Hitler and Mussolini would meet in Venice on June 14–15. Special correspondents poured into the old city, the *serenissima*, in anticipation of the historic first meeting of the two dictators.

Hitler's plane touched down at the San Nicolò airfield at ten o'clock on the morning of June 14. He emerged in civilian clothes, a yellow raincoat concealing his black jacket, chalk-striped trousers bagging over his polished shoes. The first impression was poor, redolent of unease; it was not helped by his nervous worrying of the maroon hat in his hands. He was encircled by officers and SS men, including Sepp Dietrich; had it not been for his eyes, he would have been indistinguishable from any second-rate functionary.

Mussolini was resplendent in his uniform with his fringed fez, his spurred boots, the dagger at his belt. The contrast was striking. The dictators boarded a motorboat and were taken through the city amid cries of *Duce! Duce!*

At one o'clock there was a luncheon in the royal villa of Stra, where Napoleon once stayed. From two until four the dictators were alone with each other. At one point Mussolini appeared at a window and gestured with his hand as if to indicate that Hitler was mad. At ten in the evening a concert was given for Hitler and Mussolini in the magnificent palace of the Doge, but all through the concert the cheers for Il Duce drowned out the music.

The next day the dictators again spent two hours together at the Alberoni golf club. "They barked at each other like two mastiffs," according to Baron Konstantin von Neurath, then Hitler's Foreign Minister. Struggling to understand Hitler's jerky speech, Mussolini sat through his impassioned tirades; later Il Duce was to remark:

"He recited his whole *Mein Kampf* to me from memory. What a bore! What an oaf!"

In the afternoon an enthusiastic crowd packed itself into Piazza San Marco, pressing under the arcades and extending all the way to the bank of the Grand Canal. Il Duce spoke from the balcony of the Doge's palace. The crowd did not once shout Hitler's name, but *Duce! Duce!* resounded from beginning to end of the speech. Young Fascists even broke down the doors in their eagerness to embrace Mussolini, who, Aloisi noted, was "pale with emotion."

In the evening Hitler was host at a dinner, which was followed by a ball. The meeting was obviously a failure. Aloisi, with the sober sensitivity of a *grand seigneur*, remarked mournfully after these two days of meetings: "I have given a great deal of thought to the men who were round me. Never have I come so close as today to human wretchedness. Tomorrow Venice will take back its countenance and its charm in silence."

For the two dictators had not reached any understanding. Europe breathed again. Between Hitler and Mussolini there was a clash—minor, it is true—of temperaments: the satisfied cynic ensconced at the summit of his glory and power, face to face with the puny, garrulous visionary whose whole career was still to be made. To add to the opposition between them there was Austria, whose annexation—*Anschluss*—to the Reich was demanded by Hitler and which, under the government of Chancellor Engelbert Dollfuss, had become an authoritarian Catholic bastion, the faithful liege of Fascist Italy. This was the apple of discord between Hitler and Mussolini.

Mussolini was often host and counselor at Riccione, south of Rimini on the Adriatic, to little Dollfuss—Millimetternich, the Viennese called him—and his beautiful wife, whom certain gossips rather hastily made the mistress of Il Duce. On July 25, 1934, when Frau Dollfuss and her children were at Riccione, a telephone call from Vienna announced that the Nazis had attempted to seize power and had murdered Dollfuss. Mussolini was revolted by the death of the Chancellor and the *Putsch* that failed. "Hitler is the murderer of Dollfuss. . . . He is a loathsome sexual degenerate, a dangerous madman," he said.

He strode up and down in his villa; then—it was four in the afternoon—he decided to send two Italian divisions to the Brenner. But for three hours the Nazis' failure had been patent; so Mussolini was playing a sure thing, knowing that he could not lose. The news of the troops' departure was given maximum publicity, and Hitler, who had perpetrated a major error, was compelled to withdraw, seemingly yielding to Italian military pressure. The

Italians stood unanimously behind Il Duce. When Frau Dollfuss left Riccione, people lined both sides of the road in an impressive silent tribute. The church strongly condemned "the challenge hurled at Europe and the civilized world."

The Fascist press was let loose. On July 29 *il Popolo di Roma* trumpeted: "What are the Nazis? Assassins and pederasts—nothing more." When Mussolini received Lagardelle, he said of Nazism: "The Germans are apes." Standing atop a tank at the Levant Fair in Bari, he exclaimed: "Thirty centuries of history entitle us to look with a sovereign pity on certain doctrines from beyond the Alps, doctrines upheld by the descendants of peoples who had not yet learned to write . . . when Rome had Caesar and Virgil and Augustus."

Mussolini had never gone so far in his opposition to Hitler's Germany, and Paris and London alike were more confident than ever that they could play off Il Duce against Hitler, Fascism against Naziism.

In a black overcoat and top-hat, Mussolini entered the Stazione Termini in Rome at seven o'clock on the evening of January 4, 1935, and greeted Ambassador de Chambrun. Together they went out to the platform, where the carabinieri in dress uniform were arrayed. At that exact moment the train from Paris came into the station. "A brown-haired man with a white necktie, waving and smiling, leaped from the train while it was still moving, like a flash. There was time to see something unheard-of: Monsieur Mussolini, that man of such perfect self-control, that stone face, was visibly flushing with happiness."

So the major French newspapers described the arrival of Monsieur Pierre Laval, Minister of Foreign Affairs. At the risk of a discordant note in the universal hymn of joy, Léon Blum said in *Le Populaire*: "For the first time a French minister is the guest of the man who killed Matteotti, for the first time a representative of the Republic of France recognizes the tyrant of Italy as a head of state." His was a lone voice.

Installed in the Hotel Excelsior, Laval was honored with a dinner in Palazzo Venezia. In his toast he hailed "the great man who presides over the destinies of Italy." He turned toward Il Duce: "You have written the finest page of modern history." The next day, in the magnificent Palazzo Farnese, the seat of the French Embassy, Mussolini and Laval held a long private meeting. Just before midnight, as he was leaving, Mussolini said: "We will sign tomorrow."

On January 7, 1935, in Palazzo Venezia, both men initialed the

French-Italian agreements intended to open an "era of close collaboration between the two countries." France gave up territories in Africa (bordering on Libya and Italian Somaliland) and guaranteed the privileges of Italians in Tunisia until 1965. As to Europe, the two states decided to consult each other periodically in order to analyze conditions; and they reaffirmed the necessity of Austrian independence.

The French press sang laudation to Il Duce, his "handsome peasant emperor's head," "that face of stone that speaks." "When the two men clasped hands," Louis Gillet of the Académie française wrote, "it was indeed the pact, it was in truth the embrace of France and Italy."

Soon military talks were initiated between Generals Pietro Badoglio and Maurice Gamelin: two thousand French war veterans paraded before cheering Roman throngs and a French naval squadron paid a call at Naples. The alliance between "the two Latin sisters" was becoming a reality.

Even better, there was a conference in Stresa on April 11, 1935, that brought together French Premier Étienne Flandin, Laval, Mussolini, Prime Minister Ramsay MacDonald, and his Foreign Secretary, Sir John Simon. England, then, had joined the "Latin bloc." The three powers seemed to be creating a common front— the Stresa Front—against Hitler's Germany, which, in violation of the Treaty of Versailles, had reinstituted compulsory military service on March 16. Mussolini seemed indeed, as Laval had told him, to have put "his prestige at the service of Europe and contributed an indispensable support to the preservation of peace."

Two items in the news from Italy immediately after the accords with Laval aroused astonishment. On January 16 General De Bono, the quadrumvir, was appointed High Commissioner to Italian East Africa and Mussolini made himself Minister of Colonies—his eighth portfolio. Why? It was well known that since the autumn of 1934 there had been a steady rise in incidents between Italy and the Empire of Ethiopia, which was a member of the League of Nations: the Italian consulate in Gondar had been invaded; on December 5 the Ethiopians had attacked the Italians in Wal-Wal with machine guns and artillery; there were frequent clashes over the demarcation of the border separating independent Ethiopia from Italian Eritrea and Somaliland. These facts stirred apprehension.

It was rumored in Paris that during his January talks with Il Duce Laval had left Fascist Italy "a free hand" in Ethiopia; this was supposedly the price demanded by Mussolini for his backing in

Europe. Moreover, in Stresa, when it was time to sign the treaty that "guaranteed peace," Mussolini had taken a pen and inserted *in Europe*; neither Flandin and Laval nor the Englishmen, MacDonald and Simon, had said a word. Laval, in fact, had smiled. Mussolini's implication was actually quite clear.

Day after day it became more obvious that Mussolini had fixed his choice on the last of the free states in Africa, where in the past, at Adowa, the armies sent by Crispi had been defeated by the gaunt warriors from the high plateau. On May 25 in the Chamber of Deputies Mussolini issued a warning "to those who would like to immobilize us at the Brenner in order to prevent us from moving elsewhere."

It could not have been put more clearly. In fact, Mussolini had initiated his policy of encircling Ethiopia as early as 1932; a military committee had been created in 1933, but it was only after the Laval agreements that the decision to act was made: on January 29, 1935.

On February 1 Mussolini held an impressive review of the Fascist Militia in the main square of Siena, where he decorated the troopers. It was an imposing spectacle against the matchless background of the old medieval city. "I want to build a nation of workers and soldiers," Il Duce declared. "Relations among nations are based on force, the force of arms."

On February 6 an army corps sailed for Ethiopia and new classes of conscripts were called up; on February 11 two more divisions sailed and volunteer enlistments began to mount. On March 23 Il Duce thundered in Piazza Venezia: "We are prepared for whatever duty our destiny may impose on us . . . the millions of bayonets borne by the people of the Black Shirts back up our genuine desire for European collaboration."

Now that he had his war, Mussolini had no interest in anything else and all other matters were neglected. France and England were in a delicate position with respect to the ambitions of Il Duce: Ethiopia was a member of the League of Nations and she could not be abandoned to destruction through aggression without a loss of face; on the other hand, Mussolini was valuable in Europe, against Hitler. What was to be done?

In Italy Mussolini reiterated his warnings. Troops in "African" battle dress—pith helmets, khaki uniforms—were being shipped out every day: the recalls of individual soldiers and of three entire classes testified to the resolve of Il Duce. "No one but Italy," he said, "can sit in judgment on so delicate a matter."

It was as if Mussolini were rushing into decisions so that he would be unable to draw back. He rejected a compromise plan put forward by Anthony Eden. In August, Galeazzo Ciano left for Africa as a captain in a bomber squadron, and the party's branch secretaries enlisted. Mussolini harangued a hundred thousand soldiers. Peddlers in the harbors sold postcards portraying attractive Ethiopian women, and *Facetta nera* (*Little Black Face*) was the song all the troops sang.

"The mere thought of war makes me shudder," the Pope asserted. ". . . The right of defense is subject to limitations and reservations that should be observed, even if the need of expansion is a fact that must be taken into account." But his voice was stifled by the managed press. Besides, the Catholic hierarchy showed its approval of the war: bishops blessed the troops as they embarked, and priests in their sermons emphasized the civilizing mission of the conquest that was to come. Little by little, international opinion began to stir. Negotiators were busy at the Palace of the League in Geneva. Laval tried to break down British opposition to concessions, but Mussolini scorned negotiations: he coveted Ethiopia, unquestionably, but in addition he wanted a total and incontestable victory; he was seeking prestige as much as profit.

On August 9 he received his Under-Secretary of State, Fulvio Suvich. "I want no agreements," he said, bringing down the flat of his hand on his desk while Suvich stood listening in silence. "Unless I get everything, including the Emperor's surrender!" He gave each word emphasis and his voice rang through the huge room. "I have to prepare for war, and even for a general war. So let them try to gain time. That's all."

In the mind of Il Duce, the means—war—had irreparably supplanted the end. On August 10 he attended aerial maneuvers; the next day he saw Aloisi, who was about to leave for negotiations in Paris with Laval and Eden. "I have a great deal of misgiving about your journey," Il Duce said at once. "You must act more like a warrior than a diplomat, a Fascist rather than a negotiator." And, losing his head, he made a major admission: "Even if they gave me everything, I would rather avenge Adowa." The logic of dictatorial power and exacerbated nationalism were leading Mussolini and Fascism quite consciously to war.

September 8, 1935. Twenty thousand *Avanguardisti* marched down via dell'Impero. "We will carry through to the end," Mussolini pledged.

September 10. The Italian secret service (Servizio informazioni militari: SIM—Military Intelligence Service) informed Mussolini that Britain's Home Fleet planned to mass in the Mediterranean, but His Gracious Majesty's ships were not ready for combat—a mere political bluff that could be ignored.

September 20. The British naval concentration got under way. The Italian press was indignant: the British Empire was denying proletarian Italy a wretched possession, her place in the sun.

September 28. The Negus of Ethiopia ordered mobilization.

October 2. At three-thirty in the afternoon the sirens wailed and the church bells tolled in every town and village in Italy and crowds gathered in the squares. At six o'clock the officials of the ministries marched through Rome to Palazzo Venezia. An hour later Mussolini appeared on the balcony; his jaws clenched, he stared down at the cheering crowd. "We have been patient with Ethiopia for forty years," he began. *"Basta—enough!"*

The crowd broke into a frenzy. Posters and banners waved wildly. Mussolini added: "Let no one suppose that we can be made to yield without a bitter fight."

October 3. The war began. Ciano and Mussolini's sons took part in the first aerial bombardment. In the League of Nations the Negus denounced the slaughter of women and children. Aloisi noted in his diary with a certain contempt: "Galeazzo Ciano's arrogance and vanity are beyond measure. He is going to be very expensive to Italy."

October 6. Adowa was occupied. The defeat of 1896 had been avenged, the Italian press shrilled.

October 10. Fifty member states of the League of Nations voted economic sactions against Italy, which was found guilty of deliberate aggression.

The most serious international crisis since the end of the First World War had been provoked on the instance of Mussolini. It was the overture to the Second World War and it was the work of Mussolini, once more a step ahead of Hitler.

So now Fascist Italy was at war, her first war, and the international situation seemed extremely dangerous: England was apparently resolved to act, and her enemies suggested that the SDN that the United Kingdom hoped to protect—in Italian, the League of Nations was the *Società delle nazioni*—was the *Sorgenti del Nilo:* the sources of the Nile.

As for Mussolini, he looked ahead to the future with confidence and irresponsibility. Receiving Ambassador Charles-Roux on October 8, the Pope confided to him: "Mussolini says he is convinced that in the end there will be war between the English and the Italians, that it will spread quickly to the rest of Europe, that the Germans are counting on celebrating Christmas in Vienna. . . ."

Then Pius XI added insidiously: "He talks as if all that amounted to no more than drinking a morning cup of coffee."

Aloisi, who was with Il Duce every day at this period, had the same impression: "Mussolini believes that war with England is inevitable," he noted. It was true that Eden was holding out for firmness, but the other members of the Cabinet, and especially Neville Chamberlain, favored conciliation that would make it possible to satisfy Italy and at the same time preserve appearances. Dino Grandi, now Italian Ambassador to England, had close contacts with members of the Cabinet and even with the Prince of Wales, who was quite pro-Italian.

In France mediation was attempted by Laval, backed by a *Manifesto of French Intellectuals for the Defense of the West and of Peace in Europe.* "It is proposed," the signers of the Manifesto wrote, "to hurl the peoples of Europe against Rome on the pretext of protecting an amalgamation of uncivilized tribes."

Clearly the Ethiopian war was revealing the split in public opinion in the democratic countries; it was the first test of resistance to the aggressions of the totalitarian countries; it also made it possible to establish contact with the leading groups and individuals disposed to collaboration with the strong governments. Italy's agents were efficient. According to a high official of the Quai d'Orsay, the Italians transferred one hundred thirty-five million francs to French newspapers during the Ethiopian war. British opinion was more reserved: a leak by two French journalists, Pertinax (André Géraud) and Geneviève Tabouis, caused the collapse of a Laval-Hoare mediation project because of British resistance; Foreign Secretary Sir Samuel Hoare resigned on December 19, 1935, and was replaced by Eden. The war went on.

From the beginning Mussolini played the great military leader. He was never out of uniform. Every day General Federico Baistrocchi brought him the latest reports, and Il Duce, a ruler in his hand, spent his time poring over a large topographical map dotted with little flags. One day, impelled by curiosity, Navarra was examining the map, which was marked everywhere by red and green arrows, and inadvertently he knocked over the flags, which he put back upright at random: Il Duce never noticed the difference. For in fact General De Bono and particularly Badoglio, who replaced him on November 16, exercised the sole command of the four hundred thousand men of the expeditionary force. Dispatches from Palazzo Venezia rained down on Badoglio, who invariably replied: "Leave the plan of campaign to me. Things will go well, as they have gone well thus far."

Mussolini's real campaign was that of the home front, the stage management, the selection of propaganda themes, and in these matters, which were his specialty, he scored one success after another. For the war was not unpopular: thirteen years of nationalist and Fascist propaganda on the necessity for expansion had impressed men's minds; in addition, the economic sanctions inspired by England and France, both endowed with colonial empires, seemed the peak of injustice. Fascist propaganda extended itself to paint a picture of a besieged Italy (although oil, which was essential to the mechanized Italian army, and airplane engines were still being delivered, and the Suez Canal had not been closed). The effective date of the sanctions, November 18, was proclaimed as a "day of shame and iniquity in the history of the world." Il Duce received eight hundred fifty women whose sons or husbands had been killed in the war and swore them to resist "the ignominious economic siege that encircles Italy."

Voluntary enlistments mounted; some anti-Fascists, such as Arturo Labriola, asked permission to return to Italy and others sought to join the army. Orlando wrote to Il Duce: "At this moment every Italian should be available for service." In the view of almost all Italians Il Duce was the incarnation of "resistance to the rich nations," of the determination to "conquer the earth for the *disoccupati*." "This is the war of the poor," Il Duce cried, "the war of the disinherited, of the proletariat. We are opposed by the ranks of conservatism, selfishness, and hypocrisy."

The church rode the tide of national unanimity and its exalted prelates conferred their blessings on the undertaking "that at the price of blood is opening the gates of Ethiopia to the Catholic faith and Roman civilization" (Cardinal Schuster of Milan). The party manipulated and aroused enthusiasm through skillful propaganda. Starace supplied its branches with topics for discussions, particularly among women. "Avoid the traditional lecture," he instructed; "stimulate exchanges of ideas." These phrases, taken from the parties of the left, were carefully chosen. Starace offered this illustration of indoctrination intended for women: "The duty and necessity of establishing a 'single front' of resistance at home in which all women should take part in order to speed the victory that will assure the prosperous future of their children."

On December 18 Mussolini launched the "rite of the wedding ring": in other words, the collection of all gold owned by individuals. Women contributed their wedding rings to the Fatherland and received steel rings in exchange. In a solemn ceremony Il Duce stood erect and plunged his gloved hand into a helmet filled with hundreds of rings, for the "rite of the wedding ring" was an unqualified success: two hundred fifty thousand wedding rings were turned in by Romans alone, one hundred eighty thousand by Milanese. Often it was the poorest women who were the first to contribute; naturally Rachele Mussolini and the ladies of the royal family were also in the van. Despite his scornful opposition, Croce, the philosopher, surrendered his senatorial emblem.

In this climate of patriotic ardor there was no grumbling at sacrifices and price rises. And prices rose rapidly, for the economy was becoming more and more autarchic, though this did not stand in the way of an unprecedented boom in industry, which was concentrating on the manufacture of war materials: dividends mounted steadily from an average of .8 percent of capital in 1931 to 7.28 percent in 1936.

Italians as a whole, of course, knew nothing of these statistics, just as they did not know that in the wake of the army in Ethiopia the hierarchs and the business men were making overnight fortunes. Hence the appeals of the anti-Fascists evoked little response during this period. Only the already converted were moved by proclamations to the Italian people, by such slogans as "Down with the Fascist rape of the Ethiopian people" and demands for "a military defeat of the Fascist government planned and executed by the Italian people."

On February 27, 1936, some members of *Giustizia e Libertà* were sentenced to terms of five, eight, and fifteen years in prison despite the lack of any evidence on which to ground serious charges against them. The public knew absolutely nothing of their trial. It seemed that anti-Fascism, which had made a hesitant forward step just before the Ethiopian war, had again been thrown back and isolated still further by the government's gains.

For the war was indeed well run; it was already a lightning war employing tanks, trucks, and, very systematically, planes. Ciano distinguished himself with his "death's-head"—*disperata*—squadron; Mussolini's sons won silver medals for "their unflawed courage." Confronted with this mechanized war, Ethiopian resistance weakened progressively. The Italians even used gas; from the air they machine-gunned infantry columns that scattered over the fields like terror-stricken sheep. The press extolled the heroism of Starace, who commanded a motorized assault force; Farinacci, De Vecchi, and Marinetti, the Academician, if the newspapers were to be believed, were also in the front lines with the Black-Shirt divisions. Correspondents asserted that the soldiers preferred to die of dysentery rather than leave the front: each grave was marked simply "A Soldier of Il Duce" and a sketchy cross was set up. The correspondent of *Le Temps* did not hesitate to report that the guaranty for victory was "these men in perfect health, accustomed to a frugal diet based on minestrone, polenta, pasta, fruits, and vegetables."

At 4 P.M. on May 5, 1936, the Italians entered Addis Ababa. The European population hailed them, for undisciplined Ethiopian troops and ordinary bandits had begun to loot the city. The walls of Rome were covered with big posters: "Mussolini has conquered. The Tricolor sheds its rays over Addis Ababa." In Piazza Venezia that day Mussolini delivered a major speech that was broadcast to crowds assembled in all the squares in Italy. Il Duce measured all his words: "I proclaim to the Italian people and the entire world that peace has been restored—our peace, Roman peace. Ethiopia is Italian."

The enthusiasm was indescribable. In the crowds there were a few young men like Zangrandi and Carlo Cassola, now an important novelist, who retained their balance, and to them this enthusiasm was a source of fear and anguish: where was Italy going?

On May 7 Mussolini was awarded the Grand Cross of the Military Order of Savoy. Two days later, at exactly ten-thirty in the morning, he appeared in uniform before a joyous throng that filled Piazza Venezia and the neighboring streets. Trumpets blared and the cries of *Duce! Duce! Duce!* rolled through the crowd. Leaning on the railing of the balcony, Mussolini read aloud a decree: "The title of Emperor of Ethiopia shall hereafter be borne by the King of Italy and his successors."

When the shouts had subsided, Mussolini intoned, as if in incantation: "Lift high your banners, your weapons, and your hearts, O legionaries, to hail the reappearance of the empire on the sacred hills of Rome after fifteen centuries." Exultation filled every square in Italy, for Italy was celebrating peace regained, national pride, and the end of a long series of military humiliations.

But the joy was a veneer over the major fissures in the structure of international relations that had been caused by Mussolini's policies. The League of Nations had been thoroughly flouted, made almost ridiculous with its declaration of unenforceable sanctions. One of its members, Nicolae Titulescu of Rumania, declared: "The Italians want to force us to eat shit. Very well; we will swallow it. But they also want to make us call it attar of roses. That is a little too much" (Baron Aloisi's diary).

The League of Nations was indeed dead after what Fascist Italy had done. In addition, Germany had profited by the Ethiopian war to advance her pawns: on March 7, 1936, to the shrill of fifes, soldiers of the Reich occupied the Rhineland. At a time when some quarters sought the broadening of oil sanctions, this created a new area of tension and left Mussolini's hands free. Furthermore, during the period of sanctions, Germany had supplied Italy with coal, and economic and financial agreements had been concluded; Count Volpi, who represented Italian business circles, promised that "Italy will never forget the loyal and honorable position of the German people during the sanctions."

It was learned also that Bocchini, the head of the police, had gone to Germany in March, 1936, and established friendly relations with *Reichsführer* Heinrich Himmler. In June Hitler himself escorted Mussolini's daughter on a motorboat tour of the Berlin lakes during her official visit.

Thus the alliance between Fascism and Naziism was accelerating. On July 11, 1936, an agreement approved by Mussolini was signed by Hitler and Chancellor Kurt von Schuschnigg of Austria, which was described in the document as a "German state"; hence Austria was no longer a stumbling block to Italian-German rapprochement. Enrapt in Ethiopia and the African chimera, Mussolini gave ground on the Brenner.

Could sanctions and the policy of Great Britain and France be held responsible for this evolution of Mussolini's policy? Only partly, for Germany too had taken a rather reserved position at the start of the Ethiopian venture. Indeed, on June 18, 1935, she had signed a naval treaty with England. Hence it was, rather, a natural tendency that led *il Duce dell'Impero* and Fascism toward Hitler and Naziism when Popular Fronts were triumphing in France and Spain.

It was the need for glory and military prestige, the similarity of ideologies, the hunger for a sweeping program, and the exigencies of an economy of rearmament that impelled Mussolini, after the end of the Ethiopian war, to join Europe's other "claimant" state, the Third Reich. The "policy of sanctions" was only an added stimulus, a welcome subject for propaganda.

In April of 1936 Il Duce was sitting in a plane at an altitude of more than thirty thousand feet watching a bombing attack, and he concluded that similar planes could reach London without detection. A few days later, he called together one hundred twenty generals and told them of his plans for a war on the western front. He flaunted his contempt for the democracies and their leaders: France no longer had any politicians worthy of the name— Flandin, for instance, was a moron; England was decadent. He ordered his statistical staff to make a study of Britain's population situation: inasmuch as there were eleven million persons over fifty years of age, the country was doomed; and besides who in England had any thought of war?

These views were elaborated by the innumerable army of imitators, sycophants, and fanatics to whom, with the help of his propaganda, Il Duce was more than ever "a hero and a prophet." The most highly official publications predicted the domination of the world by Italy: "Italy and Rome, Africa, Asia, Australia. . . . The Mediterranean is the heart of the great Eurafricaustralasian system . . . and, thanks to the conquest of Ethiopia, that chain has been made Italian."[2]

Before he issued his proclamation of empire, Mussolini told the throng in Piazza Venezia on May 5: "I am more than ever convinced that to trouble Europe's peace would be to drag her to annihilation." But this had somewhat the ring of Napoleon III's "the empire is peace."

When Galeazzo Ciano, the hero of the Ethiopian war, was appointed Foreign Minister on June 9 at the age of thirty-four—a post turned over to him by his father-in-law—it was generally recognized that the dilettante playboy could be no more than the mouthpiece of Il Duce, whom ostensibly he was replacing. Furthermore, Ciano's appointment was accompanied by the departures of career diplomats. Overwhelmed with honors and praise, Baron Pompeo Aloisi left his position as executive secretary. Il Duce presented him with a huge signed photograph.

Not long afterward, during military maneuvers, Mussolini burst out: "We can mobilize eight million men at any time in a couple of hours on a single order from me." For Italians, in fact, the war was to go on under other guises and in other places.

[2] Quoted by M. Vaussard, *De Pétrarque à Mussolini* (Paris: Colin), pp. 264–265.

Part III
ITALY
IN TURMOIL
(1936–April 29, 1945)

13

The Road to War

(1936–1940)

"I would rather see Italians terrify the world with their aggressiveness than charm it with their guitars."—IL DUCE (1937)

THE INHABITANTS of the village of Berkrane, in French Morocco, were astounded to see two heavy planes fly very low overhead on July 29, 1936, their engines frequently missing, and then come down unskillfully just beyond the farthest shacks; one of the planes ground-looped. Soon a lighter machine painted in the Spanish colors flew over them almost at ground level and dropped a package, which the French police picked up. It contained Spanish army uniforms and a note that said, in Italian: "Put on these uniforms and tell the French that you belong to the Legion stationed at Nador."

The two planes on the ground were Italian heavy bombers— Savoia S-81's—on their way to Spanish Morocco, where twelve days earlier a military revolt against the lawful government in Madrid had broken out. One of the Italian pilots—wearing civilian clothing—was found to be carrying orders dated July 15, the original choice of the Spanish generals for the eruption of their insurrection, that pronunciamento that was to become the cruelest of civil wars. Mussolini, then, had chosen from the outset to commit Fascism to General Franco's side.

The bonds between Il Duce and conservative and military circles in Spain were of long standing. General Primo de Rivera, dictator of Spain until 1930, had gone to Rome in 1923. In 1932 Italo Balbo had supplied arms to support General Sanjurjo's uprising. At four o'clock of the afternoon of March 31, 1934, four Spanish leaders of Comunión tradicionalista and Renovación española (Traditional Fellowship and Spanish Revival) had been ushered into the Hall of the Mappamondo in Palazzo Venezia, where Mussolini and Balbo were waiting for them.

Il Duce asked for a summary of the situation in the new Spanish Republic and expressed his readiness to support a regency and above all to supply at once twenty thousand rifles, the same number of grenades, two hundred machine guns, and one and a half million pesetas in cash. This help, Il Duce said, was purely preliminary in nature: "Substantial backing will follow at the right time, to the extent warranted by the work accomplished and in the event that circumstances make it necessary."

The Frente popular won its victory in Spain on February 16, 1936, and the generals' conspiracy soon followed. But, when General Franco, who had assumed the leadership of the rebellion, turned to Mussolini, Il Duce hesitated: that was the nature of the man—to commit himself and then at the last minute to be apprehensive. Franco's emissaries had to labor long with Mussolini, and it was only after their third appeal that he decided to allow the Savoia bombers to take off. On August 4, they went into action against the Spanish Republican fleet and two days later, in a decisive mission, they flew cover for the five ships carrying Franco's Moroccan army across the Strait of Gibraltar from Ceuta to Cadiz. Mussolini was later to tell the story of those fateful days. "The Ethiopian war was barely over," he said, "when we received . . . Franco's appeal. . . . Could we as Fascists allow that cry to go unanswered and could we remain indifferent to the continuing bloody outrages of the so-called popular fronts? No. Thus the first squadron left on July 27, 1936, and on that same day we suffered our first losses on the field of honor."

What Il Duce was really aiming at by way of the Spain of the Frente popular was the France of the Front populaire: Franco's victory would leave France exposed at the rear and facilitate Italy's Mediterranean expansion. Hence Il Duce committed himself firmly to intervention.

His bombers went into action first; they were followed by the so-called volunteers: Black-Shirt battalions on their way home from Ethiopia and diverted to Spain, augmented by the unemployed from southern Italy who had left home as colonists of empire and who, unloaded at Cadiz, were offered a dollar a day plus two Spanish pesetas if they would serve the cause of Il Duce shoulder to shoulder with General Franco's Moors. At the end of August the former squadrista, Arconovaldo Bonaccorsi, a red-haired, red-bearded giant, set up his headquarters on Mallorca with a fighter squadron known as "The Dragoons of Death" and three bombers. Wearing a white cross beneath his black shirt and using the name of Count Rossi, Bonaccorsi was soon the master of the island, where wounded and captured Republicans were methodically finished off. Bonaccorsi posed for the photographers with his foot planted on one of the bodies. *"Il bel tempo è tornato,"* he said— "Happy days are here again."

Soon there were almost thirty thousand Italian troops in Spain— men of the regular army with abundant supplies. This fact, however, did not deter Italy from agreeing on August 21 to the French proposal of "non-intervention" in the Spanish war. When Ambassador de Chambrun questioned him about the planes that had landed in Morocco, Ciano replied off-handedly: "Those were planes that private industry had sold to Spanish citizens. The government knows absolutely nothing about the matter."[1]

The farce of non-intervention began, affording young Ciano, with his rather heavy face, his black hair carefully slicked back, and his general air of a man aware of his looks, the opportunity to make his first moves as a minister with great care—and effectiveness. The democracies, which—in essence—fulfilled the obligations that they had signed, stopped shipping arms. The only help available to the Spanish Republic in its struggle was the volunteers from abroad.

Italian anti-Fascists were in their front lines, and in this fashion too the Spanish civil war played a part in the history of Mussolini's Italy. For the Italian exiles the struggle in Spain was the continuation of the battle that they had fought in Italy and in addition the presage of future battles. *"Oggi in Spagna, domani in Italia*—Today in Spain, tomorrow in Italy," Carlo Rosselli, the fugitive from Lipari, declared in Paris on August 28. One month later to the day, at Monte Pelato, the Italian volunteers fought their first victorious battle: the Rosselli brothers transported munitions all the way to the fighting lines in their old Ford. Soon a Garibaldi Battalion was formed within the International Brigades. So Guido Picelli, who had defended Parma in 1922, Pietro Nenni, Palmiro Togliatti, Luigi Longo, Giuseppe de Vittorio, Randolfo Pacciardi, and many others found themselves face to face with the squadristi, Mussolini's generals—Mario Roatta, Berti, Gambara, Bergonzoli—and the Black Shirts. For the Italians Spain became the lists in which they carried on the struggle for or against Fascism that had begun in 1919.

[1] Count Ciano's *Diplomatic Papers* and his *Diary* are indispensable sources for this period from 1936 to 1939.

The Road to War

This was equally true of the Germans. Ciano received Ambassador Ulrich von Hassell on July 25. The son-in-law of Il Duce was at that time a firm believer in the German alliance, and in the vast office in Palazzo Chigi the two diplomats confirmed "once more the absolute parallelism of German-Italian policy." Ciano reported: "I told von Hassell that we shared the Reich government's concern lest the Soviets establish themselves at the gateway to the Mediterranean."

Military collaboration got under way the next day: Colonel Walter Warlimont of the Wehrmacht and the famous Admiral Wilhelm Canaris conferred with General Roatta of the SIM, the Italian secret service. It was an Italian cruiser that carried Warlimont to Tetuan. As Rosselli wrote: "Attention! The European war is being prepared. We have reached the time when two worlds in conflict, the world of freedom and the world of authority, are going to stand face to face with weapons in their hands."

And, from the first moment of German-Italian collaboration, Mussolini and the Fascists were the gulls of Hitler and the Nazis. The eminent Ambassador von Hassell, who incited Ciano to act in Spain, wrote in a report to the Wilhelmstrasse in December, 1936: "The Spanish war could play the same rôle as Ethiopia in Italy's relations with France and England. . . . It will only make all the clearer to Italy the necessity of standing shoulder to shoulder with Germany in confronting the Western powers."

Hitler at once furthered this policy with great skill, even supplying arms to the Republicans. "A hundred-percent victory for Franco would not be desirable from the German point of view," Der Führer told his generals in a meeting on November 5, 1937; "It is rather to our interest to see the war continue and to maintain tension in the Mediterranean." For, as it went on, the war in Spain finally isolated Italy from the Western powers.

But Hitler merely exploited a situation created by Mussolini and Mussolini alone. For, after the war in Ethiopia, Il Duce fell deeper than ever into errors, while the Fascist system began to show its flaws. Mussolini was incontestably the captive of the cocksure character that he had assumed: had he not just achieved "a lasting victory over the Ethiopian enemy and the fifty-two nations that had voted sanctions"? Such Nazi leaders as Frank and Goering sought his counsels; the English and the French sought his allegiance. He could lay down the law to Europe.

When Goering visited him on January 23 and asked why Italy did not withdraw from the League of Nations as Germany had done, Il Duce replied: "The Ethiopian question does not seem to have been settled yet. The recognition of the conquest that Italy wants from the League is still lacking. That, so to speak, is the glass of castor oil that sooner or later the League of Nations will have to swallow."

Such a statement was a perfect epitome of the equivocation, the hesitations, and the dangers of Mussolini's policy, and at the same time the epitome of the man's character. He wanted to have his empire—which was limited to Ethiopia—certified by the League as routinely as any power that respected that international body would have presented some routine question. But, even while he was seeking this guaranty, he wanted to humiliate the League and take personal vengeance on it in the style of the squadrista outrages.

This man who handled international relations as if he were leading a raid on a Po Valley village aged rapidly during those crucial years of 1936–39. Some of his old war wounds began to give him trouble again; his strict diet did not protect him against stomach disturbances, which grew worse with the years and the stresses, for they were basically of nervous origin. He was already subject to violent depressions; often he vacillated under opposing pressures and made his decisions in terms of the most recent; and this tendency was all the more ominous because Italy was going to have to choose between war and peace.

His egocentricity and his cynicism fed on each other. Since he identified himself with Fascism, the slightest personal attack made him change the country's policy. His contempt for others and his indifference to their sufferings increased. When Franco's troops captured Italian anarchists and Communists, he gave orders that all of them be shot: "Dead men do not write history," he commented tartly. And more than ever he believed in the virtues of violence and the "curative" power of war. "When the war in Spain is over," he said, "I shall have to find something else: the Italian character must be shaped in battle."

The rapidity of his aging may also have been influenced by his affair with Claretta Petacci. She was twenty-four when she became his mistress in 1936. On Mussolini's advice she had married Lieutenant Frederici of the air force, who had afterward been posted to Tokyo as air attaché. One day when she went to visit Mussolini, she found him in a rage. "I respected you," he bellowed, "and you are unfaithful to your husband." He insulted her and slapped her face, and finally, in tears, she fell into his arms. Thus Claretta Petacci became the mistress of the fifty-three-year-old man who ruled Italy.

It was a serious affair, virtually semi-official, and soon Rachele Mussolini was the only Italian who was ignorant of it. Every afternoon Claretta Petacci entered Palazzo Venezia through the little gate in via Astalli and took a private elevator to her own apartment there, known as the Cybo suite, which was composed of two scantily furnished rooms. There, stretched on a couch in the Zodiac Room and wrapped in a stridently garish dressing-gown, she waited patiently for Mussolini. The signs of the zodiac painted in gold on the domed ceiling were ideal for the fantasies of a superstitious woman; or she would kill time playing solitaire, drinking tea, and chattering with Navarra. At last Mussolini would join her and, dropping his Caesarean mask, talk about his day, his past, and his plans. Il Duce was simply talking to himself in the admiring presence of Claretta. He dominated her with his experience, his power, his titles, his age; and the girl's humility and malleability were completely acceptable to this man who could not endure anyone's standing up to him.

As time went on, there were quarrels, especially as Claretta's own personality began to assert itself, though without ever emerging from submissiveness. One day he hit her with his fist and left her lying half-unconscious on the floor; her physician father was summoned.

Yet there should be no misunderstanding: Mussolini had a genuine attachment to Claretta. He would telephone her from Germany; when he held a review, he wanted to be able to see her in the crowd; she was a compensation for the isolation in which he was more and more shut off; she had become his thing, wholly at his disposal, and he was unaware of his cruelty to her: he liked to make her suffer, telling her of his adventures with other women although he knew that she was jealous; he offered her nothing, he behaved with indifference; in sum, he found it quite natural that women should love him because he was Mussolini.

Italy was quickly filled with rumors about "the Favorite"—supposedly she was overwhelmed with gifts, she had two thousand pairs of shoes. When the Petacci family began building a magnificent house, the high point of which was to be Claretta's bedroom, on Monte Mario, it was assumed that Il Duce was paying for it. In actuality he was a niggardly lover, quite capable of asking his mistress: "How do you manage for money? Does your father do well?" It was others who paid for the pleasures of Il Duce.

Claretta, undeniably, was not concerned with security for the future; but her brother, Marcello, her sister, Myriam, and the other members of the family exploited their position by selling their influence. Out of secret funds the Under-Secretary of State for the Interior, Guido Buffarini-Guidi, gave Claretta about ten thousand dollars a month for charitable contributions. It was a huge sum and, even if Claretta used most of it for manifold contributions, she must also have dipped into that bottomless well that was constantly replenished. Thus Buffarini shrewdly assured himself of a solid support. Industrialists, fashionable dressmakers, businessmen seeking the monopoly of a market or the abrogation of a law dealt with Marcello Petacci: he was a power. A special board of examiners was convoked at a special time in order to award him his doctorate. Thus corruption spread its roots, through the Petacci clan, into that private apartment where Claretta, at once innocent and debauched, lived her daily dream.

In truth the relations among influential persons and the web of jealousies, gossip, hatreds, calculation, and self-interest were beginning to envelop Palazzo Venezia and the régime in that intrigue-saturated atmosphere that was so well known to the princely courts of Renaissance Italy. Bocchini, the head of the police, a skeptical sensualist; Starace, with his fanatical, limited, dogmatic mind; little black-haired Buffarini-Guidi, ambitious, crafty, and self-seeking . . . all of them absorbed themselves in schemes and wiretaps, each spying on the others in the defense of his place.

Beginning in 1936, however, Galeazzo Ciano, the son-in-law of Il Duce, was placed above them all and each had to report to him as all had to report to Mussolini. Ciano was the dispenser of offices, the inviter of confidences, the font of advice on everything: in a word, he was apparently the chosen successor. An intelligent man, he seemed to be successful in all matters, from career to women. Like an heir, a crown prince, he was always surrounded, and his heavy, rather soft face was constantly smiling in satisfaction. At the beaches and the golf clubs he was sought out by pretty women; young diplomats aped him as he aped Il Duce, whom he genuinely admired.

But from top to bottom, along those capillary vessels of a totalitarian society that are formed by its party and its departments, corruption was advancing. Starace, who was held out as a glorious hero of the Ethiopian war whereas he had been the leader of an operation devoid of danger, and Farinacci, also a hero of the empire by virtue of having lost one hand while catching fish with grenades in Ethiopia, posed as pillars of virtue. "Very often I receive *raccomandazioni* for young Fascists or officers or, even worse, persons who do not belong to the organization, with requests that I do something for them in competitive examinations," Starace said with much indignation at the same time when Marcello Petacci was so easily becoming a doctor.

The "stabilization of the empire" opened the way to other abuses:

clever hierarchs and business men with good connections drained the public funds for their own purposes, while courses continued to be given in the School of Fascist Mystique in Milan and, in Palazzo Vidoni, the headquarters of the PNF, Starace worked in an imposing office adorned with stuffed eagles, shields, and lances, as if he were a real hero. He told one young Fascist[2] whom he had summoned to his office: "Whenever Il Duce telephones me, I—the secretary of the Fascist Party—stand at attention while we are talking."

And what the government sought was indeed to keep all Italy standing at attention. The young were consolidated into a single organization attached to the party: the Gioventù italiana del littorio (Italian Youth of the Lictor), whose secretary was Starace. The *sabato fascista* (Fascist Saturday) was inaugurated: every Saturday afternoon all Italian males were supposed to be in the stadia or the parade grounds of the barracks. Starace issued a great number of orders on this point—"There is only one Saturday: the Fascist Saturday"—but these reiterative injunctions availed little against the passive resistance of the majority of Italians.

"Fascist style" was the incessant theme of the press and of meetings; "gagas"—long-haired young jazz enthusiasts—were pariahs. In wretched villages in the *Mezzogiorno* where the houses lacked even fireplaces—to say nothing of running water—huge posters dominated the flat roofs: "*Abbasso i gagà*—Down with the jazz-hounds." Starace reminded the nation that "shaking hands has been abolished" and "the new man of the Mussolinian century is now being born."

This new man was under constant surveillance—one resident of each building was designated for the purpose—and his reading was regulated. The Ministry of Popular Culture issued detailed, if unexpected, directives to the press. A few examples:

June 28, 1935. Do not publish photographs of Primo Carnera (a heavyweight boxing champion for a brief time) after knockdowns.

June 18, 1936. Nothing is to be printed about the death of Maxim Gorki.

December 26, 1936. Albert Einstein is never to be mentioned.

Now for the first time large masses began to look on this increasingly oppressive system with skepticism, the first step toward a stronger form of opposition. In spite of the oratory, in spite of the empire and corporativism, prices continued to rise, income lagged far behind, unemployment persisted, and in 1938 farm workers

[2] Ruggero Zangrandi; see Selective Bibliography.

were exported to Germany. By now the corruption at high levels and the innumerable "village Staraces" were common knowledge. Soldiers back from Ethiopia made disclosures: they had seen the disorganization of certain branches of the military, they had been silent witnesses to the publicity shams, and they compared what they had seen with the colorful accounts in the newspapers. Some, either under duress or more or less as volunteers, went off again to Spain: so the war was not over. The reasons that Il Duce advanced for drenching Ethiopia with Italian blood could be understood; but Spain was another matter. The struggle against Bolshevism had no clear meaning for the landless peasant in Apulia. The young students who believed in *universalfascismo* as a force for peace, a corporative revolution transcending Socialism and capitalism, suddenly found the Fascist system allied with the conservative landowners of a rigidified Spain.

Doubt crept in wherever Starace's directive intruded. It took the form of a song—

> Starace rapace incapace
> Requiescat in pace.
> (Rapacious incompetent Starace,
> Requiescat in pace.)

—or another—

> L'aquila che è rapace,
> La lupa che è vorace,
> L'oca che è Starace.
> (The eagle is rapacious,
> The she-wolf is voracious,
> And the goose is Staracious.)

Italians began listening to the broadcasts from Madrid and Barcelona, which included appeals by Nenni, Rosselli, Randolfo Pacciardi, and others. "Comrades, brothers, Italians—listen: this is an Italian volunteer talking to you on Barcelona Radio," Rosselli said. "Italians, a dictatorship is only a parenthesis in the life of a nation." The Communist Party issued proclamations calling for a broader unity: "Give us your hands, Fascists and Communists, Catholics and Socialists, for the salvation of Italy and the reconciliation of the Italian people."

There were demonstrations in favor of Republican Spain; sabotage began: bombs fell on Barcelona, but did not burst because the Italian workers who made them had filled them with sawdust instead of explosive. But it would be fallacious to think that there

The Road to War

was a widespread rebellion against the Fascist system. While anti-Fascist militants began at last to hope and many young intellectuals were dismayed and anguished by the loss of their illusions, all that the majority felt was still only a general disenchantment. But the position taken by Fascism toward Naziism was to intensify the process of disaffection and opposition to the regime.

On September 23, 1935, Hans Frank, the most cultured of the German ministers, paid a visit to Mussolini. Frank knew Italy well, and the future governor- (and executioner-) general of Poland prided himself on his musical, literary, and artistic pretensions. He began by inviting Mussolini to Germany. Skillfully then he drew out Il Duce.

"France is sick and senile," Mussolini said. "All that anyone thinks of there is food. It is a country where cooking has become a state art. The population decline is appalling. France is losing two thousand inhabitants every week."

Frank listened quietly, now and then putting a question: "How did Italy manage to normalize her relations with the church?"

"Fighting religion is useless," Il Duce replied. "Religion is as intangible as fog." He went on to develop his ideas, proud to display his political genius. The conversation, Il Duce pointed out with satisfaction later, in fact opened the way to that "German-Italian front already set up in Spain."

But relations between Italy and Germany were still burdened with suspicion. Each feared that the other would desert her for an alliance with England. In order to eliminate misconceptions and prepare the way for the future, Ciano visited Der Führer on October 24, 1936, in Berchtesgaden. The conversation lasted two and a quarter hours. Hitler spoke slowly, in a low voice, with violent outbursts when he dealt with Russia and Bolshevism. "In Spain," he said, "the Italians and the Germans together have dug the first trench against Bolshevism."

"Mussolini has held aloft the anti-Bolshevist standard for the world since 1919," Ciano pointed out.

"Il Duce," Hitler replied, "is the world's leading statesman, and no one has the right to compare himself with him, even remotely."

Ciano then gave Der Führer a secret file that Dino Grandi had cleverly managed to procure in London. Under the title of "The Nazi Danger," Eden had collected thirty-two documents, in particular a report by Sir Eric Phipps, the British Ambassador in Berlin, that showed that the government of the Reich was composed of dangerous adventurers. There was a silence, and then Der Führer burst out: "According to the English there are two countries in the world today that are governed by adventurers: Germany and Italy. But England was also ruled by adventurers when she built her empire. Today—" he made a grimace of contempt "—she is ruled by mere incompetents."

Der Führer had hit his stride, and his animation rose. "Germany will be ready in three years," he told Ciano, who was delighted. He noted in his diary: "Der Führer treated me with remarkable cordiality. He telephoned to Munich twice to get a full report on the reception that was given to me there."

On his return to Rome, Ciano reported to Mussolini, and both rejoiced at having troubled the relations between Germany and England and signed a secret protocol with Germany. Thereafter, with a certain bombast, Mussolini was in a position to harangue a crowd in Piazza del Duomo in Milan and to baptize the new alliance with a word that was to have a long career: "The Berlin-Rome line is no longer a diaphragm: it is an *axis* round which all European states can unite." He added: "No one will be surprised if we raise the flag of anti-Bolshevism today: that is our old banner, the sign under which we were born."

In the ensuing months, therefore, he committed himself increasingly to the war in Spain, thus binding himself to Germany at the same time when Hitler, who wanted to keep a free hand, was limiting his participation. By January, 1937, there were almost forty-five thousand Italians in Spain, equipped with the best that the army could provide, so that after Ethiopia its reserves were wholly depleted. All that Italy asked of Spain in return for such valuable help was a policy of friendship (the treaty of November 28, 1936). Day after day Mussolini swallowed more of the bait of this policy: on January 23 he received *Minister-Präsident* Goering and told him again: "The common front of our two countries has already found its expression in our common military front in Spain."

Goering made a great display in Italy. He was a guest of the King; he visited Naples and Capri. Il Duce had the impression that German backing would not be lacking if he embarked on an ambitious program in Africa. His imagination had free rein.

Sitting astride a horse in Libya on March 18, 1937, his legs outstretched in the stirrups, under a blazing sun he waved "the sword of Islam," which had just been presented to him by the assembled Arab chieftains. He issued a call to all Islam in the midst of the shouts of *Uled!* that rose from the mass of picture-book horsemen. He seemed to have reached the apogee of exultation, turning his head from right to left in a pose that he assumed to be virile; but a few hours later, in a rage, he left Libya for Rome. A dispatch had just informed him of the defeat at Guadalajara.

The Road to War

Thirty thousand Italians—the Black Shirts, the Black Flames, the Black Arrows, the Littorio Division, two hundred fifty tanks, seventy trucks, plus planes—had all together, as Mussolini had ordered, attacked the International Brigades and especially the Italians in the Garibaldi Battalion. It was a symbolic battle that admirably fitted the image of the story of Fascist Italy. Nenni, Pacciardi, and Ilio Barontini gained the upper hand over Generals Roatta, Coppi, and Nuvolari. Weather conditions hampered the Fascist fliers, but, more than that, the Garibaldi Battalion had mastered the weapon of propaganda. Its planes dropped thousands of pamphlets over the Fascist lines; its loud-speakers played *Bandiera rossa* and then declared: "If you surrender, you will be welcomed as brothers."

Pacciardi announced on Radio Madrid: "The anti-Fascists of the Garibaldi Battalion and the Fascists of Mussolini's divisions have met on the battlefield. . . . We were the victors: better, the idea that we represent was the victor."

To Mussolini the insult and the challenge were personal, resented as if he had been flogged. On March 23, the eighteenth anniversary of the inception of the Fasci, he snarled: "We must remember and prepare." Arrests multiplied in the major cities of Italy and teams of squadristi, brought back into action, hunted down and assaulted everyone who listened to the Spanish radio.

In April Mussolini saw Goering, and a few days later, with his characteristic pleasure in prophecies, he said mysteriously to Lagardelle: "After 1940 Europe will blow up, you will blow up, and I shall blow up too." In May the German Foreign Minister, Konstantin von Neurath, arrived; in June it was the Minister of War, Marshal Werner von Blomberg. To the considerable terror of the marshal, Il Duce insisted on serving as his pilot. In Naples Blomberg took part in an impressive naval review.

The wind of Guadalajara was still blowing. On June 11, 1937, behind a hedge in Normandy, the bodies of the Rosselli brothers were found—thirteen years after Matteotti, two months after the defeat at Guadalajara. They had been attacked near their old Ford that had served as a munitions carrier at the battle of Monte Pelato in Spain. In spite of Italy's denials, the whole world saw her signature in the murders. Roberto Navale and Santo Emanuele, agents of the SIM, had unquestionably been ordered to act by Ciano and Filippo Anfuso and had approached members of the *Comité secret d'action révolutionnaire* (CSAR: Secret Revolutionary Action Committee), the French extreme-right group attached to the *Cagoule* (literally, The Hood, one of the terrorist organizations of pre-war French Fascism).[3] Feeling was intense everywhere: in that Paris of the Popular Front two hundred thousand persons marched behind the two coffins; but the loss was tragic for anti-Fascism. Carlo Rosselli, the fugitive of Lipari, the organizer of the first Italian volunteer group in Spain, was dead. By Mussolini's psychology, Guadalajara was avenged.

And the war went on. Italian submarines sank English and Russian ships supplying the Republican forces. In spite of Franco and on Mussolini's direct orders, the Savoias bombarded the workers' quarters of Barcelona and Mussolini vaunted his delight at the results. When the Black Shirts took Santander, all prisoners were murdered. "I should rather," Mussolini said, "see the Italians terrify the world with their aggressiveness than charm it with their guitars."

That was the attitude with which he set out for Germany on September 23, 1937, for his second meeting with Adolf Hitler.

Ciano, Starace, and a hundred other dignitaries accompanied Mussolini. Il Duce wore a uniform designed for the occasion, and he had personally seen to it that all the Italians made an impeccable appearance. Der Führer too had devoted meticulous attention to appearances: his reception of Mussolini was to be a revenge for the humiliation suffered in Venice in 1934; besides, Hitler must have known how superficial and impressionable Il Duce was, and he had resolved to make a display of his strength. All the Germans were in uniform. In Munich Der Führer himself wore the visored cap, the black trousers, the brown tunic and shirt. Hess, Frank, and Goering greeted the Italians. The SS paraded, goose-stepping, and these black automata, the product of the whole history of Prussian militarism and apocalyptic Nazi stage design, fascinated Mussolini.

He watched the *Reichswehr* in maneuvers with live ammunition in Mecklenburg; he visited steel mills; everywhere he was shown the power of Germany, and he who admired Nietzsche, who like every Italian regarded German power with a mixture of superiority and admiring anxiety, was intoxicated with this Germany that seemed to be offering herself to him.

On September 28 a million persons were waiting for him in Berlin. Mussolini was impatient; until the last minute Goering had kept him playing with the model electric trains of which the German minister was so fond, and hence Il Duce had had no opportunity to review the manuscript of the speech that he planned to deliver in German. When Il Duce at last appeared beside Der Führer on the platform in the Maifeld, the crowd—a crowd on the

[3] See J. R. Tournoux, *L'Histoire secrète* (Paris: Plon), documents on pp. 310 ff.

The Road to War

German scale, such as Il Duce had never seen—burst into prolonged cheering. In his rasping voice Hitler cried: "Here is one of those rare men . . . who are not made by history but by whom history is made."

Then, in his textbook German, Mussolini addressed the throng, on which a cold, heavy rain had begun to fall. The public-address system was not working properly and Mussolini's voice was often inaudible. "When the Fascist has a friend," he said, "he marches beside that friend to the very end." Much of the rest of the speech was lost, but the crowd could hear the conclusion: "The two greatest and most genuine democracies that exist in the world today are the German and the Italian. . . . Tomorrow the whole of Europe will be Fascist. . . ."

The drenched crowd cheered lustily and then quickly scattered in the downpour, while Mussolini, wet to the skin and lost in the confusion, went back alone to his hotel. Yet he was quite satisfied. That evening he telephoned to Claretta Petacci: "It was a triumphal success."

It must have seemed to him that at last he had the upper hand over Nazi Germany. Hitler, the SS, and the Wagnerian-opera atmosphere of the ceremonies had conquered the man who stood in Palazzo Venezia and checked the behavior of the policeman on the Corso or directed the musical comedy of the black musketeers. Psychologically Il Duce was now a subjugated ally, and Ciano too was conquered.

When he returned to Italy, Mussolini played the German card and demanded a place for the Reich in "the sun of Africa." On November 6, 1937, Italy signed the Anti-Comintern Pact with Japan and Germany.

Apparently Mussolini did not know that on the previous afternoon Hitler had convoked the leaders of the Wehrmacht in order to disclose his intention of moving as quickly as possible against Austria and Czechoslovakia: they were to be ready in 1938. Der Führer knew that he need no longer fear Italian opposition to his plans for Austria.

After November 6 he had Joachim von Ribbentrop's corroboration of that. That evening Ribbentrop, soon to be Germany's Foreign Minister, had had an audience with Mussolini, who told him during their conversation: "The Austrian question should not be regarded as a problem between Italy and Germany. I am tired of standing guard over Austrian independence."

Thus Italian diplomacy took a radical new direction. In his eagerness to please the Nazis in advance, Mussolini told Ribbentrop confidently: "We are carrying on a very clear campaign of anti-

Semitism, constantly intensifying, under a man who is very popular in Italy, *l'onorevole* Farinacci." That was another turning point: Fascism, at the heels of Naziism, took to the road of racism. And five months earlier, as host to Austrian Chancellor Kurt von Schuschnigg, Mussolini had declared with equal emphasis: "There are obviously substantial differences between Fascism and Naziism: we do not accept racist theories."

Once more Il Duce was rushing into the camp that he thought was the winner's; convinced that his judgment was sound, he would henceforth recognize no limits. Ciano was to be one of the first to learn that.

Foreign Minister Galeazzo Ciano had frequent conversations with Il Duce. These were conversations during which Mussolini allowed his thoughts to wander aloud from one idea to another in the presence of his son-in-law and confidant. When Ciano returned to his office, he would transcribe what Il Duce had said and his own replies, and this *Political Diary*, which was kept scrupulously, is one of the most valuable documents available to us for the study of Fascism and its policies between 1937 and 1943.

On December 21, 1937, without introduction, Il Duce said in a threatening voice: "I am preparing Italians for a tremendous surprise. As soon as Spain is out of the way, I will issue a communiqué that will be a classic."

Ciano had no doubt what was planned: Mussolini was contemplating a surprise attack on the British Mediterranean Fleet, and for several weeks Il Duce discussed, analyzed, and elaborated such a plan of action. In the light of the condition of Italy's military forces, this plan was obviously a pure chimera, but these bellicose divagations were to become the basis for the workings of Mussolini's imagination and action. And it was indeed the end of 1937 that marked the irruption of the most unexpected moves under pressure from Il Duce.

An enormous bronze statue, the *colosso Littorio*, was begun: it was to be erected on Monte Mario and to portray Hercules wearing a lion skin and giving the Roman salute. Two elevators would take visitors up more than two hundred feet to the figure's huge nostrils, which would also serve as terraces for a panoramic view. To Mussolini's great satisfaction, this Hercules was going to look like him and rise higher than the dome of St. Peter's. The war prevented the completion of this work of art, but other things were accomplished, to the accompaniment of general stupefaction and, soon, anger.

One such occurrence dealt with everyday speech. Normally the formal third person in Italian is *Lei*, which is like the German *Sie* (the usage was introduced in Italy during the Spanish occupation) in that it can be either the formal second person or the normal third person. Mussolini ordered *Lei* abolished in favor of *voi*, which, like the German *ihr*, can serve either as the familiar second person plural or, capitalized, as a semi-formal but not intimate second person singular. Mussolini's reasons for the change were the virility of the language and a return to its national sources. Originally suggested by a journalist, the idea appealed to Mussolini, and soon Starace issued the orders. In his magazine, *Critica fascista*, though it was known for its independent spirit, Bottai wrote: "Now that the Revolution has restored our national pride, let us go back to *tu* [the intimate second person singular], the expression of Roman and Christian universality, and *voi*, the symbol of respect and hierarchy."

Outside the army and the party, in which it was mandatory, and official correspondence and the press, where it was to be expected, obedience to such a measure was of course impotent against old habits. And in any case it was an irritant because it was an attempt to regiment even the language.

Even more revealing, and more sharply criticized by Italians, was the adoption of the *passo romano*: the "Roman step" was Mussolini's name for the German goose-step. Its adoption is an insight into the psychology of Il Duce and his increasingly unmistakable lack of realism, his desire to imitate the Nazis *ad absurdum*. Stiff-legged, he himself practiced the *passo romano* in the Hall of the Globe and at home. The step delighted him because he found it virile. "It is not my fault," he said smugly to Ciano, "if the King is a half-pint; of course he cannot do the parade step without looking ridiculous."

On February 1, 1938, outside the Coliseum, Il Duce reviewed the first parade in which the Militia and the army used the new step. It was "the firm, sure, inexorable stride of the legions, with which every march is a conquest," Mussolini concluded afterward. But in fact public opinion was stubborn and humiliated in the face of this abject imitation of the Nazis; military circles were antagonized by it, but they did not voice their opposition: Fascism had ruled for fifteen years and servile acceptance had become second nature; the King, Marshal Badoglio, and other officers made a point of expressing their satisfaction at reviews. The reaction was identical when, again in imitation of Naziism, Il Duce decided to replace the Militia fez with a tall helmet bearing a menacing eagle, varied according to rank. Thus hatted, booted, and buckled into their black uniforms, the Fascist hierarchs showed greater and greater resemblances to the Nazi dignitaries.

Starace went to the extreme of resolving to require an equivalent of *Heil Hitler*. He issued an order that all letters and official conversations be concluded with *Viva il Duce*. For once Mussolini rebelled. He ordered Starace to appear in the Hall of the Globe, where, in a thundering voice, Mussolini declaimed: "Dear Sir: I wish to inform you that your son, Corporal So-and-So, has broken his leg. *Viva il Duce!* Dear Sir: I wish to inform you that you have been dismissed. *Viva il Duce!*" The order was rescinded, but this isolated reaction could not conceal the fact that Mussolini had become an imitator of the Nazis; enlisted in their train, he lost more initiative every day.

Events began to move more quickly. On February 4, 1938, the German radio announced a message from Hitler. "As of this date," Der Führer declared, "I am assuming personal command of the armed forces."

The *Oberkommando der Wehrmacht*—OKW: Armed Forces Supreme Command—was established, and Mussolini sent a message of congratulations. "This step," he wrote, "is bound to strengthen the relations of comradeship between our armed forces and our governments."

On February 12 it was learned that Chancellor von Schuschnigg had been summoned to Berchtesgaden and faced Hitler and Generals Wilhelm Keitel, Walter von Reichenau, and Hugo Sperrle. So Hitler had made up his mind: *Anschluss* was imminent. Mussolini and Ciano were apprehensive: for the first time they were learning that Hitler could confront them with the accomplished fact. Now Ciano attempted a reconciliation with England, but it was very late. Dino Grandi received the following instructions from his minister:

Dispatch No. 1558   Rome, 16/2/38
Secret—Personal
My dear Dino,
   The new development is the conversation at Berchtesgaden and what has come out of it. The Nazification of Austria can now be considered, if not complete, in any event well under way. . . . To repeat what Il Duce said, we are now in the intermission between Act IV and Act V.
   Time is pressing, and not all the cards in the deck can remain always and only in our hands and theirs.

Clever Dino Grandi, whose mannered simplicity and round face with its veiled look, barely perceptible goatee, and rather overforced smile hinted at his crafty, tortuous character, had been able to make many connections in British political circles, and he moved. At eleven-thirty on the night of February 18 he was received at Downing Street by Prime Minister Neville Chamberlain; Eden was also present.

"The situation in Europe and above all the new events in Austria are very disturbing, don't you think?" Chamberlain began. Then the conversation, which was tense, focused on Grandi's demand for recognition of the Italian empire in return for Italian support in Europe. Soon Eden, who was an advocate of firmness, and Chamberlain were debating sharply in Grandi's presence—"as if I were not there," he observed with satisfaction.

Mussolini spent Sunday, February 20, at Terminillo, in the Abruzzi not far from Rome, closely guarded as he skied. Claretta Petacci was with him. Just after ten o'clock that evening there was a call for him from Palazzo Chigi with urgent news: Eden had resigned. Mussolini was jubilant. First of all, a reconciliation with England would now be easier; in truth Il Duce felt that the democracies were yielding and would always yield, and, therefore, victory for Der Führer was sure. He plunged in all the way.

On February 28 it was announced that Hitler would make an official visit to Rome during the first half of May. Thereafter Il Duce thought of nothing but that journey. He gave orders for the whitewashing of all the old houses that bordered the railway the whole distance from the Brenner to Rome; *passo romano* parades were stepped up. The visit was in fact a master stroke by Hitler. By announcing it as early as February 28, Der Führer kept Mussolini paralyzed during the critical weeks when the fate of Austria would be settled. In vain Schuschnigg sent his envoys to Rome to call on Mussolini to succor his country, and to announce that on March 13 he would hold a plebiscite on the annexation of Austria to Germany; nothing worked.

"You are making a mistake," was all that Mussolini replied to the Austrian Chancellor.

On March 11, when Nazi troops were already marching toward Austria, Prince Philipp von Hesse, Nazi Party member, *Obergruppenführer der SA* and husband of Mafalda, second daughter of Vittorio Emanuele III, boarded a plane for Rome. A few hours later he handed Mussolini a personal letter from Der Führer:

Excellency,
   I am now determined to restore law and order in my native country. . . . I wish to give Your Excellency, as Duce of Fascist Italy, the following solemn assurances:
   1) Consider my decision solely a legitimate defense step.

2) At a critical time for Italy [this was an allusion to the Ethiopian adventure] I gave you proof of the unshakable constancy of my attitude. Rest assured that in the future my position will never change.

3) I have drawn a clearly marked frontier between France and Germany and I am drawing another between Italy and us: it is the Brenner.

This was small consolation for the fact that at dawn of March 12 German troops crossed the Austrian border: fifteen years of Italian and Fascist diplomacy were swept away. At 10:25 that evening Prince Philipp put in a telephone call to Der Führer from Rome. "I have just come from Palazzo Venezia," he said. "Il Duce says that the fate of Austria does not matter to him."

"Be good enough to tell Mussolini that I will never forget—never, no matter what happens," Der Führer replied emotionally. "If ever he is in danger, he can be sure that I shall be loyal to him, whatever happens, even if the whole world is in league against him."

In order to avoid having to reply to Schuschnigg's pleas, Il Duce had retired on March 11 to his estate at Rocca della Caminate and given orders that he was not to be disturbed. But, though the fate of Austria was of little moment to him, the diplomatic defeat and the condescending off-handedness of the Nazis after the event were obvious.

Eyes opened in Italy, and the prestige of Il Duce was struck a heavy blow. It was learned that, though the Germans had promised to send their troops no farther than Innsbruck, they were establishing themselves on the Brenner. The commanding officer of the first regiment, Colonel Schoerner, had won Germany's highest award, *Pour le mérite*, for his brilliant comportment during the battle of Caporetto; now, with insolent innocence, he asked to salute the Italian troops.

Far more than the adoption of the *passo romano*, these events awakened public opinion. At the University of Rome students debated with Virginio Gayda, the official journalist who in 1934 had hailed the sacrifice of Dollfuss and the dispatch of Italian troops to the Brenner to defend Austria's independence; in the lecture halls there were brawls with the leaders of the GUF. The Pope, who had criticized Naziism in his encyclical *Mit brennender Sorge* (*With Burning Sorrow*) on March 14, 1937, repudiated the Austrian bishops, who had approved Hitler's action.

Mussolini felt that he was in a trap: 1934 was not so far in the past, and in Italy and the rest of the world it was still remembered that he had declared: "The independence of Austria is a principle that has been and will be defended by Italy." On March 16 he found it necessary to offer the Chamber an explanation, but it was an embarrassed speech. "When an occurrence is inevitable," he began, "it is better that it take place with you rather than in spite of you or, even worse, against you . . . millions of Germans too are listening to us. The time has come to make what might be called the test of the Axis."

The deputies and the Fascist Party threw themselves into an orgy of praise for Mussolini, as if to bury the real defeat beneath a surfeit of honors and flattery. From the speeches and the Italian press it would have seemed that it was Il Duce who had annexed Austria and scored an unprecedented diplomatic success. "Foreign policy is Mussolini's masterpiece," one deputy said. "He is not to be questioned: he is to be exalted."

A few days later, on March 30, in still another imitation of Hitler, Mussolini announced to the Senate: "In Italy war will be waged by one man alone, the man who is addressing you." The Senators rose, and in the midst of their cheers Costanzo Ciano moved a new decree:

"Article I: The rank of First Marshal of the Empire is hereby created.

"Article II: This rank is hereby conferred on His Majesty the King and Emperor and on Benito Mussolini, Duce of Fascism."

A "spontaneous" demonstration broke out at a signal from Starace: spectators from the galleries mingled with Senators and deputies. When it had subsided, it was found that all the prints that adorned the staircases of Palazzo Madama had been stolen and the Senate's tobacco shop had been robbed bare.

It gave the King no pleasure to see Mussolini take over the supreme command and thus become his peer; he protested and, as was his custom, gave in. His feeble resistance, however, had been enough to revive anti-monarchist stirrings in Mussolini. "*Basta*," he told Ciano, "I've had a bellyful. I work and he signs. . . . When we have finished with Spain, we shall see."

Mussolini also had a few threats for the church. "I am prepared to dust the priests' backsides with *manganelli*," he said. "It would be easy, because the Italians are not religious. They are merely superstitious."

So violence was still the last resort, the final argument; but, since opposition was spreading to broad masses, violence was no longer aimed at anti-Fascists alone but at the whole people. It would not be long before Mussolini would rail against "the human material with which I work" and contemplate setting up concentration camps in order to make Italians "hard, implacable, hateful, to make lords of them." And at the end of 1938 he confided to Ciano: "Italy will never be sufficiently Prussianized. I will never leave the Italians in peace until I am six feet under."

It was true that the people were slipping away because with every new day there was fresh evidence that Mussolini and the Fascist system were plunging Italy into a policy contrary to her most elementary interests. There were times when Mussolini and Ciano themselves had flashes of insight, and at such times they recognized the reality of the Nazi danger. On April 16, 1938, for example, Anglo-Italian naval accords were signed; five days later Il Duce said: "If those Germans think that they can move the boundary markers back a single yard, I will unite the whole world against Germanism. And we will smash Germany for at least two centuries."

But in fact Il Duce and Fascism were prisoners of their own ideology, of the verbal violences of fifteen years, of economic interests, and perhaps also of fear. It was rumored that in the imperial archives in Vienna there were records that compromised Mussolini and that had been seized by the Nazis. In sum, Fascist Italy's choices were determined by the history of Fascism, the psychology of Il Duce and the hierarchs, Nazi cunning, and belief in the invincible power of Hitler's Germany.

The solution evolved by Ciano in response to the *Anschluss* was action in Albania and the occupation of that small independent country: in short, a miniature Balkan *Anschluss*. On May 2, 1938, Ciano was invited to Tirana for King Zog's wedding. He saw the quiet, rural life of the capital, with its Zog Boulevard and its Mussolini Boulevard, and at once he thought of annexation. With cold realism he recalled the operations of Italian submarines during the Spanish war and wrote: "I do not think that a few machine-gun volleys in the ravines of the Mirditia or the Mathi would upset a world that ignored the explosion of torpedoes between Malta and Tunis."

The degree to which the policy of appeasement was stimulating the Fascist leaders to act was clear. When Ciano returned to Rome, Hitler arrived for his official visit.

Ribbentrop, Goebbels, Hess, Keitel, Frank, Himmler, Sepp Dietrich's SS, and the uniformed journalists arrived with Der Führer on four special trains: they were welcomed by the King, Il Duce, and Ciano, but there was a humiliation for Mussolini: he had to take second place behind the King, who had the honor of escorting Hitler to the Quirinal in a horse-drawn carriage. "The

The Road to War

crowd," Mussolini was later to write, "looked in vain for Il Duce. He had gone back to his office through the side streets of the Testaccio."

The King was hardly more pleased by having to play host to the Austrian corporal, whose table manners were poor. Hitler himself complained that he was neglected in the Quirinal. "Tell Der Führer to be patient," Mussolini said; "I have been patient for sixteen years."

On several occasions Hitler asked Mussolini to appear beside him on the official platform, although protocol required Il Duce to stand behind the King; to make matters worse, Pius XI ordered the Vatican Museum closed for the duration of Hitler's stay in Rome, and he himself went off to Castel Gandolfo. And some students hurled insults in Roman dialect at Nazi officers parading through the avenues of the city; other students slashed the tires of the Germans' official cars.

In other respects, however, everything went off well. Hitler was not spared a single museum, but on the other hand he was genuinely interested in all of them. In Palazzo Venezia he paid a vigorous tribute to Il Duce: "Today, thanks to your historic undertakings, Benito Mussolini, the Roman state is rising into new life founded on its ancient traditions."

At Naples Hitler attended a massive naval exercise—dozens of submarines surfaced at the identical instant in a straight line. On May 9, the day of his departure, he discovered Florence, the "city of his dreams," where the reception by the population was more cordial than in Rome, and so the visit ended in a climate of mutual satisfaction.

Once again Mussolini had responded to Hitler's flattery, and, in spite of verbal reservations, court and party circles had bowed to the exigencies of protocol. Mussolini could go forward. Though he had still held out against Hitler's and Ribbentrop's requests for a definite military alliance, his whole attitude had made it clear that in time this decisive step would be taken.

Meanwhile there were further evidences of the closer ties between Germany and Italy. Farinacci, a partisan of the alliance, was made Minister of State by the King; exchanges of delegations with Germany increased; to crown these symbolic gestures, the *Discobolos* of Myron was given to the Reich because during his visit to Rome Der Führer had much admired the sculpture. Naturally the tightening of the bonds influenced the Fascist movement, and in matters other than the style of uniforms and marching.

First of all, party discipline tended toward greater rigor. Starace required that all the hierarchs engage in physical exercise;

he himself, his face unshakably solemn above his naked torso, would leap from a white horse while a half-dozen assistants arranged themselves to catch him: or, in a bathing suit, he would take a collective swim in the center of the hierarchs.

Another revealing and much more important event was the publication of the *Manifesto on Race* on July 14, 1938. Signed by ten eminent professors, this was the first official document to proclaim anti-Semitism and formal alignment on Nazi bases. In its ten points the *Manifesto* declared that:

1) There are various human races. . . .
4) The population of Italy is of Aryan origin and its civilization is Aryan. . . .
6) There now exists a pure Italian race. . . .
7) The Jews do not belong to the Italian race. . . .

The *Manifesto* was a bombshell. The Jews—some fifty thousand of them—were completely assimilated in Italy; besides, the desire to imitate the Nazis was so obvious that many Fascists could not help feeling shame. The Pope protested. But the party and men like Starace and Buffarini-Guidi poured out statements: anti-Fascism, it was argued, had always been the doing of the Jews. As for Mussolini, on July 30 he declared with an assurance that deceived no one except perhaps himself: "To say that Fascism has imitated someone or something is simply absurd."

Actually, while the laws were new and the Nazi odor was strong, it could not be denied that for some time Mussolini and Fascism had been characterized by an extreme chauvinism that easily lent itself to the growth of racism. Baron Aloisi had noted on April 2, 1934, that Mussolini was particularly incensed by the publication of *Black Love*, the story of a romance between an Italian and a black woman: this was unthinkable, Il Duce said, for a nation that intended to build an empire in Africa.

In any case, the first step was laws for the exclusion of Jews from the schools. Mussolini even ordered an investigation into Ciano's ancestry; it was reassuring enough to enable him to declaim: "I am a Nordic, my daughter married an Etruscan, my son married a Lombard; I myself feel an affinity with the English and the Germans." Such rhetoric and such measures naturally aroused increasing opposition and sharper recognition of what was going on.

When Hitler visited Italy, it had been necessary to make a large number of preventative arrests; now public anxiety and bewilderment were heightened by the threats of war and by the reiterated solidarity between Duce and Führer. Indeed there were many things in common between them, such as their shared contempt for the democracies: "Only a cowardly, ugly, insignificant country can be democratic. . . . All that we can expect from France or England henceforward is decay," Mussolini told Ciano. He also told his son-in-law that he had resolved to move with Hitler, who was inexorably following out his plans.

After Austria it was Czechoslovakia. On May 30 Der Führer completed *Fall Grün* (Case Green) and set its execution for no later than October 1, 1938. As usual, nothing was said to the Italians. But a large delegation of Fascists, headed by Farinacci, attended the Nazi Party congress at Nürnberg on September 12, when Hitler demanded the right of self-determination for the Sudeten Germans. Mussolini approved. He threw himself into a speaking campaign that would "warm up" Italian opinion.

"Italy has made her choice," he bellowed. "We prefer to be feared, and we are unconcerned what hatreds we arouse: we reciprocate them." The crowd would respond in rhythm: "We are ready, we are ready, right away, right away!" and Mussolini replied: "No one has stopped us, no one shall stop us."

In Padua on September 24 he disclosed the time limit secretly set by the Germans in their ultimatum to Prague—six days. Was this done out of stupidity, out of error? Perhaps; but also, undoubtedly, out of a desire to avert a war, for he was keenly aware that the Italian forces were in a state of glaring unpreparedness. As Raffaele Guariglia said, such speeches were a political bluff of unreasoned audacity, which succeeded once more because Chamberlain was willing to be made a fool of.

September 28, 1938. The German ultimatum to Czechoslovakia expired at 2 P.M. on this gloomy Wednesday. News of mobilizations came from everywhere. War hung over Europe.

At ten o'clock that evening Mussolini received a message from Chamberlain: "I have sent a final appeal to Hitler today asking him to refrain from using force for the solution of the Sudeten problem. . . . I have offered to go myself to Berlin at once. . . . I hope that Your Excellency will be good enough to inform the German Chancellor that you are willing to be represented."

An hour later there was a telephone call from Rome for the Italian ambassador in Berlin. Mussolini himself was calling. "This is Il Duce," he said. "Can you hear me clearly?" Ambassador Bernardo Attolico could, and Il Duce continued: "Ask for an immediate audience with the Chancellor." Mussolini summarized Chamberlain's suggestion and added: "Tell the Chancellor that Fascist Italy and I stand back of him. It is up to him to make the decision. But tell him that in my opinion he ought to accept the suggestion."

When Attolico arrived at the Chancellery, it was almost midnight, and Hitler was conferring with André François-Poncet, the French Ambassador, but he interrupted the meeting at once when Attolico was announced. "I have an urgent message to give you from Il Duce," the Italian said as he entered the room.

Hitler reacted quickly: "Tell Il Duce that I accept his suggestion." German mobilization, already under way, was officially delayed; war had been postponed and the Munich Conference was about to begin.

September 29: Hitler went to Kufstein to welcome Mussolini at what had been the German-Austrian border. In the train that took them all on to Munich, Der Führer said: "The time will come when we shall have to fight side by side against France and England."

Mussolini agreed. Attolico, meanwhile, was showing him a German document—in Italian translation—that set forth the German demands; but, the Ambassador pointed out, Ribbentrop would unquestionably put forth new and more exigent claims. Mussolini kept the Italian text.

At 12:45 P.M. the conference that brought together Hitler, Mussolini, Daladier, and Chamberlain began in the *Führerhaus* on the Königsplatz. Ciano, Mussolini, and Hitler were in uniform; Chamberlain, his face grave above his white wing collar, and Daladier, looking frightened above his striped necktie, wore dark suits. The contrast between the arrogance on the one side and the lifeless defeat on the other was crushing.

His chest thrust forward, Mussolini ran the proceedings. It was his last diplomatic triumph. He let Hitler and Chamberlain speak first; then he drew from his uniform pocket the paper that Attolico had given him in the train and read it aloud as if he were stating his own claims, whereas these were the German demands as of the day before, without the last-minute revisions. Then he sat down, relaxed in his chair, and seemed to remove himself from the discussion.

At three o'clock the conference broke off for almost three hours. When it was resumed, Hitler kept silent most of the time. Mussolini, in contrast, spoke in English, French, and German—not fluently, it was true, but well enough to make himself understood. Hitler's eyes seemed never to leave Mussolini's face, whose lively expressions, sharp eyes, and confidence seemed to confirm his mastery of the meeting and his function as the savior of peace, the great man of the age.

At one-thirty the next morning, when the four men were affixing their signatures, Il Duce told Daladier: "When you return to France, you will be a hero." Daladier looked skeptical.

Then, when Chamberlain and Daladier were on their way back to the Hotel Regina-Palast, confident that they had assured "peace for our time," Hitler and Mussolini descended the stairs of the *Führerhaus*. In his hotel room Ambassador Voitech Mastny of Czechoslovakia wept for the death of his country.

Throughout his journey home Mussolini was acclaimed; all Europe looked on him as the mediator although he had been the spokesman for the German demands. Furthermore, the real inspiration for Munich was Chamberlain, and, from an objective point of view, it is clear that the Anglo-German agreement over the dead body of Czechoslovakia had to have a justification: Mussolini's mediation.

Nevertheless his triumph, built once again on the actions of others, added still more to his stature and ostensibly set Rome at the center of the international situation, whereas already it had become no more than an echo, more or less delayed and more or less submissive, of what was decided in Berlin.

The whole corps of the hierarchy was waiting to welcome Mussolini in Rome, and a long procession started out amid cheers toward via Nazionale, where Starace had prepared a triumphal arch covered with laurel branches. Mussolini was furious. "Who dreamed up that carnival?" he roared.

He was already beginning to discover that his rôle as *salvatore della pace* (savior of peace) did not fit his historical character and that the people had cheered enough for the preservation of peace. This might foster illusions that he would have to combat.

On October 21 the "Legionaries" home from Spain paraded before the King and a huge throng. The newspapers proudly listed the Italians' losses, which were higher than those of the Ethiopian campaign. Italy paid high for General Franco's friendship. The parade and the tone taken by the press showed that the Munich conference had not inaugurated an "era of peace." That was quite clear to the Pope. In an audience with some Italians who were congratulating themselves on the Munich agreement a few days after Mussolini's return, the Pope burst out: "It is a fine peace that is patched together at the expense of the weakest party without even consulting him. It is an unjust peace. You can say as much on my behalf to the head of the Italian government."

Pius XI was not mistaken. One month after Munich almost to the day—on October 28, 1938—the German Foreign Minister, Ribbentrop, that cold-faced man whose look seemed at first to be merely ironic but was really merely contemptuous of whoever was with him, demanded an audience with Il Duce, who received him in Ciano's presence. The three men exchanged congratulations and then got down to business.

Ribbentrop spoke first. "Der Führer is convinced that we have to view a war with the Western democracies as inevitable in a few years—perhaps three or four."

Il Duce agreed. "That is part of historic dynamism. An unbridgeable gulf has been opened between the two worlds."

Then Ribbentrop turned to the purpose of his visit. "After what happened in Munich, the Axis is in an extraordinarily good position, and a possible alliance along the lines laid down by our proposal. . . ."

The Nazis sought to go beyond the Axis and establish a real alliance with clearly defined commitments. But Mussolini hesitated, and he stated his reasons: "The Italian people has reached the stage of an axis, but not yet that of a military alliance." He made a reassuring gesture and added: "On the other hand, that may come very quickly."

Then, just before eight at night, when the meeting was almost over, Il Duce made a statement in the secrecy of Palazzo Venezia, barely a month after Munich: "We should not enter into a purely defensive alliance. There is no need for that, because no one dreams of attacking the totalitarian states." Playing schoolmaster to Ribbentrop and eager to show himself more resolute than the Nazis, as had become his habit, at least in the realm of talk, he shot out his words like bullets: "We want to make an alliance so that we can change the map of the world. Therefore we shall have to establish objectives and choose conquests. As far as we are concerned, we know now where we ought to go."

The resolution on conquest, then, was deliberate, and one established objective was Albania; but was that all?

Smug and aloof, Ciano received the new French Ambassador, André François-Poncet, on November 9. In his earlier capacity as Ambassador to Berlin, this brilliant diplomat, known for his careful elegance, had been present at the Munich Conference: the sight of Il Duce conducting the negotiations as Hitler watched in admiration had led him—somewhat precipitately—to the conclusion that the key to all the problems of Europe was in Rome. He had managed to be transferred there, and the French government, which for two years had refused to accredit an ambassador to Italy in order to avoid recognizing the conquest of Ethiopia, had agreed to address his credentials to "His Majesty Vittorio Emanuele III, King of Italy and Emperor of Ethiopia." André François-Poncet's attitude was friendly and Galeazzo Ciano's was condescending: after all, this meeting was in his view a minor Canossa for France.

Five days later Ciano wrote to Dino Grandi, who was still in his London post:

My dear Dino,

As you can well imagine, our leader has no intention of halting even for a moment.

A new problem has arisen that we should examine from the point of view of the latest imperial accomplishments of the régime. I mean our relations with France. The demands that we have been holding in reserve can now be laid on the table in a short time.

After Albania, then, France was one of Mussolini's objectives. France's retreat in Munich unleashed the hatred and the ambitions that had mounted behind the smiles during the fifteen years of Fascist rule; that hostility had its roots in the old core of Italian chauvinism of which Il Duce was the heir. François-Poncet was to come face to face with it, to his cost.

On November 30 he went to Montecitorio and took his place in the diplomatic gallery. Ciano had notified him that he was going to deliver an important speech. Against an accompaniment of applause the young minister began to speak: "We intend to defend the natural interests of the Italian people with inflexible firmness." Deputies rose and shouted, and for a time all that could be heard in the august hall of Montecitorio was cries of "Tunis! . . . Djibouti! . . . Corsica! . . . Nice!" without any interruption from any member of the government. The French Ambassador sat motionless. Finally Ciano could resume his speech; after the session, François-Poncet said to his German colleague: "Perhaps the deputies have forgotten that the road to Tunis has to lead through forty-five million Frenchmen."

Regardless of that, it was an important development. It marked the initiation of an anti-French campaign: quite obviously the deputies' demonstration had been organized from above, by Il Duce himself. "This," he said, "is how one states a problem and arouses a people."

France seemed to have become his obsession, the target of his scorn, the preferred area of his demands. "We need Tunisia and Corsica," he told the Fascist Grand Council. "Furthermore, the [French-Italian] border should be moved backward to the Var."

Until he declared war in June, 1940, there was not to be a week when Mussolini did not voice his virulent hatred. And many Italians shared it, the King above all; but many segments of the population, and especially the young, were also carried away by the propaganda that had them shouting: "*Nizza nostra*—Nice is ours." In many ways it was like the manifestation of an inferiority complex, the attitude of someone close to a person whom he despises, or that of a younger brother who shows his resemblance through his aggressions. All this was rooted in an old Gallophobic tradition, hatred of a France that was democratic and faithful to the spirit of 1789 and that offered asylum to the *fuorusciti*. "One day," Il Duce told Ribbentrop, "we shall have to settle many scores with France that we have been holding back and that cannot be liquidated without a war. The only peoples that France respects are those that have defeated her."

Ciano assumed the task of provoking massive anti-French sentiment. "Anti-French propaganda among the workers must be given a social color," he said. "France is a middle-class state, a defender of privilege."

Ciano assigned Starace to mobilize opinion round this thesis, to arouse "a wave of hate." How clearly the son-in-law revealed himself to be the servile flunkey of Il Duce, how unthinkingly he embraced his father-in-law's passions and hostilities. When at last he did make up his mind to resist, it was too late. In Mussolini, hatred of France was also an expression of personal feelings. If a French newspaper hinted at his private life, he ground his teeth and said to Ciano: "Those French will be the first to go down. Some insults have to be wiped out with cannon and bombs."

He made a great show of refusing to speak to François-Poncet, who was supposed to have remarked in a private conversation— assiduously reported to Il Duce by the Uruguayan minister—that Mussolini had fallen into a period of intellectual decline. "In Germany," François-Poncet supposedly added, "I had to deal with real leaders; here, however, I do business with lackeys turned masters." True or false, the rumor of such remarks was enough to make Mussolini write in *Il Tevere* (*The Tiber*), a Roman publication financed by the German Embassy, an anonymous article entitled "Francia da sputi (France Is a Spittoon)."

He often told Ciano that the French were "a low people." He would add: "When I have beaten them, I'll show how peace is made in Europe. I will demand nothing, but I will destroy everything and I will sow the site of many a city with salt."

In spite of the Carthaginian fate threatened for so many French cities, Georges Bonnet, the French Foreign Minister, and Daladier, who, however, clung to a firm position in his public utterances, embarked on negotiations. Paul Baudoin, a banker and director of the Somali Salt Mines, arrived in Rome on February 2, 1939, with proposals that were essentially economic and colonial in nature. The reason for this was that, face to face with Germany, the stubborn French and English statesmen always continued to look on the Italy of Il Duce as a kind of recourse. Neville Chamberlain and his Foreign Secretary, Lord Halifax, even went to Rome in January, 1939, at the height of the anti-French campaign. The solemn Englishmen were full of reassurances; "they had never doubted the good faith of Il Duce"; they recognized that the Axis "represented the fundamental basis of Italian policy"; they "intended to do nothing against it." One evening they were received at Palazzo Venezia. In a corner of the room Il Duce and Ciano were talking.

"These men have nothing of the stuff of Francis Drake and the other glorious adventurers who created the empire," Mussolini said. "These men are the tired descendants of a long line of rich generations. As for the empire, they are going to lose it." And their humble approaches and their concessions reinforced Mussolini in his aggressive stand and, above all, impelled him to strengthen his ties with Nazi Germany.

Ciano punctiliously reported the tenor of his talks with Baudoin to the German Ambassador, Hans-Georg von Mackensen. On January 12 Ciano wrote in his diary, with the unconcealed satisfaction of one who thinks that he is on the right road: "German rearmament weighs on the English like a lead blanket. This profound anxiety in the English has convinced us of the necessity of the three-power alliance [Italy, Germany, and Japan]. With such a tool we shall be able to get everything we want. The English do not want to fight. They are trying to back down as slowly as possible."

Ciano's political blindness was to be cured in a few months: for the moment, like Il Duce, he was drunk on success. Chamberlain sent Mussolini the text of a speech even before he delivered it in the House of Commons—a report on his journey to Italy. Contemptuously Il Duce remarked to Ciano: "I think this is the first time that a head of the British government has submitted proofs of one of his speeches to a foreign government. It's a bad omen for them."

French and British statesmen, it is conceded, did not have the privilege of sharing Mussolini's secret confidences. The fact remains that from the newspapers, the public speeches, and, especially, the course taken by his rule, they had available sufficient data to enable them to understand what Fascist Italy's foreign policy might be.

Day after day the régime was straightening its alignment with Naziism. On November 10, 1938, the anti-Semitic legislation was promulgated, and Jews emigrated in increasing number. Enrico Fermi, the famous physicist, left for the United States because his wife was Jewish. Formigini, a Jewish publisher, leaped to his death in December from the Ghirlandina tower in Modena. Colonel Segre was in charge of training exercises at Vercelli when an envelope was delivered to him: he called his troops together and, astride his horse before them, he shot himself to death: he was a Jew and the envelope contained notice of his dismissal from the army. The population and the church made every effort to protect the Jews, but Starace was an assiduous persecutor; Olivetti, the industrialist, despite his liking for Fascism, was uneasy. On June 7 the party secretariat issued a general bulletin entitled: "There Are Still Some Who Give Jews *Raccomandazioni*."

Buffarini-Guidi grew rich on the spoils. There was a decided intent to launch total persecution throughout the country, and it might have been cruelly successful had it not been for the passive resistance of the Italian people and of a large number of Fascists.

In a telegram dated January 4, von Mackensen reported to the Wilhelmstrasse on a conversation with Il Duce and Ciano. "To a question about the Jews," he wrote, "Mussolini answered immediately. Racial legislation is a *noli me tangere*. And Ciano added that the screws would soon be tightened a little more in Italy."

Once again Ciano outstripped Il Duce when he explained: "As things stand today, Europe is seeing a radical division between the Aryan world and the non-Aryan world."

This Hitler-styled anti-Semitic campaign aroused harsh criticism in Italy. Pius XI, it was said, planned to deliver a speech frankly hostile to the course taken by Fascism; the speech was scheduled for the anniversary of the Lateran Accords, but he died on February 10, 1939, and Eugenio Cardinal Pacelli became Pope Pius XII.

Nor was the church alone in reacting. The ordinary middle class, which had hitherto been extremely amenable to Fascist demagogy, and even the upper middle class, became more and more apprehensive in direct proportion to the sound of boots and the rise in identification with the Nazi system. The Vatican's newspaper, *l'Osservatore romano*, soon became the most widely read daily in Italy, and Starace sent out little parties of thugs who manhandled its sellers and burned their papers. The party staged a *Mostra anti-borghese*, an anti-middle-class fair, which caricatured everything bourgeois.

But, while there was hesitation, it was too early to speak of opposition between the middle class and the Fascist system. That system was still the basic framework of the social order; every day autarchy created closer bonds between the ruling circles and the industrialists who were making profits out of arms contracts. When the Fascist government dissolved the Chamber of Deputies on January 14, 1939, and replaced it with the Chamber of Fasci and Corporations, whose members were appointive rather than elective, the fusion of the party's political personnel, the state officials, and the representatives of the world of business and industry was complete.

It was all the more facilitated by the fact that what Il Duce did often resulted in rich gains: the conquest of Albania, for instance, was a matter not only of prestige but also of iron mines. The Ciano family owned the Terni foundries, and the conquest of Albania was to be the work of Galeazzo Ciano, the Foreign Minister. Rodolfo Benini, an industrialist and national councilor in the Chamber of Fasci and Corporations, was as deeply involved as Ciano. It was no accident that he became Under-Secretary of State for Foreign Affairs.

But what assured the adherence of the ruling classes to Fascism more than anything else was its success. And it seemed that for Naziism and Fascism everything was a success.

On March 15, 1939, Prince Philipp von Hesse arrived in Rome again with a message from Der Führer: at six o'clock that morning German troops had entered Bohemia. That night Hitler slept in Prague, in the Hradschin Palace, over which the *Hakenkreuz* waved. Once again, as in the case of Austria, the Italians were informed after the event. "The Axis," Ciano observed, "functions only in favor of one of its partners, who assumes a disproportionate importance and acts on his own exclusive initiative."

Il Duce acknowledged the blow. He wanted no public mention of Hesse's arrival. "The Italians would laugh at me," he said. "Every time Hitler takes another country, he sends me a message."

For several days he was depressed; he aged considerably. Now and then he had outbursts of anti-Germanism, and he was afraid of a German thrust to the Adriatic by way of Croatia. "Even the stones would be upset by a German alliance," he said. He kept to the solitude of the Hall of the Globe, watching through the blue curtains as the Militia units drilled, correcting the gestures of the band leader; he was incapable of decision, and his stomach troubles grew worse; suddenly he exclaimed: "We cannot change our policy because we are not whores."

On March 21, in a voice loaded with anger and contempt, Italo Balbo told the Fascist Grand Council: "You are licking the Germans' boots." Ciano made an irate defense of Mussolini's policy, and Il Duce said tartly: "Balbo will always be the same democratic pig he always was." For it was too late for either the system or its leaders to take a backward step; both their successes and their hopes forced them forward.

On March 28 Madrid fell into Franco's hands. "This is a new and tremendous victory for Fascism," Ciano exulted. That evening Mussolini appeared on the balcony of Palazzo Venezia, holding an atlas opened to the map of Spain. "It has been opened like this for three years," he declaimed, pointing majestically at the atlas. "Now it is enough. But I know already that I must open it at another page."

The mass of party members waved and clapped, shouting: "Duce! Duce! Duce!"

The next page was Albania's.

As we have seen, this enterprise had long since been prepared by Ciano. He did not scruple at playing on any feeling in order to succeed. "Zog will give in," he wrote. "I rely largely on the approaching birth of his child. Zog loves his wife. . . . Frankly, I cannot picture Geraldine fleeing through a battlefield and over the mountains in her ninth month."

Hitler's seizure of Prague accelerated Italy's preparations. The occupation of Albania would also be a means of blocking the German advance, as well as a satisfaction and a compensation. Marshal Badoglio, who did no more than ask for reinforcements, the King, and all the ruling circles were in agreement. But in Bologna a Bersaglieri battalion mobilized for the Albanian campaign staged a demonstration, chanting: "We want peace, not war." This was the first sign of a deep disaffection that was later to penetrate the regular army as well, but that was not yet strong enough to hamper the policy of Il Duce.

On Good Friday, April 7, Ciano watched from a plane in the warm, clear air as Italian troops occupied Tirana on the first day of the invasion. "A magnificent spectacle," he wrote.

King Zog fled to Greece with his three-day-old child. Military operations met little resistance in the tiny kingdom, and on April 16, in the halls of the Quirinal where King Vittorio Emanuele sat enthroned, wet-eyed Albanian warriors tendered him the crown of Albania. Il Duce stood beside the King, and Ciano, carried away by his enthusiasm, likened his master to a "bronze giant."

This easy and anything but glorious victory over Albania could only entrench Mussolini in his convictions. When Ciano, on April 15, handed him a message from President Roosevelt, who suggested a ten-year truce among all the nations of Europe, Il Duce refused at first to read it; then he glanced through it and pushed it aside contemptuously. "This is the result of his spreading paralysis," he smiled scornfully.

Now he was prepared to commit himself to the limit, but as always the final decision would be taken on an impulse.

Ribbentrop and Ciano conferred in Milan on May 6 and 7. Enthusiastic—and well-organized—popular demonstrations greeted the two ministers when they appeared together in uniform, relaxed and smiling like a pair of intimate friends on a holiday. Mussolini had ordered the meeting held in Milan because the foreign press had so often spoken of the Lombard capital's anti-German atmosphere. After their exchanges of views the ministers were dining on the Saturday evening in the Hotel Continental when Ciano was notified of an urgent telephone call. It was Il Duce, who barked an order at Ciano to ask Ribbentrop for the immediate signature of a German-Italian military alliance. This was Mussolini's reaction to reports in foreign newspapers that there had been anti-German demonstrations in Milan.

So it was an emotional impulse that was midwife to the Pact of Steel; but, though the actual signature was determined by chance, the treaty itself was the product of the long and logical evolution of Fascism. Mussolini was so thoroughly convinced that Naziism would triumph that—and this is extremely rare in the history of diplomacy—he allowed the Germans to draft its entire text, which the Italians merely signed. Ciano read the German draft on the train that took him to Florence on May 13, and he noted: "I have never seen a treaty like it—it is real dynamite." In fact, the Pact of Steel was an accord not so much between the two nations as between the two régimes, "tightly bound to each other by the internal affinities of their views of the world."

It was the ambition of Fascism and Naziism alike "to dedicate themselves, in the midst of a disordered, disintegrating world, to the task of perpetuating the bases of European culture." Fascist Italy and Nazi Germany assumed the obligation of regimenting Europe. In what way? Article III was of unprecedented moment: it stipulated that the two powers "pledged themselves to support each other without a separate peace or armistice in the event of warlike confrontations with one or more powers, immediately and with all their military forces." Thus Italy would automatically have to enter a war if it came: the only qualification—and it was minimal—the only governor on the engine was "reciprocal consultation between the two parties." There had never been such a treaty in all the history of diplomacy.

It was ratified with great pomp in Berlin on May 22, 1939, in the presence of Hitler, Goering, and Grand Admiral Erich Raeder.

Ciano had presented Ribbentrop with the Collar of the Annunziata in the name of the King: Goering's eyes had filled with tears of jealousy and he had made a scene with von Mackensen, the Ambassador to Rome, for it was he, Goering, who had brought about the German-Italian alliance and now someone else was collecting the reward for his patient endeavor. Ciano promised to use his influence with the King, and Mackensen managed to console Goering.

When Ciano returned to Rome on May 24, he was welcomed in triumph: a mass of hierarchs clustered round him; the cheering squads did their work with zeal at the train station and the press made huge headlines of the Italian people's enthusiasm for the Pact of Steel, which, the papers said, would make it possible for Italy to bring vast projects to reality.

Mussolini was already expediting the highway construction that would enable his troops to move from Albania into Greece, which, Ciano wrote, he intended to attack as soon as possible. And Il Duce behaved with more and more assurance. He humiliated the British Ambassador, Sir Percy Loraine, who came out of Palazzo Venezia "red-faced and excited, trembling nervously, and looking like a man who has just been slapped in the face."

What was there for Mussolini to fear? at worst, another Munich. In a thoroughly sincere tone Ribbentrop had told Ciano in Milan: "Germany is convinced of the need for a period of peace that should be not less than four or five years."

In Berlin he reduced this figure to three years. This was exactly the time required by Mussolini for the rebuilding of his army, worn down by Ethiopia and Spain, and it would expire in 1942, the twentieth anniversary of Fascist rule and the date set for a world's fair in Rome. On June 30 General Ugo Cavallero gave Der Führer a memorandum in which Il Duce insisted on the necessity of preserving the peace until 1943. Hitler accepted the memorandum, which, he said, he had "read with great interest." Actually, *Fall Weiss* (Case White) had been under way since April 3—in other words, even before the ratification of the Pact of Steel. Der Führer had instructed OKW to prepare the Polish campaign: "Plans should be made in such a way that the operation can be launched at any time after 1. IX. 1939."

The day after the ratification of the pact, Hitler had told his military leaders in the Chancellory: "It is not Danzig that is the reason for the war. It is a question of enlarging our living space in the east. . . . There is no thought of sparing Poland. . . . England is against us and we have to make war on her. . . . French blood will not be spared." Clearly Der Führer faced the prospect of a

The Road to War

general war; he concluded: "Secrecy is an essential condition of success. Italy and Japan will not be told of our plans."

Within twenty-four hours of its signature Italy had been duped by the Pact of Steel. Il Duce, Ciano, and the hierarchs were to be brutally awakened to the realities of Nazi policy, and the Pact of Steel was to deserve the name that Il Duce later gave it: *Patto di sangue*—Pact of Blood.

At the beginning of July, however, everything seemed quiet. Diplomats in Rome went off to their summer homes, and the Danzig issue and the Polish question no longer seemed serious. Reassured by Hitler as to the likelihood of war, Mussolini received Loraine, the serious-faced, friendly British Ambassador, on July 7: Loraine presented a message from Chamberlain. Mussolini read it quickly and repeated over and over to the Ambassador: "Tell Chamberlain that, if England is ready to fight for the defense of Poland, Italy has decided to take up arms for her ally, Germany."

The same evening Ciano told von Mackensen the gist of this, and the German seemed highly satisfied. The Italians' firm stand was based on their conviction that there would still be three or four years of peace. Hitler and Ribbentrop had said so more than once, and Mussolini was risking nothing by displaying his resoluteness to Loraine. Then the situation changed brutally: when Ciano returned to Palazzo Chigi from Spain at the end of July, he found a mass of dispatches from his Ambassador in Berlin, Attolico. Near-sighted as that smiling man might be, his eyes were sharp enough to see what game the Germans were playing. He believed that war was near. Ciano, occupied with his golf games, his beach parties, his trips to Capri, and the matter of the Collar of the Annunziata that the King wanted to award him for the conquest of Albania, did not understand. "Attolico's insistence bewilders me," he wrote in his diary. "Either the Ambassador has completely lost his head or else he sees and knows something that totally escapes us. The evidence inclines me to the former hypothesis, but events must be followed with care."

Since "Attolico's alarmist bombardment" was continuing, Ciano decided to confer with Ribbentrop. "It is essential to show the Germans that war would be insane at this time," Il Duce told Ciano. "We have only a fifty-percent chance; in three years it will be eighty percent." Mussolini also suggested the possibility of an international conference, a super-Munich that would be as profitable as its predecessor. Ciano was instructed to present these views to the Nazis.

He arrived in Salzburg by plane on the morning of August 11. Ribbentrop took him to his private estate, Schloss Fuschl: in the solemn setting of the castle, confiscated from its former owner, who was now in a concentration camp, Ciano and Ribbentrop faced each other for almost ten hours, beginning their talks in the garden. Ciano recorded the meeting in his diary.

"Well, Ribbentrop," he began, "what in sum do you want: Danzig or the Polish Corridor?"

"More than that," Ribbentrop replied, staring coldly at Ciano like a figure in a wax museum. "We want war."

Ciano was brought cruelly face to face with fact: panic struck him because he knew that he was powerless against German determination; he was up against a blind resolve that threatened to drag Italy in; he was in panic, too, because he knew very well within himself that Fascism, Il Duce, himself—Ciano, Minister of Foreign Affairs—had been made fools of and were responsible for this irremediable situation. It was no longer a business of receptions and speeches, parades and decorations: it was a business of war. Ciano was pale and shaken. When the Ministers went to lunch, there were frequent intervals of total silence broken only by some comment on what they were eating. Ciano whispered to his brother-in-law, Count Massimo Magistrati, a diplomat who was with him: "We are at swords' point."

Ribbentrop turned aside every argument by the Italian with a general statement: the war against Poland would not spread; if that did happen, improbable as it was, France and England would be smashed. During dinner in the Österreichischer Hof in the town, Ribbentrop offered a bet: if France and England did not act, Ciano would give him an Italian painting; if they did, Ribbentrop would give Ciano a collection of ancient weapons. No one smiled.

On August 12 and 13 Ciano conferred with Der Führer. Hitler was standing in front of a number of large-scale maps: he was already the wartime leader, backed up by Ribbentrop and two SS officers, Martin Bormann and Eugen Dollmann. "The best time for the operation," Hitler said, "is between now and October 15. But," he insisted, "it will be a localized war."

In order to impress Ciano, Hitler showed him a copy of a telegram from Moscow that announced the initiation of negotiations between Nazi Germany and the Soviet Union. While the telegram accurately represented Hitler's hopes, at that time it was still meaningless and without binding effect, but the gesture must have reassured Ciano.

That evening the Italians held a private conference in the bathroom of Ciano's hotel suite: all the taps were opened in order to

The Road to War

drown out their voices, for they assumed that the Gestapo had hidden eavesdropping devices in all the rooms. It was a serious situation and raised the question whether the Pact of Steel would come into force. True, Der Führer had indicated that Italy was free to stay out of the war, but the commitments contained in the Pact of Steel were express.

On the second day of Ciano's talks with Hitler the tone was peremptory. To an explicit question by Ciano, Hitler replied: "The absolute deadline for the start of operations is the end of August." Then, to put an end to the short meeting, Der Führer lavished praise on Mussolini: "Another statesman who will go down in history as great and unique. . . . Sometime I should like him to be my guest at the Bayreuth Festival."

Ciano flew back to Rome that day—August 13—and went immediately to see Il Duce. "Given the behavior of Germany," he told his father-in-law, "I believe we have a free hand. We ought to announce that we have no intention of taking part in a conflict that we neither wanted nor brought on."

Mussolini gave Ciano a long, worried look before he spoke. After their meeting Ciano wrote in his diary that night: "At first he agreed with me. Then he said that honor required him to march with Germany. Finally he said he wanted his share of the loot in Croatia and Dalmatia."

Mussolini had been shocked into betraying the indecisiveness of his thinking and the essence of his political vision, the constant in his diplomacy: spoils. In a few months Italy was to perceive that for seventeen years she had been in "strange hands."

August 14–September 3, 1939. Europe was twenty-one days away from war. Mussolini, Ciano, the Fascist hierarchs, and Italian ruling circles knew that the Germans had decided to put an end to Poland on the pretext of Danzig, and the majority expected England and France to stand by the Poles. But, as the days and even the hours wore on, Mussolini was still hesitantly, constantly changing his mind, sending Ciano, a firm advocate of non-intervention, shuttling between hope and fear.

August 15. "It is still possible that the democracies may give in," Il Duce said, "though it would seem difficult. In that case it would not be good to irritate the Germans, because we ought to get our share of the spoils too." By nightfall and again next day, he held a different view: "This time it is war, and we cannot take part in it because we are in no position to do so."

August 20. Il Duce changed his mind again. Ciano rushed home from Albania and "fired all his ammunition" at the Axis:

"Tear up the pact and throw it in Hitler's face, and Europe will regard you as the natural leader of the anti-German crusade." But at ten-thirty the next morning Ribbentrop told Ciano that the signature of a non-aggression treaty with Moscow was imminent. Again there was hesitation. "We must wait and hold ourselves in readiness," Il Duce said, "so that if possible we can grab our share of the spoils in Croatia and Dalmatia."

August 23. "Il Duce is belligerent. He talks of arms and attacks."

Those three weeks of vacillation were the drama of the imperturbable Duce who "fights to the finish," face to face with brutal reality: a man rocked between one decision and another by events that he had not anticipated, a man whose mind could be changed by whoever talked to him cleverly enough, a nervous man who had no plan and who with every day lost more of his grasp on reality.

It was a reality that he refused even to see. The façade was cracking in every direction: the military position was disastrous and the myth of the "Fascist grand army" was evaporating. Exhausted by Ethiopia and Spain—Franco, for example, had been given nineteen hundred artillery pieces—the army was stripped. Of course it still had a surplus of generals, but for the men of fifteen divisions there were not even uniforms. The troops had barely a month's supply of ammunition, their rifles were of 1891 design, the armored attack vehicles, designated L-35, were extremely light (three and a half tons)—the soldiers called them *tascabili*, pocket editions, or sardine tins, or vanity cases—and they broke down regularly.

After seventeen years of Fascism the situation was in every respect worse than in 1915: though forty-two divisions had been mobilized, in actuality there were only thirty-seven, or the equivalent—on paper there was a figure of seventy-three, but in order to make thirty-seven it had been necessary to reduce the number of regiments in each. In the air force, which was the best branch of the Fascist armed services, there were seven hundred modern planes, but not all were in flying condition, and, besides, no one knew where they were based.

The industrial backing for this army was laughably understocked: on September 1, 1939, there was enough steel for two weeks, iron ore for six months, nickel for twenty days. Furthermore, the equipment produced by Italian industry was indescribably inefficient: the grenades did not explode, the nails fell out of the shoes and the soles wore through in a few miles; the uniforms, when they were available, were made of second-hand fabrics and gave no protection against the cold.

"And what is Il Duce doing?" Ciano asked his diary. "He concentrates on matters of form. If the troops do not present arms properly or if an officer cannot lift his leg high enough for the *passo romano*, it becomes a major problem: on the other hand, he seems to pay very little attention to shortages with which he is completely conversant. . . . Perhaps he is so afraid of the truth that he does not want to hear it."

Favor-currying generals made it a practice to reassure him with false statistics on the strength of the armed forces; as experts in the military art they could not be ignorant of their needs, but they kept silent in connivance with the government. Only a few spoke out: the noted General Alfredo Dallolio, who had been in charge of military procurement since 1915 and was unequaled as an organizer, resigned on August 28, 1939. But most shared General Roatta's view: "We generals should always be in favor of war. . . . Germany has arms enough for us too." Other generals argued for war simply because they had financial connections with the arms industries.

The lack of military preparedness was indicative of the behavior and the condition of Italian industry in this essential sector of the Fascist economy. Dishonest contracts, bribes, refusals to modernize because of the concomitant necessity of investing part of the profits in new production equipment and methods, squandering of military credits despite their vast volume—these were the realities.

There were others even more serious. A policy of self-sufficiency compels a country poor in raw materials, like Italy, to export manufactured products in order to obtain foreign exchange and import raw materials; so Italy sold what she most needed between 1938 and June, 1940 (the date of her entry into the Second World War)—namely, arms! And the Fascist system, which was driving toward war while at the same time pursuing autarchy, was also bringing on military unpreparedness; this was a contradiction that could be resolved only by remaining neutral.

Hence business circles spent these twenty-one days pressing for a policy of independence of Germany. For the signature of the Pact of Steel had entailed economic consequences too. German financial missions and engineers established themselves in Italy and sought to colonize the country: their purchasing agents cornered the market in food products and textiles and accumulated debts of seven million dollars in December, 1938, seventeen and a half million in March, 1939, and thirty-nine million in August of that year. These debts could not be paid, and the campaign for Italian neutrality resulted also from this clash between two autarchic economies: Germany was trying to consolidate a dominance of the Italian economy and to reduce it to a condition of dependency. Was it fortuitous that Ciano, with his ties to the Terni metallurgical industries and the Leghorn shipbuilders, championed autonomy for Italian policy?

In this conflict he had the King's backing. "The army is in miserable condition," the sovereign told Ciano. "The officers are not up to their jobs and the equipment is worn out and defective."

When the King bestowed the Collar of the Annunziata on Ciano, Italy was full of the most various rumors: supposedly Ciano had brought off a successful "peace mission" *in extremis* at Salzburg, or the King was relying on him to rid the country of Il Duce. Such rumors, and their persistence, showed that beneath its seeming indifference public opinion was watching the situation with apprehension.

On August 15 Starace issued a "marching order for Fascist culture," the theme of which was "preparation for total war," but it aroused no response. The day before, Ciano had asked him "not to conceal from Il Duce the clearly anti-German spirit of the country." But how was it possible to rely on Starace, the party secretary—in other words, the stage manager for Fascism since 1931—avowed partisan of the Axis, servile imitator of the Nazis, flatterer in whom fanaticism was coupled with stupidity? Ciano observed contemptuously: "Starace, with his lack of intellectual power, was not afraid to tell Il Duce that Italian women were happy at the prospect of war because they would get allotments of thirty cents a day and be rid of their husbands. What a disgrace! The Italian people does not deserve an insult as vulgar as that."

Indeed, the comment went much farther than its author, condemning the whole political system that could give the highest post in the party to a Starace. Ciano turned to Bocchini, the extremely pessimistic head of the police. "If there should be demonstrations in favor of neutrality," Bocchini said, "the carabinieri and the regular police would make common cause with the people."

Despite the screen erected by the Staraces, this economic, military, and political climate weighed heavily on the decision of Il Duce, that Duce of whom Hitler had pointed out, in his military conference on August 22, that, like Hitler's own, "his existence too is a determinant. Let something happen, and there will no longer be any certainty of Italy's loyalty to Germany. Il Duce has the strongest nerves of any man in Italy."

At this same conference Hitler set the attack against Poland for 4 A.M., Saturday, August 26. Europe had reached the eve of war.

August 24, 1939. Mussolini conferred with his military leaders.

August 25. Duce was still belligerent. Mobilization and marching orders were ready for promulgation. Some classes of reserves were called up.

At 3:20 P.M. von Mackensen brought a message from Hitler to Mussolini. It was a justification of the German-Russian treaty and an announcement of the imminence of the attack on Poland. Hitler confined himself to requesting "Italian understanding." Ciano seized on the phrase: Italy could not move unless Germany gave her very considerable help.

6 P.M. Hitler learned that Great Britain had signed a treaty of assistance with Poland: so the conflict could not be localized. At about the same time Attolico presented Mussolini's reply to Hitler: "Given the present state of military preparations in Italy, I cannot take the initiative in any warlike operations. The war was planned for 1942 and at that date I should have been ready. I feel that it is my imperative duty as a loyal friend to tell you the whole truth and to inform you of the real situation in advance." When the German translation of this was read to Der Führer, he exclaimed: "The Italians are behaving exactly as they did in 1914."

Two and a half hours later, at 8:30, *Fall Weiss*—the attack on Poland—was ordered suspended. At 9:30, in Rome, von Mackensen gave Il Duce a letter from Hitler requesting a completely detailed inventory of Italy's needs. War had been averted, then; it would not begin on August 26: the Anglo-Polish accord had been the determining factor, and a subsidiary part had been played by Mussolini's letter.

August 26. At 10 A.M. the chiefs of the Italian general staff sat down in Palazzo Venezia to compile the catalogue of their needs. "It would choke a bull if he could read it," Ciano said with pleasure: one and three quarter million tons of gasoline, coal, steel, wood, anti-aircraft batteries. With it Mussolini sent a covering letter to Hitler:

Führer,
I would not have sent you this list if I had had the time (on which we had agreed) to accumulate a stockpile and to accelerate the growth of self-sufficiency.

At three in the afternoon, in Berlin, Attolico, who was opposed to war, took it upon himself to reply to a question from Ribbentrop as to the delivery date requested by the Italians. "At once," Attolico snapped, "before hostilities begin." The shipment would have required seventeen thousand freight trains.

Two hours later Mussolini had another message from Hitler: "I will not hesitate to settle the eastern question even at the risk of complications in the west." The decision on war was irrevocable. "Il Duce is truly overwhelmed," Ciano wrote. "His military instinct and his sense of honor were pushing him into war, but his reason has stopped him. He is really suffering."

August 27. At 9 A.M. Mussolini received the message in which Hitler agreed to Italian neutrality:

Duce,
   I respect the reasons and the motives that have led you to this decision.

Der Führer requested secrecy and the dispatch of Italian workers. The die was cast: Italy would stay out of the war. But Mussolini was nervous; certain now that he would not act, he increased his military measures—recalls of reservists, blackouts in the streets of the large cities, requisitions of supplies.

August 31. Rodolfo Graziani and Umberto di Savoia were appointed commanders-in-chief of the two army groups that constituted Italy's forces. On the same day London broke off telephone connections with Italy. Was England planning a surprise attack? Had she been taken in by Mussolini's warlike actions? Ciano found himself constrained to stage a melodramatic scene with Ambassador Loraine in order to prevent any Allied action. He sent for the Briton and demanded: "Why do you want to do something irreparable? Didn't you understand that we would never take the initiative in a war against you and France?"

Hitler, in Berlin, rescheduled the attack on Poland for 4:45 A.M. on September 1.

September 1. Mussolini himself telephoned to Attolico and ordered his Ambassador to get a telegram from Hitler that expressly relieved Il Duce of his obligations to Germany. In a word, he wanted to save face. At 8:40 the telegram was sent.

At two thirty in the afternoon the Italian radio interrupted normal broadcasts for a communiqué from the Cabinet: "Italy will not take any initiative in military operations." This was immediately followed by a grave-voiced reading of Hitler's telegram to Il Duce:

Duce,

I offer my heartiest thanks for the diplomatic and political assistance that you have recently given to Germany and to her just cause. . . . I do not expect to need Italy's military aid. I thank you also, Duce, for everything that you will be able to do in the future for the common cause of Fascism and National Socialism.

Adolf Hitler

On September 2 and 3, essentially under pressure from France, Ciano and Mussolini sought to find a means of mediation on the Munich model. But Great Britain insisted on the withdrawal of the German troops who had invaded Poland, and the effort failed.

At 11 A.M. on September 3, 1939, Great Britain declared war on Germany; six hours later she was followed by France. Italy was out of the conflict. That evening, when the Second World War had begun, Hitler, who was about to leave for the front, wrote again to Il Duce, just before ten o'clock: "Though we now follow different roads, destiny will always bind us to each other. . . . If National Socialist Germany were to be destroyed, . . . the future would be cruel for Fascist Italy. I have always recognized that the futures of our two systems were joined together, and I know, Duce, that you personally share my opinion."

When Ambassador von Mackensen handed him this message, Mussolini emphatically repeated his pledge of total solidarity with Nazi Germany. Thus, as Italy went through her first night of non-belligerence (Mussolini had rejected the word *neutrality*), it seemed that this shaky peace was already threatened. Rome was still enveloped in darkness; all public places had been ordered to close at 11 P.M.; meat rationing was instituted and the sale of coffee was prohibited. When this first night was over, early risers in the workers' quarters of Rome saw crudely printed posters: "Italian workers will never fight alongside the butchers of their Polish brothers."

Two nights later the same posters were pasted up in Naples and Florence during the blackout. They had been written by young men who came from Fascist organizations. Even if these ink-blurred leaflets and posters were read by only a few Italians, the fact was both important and symbolic. It clearly showed that little by little, in this autumn of 1939, Fascism was losing all real foundation.

Certainly neutrality had been greeted with relief, but it was no longer viewed as a success for Fascism and Il Duce. Times had changed since Munich. Soldiers on leave talked more and more about the deficiencies in weapons and uniforms. No one knew the whereabouts of the eight million bayonets of which Il Duce had boasted. The whole nation was learning the vanity of eighteen years of rhetoric. Mussolini sensed this, and for almost three weeks he was silent. Irony, if only under the breath, came back to life: Mussolini became *Mutolini*, the little mute. With great bitterness he confided to Ciano on October 9: "After eighteen years of bellicose propaganda the Italians cannot understand that I become the champion of peace when Europe is in flames. They can attribute this only to our lack of military preparation, for which also they hold me responsible—me, who have always proclaimed the power of our armies."

And it was true that now Il Duce personally was at issue. There were all kinds of rumors of concerted action by the King, Ciano, and the army. Some Italians predicted the imminent collapse of the Axis and a democratic turn by Fascism; others argued that Il Duce no longer exercised any power and the King and the hierarchs were pulling the strings.

So for a few weeks there was a climate of optimism while everyone looked forward to a "fat-cat neutrality" on the Swiss model, as Ciano wrote. Barely two days after the start of the war, he observed with pleasure: "Neutrality is beginning to bear its fruits: stock prices are soaring, we are getting our first orders from France, ships are sailing again even though freight rates have doubled, and they are loaded to the gunwales."

It was a joyful autumn that was beginning. A musical comedy, *Hands in My Pockets and Face to the Wind*—its title was its own commentary—was a smash hit. Suddenly, on September 23, hopes were sent reeling.

Il Duce had convened the Fascist hierarchs for that day and, addressing those of Bologna, the Tenth Legion, he began: "The Italian nation knows that it must not distract the pilot when he is guiding the ship through the tempest, or ask him for details of the course that he has plotted." The hierarchs applauded loudly and, with more conviction, Il Duce continued: "When I appear on the balcony and summon the whole Italian people to hear me, it will not be for an analysis of the situation but rather for an announcement, as on October 2, 1935, and May 9, 1936, of decisions—" here Il Duce paused, surveyed his audience and then resumed "—of decisions, I say, of historic import."

This peroration was accompanied by denunciations, in the squadrista style, against the Freemasons, the "trash," the Jews, all of whom must be swept away. Only the day before, on via Veneto in Rome, a man had been soundly beaten for having used *Lei* instead of *voi*. So, at a pace matching the German victories in

Poland, Fascism reared up with new vigor and once again began to contemplate involvement in the war.

This step, in the view of some Italians, was inevitable for the government regardless of how Mussolini might hesitate. For the system was founded on a party all of whose functionaries, at least in words, had backed up Il Duce in his bellicose and pro-German policies. Non-belligerence meant the defeat not only of Mussolini but also of the party and the system, and, the longer inaction continued, the greater was the repudiation of eighteen years of warlike oratory and of all those who had engaged in it.

Therefore—perhaps sooner, perhaps later, but inescapably—neutrality could lead only to crisis for Il Duce, the party, and the government. Intervention on Germany's side, on the other hand, offered the chance of winning the gamble of war and hence of saving Il Duce, the party, and the system. Mussolini completely understood the problem, and the change in his views was the result of his recognition of the gravity of the situation: either way, the fate of Fascism was at stake, whether Italy entered the war or stayed out.

Undoubtedly Mussolini's vacillations were accentuated by his physical condition. His stomach troubles had come back. In February, 1940, Sumner Welles thought that Il Duce looked "fifteen years older than his age of fifty-six. He is sluggish and pretentious rather than keen, and his walk is like an elephant's." He often kept his eyes closed, and frequently sipped at hot beverages. But, if this man, "with his heavy body, his close-cropped white hair, his face falling into ripples of flesh when he was relaxed," could not make up his mind to fight, it was not so much for psycho-physiological reasons as because his military position was far too precarious as a result of the hostility of public opinion. The state of his health was an effect, and not a cause, of his non-intervention.

For now there were demonstrations in Italy. One day in October, 1939, a group of students in Milan carried a large tree-trunk into Galleria Vittorio Emanuele, in the center of the city, sawed it into four sections, and left them there. Each section bore one of the four letters of A-S-S-E (Axis), separated from the others. Other students founded a new party, the Partito socialista rivoluzionario (Revolutionary Socialist Party), and distributed leaflets. Individual acts of protest—sometimes sabotage, more often inscriptions on walls—pointed to growing opposition; what was more serious for the government was the groups that were forming in various barracks. Therefore there were massive arrests of *sovversivi* (subversives) at the end of 1939. But the major factor in keeping Mussolini out of active participation was the lack of preparation of the army. Ciano noted on January 15, 1940: "Il Duce is depressed because now he knows the true situation of our armed forces. Ten divisions are ready; by the end of January there will be eleven. The others are short of virtually everything; in some divisions the artillery supplies are down to eight percent of normal. Under such conditions it is hard to talk of war."

Mussolini, who was well aware that the fate of the system depended on a victorious war, could not in these circumstances help giving way to discouragement: "He is so crushed that he says he can feel the symptoms of a new stomach ulcer."

For Ciano and for public opinion, however, there was a new surge of optimism. On October 31 Ettore Muti replaced Starace as party secretary. Muti was the epitome of the disciplined Fascist, the strong-arm man who had served d'Annunzio as his pilot; he had the mentality of an Ardito and a squadrista, blindly loyal to Il Duce. But what interested Italy more was the dismissal of Starace. His removal was interpreted as a confirmation of neutrality and hence of the liberalization of the party.

On January 17, 1940, Mussolini told Ciano: "The Germans would be well advised to let themselves be guided by me if they want to avoid making irreparable mistakes. There is no question that politically I am more intelligent than Hitler."

But the more clear-thinking hierarchs—Balbo, Bottai, Ciano, Bocchini, Federzoni—were beginning to wonder whether Mussolini's incoherence was not of pathological origin. "Il Duce ought to get really adequate treatment for his syphilis," Bocchini told Ciano.

However well or ill founded, such a viewpoint, as we have indicated, was one-sided, for incoherence and vacillation were no monopolies of Il Duce alone; they were shared by the hierarchs, and not all these were ill. It was simply that the seriousness of the political situation was pitiless in revealing the flaws in Fascism and its leaders. Il Duce swung from one opinion to another and the hierarchs followed him, exaggerating the swings, criticizing Mussolini and clinging to him, forming alliances against him in the secrecy of drawing rooms and tearing one another apart in his presence. When Starace castigated Muti as incompetent, Mussolini said: "That is just country gossip. Basically I think Starace is jealous because Muti has received more medals than he has."

Europe was already plunged into the most disastrous of civil wars and, even as they were poised to hurl Italy into it, the Fascist hierarchs were still absorbed in their ballet of reciprocal denunciations and in their traffic in influence in that Palazzo Venezia that was becoming more and more isolated from the nation. One month after the start of the war Ciano wrote with smug self-congratulation in his diary: "The Prince of Piedmont has given me a little personal present, a small jewel to be worn with evening dress next to the Collar of the Annunziata."

This was the clearest-sighted of all the Fascist leaders. Actually none of them—Ciano no more than the rest—could stand out long against Il Duce. "I can send anyone to the gallows, with no exceptions," Mussolini warned.

Il Duce and the hierarchs almost unconsciously recognized, furthermore, that only by forming a solid unity could they hope to survive and to carry on. The hierarchs knew that Fascism, by which they lived and from which they derived their power, was nothing without Mussolini, and he was well aware that in neutrality there was nothing for Fascism but isolation and doom. Hence he must base his actions on making the best of Italian military realities—that is, enter a war that was already won and in which he need not fight. This was to be made possible by the German victories that piled up one on another in the first half of 1940.

As the German gains mounted, Il Duce altered course in proportion. For more than two hours on December 21, 1939, he held a private conversation with Himmler. "I will never permit a defeat of Germany," he is supposed to have told the head of the Gestapo and the SS.

In January Mussolini wrote to Der Führer; on March 10 Ribbentrop was in Rome. "In a few months," he told Mussolini confidently, "the French army will be annihilated and the only Englishmen left on the continent will be those in the prisoner-of-war camps."

Everyone in Rome knew that Il Duce was on the threshold of a decision. During a golf game on March 14 the Minister of the Royal House, the Duke of Acquarone, talked to Ciano. "The King knows the uneasiness that is disturbing the country," he said. "His Majesty might be compelled to act."

Ciano evaded him. Was it true, however, that in those March days he was thinking of poisoning Mussolini because of Il Duce's increasing preference for war? Supposedly he asked Bocchini for a fast-acting poison. But this may have been no more than another of the many vague notions that Ciano was always entertaining and that he never carried out.

On March 18 Mussolini met Hitler at the Brenner "with a feeling compounded with anxiety." When Il Duce returned to Italy, the railroad stations were filled with hundreds of plain-clothes policemen, Fascists under instructions to drown out any possible shouts of *Pace! Pace!* with the traditional *Duce! Duce!*

On March 31 Mussolini drafted a memorandum on intervention. "It is necessary," he told Ciano; "neutrality would take Italy out of the class of the great powers for a century, and discredit her for all eternity as a Fascist régime; Italy would become a grade-B country." This decision to join the war rejuvenated Il Duce, whose violence and contempt for the people, which he believed to be pacifist, emerged without the slightest concealment, revealing not only the coarsest cynicism but a superficial philosophy whose roots were in the cult of the leader.

"When a people is dominated by the instincts of the vegetative life," he told Ciano, "there is only one way to save it: by the use of force. Even those whom it strikes down will be grateful for it. Have you ever seen a lamb become a wolf? The Italian race is a race of sheep, and eighteen years are not enough to change it. That would take a hundred eighty years, or perhaps a hundred eighty centuries."

The idea of resorting to punishment recurred frequently. When Ciano told him that the shortage of coal was going to make heating difficult, he retorted: "It's a good thing for the Italian people to be subjected to hardships that shake it out of its age-old mental laziness." And, unmasking the heart of his political thinking, he added: "The mass must be regimented and kept in uniform from morning to night, and it needs the stick—the stick." The Milanese and the Genovese were cowards, "incurable Anglophiles, imbeciles, and criminals who think that Germany will be beaten." Mussolini's evil temper seemed to be increasing with his perception of the growing isolation of the government. On April 11 he declared: "To make a people great it must be sent into battle even if it has to be kicked in the ass."

Two days earlier German troops had invaded Denmark and Norway. "I thoroughly approve this act by Hitler," Il Duce told von Mackensen. "I will order the Italian press and people to give unreserved praise to this move by Germany." He added: "The people is a whore that goes for the strongest male."

In fact, it was above all the middle classes and the intellectuals who were won over by the German victories—the groups that had been skeptical of Germany's chances in 1939 and were now beginning to think that Italy must claim her share of the loot. Dino Grandi went to see Ciano and told him dramatically: "We have to acknowledge that we have been completely wrong and to prepare ourselves for the new era."

Industrial and financial circles, which for a time had advocated neutrality, also came round to the interventionist side. In February Mussolini refused a British offer to purchase twenty million pounds' worth of war materials and farm products. On March 1 the British blockade was extended to German ships carrying coal to Italy. The British market having thus been closed, the Italian economy was chained to the German. The coal moved through Switzerland; and Mussolini delivered to Germany thirty-five hundred tons of brass requisitioned from every possible source. "What the churches need," Il Duce observed sarcastically, "is not brass but faith."

He also contemplated the export of works of art as a means of acquiring foreign credits, and his Finance Minister endorsed the idea. "We shall be rich," he told Ciano, "and gold will no longer matter."

The industrialists were more realistic. In order to meet the economic and financial crisis that threatened Italy after the loss of her traditional outlets, they banked on German victory. The president of Confindustria, Giovanni Balella, said: "We must create new outlets to replace those that will inevitably be lost; we must penetrate new markets regardless of cost." Thus the powerful forces of Confindustria too abandoned the policy of neutrality, which had initially been profitable, and joined Il Duce and Fascism in interventionism.

When at five-thirty on the morning of May 10, 1940, the Wehrmacht invaded Belgium, Holland, and Luxembourg, it was clear to Italians that Fascism's entry into the war was near. Ciano's own wife, Edda, went to her father in Palazzo Venezia to urge him to act; on the other side the Pope, Roosevelt, Churchill, French Premier Paul Reynaud, and Daladier flooded Il Duce with messages urging him to remain neutral. It was useless. On May 13 Mussolini told Ciano: "We Italians have been disgraced enough already. Any delay is unthinkable."

On May 26 Marshal Badoglio went to confer with Mussolini. The marshal had barely entered the room when Il Duce thundered, as if he were addressing a vast amphitheater: "Yesterday I sent Hitler a statement in writing . . . as of June 5 I shall be ready to declare war."

Badoglio stopped in his tracks. "That is suicide," he is supposed to have said.

"Marshal," Mussolini retorted in a peremptory tone, "all I need is a few thousand dead to be able to sit down as a belligerent at the peace conference."

Three days later Mussolini sent for all his chiefs of staff— Badoglio, Giovoni, General Francesco Pricolo, and Admiral

Domenico Cavagnari. They would be adjutants to Il Duce, who was going to assume the post of supreme commander with the firm plan of waging a war parallel to Germany's by making the Mediterranean the main theater of operations. Every one of the military leaders in his office was thoroughly aware of the military catastrophe that was awaiting an Italian army deprived of basic needs, but none said a word. "Badoglio is putting on a good face with bad cards and getting ready for war," Ciano wrote.

When General Giacomo Carboni suggested to Marshal Badoglio on June 8 that he resign deliberately as chief of the general staff in an effort to stop the war, Badoglio replied wearily: "I believe there is really no more to be done; besides, who knows? perhaps Mussolini is right. Certainly the Germans are extremely strong, and they might be able to win a quick victory."

It was in fact the German successes, which destroyed the French army, that made possible an Italian intervention that, as Mussolini knew very well, was inconceivable except against an already defeated enemy. The date chosen was June 11. Ciano noted: "The King has also approved the date because of the brief interval that it allows us and also because it is his birthday and, as a recruit, he had the serial number of 1111."

The remark betrays an unbelievable mixture of blindness, political complicity, and faith in a short, easy war. The King never replied to the appeal that Carlo Sforza, from his exile, sent to him on May 30, 1940: "If Your Majesty lends his name and his signature to this senseless war," the former Minister wrote soberly, "Your Majesty must remember that it will mean the most terrible of destructions for Italy. The calamities will be so appalling and the loss of national honor will be so shameful that in the end they will destroy the bonds of affection and loyalty between the Italian people and Your Majesty."

On June 10, 1940, in response to a summons, Ambassador François-Poncet entered the office of Count Ciano, who was wearing his air-force uniform. "You probably know already," Ciano began their talk, "why I sent for you."

"Although I am not very intelligent, this time I understood," the Ambassador said; then he listened to Ciano's reading of the declaration of war. At the end François-Poncet said: "It is a dagger thrust into a fallen man. Thank you, nevertheless, for wearing a velvet glove." As he left, he indicated Ciano's uniform and added: "Don't get yourself killed."

A few minutes later Ciano received the British Ambassador, who kept his composure and his distance.

Meanwhile, in a black uniform, Mussolini was speaking from

the balcony of Palazzo Venezia. There was no emotion in the crowd, and only little knots of uniformed Fascists raised the cry of *Guerra! guerra!* There was nothing of the vibrant enthusiasm that had filled the square after the Ethiopian war. Party officials had jostled the crowd into ranks, from which there came shouts of *Crepa! crepa!* (Drop dead! drop dead!), but the words were drowned in the deafening blare of trumpets and bands.

"We are embarking on a battle against the plutocratic, reactionary democracies of the West," Mussolini declaimed; "we are taking up arms to resolve first the problem of our continental borders and then the problem of our maritime borders. A nation of forty-five million souls is not truly free if it does not have freedom of access to the oceans."

Shouts, which were more cadenced than fervent, and the roll of drums accompanied the shabby pretext given by Il Duce for Italy's entrance into the war. More than a year earlier, on February 4, 1939, in a meeting of the Fascist Grand Council, he had already coined the vague slogan of a "march to the ocean"—to the Indian Ocean as well as to the Atlantic.

On June 15, in command of his squadron, Ciano flew over Nice; a day later he bombed Calvi; two days later he bombed Borgo and Bastia. On June 14 the Germans had entered Paris and on June 17 Marshal Henri-Philippe Pétain assumed power; a day later Mussolini and Hitler met in Munich. Il Duce was ill at ease: "He is afraid that peace is near," Ciano wrote, "and once again he sees what has always been the unattainable dream of his life eluding him: glory on the field of battle."

On June 20, when the Germans were in Besançon and the French were requesting an armistice, Mussolini gave the order to attack in the Maritime Alps. He wanted his victory and his dead. Without preparation, without enthusiasm, poorly armed, wearing cardboard shoes, the Alpini launched their attack on the French positions: more than seven thousand Italians were killed, wounded, frozen, lost in the gorges of the Alps or the streets of Menton without the gain of a yard. Mussolini was insistent: he wanted his troops to reach Nice. It was no use. In spite of his boasts of "penetration of the Maginot Line of the Alps," he was bitter. "A people that has been enslaved for sixteen centuries cannot become a conquering people in a few years," he told Ciano with contempt.

June 23. The French plenipotentiaries arrived in Rome on German planes. The first negotiation began at seven-thirty in the evening in Villa Incisa, on via Cassia.

June 24. The armistice was signed at 7:45 P.M.

Italy's gains were minimal: the occupation of the area that she had conquered and the demilitarization of a zone thirty miles deep. Mussolini was afraid of a rupture of the negotiations, which would have displeased Hitler and created difficulties for the Italian army. Besides, his ambitious ideas (the occupation of France as far as the Rhône) were not supported by any military victory: the soldiers of Il Duce had dragged their feet. Mussolini had only his dead.

On June 30, however, he visited the Alpine front and returned enthusiastic to Rome. "Even in the matter of arms he thinks everything is going well," Ciano observed. A few minutes later Mussolini announced to his son-in-law with triumph and arrogant assurance "that the march on Alexandria and the Suez Canal was as good as done." The real war was just beginning.

14

Three Years of Defeats
(June, 1940 – July, 1943)

"Wars are necessary for an accurate understanding and appraisal of the internal composition of peoples."—IL DUCE to Ciano

EARLY IN JULY, 1940, Italian newspapers covered their front pages with huge headlines: WE DESTROY 50% OF BRITISH MEDITERRANEAN NAVAL POTENTIAL IN THREE DAYS.

The headlines were written by Mussolini himself. Actually, Admiral Cavagnari, chief of the naval staff, confided to Ciano that in the battle of Punta Stilo on July 9 Italian ships had undergone a six-hour bombardment by Italian Savoia-Marchetti 79 planes and that on July 19 the battle of Cape Spada began at 7:22 A.M. but no Italian bombing planes appeared until 12:37 P.M., when they attacked the British warships engaged in rescuing the crew of the sunken Italian cruiser *Colleone*. Almost a month earlier, on June 28, Italo Balbo had been shot down over Tobruk by the anti-aircraft guns of another Italian cruiser in the belief that the air marshal's plane was a British aircraft. The real war was off to a bad start for Fascist Italy.

Nevertheless, since the armistice with France had cheated him of the successes that he believed necessary to his government, and since he was more than ever convinced that he was on the winning side, Mussolini wanted an active war. Ciano, in uniform, represented him at the Reichstag on the evening of July 19, when Hitler, in a long speech, attempted to reopen a dialogue with England. Every time Hitler stopped for breath, Ciano jumped up and gave the Fascist salute; he "behaved like a clown," in the words of William L. Shirer, the American author of *The Rise and Fall of the Third Reich*, who was present. Ciano had forgotten his anti-German convictions (success wiped out everything): "Hitler spoke simply," he noted, "and, I should say, with unaccustomed humanity." When Ciano returned to Italy, he asked what Il Duce had thought of Hitler's oratory. "Too clever," Mussolini said. He explained to Ciano that "he was afraid that the English might find in it some pretext for initiating negotiations. This would be a great frustration for him, because more than ever he wanted war."

Mussolini pressed his generals to drive out of Libya into Egypt and out of Ethiopia into British and French Somaliland and the Sudan. Overriding General Rodolfo Graziani, who wanted to wait for a shipment of tanks, Mussolini gave the order "to attack at once"; victories were needed, he said, in order to be able to go into the peace talks on a solid footing.

The offensive was launched along the coast on September 12, and it went well. The Italians took Sidi el Barrani and Mussolini was overjoyed: he himself dictated the headlines for the newspapers, and he telephoned Ciano in the middle of the night. But the promised armor never arrived and soon the improvised offensive bogged down. Graziani wanted two months of preparation before resuming it, and Mussolini grew angry: "I tell you again," he telegraphed to Graziani, "that we will bring home only what we have won by force of arms; it was hardly worth the trouble of taking sixteen months to prepare and getting everything for which you asked if all you bring home is Sidi el Barrani."

He raged against the Italians, "who are too fond of drink and incapable of making decisions." Irrelevantly he suddenly told Ciano that "the chief purpose of reforestation in the Apennines is to make the Italian climate more severe, because this will make for better natural selection and the improvement of the race." He snapped at his generals' heels—"If Graziani does not attack on Monday, he will be replaced."

The navy was ordered to track down the British fleet and make it give battle. Il Duce played war leader without a thought for tactics or strategy, without the faintest knowledge of military problems. But now the consequences of his improvisations were no longer merely house-cleanings in embassies abroad or in the Italian provinces; the fate of thousands of men was at stake. Most often the generals put up no resistance to pressure from Il Duce. They had bowed to him on joining the war, and they bowed again, and for the same reasons. Besides, in the years of the Fascist Era careers had opened rapidly for officers who said the right thing.

Three Years of Defeats

The generals were constantly scheming: "Their jealousies are worse than women's," Ciano wrote. Clans and cliques sprang up: to keep one's job one had to please, and that meant to back Il Duce and to attack. The invasion of Greece was to bring into full prominence the flaws in the Italian army that the Fascist system had built.

On October 11 the Germans occupied Rumania. "Hitler always confronts me with an accomplished fact," Mussolini complained. "This time I am going to pay him back in his own coin. He can find out from the newspapers that I have occupied Greece. That will restore the balance." When Ciano asked whether Badoglio had been informed of the project, Mussolini replied: "Not yet, but I will resign my Italian nationality if anyone makes any fuss about fighting Greeks."

Ciano indicated his approval of the plan (later, according to Professor Salvemini, he carefully tore out of his diary all the pages that showed how he had exerted day-to-day pressure in favor of the attack). He supposed that the campaign would be as easy as that of Albania; besides, as he pointed out, had he not bought any number of Greek officers?

At eleven in the morning on October 15, Marshal Badoglio, Generals Ubaldo Soddu, Mario Roatta, and Sebastiano Visconti Prasca, and Ciano gathered in Mussolini's office in Palazzo Venezia. In theory the reason for the meeting was to prepare the attack on Greece down to the most insignificant detail. Mussolini was full of questions, and he wrote down every answer. He was in uniform and his face was grave, but the questions that he put, like the answers that he got, were almost totally superficial.

Il Duce: "How far is it from Epirus to Athens?"
Visconti Prasca: "About a hundred fifty miles on not very good roads."
Il Duce: "What is the country like, in general?"
Visconti Prasca: "Steep, high hills, quite bare."
Il Duce: "In what direction do the valleys run?"
Visconti Prasca: "From east to west, right in the direction of Athens" (sic).
Il Duce: "This is important."
Roatta: "It is true up to a certain point, because one has to cross a mountain range more than six thousand feet high."
Visconti Prasca: "There is a number of mule tracks."
Il Duce: "Have you been over these roads yourself?"
Visconti Prasca: "Yes, several times."

Mussolini himself was to publish this transcript with all its revelation of the triviality of his information. Then, in his sharpest voice, he concluded: "I advise you not to pay too much attention to whatever losses you may suffer. I am telling you this because sometimes a commander halts as a result of heavy losses."

"I have given orders," Visconti Prasca assured him, "that the battalions are always to attack, even against divisions."

While a brilliant reception was under way on October 26 in the Italian Legation in Athens in honor of Giacomo Puccini's son, who had bestowed the honor of his presence on the Greek National Theater for its presentation of *Madama Butterfly*, four long telegrams in code arrived from Rome. This was a Saturday; two days later, at three o'clock in the morning, Gazzi, the Italian consul, presented the Italian ultimatum to Premier Ioannis Metaxas, who had been roused from bed for the purpose. At six o'clock the Italian troops began to move; at eleven the sirens of Athens wailed and the first bombs fell. Most of them, fortunately, as the German military attaché was to disclose with a certain irony, fell in the sea or in open country.

That day Hitler was told in Florence by Mussolini that Italy had attacked, opening a new front for Germany, which would soon be called upon to hold it. For things went badly for the Italians in Greece from the start. The port of Durazzo, where the Italian ships put in, was completely bottled up by ten vessels, and thirty thousand tons of goods piled up on the piers. The Italian troops went ashore in disorder, many of them without their weapons, which had been left in the ships' holds or even in Italy. Front-line positions had not been worked out; the fighting was all random, sometimes attack, sometimes defense of the sector held, but all without any coordination. The Greeks advanced at once and threatened Albania. Ciano, who had so much enjoyed his participation in a text-book bombardment of Salonika on November 1, was worried now.

On November 11, completely unperceived by the Italians, a large British naval force, including the aircraft carrier *Illustrious*, moved in on Taranto. Two waves of torpedo planes took off and attacked the anchored Italian cruisers. The *Cavour* sank at once and the *Littorio* and the *Duilio* were damaged. The British force sailed away without molestation: reconnaissance planes did not spot it until two days later, when it was heading for Alexandria. Then Durazzo was bombed and the AGIP petroleum storage tanks were set afire.

In this precarious situation Il Duce raged against everyone, including Badoglio, who had let him go his way. "Even Count

Ciano has given me inaccurate information," Mussolini complained to Farinacci.

Soldiers who had just been demobilized were quickly called back to duty; the divisions were thrown into chaos by the goings and comings. Troops were hastily loaded aboard ships for which British submarines were lying in ambush. General Soddu, who even at the front was busy writing music for films, fell back on the Albanian ports. Hitler was uneasy. During a long tea in the Berghof on November 18 he filled the oppressive atmosphere with criticisms that Ciano accepted in silence. Then Der Führer wrote to Mussolini, who, having read the letter, said to Ciano: "He gave me a slap on the wrist."

But the government was shaken by these early setbacks. "All the fault lies with the leadership of Il Duce," Badoglio told Alessandro Pavolini. "He has no business exercising command; he ought to let us handle it." Pavolini repeated the remark to Il Duce and Farinacci attacked the marshal in his newspaper.

On the morning of November 26 the footmen in Palazzo Venezia ushered the leading men of Italy into separate rooms in order to avoid a general uproar. Mussolini was discouraged and physically weakened. He said to Ciano: "There is nothing more to be done. It is ridiculous and grotesque, but that is the way it is. We must ask for an end of hostilities through Hitler's intercession."

In the end the front held out until the arrival of German reinforcements, but Badoglio was compelled to resign; he was replaced by General Cavallero as chief of the general staff. Cavallero was anything but popular among the military; it was admitted that he was intelligent, but he was known as a "business general" who had twice retired from the army to join large firms: first the Pirelli rubber interests and then the Ansaldo naval shipyards. He was believed to be pro-German and also to be involved in financial speculations connected with Ansaldo's contracts for the construction of cruisers.

Thus seven months of war had made deep fissures in the régime. But the difficult period was only beginning.

On December 10 a new temblor rocked the structure: O'Connor's troops attacked in Libya and in a few months they captured Sidi el Barrani, Bardia, and Tobruk; the British vanguard thrust as far as El Agheila: Tripoli was in danger. The Italian divisions were giving ground on the whole front: at Tobruk the Australians captured twenty-seven thousand prisoners, two hundred eight cannon, eighty-seven tanks, two hundred other vehicles, and ten thousand tons of water. The Italians had not even destroyed anything: in all, the British were to take one hundred thirty thousand prisoners in their attack, at a cost of four hundred seventy-six killed, twelve hundred twenty-five wounded, and forty-three missing.

Mussolini was stricken. "Five generals captured and one killed!" he raged. "That is the ratio between Italians who have some military ability and those who have none." Brushing aside the maps laid before him, he added: "The Italians of 1914 were better than today's: that is not much to show for twenty years of power."

In actuality the Italians were engaged in a war that had been forced on them, and increasingly large groups of them were becoming aware that this was Mussolini's and Fascism's war but not Italy's. Certainly there were still high-spirited young men for whom Fascism was the incarnation of *la patria*, but, though they went off to war with the highest patriotism, the tales of older soldiers and their own discoveries of the army's plight soon showed them the swindle of the twenty years of power.

One such young man was an officer candidate in the Modena training school. In the spring of 1941 the course was suddenly halted. General Giacomo Carboni called the two hundred student officers into the auditorium and told them: "As of today you are no longer students but officers. The war is going badly. You will be assigned to mobilized units on the front. Remember that the responsibility for the army's lack of preparation lies with Fascism."

These bold words from the general (a clever way of absolving the officers of their permanent complicity with the government) were corroborated by facts. When the young officers reached their units, they found that fifty percent of the soldiers had holes in their shoes and the old 1891 rifles were in deplorable state; so some of these young officers volunteered at once for front-line combat: "In order to still believe in something, it was necessary for me to go into the line," Revelli wrote.[1]

They hurled themselves heroically into battle, as a man kills himself rather than have to repudiate twenty years of his life, their youth innocently sacrificed to Fascism.

As serious as it was among the troops, the situation was no better on the home front in those winter months of 1940–41. Even the greatest of the pessimists had been surprised by the magnitude of the defeats. Peace, which had seemed so near, was vanishing. The most important goods were placed under rationing and, at virtually the same time, on the black market. Prices rose, but salaries and wages did not follow. Suffering and hunger began to

---

[1] Nuto Revelli, *La guerra dei poveri* (Turin: Einaudi).

Three Years of Defeats

appear. Yet anyone could plainly see that Mussolini's hierarchs were still growing rich and that national solidarity was an empty platitude. In order to evade the law that restricted business corporations to dividends of seven percent of capital, the major industrial firms increased their capital in the spring of 1941: Edison by twenty-five percent, Montecatini by twenty-three percent, Terni by nineteen percent. Under these conditions, in spite of its millions of members, the Fascist Party lost all meaning; the facts were too flagrant.

Meanwhile Mussolini and his hierarchs were busy Italianizing "foreign" words: the Standard department stores became Standa. They racked their brains to fabricate successes out of whole cloth, and the example was set by Il Duce himself. When one hundred fifty parachutists occupied the island of Cephalonia, he said to Ciano: "If we have a good nucleus of parachutists, we will be able to claim a whole division of them even if they amount to no more than a regiment."

But war has its own inviolable laws, and too many Italians were under arms for the sham to be maintained. A teacher in Leghorn wrote to Ciano to protest because his eighteen-year-old son was mobilized on January 17 and sent at once to Albania before he had even learned what a firearm was.

Against these realities, the prestige of the government and its Duce began to crack. In March, 1941, he visited the Albanian front and, without any artillery preparation, he ordered an assault made for *his* benefit, for *his* victory: for five days the officers sent their men out in vain, and the word soon spread among the soldiers that Il Duce brought bad luck. He walked round among the wounded; tightly belted into his double-breasted tunic, he leaned over the stretchers with the solemn look of Napoleon after Eylau. "I am Il Duce," he would say, "and I bring you the greetings of the fatherland." Finally one soldier, his belly torn open by a grenade, replied through pain-twisted lips: "Well, now, isn't that great?" Quickly Il Duce moved on.

Back in Rome, in the Hall of the Globe, deserted by success, he was as alone as he had been amid the contemptuous indifference of the wounded. One evening the tension was too unendurable. He went to visit Claretta at La Camilluccia, her family's house on Monte Mario, and soon he was regularly spending a few hours with the Petacci family. When Claretta had had a miscarriage in September of 1940, he had been at her bedside every day; the conference schedule at Palazzo Venezia had been disrupted for more than a month. He was talkative during these visits; he took an interest in what the various members of the

Petacci clan were doing and in Myriam's desire for a film career, which he was to further with very firm orders.

All this soon became common knowledge. The gossiping hierarchs used it as a pretext for opposing Il Duce, who was no longer leading them to victory. In January, 1941, he decided to put them all into the army—members of the government and the Grand Council, of the Fasci and the corporations. "I will govern with the regular career functionaries," Il Duce told anyone who expressed apprehension.

Grandi, at the age of forty-five, went off to the Albanian front. Ciano joined his flight squadron in Bari. Though it was true enough that most of the mobilized hierarchs were far from the front lines, the order irritated them nonetheless.

In May, 1941, Starace, the former party secretary, who was now chief of staff of the Militia, was stripped of that post on the pretext that Donna Rachele Mussolini objected to his using a Militiaman to walk his four dogs. "Italy is still too disgusted by the memory of d'Annunzio's dogs to put up with Starace's," Mussolini told Ciano. But the Fascists found this an injustice. In Ciano's presence Starace wept with rage. Officially, the only charge made against him was that of having worn a wound stripe without authorization.

Sectarian divisions within the ranks of the party hardened. There were a Petacci clan and a Ciano clan. Donna Rachele herself took a hand, threatening to *fare le schioppettate* (fire a few shots): she had come under the influence of one Pater, an engineer by profession, who was known as "the miniature Rasputin." "It's the menopause," her daughter, Edda, said. Disguised as a stonemason or a peasant woman, Rachele roamed the streets of Rome to make her own personal investigations.

This climate and the military setbacks isolated the government, the party, and its chief. Mussolini reacted with contempt and violent speech. "This morning," he told Ciano, "I wanted to get out of the car and lash some officers on their way to the War Ministry because they were so unfit to wear the uniform."

When Naples, which had no anti-aircraft defenses, suffered a heavy bombardment on July 10, 1941, he declared with satisfaction: "I am glad that Naples is having such rough nights. It will make the race all the stronger. The war will make a Nordic people out of the Neapolitans." When he heard that a general in Albania had told his soldiers: "You used to be good husbands and fathers: here you can never steal enough, never kill enough, never violate enough girls," Mussolini said that this was the only general whom he respected. Indeed, the longer the war went on, the weaker the

Three Years of Defeats

régime grew, not only because it was increasingly evident that it was leading Italy to disaster but also because it was betraying itself.

German troops moved into Greece and defeated the Greeks in April, 1941. Regarded with contempt by the victors, the Italian soldiers were often confined to their barracks; German soldiers with machine guns kept them off the roads and the bridges.

In Africa General Erwin Rommel attacked in April without concerning himself with the Italians, and he scored victories. The motorized Afrika Korps poured along the desert tracks and covered the slogging, under-equipped Italian foot soldiers with yellow dust. Every German had more than a gallon of water a day, every Italian barely a quart; in that barren country there was not even fuel for heating their food.

Mussolini himself knew humiliation; Hitler would send for him peremptorily. "I do not like these interviews announced by the ring of a bell," Il Duce said drily: "that is how one summons servants. And what interviews! For three hours I have to listen to a totally boring and useless monologue." Then, after a pause, he added sullenly: "I will go on fortifying the Alpine passes—that will be useful one day." There was another pause, followed by another change in tone. "For the moment there is nothing to be done. One must howl with the wolves."

The Fascist system suffered another blow on April 3: less than five years after its capture, Addis Ababa was abandoned by the Duke of Aosta and his troops without even an effort at resistance; the empire ceased to exist. The romantic years of Fascism, as Il Duce nostalgically described 1935 and 1936, were far away, and Mussolini could only rant against those strong points in Ethiopia that surrendered to the British with all the honors of war and whose four-thousand-man garrisons, in eight weeks of war, suffered a total casualty list of two killed and four wounded.

These figures are indicative not of the cowardice of the Italian soldier but, rather, of his psychological upheaval. He had to fight this war of undefined objectives barehanded at the side of an ally whom he quickly learned to hate. Under these conditions, surrender was the best means of self-defense for the soldier; hence the lack of fighting spirit in the Italian troops should be interpreted as a spontaneous way of rejecting the goals of Fascism's war, a kind of unconscious anti-Fascism, a passive resistance, a "military strike" that played a major part in the fate of the war and the system.

Fleetingly and superficially, Mussolini himself was aware of the false position into which he had thrust his country. "Write in your diary," he told Ciano, "that I predict the inevitability of conflict between Italy and Germany." At the same time, the SIM was reporting that in all the major Italian cities the Germans were setting up "military cells" that were unquestionably making plans for a systematic occupation.

The Italian workers whom Il Duce had been exporting to Germany since 1938 were mistreated, beaten, hunted down by specially trained dogs. Edda Ciano protested to Hitler because a German supervisor had cut off an Italian worker's fingers. Aboard the trains that hauled them north they were the brothers of the forced laborers from the occupied countries, so despised were they as allies; gaunt and poorly clothed, they quietly sang their old country songs. They wanted to hear no more about Fascism.

It was futile for Mussolini to burst out: "I will not allow the sons of a race that has given mankind Caesar, Dante, and Michelangelo to be eaten by the Huns' dogs." This was only an ephemeral tantrum after a meeting with Hitler, from which in the end Il Duce returned once more drunk on the hope of victory, once more convinced of the indispensable and inevitable alliance of Fascism and Naziism.

At three o'clock on the morning of June 22, 1941, the German counselor of embassy in Rome, Prince Otto von Bismarck, brought Ciano a letter from Hitler for Il Duce. Ciano at once telephoned to Riccione, where Mussolini was staying. In a few hours Il Duce had digested the letter from Der Führer.

> Duce,
> I am sending you this letter at the moment when, after months of torturing reflection and aggravating waiting, I have just made one of the most serious decisions of my life: I have resolved to put an end to the hypocritical game of the Kremlin.

Operation Barbarossa was under way. Mussolini was angered by the way in which the news had been given to him. "I would not permit myself to disturb my servants in the middle of the night," he said, "but the Germans haul me out of bed without the slightest consideration."

Nevertheless he asked to be allowed to send troops to the Russian front from the first day, and in spite of Hitler. On June 26, in Verona, he reviewed the first units to be dispatched to Russia and he was enthusiastic. "These divisions are superior to the Germans in men and equipment," he said emphatically.

In this specific matter of sending Italian troops to the Soviet Union the responsibility was entirely Mussolini's: for everyone tried to dissuade him—Hitler, Ciano, his own general staff, each for different reasons. But he persisted, for he wanted to be on the winner's side and he wanted military glory; irresponsible and incompetent, he was bursting with extravagant statements. "The Tridentina Division is superb," he said. "I should not hesitate to say that in all Europe there are no soldiers so perfect."

He arrived at the most unreasonable judgments. In September, 1941, he told Ciano that "the unrest of the Italian people arises out of the fact that it is not taking a large part in the military operations against Russia." He was already thinking of transforming the Italian Expeditionary Corps in Russia (CSIR) into the Italian Army in Russia (ARMIR), and he issued the most astounding orders. Rome was very often roused by false air alarms, because Il Duce had ordered the sirens to be sounded in Rome whenever there was an alert in Naples: the Romans must not forget that there was a war on. Huge green, white, and red posters proclaimed *Vinceremo* (We will conquer) or *Siamo in guerra* (We are at war)—unnecessarily, at the very least, in a city where food was scarce, where iron gates were melted down for their metal, where the use of private cars was forbidden, and where almost every family had contributed a soldier.

Il Duce talked to his ministers in the same terms. In any event the Cabinet was completely superfluous: the ministers would simply salute Mussolini *romanamente* and listen to him in a religious hush. They were forbidden to take notes, and there was no stenographic record "because," Il Duce said, "I wish to speak freely." At times he would speak as long as three hours, leveling his inquisitor's look on first one and then another minister. "Let no one have any illusions," he told them on September 27, 1941, "that there will be no more bread cards in this country after the war. They will remain in force as long as I exist."

He savored the surprise that he could see on the ministers' faces, and then he added: "If anyone thinks that a half-pound of bread is not much, well, I want you to know that in the spring the ration will be reduced further, and I am glad of it, because we shall see the mark of suffering on the face of the Italian people and that will not be unhelpful when peace comes."

But the signs of suffering were already clearly visible at the beginning of the winter of 1941. Italians called the last hole in their belts the *Foro Mussolini* (*foro* means not only *forum* but *hole*, and there was already a Mussolini Forum in Rome). Certain areas were especially badly hit by want and hardship—Sicily was one. Mussolini decided that henceforth Sicilian officials could hold no positions on the island: this was his way of combatting the discontent that was appearing there.

Listening to Radio London became more and more widespread throughout Italy. Small groups of anti-Fascists sometimes re-formed ranks round a radio set. Ties with the old parties were almost non-existent, but now the clandestine militants of those parties found favorable reactions everywhere.

Communist emissaries crossed the border in July, 1941; the young members of the Revolutionary Socialist Party continued their skillful and sometimes questionable operations: they faked anti-American articles for the Fascist press and, when they appeared, sent the clippings to American correspondents; they published Fascist anti-capitalist propaganda and they provided the readers of the Fascist press with figures on the profits of certain companies; they attacked the Fascist hierarchs in the name of the Fascist revolution; in short, they contributed to keeping men's minds uneasy and making them think.

The facts that they made public carried all the more weight in the light of the increasing rumors about the fortunes being made by the hierarchs, who had flung themselves on conquered Greece like carrion birds. Everyone talked of General Cavallero's attempt to extort a gift of twenty-seven hundred fifty acres of land in Albania.

Among the exiles, the Soviet Union's entry into the war had facilitated the creation of a united front embracing the Socialist Party, *Giustizia e Libertà*, and the Communist Party. Silvio Trentin, Fausto Nitti, Nenni, Giuseppe Saragat, and Sereni signed a call for the union of the people:

Italians!
We anti-Fascists have often been divided in our appraisals of problems and situations. Today we are fraternally united for the soundest of causes: Soldiers, sailors, officers, unite to put your weapons at the service of Italian independence.

Italians!
The will of the people must and will give birth to the new Italy of Peace, Independence, Freedom, and Work.

The program proposed to Italians consisted in breaking the treaty of alliance with Hitler, concluding an immediate separate peace, and driving Mussolini out of power. Many leaflets appeared under the heading: *Via Mussolini dal Potere*—Throw Mussolini Out of Power.

The Fascist leaders themselves began to have doubts about

Three Years of Defeats

their Duce, whom the Germans called "our *Gauleiter* [district leader] for Italy." Bottai grew increasingly pessimistic. He confided in Ciano: "I remember that Balbo called Mussolini the result of syphilis and that made me angry. Now I wonder whether his opinion was not correct, or at least very close to the facts." Bottai added soberly: "Il Duce has deteriorated mentally and physically. I no longer respond at all to his charm. He has no will power; he is a creature of caprice who wants to be adored, flattered, and lied to."

In actuality, the hierarchs and the Italian ruling classes were learning Mussolini's defects in time to the military defeats, whereas it was not only the leader but the whole system that was infected.

General Cavallero proclaimed to Ciano that he had resolved the problem of mechanizing the army. How? by raising the daily marching quota of the infantry from twelve to twenty-five miles. To counter the effects of a naval defeat in the Mediterranean, Admiral Raffaello Riccardi (who was under Claretta Petacci's protection), announced that the submarine *Malaspina* had sunk two ten-thousand-ton vessels, although that submarine had been written off as missing for months. Nevertheless, when the deputy chief of naval staff read the announcement to the press, he struck out "ten thousand tons" and replaced it with "thirty thousand tons."

Such behavior could only demoralize honest officers, the victims of cliques, and their troops, for there was no escape from following these sham triumphs with word of the British offensive that had been resumed on November 18, 1941. Once again Cyrenaïca fell into British hands. Mussolini was worried: *l'Osservatore romano* published photographs of Italian prisoners in Egypt looking absolutely happy. "Our soldiers are only too eager to get themselves captured," Il Duce grumbled. "If they see that things are good on the other side, how are we going to be able to keep them on ours?" But Mussolini's humor was utterly unintentional.

When the Japanese Ambassador told Il Duce on December 3, 1941, that war with the United States was about to start, he trumpeted his delight. "So now we are coming to the inter-continental war that I predicted in September, 1939," he rejoiced. He seemed uncomprehending of the force that was represented by the United States. He was jubilant at the attack on Pearl Harbor, and the King himself was extremely happy over it. On December 11, in his black uniform, Il Duce addressed a crowd marshaled beneath the balcony of Palazzo Venezia. The short speech was delivered in a metallic voice that soon turned hoarse: Italy had declared war on the United States. "A new stage in the history of continents has begun," Mussolini explained, extolling the two hundred fifty million men and women of the *tripartito* and hailing "the soldiers of the rising sun," of whom he cried: "It is a privilege to fight at their side." For several seconds there was a cadenced response of *Giappone! Giappone!* (Japan! Japan!), in a rhythm far too perfect to be spontaneous. By way of conclusion Mussolini cried: "Men and women of Italy, to your feet once more! *Vinceremo!*"

The Fascist army, whose chief of staff had resolved the problems of mechanization by making the troops walk farther, now had as its adversary the America of the Ford factories. That seemed hardly to trouble Il Duce in those last days of 1941. He was pleased even by the German defeats in the east. "Hitler tried to dazzle everyone with big numbers," he told Ciano, waving German communiqués, "like that idiot, Roosevelt, and the results were disastrous. Besides, those two imbeciles are both the same, born of the same race of mules." He also denounced the Vatican, God, Christmas presents, and Christmas itself, "which merely recalls the birth of a Jew who gave the world a set of debilitating and anemic theories and who did special damage to Italy through the disrupting influence of the Papacy."

Disintegration at the moment was reaching into the Fascist Party above all. Its secretary, Serena, and the Minister of Agriculture traded insults and then punches in Mussolini's waiting room. Guido Buffarini-Guidi was busy scheming and surrounding Mussolini with "Petaccists."

On December 26, 1941, to universal astonishment, it was learned that a total stranger named Aldo Vidussoni had been appointed secretary of the Fascist Party. He was a young man of twenty-six who had been awarded a gold medal for his brilliant conduct in Spain, where he had lost a limb. He acted as a devoted aide-de-camp of no great intellectual merit but much dedication. Every morning when he opened the doors of the Hall of the Globe he stood at attention and then strode toward Mussolini's desk at the racing speed of the Bersagliere march. Naturally Il Duce was highly pleased with this new secretary. On January 3, 1942, he told the party directorate, composed for the most part of veteran Fascists: "We have reached the point at which the generation that carried out the revolution has grown old, weak, or ill; now it is in decline, while the new generation is on the march."

Very soon young Vidussoni found himself isolated and detested: he tried to bring about the closing of the Rome golf course, the clubs, the social organizations; he spoke of having a million Slovenes shot; he made a show of revolutionary purity in that Fascist Party where everyone was watching everyone else and scandals were proliferating.

The managing director of the Banca del Lavoro was thrown out because he opposed certain deals by Marcello Petacci. When the prefect of Venice sent Il Duce reports on Petacci's extravagances, Buffarini-Guidi intercepted them. A major gold transaction with Spain came to light, and the Petacci family was involved in it. By now Mussolini's affair with Claretta was known to every Italian, and Il Duce himself felt a need to justify himself. "No one has any right to look into another man's private life," he told Pavolini, and he ran down the list of the heroes of the *Risorgimento* to show that every one of them had had his amatory adventures.

Mussolini's statement of principle was sound enough, but he mixed together his private and his public lives. Myriam Petacci's wedding on June 22, 1942, was the great social event of Rome and gifts flowed in from everywhere. The bridegroom was Marquis Armando Boggiano, who had just been made a Knight of the Holy Sepulcher. The witnesses were Admiral Riccardi, Under-Secretary of State for the Navy; a general from the Medical Corps, another general from the Militia, and Count Seyassel of Aix. Mussolini's gift was a magnificent silver banquet service; in addition, he superintended the press reports of the ceremony as he had guided Myriam's first steps as an actress by telephoning producers at Cinecittà and editing the critics' reviews.

Granted that every country's history is rich in far more shocking episodes; but this was war time and every day of that same month Mussolini was telling the party's branch secretaries: "We should become a serious nation at all costs." The contradiction was flagrant and glaring, and furthermore it concerned not only Mussolini but all the highest members of the party.

During that summer there was a convention of the party's branch secretaries. Piva, the Venice secretary, described the atmosphere in his city during the film festival, in which one of the entries was Myriam Petacci's picture, *The Ways of the Heart.* "The hierarchs and their women shacked up for weeks in luxury apartments," Piva said bitterly; "they poured through the city like a tide of mud, an insult to the population in its war effort. If I had to say where the rot begins and ends, I certainly would be utterly lost."

The silence that followed was oppressive. Everyone knew that Piva was genuinely revolted, that he was speaking like a man who finally unburdens himself of an anger that he has long buried inside him. "My own feeling, however," he went on, "is that it is time to clean the place and get rid of this whorehouse."

This accuser was a Fascist—one of those who, loyal but disgusted, swore to settle accounts with the hierarchs after the war.

But resentment outside the party was spreading to ever widening circles. Groups came into being everywhere round young or old militant anti-Fascists. The older anti-Fascists had at last the impression that after so many years they had more possibilities of action. On March 28, 1942, in Venice the first major demonstrations brought on by the lack of bread were staged outside the bakeries.

"The saddened Duce" (Ciano's phrase) ordered the demonstrations broken up with bludgeons. There were more serious incidents at Matera on March 29: women attacked the Lictor's Club and demanded bread, and the carabinieri fired into the air. There were many protests in the railway stations, where the few trains were always full at a time when it was constantly necessary to go to the country to try to find a few vegetables.

In March, 1942, the bread ration varied, according to the kind of ration card, from five ounces to a pound. The responsible minister, Alessandro Pavolini, on orders from Il Duce, strove in vain to find journalists willing to prove that the food shortage had been worse during the First World War. In Sicily the peasants refused to deliver their wheat; they fired on anyone who tried to collect it. Discontent spread into the garrisons. When a detachment of Alpini was preparing to leave for the Russian front, a battalion of student officers amazed everyone by singing *Bandiera rossa*: a symptom that was the more serious because these were almost all young men from the régime's universities and youth organizations. But their demonstration did not prevent the troops' departure for the Russian steppe.

They left in long trains for the distant Don front. By way of preparation, the Alpini had been sent on daily marches along the Po; full climbing equipment had been issued to them, from ropes to ice axes, but nothing had been done about their thin wool uniforms or their broken shoes. They had been told over and over that "the Russian population is primitive, the same as the African —just as in Ethiopia earlier, a few trinkets will be enough to win it over." Nevertheless the Alpini set out joylessly for a front that was three thousand miles away, singing about a black flag, *Bandiera nera*:

> The mourning banner of the Alpini off to war,
> The flower of our youth lies underground.

Il Duce had insisted on dispatching them and on transforming the expeditionary corps into an army of two hundred fifty thousand men. Again and again he declared that "wars are necessary for the accurate understanding and appraisal of the internal composition of peoples."

In this spirit Il Duce had another intellectual windfall: he proclaimed himself the world's leading "pro-Japanese." He ordered civilian mobilization of all men between the ages of eighteen and fifty-five. "Then it will be the women's turn," he added sternly. He was angry at the low level of popular enthusiasm: "This war was not made for the Italian people, which has neither the maturity nor the tenacity required to endure so tremendous and decisive an ordeal. This is a war made for the Germans and the Japanese, but not for us." And his face was eloquent of all the revulsion that filled him at belonging to the inferior race.

Hope returned, however, in the spring of 1942. German and Italian troops recaptured Bengazi and then, on June 20, Tobruk. Field Marshal Albert Kesselring and the Italian general staff wanted to attempt an attack on Malta, that anchored aircraft carrier that was paralyzing the Mediterranean communications routes of the Axis. But Rommel convinced Hitler that the Axis must first push through to the Nile delta. On June 23 Hitler sent another message to Mussolini:

Duce,
    The British Eighth Army is virtually destroyed and Egypt can now be seized from England. In battles the goddess of Fortune takes the side of the *condottieri* only once, and he who does not seize hold of her then can never, as a rule, find her again.

Hitler's prophetic tone and the mirage of Egypt molded Mussolini's decision: Operation Ercole against Malta was dropped, the island continued to be a threat in the heart of the Mediterranean, and the Italian and German troops were to become the prisoners of their own successes. They were advancing steadily, and Mussolini began to pack his luggage for a triumphal entry into Alexandria. The commanders had been told to flash the code word *Tevere* (Tiber) if it became certain that the troops could reach the Suez Canal. That signal was made on June 27, and two days later, at six in the morning, five planes took off from Guidonia, carrying Mussolini and his court to Tripoli.

He established himself behind the lines and, with young Vidussoni, went on hunting trips with machine guns; sometimes it diverted him to point his gun at British prisoners of war on their way to the rear. On July 2 he sent Ciano a message calling for the opening of talks with the Germans on the future status of Europe. An Italian governor for Egypt had already been appointed and a hymn of triumph had been composed. Everything was in readiness for Mussolini's entrance into Alexandria: standing atop a tank, Il Duce would lead the march of his troops.

The tension in Italy was acute: the Japanese were at Singapore, the Germans were marching on the Caucasus, and the Italians were approaching the Nile; some newspapers even envisaged a link-up between German and Japanese troops in Burma. Then, weary of waiting, Mussolini suddenly went back to Rome on the evening of July 20. The last illusions crumbled: before El Alamein the Italian and German troops encountered fierce resistance.

Certainly Mussolini had not perceived that the turning point of the war was near: he had left his personal luggage in Libya, to which he expected to return in a few days. He was in error. For the Axis the period of attack was definitely ended. On July 24, 1942, the Allies had decided to plan their first major landing: Operation Torch against North Africa. In the Soviet Union the battle of Stalingrad had been joined.

On July 25 Mussolini left for the resort of Riccione, where he was to remain until October 7. Claretta Petacci was in Rimini, and the lovers managed to see each other: a dancing instructor, Spisani, offered the hospitality of his school. But it was impossible now for Mussolini to forget the constantly worsening situation.

Supplies destined for Africa were not getting through, in spite of all the subterfuges employed, from the hospital ship loaded with drums of gasoline to the submarine carrying drinking water. By September everyone in Rome was envisaging the future in the gloomiest hues. Bottai discovered that the war was illegal because it had not been voted on by the Fascist Grand Council. "After all," he explained to Ciano, "Mussolini is only a self-educated man."

Ciano, moreover, heard every day from visitors who kept him advised of the gravity of the internal situation and the rise in discontent. At the same time his wife, Edda, told him that her father was again subject to anguishing "stomach burning" that made him irascible and despondent. As always when events got the better of him, Mussolini was indeed ill: he had attacks of vomiting and dreadful cramps, he was losing weight, and he immured himself behind a wall of surliness and suspicion. Some of his physicians diagnosed an amoebic infection, but the illness was more psychological than microbic. The affliction manifested itself just when the home front was sagging.

"It is more essential than ever that Il Duce regain his health," Ciano told his diary. But he was deceiving himself; Mussolini's health could no longer be enough to wipe out the heavy bombing of cities and the scarcity of food.

On October 11, 1942, Himmler went to Rome to make his own

analysis of conditions there. Wearing civilian clothes and accompanied by Colonel Dollmann of the SS and his Italian informers, he inspected the city and examined Italy's political problems. Ciano, that *naïf*, interpreted the visit only as the result of "Himmler's overriding need to spend a little time in a civilized atmosphere after his long days of horror at the front; he was extremely restrained." In actuality Himmler was making his surveys for the total occupation of Italy.

This was the climate in which, on October 24, Italy learned that the troops of General Sir Bernard Law Montgomery (later Field Marshal Viscount Montgomery of Alamein) and General Claude Auchinleck had attacked at El Alamein. Il Duce ordered the Italians to hold their lines; the German command authorized Rommel to retire: the result was catastrophe. The Germans stole the Italians' transport and Montgomery's armor thrust deeply forward. Did Mussolini recognize the seriousness of the situation? "We must regard Libya as probably lost," he told Ciano casually. "From certain points of view this is an advantage, because North Africa has cost us our merchant fleet. Now we shall be better able to concentrate on the defense of our mainland territory."

But the Axis had not exhausted its woes. On November 5 the Italian general staff reported a large concentration of Allied ships at Gibraltar. Two days later Il Duce and Ciano were speculating on the destination for which these ships had just left Gibraltar. At five-thirty in the morning of November 8 Ribbentrop telephoned Ciano to tell him that the Americans were landing in Algeria and Morocco: Operation Torch was a success. Henceforth Italy seemed to be the Allies' next objective, and the Italians were well aware in that winter of 1942–43 that the last act was about to begin.

The anti-Fascists rallied: conversations were begun in Turin in September not only between the Socialist and Communist Parties but also, and this was the decisive factor, between both and the Christian Democrats. These three forces were joined by the Proletarian Unity Movement and the Action Party, the latter of which was a new activist scion of *Giustizia e Libertà*. Soon *l'Unità* could announce the formation of a "National Action Front," and this Communist newspaper, whose clandestine circulation was increasing, headlined in October: 28 OCTOBER 1942: LAST ANNIVERSARY FOR MUSSOLINI IN POWER. The sub-heads added: MUSSOLINI DRAWS RAF BOMBERS AND LEAVES POPULATION DEFENSELESS.

For bombing was becoming a daily reality in Italian cities: Genoa, Naples, and Turin were severely damaged. Everywhere there was an atmosphere of resistance coupled with a growing indifference to its concealment: the Fascist hierarchs set the example with their increasing criticisms and reproaches. As for Mussolini, he hoped to be able to hold on to Tunisia; his Fourth Army had occupied Nice and, using sailboats with auxiliary engines, Corsica. He tried to exploit these latest gains, but in vain: everyone knew how very transitory they were.

Meanwhile illness continued to undermine Il Duce: his stomach troubles grew more acute and he lived on fruit and liquids; his cheeks grew more hollow and his complexion yellowed; pessimism had taken possession of his innermost being, brightened only by occasional irruptions of energy and optimism, but these were more a reflex born of past thinking than real determination. Even Claretta Petacci made him weary. In December he talked intimately to Countess di Gangi, telling her that now Claretta was to him just an "emetic." The countess said: "He has had his belly full of Claretta and her sister and brother, but he cannot get rid of them because they are all scum who will turn at once to blackmail and scandal."

Il Duce was under surveillance from all sides: the King, the hierarchs, and the military were accusing him. It was said that he had cancer and would be dead in five or six months at most, and speculation turned to his successor.

As for the industrial community, it began to pull away. More and more financiers were journeying to Switzerland, where, in Geneva and Lausanne, they conferred with British business men. Pirelli returned from a trip to Switzerland during which he had established numerous contacts and told Ciano that it was generally believed that the Allies had now won the war.

Faced with this swift change in circumstances, Mussolini sought to find diplomatic solutions: he urged the Germans to make a separate peace with the Russians. Some of the officials in Palazzo Chigi suggested that Italy assume the leadership of Germany's allies—Rumania and Hungary—in exerting pressure on Hitler to accomplish a dramatic wartime Munich with the Western powers.

But freedom of action had long since ceased to exist for Mussolini and Fascism. Little by little the Germans were taking Italy in hand; they had their men in Fascism's ruling circles—Buffarini and Farinacci. What was more, Il Duce knew very clearly now, even more clearly than when he had joined the war, that his power could survive only if the Germans were victorious. As Farinacci wrote to Il Duce on November 19, "honest Italians are going

Three Years of Defeats

through a period of doubt, and there are traitors who would gladly envisage the defeat of our arms in order to strike at Fascism." Monsignor Montini (later Pope Paul VI), who was then Under-Secretary of State in the Vatican, told Guariglia, who informed him that Il Duce was planning to leave Rome in order to deprive the Allies of a pretext for bombing the city: "I think he will have to stage a new March on Rome if he wants to return."

This view expressed the general sentiment in December, 1942, and it could only be reinforced by the news from the eastern front. The battle of Stalingrad was still raging, and there were clear signs of the disaster that it was to be for the Germans; but it was, above all, the Italian troops who were directly stricken by the Soviet offensive. They were holding the Don under conditions that, in the light of the realities of war at the end of 1942, could well be described as those of absolute destitution. They constituted a thin screen of men along the river: one man every twenty feet, one machine gun every mile; munitions were scarce: not a shot could be fired without prior authorization from regimental command; food was in short supply, and the temperature was thirty and forty degrees below zero.[2]

Without warning, these unequipped forces were flanked on December 16 by the Soviet encirclement drive; that was the beginning of their death march, a retreat and then a rout, across the steppes swept by the icy wind. They had to abandon their wounded and battle to open a path through Soviet partisans and armor. The Germans seized the Italians' vehicles and threw the wounded Italians out into the snow in order to take over their places in peasant huts. Feet froze in the ripped shoes during the three-hundred-mile march in panic fear of capture, for there was a rumor that the Russians were shooting every prisoner they took. In actuality, Russian leaflets were dropped by plane ahead of the long black column, in which a man who had retained his weapons was a rarity:

Ukrainians!
In a short time the remnants of the beaten Italian army will be coming through your territory. Feed them, house them, take care of them. Their weapons are of wood. They are not your enemies: they are the slaves of the Germans.

These men, exposed to blizzards in temperatures of —30°, from officer to private soldier, acquired a stubborn hatred of Il Duce and the Germans. To a Wehrmacht soldier, an Italian general mattered less than a German *Feldwebel* (sergeant). Exhausted

[2] See Revelli, *La guerra dei poveri.*

and drained, having lost fifty to seventy percent of their strength (one hundred twenty thousand men), the Italian troops were still put to forced labor, like the Ukrainian civilians. At the very end, these half-dead soldiers received a few pitiful boxes from Italy: "Apples from Il Duce, sunshine from Italy." Those who survived had only one purpose when they returned to their homes: "remember and tell." Many dreamed of taking vengeance on Fascism for their dead.

Mussolini knew that he must face the rising storm, if indeed there was still time. Mastering his illness, he reappeared in public, speaking in a more subdued voice and denouncing England and Churchill. He wanted to revive the party. "This is the party's hour," he proclaimed, "because it is revolution's hour." He turned to the Fascist veterans. Carlo Scorza was appointed vice-secretary of the party. He was a former squadrista, responsible for the attack on Giovanni Amendola. But no such measures could halt the tide of disasters, and the last illusions melted.

On January 24, 1943, at Mussolini's order, the Italian newspapers proclaimed in large headlines that four British ships had been sunk. But the readers who went on to the official communiqué found that the British had taken Tripoli. Thus the oldest of Italy's possessions, won under Giolitti, was lost: the régime that had sought to build an empire abandoned democratic Italy's only colony, and Mussolini's oath to make Tripoli the Stalingrad of Africa had been no more than a pious hope.

The blow to the prestige of Il Duce and Fascism was telling. Mussolini bore the physical stigmata of the military and psychological disaster: his health declined, his gastric disturbances grew worse, he could now eat only milk and rice. Now he raged at everyone: the *bracaioli*, those slovenly cowards who were always holding up their trousers; the military; mankind in its entirety, which thought of "nothing but bread and its testicles." Mussolini's flight into sullenness and sarcasm angered the hierarchs. Lunching together, Grandi, Bottai, Farinacci, Ciano, and Scorza analyzed the situation. In the midst of the meal, his thin face brightened by a bitter smile, Bottai said: "Basically we have reached another goal. In 1911 Mussolini said we should give up Libya. It has taken him thirty-two years to keep his word."

The anger was shared, too, by the high-ranking officers who were presiding over the rapid dissolution of the army. Generals Vittorio Ambrosio, Vercellino, and Amé met frequently, and all were convinced that Germany would be defeated and that it was incumbent on Italy to "think of her own affairs." Mussolini sensed

Three Years of Defeats

the rise of this discontent, he felt the breath of "the wind of Berezina." He knew that everyone, from the King to Marshal Badoglio, from Grandi to Federzoni and even Ciano, his own son-in-law, was trying to "make himself a new, non-Mussolinian maidenhead," as Marshal Enrico Caviglia put it. So he struck.

On January 21 he returned to Rome from Rocca della Caminate; he needed a scapegoat for the military disasters, but that was no problem. He dismissed Marshal Ugo Cavallero, chief of the general staff, and replaced him with the upright and taciturn General Ambrosio. This honorable Piedmontese monarchist at first declined the desperate appointment. "In a Fascist system," Mussolini retorted, "orders are executed, not discussed." Thereupon Ambrosio forthrightly stipulated his terms: the recall of as many as possible of the Italian divisions scattered from Nice to Greece. It would be essential, he said, "to be able to show our teeth to the Germans." Il Duce let him talk: for Mussolini the counter-attack was not finished.

At four o'clock in the afternoon of February 5 he conferred with Ciano. He was ill at ease. "What would you like to do from now on?" he said sharply. Ciano saw that he was being dismissed (he was to be made Ambassador to the Holy See) with his entire staff. The news became public three hours later. Giuseppe Gorla, Minister of Public Works, who was on an inspection trip, was bewildered to see the railway men in Naples uncouple his official private car; he inquired the reason and was told that he had just resigned. Carlo Tiengo, the new Minister of Corporations, received his appointment while he was in a mental institution, to which, after a few days in his new post, he returned.

It was above all essential that the new government demonstrate that Mussolini retained the management of the country and that the pro-Axis line was being maintained.

Nevertheless the country was more and more eluding the grip of the government. Governmental measures were as ineffectual at home as on the battle fronts. Prices, for instance, had continued to rise, from 110 in 1939 to 165 in 1943, while purchasing power (calculated on the 1928 base figure as 100), fell from 90 to 80. It took a textile worker more than a month's wages to buy a bottle of olive oil on the black market, which was a daily fact of life. Under such conditions the limit of patience among the masses was soon reached.

In August, 1942, there had already been a wave of slowdown strikes in Turin and at Alfa Romeo in Milan. Naturally, by virtue of their very occurrence, there was an anti-Fascist aspect to these strikes, all the more in that in the majority of instances they were organized by the Communists. But there were not very many of these: in FIAT's Mirafiori plant, only forty-five of the two thousand workers were enrolled in the Communist Party's cell; elsewhere the ratio of Communists to total work force did not exceed one-sixtieth. But the newly favorable climate was increasing the number.

At ten o'clock in the morning of March 5, 1943, a strike was called at FIAT-Mirafiori. It spread to the major factories in Turin and soon included more than one hundred thousand workers. On March 24 *l'Unità* called on the workers of Milan to go out in support of the Turinese: a few hours later Pirelli was closed by a strike. Leaflets were circulated everywhere, Fascist hierarchs were hissed, the Militia was received with a barrage of bolts; armored cars patrolled the streets of Turin and all units of the Militia were mobilized. But, faced with the magnitude of the risings, repression was limited to nocturnal arrests: these were indeed numerous (six hundred), but they were not enough to break the movement. In addition, despite the instructions of the Fascist Federation of Industry, some factory owners granted the increases demanded by the strikers (one hundred ninety-two hours of paid work per month).

These strikes aroused national repercussions. They had mobilized almost three hundred thousand workers who had not hesitated to paralyze war industries; they made it clear to everyone, from the King to the Fascist hierarchs, that anti-Fascism had acquired a broad popular base that was ready to march. In every factory rank-and-file Fascists had joined the strikes; even the members of the Fascist Militia's Legion of 18 November at FIAT had walked out. Farinacci was apprehensive. "We must have the courage to make an example," he wrote. "We should not be concerned with what Radio Moscow or Radio London might say."

The import of these strikes was no less grave to conservative and military quarters, which, by now aware of the collapse for which Fascism was heading, recognized too that they must act swiftly against Mussolini to avoid the risk of a new Bolshevik peril in the country. On March 15 Marshal Caviglia sent a memorandum to the King in the hope of stimulating Vittorio Emanuele III to commit himself firmly against Fascism. "If the situation could be settled under the aegis of the dynasty," Caviglia wrote, "the solution would have a quality of legality and order, provided that the troops would still obey their commanders. If there should be other leadership, if the troops should refuse to obey, if there is an internal revolution with or without Soviet influence, then it would be impossible to predict what might happen."

In addition the events of March, 1943, provided a forceful impetus to all the anti-Fascist groups. Ivanoe Bonomi, the former minister of 1922, was at the head of the Roman organization, which also included the group of Christian Democrats under Alcide De Gasperi. In Milan contact was made with the Communists by Piero Calamandrei and Luigi Salvatorelli. Thus the course of battle and the strikes at home combined to forge an alliance in fact among men of the most varied allegiances. But once again, as in 1922, 1924, or 1940, what was essential was the King's position.

Complete information was laid before him at the beginning of April by the "Duce of the Sea," Admiral Thaon di Revel, once a minister under Mussolini. Vittorio Emanuele III did not turn a hair. Belted into his uniform, staring vacantly out of his parchment-skinned face above his white moustache, he was like a scrupulously maintained wax image in the setting of the royal apartments. It was as if he did not hear the man who was speaking to him; his fingers twined and untwined almost imperceptibly. Finally his piping voice was heard. He could not move against Il Duce, he said, unless Parliament gave him the opportunity to do so. Parliament—the Chamber of Corporations and the Senate—belonged to Mussolini after twenty years of the Fascist Era. For the sovereign, constitutional fictions were immortal.

But events were to overturn plans and reservations and speedily impel even the most luke-warm and the most cautious to act. The battle of the Mareth Line in Tunisia had begun on March 16. General Giovanni Messe commanded the Italian troops, who held out valiantly against Montgomery's attacks. Nevertheless the Italians and the Germans were locked in a trap with their backs to the sea, and soon some of the officers—particularly the Germans, Messe said—were gripped by a "psychosis of repatriation," making use of the last planes to get themselves out and deserting their troops without even notifying the over-all command. Everyone in Italy saw that the battle of Tunisia was in its last stages.

General Ambrosio, the chief of the general staff, was especially clear-sighted. On the afternoon of April 6 he and Mussolini were aboard a special train on their way to Salzburg, where Der Führer was waiting for them. The two delegations met in Schloss Klessheim, whose rugs, furniture, and tapestries had come from France. During the whole journey Mussolini had twisted and turned in pain. "There is a name for my disease," he told Dino Alfieri, now Italian Ambassador in Berlin. "It is trains."

When the two dictators came down the staircase of the castle, everyone was astonished at their appearance: both were pale, their eyes were tired, they walked laboriously. "Like two sick men," an Italian murmured to a friend, who replied: "You mean two corpses."

The Germans were apprehensive over the Italians' state of mind. To them General Ambrosio's detailed questions were full of barely hidden hostility. Moreover, the March strikes had demonstrated the gravity of the situation in Italy; the secret service of Walter Schellenberg, a deputy of Himmler, was already under orders to operate directly in Italy.

During a conference that had been requested by Mussolini, Himmler gave Il Duce advice: "Forced labor and concentration camps are entirely satisfactory, but they are not indicated for Italy. It would be better to create a personal bodyguard for Il Duce on the model of the SS." Himmler offered to fit out an entire division with the most modern weapons. Il Duce accepted eagerly, brought back to life by the assurances that Der Führer and all the Nazi dignitaries had given him on the outcome of the war. Later Hitler was to remark with smug condescension: "When Il Duce came out of the train at Klessheim, he looked like a beaten old man. When he left, he was full of energy, ready for anything."

Those among the hierarchs, the officers, and the circles close to the crown who had hoped for some possible show of independence by Il Duce went home disheartened. Most certainly it seemed that they must rid themselves of Mussolini: as soon as he returned from Klessheim, General Ambrosio set General Giuseppe Castellano to preparing a plan for Mussolini's arrest. But Il Duce seemed resolved not to prolong his inertia: encouraged by Hitler and counseled by Himmler, he moved.

First of all he attempted to regain personal control of the police and the party. Carmine Senise, the shrewd Neapolitan head of the police who was adept at taking all sides, was discharged because he had not put down the March strikes: he was replaced by Renzo Chierici, a squadrista. Then it was the party's turn. On April 17 Il Duce convened the party's directorate in Palazzo Venezia. His manner was sharp and confident.

"Vidussoni is no orator," he began. "I have decided to replace Comrade Vidussoni with Comrade Carlo Scorza." There was a burst of applause. Il Duce resumed: "He will execute my directives in the party with the pace and the spirit of the Bersaglieri."

There was more applause. At first sight that assembly might have seemed proof that Fascism was a homogeneous whole capable of standing up to all assaults. The sight of this gathering of men in black uniforms, their chests covered with decorations, seemed to comfort Il Duce. In a firm voice he talked of the March strikes. "This totally unwelcome episode," he said, "is exceptionally deplorable. At one stroke it has put us back twenty years." Mussolini explained it by the international situation and the workers' hope that *il Baffone* (the Big Moustache—Stalin) would soon arrive to liberate Italy.

Then he attacked the police and the inadequate repressive measures. "If the armored cars had fired," he said, banging his hand against the lectern, "I would have assumed complete responsibility for the decision. When Italian workers murder our fighting men, I open fire!" The whole directorate rose in unison and applauded deafeningly.

Italy, Il Duce resumed, must develop SS units, politicalize the army, and forget about public opinion, for of course there had never been a popular war. When he had finished, there were congratulations from all sides. He had made a tough speech, the program speech of war to the limit. "Comrades," he cried, "we must have the courage to take the defeatists by the neck and turn them in."

Carlo Scorza, the new party secretary, organized *Squadre dei Manganellatori* (Bludgeon Squads), whose assignment was to club anyone who was not wearing the Fascist emblem: he insisted to Il Duce that each party branch should have available an armed squadra, *la guardia ai labari*—a guard with banners.

In this seemingly favorable climate that apparently foreshadowed a fresh start, Mussolini found the courage to resolve a personal problem. On May 1, 1943, Claretta Petacci arrived as usual at Palazzo Venezia, but the police refused to admit her. She raised her voice, tried to push the policemen aside, insulted them, and finally got through. When she reached Mussolini's office, he said to her without emotion: "The cycle is over."

Assailed by her recriminations, he told her glibly that he might agree to see her again; but actually he had spoken his mind honestly: the cycle was indeed over. But it was more than a love affair, it was a whole part of his life that was dying.

Four days later he made his last speech from the balcony of Palazzo Venezia. His audience was a group of Fascists who had just come from a meeting in Palazzo Adriano. "I know that millions and millions of Italians are stricken with an indefinable sickness," he shouted hoarsely, "and the name of it is the African sickness." His voice rose and became strangely shrill. "There is only one way to cure it, and that is to go back there. And we will go back there." The crowd howled back: *"Ritorneremo!—We will return!"*

"In your voices," Il Duce resumed, "I hear the old incorruptible faith and a supreme certainty: faith in Fascism, certainty of victory. *Vinceremo!"*

"*Vinceremo! Vinceremo! Vinceremo!*" the throng replied.

But in actuality, aside from that group of the faithful enraptured by the rediscovered voice and the momentarily restored atmosphere, who could believe in victory? Only a few hours earlier, Scorza himself had said in Palazzo Adriano: "If we have to fall, let us vow to fall splendidly."

On May 12 the Italian troops in Tunisia laid down their arms. In spite of having been captured, General Messe was made a marshal by Il Duce. Two days later, without the least irony, the Fascist newspapers headlined: ALL RESISTANCE ENDS IN TUNISIA ON ORDER OF IL DUCE.

But, on the same day as Tunisia, the island of Pantelleria, a veritable natural fortress, surrendered with its twelve thousand men: thirty-five were killed. The island was the springboard for Sicily. "They are knocking at the gate," Mussolini commented.

On June 19, Count Vittorio Cini, a minister who represented the industrialists, asked to see Il Duce. He expounded on the gravity of the situation and the necessity of contemplating compromise solutions. Il Duce brutally closed the door on any possibility. "Italy's only alternatives," he said, "are to conquer or fall at Germany's side." Three days later Cini resigned: a step that was highly significant of the business leaders who were deserting Il Duce before the shipwreck.

But on June 24 Mussolini again received Scorza and the party directorate, with their solemn presentation of the latest party statistics: 4,770,770 members, 1,217,036 members in its women's organizations, 4,500,000 participants in the *Dopolavoro*. Mussolini commented on these impressive figures with great satisfaction; then he hinted at the possibility of an Allied landing in Sicily. "The minute the enemy starts to debark," he ordered, "he must be stopped stone cold on the line of the *bagnasciuga* [the strip of sand where the water ends and the land begins]."

On the night of July 9–10 the first Allied parachutists were dropped on Sicily, and a few hours later the landing craft hit the island's beaches. The knell was tolling for the Fascist régime and for Mussolini, who had made a fool of himself with his *bagnasciuga* talk.

Three Years of Defeats

15

The Fall of Fascism and
the Return of Mussolini
(July, 1943 – October, 1943)

"A perfect organization of the state, four hundred thousand men in a loyal and seasoned militia, three million members, a mass that respects and fears this power, the leader standing firm at his post, more resolute than ever. . . ."
—IL DUCE (a few days before his fall)

ON THE MORNING of July 10, 1943, Il Duce was in Sette Vene, twenty-five miles from Rome. Surrounded by a much decorated staff, in which German uniforms were plentiful, he took the salute of the "M Division," an élite formation made up of Fascist Militiamen of the first water. Himmler had kept his promise: the best German arms, thirty-two Tiger tanks, and the SS instructors had arrived on time, and the M Division made an excellent impression. Now Il Duce had an obviously highly effective pretorian guard. But General Ambrosio, who was present at the review, insisted to Mussolini that these troops should be sent to the Sicilian front, and in the presence of his officers Il Duce agreed; a few days later the M Division was transferred from the Fascist Militia's control to the army's. General Ambrosio had won a well-played hand— or at least he had half won: the M Division did not go to the front, but the pretorians of Il Duce were now under the general's orders.

Like many other officers—from Marshals Badoglio and Caviglia to Generals Giacomo Carboni, Giuseppe Castellano, and Antonio Sorice—General Ambrosio believed that at all costs Italy's fate must be divorced from Germany's. The currents among the people and the Allies' landings and quick successes in Sicily confirmed him in this view. Little by little he was beginning to contemplate the overthrow of Mussolini.

General Roatta had assumed command of the military district of Rome on June 1, at which time Ambrosio had indicated to him that a change in government was possible and that mobile units must be concentrated round the capital in anticipation of any reaction by the Fascist Militia and the Germans. Ambrosio's anxiety at the presence of the M Division near Rome was quite understandable. But in essence this attitude among the generals was a reflection of the change that had taken place in the man who was still the ostensible head of that army in which the Piedmont tradition was so strong, the man to whom the officers still swore allegiance: King Vittorio Emanuele III.

The sovereign was indeed the archetypical representative of the Italian military class with its strong conservative psychology that had led it to foster and accept Fascism, its honors and its wars. But when disappearance threatened the state and the social order, the King, confronted by the blindness of the upstart, Mussolini, regained the rationality and the aloofness of an old monarchy versed in skillful turnabouts, and its caution as well, for it was essential to bet only on a sure thing: what was at stake was the future of the dynasty, and the situation was complicated and fluid.

First of all there was the state of war; then there was the presence of the German ally on Italian soil; there was also, and undoubtedly this was the major determinant, the King's desire to preserve Fascism's conservative gains. All these factors were reasons for Vittorio Emanuele's slow progress in his preparations. Ideally he would have liked to be able to retain Mussolini, with whom the court, the officers, and the business world had collaborated for twenty-one years. Later, however, the King was to write to the Duke of Acquarone, the Minister of the Royal House, who was consistently kept informed of the monarch's plans:

Dear Acquarone,
I hereby authorize you to state that as of January, 1943, I had definitively decided to put an end to the Fascist régime and to dismiss the head of the government, Mussolini.

But was not Vittorio Emanuele III distorting reality by transforming what was only a possibility into a decision? Actually, in 1943 as in 1922 or 1924, the King was under the most varied pressures. The old notables of parliamentary Italy—Bonomi and Soleri—tried, one after another, to influence him into a decision and to learn what he intended to do, but in vain. On June 2, 1943, Bonomi had an audience that left him disappointed. "In substance," he wrote, "the King ignored every proposal. He did not discuss, he did not oppose: he contemplated, with the arrogance of an unbeliever who regarded the thing as impossible. He fell back on sarcasms about Roosevelt, the President of a plutocratic republic that was now an ally of Communist Russia."

In fact the King's attitude was overly clever, and it was based not so much on subtlety (which was real) and caution (which was unremitting) as on political contradictions. In the words of the liberal, Soleri, who tried to convince him of the necessity of an armistice with the Allies, "emotionally the King is against the Anglo-Americans and he is still living in the atmosphere of the Axis."

Could Vittorio Emanuele III forget that Mussolini had made him Emperor of Ethiopia and King of Albania? On June 18, 1943, he was still saying of Mussolini to General Paolo Puntoni, his faithful aide-de-camp: "And yet the man has a first-class mind."

But events were developing on the battle fronts and the home front. The King, who had excellent sources of information, knew that anti-Fascism was acquiring an increasingly broader base and that it was often republican in tendency. Princess Marie-José and the Prince of Piedmont established contacts with the moderate anti-Fascist groups and the officers, and very soon Marshal Badoglio emerged as the candidate designated to succeed Mussolini. "Caviglia," the King said, "is too old, and Ambrosio is a professional."

It was Ambrosio, however, who was in daily contact with Il Duce, who openly committed himself. Immediately after his return from Klessheim, as we have seen, he had instructed General Castellano, who was intelligent and strongly anti-German, to work out a plan for the arrest of Il Duce and the major hierarchs, plus defensive measures to be adopted against the Fascists and the Germans. General Ambrosio too thought that the new government should be headed by Badoglio, but that it should take the form of a national-union government that would include Soleri, Bonomi, Luigi Einaudi, and even such men of the left as the syndicalist, Bruno Buozzi.

But this political government was not acceptable to the King. On July 15 he received Badoglio in Villa Savoia, one day after the marshal and Bonomi had completed their project for a coalition government. "The King," Bonomi wrote, "did not accept Badoglio's plan. He said that no *coup d'état* with a fixed date ever succeeded. No one in Italy had ever learned the habit of keeping a secret: in two hours everything would come out and the plans would be known to those who had every reason to thwart them."

This "technical" criticism was well founded; it explained the King's cautious procedure; but what was essential was what Vittorio Emanuele said next in his impersonal voice, in that detached tone that could be deceptive but in which nevertheless one could detect a well-thought-out resolution and matured conviction.

"It is wrong to set up a political ministry," he said. "That would mean conflict with too many men and things, and, given the fact that it would be composed of old men, of ghosts, it would give the impression of a pure and simple return to the past."

"But, Your Majesty," Badoglio replied, "both of us are also ghosts."

In fact the ages of the ministers mattered less than the conservative preferences of Vittorio Emanuele III, who wanted a government of military men and experts. Bonomi was the more uneasy because the King's confidant, Acquarone, had said: "We must proceed by stages: overthrow Mussolini, yes, but not tackle the whole of Fascism." And this seemed feasible, for men like Grandi, Ciano, Bottai, and Federzoni were playing their own game against Mussolini in order to save themselves and Fascism. Ciano's loose talk on the golf course or in the drawing rooms of the Roman aristocracy, Grandi's contacts with the members of the court, and Bottai's opinions, were all common knowledge in Rome. Hence, at the end of April, General Castellano had no hesitation in showing Ciano his plan for the arrest of Il Duce. Ciano displayed great interest.

On June 3 the King conferred with Grandi. For some time the former Ambassador to London had been the spokesman for a tendency that was favorable to an understanding with the Western powers. Grandi explained to the King why it was necessary to break with Germany, and then, alluding to the history of the House of Savoy, he said: "Your Majesty, there is no choice: it is either Novara*—in other words, abdication—or a change of front on the model of Vittorio Amedeo I of Savoy, who, though he was allied with the King of France, did not hesitate to go over to the empire and thus saved Turin."

The King was silent for some time; then, calmly, with quiet confidence, he said to Grandi: "The time will come, and I know I can count on you. Let your King choose the right moment, and in the meantime help us to find constitutional means."

* The site of Carlo Alberti's defeat on March 23, 1849, by the Austrians, which led to his abdication.—Translator.

After this conversation Grandi retired to Bologna and waited.

Meanwhile the pace of the war was heightening. For the first time, on the night of July 3–4, there was bombing in the vicinity of Rome, at Ostia and Fiumicino. On July 12 the Sicilian base of Augusta surrendered; to the immeasurable shock of the Germans, the Italian admiral had blown up all the coastal defenses before he had even seen a single enemy soldier. Was there an agreement between the Italian naval staff and the Allies? Some thought so; there is no question that between June 25 and the armistice of September 8 not one gun was fired by the Italian navy and not one Allied bomb fell on the Italian ships anchored at La Spezia and Taranto. Other cities, in contrast, suffered the results of the harsh Strategic Bombing Policy. After the warning of July 4 there was reason to wonder whether Rome's turn had not come.

As if to counter these developments, Scorza wanted to organize a vast series of warlike speeches in all the provinces, sending the hierarchs to the major cities. Scorza brought this plan to completion on July 13, but Grandi refused; Bottai, one of the most intelligent of the Fascist leaders, presented another plan of action to Scorza: the Fascist Grand Council must be convened, he said, and the Fascist constitution must be applied, so that military ministers would be appointed and Il Duce would be restricted to his position as chief of government; or else, if the situation was too serious, the King must be allowed to act. Bottai concluded: "Mussolini should, and only he can, get a German commitment, *in extremis*, not to ravage the country. The King could get the same thing from the other side, the Anglo-Americans." Thus the idea of convening the Fascist Grand Council appeared for the first time in this meeting on the afternoon of July 14, 1943.

A day later, as we have seen, the King informed Badoglio of his desire for a government of soldiers and technicians after the overthrow of Mussolini. Thus in mid-July there were two conspiracies against Mussolini: that of the King and the generals, leading to a Badoglio government, and that of the hierarchs, which was less precise. Dino Grandi aspired to be the new Premier, and he had already thought of the industrialist, Pirelli, as his future Foreign Minister. But the royal conspiracy enjoyed the advantage of knowing about its rival, while the Fascist leaders knew virtually nothing of the King's intentions; in addition, and this was the greatest weakness in their scheme, the hierarchs had to work through the sovereign; at the last minute he might betray them.

On July 16 some fifteen hierarchs waited on Mussolini in Palazzo Venezia late in the afternoon to ask him to summon the

Grand Council. Full of suspicions, Il Duce stared in a long silence at the Fascist leaders, then shrugged. "Very well," he said, "I will convoke the Grand Council. On the other side they will say that it is meeting to discuss a capitulation. But I will call it."

At this time, however, nothing definite had yet been decided on, for both conspiracies shared a common characteristic: the persistent hope that they would not have to combat Mussolini. They hoped that they would not have to get rid of him because the men behind them were so closely bound to him and to Fascism by their pasts and their prospects.

On the morning of July 18 Ambassador von Mackensen brought Mussolini an urgent summons from Der Führer. It was quickly decided that they would meet in Italy, in an eighteenth-century villa near Feltre. That evening Mussolini left by plane for Trevisio with his physician and his secretary. General Ambrosio traveled by train with the Secretary of State for Foreign Affairs, Giuseppe Bastianini. In Rome the conspirators stood still; as on so many other occasions, the hope of a resolution of the crisis by Mussolini held back the King, his advisers, and the hierarchs. Meanwhile, at the Trevisio airfield, Il Duce stood watching Hitler's plane, which was circling overhead until it should be nine o'clock, the time officially set for their meeting.

July 19. The early-morning pedestrians in the streets of Rome found leaflets warning that a bombardment of the city was imminent. "The crews chosen for the operation," the leaflets said, "have been meticulously briefed and are familiar with the city." Few Romans took the warning seriously: no one could bomb the Holy City. The sky was blue and clear.

Hitler's plane was standing on the Trevisio airfield. The air was heavy. The two dictators went by train to Feltre and then in an open car to Villa Gaggia, a veritable maze of corridors or, as Mussolini called it, "of petrified crossword puzzles."

The two delegations assembled at eleven o'clock in the outer drawing room and Der Führer launched into a long monologue. Mussolini, sitting on the edge of an armchair that was too deep for him and resting his hands on his crossed legs, waited patiently without altogether catching the meaning of the impassioned oratory filled with reproaches for the Italian army, "whose organization is manifestly bad." Then Der Führer raised his voice: "The war can go on indefinitely: it comes down to the problem of manpower, and also the question of will power."

At noon Mussolini's private secretary came into the room with a note, which he handed to Il Duce. In a voice full of emotion,

Mussolini read it aloud, translating into German: "At this moment the enemy is heavily bombing Rome."

The sirens had begun to sound at eleven o'clock in the capital. Five minutes later the Flying Fortresses and the Liberators dropped their first bombs on the railways, the station, the workers' quarters of San Lorenzo, Tiburtino, and Appio Latino and the airfields of Littorio and Ciampino. The anti-aircraft guns, which on orders from Il Duce had so often fired at nothing, simply in order to create a wartime atmosphere, did not hit a single plane, though the attackers flew quite low and some of them even machine-gunned the streets. There were four waves of planes in three hours, and the toll was more than fourteen hundred dead and six thousand wounded.

In Feltre, unmoved, Der Führer resumed his monologue, giving Mussolini a veritable lecture and humiliating Il Duce before his associates. They were outraged. At one o'clock, when lunch was about to be served, they clustered round Mussolini. White with anger, General Ambrosio played his last card, without circumlocution, in what amounted to an ultimatum. "You have to speak clearly to the Germans," he told Il Duce; "they want to use Italy as a rampart and they don't give a damn if it ruins her." His head bowed, Mussolini said nothing, and Ambrosio added: "You are Der Führer's friend; make him understand our thinking—we ought to break loose and think of our own problems." In a tone that admitted of no reply and in words each of which was like a shot, Ambrosio concluded: "We must be out of the war within two weeks."

"Are we ready to erase twenty years of power at one stroke?" Mussolini protested.

It was a complete avowal: Fascism was bound to Naziism, and its fate depended on the outcome of the war; this was a basic premise that those who still hoped in Mussolini had not grasped. Did Il Duce indeed appreciate the gravity of Ambrosio's ultimatum? What seemed to concern Mussolini more than anything else was what the Romans would think of his absence from the city when bombs were falling on it. "I would not want the Romans to think . . .," he began again and again, but he never finished the sentence.

At five in the afternoon Hitler and Mussolini were back at the Trevisio airfield. As Der Führer was leaving, Mussolini cried: "We have the same cause, Führer!" Then he turned to Field Marshal Wilhelm Keitel and added: "Send us everything we need; remember that we are both in the same boat."

As long as Hitler's plane could still be seen, Mussolini kept his arm raised in the Fascist salute. Then, as his men gathered round him, he started to leave, saying in a low voice: "There was no need for me to make a speech to Hitler."

This time Ambrosio understood: Mussolini could no longer be relied on. The general said to Bastianini: "He did not take what I said seriously. But he is mad. I tell you, he is mad. What I said to him was a serious matter, very serious."

So the decision would be made in Rome by the King. When in mid-afternoon he went to visit the areas destroyed by the Anglo-American bombs, the fires were still burning and the wounded were still moaning where they lay; no one had taken charge of rescue operations. At the Ciampino airfield the entire personnel had fled when the first bombs exploded. But what most struck the King was the glacial silence with which he was received: not a cheer, only silent reproach. A few minutes later, however, Pius XII was hailed with the utmost fervor.

The frigidity of the popular attitude, the more significant in the light of so many other signs of the course that the country was taking, and General Ambrosio's report on his return from Feltre made up the King's mind. It was probably to Ambrosio and Colonel Giuseppe Cordero Lanzoldi Montezemolo, both of whom went to him directly from the station, that the King announced his intention of removing Mussolini.

Pale and nervous, the King received Il Duce on July 22. "I tried to make Il Duce understand," the sovereign told General Puntoni, "that now his person alone stood in the way of the country's recovery. It was like talking to a wall."

In Sicily that night Palermo and Trapani fell to the Allies. In most instances Italian troops were laying down their arms without a fight.

Also on July 22, Acquarone sent for General Castellano and told him that within six or seven days the King would appoint Marshal Badoglio to succeed Mussolini. Officially there was no question of arresting Il Duce, but the duke knew that Castellano had a plan for his arrest ready for execution. Undoubtedly the dismissal would take place on July 26, a Monday, which was Mussolini's weekly audience day. Senise, the former head of the police, and General Angelo Cerica, commander of the carabinieri (the police force traditionally attached to the Piedmontese monarchy), were alerted.

The carabinieri were to look to the occupation of the telephone exchanges and the arrest of Mussolini; they were to be prepared for possible resistance by the forces of the Fascist Militia; a list of hierarchs to be arrested was prepared, and General Carboni, who was reliable, was put in command of an armored corps that was to assemble in Rome. The troops would assist the carabinieri.

On the morning of Saturday, July 24, Acquarone and Generals Ambrosio and Castellano went to Marshal Badoglio and informed him that the King had designated him to succeed Mussolini. They gave him a proclamation that Orlando had written for Badoglio to read over the radio.

"Everything is in order," Badoglio said.

That Saturday had not been selected at random. At five o'clock that afternoon the Fascist Grand Council was to meet in Palazzo Venezia in accordance with Mussolini's agreement of July 16. Farinacci, who stood for even greater submission to Germany, and Grandi and Bottai, who were looking for ways to a separate peace, were equally insistent on this session of explanation and decision.

Grandi, Bottai, Giuseppe Albini, and Federzoni had drafted the text of a resolution. Grandi, who was to assume its paternity for the historical record, submitted it to Il Duce on July 22. That act shows how basically bound to Il Duce the Fascist chiefs still were and how strongly they still hoped that he would accept their common-sense proposals. If, furthermore, they were moving so cautiously along the road of opposition to Il Duce, it was because they knew only too well that his fall threatened to drag down all Fascism with him.

But Mussolini was confident. "You would be right," he told Grandi, "if the war were sure to be lost, but it will be won. In a few days the Germans are going to bring out a weapon that will change the whole situation." He escorted Grandi to the door of the Hall of the Globe and with a relaxed smile he greeted Marshal Kesselring, who had been waiting for one and a half hours.

Thereupon, the last approach to Mussolini having failed, Grandi —who also had his own ambitions and thought of himself as the chosen crown prince—sent the text of his resolution to the King at four o'clock on the afternoon of July 24, one hour before the Grand Council's meeting. "We are preparing ourselves to fulfill our duty," Grandi wrote to Vittorio Emanuele III. "I am confident that the King of May 24 and Vittorio Veneto will save the fatherland."

Grandi's move was one more card in the King's hand: if Grandi's resolution threw Mussolini into the minority in the Grand Council, the King would have that constitutional pretext for which he was seeking as a ground for his action. It is impossible not to admire the King's skillful game; he moved his pieces only when he could be certain of the sequel, and he held them poised in his hand for a long time before he placed them, like a prudent chess player. His men were all in place, Mussolini's successor had been chosen, and the Fascist hierarchs had put themselves at his disposal, quite obviously hoping to be rewarded and already working for that Marshal Badoglio who already had in his possession the appeal that he would read on the radio.

What was astounding was Mussolini's blindness. When Farinacci or Scorza told him that the generals or Grandi or Bottai were plotting against him, he burst out: "That sounds like a detective story." A few days before the Council meeting, Ottavio Dinale, a journalist, went to see him. Dinale took him by the right hand and embraced him, saying: "God bless you, Mussolini."

For a moment Il Duce was stunned. "God bless you too, Dinale," he said at last.

"You first of all," the journalist replied.

"In God's blessings there is no hierarchical precedence," Il Duce said.

After this edifying exchange, Dinale told what he knew of the rumors of plots that threatened Il Duce, who replied emphatically: "I cannot admit that anyone would think that a system like the Fascist system could be brought down by forty or fifty conspirators." He raised his hand confidently and added: "A perfect organization of the state, four hundred thousand men in a loyal and seasoned militia, three million members, a mass that respects and fears this power, the leader standing firm at his post, more resolute than ever—come off it! Let's not make jokes."

Carried away by his own words, he told Dinale that perhaps luck would give him the opportunity, thanks to these conspiracies, to rid himself of the obstructionists, and the law would be on his side, he would be acting in legitimate self-defense.

Such blindness just before the meeting of the Fascist Grand Council was the product of the man's character, but in addition and above all of the fact that Mussolini, sealed into his fictitious universe, had lost all touch with reality years before. Ever since the war in Spain he had been the master of history only in his speeches.

But Mussolini's blindness was matched by that of the hierarchs who hoped to get rid of Il Duce and remain in power to preserve the essence of the system and their own privileges. These contradictory and complementary illusions demonstrate for the same reason that Fascism was doomed and that already it was no more than a semblance, a fictitious survival. A push would be enough to shatter it all.

It was five o'clock in the hot Roman summer afternoon of Saturday, July 24: in a moment the Fascist Grand Council would open its meeting in Palazzo Venezia. A few minutes earlier Rachele Mussolini had said to her husband, speaking of the hierarchs: "Have them all arrested." It would have required the arrests of many Italians indeed to save Il Duce.

Grandi and Federzoni had gone to confession and Grandi had also made his will; he was carrying two grenades. Many more of the twenty-eight members of the Fascist Grand Council were armed, and almost all of them knew that this meeting would be decisive.

Piazza Venezia was deserted: no Fascist banner floated from the balcony, no black-uniformed musketeer of Il Duce stood the traditional guard outside the Grand Council's meeting place. Empty of all traffic, the streets round the Palazzo were silent in the blistering heat of that Saturday, July 24, 1943.

When Grandi entered the courtyard of the palace, he was afraid. "This is the end," he thought, as he wrote later. The old courtyard was crowded with armed Militiamen, and almost two hundred policemen were distributed inside the building. Grandi went up to the meeting room: many of the hierarchs had already arrived, and he began moving from group to group to collect signatures for his resolution. It was just five o'clock.

All these men dressed in the same black desert uniforms, these twenty-eight members of the Fascist Grand Council bound for years to Fascism and its chief, gradually took their places at the long table on which, as in a classroom, Mussolini's desk looked down. There were Grandi, Bottai, Scorza, Farinacci, De Vecchi, who in the brawling days of squadrismo had led the attacks on the peasant organizations by those squadre of young men who had raised Il Duce to power; there was Federzoni, the eminent president of the Academy of Italy, who had opened the avenues of legality to Fascism and served as its link with the throne; there was Antonio Tringali-Casanova, the presiding judge of the Special Court that had imposed thousands of years of prison sentences on anti-Fascist suspects and militants; and there was General Enzo Galbiati, the commander of the Militia. There was also Galeazzo Ciano, unshakable in his self-satisfaction, the Ambassador to the Holy See and former minister, who, between two diplomatic conversations, between two golf games, between two adulteries, went off to bomb Tirana or Salonika at the head of his squadron. All these men were there, and others as well: the old quadrumvir, Marshal De Bono; Giovanni Balella and Tullio Cianetti, the industrialists; Buffarini-Guidi, the schemer—all sitting together in the gloomy room of the Renaissance *palazzo* and waiting for Il Duce.

They seemed cut off from Italy, these twenty-eight men in this austere setting, under these high ceilings, like a brotherhood in sober uniform, a brotherhood shut into the *palazzo* and surrounded by the silence and the bright hot light of summer. But the isolation was only an illusion; the *palazzo* and the Grand Council's meeting room were rocked in the turmoil by which these twenty-eight men had chosen or permitted Italy to be scourged, by the defeats that had been accumulating for three years from the Alpine front to Sicily, from Ethiopia to the Don, by those offenses to the nation's honor, by this war in which incredible and comical unreason contested with tragedy, by everything in the twenty-one years of Fascist rule that little by little, from the factories of Turin to the general staff of the army, had begot and conceived and nurtured contempt, reproval, and condemnation.

Twenty-eight men sat waiting for Il Duce. Some among them thought of an invasion of their country; the majority was striving to evade its responsibilities and the judges who might one day be waiting for it. The most resolute—Grandi and Bottai—must certainly have felt that within the next few hours they were going to decide the fate of Italy and the system. In reality, the destiny of Fascism had been settled on the picket lines of Turin, on the beaches of Sicily, and in the drawing-room of Vittorio Emanuele III in Villa Savoia.

At five minutes after five Mussolini entered. "*Saluto al Duce!*— Hail to Il Duce!" Scorza, the party secretary, cried. All twenty-eight raised their right arms in the Fascist salute.

Mussolini's ill temper was almost palpable. He set a thick folder on the desk before him and began his summary of the military situation in a dry, bitter, arrogant voice; he discussed the question of the supreme command, asserted that he had never wished to assume it, and declared confidently, speaking of himself in the third person: "Mussolini contemplated relinquishing the military command, but he did not do so because he thought it improper to abandon the ship at the height of the tempest. He preferred to do so after a day of sunshine, which has thus far not appeared."

He laid the blame for the defeat on Badoglio, Rommel, the general staff, the troops, and the Sicilians; he praised Germany, "which has come to our aid in generous fashion." Then he raised his head and looked in turn at each of the twenty-eight men at the table; they knew that he was about to attack.

"A war is always one man's war," he said: "the war of the man who declares it." He allowed this to sink in in silence before he went on. "I warn you, comrades, that Grandi's resolution may jeopardize the existence of the régime. Reactionary and anti-

Fascist circles and those groups devoted to the Anglo-Saxons are pressing in that direction."

Il Duce had finished; he had spoken for one hour and fifty minutes. He sat down and raised his hand to his eyes like a visor. The debate began.

Marshal De Bono defended the army; Farinacci denounced the general staff and especially General Ambrosio; Bottai posed the problem of peace or war. Then Dino Grandi rose. He spoke with virile eloquence. "It is dictatorship, not Fascism, that has lost the war," he said. Then he read his resolution:

> The Grand Council first of all salutes the heroic combatants of all branches who, at the side of the proud Sicilian population, have renewed the noble traditions of ultimate courage and the unbeaten spirit of sacrifice.
>
> The Grand Council calls on the chief of the government to pray His Majesty the King and Emperor, in pursuance of Article V of the Statute of the Realm, to assume the supreme power of decision through the active command of the armed forces.

Thus Mussolini was to be stripped of his military powers in favor of the King, while at the same time, by calling on the old Statute, Grandi's resolution seemed to nullify the Fascist constitution.

Grandi was to go on speaking in his hoarse voice for almost an hour. It was no longer the polished ambassador who stood before Mussolini but an accuser who allowed his passion to have its head, who shook off years of repressed angers and humiliations. "You think yourself a soldier," Grandi cried; "permit me to inform you that Italy was ruined the day you took your marshal's insignia."

Mussolini did not react, except occasionally to shake his head or to mutter something. Bottai and Ciano backed Grandi. Mussolini's son-in-law spoke without violence, but his detailed account of Italian-German relations was only the more shattering. "In no instance have we been the traitors," he concluded; "in every instance we have been the betrayed."

Farinacci defended the Germans, but at the same time he asserted that power should be exercised by organs of the government and not by Il Duce alone. So the conflicting tendencies in the Grand Council were united in their determination to curb Mussolini's powers.

Toward midnight Il Duce asked that the debate be adjourned until the next day. Grandi vigorously refused, Mussolini gave in, and there was merely a fifteen-minute recess. Scorza, Buffarini, Alfieri, and Galbiati gathered round Il Duce, who had left the room; Grandi had remained behind to try to convince the remaining waverers.

"Let's arrest them all," Buffarini said to Il Duce; "it's a conspiracy."

Mussolini shrugged. Did he grasp the gravity of the crisis? It is to be doubted. Basically he knew very well that the Grand Council was a body devoid of any representative character; let the hierarchs adopt Grandi's resolution—then what? Mussolini thought that he would go on governing as in the past, for who could prevent him? The King? but the King was safe. That was what led him to under-estimate the importance of the Grand Council's vote. Yet Grandi's vehemence had shaken him—not on the level of the political future but psychologically: most of the time Mussolini had known only subservient approval, and he did not know how to stand up toe to toe to an opponent. In his shock he had let Grandi go on without daring to interrupt him, though Mussolini was heard to murmur: "Unquestionably luck has turned its back on me."

The session was resumed at fifteen minutes after midnight; it had already lasted seven hours. Now Mussolini had to endure the attacks of Bastianini; his only reply was that the hierarchs had made scandalous fortunes. Then, regaining assurance, he said: "I am sixty years old; after all, I could call these twenty years the most marvelous adventure of my life, I could put an end to the adventure; but I will not step down. The King and the people are on my side."

With this remark Mussolini revealed both his deep-seated individualism and that egocentricity that had made those twenty years of the Fascist Era his "personal adventure." The remark also confirmed his blind confidence in the King.

"What will happen tomorrow," he concluded ominously, "to all those who have opposed me tonight?"

General Galbiati and Antonino Tringali-Casanova supported Il Duce. Scorza, who had momentarily given assurances to Grandi, now offered a resolution that would confirm Mussolini in power; Farinacci presented one of his own. About two o'clock in the morning Tringali-Casanova shouted above the confusion: "You will pay for this treason with your heads."

Galbiati threatened to call the Militia. Sitting comfortably at the door, the heads of the police and the security service followed the discussion attentively. Suddenly someone pointed to Gaetano Polverelli, Minister of Popular Culture, and addressed Mussolini: "Whenever you had to choose among a half-dozen men, you always took the biggest idiot, and this one is an example."

Then Grandi rose, summarized his arguments, and concluded dramatically: "Duce, we will follow you forever because you are our leader and the best man among us all. Take off that uniform, tear off those eagles, go back to the simple shirt of our revolution."

Mussolini made a gesture of weariness and then he told Scorza to put the resolutions to the vote. There was absolute silence as Scorza counted: "On the Grandi resolution: nineteen votes in favor, seven against, one abstention."

Mussolini rose and leaned heavily with his clenched fists on the desk. His face was drawn and his movements were the slow movements of a weary man. He collected his papers and brutally it seemed to strike him that an irreparable event had just occurred.

"You have brought on the crisis of the régime," he said in a dead voice. As Carlo Scorza was about to shout the traditional *Saluto al Duce*, Mussolini stopped him with a gesture.

Tringali-Casanova went up to Ciano. "Young man," he said, "you will pay in blood for what you have done tonight."

One after another the members of the Grand Council left quickly, surprised that they had not yet been arrested. It was 2:40 A.M. Little by little the dawn was silhouetting the *palazzo* in which, on this Sunday, July 25, 1943, Mussolini was beginning his last day as chief of government.

A few minutes after the Grand Council had adjourned, he conferred in the Hall of the Globe with his closest retainers: Scorza, Galbiati, and Buffarini-Guidi. He no longer seemed concerned; when Buffarini-Guidi assured him that Grandi's resolution was unconstitutional, he agreed. Then, with Scorza, he went to his home, Villa Torlonia. His wife was waiting for him. "Did you have them all arrested?" she asked. Supposedly he replied: "I will, if it is not too late."

Then he was suddenly overcome by one of his surges of realistic pessimism. "There is nothing more to be done," he said. "They all want to destroy me. I am afraid that what I want no longer matters."

At the same time—it was about three-thirty in the morning—Acquarone and Grandi met at the home of Marquis Anteo Zamboni. Still gripped in the tension of ten hours of contest during what to a degree was his night in history, Grandi spoke for almost three hours more, describing the Grand Council's meeting for Acquarone and then moving on to political proposals: the King should designate Marshal Caviglia as the head of a government of sacred union; Grandi himself would assume the task of negotiating with the Allies. That was when Acquarone told him that the King had already made his choice—Badoglio—and Grandi began to see that Vittorio Emanuele III had worked out a plan of campaign.

At eight o'clock that Sunday morning Mussolini was at his desk in the Hall of the Globe. He conferred with General Galbiati, who suggested the mass arrest of the nineteen signers of Grandi's resolution. Mussolini refused. "In a few hours I will talk with the King," he said. "I will see what happens."

Then he received the Japanese Ambassador; after that he discussed Goering's arrival in Rome, which was scheduled for July 29 and the celebration of Mussolini's sixtieth birthday. Perhaps Il Duce still clung to the hope, chimeric as it was after Stalingrad, that a separate peace with the Russians was possible and that he could convince Goering of its indispensability.

At ten minutes before eleven that morning General Puntoni and the King met in Villa Savoia. Vittorio Emanuele told Puntoni that Mussolini's dismissal had been decided on and that it would take place the next day—Monday, July 26—which was Mussolini's audience day.

At 12:15 P.M. Mussolini's secretary, Nicolò De Cesare, telephoned Villa Savoia to say that Il Duce would prefer that Monday's interview be held Sunday afternoon at five o'clock. In that event all plans would have to be advanced twenty-four hours. But Acquarone and the King did not hesitate, because the Grand Council's vote had given the King his constitutional justification.

Once again Acquarone and Generals Castellano, Cerica, Ambrosio, and Carboni reviewed and polished the various phases of what was to be done: the occupation of the telephone exchanges, the ministries, and the broadcasting facilities and the neutralization of the Militia units. It was true that Vittorio Emanuele III had not officially asked that Mussolini be arrested, but he had expressed no opposition to such a possibility; this was typical of his cautious way of never committing himself to the full. The generals took it on themselves to decide on the arrest of Il Duce inside Villa Savoia; the King preferred the arrest to be made outside—he did not wish to know about it—but he nodded assent when the officers set forth their technical arguments.

About three o'clock the King sent for Puntoni. "Since I cannot foresee how Il Duce will react," the sovereign told the general, "I should like you to remain at the door of the room where we will have our private talk. If the necessity should arise, come in."

Meanwhile Mussolini and General Galbiati were inspecting the damaged areas of Rome. Aside from the Militiamen posted here and there by the general, as well as a few naval cadets, no one pretended enthusiasm. After the tour Il Duce went back to Villa

Torlonia, where he lunched and chatted with his wife, who was apprehensive and begged him not to go to see the King. He shrugged.

At five minutes before five his car entered the gardens of Villa Savoia through the great gate. Il Duce was wearing a midnight-blue summer suit; the King greeted him in a marshal's uniform. Their private talk lasted twenty minutes. General Puntoni tried hard to listen from his post at the door, but it was difficult to catch the entire conversation, which was held in low tones.

"I am sorry," the King concluded, "but no other solution was possible."

"Then it's all over," Mussolini mumbled; "it's all over. What is going to happen to me and my family?"

"I will answer with my life for your personal safety," the King said. He accompanied Il Duce to the door and they shook hands.

In the garden a captain of carabinieri asked Il Duce to enter an ambulance parked there. The captain and two of his men followed. Two carabinieri armed with machine guns mounted the running boards. When Mussolini seemed to balk, the captain assured him: "It is for your own safety." The ambulance moved off fast; a half-hour later it stopped at the Pastrengo carabinieri barracks in via Legnano.

It was 6 P.M. on July 25, 1943. After twenty-one years there was no longer a Duce.

Nothing of this was known in Rome. Newspaper offices had heard some rumors after the Grand Council's meeting, but, as the long twilight of July 25 deepened, contradictory stories began to circulate. Soon the atmosphere was tense. At the Caffè Aragno on via Veneto, according to Paolo Monelli, a journalist, a general scuffle over nothing broke out between Militiamen and newspaper men. Suddenly there was a shout: "Mussolini has been arrested!"

Outside everything was silent; occasionally an official car broke the blacked-out emptiness of the streets. At 10:45 P.M. a radio program of light music was interrupted, but for a long interval nothing followed. Then came the voice of the announcer employed for major occasions, Giambattista Arista—he was known as the Voice of the Lictor—who spoke without emotion: "His Majesty the King and Emperor has accepted the resignation of His Excellency *Cavaliere* Benito Mussolini from his duties as chief of government, prime minister, and secretary of state, and has appointed *Cavaliere* and Marshal of Italy Pietro Badoglio to be chief of government, prime minister, and secretary of state."

There was another interval, and then Arista read two proclamations. The first was that of the King, who announced that he was assuming the command of the armed forces: "No deviation can be tolerated; no discussion can be permitted." The second proclamation was Marshal Badoglio's: "The war is continuing. Italy, the jealous guardian of her age-old traditions, remains loyal to her pledged word."

"The war is continuing." But who paid attention to those few words that were to weigh so tragically on Italy's destiny? All that Rome heard was the first announcement, and her population poured out into the streets in that summer night when no one gave a thought to the blackout. For in every mind the fall of Mussolini implied the end of his war as it did the end of Fascism. In the workers' quarters the "Fascist circles" were attacked, the busts of Mussolini were shattered, his portraits were burned; *il Messaggero* put out a special edition; everywhere clusters of half-dressed people greeted one another with joyful shouts; an actress in pajamas was carried in triumph on men's shoulders. "Death to Mussolini!" the Romans cried. "Down with Fascism! *Evviva il re!* Up the army!"

Men who an hour earlier had worn in their buttonholes the Fascist emblem—known to the people as *la cimice*, the bedbug—tore it out and trampled on it. The demonstrators went in search of the hierarchs, but Carlo Scorza, the party secretary, had vanished; Farinacci and Pavolini sought asylum in the German Embassy, which, as Colonel Dollmann of the SS said, was turning into a travel agency: in desperation after Mussolini's arrest, Grandi, Ciano, and Bottai were hiding there. This was something that they had not anticipated.

"What a calamity!" Ciano lamented. "Everything is collapsing. Now they are going to put us in chains too."

"There was no reason for this," Grandi protested; "it is further proof of the lack of courage and of the slightest political judgment."

But not one man rose to defend Mussolini and his régime. General Galbiati, Scorza, the prefects, the Militia, the M Division . . . all made their act of submission to the King and the army. Some turned to the police for protection against the fury of the people. Guglielmo Pollastrini, a Roman squadrista of infamous reputation who was to distinguish himself further under the German occupation, survived only because of the intervention of the carabinieri. Inevitably there was violence: some local Fascists of neighborhood reputation were thrashed, but—and the fact deserves emphasis—not one was killed. The only death arising out of the events of July 25 was that of Senator Morgagni, the head of the

Stefani news agency, a native of Forlì and a lifelong comrade of Mussolini: Morgagni shot himself in the head. A note on his desk said: "Il Duce has resigned. My life is over. *Evviva Mussolini!*"

This single death is evidence enough that the régime had already lost virtually all its support. Even before the conspiracies and the Grand Council's meeting, it had become no more than a house of cards, a political skeleton divorced from reality, held together by inertia, reduced to being only Mussolini, Mussolini without either followers or social forces to back him. And the arrest of Il Duce was sufficient to make it clear to everyone that as a deep national reality Fascism had ceased to exist, even if its imprint was still sharp and lasting in many aspects of behavior and thinking.

Monday, July 26, was a holiday. Rome was thronged with flag-decked processions. A crowd filled the courtyard of Palazzo Venezia. Demonstrators in clusters clung to trucks that coursed the streets, stopping at official buildings, where young men would jump down, then scale the façades and smash the lictor's fascio, the emblem of Fascism, to bits with sledge-hammers. The same scenes took place throughout Italy. In Milan the monarchists tried to parade the old Count di Torino on the balcony of the royal palace, but he was stupid enough to declare: "The war goes on. *Credere, ubbidire, combattere*—Believe, obey, fight." At the shouts of the crowd he fled inside.

Above the demonstrators' heads rose a huge portrait of Matteotti, carried by young men, and it was almost as if the most illustrious of Fascism's victims, in spite of death and time, were presiding over the great victory celebration. The atmosphere in Turin was the same. The *Casa del Fascio* was wrecked. Thousands of workers stormed the New Prisons and soon a truck broke down the gate: all the political prisoners were set free. This was the case also in Milan, Genoa, and Bologna, as well as in smaller towns. Cuneo, in Piedmont, was aroused with shouts: "Fascism is destroyed! Hurrah for the army! Hurrah for Badoglio!"

The homes of the best-known Fascists were sacked and their furniture was thrown out the windows. The prefect of Cuneo was beaten. At eleven o'clock, in Piazza Vittorio, a lawyer named Tancredi Galimberti, a member of the Action Party whose Resistance alias was Duccio, delivered the first speech under the new freedom. But it was a warning, a call to arms: "The war goes on, yes; but against Germany. For this there is only one means: popular insurrection."

Most of the crowd listened in amazement: was not the fall of Mussolini the signal for peace?

There were other grounds for amazement, however. In Piazzo

Torino in Cuneo the troops opened fire on the demonstrators. In Milan a state of siege was proclaimed and a hundred soldiers with fixed bayonets and tank support fired into the air to break up a rally. In Rome government forces began to act at noon on Monday.

Then came the news that, instead of having been disbanded, the Fascist Militia had been incorporated into the regular army and that the military authorities were assuming full powers. A curfew was established at 9:30 P.M. and it was enforced to the letter. All meetings were prohibited. General Roatta, who had commanded the expeditionary corps in Spain and played a part in the murder of the Rosselli brothers, issued an imperative general order to all the armed forces on July 27: "In the event of demonstrations action must be taken against the population as against the enemy, with mortars and artillery. No one is to fire into the air: shoot to kill, as in combat."

There were twenty-three dead and seventy wounded in Piazza Roma in Bari. Such events were easily to be understood. The King and certain sectors of the military had too long been linked with Fascism not to fear that they too in their turn would be dragged down by its collapse. Their ideal was still that of authoritarian government without Mussolini and without Fascism, since Fascism had lost its last support. In addition conservative circles feared insurgency from the left. Indeed, anti-Fascist Opposition Committees had been established everywhere, and on August 3 Bonomi called on Badoglio in the name of six political parties (Christian Democratic, Socialist, Action, Communist, etc.) to request the end of the war and the denunciation of the alliance with Germany. For the Germans—and this was the final reason for the firm stand taken by the authorities—were in Italy, and they could move at any moment.

Specifically, the greatest weakness in the royal-military conspiracy was the fact that it had made no plans for getting out of the war.

"The war goes on," Badoglio had said; and this made no sense once Mussolini had been arrested and (on July 28) the Fascist Party, the Special Court, the Grand Council, and the Chamber of Fasci and Corporations had been dissolved. But Badoglio's government (one marshal, one admiral, five generals, one ambassador, one prefect, the director general of the Bank of Italy, and some high officials), the prisoner of its own dreads, of its calculations, and of the pasts of its members, hesitated.

Caught between a nominal enemy (the Anglo-Americans) who was advancing through the national territory and an ally (the

Germans) who was henceforth the natural enemy once Fascism had been overthrown, the government limited itself to sending two diplomats, followed by General Castellano, to Lisbon to sound out the Anglo-Americans.

Now time was of the essence. On the morning of July 26 the first German troop trains passed through the Brenner. Two SS divisions—the Adolf Hitler and the *Hoch und Standarte*—were moving forward in battle order. Some of the soldiers had painted *W Mussolini* in white letters on their helmets. How could Hitler not have recognized that the ouster of Il Duce must sooner or later take Italy out of the war? Hence his soldiers, automatic weapons in hand, were advancing through the Alps in execution of his *Asche* and *Schwarz* (Ash and Black) plans, which called for the total occupation of Italy, the destruction of her army, and the capture of her fleet. In addition Der Führer was planning the execution of two other operations: *Student* and *Eiche* (Oak), the first for the restoration of Fascism and the capture of Rome, the second for the liberation of Mussolini.

By the end of the first week of August there were seven new German divisions in Italy. Already the soldiers had gained control of power stations, railway stations, and tunnels; often they paid for what they bought with occupation marks. The fiction of the alliance was stone dead.

But for Badoglio's government "the war went on." Italy's tragedy had begun.

The danger for Badoglio's Italy could not come from Mussolini or Fascism. Locked in the bedroom of the commander of a garrison of student carabinieri, Il Duce had not shown the least sign of resistance, aside from a mere burst of temper when he was denied the use of the telephone. Soon afterward he began to talk to whoever would listen, the barracks physician or his guards, descanting on the "superficial" Italian people and then dropping off to sleep. At one o'clock on the morning of July 26 he was awakened by General Ferone with a message from Marshal Badoglio:

To *Cavaliere* Benito Mussolini,
    The undersigned, chief of government, hereby informs Your Excellency that all the measures taken with respect to you have been based on your own personal safety.

Badoglio pledged himself to move Mussolini to any place of his choosing—a promise that was not to be kept. At once Mussolini dictated a four-point message to General Ferone:

1) I should like to thank Marshal of Italy Badoglio for the precautions that he has been good enough to take for my person.
2) The only residence available to me is Rocca della Caminate, to
which I am ready to go at once.
3) I should like to assure Marshal Badoglio, especially in memory
of our labors carried out together in other times, that for my part
not only will no difficulty be created for him but all possible
collaboration will be made availabe to him.
4) I am happy that the government has decided to carry on the war.
I offer my best wishes that success crown the onerous task to
which Marshal Badoglio has dedicated himself on the order and
in the name of His Majesty the King, whose faithful servitor I
have been for twenty-one years, and still remain.

Mussolini took the pen that General Ferone handed him, signed
nervously, and added: *"Viva l'Italia!"*

Beneath the rolling phraseology, like that of a military proclamation, there was in fact the most complete renunciation. In this
sense the letter was a declaration of submission, and the martial
dictator was behaving like General Galbiati or any ranker in his
Militia. Undoubtedly common sense and exhaustion played their
parts, but there was also undoubtedly relief at this personal outcome of an insoluble situation.

The next day Mussolini was taken to Gaeta; from there he was
moved to the island of Ponza. It is among the ironies of history
that that island was one of the places of exile for anti-Fascists.
During the voyage aboard the corvette *Persefone*, Mussolini spoke
incessantly with Admiral Francesco Maugeri, complaining that he
was being sent to Ponza when it was still the place of confinement
of Tito Zaniboni, the Socialist deputy who had made the first
attempt to assassinate him. While Mussolini was on the island, he
translated Giosuè Carducci's *Odi barbari* (*Savage Odes*) into German, made notes, read a biography of Jesus, had discussions with
a priest, and, on July 29, celebrated his sixtieth birthday.

All his thoughts had turned toward the past; explanations and
justifications came one after another. He seemed to take no interest in the present and still less in the future. He did not even
complain against Badoglio or the members of the Grand Council;
he submitted, outside history, and he elaborated his legend,
undoubtedly reflecting on that other prisoner with whom at an
earlier time, in Ludwig's presence, he had been pleased to be compared: Napoleon I.

On August 7 he was moved to the island of La Maddalena, off
the Sardinian coast. There he received a fine twenty-four-volume
edition of Nietzsche's works, a gift from Hitler. He went on talk-

ing and writing, and now he was fearful for his own future, for he could read the Italian newspapers with their revelations of his private life, their forthright attacks on the Fascist system, the hierarchs, and Il Duce, and their demands that he be brought to trial with his collaborators.

On August 18 a German plane made a low-altitude flight over the island. One of its occupants was SS Colonel Otto Skorzeny, whom Hitler had instructed to find where Mussolini was being held. On its way back to its base the plane fell into the sea, but Skorzeny was rescued by a torpedo boat of the Italian navy. Karl Student, the parachute general to whom Skorzeny turned over his information, began to plan a combined operation against the island, but on August 26 a Red Cross plane transferred Mussolini to the Gran Sasso, some sixty-five hundred feet up in the Apennines.

The only access to the peak was by way of a funicular railway. Guarded by two hundred fifty carabinieri, Mussolini lived in the Hotel Campo Imperatore. He would read in the hotel's main lobby, talk with his custodians, play cards; he adopted a grape diet; he went endlessly back and forth over his explanations and excuses. Or he would listen to the radio, or offer confidences to Gueli, the police inspector assigned to watch him, repeating that the English would never get him alive and that, as he had already told Admiral Maugeri on the voyage from Ponza to La Maddalena, "to be set free by the Germans would mean my return to the government under Hitler's bayonets. That would be the greatest humiliation that could be inflicted on me."

Weary, old, out of control of events, he endured his lot without too much suffering, accepting the rôle of a retired dictator who talks about his past to anyone who will listen, delivering long monologues, finding a childish pleasure, as he was to write later, in the thought that he was being kept in "the highest prison in the world." This garrulous man cut brutally down to his real size was once more to be thrust into the spotlight by history, to his and Italy's grief. For history too was continuing.

Hitler and his staff had not limited their concerns to the search for Mussolini and the furtherance of the SS divisions' advance into Italy. They were scouring the peninsula for men with whom they could try to rebuild a semblance of a Fascist state.

Farinacci, who had fled Italy in the uniform of an SS officer, reached Hitler's headquarters. But Farinacci attacked Il Duce in Hitler's presence, and Goebbels noted sadly: "This man cannot be used by us for major undertakings. For the moment Der Führer has turned him over to Himmler's care."

After talks with a number of other Italians—including Giovanni Preziosi, a fanatical anti-Semite—Hitler soon recognized that there was no one in Italy who could take Mussolini's place. Hence Mussolini must be freed regardless of the cost and Italy must be occupied. "But we should move suddenly," Hitler told his generals; "otherwise the Anglo-Saxons will defeat us before we start by occupying the airfields."

Rome had premonitions of the German decision; there were fears of a sudden attack, a St. Bartholomew's Day massacre of the Badoglio government and the anti-Fascists, as well as the arrest of the royal family. The danger was real, for Hitler was contemplating such moves; he was no stranger to those "nights of the long knives," but under pressure from certain advisers such as Dollmann of the SS and the German military attaché in Rome, General von Rintelen, to whom "only the Badoglio government can prevent Italy from slipping into Communism," he preferred to move cautiously, sending fresh divisions across all the borders: he wanted to back a sure thing and to gain time.

That was also the great concern of the Badoglio government. That government had to confront the most serious and the most confused situation that Italy had ever known, and for forty-five days, from July 25 to September 8, it attempted to govern.

The single basic problem was still that of knowing how Italy would emerge from a war that she could no longer carry on and that had lost all purpose. General Castellano, who had had a talk in Madrid on August 15 with Ambassador Hoare of Britain, went off to Lisbon. There he met General Walter Bedell Smith, General Eisenhower's representative. Smith spoke with brutal frankness: there could be no talk of armistice; surrender must be unconditional.

The situation in Italy was developing swiftly. The Germans had cut off coal shipments. In Rome, where this was often the only fuel in poor homes, housewives began lining up at three in the morning in endless queues in order, with luck, to get two and a quarter pounds of coal; then they had to line up again for bread and a third time, in the hot August sun, for vegetables. The enthusiasm of July 25 and 26 soon faded and was replaced by dismay at the continuance of the war, crueler now than ever.

Throughout August there were "terror" bombings of Milan, Turin, Genoa, Bologna, and Rome. Incendiaries and two-ton bombs destroyed Palazzo Madama and Palazzo Carignano in Turin, as well as workers' houses, churches, and hospitals.

The newspapers were always filled with this senseless war. On August 14, for instance, communiqué No. 1175 announced counterattacks by Italian and German troops in Sicily once more. Three days later, however, that *"italianissima—super-Italian"* island, as *La Stampa* called it, was abandoned. At eight-fifteen in the evening of August 17 Marshal Badoglio took to the radio: "Italians! I am speaking to you for the first time in order to address our beloved brothers in martyred Sicily. After a vigorous defense that did great honor to the Italian-German troops, all the sacred territory of the island had to be abandoned."

The population, thus compelled to endure cruel bombardments, warlike proclamations, and the presence of the Germans, whose infiltration was glaringly apparent, could not understand. To the people the fall of Fascism meant peace. The contradiction between the state of war and the meaning of the events that had taken place was all the more flagrant because the government continued its anti-Fascist activities. On August 17 the newspapers disclosed that "the inquiry aimed at expropriating the hierarchs' fortunes will be broadened to the property of members of their families."

Soon it was learned that Starace, Generals Soddu, Galbiati, and Attilio Teruzzi, Marshal Cavallero, four hierarchs—Bottai, Buffarini, Pollastrini, and Raffaello Riccardi—and Mussolini's secretary, De Cesare, had been arrested. Ettore Muti, the former party secretary, was killed by carabinieri when he tried to escape. The SIM, which was now under the command of General Carboni, was responsible for these arrests, the purpose of which was to throttle an attempt, supported by the Germans, at Fascist reaction against the government.

At six o'clock in the evening of August 12 carabinieri appeared in the villa at Meina, on Lago Maggiore, in which the terror-stricken Petaccis were hiding. While Marcello Petacci managed to escape, the other members of the family were arrested on charges of "fraudulent conversion and theft." They were sent to the Novara prison, an old ivy-covered castle. There they received no special handling; they were searched, and Mussolini's letters to Claretta, which she had with her, were seized.

All these arrests were indicative: with more or less adroitness Badoglio's government was trying to prove that the "old order" was dead. It adopted social legislation; the old syndicalist, Bruno Buozzi, was chosen with a Communist and a Christian Democrat to head the industrial workers' union. Moreover, there were some genuine anti-Fascists in the government itself (Leopoldo Piccardi and Leonardo Severi); and National Front Committees to support them had been formed throughout the country. In Rome there was a Central National Front Committee with which Badoglio himself had dealings. The more or less underground newspapers of the anti-Fascist parties increased their pressure on the government. "Cry *Peace and Freedom* in the public squares," *l'Unità* urged on July 27. "Demand a democratic government." *L'Italia libera*, the Action Party's newspaper, said in a special edition on August 5: "We have scored an initial success, but one swallow does not make a summer."

There can be no doubt that the Fascism-steeped segment of the government was strong. True, the words *Fascism* and *Duce* were scorned as appurtenances of an obsolete past, but the spirit survived. The King was uneasy and felt threatened. He told General Puntoni on August 15: "Badoglio makes it look extremely grim. With his mania for striking at everyone, it seems that he wants to create a vacuum round the monarchy." On August 30, undoubtedly reflecting the King's thinking, Puntoni wrote: "The government has hurled itself into useless persecutions." Earlier, on August 16, the King had issued a sharp warning: "The elimination of all former members of the Fascist Party from all political activity must absolutely stop. If it does not, we shall reach the ridiculous situation of seeing the King's actions judged and condemned." Vittorio Emanuele III, Emperor of Ethiopia and King of Albania, was quite well aware that one day he might be called on to render an accounting.

He had the support of former ministers under Mussolini who were now in Badoglio's Cabinet, such as Generals Roatta and Adami-Rossi. Adami-Rossi, commander of the Turin district, had had batteries of machine guns set up inside the FIAT plants: fifty-four arrested workers had been tried by a military tribunal and the officers who had given the command to fire on them had been congratulated. On July 30 Second Lieutenant Carmine Massarelli of the First Infantry Regiment was cited in an order of the day in these terms: "Against a group of recalcitrant workers who refused to return to the work that they had unreasonably abandoned and who stated in mocking terms their belief that the troops would not dare to shoot, he ordered the unit under his command to open fire, with the result that many workers were wounded."

The army still contained many officers whose minds were so attuned. This was the result of Fascism, but in the more honest it was also the result of inability to understand the situation and of bewilderment. A captain who had left men dead behind him in the Russian steppe or the desert dunes felt that they had died for nothing and that all the sacrifices had been made in vain, and at times, in an excess of emotion, the captain obstinately wanted the war to go on out of loyalty to three years of alliance and suffering. Another, turned anti-militarist by his experiences on the Russian front, could not contain himself when someone spoke of war against the Germans: "What, desert our people in the Balkans, in Africa, in Greece? Leave them to their fate, as we were deserted on the Russian front?"[1]

And it was true that the situation was agonizing and insoluble, the more so because the government was trying to deceive and outwit the Germans. It had not issued that blazing proclamation that some had expected in the joyous days of July 25 and 26: "Immediate peace, a mass rising against the Germans if they oppose peace, alliance with the United Nations." This government was the prisoner of its prudence and its fear. "I do not wish to run the risk of ending like the King of the Belgians," Vittorio Emanuele said time and again.

Therefore he gave orders to make all preparations for a possible evacuation of Rome, while Foreign Minister Raffaele Guariglia and General Ambrosio went to confer with Ribbentrop and Keitel at Tarvisio on August 6 in an effort to divert the Nazis. The Germans made no secret of their distrust: they arrived in an armored train. The SS took over the station and surrounded the villa in which the talks were held. General Ambrosio sought to obtain permission for the Italian troops stationed in France and the Balkans to return home, and this confirmed the Germans' suspicions: the Italians were negotiating with the Allies. Ribbentrop thereupon demanded that the King, the Crown Prince, and Badoglio go to Germany for talks with Der Führer. This trap was too obvious for the Italians to fall into it, but Ribbentrop's request set the tone for the meeting.

Meanwhile the Allies' bombardments were continuing, and no major Italian city escaped. The atmosphere became still more charged. A new German Ambassador arrived in Rome: Rudolf Rahn, an expert in dealing with the governments of occupied countries. Rumors of pro-German conspiracies grew; there were increasing arrests of former Fascist leaders. Frightened, the Ciano family attempted to flee to Spain; on Himmler's orders, Colonel Dollmann and Lieutenant Colonel Herbert Kappler, the head of the German police in Rome, persuaded them to seek refuge in Germany: from there it would be easier to get to Spain. Ciano agreed: he thus leaped into the lion's mouth, and this step, which cost him his life, gives the measure of his political blindness.

The Allies' bombardments grew worse, and a choice had to be made quickly. General Castellano returned from Lisbon on August 27 with the Allies' terms and a radio transmitter for direct

---

[1] Revelli, *La guerra dei poveri*, p. 125.

communication. On September 1 Vittorio Emanuele III agreed to unconditional surrender. Castellano at once established contact with the Allies' headquarters in Cassibile, Sicily, less than ten miles south of Syracuse.

At five o'clock the next afternoon Castellano arrived in the dense olive grove in which Allied headquarters was hidden. Wearing elegant dark civilian clothes, he entered the huge tent where the generals were waiting. Fifteen minutes later the text of the armistice had been signed by Castellano and General Walter Bedell Smith, representing Eisenhower, in the presence of Commodore Roger Dick and Brigadier Kenneth W. D. Strong. The document provided that the armistice would be announced by radio on a day to be set, coinciding with an Allied landing; Anglo-American parachute troops would take over the Roman airfields with the help of Italian troops.

Castellano went back to Rome immediately after the signing. That night the Romans heard the engines of huge waves of bombers: their targets were Bologna, Trento, and Bolzano. A few moments earlier Naples had been heavily damaged. These last-minute attacks were evidence of the Allies' distrust of Badoglio's government. They had set September 12 as the probable effective date of the armistice; in fact, they wanted to mislead the Italians, who, they thought, might warn the Germans. As General Smith wrote, the Anglo-American general staff wanted to conceal behind a "gigantic bluff" the true date for the armistice, which would also be that for the landing. The Italians, for their part, tried to deceive the Germans.

On September 3, after the armistice agreement had been signed, Badoglio received Ambassador Rahn, who was uneasy at the Italians' attitude. Badoglio's pleasant face broke into a sad smile: "I am Marshal Badoglio, one of the three oldest marshals in Europe. Yes, [August von] Mackensen, Pétain, and I are Europe's oldest marshals. The Reich government's distrust of me is beyond my understanding." The old marshal paused a moment, as if to emphasize his pained astonishment; then he added in a firm tone: "I have given my word and I will honor it. I ask you to trust me."

These first days of September, which were among the darkest in Italy's history, went by in this aura of mutual deceit, for on August 30 Keitel had sent the following order to all German units: "The most important task is that of disarming the Italian army as quickly as possible."

This order was to be carried out on September 7. On that day a massive Allied convoy was observed in the Mediterranean, heading for the Italian coast. Also on that day General Student, acting on information from the German police, which may have suborned some Italian officers, began preparing Operation Free Mussolini.

And on that same day, early in the morning, General Maxwell D. Taylor and Colonel William T. Gardiner left Sicily. At four-thirty in the afternoon they landed at Gaeta, accompanied by Italian naval officers: they had come to prepare for the operation called "Giant Two," the launching of two thousand parachutists onto the Roman airfields. But these were already held by the Germans, who in addition controlled the gasoline dumps of the Italian troops who were theoretically intended to assist the Allies' operation. Taylor and Gardiner left Rome in an Italian plane. At 5:30 P.M. on September 8, just before the deadline for the start of the airborne operation Giant Two, they landed at Tunis.

Fifteen minutes later the American radio announced the Badoglio government's surrender. Two and a quarter hours after that, the Italian radio interrupted its regular programming to announce that there would be an important communiqué by Marshal Badoglio. A few minutes later the marshal's heavy, uninflected voice began to speak:

> Recognizing the impossibility of continuing an unequal struggle, the Italian government has asked General Eisenhower for an armistice. The request has been granted. All acts of hostility everywhere against the Anglo-American troops on the part of the Italian forces are to cease. The Italian forces will reply, however, to attacks from other sources.

Sitting beside the radio in the lobby of the hotel on the Gran Sasso, Mussolini said nothing.

In the streets of Rome and the cities of Italy there were a few cries of *Viva la pace!* Pedestrians gathered in front of the cafés to hear the rebroadcast of Badoglio's message. Soldiers sang and embraced, throwing their caps in the air. Then the streets emptied.

The first sound of cannon was heard in Rome toward midnight, and it was very near; in other cities German patrols went into action within an hour of the news of the armistice, disarming the bewildered Italian troops and handling them roughly. "Il Duce will go down in history as the last of the Romans," Goebbels wrote, "but behind his powerful figure a nation of gypsies will ultimately rot away."

The royal family and Badoglio took refuge in the Ministry of the Interior with the greater part of the generals. They were all gripped by the fear of German reprisals. About five o'clock next morning, in an atmosphere of anguish, the King and his court left

Rome, driving to the port of Ortona. Over and over Badoglio was saying: "If they get us, they will cut off all our heads."

The King was calm, but he grew angry when at the dock he saw the number of higher officers who had followed him. General Roatta was there, an automatic rifle on his civilian-clad shoulder; the King looked at him and shook his head. This sovereign on the pier in the pre-dawn dark, this worried marshal, these officers—they were the image of a disintegrating Italy.

Certainly the flight of the King, who established himself at Brindisi, far from the German occupation, preserved the continuity of the state and would foster the struggle against the Germans and resurgent Fascism by showing where legality resided. Thus the Italian fleet in a body, in spite of heavy attacks by German planes, which sank the flagship, obeyed the King's orders and sailed to Malta.

But the hasty flight of the King and Badoglio, leaving the general staff and the ministers without any clear-cut instructions, made it easier for all those in the army—the majority of the officers—who rebelled at resistance to the Germans. And the Germans moved quickly, shooting generals, firing without warning, while Italian generals and ministers learned *only* from the radio, at the same time as the public, that there was an armistice. It would have required much resolution and foresight for officers and soldiers to resist the violence of the Germans. Besides, twenty years of Fascism, three years of defeat, and forty-five days of uncertainty had exhausted men's will power.

The Italian army melted in a few hours. The Italian Fourth Army, stationed in southwestern France, headed for Italy in disorder, stealing bicycles, throwing away weapons; in the last French villages before the border officers and soldiers alike tried to buy civilian clothes without regard for price: there were generals dressed as nuns, and the mountain roads were littered with uniforms, weapons, and regimental records. The laughing French watched the passage of this panicked army with its columns of mules, and now and then the village children would shout: "*I Tedeschi!*—The Germans!" to see the Italians break into a run.

In Italy the army's supply dumps were looted. In Cuneo, great cheeses, barrels of wine, sacks of rice and flour, and even trucks were taken over by civilians who had made their way into storehouses and barracks left open to the four winds. The officers were often the first to run, to hand over their unarmed men, to order them to give way to the Germans. Four Wehrmacht motorcyclists were sometimes enough to disarm an entire regiment, which was soon beaten into cattle cars with rifle butts and shipped off to the prison camps of Germany. The Germans had painted the cars with the legend *Badoglio Truppen*—Badoglio's Troops, and throughout the northward journey the trainloads of German soldiers pouring south into Italy spat insults at these former allies, these tattered, battered "traitors." In a few days seven hundred thousand Italians had been shipped off to the Reich.

In the wake of the Germans the Fascist hierarchs slunk back, shouting of Badoglio's betrayal, calling on all veterans of the desert and Russia to remain loyal to the alliance and to the dead. At the same time the British radio kept broadcasting the appeals of Churchill and Roosevelt: "Italians, the destiny of your country will depend on what you can do with it to aid the victory of the free peoples."

Some Italian units had not needed such appeals. Where officers had been able to galvanize their troops and join their operations with those of the local populations, it was possible to resist the Germans.

In Corsica the Seventh Army Corps fought shoulder to shoulder with French troops and underground fighters; five hundred Italian soldiers died for the liberation of Bastia. Some units in the Balkans merged with the Partisans. The troops on Corfu resisted for days without any help from the Allies.

In Cephalonia the general decided to lay down his arms; but during the night other officers took over the Acqui Division and the soldiers approved in a tumultuous meeting. They organized a defense, but it was wrecked by the lack of ammunition, and in one day the Germans shot four hundred fifty officers and soldiers and left their bodies unburied. "Italian rebels," the German major said, "do not deserve burial."

On the Italian mainland itself resistance began to take shape. In some instances it was individual resistance by veterans who had learned to know their German ally on the front. Officers who had gotten out of Russia tried to rally disbanded units, to rouse the consciences of other officers; then, collecting abandoned weapons, they took to the mountains. At night, civilians sneaked furtively through towns to gather the arms and munitions that the soldiers had abandoned. Some of the men of the Fourth Army formed new units of their own on the wooded slopes of the Piedmont mountains. Every morning they saluted the colors. These tiny units foreshadowed the formation of autonomous Partisan forces.

Tancredi Galimberti (Duccio), the Cuneo lawyer, also took to the mountains after a long, futile effort to win over a general of that same Fourth Army. "What shall we do, then?" Galimberti asked.

"I spent the whole night weeping," the General replied.

"Well, you keep on weeping; I haven't the time."

Soon Galimberti's inspiration and guidance were to bring to life the Partisan divisions of *Giustizia e Libertà*. But on September 22 the Piedmont village of Boves was burned by the Germans in their first reprisal. The bitter, cruel Partisan warfare was beginning in Italy too. It was to be merciless. As the Germans saw it, Italy had to pay for her betrayal, and some officers announced that they would turn her into another Poland.

There were demonstrations in Turin and Milan; in Piombino sailors, soldiers, and workers seized the factories and the coastal batteries and held out for several days, inflicting almost a thousand casualties on the Germans.

Resistance began in Rome too. The troops fought at first: a grenadier regiment and the Ariete Division fought hand to hand at Porta San Paolo, and the artillery fire heard at midnight of September 8 was theirs. General Carboni, furthermore, took it upon himself to distribute arms to the Central Committee of the National Action Front, which on September 9 became the Committee of National Liberation (CLN). Sandro Pertini, a Socialist, Luigi Longo, a Communist, and Ugo La Malfa, of the Action Party, with others who had recently gotten out of prison, went into the workers' quarters to form anti-Fascist units and distribute several truckloads of weapons. The struggle against the Germans was bitter and unequal, and rich in acts of courage like that of Second Lieutenant Rosso of the engineers, who saw a group of German high officers coming as he was mining via Cassia: in danger of arrest, he jumped with both feet on a mine and blew himself to bits.

On September 10 Kesselring forced the Italian troops in Rome to surrender. Nevertheless civilians went through the empty, silent city shouting: "Give us rifles: the Germans are coming." Soon the streets echoed to the exhausts of German motorcycles. A shot sent one of the Germans zigzagging until he fell in his own blood, covered with leather and steel, still astride his cycle, whose engine went on pulsing, more slowly, like a heart, in front of the office of Mussolini's newspaper, *il Popolo d'Italia*.

Then there was silence, suddenly broken by the bursts of grenades, hurled at random from a distance by the Germans to cow the city. The next day small groups of Wehrmacht troops appeared, having received authorization for twenty-four hours of pillage in the city that was the symbol of betrayal. They arrested any civilian who ventured out; they snatched watches from wrists and showed their thanks with a kick or a blow from a rifle butt. The radio resumed broadcasting popular songs and light music, interspersed with a voice that repeated regularly in a German accent: "Desert the traitors! Come back to your German comrades!"

On September 9, while fighting was going on in Rome, the Allies had landed at Salerno in Operation Avalanche under General Mark W. Clark. The eighteen-mile beach dominated by heights was curtained by German fire, but under a powerful aerial umbrella the Allies dug in despite counterattacks by Kesselring and extremely bitter combat. Naples was the Allies' first objective, while Montgomery's British forces, fresh from Sicily, were fighting their way up the Italian boot to reinforce the sea-borne forces.

But on the very day of the Allies' landing at Salerno DNB (Deutsches Nachrichtenbüro—the German News Agency) issued the first proclamation by a new Fascist government. Vittorio Mussolini, Alessandro Pavolini, and Renato Ricci had rejoined Roberto Farinacci and Giovanni Preziosi at Hitler's headquarters. "Treason will not succeed," they declared in their statement. "A national Fascist government has been established and it is functioning in the name of Mussolini."

But the German leaders were not satisfied: the new Fascist government contained no one of sufficient stature to make an impression on Italian opinion. Goebbels wrote regretfully: "We should like to publish the membership of the new Fascist government, but unfortunately we cannot announce these names because they are so unimportant." But General Student's parachutists and Otto Skorzeny's SS were about to give Der Führer Benito Mussolini.

On the Gran Sasso, Mussolini was sitting at his window at about two o'clock in the afternoon of September 12 when suddenly he saw a glider land a couple of hundred yards from the hotel. Armed men sprang out. Soon seven more gliders landed; another crashed as it came down; three more missed the landing area and smashed into the surrounding precipices.

The soldiers moved in on the hotel and the carabinieri hesitated to fire, for at the head of the parachutists was marching their own General Ferdinando Soleti, whom Student's men had abducted the day before. General Soleti had attempted suicide, but the Germans had prevented him and forced him into the leading glider. Soon the Italians had been disarmed without the firing of a single shot.

Mussolini seemed thinner and looked old. He thanked Skorzeny and asked to be taken to his house at Rocca della Caminate. But history had a final trick to play on him: it was too late to let him escape his mission; the Germans had strict orders that Mussolini was to be taken back to the air base of Pratica di Mare.

A *Storch* scout plane landed near the hotel. In black hat and overcoat, Mussolini went aboard and sat between the massive legs of Skorzeny. The plane bumped along its short improvised runway and fell into a hollow that cut across the sloping ground; for a moment the plane dropped, but then its pilot, Gerlach, a Luftwaffe ace, straightened it out and gave it full throttle. Operation Oak was a success. The Germans had a big name for the national Fascist government.

Actually, the most difficult phase of the liberation of Mussolini had been the landing of the gliders and the take-off of the *Storch*, for neither Police Inspector Gueli—who had ordered the carabinieri not to shoot—nor Police Chief Senise wanted to stand up to the Germans.

At one-thirty, a half-hour before the first glider came in, Senise —and let us remember that he headed the police in Mussolini's government until April, 1943—counseled Gueli that he would do well to "observe the maximum of prudence." Senise was quite capable of helping the Germans free Mussolini. In any event he did not impede them: that was the least that could be done by the policeman who had climbed every rung on the ladder under the Fascist system; for that matter, so had most of the top police officials.

As for Marshal Badoglio, he had indeed proclaimed that Mussolini would never leave his prison alive, but, when the marshal precipitately departed from Rome at dawn on September 9, he left no instructions. And so now Mussolini was free, in the hands of the Germans.

A Heinkel took him from Pratica di Mare to Vienna, where he arrived at about midnight. Almost prostrate with exhaustion, stripped of everything, he spent the night in the Hotel Continental. On September 13 he was taken to Munich, where he was reunited with his family, who until then had been interned at Rocca della Caminate; he spent a day with his wife and his sons while the hierarchs who had been liberated by the Germans' arrival in Rome were on their way to Munich. Thus the survivors of Fascism came together in the capital of Bavaria; in the same city there were also, in isolation, the Cianos, who were in the midst of their enemies.

Der Führer received Mussolini in his headquarters on September 14. They clung together in a long embrace, in a renewal of that bond between them that had been forged in their many meetings and that had made Hitler the unchallenged leader. For two hours they talked in Der Führer's bunker.

Did Mussolini insist that he wished to withdraw from political life? did he agree to resume the leadership of a Fascist government only under the threat of harsh German reprisals against the Italians (the use of gas and the occupation of the Po Valley by the Reich)? Mussolini was to insist in 1945 that this was indeed the case. It was an easy defense, even if there was some element of truth in the reference to Hitler's intentions and in Mussolini's statement that he wanted to leave the stage.

But Mussolini was not making his first surrender to Hitler, and this latest one was in no way surprising. He was under the threat and the ascendancy of the man whom he had chosen to follow, and above all he must have fallen victim again to the illusion that somehow the course of events would turn. And besides, isolated in this hidden bunker concealed in the gloomy forest of central Europe, alone with Hitler, had he a choice?

He had been brought to this point by his repudiations since 1937 and, even more, by the Fascist system of which he was the inspiration and the symbol. What could he do, give in? The only other avenue, at the point that he had reached, was suicide. But he had always clung to life and he had never had principles enough to reject it for their sake. Then too, as an old hand at politics, he imagined that there was always the possibility of a stroke of luck, that there was no damnation in politics, that sometimes holding on was enough to mean salvation. And, of course, there was power, even if it was only a semblance now.

So he surrendered. Hitler even had his personal physician, Dr. Theo Morell, examine him.

Already the scheming rivalries of the Fascist leaders were twining again round Mussolini; from Pavolini to Farinacci, each of them put himself forward as the spokesman for the Nazis. Once more among them, Mussolini had regained his past, he was again Il Duce.

On September 15 DNB announced: "Mussolini has resumed the leadership of Fascism in Italy." This announcement on the radio was followed by the reading of five decrees, the *Fogli d'ordini* (order sheets). The first was addressed "to loyal comrades in all Italy: As from today, September 15, 1943, Year XXI of the Fascist Era, I resume the supreme leadership of Fascism in Italy. Benito Mussolini." The second appointed Alessandro Pavolini "provisional secretary of the Partito nazionale fascista, which as from today shall be known as the Partito fascista repubblicano (PFR)."

The other decrees provided for the establishment of all the old party branches in the new Fascist Republican Party.

As they read their newspapers, Italians said nothing. For some it was the dissolution of a dream; for others, the small number of Fascists, it was escape from a nightmare. Il Duce had returned, and these Fascists were going to exact a high price for the fear with which they had lived for fifty days. They put on their black shirts and their buttonhole insignia again, they went knocking on doors, they provoked reaction, and many Italians went back— though this time with fury in their hearts—to their masks of aloofness and humility, while the few Fascist *prepotenti* (bullies) strutted.

This was the situation throughout central Italy and the Po Valley, for the Allies held only the southern part of the boot, below the Garigliano, some hundred twenty miles south of Rome.

On September 18 Mussolini broadcast from Munich. His voice was weak and weary. "Black Shirts! Men and women of Italy! After a long silence you hear my voice again, and I am sure that you recognize it." (It was 9:30 P.M. At the Ghedi airfield, near Brescia, Claretta Petacci, who had been freed by the Germans and who was on her way to Munich under their escort, listened, wept with joy, and fainted.) Mussolini summarized what had happened and offered explanations. "The word *loyalty*," he said, "has a profound, an eternal significance to the German soul." He attacked the King, Badoglio, all the traitors, and the liars; he reaffirmed the necessity of the German alliance; then he concluded: "The parasitical plutocrats must be annihilated! Workers, peasants, little people, the state that will be built shall be yours!"

The voice had no warmth, the rhetoric was shabby, and the demagogy was unrestrained and absurd.

The Germans refused to allow Mussolini to live in Rome, which was an open city. He had to go to Salò, on Lake Garda and considerably more accessible to the Reich. There he had with him Tringali-Casanova, Buffarini-Guidi (now Minister of the Interior), Pavolini, and Marshal Graziani, who had accepted the Ministry of Defense out of hatred of Badoglio and loyalty to Germany and Il Duce. But to rebuild a Fascist army was not easy: the Germans needed Italian laborers more than unreliable Italian soldiers; besides, the potential recruits were fleeing to the mountains and the officers were in hiding.

Each of the ministers of the new Fascist Republic set up his own defense force: Ricci had the Militia, Pavolini had the Republican National Guard or *Brigate nere* (Black Brigades), Buffarini had his police force; there was also the Muti, an independent repressive organization that had adopted the name of the former party secretary, elevated to the rank of Martyr of Fascism after he had been killed by Badoglio's carabinieri. The new government also used the naval commandos, the Tenth Squadron under Prince Valerio Borghese,* who commanded some four or five thousand men and organized them into an independent group with decided political ambitions.

There were also, mixed into these various ranks, a few youngsters who wanted to defend their country against the invader, a few veterans loyal to comrades who had died in the three years of war, and the swarm of disreputables that gathers round every imposed government, a little army of fifteen- to seventeen-year-old ruffians whose minds were set on murder and rapine and who vanished when there was real fighting to be done.

This half-world, which was only the ghost of the Fascist régime, was dominated by Colonel General Kurt Wolff's SS and the German spies: even telephone calls were under their surveillance. They protected and controlled. They were in a conquered country, and Mussolini's government was not even a screen for their domination.

The newspapers teemed with "ordinances from the German command." On October 2, in the middle of its front page, *La Stampa* published pictures of the occupation mark, for which the rate of exchange was fixed at ten *lire*. Officially northern Italy was now nothing but a territory under military occupation. But on the same day when German currency was portrayed in one of the major newspapers of the Salò republic, the greater part of the population of Naples attacked the Germans with weapons that had been taken from them or that had been abandoned. There was shooting in the Vomero quarter and in Piazza Nazionale; after four days of battle Major Scholl and his staff were compelled to surrender. The great capital of the Mezzogiorno was already free when the Americans entered it.

These four days of Naples were one of the indications that in Italy occupation would not be merely endured but would always be challenged. Mussolini and the Salò Republic were storing up dark days for themselves.

The climate of July 25, when a few slaps were vengeance enough for the laughing Romans against the Black Shirts, was gone. On July 25 no one had been killed in Italy. Many lives would be claimed in the final act that began in the autumn of 1943.

* With another veteran of Salò Giorgio Almirante, Borghese now leads the frankly Fascist and growing *Movimento sociale italiano*—Italian Social Movement—and its new squadre.—Translator.

16

The Social Republic of Salò
(October, 1943 – January, 1944)

"Reasons of state transcend any other conflicting consideration today. Now we must carry through to the end."—IL DUCE (before the Verona trial)

MUD! DAYS AND NIGHTS of heavy, stubborn rain, of clouds clinging to the flanks of the Abruzzi, water tumbling over helmets, fog filling the depths of the narrow valleys and mud rising occasionally over the tents, the blackish mud up to the hubs of the skidding jeeps; and war-tested German troops along the whole fortified Gustav Line and regularly relieved—these were the obstacles faced by the British and Americans during the autumn and winter of 1943–44. From Cassino to Ortona the front was motionless, and the Americans and the New Zealanders sat and waited in a war in which it seemed that men were dying for nothing, for a yard of rocky ground, as in the past. But that unmoving front was a living wound in Italy's side.

True, the south, approximately a third of Italy, was free. Free to die of hunger. Naples knew the nadir of suffering in that winter of 1943–44. For days the buildings that the Germans had mined were exploding, strewing desolation and terror everywhere.

Every night the German bombers battered the big harbor, and there was fresh panic, more death in the quarters already disemboweled by the Allies' bombs. The city was attacked as well by an epidemic of typhus: running water was a luxury, and so was food. Communications were difficult; the railway lines had been destroyed. In Lucania an overloaded train was compelled to stop in a tunnel; the frightened passengers left the cars and stood in a pungent smoke that blinded them and suffocated them; the dead were counted by the hundred. The roads were congested with persons of all ages loaded with objects of every kind that they hoped to be able to offer the peasants in exchange for vegetables. These would be resold in the streets of Naples, where, in fact, everything was on sale. Prostitution was endemic, robbery was incessant. Trucks, whole trains, even, it was said, a ship disappeared. American Negro soldiers were made drunk and then sold over and over again and progressively despoiled. Misery, corruption, and despair ravaged the south under the Allies' military government.

Yet the King and Badoglio's government had established themselves at Salerno. On October 13 they had even declared war on Germany.

In front of the little railway station of Trani, bare-chested Allied soldiers in shorts laughed at the spectacle as the King held his first review of his troops: three or four hundred officers and men stood at attention while Vittorio Emanuele III, in the midst of seventeen high officers, saluted the flag. The band played the royal march, a rousing musical mockery for the few soldiers and the small apathetic audience of children and priests.

The Allies, moreover, were not prepared to permit Italy to take an active part in the war, though in December one unit was formed: the "Italian Motorized Group," which was successful in combat. But Allied Headquarters in Caserta was not eager to expand the experiment. Let Italy keep her place as a conquered enemy; it would be so much the easier to settle her fate. In Sicily there were already one party calling for the island's independence and another, the Forty-ninth Star Party, which wanted annexation to the United States or even, failing that, to Great Britain.

In addition there was sharp political conflict in this liberated third of Italy. The anti-Fascist parties assembled in the CLN refused to recognize the authority of the King—the Emperor of Ethiopia—and Badoglio—Duke of Addis Ababa. On January 28–29 the CLN parties held a major congress in Bari and called for the immediate abdication of Vittorio Emanuele and the convocation of a Constituent Assembly. While some children were selling their bodies and while others were organized in gangs that rifled every American truck parked in a street, these political struggles seemed premature, at the very least, and all the more so when there was another Italy on the other side of the static front: Mussolini's Social Republic.

The Germans had set up Mussolini's new régime on the western shore of Lake Garda in a quiet countryside ambiance where luxurious villas nestled among southern trees and flowers. The ministries were spread out along the lake shore from the little town of

Salò to Gargnano, where Mussolini lived. This was where d'Annunzio had spent that gilded exile to which Il Duce had restricted
him. So once more the play and the irony of history brought Mussolini together with the shadow of the poet who had contributed
so much to the birth of Fascism.

The whole region was sealed off by the Germans. SS patrols
controlled the streets, the highways were blocked with complicated barricades, and the garden of the Villa Feltrinelli was filled
with armed sentries. On the roof of the villa there was an anti-
aircraft gun.

In the beginning this huge, beautiful house was Mussolini's
home and office. Rachele wandered through it, full of jealousy.
After July 25 she had learned the whole story of the long affair
with Claretta Petacci. The grandchildren of Il Duce shouted on
the stairs; Romano played his accordion; cousins, grandnephews,
a whole army of distant relatives descended on the villa to clamor
for money and wheedle for alms, scheming and maligning.

Distributed on the various floors of the house, thirty SS men
from the personal guard of Der Führer observed the swarm and
listened to the noisy voices amid which Mussolini was supposed
to be governing Italy. In order to maintain a better watch, a
Lieutenant Dyckerhoff lived in the villa; always in evidence, over-
hearing every conversation, he reported everything to a Colonel
Jandl, assigned to Mussolini's person, who in turn informed
Ambassador Rahn or SS General Wolff. Toward the middle of
November Mussolini decided to move his office to the Ursulines'
villa, a little more than a half-mile from Villa Feltrinelli. Colonel
Jandl took up a midway position, while Dyckerhoff went on living
in Villa Feltrinelli.

Under constant observation, reduced to moving from one villa
to the other in this tourist resort where a German profile marked
every yard of distance, Mussolini in dead earnest played at governing. He was at his desk at 8:45 every morning; until 2 or 2:30
P.M. he received visitors, and then, after an hour's rest, he went
back to work, ending his day at 9 P.M. He devoted himself to reading newspapers and marking them with his blue pencil; he wrote a
series of articles for *il Corriere della Sera* to unmask the monarchy's conspiracy and betrayal; above all he talked, with anyone—
with his visitors, of course, but especially with those round him.
The two specialists sent by Morell, Hitler's physician, were his
confidants. One of them, Captain Georg Zachariae, had to endure
lengthy nightly monologues on literature and history; the other,
Horn, did his listening during the day, when he gave Mussolini a
massage. Undoubtedly Horn was working for the Gestapo. Even

Quinto Navarra, who had also managed to reach Gargnano, found himself raised after twenty years to the rank of listener. Mussolini seated his visitors and then the talk, which was most often a monologue, began. And indeed what else was there to do in Gargnano?

Any journey was discouraged by the Germans, who brought up the danger of assassination attempts and air assaults. What choice was there but to accept their counsels when everything was quite officially in their hands from the telephone switchboard to the SS guard round Il Duce, from the railways to the management of the Italian economy? The power of Mussolini and his ministers ceased to exist at the door of his office in the Ursulines' villa or at the steps of the royal train, abandoned on a siding and used as the headquarters of the Ministry of Popular Culture, or at the door of some hotel where another ministry was quartered.

The Social Republic was like a caricature—a gross, grimacing caricature—of the Fascist system in its days of splendor. An old, loquacious Duce let himself go in the most irrational fantasies, as when he said to Navarra: "I and I alone—do you understand?—will really establish Socialism in Italy." Those exigent masters, the Germans, were everywhere. From one villa to the next the scheming multiplied like a fly swarm among these men all torn by dread.

With various of his relatives and his incompetent sporting friends Mussolini's son set up a political secretariat that was jealously watched and battled by the special secretariat in the hands of Giovanni Dolfin, consul of the Militia. Pavolini, the secretary of the Republican Fascist Party, was the rival of Guido Buffarini-Guidi, who was still Minister of the Interior. Ricci and Preziosi played their own game, the latter having, in the eyes of the Germans, the advantage of being a dedicated anti-Semite.

Donna Rachele seldom left her quarters. Buffarini and a corps of servants, policemen, and clerks kept her informed. She had as well a retinue of her own. It did not take her long to learn that Claretta Petacci had arrived at Lake Garda. Claretta lived in Villa Fiordaliso, in Gardone; the third floor was occupied by officials of the Japanese Embassy. Mussolini, when he visited her, left the Ursulines' villa by a side door and was driven in a small car to Gardone. Villa Fiordaliso was also under guard by the SS, and Hitler himself had seen to it that Claretta should be near Il Duce: she had gone to prison for him and he had no right to abandon her.

Nevertheless the majority of the hierarchs showed open hostility at her arrival. Claretta threatened to undermine the popularity of the nascent government through her association with the old Roman corruption. All the more, indeed, because she had not come alone: her parents and her brother and sister were with her. But the hierarchs quickly fell back into their old habits, and the comings and goings and connivings round the favorite were resumed. For all his confidential relation with Rachele Mussolini, Buffarini made semi-weekly visits to Claretta Petacci, with whom he was on the best of terms. Claretta herself was constantly reproaching her Duce: he did not visit her often enough, and every day she wrote to him and telephoned him.

In March, 1944, she learned that he had had a private audience with a young blonde party worker from Maderno, Elena Curti. Was she the daughter of some former mistress of Il Duce? Was she Mussolini's own daughter? Whatever the truth, Claretta's jealousy broke its bonds, and so did Rachele's.

In October, 1944, in spite of Buffarini, Donna Rachele went to Villa Fiordaliso and the two women met face to face. Claretta listened to the invectives and the outcries of the legal wife, then showed Rachele the copies of her letters to Il Duce, and the whole affair ended in tears. That night Mussolini found it more advisable to sleep in his office in the Ursulines' villa.

Calm was restored, and three days later, in commemoration of the twenty-second anniversary of the March on Rome, Mussolini reviewed the M Division, whose members saluted him with drawn daggers in their raised hands. Mussolini moved slowly, his jaw out-thrust as in the old days. But his face had aged. He was followed by Marshal Graziani, who had lost weight and whose face looked withered. The commander of the M Division, in his German cap, assumed a martial manner; nearby, in a soiled grey suit with baggy trousers, Francesco Barracu, under-secretary to the Premier, smiled. He was wearing a black shirt and a monocle screwed into his right eye, and he looked uncomfortably like a gangster. Then Mussolini mounted a low platform and made a little speech to his legion before he presented it with a *gagliardetto* marked with an M. Behind him, General Wolff smiled discreetly to the SS officer at his side.

With their telephone taps and their reading of every letter, even Rachele's, the Germans knew whatever was to be known of the little world of Republican Fascism, and to them the Social Republic was merely a stage set and Mussolini was an old actor who had to be kept on his feet until he was no longer of use.

For the moment he still had some value. The fiction of the revival of Fascism kept the German people from feeling isolated. In Italy the Black Brigades, the Republican National Guard, and the little groups of men in every town who had gotten themselves in too deep to draw back could be relied on for valuable services: they did the dirty jobs, the arresting and torturing and killing. Booted and belted into their black uniforms, they patrolled the streets; at their belts they wore daggers, grenades, and pistols in cowboy style; their helmets and their lapels flaunted the death's head. They were hated and therefore loyal. But their collaboration was not supposed to go too far. For many months, as we have noted, the Germans opposed the reconstruction of a Republican army; then they agreed to train four divisions in Germany. To man these, appeals were made to the seven hundred thousand Italian soldiers held in captivity in Germany: exactly 1.03 percent volunteered to serve in the Republican ranks, and many of them were concerned above all to return to Italy, prepared to desert in whole companies with all their arms and equipment.

The gap had to be filled by conscription, against which sixty to seventy percent revolted, and by recruiting boys of fifteen to seventeen, sometimes even younger. Side by side with the old squadristi and not a few avowed criminals freshly out of prison, then, there were children.

One day a Partisan group ambushed a Fascist Militia truck on a road in Piedmont. The truck ran into a ditch and the first Militia-man to come out of it was a thirteen-year-old in an over-sized uniform, a boy old before his time who told without emotion of the tortures that he had witnessed and who offered, in exchange for his release, to poison all the officers in his Militia unit. A Fascist newspaper, discussing the age of the young Militia recruits, commented: "It is said that they are all children, but that is not true. Yet what if it were? They know how to obey and, if the need arises, to make others respect the law, to maintain order, and to protect honest citizens."

Besides, the Fascists had few other resources. In 1944 conscription should theoretically have recruited one hundred eighty thousand young men between eighteen and twenty. Only eighty-seven thousand were found, and more than half of these were immediately requisitioned by the Germans; twenty-five thousand were assigned to the Republican National Guard for action against the Partisans; the few thousand left over were put into the army, but what happened to them made Marshal Graziani indignant. "It is sad, and unworthy of us," he wrote, "to see Italian soldiers set to caring for the flowerbeds and kitchen gardens of villas requisitioned by the German commanders, or carrying gasoline tins, washing Germans' cars, and performing other similar tasks." Marshal Graziani's revolt did not go beyond regret. Like the other

Fascist chiefs enlisted with Mussolini in the final adventure of the Social Republic, he had to accept humiliations and irritations.

For to the Germans Italy was only a reserve, and above all a source of labor. Fritz Sauckel was the managing director of what Ambassador Rahn himself called "this modern slave trade." The Germans rounded up not only conscripts but also young men in bars and streets. On June 16, 1944, the Militia sealed off the central area of Genoa and every able-bodied man found in the streets was shipped off to Germany.

But that was not all. In every town and every sector of the economy, the *Militärverwaltung* (military administration) set up an efficient network that regulated production and the entire economy down to the smallest detail. It was a methodical spoliation that was in operation on the territory of the Fascist Republic. On November 19, 1943, Hitler said brutally: "Whether it is we or the English who take their trousers, it comes to the same thing."

Requisitions affected every area from shoes to medicines. From captains to corporals the local commands lived on the country as so many soldieries had done on that soil kneaded by history. They carried off poultry, vegetables, bedclothes: *"Paga Badoglio* [Badoglio will pay]," they laughed.

This was merely the daily behavior, which might be thought of as natural. What was more important was the removal of the gold reserves of the Bank of Italy—ninety-five tons—to Germany and the plans for dismantling the major factories and transferring them to Germany.

Angelo Tarchi, the Fascist Republic's Minister of Corporations, attempted to oppose this dismantling, but how could he succeed when Il Duce himself was unable to obtain the allocation of a few trucks? On September 21, 1944, Mussolini wrote to Ambassador Rahn: "It would be really unpleasant and the consequences would be grave if the lack of a few dozen trucks resulted in famine and hence in revolt. This minor problem has been discussed for ten months without the least action. FIAT turns out fifty trucks a day. If we could have at least three of them, we should soon be in a position to make regular food distributions to the population. And let there be no requisitioning of those few old trucks that it is still possible for us to find."

"FIAT turns out fifty trucks, let us have at least three": nothing could better define the degree of independence granted to Il Duce and his government by the German military authorities.

It would be understandable that, in the humiliating, impotent, verbose inactivity that he had accepted, Mussolini might have called down a few imprecations on the Germans in anyone's pres-

The Social Republic of Salò

ence, as he occasionally used to do with Ciano. But he knew better, for Adolf Hitler's SS was standing watch in the garden to protect him. In his dealings with the Nazis he adopted an attitude of vexed humility: for instance, he wrote to Rahn: "I urgently beseech you to be good enough to devote ten minutes of your valuable time to reading Report No. 7 on the problem of the Partisan bands."

He flattered Kesselring and Hitler; at times he protested; neither course was any more effective than his request for trucks. Indeed, the government of the Fascist Republic was constrained to pay the costs of the German occupation: seven to ten billion *lire* per month. But the Nazis had in reserve a final slap for Mussolini and Fascism. On September 23, 1943, Goebbels wrote in his diary: "According to the thinking of Der Führer, we ought to advance to the borders of Venezia, and Venezia itself should be incorporated into the Reich under an autonomous government."

Venezia! This brought Italian unity into peril. The Germans had already driven the Italian authorities out of the South Tyrol and Venezia Giulia. Even the Fascists were barred from those areas: their carabinieri and policemen had been interned in Germany. The Germans installed two *Gauleiter*, Franz Hofer and Friederich Rainer, old officials who had served the Austro-Hungarian Empire. Trieste, of course, was occupied, and the Germans dynamited its monuments to Italians killed in the First World War. Vittorio Veneto was wiped out and all that Mussolini could get by way of concession was the right to keep a telephone line to Trieste.

For the man who had said to King Vittorio Emanuele III on October 30, 1922: "I bring Your Majesty the Italy of Vittorio Veneto," the man who since 1915 had made himself the champion of nationalism, the apostle of war for the "unredeemed lands," this Duce who had trumpeted his desire to build "Greater Italy," defeat and humiliation were complete.

With these territorial dispositions Hitler and the Germans made clear all the contempt with which they viewed this government of beaten men ready to submit to anything in the hope of saving their power and their lives.

In one domain, however, at least for a few months, the Germans allowed the Fascists to operate freely: the domain of words. For it was essential that this government have some activity, some means of entering into Italian reality aside from its police functions: the Republic of Salò should ostensibly function. All that was asked of it was to *be* Mussolini's government, with ministers, a few military reviews, a few speeches—what difference if there was nothing behind the façade? for a while it could create the illusion. Hence it was in the realm of rhetoric and plans that the essence of the Salò Republic's non-police activity was to take place—activity that must inescapably be described as demagogic.

Thereupon Mussolini played his last card, which, in the light of the German grip on the economy, was risible. This was the card of socialization. The Fascist Republic was officially entitled "Social," and, since the monarchy had deserted it, Mussolini asserted that at last Fascism had returned to its true character, which was republican and social. He spoke of the "return to the sources," sources obviously viewed through the distorting prism of the Mussolinian legend.

There were a few hack writers gathered round Mussolini— Edmondo Cione and Concetto Pettinato, who were journalists; Carlo Silvestri, a former Socialist; Nicola Bombacci, who had the face of a prophet, a former Communist deputy and, like Mussolini, a former teacher in the Romagna. All of them took up the quasi-Socialist vocabulary of Mussolini's early days. They castigated the "Masonic conspiracy" and the "international plutocracy." The press devoted column after column to analyzing the problems of "labor." Finally the Republican Fascist Party held its first congress on November 14, 1943, in Verona.

In the famous medieval city enveloped in the fog that clings to the Adige at that season the delegations of all the party's organizations assembled. Old squadristi of 1920, decorated veterans, scheming slackers, newly recruited young fanatics gathered for the first time since July 25. The meeting was held in Castel Vecchio, an impressive structure on the bank of the Adige opposite the old Scaligero bridge. This was the heart of fourteenth-century Verona, violent, passionate, and cruel. Il Duce did not attend the congress, but he set its tone in a message: "The people once more in arms must go to the baptismal font bearing our Social Republic —in other words, Fascist in the original meaning of our revolution." As in the old days, the audience rose to its feet and shouted *Duce! Duce!* Then Pavolini, the party secretary, began his speech. "Squadrismo was the springtime of our lives," he said, "and a man who was once a squadrista is a squadrista forever." He promised that a Constituent Assembly would be convened, paid tribute to the memory of Ettore Muti, and concluded by leading the congress in the singing of *Giovinezza*.

In reality the state of mind of the participants in the congress did not lend itself to political speculations. Those men were frightened. They felt isolation at their jugulars, and, while some of them had once risked their lives, they were older now and, in spite of German protection, they knew that they might fall under Partisan attacks.

While debate was continuing in the afternoon, a note was handed to Pavolini. Soon, in the silence, the entire audience was on its feet with suspense. In a solemn voice Pavolini announced: "The federal commissar of Ferrara, Comrade Ghisellini, three times winner of the silver medal, three times winner of the bronze medal, has been murdered with six revolver shots. He will be avenged at once."

"To Ferrara! everybody to Ferrara!" the audience howled. Pavolini restored order and then decreed that the Fascists of Ferrara, Padua, and Verona would leave with their squadre to avenge Ghisellini. The squadristi and the Republican National Guard arrived in Ferrara that night. In a short time the main square held seventeen corpses—known anti-Fascists, prisoners, and workers who had been hunted down in the streets—under guard by armed Militiamen who shot on sight.

This bloody reality set the tone better than the speeches in the congress. The "historic assembly of Castel Vecchio," however, required a conclusion other than these seventeen deaths. Pavolini quickly read off eighteen points that represented the party's program: they were adopted in tumult by acclamation. They set forth in detail the provisions for the convocation of the Constituent Assembly and proposed the idea of a "European community," but the major emphasis was in Point No. 9: "The foundation of the Social Republic and its primary object are manual, technical, and intellectual labor in all its manifestations."

Point No. 11 proclaimed: "Everything in the national economy that, by reason of its importance or its function, transcends private interest to become part of the collective interest belongs to the sphere of action that is in the highest sense that of the state." The final sentence of the program was like a trumpet call: "There is only one means of attaining all these social goals: to fight, to labor, and to conquer."

These eighteen points were to become the themes of the whole press: socialization was in sight. On Thursday, November 18, *La Stampa* carried a huge eight-column headline: PARTY PROGRAM LAID DOWN ON EVE OF CONSTITUENT ASSEMBLY: *ABOLITION OF CAPITALIST SYSTEM AND WAR AGAINST WORLD PLUTOCRACIES.*

It goes without saying that the Social Republic never had the chance to convene a Constituent Assembly or to touch the country's economy, which was solidly in German hands. Yet some men did believe in these fantastic phrases: some because they were frightened by them (Farinacci and a few German officers), some, like Angelo Tarchi, because they congratulated themselves on the fantasy that they could be realized. "The old Fascist Party," Tarchi told Ambassador Rahn, "was always making promises that it did not keep. That must not start again. The new socialization law would represent a severe blow to Communist and Bolshevik influences, to which the Italian workers are far more exposed than their German counterparts."

In fact, even while the party congress was under way and the Fascist program was adopting revolutionary trappings, major strikes were taking place in Turin, Milan, and Genoa. Secret agitational committees composed of Socialists and Communists were at work everywhere. In addition, the armed *Gruppi di Azione patriottica* (GAP—Patriotic Action Groups) were protecting the strikers, and thus these movements had a clearly anti-Fascist meaning.

By 1943, after twenty-one years of Fascism and the collapse of July 25, it had become difficult to build a policy on words alone. Acts too were needed.

The *repubblichini* (sham republicans) were able to produce one: a show trial in which hatreds and vengeances would be slaked and that was supposed also to prove that Fascism had changed its character because it did not hesitate to strike at its own: and Il Duce handed over his own son-in-law to the executioner. What better evidence of an incorruptible revolutionary policy? So the Verona trial began on January 8, 1944. The six defendants—Galeazzo Ciano, Marshal Emilio De Bono, Giovanni Marinelli, Carlo Pareschi, Luciano Gottardi, and Tullio Cianetti—and thirteen others being tried *in absentia*—were called on to answer for their votes in the Fascist Grand Council on the night of July 24–25, 1943. In order to explain how Fascism could have collapsed overnight, it was essential to find traitors. They were locked up in the Scalzi prison, an austere former cloister. Arrested at various times, these six men were reunited in the January cold in that ancient structure. Two SS men stood guard at the door of Ciano's cell. "Oh, this stinks of death!" he exclaimed when he saw them. He had been fetched back from Germany, and he stood up to the prospect of death with somewhat bewildered courage.

"In a few days," he wrote in his diary on December 23, 1943, in Cell 27, "a tribunal of puppets will announce a sentence handed down by Mussolini under the influence of that gang of prostitutes and procurers who have poisoned Italian political life for years and led the country to its destruction."

Ciano had the friendly and soon compassionate attentions of a young blonde woman, Frau Hildegard Berger, whose Gestapo name was Felicitas Beetz and who dedicated herself to his welfare and had free access to the former Foreign Minister's cell. She soon disclosed her objective: possession of the "political notebooks" in which from day to day Ciano had reported his conversations with Mussolini, Ribbentrop, and Hitler. The young Foreign Minister, whose susceptibility to beautiful women the Germans knew well, the woman, the other dignitaries in the damp, dark old cloister, all evoked the atmosphere of the Renaissance, in which debauchery and honors broke bread with death.

The trial was held in the same Castel Vecchio in which the party congress had taken place. Above the long table behind which the judges sat, there was a black banner in which the white *fasces* of the lictor was centered. The audience was composed chiefly of Fascist Militiamen, some of whom were armed, who had come to see justice done to the traitors.

"The *coup d'état* of July 25 exposed Italy to the greatest betrayal in the memory of history," the government declared in its proclamations establishing the special court. In the courtroom Frau Beetz and two SS officers followed the proceedings, but there is no evidence that the trial was inspired by the Germans. No doubt it pleased them and they kept their hands off, but there was no occasion for them to interfere. The survivors of Fascism who were ruling the Social Republic needed the blood of a few traitors and the Verona trial was a demagogic maneuver as well as a settlement of accounts. Besides, Mussolini had not lost his passion for vengeance, his pleasure in heroic "Roman" attitudes, which in fact cost him little, for the exercise of power had robbed him of every vestige of friendship, the capacity for pity, humanity, and a sense of proportion.

When the members of the tribunal, in civilian clothes with black shirts, entered the courtroom at 9:15 A.M., Ciano and his fellow-defendants stood at attention and, like everyone else in the room, gave the Fascist salute. After the names of the accused had been read off, Marshal De Bono, the aged quadrumvir linked to Mussolini by twenty-three years of activity, walked to the bar to defend himself. He had not favored the removal of Il Duce. All the defendants were to repeat this statement in virtually the same terms, and for them it undoubtedly represented the truth. "The position of Il Duce was not at issue," Ciano was to declare. Only Marinelli shuffled to the bar in tears. He explained that because of his deafness he had not been able to follow what was being said in the Grand Council and he had voted for Grandi's resolution without knowing what was in it.

At 1:40 P.M., in an inaudible voice, the presiding judge pronounced the sentences: eighteen death sentences, five of which involved the six men present in the dock. Ciano turned to De Bono and pointed to Cianetti: "He is the only one to get out of it; for the rest of us it's all over." He crossed himself. Cianetti was sentenced to thirty years in prison; immediately after the Grand Council's vote he had switched sides and joined Mussolini.

"What did they decide about me?" Marinelli asked: he had heard nothing.

"Death, the same as for us." Marinelli fainted.

Squadristi were on guard outside. There were cries of "Kill them! Kill them!" The white-faced, resigned doomed men had to be kept in Castel Vecchio for more than two hours, until the Fascist sections had left the city.

Mussolini had spent the day alone. When Dolfin brought him the news, he also described the behavior of the defendants. "Marinelli will never make it to the firing squad," Mussolini said tartly, "they will have to carry him." Then he went into explanation and self-defense: "The dilemma that I set before the Grand Council was clear. Voting Grandi's resolution meant bringing about a government crisis and my succession. Grandi, Bottai, and Federzoni knew that. Ciano played this crucial hand with them."

There was no clemency. Pavolini ordered the rebuff of the attempt made by a Militia general, thus sparing Mussolini from having to declare himself in Ciano's case. But Mussolini had already said: "For me Ciano has been dead a long time." Edda, Mussolini's daughter, and Ciano's wife, tried with the help of Frau Beetz to save her husband's life; with the strength of desperation she was ceaselessly busy. She wrote to Der Führer and to Il Duce, offering to buy Ciano's life with documents that were in her possession. To her father she wrote:

Duce,
I have waited until today for you to show me some minimal sentiment of humanity and friendship. Now this is too much. If Galeazzo is not in Switzerland within three days under the conditions that I have established with the Germans, everything that I know, with supporting proofs, will be used without mercy. In the contrary case, if we are left in peace and security (from tuberculosis to automobile accidents), you will never again hear of me.
Edda Ciano

In the middle of the night Mussolini telephoned to General Wolff to have his counsel. The general refused to take any position, but he did order the two-hour withdrawal of the two-man SS guard outside Cell 27, which was Ciano's. It was too late, however, for Mussolini to make a decision. For him it was easier to let events take their course and not to interfere. He waited.

In the Scalzi prison Don Chiot and a Franciscan, Dionizio Zilli, were already busy consoling the prisoners, who had all been put into one cell. At the last moment Ciano had tried to poison himself, but the drug supplied by Frau Beetz was harmless. At five o'clock in the morning of January 11 the prisoners awakened to begin their final wait. Marinelli, who had almost collapsed, moaned feebly. It was a slow, icy winter dawn. The very length of the wait revived hope; all the men had presented petitions for clemency and they hoped that Mussolini would grant them. But, after four hours of uncertainty, the judges, the police, and the Fascist leaders appeared in the cell at nine o'clock: clemency had been refused.

The prisoners were chained together and surrounded by armed Militiamen. So Ciano and De Bono, who had been among the highest officials of the Fascist government, were to die under Fascists' bullets. History had often hovered over the man who had seemed to be fortune's favorite, this Count Ciano caught up in the whirlwind of adulation, strutting through Hitler's Berghof, flaunting himself on the golf course or on the airfields in his rôle of a bomber captain ready to take off for Albania or Greece, this son-in-law of Il Duce, this young man about to die. When violence is the mainspring of a system, who can hope to escape its reach? Not even those who used violence in behalf of that system—Marinelli, secretary of the Fascist Party, De Bono, the quadrumvir, or Ciano, the aviator-minister.

Twenty-five men, all volunteers from the Militia, stood ready on the firing range of the fortress of San Procolo; a few judges, some Fascist leaders, and a number of officers of the Republican National Guard were also present. The doomed men were seated backward on chairs, their backs to the firing squad and their arms bound to the backs of the chairs. Marinelli struggled; "This is murder," he cried. He had to be bound by force, and several Militiamen did the job. The other condemned men were calm and firm, but somewhere in every face there was still a certain terror, a stubborn unbelief. They, the leaders of Fascism, were there to be shot by a Fascist firing squad.

The Militiamen stood fifteen paces away. Those in the first row were kneeling. Ciano and De Bono turned their heads several times, and, just as the command to fire was given, one of the five men on the chairs was heard to cry: *"Viva l'Italia, evviva il Duce!"* The volley cut the cry short in the icy air. Four men fell; one chair still stood upright and undoubtedly its occupant had not been hit. There were still sounds and movements from the four who had fallen. A new volley had to be fired at the prisoner who was still seated and the four who lay on the ground. Then all five were finished off with pistols. The entire scene was recorded on film.

Later that day the radio announced that there would be an important communiqué. After a reference to the death sentences, the announcer added: "The sentences were carried out at 9:20 A.M. The five guilty men have been shot." The words were immediately followed by the rousing Fascist anthem—*Giovinezza, giovinezza, primavera di bellezza.* . . .

When Mussolini heard the broadcast, he burst out: "In all situations the Italians love to act like savages or clowns." Indeed, after this savage and clownish execution by a firing squad that could not even kill five poor devils at fifteen paces with one volley, the government and Il Duce tried to clear themselves and give themselves absolution. On January 12, under a large headline— 18 MEMBERS OF GRAND COUNCIL SENTENCED TO DEATH —*La Stampa* proclaimed: "The axe has fallen. Twenty years of indulgence acknowledged with betrayal and ingratitude is too much. Pardon is a luxury. The doomed men of Verona paid for their criminal destruction of the national edifice arduously erected with the money and the blood of the people. They paid for the division of their country, for bringing war to the heart of Italy."

In short, all the sins of Fascism were laid on the heads of the doomed men of Verona, and Mussolini tried to pay with their blood for his own and the whole system's mistakes. But he was seeking as well to give himself a quiet conscience. He questioned Don Chiot and, when they had talked of Ciano, Mussolini said: "Pray for him and for me." He swore to Ciano's lawyer, his mother, and Edda that he had not been informed of the clemency petitions. "It was the ones who wanted the trial who refused to forward the petitions to me," he said, "because they were afraid I might grant them."

Nevertheless the executions were a desperate effort by him and by Fascism at once to assert their innocence and to make new threats. The January 12 issue of *La Stampa* said also: "*Salus Reipublicae suprema lex*—The safety of the republic is the highest law. The judgment of Verona is proof that the Republic will fight to the finish. Let the warning be understood by those who need it, and let it summon the entire country to return without delay to the clear recognition of its own duties and of the superior rights of the Fatherland."

The warning was as clear as an order: let the citizen bow if he did not wish to undergo Ciano's end. For, if Ciano could be shot, anything was possible now. The executions in Verona were indeed a necessary alibi and justification.

17

Reprieve: The Year 1944

"We intend to defend the Po Valley tooth and nail."—IL DUCE (December 16, 1944, in Milan)

ONE MORNING TEN DAYS AFTER the Verona executions—on January 22—long columns of German trucks loaded with helmeted parachute troops drove rapidly across Rome, preceded by motorcyclists with sub-machine guns strapped to their backs. They were heading for the sea at Anzio, thirty-six miles from Rome, where at two in the morning the Allies had landed by complete surprise. Operation Shingle had succeeded.

When the news became known a few hours later, Italians and above all Romans felt that their liberation was at hand. Anxious activity already filled Palazzo Widekind, the Fascist Party's headquarters, which was protected by machine-gun batteries and armored cars; some of the Fascist leaders left Rome for north Italy. Even in Kesselring's headquarters officers were ordered to be ready to leave within four hours.

But very soon both hope and fear subsided. As it grew dark, the roads and railways round Rome were choked with great military convoys rushing five German infantry divisions from France, north Italy, and the Balkans. The excessive caution of the Allies, who had not exploited the advantage of their surprise, had worked to the benefit of the able Kesselring: the landing had succeeded, but it had done no more than create a beach-head. On February 17 the Wehrmacht launched its first attack along the entire front from Anzio to Nettuno.

This was a new respite for the Fascists. Behind the stabilized fronts they could defend themselves against their enemies: the Partisans.

Partisans had organized everywhere in that mountainous country. The Communist Party's Garibaldi Brigades, whose high command was in Milan, dated from November, 1943; they were soon followed by the GAP and then the *Squadre di Azione patriottica* (SAP—Patriotic Action Squads), and all these groups were broadening their operations and accelerating their attacks. By the end of November almost twenty-eight hierarchs had been killed by the "*gappisti*—the men of the GAP"—who used only side-arms, attacking in the streets and making their escapes on bicycles. Many of them had fought in Spain and with the French Forces of the Interior and other French resistance forces. On December 19 the head of the Milanese Fascist branch, Resegna, was slain; on April 15, 1944, it was the turn of the philosopher, Gentile, in Florence.

To the Fascist press and the Germans these were ordinary murders, criminal acts that had nothing to do with the war. Some Resistants also condemned these methods, for each successful attack was paid for in the lives of hostages. To those—and they were many—who denounced the execution of Gentile, the Partisans of *Giustizia e Libertà* sought to reply with leaflets and articles in the clandestine newspapers. One of these said: "He was an honest man, an educated man. But today the Italian people is fighting for life and death, without hesitation and without pity. This is a struggle without quarter, as exalting and terrible as the unhesitating moral necessity that directs it and the pitiless historic justice with which it is carried out."

In Italy as indeed in the whole of warring Europe the eternal, cruel problem of violence had to be faced. The conflict deepened. Partisan units multiplied: the Socialists' Matteotti organizations, the *Giustizia e Libertà* groups, the independent Catholic and officer-soldier bands. In order to protect their lines of communications the Germans were compelled to resort to vast *rastrellamenti* —dragnet arrests. German armor patrolled the roads that bordered the rivers of the Piedmont Valley and scout planes directed German mortar fire; expert mountain troops stormed the peaks. The Partisans moved from one valley to another, shooting while villages burned and the SS blew up the houses of its own informers with all their occupants and cattle locked inside.

Sometimes the entire population of a village would be rounded up in the square and the priest would be the last to be brought down by the machine guns, falling on the piled-up bodies of his parishioners—old men and babies with all their relatives: such was the fate of the villages of Marzabotto and Sant'Anna, among others. Dozens of hanged men (in one single instance, fifty-three) marked the route of one "accursed battalion" of the SS; crematory ovens were kept busy at the gates of Turin; Jews in hiding in the mountain villages were hunted down, and escaped Allied prisoners were recaptured. The SS units included Russians from the renegade General Vlassov's pro-German army, drifters who killed and looted out of habit and despair.

There were also the Fascists. Every town had its "torture house": Villa Tasso in Rome sheltered Pollastrini after July 25, 1943; or sometimes an ordinary apartment in an ordinary apartment building, where little commandos of torturers operated under a leader's orders and ran their own campaigns independent of all control. The insensate horror attained inhuman abysses: eyelids were torn off, temples were compressed between steel clamps. This was how the *questore* (police chief) Pietro Caruso and his German counterpart, Kappler, maintained order in Rome.

In Milan the SS and the Fascists worked out of the Hotel Regina. In Florence, Carita "invited" his victims to watch the most extreme orgies after they had been tortured. General Kurt Maelzer in Rome was also an adept of debauchery. In that era of death, unbridled violence stripped the torturers of the last vestige of humanity and eroded the morality of many Italians. During a savage interrogation Captain Saeveki of the SS shouted at one Resistant: "You are angry at us—be angry at your fellow-citizens. Every day my desk is piled high with letters informing on patriots."

For the spies were beyond counting. Convinced Fascists or poor co-opted devils, they listened and they gave names. In a train carrying workers to their jobs in Milan one gloomy morning, a loose-lipped woman remarked: "If I were a man, I'd be a Partisan." Someone persuaded her to talk further. Suddenly the train stopped in open country, Fascist Militiamen entered the compartments, and the man who had been pleasantly chatting with the woman denounced her: she was machine-gunned to death beside the track. Elsewhere other spies coursed through the mountains and the valleys on the hunt for the Partisans' hiding-places.

For the Partisans the Fascists had no mercy. They knew that they were facing the enemies whom they had been battling since 1919 from Milan to Turin, from Guadalajara to Barcelona, the enemies whom they thought they had killed in the person of the anonymous *capolega* (peasant-league chief) murdered in Emilia, of Matteotti and the Rosselli brothers, and who were rising again with greater strength and zeal. General Mischi, who had already learned his business by fighting the Partisans in the Balkans, suggested that German planes bomb factories where workers were on strike. "Now," he said, "our lives are beyond any conditions of victory or defeat."

Mussolini belabored Graziani with personal orders to put an end to the "banditry." "Fascism's achievement," he wrote, "should be the Social Republic's march against the *Vendée*.* Since the center of the monarchist-reactionary-Bolshevik *Vendée* is Piedmont, the march should consolidate all its forces in Turin and start with Piedmont. It should fan out from Turin into all the provinces, clean them out thoroughly, and then move at once into Emilia."

With its reference to the *Vendée* this document is one of the best self-caricatures of Mussolini's style of thinking. Stripped of its revolutionary rhetoric, however, it belongs with the order issued by Marshal Kesselring's headquarters: "Action must be undertaken in the most forceful fashion possible against the armed bands of rebels. All persons found responsible should be hanged in the public squares. . . ."

But that was a strenuous task, and the immutable logic of repression led only to further assaults by the Partisans. In the spring of 1944 Committees of National Liberation (CLN) appeared in the majority of the cities; these were soon followed by the national CLN's military organization for north Italy, the Corps of Volunteers for Freedom. Its head was General Raffaele Cadorna, a smiling, slender man and a career officer, appointed because it was supposed that he would inspire confidence in the Allies. On September 20, 1870, his grandfather had conquered Rome, and his father had played a highly important part during the First World War. This nervous, resolute man was indeed a symbol, the culmination of a national military tradition. He had to make his way into north Italy in order to assume his dangerous command.

On August 11, 1944, he parachuted from a Halifax aircraft with a Briton, Major Oliver Churchill. He was hurt, but he had to go into battle at once, because the little group of Partisans waiting for the general was encircled by the Republican National Guard. A few weeks later he acquired two "political" assistants, Ferruccio Parri of the Action Party and Luigi Longo of the Communist Party.

This triumvirate was the true mirror of the Italian Resistance. When the Fascist Militiamen who had surrounded the Turin cathedral on Friday, March 31, 1944, arrested, one by one, the members of the Piedmont Military Resistance Committee, which was to have met in the church, they found that their prisoners

---

* The name given to a mass French counter-revolutionary rising in 1793 because the Vendée was the area of its start and later its stronghold.— Translator.

included one general (Giuseppe Perotti), two lower officers, one Christian Democrat, one Socialist, and one Communist. When the judge pronounced the sentence of death on all of them, General Perotti rose and said firmly: "Officers, attention!" His whole committee rose. *"Viva l'Italia!"* the general said, and *"Viva l'Italia!"* the committee responded.

It was indeed a new Italy that was rising out of the abyss of September 8, 1943. A new *Risorgimento* was inspiring the people of the peninsula, but more profoundly than the resurgence that had led to unity in 1870: now the worker and peasant masses had entered the arena side by side with those officers and intellectuals who had in the past been the figureheads of the first *Risorgimento*.

On March 1, 1944, the workers of Turin and Milan went out on strike again in spite of the Germans and the Fascists. In June the strike was resumed at FIAT in order to prevent the disassembly of the machinery and its shipment to Germany. The industrialists often supported such activities, even if in other respects they continued doing business with the occupation authorities.

This national unity that was daily increasing the isolation of the *repubblichini* had had a prelude in the south. When Palmiro Togliatti, the Communist leader, returned from the Soviet Union, he had occasioned considerable surprise by agreeing to join a Badoglio government, and this brought in the other anti-Fascist parties behind him. As for the King, in order to preserve the principle of monarchy he decided to make way, after the liberation of Rome, for his son, Umberto, who would act as Lieutenant General of the Realm: thus the question of choosing national institutions was postponed until there should be peace.

But at the moment there was war. Colonel Giuseppe Cordero Lanza di Montezemolo, a monarchist of great courage, was working in occupied Rome under the alias of Giacomo Cataratto-Martini, engineer, with Bruno Buozzi, the Socialist, and Giorgio Amendola, the Communist son of the former liberal leader murdered by the Fascists. Certainly none of them had surmounted all his mental reservations, but the significance of this joint undertaking was greater than the differences among them. At the moment there was war, and war is cruel.

Spring was splendid in Rome in March of 1944. On March 12 Pope Pius XII made a speech, and the crowd massed in St. Peter's Square cried *Pace Pacelli*. The Militia arrested a few Partisans, who mingled with the pilgrims to distribute leaflets and shout: "The Germans are at the gates!" The sky was cloudless; every shrub, every blade of grass in the gardens of Villa Borghese was vibrant and gay with life.

On March 23 a street-cleaner was doing his work in via Rasella. Round a corner came a detachment of the *Südtiroler Ordnungsdienst*, a voluntary militia from the South Tyrol. The street-cleaner lighted a wick in his wheeled barrel and ran. He was Bentivegna, a *gappista*; other *gappisti* got the local children out of the way. A minute later the neighborhood was rocked by an explosion, and fifty soldiers lay in the street. The *gappisti* fired on the remainder of the column and then fled.

Rome was wrapped in silence again. It was three-twenty-six in the afternoon. Already the light was softer above the roofs and the golden ochre domes. Soon the SS swept through every house in via Rasella, via dal Traforo, and via delle Quattro Fontane. The residents were manhandled and carried off. The story of the attack began to spread through the city. General Maelzer, the commander of the Rome military district, Kappler, and Marshal Kesselring telephoned the headquarters of Der Führer. Hitler requested that the whole quarter and all its inhabitants be blown up, but finally it was decided to fall back on the hostage method. Caruso, the *questore*, said that he was already holding a number of political prisoners under death sentences: it was decided to execute them in the ratio of ten hostages for every German killed. In practice the Germans merely selected political prisoners and Jews without inquiring whether they had been tried. They were hastily loaded on to trucks, with the result that a mistake was made: instead of three hundred thirty hostages (thirty-three Germans had been killed), there were three hundred thirty-five. These five extra men represented despotism at its depth.

The trucks headed for via Ardeatina, where tunnels had been cut into the quarries. One at a time, the three hundred thirty-five hostages—Colonel Montezemolo, various generals, Jews, workers, journalists, film directors—were dispatched with a bullet in the back of the neck. As the work progressed, the later victims were compelled to climb on top of the bodies of the others in order to reach their appointed places and wait for the shots that would set them free. The butchery lasted from the evening of March 24 until nine o'clock the next morning. Then the tunnels were mined, and there was the sound of heavy explosions, which brought great masses of rock down to bury the bodies. Later in the morning the Partisans' attack and the reprisal action were officially announced by the German command. Even the Fascist newspapers said nothing: three hundred thirty-five persons were almost the population of a whole village.

Rome was draped in a heavy cloak of horror and terror. The city did not rise. Perhaps that was what the Germans wanted: the capital just behind the battle line should submit to occupation without rebelling; undoubtedly too they sought to create conflict over the methods of underground resistance between Badoglio's military command and the Communist *gappisti* by showing the population of the Holy City the high price of German blood. In any case, the tragedy of the Ardeatine Tunnels shocked all Italy. It demonstrated the essence of the conflict that was raging in that miserable country. Even in Rome, even in spring, war is cruel.

And the war went on, feeding indeed on its own duration, seeming to repeat the same events as if the tragedy were never to end and Mussolini and Hitler, through reprieve after reprieve, would be able to govern forever. On April 22 those two men met in the same castle in Klessheim where Ciano had once dined with Ribbentrop. Nervous and looking old, Hitler munched endlessly on pills provided by Dr. Morell. Mussolini set forth his grievances and for once Der Führer allowed him to talk without interruption. By now Mussolini's opinions and counsels were so unimportant! Marshal Graziani presented a list of the Italian Republican army's needs and dwelled on the imperative necessity of its reconstruction. Hitler's only reply was to remind the Italians of the collapse of Fascism on July 25, 1943.

Humiliated, Mussolini had to justify himself once more. "The Fascist Party's strength," he said, "was all with the armies at that time. At home we had nothing but women, children, and old men." Then, even while he spoke, Mussolini took leave of reality again, falling back on his dreams of conquest, Egypt, Africa, everything that had been lost because of the generals and the King. But this would not happen again, he promised. He was delighted that the interned Italians would remain in Germany; he was ready "to call up the class of 1914 for *Gauleiter* Sauckel and the classes of 1916 and 1917 for Marshal Goering—twenty classes, if necessary, to fill out the labor battalions."

Spoken to make it appear that he was still in control of Italy, these words meant that men would be forcibly loaded on to trucks from the streets of Genoa and Rome and from the villages of the Po Valley. These words included thousands of men who had fled to the mountains in order to escape deportation to Germany and were to supply the great body of the Partisan movement's troops. In the summer of 1944 more than 100,000 men were in the Alps and the Apennines. But these men driven into battle by necessity matured quickly; they became political and from the old anti-Fascists they learned to know what they had not known: the other side of the Fascist Era.

High in the Alps, Nuto Revelli, a former member of Fascist

organizations and once an officer on the Russian front, listened as one Livio set forth his lucid political thinking. "When he talks to me of Rosselli in Spain, of militant anti-Fascism," Revelli wrote, "he transports me into a world of which I knew nothing, or a world that I knew badly. But the world of my Fascism, of my war in Russia, was in large part unknown to Livio."

This was how an Italy of good faith was reconstructed through men and the Resistance. Carlo Levi, a former *confinato* (political prisoner exiled within Italy), wrote:

> We lived together
> And together we became men.
> In a world divided
> Our hearts were united.
>
> We learned to know one another,
> A new people . . .
> Was born with new names.
> This was the Resistance.

Round their campfires at night in the upper valleys, while some of their fellows stood guard near the *baite* (mountain huts), they sang in spontaneous harmony, songs in which these former Alpini, these mountaineers, and these woodsmen blended melancholy with violence:

> A black flag floats above the mountain,
> A Partisan's gone to his death in the war,
> Another Italian lies under the ground,
> Beside an Alpino killed on the Don.
> Germans and Fascists, get out of Italy!
> For mercy is dead, mercy is dead.

This Resistance, whose men called on the memories of the soldiers of Fascism killed on the Don as well as the patriots slain in the mountains, was to draw new vigor from the Allies' offensive of the spring of 1944.

The battle of Rome began on May 11. Monte Cassino was taken a week later. On May 23 the United States Fifth Army made its junction with the troops landed at Anzio; General (later Marshal) Alphonse Juin's French Expeditionary Corps broke through on the Garigliano. On June 2 the Allies were only a dozen miles from Rome. Two days later General Maelzer was drunk in the German headquarters and long lines of Fascists' trucks were heading north. Electricity had been cut off. Fascist policemen were busy removing their insignia and replacing them with the *stelletta* (little star) of the King's army.

Rome was quiet. There was no insurrection. The intricate schemes and counter-schemes, the rivalries between the CLN and followers of Badoglio, the crushing tragedy of the Ardeatine Tunnels, Vatican diplomats' justified preoccupation with preventing death and destruction in the Eternal City . . . all these factors had averted any street fighting against the retreating Germans. Mussolini demanded a fight to the finish, but Kesselring's troops were withdrawing, and who would fight after that?

At the same time, without any interference, the SS was able to evacuate all its captives from Villa Tasso and machine-gun them in the suburbs, near La Storta. One of them was Bruno Buozzi, the old Socialist and syndicalist leader, who had survived twenty years of the Fascist Era.

Rome was liberated on June 4. The next day Juin could telegraph to General de Gaulle: "Population delirious acclaims French especially." On June 17 the French colors were raised at Villa Incisa, where the armistice had been signed in June, 1940.

Once again Fascism's final hour seemed to have struck. The news of the June 6 landing in Normandy confirmed every hope. Four days later Bonomi formed a government with the six leaders of the parties in the CLN; it included Benedetto Croce, Alcide De Gasperi, Giuseppe Saragat, and Palmiro Togliatti. Vittorio Emanuele III made way for Umberto, Lieutenant General of the Realm. For Italy the end of the nightmare seemed near. There were strikes in Turin and Milan; Partisan units stepped up their attacks. Mussolini issued a proclamation to the nation:

> Italians! The Anglo-American invaders, to whom the infamous treason of the monarchy opened the gates of the Fatherland in Sicily and at Salerno, have entered Rome.
> Workers and peasants, to your posts.
> The Republic is endangered by plutocracy and its mercenaries of every race. Defend it.
> Long live Italy!
> Long live the Italian Social Republic!
>
> Benito Mussolini

On June 21 the party was militarized and mobile Black Brigades were created. Their purpose was obvious: to smash the Partisans at all costs. Mussolini wrote: "I am sure that words will be succeeded by deeds. We must free ourselves of this loathsome evil with fire and sword."

But the Allies continued to advance. An Italian Liberation

Corps went into action in their ranks, and the Partisan movement continued to grow. Whole valleys were liberated and the Partisans set up their own border posts with full inspection of travelers' documents. After twenty-two years of Fascist rule there were free elections in villages.

The position of Fascism was grave.

On July 15 Mussolini left Gargnano for Germany, accompanied by his son, Vittorio, and Graziani. They traveled in a special train, but Germany had long since ceased to be a sanctuary beyond the reach of Allied planes. The train stopped in open country: everyone had to leave the cars and crouch in ditches to wait for the thick formations of Flying Fortresses to pass overhead on their way to their targets. The cities through which the train traveled were half destroyed, shattered by explosions. It was a long journey. Il Duce insisted that he must visit the four Italian divisions under training in Germany—the Monte Rosa, the Italia, the San Marco, and the Littorio.

He was greeted with enthusiasm everywhere. Standing before the troops, his cap settled firmly on his shaved skull, he gave them optimistic predictions. "There is only one road," he cried: "the road of battle and honor." But his voice was weaker, his face was older, and Vittorio and Graziani showed strain. The Allies' advance was accelerating.

Mussolini went on with his journey to East Prussia, where he was to meet Der Führer at Hitler's headquarters. The train was supposed to go to Goerlitz, the code name for the little station; but there was a long stop on a siding, after which the journey was resumed at reduced speed. The passengers had been given strict orders: all windows were to be closed and blacked out. The Germans accompanying Mussolini seemed to be terrified. Der Führer was waiting at Goerlitz, his arm throbbing with a nervous tremor; Ribbentrop, Himmler, and Bormann stood behind him. The platforms and the tracks were filled with SS. It was four o'clock in the afternoon of July 20, 1944.

Hitler stepped forward. "Duce," he said, "a short time ago I was the target of a bomb." It was actually about 12:40 P.M. when Lieutenant Colonel Klaus Graf von Stauffenberg's bomb exploded, to no avail.

Once again the two dictators were together at a critical point in their history; their lives were inextricably intertwined. Hitler took Mussolini to the room where the explosion had occurred. The doors, the roof, the girders, and the rubble on the floor impressed Mussolini; the survival of Der Führer seemed a miracle.

Reprieve: The Year 1944

"What happened today is an omen of destiny," Hitler said. "The great cause that I serve will triumph."

In the same tone Il Duce replied: "After this miracle it is impossible that our cause should know defeat."

Then Mussolini attended a meeting of the German leaders. The tension was still high. Il Duce was stupefied at the spectacle of the wild beasts that howled at one another in this headquarters of Der Führer that was in fact called *Wolfschanze*—the Wolf's Lair. Ribbentrop and Goering insulted each other. Grand Admiral Karl Doenitz accused the air force and the army of incompetence. Long silent, Hitler lost his temper at last, screaming and raging against the plotters: "I will have their wives and children thrown into concentration camps."

Thus for the first time, without masks and in the verity of fear and hatred, Mussolini and the Italian delegation really saw the group of men to whom they had bound their destinies and delivered Italy. But then Hitler spoke of secret weapons that would radically alter the military position; he gave Il Duce the concession of returning two divisions that had completed their training to Italy. Then he accompanied Mussolini to the train. "I know that I can count on you," Hitler said, taking his arm, "and I beg you to believe me when I say that I consider you my best friend and perhaps my only friend in the world." When Mussolini had entered the train, Hitler turned to Ambassador Rahn. "Be very careful," he said in a low voice. Did he fear a turnabout by Mussolini or an attack against Il Duce? Either hypothesis was plausible.

The train left the station at about seven in the evening, and again it had to be blacked out. The atmosphere was heavy in the badly lighted carriages. Mussolini's sole consolation was that now he could speak of the betrayal of Naziism by German officers, similar to the betrayal of Fascism by Italian generals. As soon as he had arrived at Gargnano, he telephoned to Claretta Petacci and told her with much satisfaction: "Der Führer has his traitors too!"

At a time when Siena, Arezzo, Leghorn, and Pisa were falling into the Allies' hands, however, that was a rather fruitless discovery. The battle of Florence began in August, and the Allies, the Germans, and the Fascists found a new Italy, resolute in battle and a presage of the north with its large Partisan formations and its industrial cities ready to rise in revolt.

For a month Florence calmly battled the Germans: the bridges over the Arno were blown up, drinking water and food were scarce, but the Partisans' military and political organization waged the battle, maintained order, and assured the distribution of food supplies. The city was liberated on August 11 and the CLN named a Socialist mayor whom the Allies had no choice but to accept.

The announcement of the Allies' landing in Provence on August 15 inflamed all Italy; then the front was brutally stabilized once more on the Gothic Line. Political imperatives (the Russians had demanded the opening of a new front in southern France) and strategic considerations (in the multiplicity of theaters of operations, Italy was a secondary sector; besides, the Allies' command in Italy was cautious to the extreme) bogged down the Allies.

General Juin did not sweeten his words. "It is a rare thing in history," he said, "to see the leaders of a war coldbloodedly decide that a victory will not be exploited and deliberately allow two enemy armies to get away and be reconstituted. History will be the judge."

The Germans dug in on the Gothic Line, backed up by the Apennines. From September 10 on, the Allies' assaults were shattered by this line of resistance. Behind the front held by Kesselring's troops, the *rastrellamenti* against the Partisans, many of whom had come out into the open in the euphoria of the victorious summer, were resumed, and always without mercy. Mussolini and the Social Republic had been granted a new and unexpected reprieve.

Mussolini and Pavolini decided to prepare a "Republican redoubt" in the Alps. The main thing was to hold out until the Allies destroyed one another, and this was bound to occur. The British and the Partisans had already come to blows in Greece, and anything was possible because the Gothic Line was holding and another winter was beginning—a new winter that would settle on northern Italy like despair after a mirage.

As cold weather settled over all the wooded areas and the heights, as German units moved along the valley roads, as the Fascists burned down villages, on November 13 General Sir Harold Alexander issued a proclamation to the Italian Partisans. First pointing out that they must not expect an Allied offensive during the winter nor even the parachuting of weapons, the British general issued two orders, among others: (1) to cease all operations organized on a large scale; and (2) to await new instructions. The order of the day was to remain on the defensive.

This proclamation was virtually tantamount to an order of demobilization for the Partisans. The instructions might be justified on the purely military level; nonetheless they intensified the crisis of the Partisan movement, already severely damaged by the German and Fascist *rastrellamenti*. Besides, how could they demobilize when thousands of men had joined their armed bands and were being hunted and threatened with summary execution? At the same time, how were these men to be clothed and fed through the winter without the Allies' aid?

There was no choice for the Committee of Liberation of Northern Italy but to disregard Alexander's proclamation. All the parties represented in the CLN issued their own appeal: "Italians! Let us mobilize the conscious will of the people against a waiting policy."

The military command of the Corps of Volunteers for Freedom replied to Alexander in sober terms that, over and above military imperatives, placed the emphasis on the psychological value of the insurrection: "For the Italian people and for every combatant, the Partisans' struggle has not been a whim or a luxury that can be abandoned whenever one likes. It has been a necessity."

Time and the Italians' tenacity were to make it possible to overcome the crisis. On December 7 General Sir Henry Maitland Wilson signed an agreement with representatives of the CLN in which he recognized the Resistance on condition that, when liberation was a fact, the military command would be turned over to the Allied military authorities. On December 26 Bonomi's government also recognized the CLN's authority in north Italy and made it the official representative of the Rome government in the north.

A rupture had been averted, but these weeks had weighed heavily on the lives of the mountain fighters in constant prey to winter and attacks. These weeks had also restored Fascism's confidence. On December 16 Mussolini spoke in Milan. Cheered as in his years of glory, he orated at length to an enthusiastic audience. "Comrades, dear comrades of Milan!" he began. "England is already beaten, for the Russian armies are on the Vistula and the Danube." He spoke of the Greek Partisans' struggle—against the British—the Sicilian separatism fostered by the Allies, the age of labor, the great Japanese victories, and Germany's new weapons.

> Comrades, the Fascist idea cannot be destroyed! Our faith in victory is absolute. Millions of Italians from 1922 to 1939 have lived what can be called the epic of the Fatherland. These Italians still exist and still believe, and they are ready to close ranks to resume their march and reconquer what has been lost!

The audience was on its feet and the cries of *Duce! Duce! Duce!* resounded.

Outside it was still the winter of 1944. France had been liberated, but from Venice to Genoa, from Bologna to Milan and Turin, Italy was still living under Fascism. In these large cities there were free distributions of pamphlets, whose covers, in white letters against a background of flames, bore what seemed to be a slogan: "Rebellion against the Germans!" Abundantly illustrated with photographs, the pamphlets described how the Germans had crushed the Warsaw revolt of August, 1944. The streets were heaped with corpses and tens of thousands of residents were shipped to the camps. "This," the text concluded, "is the tragedy of a people that had no lack of courage but that trusted Moscow, London, and Washington."

It was a well-prepared document and its insidious propaganda was a truthful reflection of that winter of 1944–45 when it seemed that Fascism would never have to die.

On December 16, while Mussolini was delivering his last speech in Milan, Field Marshal Gerd von Rundstedt launched his armor into the Ardennes beneath a somber sky, and this last attack seemed to be succeeding.

Yet Paris and Brussels were already forgetting the occupation. In Rome the GI's and the Tommies strolled along the Corso, and the cafés of via Veneto were never empty.

But Mussolini was still in Gargnano. How in that winter could he not have hoped that he would win another reprieve, how could he not have believed in some new miracle?

18

The End of Fascism and
the Death of Mussolini
(January—April 29, 1945)

"It would indeed be stupid of me to ask to be let alone after my death. Over the graves of the leaders of those great transformations that are called revolutions there is no peace."—MUSSOLINI: *Vita di Arnaldo* (*Life of Arnaldo*), 1932

GRIPPED IN AN ICY FOG, Milan entered a new year of war on January 1, 1945. There was little traffic: now and then a police car or a Wehrmacht vehicle, its headlights painted blue, slid almost noiselessly through the gloom of a city beset by shortages, blackout, anxiety, and bitterness.

Film theaters started their last showings about seven in the evening so that they would be over before the curfew. All of them were filled, for life went on and it was cold in everyone's home, and besides it was New Year's Day. Suddenly there was turmoil, at exactly the same moment, outside the theaters in many sections from Porta Ticinese to via Vitruvio. Armed, masked Partisans leaped to the stages of the theaters as the audiences wondered what was happening; other Partisans posted themselves on guard in the aisles, and speakers called on everyone to join the Resistance.

A few days later the same scene was repeated in the Goldoni Theater in Venice, which was playing Pirandello's *To Clothe the Naked*. Each time Germans and the Italian police officers sat motionless in their seats, paralyzed by the muzzles of sub-machine guns. In spite of everything, hope had changed sides.

On February 28, in Gargnano, Mussolini decided to mark the seventh anniversary of d'Annunzio's death. He went to the Vittoriale and, before a crowd of armed Militiamen, he paid tribute to the poet in a failing voice; it seemed to many that Mussolini was already telling of his own legend. *"Comandante,"* he orated, "you are not dead and you shall not die as long as there is set into the heart of the Mediterranean a peninsula that is called Italy, as long as there is a city to which we will return and that is called Rome."

Everyone who visited Mussolini in these early days of 1945 found him thin, pale, old, in the grip of an aching, anxious melancholy. Perhaps toward the end of February he had made a final journey to Germany and met Hitler for the last time; there is still debate on the matter. Supposedly, the two dictators toured secret laboratories in Bavaria and for a few days Mussolini seemed to have got back his courage. "I saw things that will astonish the world and change the face of history in a few days," he was reported to have said. And, when the Militiamen at a road-block along Lake Garda saluted him, he barked: "Hold fast, boys, we've won the war already!"

But this excitement soon subsided, leaving him even more helpless in the face of reality. Partisan attacks were extending now even to the shores of the lake. The Foreign Ministry's villa was surrounded, its occupants were disarmed and some of its files were carried off. Officers of the Japanese military mission were abducted. Even if it was proceeding slowly, this was unalterably the death agony.

Mussolini was aware of it, even if he clung in his heart to the irrational, unvoiced hope that at the last minute, as so often before, he would find a way out. He vacillated between desperation and attempts by any action whatsoever to shatter the reality against which there was no defense. More often, however, it was discouragement that had the upper hand. He unburdened himself to a young woman writer who went to interview him: "I am finished, my star has set, I am waiting for the end of the tragedy. I went wrong and I will pay with my wretched life if that can be a payment."

But he was not a man to accept punishment, to be willing to give his life. He clung to his skin in very common, very human fashion, because on most occasions in his political life he had made decisions on the basis not of principle but of personal ambition, because he was neither a mystic nor a madman and he was incapable of anticipating and preparing his death so that it would be a success. So he clung to life, to all those fleeting ideas made up of recollections, of hopes wrongly encouraged by advisers who themselves were the victims of their own chimeras. General Wolff of the SS was systematically arranging for the surrender of the German forces in Italy, dealing with the Allies' secret services in Switzerland and particularly with Allen Dulles. Wolff's colleague in these efforts was Ildefonso Cardinal Schuster, Archbishop of Milan, and as proof of his good faith he procured the liberation of the CLN's chief for northern Italy, Ferruccio Parri. In his own residence in Milan the SS general even installed an Allied radio transmitter in order to facilitate communication with the American secret service. It was true, of course, that the troops under Wolff's command represented a medium of exchange. As for Mussolini, he no longer had anything to offer; he could go only from one solution to the next.

With Pavolini he went back to the project of an "Alpine redoubt" at Valtellina: three thousand Black Shirts would defend their Duce to the death. But the area was already infested with Partisans and the *rastrellamenti* were ineffectual.

The German general staff estimated the number of Partisans in uniform at this time at two hundred thousand, for parachute drops had notably increased. Scarves knotted over battle-dress identified the formations: green or red for the *Garibaldini* or the *Giellisti* (the men of GL—*Giustizia e Libertà*), blue for the independent units. The Partisans had arrived by now at a genuine home-army organization. Ranks were officially assigned and police, supply, and even health services were regularly maintained. Home guards controlled the liberated areas; other groups were specifically assigned to prevent the destruction of factories or other installations by the Germans. These Partisan units fought more and more in the open, and soon the Wehrmacht soldiers had a song about them:

> Here where Il Duce reigns without peace,
> Here where the Partisans give us no rest,
> Here where at night every corner is death,
> Here where the trains are blown sky-high,
> In Italy—
> To hell with this damned country.
> Führer, do not leave us here,
> Take us back to our own land,
> Back to our own Reich.

This state of affairs, obviously, was damaging to the prospects for an Alpine redoubt. Besides, as his whole history showed, Mussolini was not a man to make a frontal resistance. So he listened to Silvestri, the renegade Socialist, who urged him to accelerate his "socialization" in order to win over the masses, but also, undoubtedly, to hold a club over the Allies. How could the Anglo-Americans not be apprehensive over the birth of a Socialist republic in northern Italy? Perhaps the hope of aborting it would induce them to treat with Il Duce.

On January 19, 1945, Mussolini created a Ministry of Labor. In February the first socialization measures covering Montecatini, FIAT, and the Lombardy Steel Mills were decreed. The Swiss, who had heavy investments in northern Italy, were worried, but the companies' shares did not drop on the Swiss exchanges: these realistic businessmen had already discounted Mussolini's fall. Nonetheless he pushed ahead with his efforts. He wanted to leave behind him, he said, "the explosive myth of Fascist Socialism." In actuality, as so often before, he was desperately looking for a way to escape, and ideology had nothing to do with his plans.

"What cards can still be played?" he asked General Wolff. Completely absorbed in Operation Sunrise—the surrender to the Allies —the SS officer, who had never told Il Duce even of his talks with Dulles, replied: "Establish socialization and bargain with Western capitalism." For that—on the assumption that bargaining would have been possible—there must be at least some concrete effort at socialization. But all that the Republic of Salò could do was to issue decrees.

When the workers at FIAT were summoned to elect internal committees for the socialized factories, only two hundred seventy-four of the 29,229 factory and office employes voted—less than one percent of the payroll. The defeat was so glaring that Farinacci, the old Verona squadrista who had never stopped advocating Fascist extremism and harsh methods, declared that "the masses have betrayed their cause and the Fatherland's by not giving the Fascist government all the support that it needed."

Now a stand had to be made quickly, very quickly.

At dawn on March 7 the Rhine was crossed by way of the undamaged bridge of Remagen and the Russians were within sixty miles of Berlin. On that day Mussolini reviewed four hundred officers of the Republican National Guard. He made a brief speech, which the newspapers described as "illuminated words" and "instructions of steel."

"We have pledged," Mussolini shouted, "to defend the Po Valley town by town, house by house. This is our sacred duty. The legionaries must be prepared for this defense." At the top of his voice he added: "The Italians who are not afraid to risk their skins are many, more than anyone thinks."

In actuality Mussolini was afraid, afraid "for his skin." He had told his officers: "The gun is a big mouth whose voice everyone understands"—Mussolini above all.

In spite of executions the Partisans' open warfare was increasing. There were reports of Allied troop movements on the Apennine front that foreshadowed an early offensive; artillery preparation all along the Gothic Line was intensifying and aerial reconnaissance was increasing. In Germany Hitler had just issued orders for the destruction of all industrial installations; then, entrenched in his Berlin bunker, Der Führer prepared himself for the final act of his life that would submerge the Third Reich in the twilight of the gods.

Mussolini was frightened. On March 13, six days after his bold words to the officers, his son, Vittorio, left for Milan, where he was to confer with Cardinal Schuster, who in the happier days of the Fascist triumphs had likened Mussolini to the Roman emperors. The thin, mystic-looking cardinal, whose huge forehead almost obliterated the lower part of his angular face, received a document from Vittorio; it was entitled *Proposals of the Chief of State for Negotiations.*

Beginning with a statement that "the armed forces of the Italian Social Republic" were "aware that anti-Fascist hatred left them no other choice than battle to the last man and the last bullet," Mussolini proposed negotiation. But the various points envisaged by Il Duce betrayed the apprehension of the Fascist leaders as to the fate that Italians planned for them. No carabinieri, no Badoglio troops, and above all, no Partisans were to enter the Po Valley. Only the Allies were acceptable. Mussolini tried to win over the Allies' command by writing: "Any undisciplined and extremist action on the part of irregular formations or any action in the streets (provoked by Partisan and Communist bands—strike movements, rallies, etc.) will be suppressed by the Republican armed forces and the Allies' forces. The clergy will devote itself to furthering universal pacification."

This was nothing less than an alliance between the Fascist troops and the Allies' soldiers against "the subversives and the extremists." In 1945, as earlier in 1919, 1922, and 1924, the secret of Mussolini's policy was the bugaboo of Bolshevism and revolution. Mussolini stated that this proposal was intended to show that "love of Italy was above all party interest." Actually one sentence unmasked the intentions of Il Duce: "We should like to know what dispositions are contemplated for the members of the government and those who have held positions of command in the Italian Social Republic (arrest, concentration camp, exile?)."

He did not even think of death; he seemed unable to conceive that an Allied tribunal might regard him as one of the men responsible for the war and its atrocities. Of course he had recognized that the Italians would have no mercy, but he did not believe that the Allies genuinely contemplated the destruction of Fascism and the doom of its leader.

On April 13, after Roosevelt's death, Mussolini, like Hitler, hoped again: he knew Churchill, who had once supported Fascism and whose fear of Communism should lead him to end the war by diplomatic means. He did not understand that the conflict between the Western democracies and Communism was a thing of the past and of the future, that what was controlling in 1945 was still (even if it was charged with mental reservations) the struggle against Naziism and Fascism.

Operation Grapeshot, the Allies' final offensive in the Apennines, was initiated on April 9. In most of the cities of Italy the economy was paralyzed by innumerable strikes. On April 10 the Italian Communist Party issued "insurrectional directive No. 16" and the CLN for North Italy set up an insurrectional committee.

On April 13, 16, 17, and 19 the CLN, in which all parties were represented, issued decrees, a call for a railway strike, and directives dealing with "national insurrection." It asserted that "places of work constitute the centers of mobilization and the fortresses of the national insurrection."

In Germany the Wehrmacht was coming apart; on April 11 the United State Ninth Army reached the Elbe. Two days later Vienna was occupied. On April 16 Nürnberg, the city of pomp and torchlight parades, fell into American hands. It was the end.

On that day Mussolini called the Cabinet of the Italian Social Republic to meet in Gargnano in the penultimate session that it was to hold. Mussolini announced that he intended to go to Milan. There the bulk of the Fascist forces was still concentrated; in addition, from Milan it would be possible to organize a retreat toward Valtellina or Switzerland. "In any event," Mussolini told Marshal Graziani, "whatever the place, Fascism must die heroically."

But again he was hoping to survive: Mussolini had complete faith in Schuster, the cardinal-archbishop of Milan, and, since the city was also the seat of the CLN, some last-minute negotiation might be possible. All these reasons impelled Mussolini toward the capital of Lombardy, which had been the birthplace of the first Fascism: the San Sepolcro meeting of March 23, 1919, twenty-six years earlier.

Five heavily loaded cars set out from Gargnano, followed by a detachment of SS. In Milan Mussolini established himself in the prefecture in via Monforte. The atmosphere was that of the end of a reign, of the eve of disaster.

Armed men came and went; crippled veterans demanded to see Il Duce. The SS stood guard outside his office, where he sat soliloquizing, arguing, skipping from one project to another. Pavolini was insistent on the necessity of withdrawing to Valtellina and fighting to the end. Motorcycles sputtered in the courtyard of the prefecture; Militiamen sat watchfully at their machine guns; elsewhere booted men lay on the ground, their rifles beside them; now and then a naval officer of the Tenth Squadron appeared; members of Pavolini's Black Brigades dotted the courtyard. Ugo Bassi, the prefect; Graziani and General Diamanti, the military commander, one after another, presented varying counsels to Il Duce. He was thinking of turning the prefecture into the "Monforte strong point," an impregnable fortress that would be the last redoubt of Fascism; this, he said, would be a highly symbolic act in the city of the *Covo* and *il Popolo d'Italia*.

But Mussolini was not a fighter. He was still the demagogic politician who, as in a dream, had allowed himself to be fitted with the boots of a *conquistador*. Then he proposed a great mass in the Duomo for all the war dead, a mass of reconciliation that would be crowned by a solemn address, a last appeal to Italy.

Already in the suburbs there was firing—this was the hour of arms that he had so ardently extolled, the hour of battle, of the final torment, of violence. War was pounding on his door and he was politicking, because he was still a man afraid to die and he had never fought except when he was sure of winning.

The days were gone when Fascism meant besieging a' newspaper or a peasant's house, or raiding a village on Good Friday. The wheel had turned. It was time now to settle the accounts. But Mussolini was still trying to squirm out. He offered power to the Socialist Party and at the same time he was trafficking with the Christian Democrats. He moved right, he moved left, throwing down his cards in a rising inner panic even if his face seemed unmoved. Only his pallor and the bewildered eyes of a hunted man who feels the net tightening slowly round him betrayed his anguish.

The Germans did not even keep him informed of their last efforts at mediation: every man for himself. At the end of a dinner in Gargnano, without a word, Ambassador Rahn handed Marshal Graziani a pistol. This was the Nazis' tacit counsel to the Fascists.

For the situation was indeed desperate. On April 21 the Allies entered Bologna, which was already in arms; three days later they were in La Spezia. The night before, Genoa had taken up arms. In Milan the railway workers had been on strike since April 18.

In the evening of April 24 a Partisan brigade attacked a Fascist garrison in the suburbs. By dawn of the next day the factories in the outskirts were transformed into fortified camps, and little by little the insurrection spread to the center of the city. In most instances the members of the Republican National Guard surrendered without resistance.

On that April 25, too, the Allies crossed the Po and French troops reached the Italian border after bitter fighting in the heights of the Authion.

At eight-thirty that morning in Milan the CLN for North Italy held its last clandestine session in the Salesian seminary. It was a decisive meeting, and the representatives of the various parties were extremely sober. By decree, the CLN, recognized since December, 1944, by the Allies and the Rome government as the official government of northern Italy, assumed all civil and military powers "in the name of the Italian people."

A state of emergency was proclaimed. Councils of War and People's Courts of Assizes were established. Every member of the CLN knew that, when he approved the publication of Article V of the decree on the administration of justice, he was sealing the fate of Mussolini and the hierarchs. Article V stated: "The members of the Fascist government and the hierarchs of Fascism, guilty of having contributed to the suppression of constitutional guaranties, destroyed public liberties, created the Fascist system, and compromised and betrayed the destiny of the Nation, and guilty of having led it to the present catastrophe, shall be punished with the penalty of death or, in less serious cases, forced labor."

It was further provided that all Fascists of the Salò Republic captured with weapons in hand or attempting to resist would be liable to the penalty of death and the sentence could be carried out forthwith.

But, though it had thus been legally determined that Mussolini must die, at 10:30 on that same morning of April 25 he agreed to a proposal by Gian Riccardo Cella, the industrialist: this involved a meeting in the archbishopric with delegates of the CLN to discuss possible conditions of surrender. The Resistance also agreed to the proposed meeting, and chose as its delegates General Cadorna, Achille Marazza, a Christian Democrat, and Riccardo Lombardi of the Action Party. They were under instructions to accept only unconditional surrender by Mussolini.

For him this was the last-chance negotiation. At three in the afternoon, against the counter-point of distant grenade explosions and the sharp rattle of automatic-weapons fire, he left the prefecture in a car dispatched by Cardinal Schuster. Barracu, Bassi, and Paolo Zerbino, a minister, were with him. Just as the car was starting, the SS lieutenant in command of Mussolini's private guard forced his way into it. Marshal Graziani was to join the delegation later.

Mussolini was the first to arrive at the archbishopric in Piazza Fontana. The cardinal received him alone, greeting Il Duce cordially, and for more than two hours they talked together.

"So you intend to carry on the war in the mountains?" the cardinal asked.

"For a while; then I will surrender." When the cardinal impressed on Il Duce that history would respect an act of immediate surrender to save north Italy, Mussolini lost his temper: "History? Do you talk to me about history? All I believe in is ancient history. History written without passion, and long after the event."

The delegates of the Committee of National Liberation for North Italy were announced, and soon Fascists and members of the Resistance were face to face in the cardinal's office. Mussolini and Schuster sat together on a couch at one end of a long table. Along one side, below Mussolini, there were Lombardi, Cadorna, and Marazza; on the other there were Barracu, Zerbino, Graziani, and Bassi. It was five o'clock.

It was a strange encounter in the muffled atmosphere of the archbishopric between two groups of men that had condemned each other to death, resolute antagonists together in this room; those on one side knew that they might be deciding life or death for hundreds of combatants, because the Fascist forces in the city were still large. A strange encounter that set Marshal Graziani and General Cadorna in opposing camps. A strange encounter that was like an interlude before the end of the drama.

There sat Mussolini beside the cardinal who had once lavished adulation on him, the thin cardinal with the veined hands who symbolized the church that survives though men tumble from the heights to death. The delegates of the Resistance stared in amazement at the old man whose heavy countenance was only the face of a man who feels the terror of death rising and who struggles desperately. Riccardo Lombardi, the Socialist, and Marazza, the Christian Democrat, undoubtedly felt a great pity for this man, so close to them in the room, whose husky voice, when he was told that the Germans were treating with the Allies, said with an element of sincerity: "Ah! the Germans. They have betrayed me. They have treated us as servants."

It was a strange encounter and perhaps it made it easier for the

Resistants—Lombardi, the engineer; Marazza, the lawyer; Cadorna, the soldier—to recognize that Fascism could not have been merely that man before them, devoured by cynical ambitions, but a whole system with economic and military components, a whole web surviving on profits, violence, and prejudices. And the system of Fascism, now in its death agony, had to be destroyed. But Fascism was also Mussolini.

"Basically he is pitiful," Lombardi whispered to Cadorna.

The general looked at Mussolini and then at Marshal Graziani. Cadorna was thinking of the Alpini of Piedmont and Trentino whom Il Duce had shipped to the Don, who had lain down rolled up in their shoddy wool blankets and been gradually covered over by the snow; he was thinking of the officers shot at Cephalonia by the Germans, of the children of Marzabotto to whom the SS had said: "You're going to have your pictures taken" and whom they had then butchered with machine guns concealed in tents; he was thinking of the hanged men in so many cities, the youths rounded up by the *Milizia* Mussolini and turned over to the Gestapo for shipment to Mauthausen; of the Jews tracked down by Pavolini's Black Brigades and of all the host of other young men tossed into a lost war to the cry of *Vinceremo*. And Cadorna was thinking too of the erosion of consciences, of those officers who lied to please Il Duce, who ordered an attack for Il Duce, this Duce who had played warrior chief with other men's bodies for nothing but glory.

Fascism was also Mussolini. And Mussolini and Fascism were condemned to death.

Mussolini rose. He wanted to think; he could not accept unconditional surrender. He left the archbishopric and went back to the prefecture. Throughout Lombardy and Piedmont the insurrection was growing. In a flurry of shouts and commands and countercommands, an automatic rifle slung over his shoulder, Mussolini decided to go north to Como and the Alpine redoubt, or Switzerland. Ten cars were soon made ready. Men called: "Duce, don't go!"

At 8 P.M. on April 25 the column set out for Como. That night the last of the Fascist forces collapsed. All that was left of the Republic of Salò was these ten cars driving fast toward the north.

An hour later they were parked side by side in the courtyard of the Como prefecture, which was a camp of armed Militiamen. The windows of the building were brightly lighted. In the cars and trucks drivers slept, resting their heads on their steering wheels; other men stood guard duty, sub-machine gun in hand.

Mussolini was weary and almost haggard; yet at times it seemed that he did not grasp the seriousness of the situation; he was worried over the safe arrival of the truck carrying his personal archives. Then in a flash he returned to the world round him, that world that was disintegrating, those unshaven men, in their incongruous uniforms with their flaunted weapons, and again he was seized with apprehension; then he leaped from one plan to another as he had done so many times before, trusting in Pavolini, who had promised to join him with a column of five thousand Militiamen prepared to die for their Duce.

He managed to be alone for a few minutes, eluding his advisers, and he wrote to Rachele with that blue pencil with which he had marked so many newspaper articles:

My dear Rachele,
Here I am at the last stage of my life, the last page of my book. Perhaps we shall not see each other again. I ask your forgiveness for all the harm that I have done you without meaning to.
As you know, we are supposed to go to Valtellina.

He wrote the date—April 25, 1945, Year XXIII of the Fascist Era—and signed with a red pencil. At that moment Claretta Petacci's car stopped in front of the prefecture. Against everyone's advice she had insisted on joining Mussolini. When Il Duce was told that his mistress had arrived, he mumbled almost to himself: "In situations like this women should stay home."

At three o'clock the next morning the column of cars and trucks left Como. Mussolini could wait no longer for Pavolini and his five thousand Militiamen.

It was dawn. A light fog hung over the lake, the west bank of which the road followed. The Swiss frontier was a couple of miles to the west, at Chiasso. But the road led also, in a northerly direction, to the Maloia and Spluga Passes. Behind there was Switzerland. A road to the east, above the lake, led to Valtellina. And these roads seemed to symbolize Mussolini's vacillation between flight and resistance in an impregnable but mythical redoubt.

Some thirty-five miles from Como the convoy stopped at Menaggio, beside the lake. From there a road leads to Porlezza, at the foot of the Lake of Lugano and the gates of Switzerland. Buffarini-Guidi begged Mussolini to take that road. They would be sure to get through, he said; the Italian and Swiss customs men would let them go; all they had to do was to head for peace and neutrality and safety. But there were many skeptics: what could be counted on when everything was dissolving, when even Mussolini's driver had deserted them? Near Como, only a few hours behind the fugitives, the Partisans were already in action; at times gunfire could be heard in the distance, and, the farther they progressed along the narrow road beside the lake, which was ruffled now by a light wind, the deeper they seemed to be going into a mousetrap. On one side there was the lake and on the other there was the mountain. And there was nothing else but these roads—the one clinging to the rocks and overlooking the dark water, the other running among the hills to Porlezza and Switzerland.

Finally Mussolini agreed to take the road for Switzerland. The cars stopped at Grandola, on the road to Porlezza. The little village was invaded by the armed men who got out to stretch their legs and talked in loud voices, whereas for months the village had seen no one but cautious travelers who were fleeing the war—Jews, escaped prisoners, and deserters.

Mussolini and the hierarchs repaired to an inn where a number of Fascist Militiamen had already halted. Actually Il Duce had not yet settled finally on his road; he was still hoping to see Pavolini and his five thousand. Some motorcycle couriers went back toward Como, but they could find nothing; there was no Pavolini detachment.

The weather was bad. The nearby peaks were covered with clouds, and at times a sudden downpour clattered against the roof of the inn. In the afternoon Buffarini-Guidi and a few others decided to scout the road toward Porlezza and Switzerland. Two of the cars left Grandola on a little unpaved road, and soon the dust that they had raised was lost in the void and the silence.

Less than an hour later, Mussolini and the hierarchs saw one of this party coming back: the man was alone, and he was running. The *Guardia di Finanzia* (customs force and border patrol) at Porlezza had gone over to the Partisans and arrested the Fascists. The road to Switzerland was closed. Everyone piled pell-mell into the cars: there was no choice but to go back to Menaggio while it was still possible.

At Menaggio indecision became endemic. Everything was collapsing and hope was fading. Anxiety manifested itself in every word, every gesture. There was no time now to be concerned with archives and justifications: all that mattered now was life. Some of the Militiamen threw away their weapons and tore off their uniforms; in peasant shirts and trousers they set off alone to try their luck. They left Menaggio, they fled Il Duce and the hierarchs as in the ancient tragedies men abandoned those who had been marked by death.

From their doors and windows the residents of Menaggio watched the feverish bustle of these armed men yelling to one another, running back and forth, buying food and clothes regardless of price. A few more cars were coming up from Como. With a great shriek of brakes, a luggage-laden Alfa Romeo *superleggera* pulled up, and a worried-looking blond heavy-set man got out. He was Marcello Petacci. Two women stayed in the car. One, wrapped in a beaver coat with the collar high, her hair concealed in a turban, was Claretta Petacci. The other was Marcello's mistress, who had her two blond children with her.

They waited. They had to wait. For what? the end? Not one of the hierarchs dared to start out again alone. They were there in a group round Il Duce, who sat among them with his head in his hands, and they all talked at once, suggesting and arguing, unable to make up their minds to abandon the man who had been "their good luck" and without whom, unquestionably, they would have been nothing but nameless shadows in Italy's millions.

The hours went on. For them Italy had shrunk to this congested village, gradually embraced in the evening fog, and hope was the road that should bring Pavolini and his five thousand Militiamen. With them it would be possible to resist at least until the Allies arrived, and then the surrender could be made.

They waited. Mussolini talked with Bombacci and showed everyone the secret documents that he was keeping in a black bag. With these, he insisted, he could clear himself. At about eleven o'clock, with much furor, Pavolini arrived. He was alone. There were no more Militiamen, or Black Shirts, or Italian SS. There were only, in glacial isolation, the chiefs, those who had held the center of the stage and occupied the front rows, and who, in a rare exception to the ways of history, found themselves reduced to their own number.

Anguish gripped Mussolini and the hierarchs in Menaggio. Power had accustomed them to the interposition of the multiple apparatus of administration between themselves and the adversary, the bodies of regiments, the defense of solidly entrenched ministries, and here they stood brutally stripped, limited to themselves and drained by fear.

And Mussolini more than anyone. He knew too well that now there would be no flight to some golden isle, no German parachutists. He had bet his last chip, and he had lost.

At dawn on April 27 the village of Menaggio was awakened by the roar of engines, the clashing of gears, the squeal of brakes. A German convoy of twenty-eight trucks loaded with helmeted soldiers was on its way to Switzerland or Germany. On the roofs of the trucks the heavy machine guns and the anti-aircraft guns were in firing position. For Mussolini and his group of Fascist leaders this organized, armed, disciplined fragment of the Reich was a new incarnation of hope. The commanding officer, an air-force captain, agreed to allow the Fascists' cars and trucks to follow his column.

Soon the convoy started out along the lake, leaving Menaggio just as the sky was beginning to brighten. At reduced speed the trucks took the corners and rolled through the little villages while the breeze roused the sleepy soldiers. In a huge armored car behind the trucks, Pavolini, Barracu, Bombacci, and Mussolini sat together in the midst of Militiamen armed to the teeth. Then came Marcello Petacci's car, followed by others packed with Militiamen. Some of the younger ones were singing. The morning fragrances of a stormy springtime spread over Lake Como.

At six-thirty that morning, in the little lakeside village of Domaso,[1] two Partisan leaders, Bill (Urbano Lazzaro) and Pedro (Pier Luigi Bellini delle Stelle), were roughly roused out of sleep by messengers: a German column had been spotted heading for Dongo, a village about three miles to the south. A few minutes later Bill and Pedro were on their way to Dongo and the little village of Musso. They heard a few volleys of automatic arms and then everything was silent again. The column had stopped at a road-block set up by Partisans of the Fifty-second Garibaldi Brigade, and there had been some exchanges of shots between the Partisans and an armored car. A peasant in his field fell, mortally wounded by one of the volleys from the car. He died a few minutes later: the last victim of Fascism in Italy.

Not long afterward the Germans asked for a parley.

On this April 27 Marshal Zhukov's troops had reached Berlin and shells were falling without interruption on the bunker housing Der Führer. Officers and soldiers of the Wehrmacht had no further wish to die beside this Italian lake a few days before the inescapable defeat of their Reich.

The Partisans bluffed magnificently: more barricades sprang up rapidly along the road taken by the German officers sent to negotiate with the leaders of the Garibaldi Brigade. On the near-by embankment armed men had taken up very prominent positions. The German captain contemplated this impressive deployment with disquiet. Finally Pedro dictated his terms to the captain as he stood facing the German in the road:

1) Only German vehicles and soldiers would be permitted to pass through. All Italians and all civilian vehicles in the column must be surrendered.

[1] An indispensable source is P. L. Bellini delle Stelle and U. Lazzaro, *Dongo ultima azione* (Milan: Mondadori, 1961).

2) All the German cars and trucks would submit to inspection at Dongo.

"I should like a half-hour in order to confer with my officers," the captain said. He walked down the road past the motionless heavy trucks until he came to the armored car. He could be seen in discussion with men in civilian clothes. At the same time a resident of Musso, the little village to which the last vehicles in the column reached, came through the fields and approached the Partisans' road-block, where he asked to speak to Pedro.

"The last cars have ministers from the Salò government," he said. He added that shortly after noon two men had gone to the parish priest in Musso and one of them said: "I am Bombacci. I am surrendering. Call a Partisan." Then the old demagogue added in a weary voice: "I am the victim of my own simple-mindedness and it is going to cost me my life."

In a few minutes the German officer announced that he agreed to the Partisans' conditions. The military convoy started up and the German soldiers punctiliously saluted the Partisans.

The armored car and a few civilian vehicles still stood in the middle of the road. A long argument with the Partisan leader began. Barracu, Under-Secretary of State to the Premier, demanded that the group be allowed to pass. In a solemn voice he said: "I have sworn to go to Trieste to defend the city against the Slavs, who are advancing and want to annex it." When this did no good, Barracu grew insistent: "I beg you once more to allow me to pass so that I may fulfill my last duty." This Fascist leader who, whether from genuine belief or superficial demagogy, tried in this way to play on the Partisan's patriotic feelings seemed indeed to have lost all contact with reality: at best he was forgetting that the Germans had been the masters of Trieste for more than a year.

Colonel Casalinuovo sprang out of the armored car and stood face to face with the Partisan, shouting: "Well, are you going to pass us through or not? Be careful: we're prepared for anything and we will never surrender! Let us through or it will be the worse for you."

At three-fifteen the armored car tried to run through the barrier. It met a curtain of gunfire, and the car was halted by the explosion of a grenade beneath it. Soon the hierarchs were prisoners. Only Pavolini got away, hiding among the rocks near the lake, and he was caught later. There was not a sign of Mussolini. The prisoners were taken to Dongo. In the middle of the road, near the blackened, half-overturned armored car, a young Militiaman writhed in agony, his face shattered.

At the same moment, the German trucks were standing in the main square of Dongo. The Partisans checked each soldier's papers individually and inspected the trucks. Suddenly a Partisan summoned Bill. He said that he had seen Mussolini in a German uniform. Bill went up to the truck pointed out by his comrade. Inside, just behind the cab, a man lay outstretched, his helmet over his face and the collar of his German army overcoat turned up. Just a drunken soldier, the other Germans in the truck said.

"*Camerata!*—Comrade!" Bill shouted. There was no reply. "*Eccellenza!*—Your Excellency!" Still no reply. Bill shouted more forcefully: "*Cavaliere* Benito Mussolini!"

The man made a barely visible movement. Bill removed his helmet. There was the shaven skull, a skull that Italians had seen so many times that they would recognize it among a thousand. Mussolini lay quite still. Bill removed Mussolini's sun-glasses and turned down his coat collar. Still Il Duce did not move. Bill removed the automatic rifle that was between Mussolini's knees. Still there was neither a movement nor a word from Il Duce. Was it fear, was it panic that paralyzed him? No doubt; but perhaps he was beyond both those emotions and merely numb.

The plunge had been too brutal. Less than forty-eight hours ago he was still Mussolini, surrounded by apparently devoted men, and now here he was constrained to put on a soldier's heavy cap, smelling of coarse wool, constrained to lie on the bed of a truck and act the drunken trooper in front of twenty private soldiers of the Wehrmacht who sat openly staring at the clandestine stowaway at their feet. He was Il Duce, whom Chamberlain and Hitler had taken by the hand, whom the Pope had received; he was Il Duce, the peer of the greatest, with the kings, the marshals, the heads of states round him, and the crowd like a sea beneath the balcony of Palazzo Venezia; and he was a hunted man in a corner of a foreign truck, less than any of these foreign soldiers.

Bill had to help him to his feet: they stood face to face. A crowd had gathered round the truck, for the news had run like a powder train through the village: "They got Mussolini!" The crowd began to shout; now the German soldiers in the truck were frightened, and they surrendered their weapons.

Bill and Mussolini were face to face. Quite spontaneously the political commissar of the Fifty-second Garibaldi Brigade announced: "I arrest you in the name of the Italian people." Then Bill and another Partisan took Mussolini by the armpits and helped him down to the road. They made a passage through the yelling crowd and took Mussolini to the town hall, where the mayor said reassuringly: "Don't worry, you will not be harmed."

"I am sure of that," Mussolini said slowly, "the population of Dongo is generous."

In a few minutes the hierarchs from the armored car also arrived at the town hall. When they saw Mussolini, they stood at attention and said together: "*Salve* [hail], *Duce*."

Mussolini nodded in reply. He could hear the shouts from the crowd outside and from time to time he looked toward the door with anxious eyes, as if he feared to see it smashed at any minute by men determined to kill him. Little by little, however, as he saw that he was being treated with consideration, he seemed to recover his self-control; he argued, answered various questions, tried to justify himself. Matteotti? He had had nothing to do with that. The war? All the doing of the Germans.

The documents in his black bag were checked, but they seemed to contain nothing of major importance. At the bottom of the bag the searchers found some sterling and drafts on Swiss banks for several million *lire*.

Pavolini was brought to the town hall in the evening. Wounded during his flight, he had been recognized by the crowd and had almost been lynched: he was hated as the chief of the Black Brigades, and the *Garibaldini* had barely been able to protect him. He was soaked, bleeding, shaking, terror-stricken. But he too, when he entered, mustered the strength to give Il Duce the Roman salute.

By now it was dark in Dongo, but there was no lull in activity. The Partisan leaders conferred. Theirs was a grave responsibility: they wanted at all costs to prevent a summary execution and at the same time they wanted to keep Mussolini out of the Allies' hands: Il Duce should be tried by the Italians. That night Mussolini was taken to Germanesino; then, in order to keep his place of detention secret, his head was covered and in a blinding rain he was taken to a peasant house in Bonzanigo in the commune of Mezzagra. There he was joined by Claretta Petacci.

She had been arrested at Dongo in her brother's car: he had claimed to be the Spanish consul in Milan. Mussolini had asked Pedro, the Partisan leader, to convey his greetings to her, and Claretta had succeeded in persuading Pedro to allow her to rejoin Il Duce. Together he and she, in that evening of April 27, 1945, clambered up the mountain road that led to the house of a peasant, De Maria. They were given the bedroom on the second floor, and two young armed Partisans were posted at the door.

It was cool and rainy.

Late in the evening the news of the capture reached the high command of the Corps of Volunteers for Freedom (CVL). As of

April 25, Article V of the code of justice promulgated by the CLN provided the death penalty for Mussolini and the hierarchs as for any Fascist taken armed. For Il Duce and the hierarchs there was no salvation.

But a race got under way. The Partisans, especially on the extreme left (Communists and Socialists), were afraid that the British and Americans would get hold of the Fascist leaders and save them from the ultimate penalty. In addition, one of the clauses of the September 8 armistice stipulated that Il Duce was to be turned over to the Allies. But the whole left Resistance approved when Sandro Pertini, a Socialist, exclaimed: "Mussolini deserves to be shot like a mangy dog!"

Meanwhile the Allies were driving northward and quick action was imperative. An American officer of Italian origin, Captain Daddario of the staff of the United States Fourth Army, had already reached Milan from Switzerland and Graziani had managed to surrender to him (and thus to escape execution). The CVL leaders decided to precipitate matters: most of them were Socialists and Communists. Colonel Valerio (who is now Walter Audisio, a Communist deputy) obtained from Captain Daddario and the Resistance military authorities (General Cadorna) the passes and other papers necessary to his mission.

Though the American captain was not informed of the colonel's purpose, General Cadorna was aware of it. But at that time he was primarily concerned with the German divisions that were withdrawing northward in good order. Besides, like every Italian in the Resistance, he did not want Mussolini to be handed over to the Allies, not so much out of fear that he would escape punishment as out of concern for national independence and dignity. The matter of Mussolini was the business of Italians. The Italian people was a mature people that stood in no need of lessons from the Allies. Such was Cadorna's thinking. Hence he kept his hands off: he did not assist Valerio's mission, but he did not impede it.

Valerio left Milan in a FIAT 1500 at two-thirty in the morning of April 28, followed by a truck carrying fifteen reliable Partisans. The first stop was Como, which they reached during the morning. There Valerio learned that two men had left Como, under the auspices of the town's CLN, to identify the prisoners and bring them back to Como. And the Allies' advance guard was entering the town even as Valerio was leaving it with his men.

Valerio raced along the lake-side road, even crashing a road-block erected by the Partisans. About one-thirty in the afternoon he and his men reached Dongo. The fifteen Partisans from Milan lined up in front of the town hall. Pedro, the local commander of the *Garibaldini*, tried to question Valerio's orders for the execution of the Fascist chiefs. Valerio had decided even to execute Claretta Petacci, and he was adamant. "I am not the one who sentenced her," he said. "She was condemned earlier. Remember, I am carrying out an order and you ought not to meddle. I know what I am doing and I am the one who will decide what I have to do."

The fate of Mussolini and Claretta Petacci was now sealed. Valerio and some of his men went to De Maria's house. "I have come to liberate you," he told Mussolini, "let's make it fast."

His manner admitted of no reply. Without a word Claretta and Mussolini followed the group of Partisans. Mussolini was wearing a workman's heavy cap; Claretta was clinging to him. After a short car trip, Valerio got out in front of the gateway of a villa. "Hurry up," he said, "get into that corner."

Stunned, his back to the wall, Mussolini stared. Suddenly Valerio said in a tight voice: "By order of the high command of the Corps of Volunteers for Freedom I am instructed to do justice for the Italian people." Mussolini almost collapsed and Claretta threw her arms round him.

"He must not die," she said.

"Back where you were," Valerio replied. She went back.

There was one volley, then a second. Mussolini and Claretta Petacci were dead. It was April 28, 1945.

Two Partisans stayed with the bodies while Valerio went back to Dongo, where the fifteen hierarchs were waiting in the park along the parapet that overlooks the lake. When Valerio tried to put Marcello Petacci among them, they raised a unanimous protest. "Get out, get out! Not with us, that one's a traitor! He should not be shot with us."

Marcello was removed. Someone cried *Viva l'Italia* and a few others gave the Fascist salute. "Half turn," the commander of the firing squad shouted. The doomed men faced the lake, whose water mirrored the April sky, with its shifting fantasies of blue areas and dark clouds clinging to the steep slopes of the mountains rising above the shore.

"Fire!" They fell, their twisting bodies resting on one another. "Fetch Petacci," Valerio ordered.

Petacci struggled and managed to work free, running through the narrow streets like a maddened animal; then he leaped into the lake and everyone began to fire at him. It did not take many shots to make him sink.

The rest of the bodies were slung into Valerio's truck: Mussolini's and Claretta's were on top of the others. The truck got back to Milan the next day, April 29. All seventeen corpses were thrown on the sidewalk of Piazza Loreto beside the garage in which the Germans had shot fifteen hostages on August 14, 1944. Soon all Milan was crowding round to view them. People wanted to see, to be reassured by the gruesome spectacle, to see and to touch: some trampled the bodies, others spat on them, shoved a mocking scepter into Mussolini's hands, made jokes. "Petacci," someone shouted, and someone else held up her corpse to show it.

Starace was taken alive in Milan and brought to the same square, where he was shot and left with the others. A Partisan had the idea of hanging all the bodies by the feet from the rafters of the garage for everyone to see. A placard with the victim's name chalked on it was attached to each corpse.

And this profanation of death seemed to serve as a magic ceremony, collective and primitive: the end of a bewitchment, the resolve to understand that in truth Il Duce and his hierarchs had been only men.

Men even poorer than the rest, even viler, for their bodies were there, offered to sneers and obscene gestures, hanged head down. And the crowd pressed in and revenged itself on them—a huge crowd of the jubilant, the hateful, and the merely curious, all discovering from these poor shapes of men reduced to bloody puppets that Il Duce and his hierarchs had had neither enough champions nor enough personal courage to save their bodies from the gallows. This April 29, 1945, concluded in violence what March 23, 1919, had inaugurated in violence.[2]

[2] I have deliberately excluded from this account of Mussolini's death the contradictory speculations on the documents and the treasure that he was supposedly carrying—documents and treasure that, allegedly, were either stolen or smuggled into Switzerland.

Epilogue

THE MERA IS a little river that empties into Lake Como. On April 27, 1945—the same day when Mussolini and the hierarchs were arrested by the Partisans at Musso and Dongo—a fishermen in a boat on the Mera saw the glitter of something metallic on the bed of the stream. He began to dredge.

In a few hours he had collected almost eighty pounds of gold —gold that hierarchs, Militiamen, or Germans had deemed it advisable to relinquish. These eighty pounds of gold were composed of wedding rings, hundreds of wedding rings engraved on the inside with the names of the spouses, the dates of their marriages, and the names of the cities where they had been celebrated.

There were wedding rings from every town in Italy, from Palermo to Reggio Emilia, from Mondovì to Bari, from the large cities and from the villages. In addition to these rings the fisherman also brought up earrings, decorations, and brooches. This was the "gold of the Nation," the gold of the "rite of faith," gold that had been collected in 1936 at the time of sanctions and that Mussolini, from his platform, had displayed running through his black-gloved fingers.

And the gold had finished there, in the bottom of the river. It had never been used and yet it represented the gift of ingenuous trust that had led millions of Italians to submit so long to Fascism. So the gold had been nothing more than burdensome loot to the government, diverted from its purpose and finally stolen, then thrown into the river as sometimes a criminal in flight hurls away some damning piece of evidence that must be hidden at any cost.

433

SELECTIVE BIBLIOGRAPHY

The following is not intended to be a complete bibliography of Fascism and Mussolini nor yet a listing of the books, periodicals, and documents that I have consulted. It is merely a guide to the reader of major sources for the study of the period.

Alatri, P, *L'Antifascismo italiano*, Rome.
———, *Le origini del fascismo*, Rome, 1956.
Aloisi, Pompeio, *Journal du Baron Aloisi (25 Juillet 1932–14 Juin 1936)*, Paris, 1957.
Bellini delle Stelle, Pier Luigi, and Lazzaro, Urbano, *Dongo Ultima azione*, Milan, 1961.
Chabod, Federico, *L'Italia contemporanea (1918–1948)*, Turin, 1961.
Ciano, Count Galeazzo, *Diary 1937–1938*, New York, 1952.
———, *Diary 1939–1943*, New York, 1947.
———, *Diplomatic Papers*, edited by Malcolm Muggeridge, London, 1948.
Deakin, F. W., *The Brutal Friendship*, London, 1962.
Gramsci, Antonio, *Opere*, Turin, 1947–1960.
Guérin, D., *Fascisme et grand capital*, Paris.
Jemolo, Arturo Carlo, *Chiesa e stato in Italia negli ultimi cento anni*, Turin, 1948.
Monelli, Paolo, *Mussolini, the Intimate Life of a Demagogue*. Translated by Brigid Maxwell. New York, 1954.
———, *Roma, 1943*, new edition, Milan, 1963.
Mussolini, Benito, *Opera omnia*, edited by Edoardo and Duilio Susmel, thirty-two volumes, Florence, 1951–1961.
Salvatorelli, Luigi, and Giovanni Mira, *Storia d'Italia nel periodo fascista*, Turin, 1961.
Salvemini, Gaetano, *Mussolini diplomatico*, Bari, 1952.
Smith, Denis Mack, *Italy, A Modern History*, Ann Arbor, 1959.
Wiskemann, Elizabeth, *The Rome-Berlin Axis*, London, 1959.
Zangrandi, Ruggero, *Il lungo viaggio attraverso il fascismo*, Milan, 1962.

Two works of literature deserve to be cited for the special light that they cast on the Fascist Era from within:

Levi, Carlo, *Christ Stopped at Eboli*. Translated by Frances Frenaye. New York, 1947.
Pratolini, Vasco, *A Tale of Poor Lovers*. New York, n.d.

Index

437

and Hitler, 274–275, 282, 287–289, 299–301, 318–319, 334
in Libya, 322–323
in Mediterranean, 318, 321–322, 330
and Poland, 302, 306, 308
See also Allies; Anglo-Italian relations
British Labor Party, 81
Buffarini-Guidi, Guido, 270–271, 287, 295, 331–332, 337, 356, 358–359, 360, 370, 381, 386, 422, 423
Bülow, Prince von, 41, 42, 44, 102
Buozzi, Bruno, 105, 106, 348, 370, 402, 406

Cadorna, General Raffaele, 41, 47, 50, 52, 160, 401, 419, 420–421, 429
Cagoule (The Hood), 276–277
Campo Dux, 221
Canaris, Admiral Wilhelm, 268
Capello, General, 49, 51
Capitalism, 7, 9, 57, 199, 223–224
Caporetto, 49, 51–52, 54, 75, 82–83
Carboni, General Giacomo, 315, 323, 346, 353, 361, 370, 377
Carducci, Giosuè, 367
Carli, Mario, 63, 69
Carnot, Sadi, 10
Carosi, Sandro, 117
Carroci, Cesira, 177, 194
Caruso, Pietro, 400, 403
Casa del Fascio, 231, 232, 364
Casalini, Armando, 191
Casalinuovo, Colonel Vito, 426
Casa del Popolo, 45
Casati, Alessandro, 39
Castellano, General Giuseppe, 343, 346, 348, 349, 353, 354, 361, 366, 369, 372–373
Catholic Action, 232
Catholicism and the Catholic Church
Church and State, 230–232
and Fascism, 142–144, 150, 160, 165, 167, 172, 198, 230–232
Italian politics, 5, 29, 40, 67–68, 88–91, 93, 97, 120, 170, 179–180, 189
and peasants, 5, 105
See also Vatican
Catholic Popular Party (PPI), 71, 80, 103, 105, 110, 120, 122, 125, 132, 136–137, 178–179, 189
birth of, 29, 67–69, 88–91, 93, 97
and Mussolini, 123, 142–144, 150, 160, 165, 167, 172
Cavagnari, Admiral Domenico, 315, 318

Cavallero, General Ugo, 299, 322, 329, 330, 331, 340, 370
Caviglia, General Enrico, 54, 73, 114, 341, 346, 348, 360
Cavour, Camillo Bensodi, 4, 148, 162, 176
Ceccherini, General Sante, 86, 149
Cella, Gian Riccardo, 419
Cerica, General Angelo, 353, 361
Cerutti, Vittorio, 245
CGL (Italian Federation of Labor), 25, 30, 59, 60, 81, 97, 103, 106, 107, 123, 125, 143, 155, 160, 165, 199
Chabod, Federico, 66
Chamber of Fasci and Corporations, 296, 365
Chamber of Corporations and the Senate, 342
Chamberlain, Austen, 256, 282, 288, 289, 294, 300
attitude toward Mussolini, 201–202
Chambrun, Charles de, 247, 251, 267
Charles-Roux, François, 87, 137, 255
Charter of the Carnaro, 99
Chierci, Renzo, 343
Chiesa, Lieutenant Damiano, 72
Chiot, Don, 396, 397
Christian Democrats, 336, 342, 365, 370, 402, 419
Churchill, Major Oliver, 401
Churchill, Winston, 211, 213, 245–246, 314, 376, 417
Cianetti, Tullio, 356, 393, 395
Ciano, Costanzo, 152, 160, 216, 284
Ciano, Edda. See Mussolini, Edda
Ciano, Galeazzo, 23, 216, 254, 255, 258, 279, 340, 349, 356, 358, 360, 363, 372, 379
arrest and trial, 393–396
execution, 396–397
as Foreign Minister, 261, 267–268, 274–277, 279, 280–282, 285, 287–322 passim, 325, 328, 330, 333–337, 339
Political Diary, 279, 300, 304, 394
Cini, Count Vittorio, 345
Cione, Edmondo, 391
Cittadini, General Arturo, 138, 154
Clark, General Mark W., 378
Clemenceau, Georges, 75, 79
CLN. See National Committee of Liberation
Colleone, Bartolomeo, 205
Colonna, Prince Prospero, 31, 77, 78
Committee of Alliance and Action, 81
Committee of Liberation of Northern Italy, 410, 420

439

fate of, 185, 191, 233, 246–247, 268, 311

financial support, 39, 118, 126, 127, 128

and financiers, 132, 165, 235–236, 296, 314

and Fiume incident, 84–86, 87, 114–115

foreign policy. See Mussolini, foreign policy of

vs. Freemasons, 176, 196, 309

ideology of, 218–220, 222, 224

and the intellectuals, 194–195, 198, 203, 230, 240

and interventionism, 40, 43, 46, 58–59, 313–314

and the invasion of Austria, 283–284

invasion of Cremona, 135–136, 146

and labor. See Labor, and Fascism

laws of, 197–198, 202–203, 237

March on Rome, 84, 87, 142, 144, 152–154

and middle-class opposition to, 295–296

and the monarchy. See Mussolini, and the monarchy

Mussolini's control of, 123–127, 129, 178, 224–225

and nationalism, 20–22, 40, 67, 71, 98, 197, 199–200, 204, 222, 247, 254

and Naziism, 176, 246, 260, 268, 275, 278, 352

and Pact of Steel, 298–299, 302

vs. Partisans, 398–402, 403–404, 406

patriotic theme of, 98, 103, 122–123

popular support for, 108–109, 113, 118, 134, 136, 142, 229–230

programs of, 232–235

and repression, 194–195, 202–203, 237–238

second wave of, 187, 190–191, 194

and Socialists, treaty of peace with, 125–126, 127, 129

and Spanish civil war, 265–267, 275–276

Special Court of, 203, 236–237, 239, 365

spiritualism of, 219–220

and squadre, 108, 109–110, 113–114, 115–116, 169–170, 344

strength of, 205

suppression of the press, 173, 179, 180, 190, 191, 193, 197, 272

symbol of, 204

themes of, 21–22, 44, 48, 53–54, 71

totalitarianism, 20, 40, 43, 48, 169, 172, 195, 197, 202–203, 219, 224–225

and the Vatican. See Mussolini, and the Vatican

and warrior mentality, 220–222, 248

weaknesses of, 169–170, 191, 204, 268, 311

and world domination, 200, 219–220, 242–243, 246–249

See also Mussolini; PNF

Fascist Federation of Industry, 341

Fascist Grand Council, 170, 209, 224, 245, 248, 292, 296, 316, 325, 335

convocation of, 1943, 350–351, 354–361, 393–397

dissolved, 365

Fascistissime (ultra-Fascist law), 197, 198, 202–203, 204, 237

Fascist Labor Union, 118, 220

Fascist Militia, 129–130, 190, 191, 193, 196, 220–222, 225, 236–237, 253, 341, 346, 363, 365

of Republic of Salò, 381, 388–389, 422–423, 423–424

Fascist Republican Party, 380–382, 384–386, 388–391, 407, 408, 409, 410

Hitler's plans for, 366, 368–369, 370, 378, 387, 404

on socialization, 391–393, 415

Verona trials, 393–397

Fascist Saturday (sabato fascista), 272

Fascist State, 190, 197, 203, 204, 219, 220, 227, 228, 234, 235–236

corporativism, 222–224, 230, 236

corruption in, 227–229, 270–272, 273, 324, 329, 332

education in, 220–222, 228, 230, 272–273

propaganda, 222–223, 230, 232, 257, 293

social mobility in, 227–229, 319–320

social rules in, 43, 225–229, 272, 279–280, 286–287

Fascist University Groups. See GUF

Federation of Labor. See CGL

Federzoni, Luigi, 22, 29, 77, 80, 153, 160, 187, 191, 193, 194, 224, 311, 340, 349, 354, 356, 395

Fera, Luigi, 116

Ferdinand, Archduke Franz, 32

Fermi, Enrico, 229, 295